OXFORD ENGLISH DRAMA

General Editor: MICHAEL CORDNER

Associate General Editors: PETER HOLLAND · MARTIN WIGGINS

THE COUNTRY WIFE

AND OTHER PLAYS

WILLIAM WYCHERLEY was born in the spring of 1641. He was educated first at home, then for some years in France, and briefly at Oxford and the Inner Temple. Settled in London, after active service in the Second Anglo-Dutch War, he launched his literary career with a verse parody, *Hero and Leander* (1669), and established himself as a brilliant comic dramatist with *Love in a Wood* two years later. The play's success gained him a rapid entrée into court circles, and the attention of the Duchess of Cleveland. His next play, *The Gentleman Dancing-Master*, was a disappointment. But in 1675 came *The Country Wife*, and in the following year *The Plain Dealer*, greatly admired for its hard-hitting satire.

Thereafter Wycherley's fortunes declined. A bout of severe ill-health left his memory permanently impaired; a secret marriage to the Countess of Drogheda lost him the king's favour, and embroiled him in legal and financial difficulties. And the publication of *Miscellany Poems* (1704) did nothing to enhance his reputation. He died on 31 December 1715.

PETER DIXON has taught at the University of Adelaide, the Queen's University, Belfast, and the University of London, where, before his retirement, he was Professor of English at Queen Mary and Westfield College. His publications include books on Pope, Goldsmith, and rhetoric.

MICHAEL CORDNER is Ken Dixon Professor of Drama at the University of York. He has edited editions of George Farquhar's *The Beaux' Stratagem*, the *Complete Plays* of Sir George Etherege, and *Four Comedies* of Sir John Vanbrugh. His editions include *Four Restoration Marriage Comedies* and Sheridan's *The School for Scandal and Other Plays*.

PETER HOLLAND is McMeel Family Professor in Shakespeare Studies at the University of Notre Dame.

MARTIN WIGGINS is a Fellow of the Shakespeare Institute and Senior Lecturer in English at the University of Birmingham.

OXFORD ENGLISH DRAMA

J. M. Barrie
Peter Pan and Other Plays

Aphra Behn
The Rover and Other Plays

John Ford
'Tis Pity She's a Whore and Other Plays

Ben Jonson
The Alchemist and Other Plays

Ben Jonson
The Devil is an Ass and Other Plays

Christopher Marlowe
Doctor Faustus and Other Plays

John Marston
The Malcontent and Other Plays

Thomas Middleton
*Women Beware Women and
Other Plays*

*A Mad World, My Masters, and
Other Plays*

Richard Brinsley Sheridan
The School for Scandal and Other Plays

J. M. Synge
*The Playboy of the Western World and
Other Plays*

John Vanbrugh
The Relapse and Other Plays

John Webster
*The Duchess of Malfi and
Other Plays*

Oscar Wilde
*The Importance of Being Earnest and
Other Plays*

William Wycherley
The Country Wife and Other Plays

Court Masques
ed. David Lindley

Eighteenth-Century Women Dramatists
ed. Melinda Finberg

Four Jacobean Sex Tragedies
ed. Martin Wiggins

Four Restoration Marriage Plays
ed. Michael Cordner

Four Revenge Tragedies
ed. Katharine Maus

*London Assurance and Other
Victorian Comedies*
ed. Klaus Stierstorfer

*The Roaring Girl and Other City
Comedies*
ed. James Knowles and Eugene
Giddens

*She Stoops to Conquer and Other
Comedies*
ed. Nigel Wood

*A Woman Killed with Kindness and
Other Domestic Plays*
ed. Martin Wiggins

OXFORD WORLD'S CLASSICS

WILLIAM WYCHERLEY

Love in a Wood
The Gentleman Dancing–Master
The Country Wife
The Plain Dealer

Edited with an Introduction and Notes by
PETER DIXON

OXFORD
UNIVERSITY PRESS

OXFORD
UNIVERSITY PRESS

Great Clarendon Street, Oxford OX2 6DP

Oxford University Press is a department of the University of Oxford.
It furthers the University's objective of excellence in research, scholarship,
and education by publishing worldwide in

Oxford New York

Auckland Bangkok Buenos Aires Cape Town Chennai
Dar es Salaam Delhi Hong Kong Istanbul Karachi Kolkata
Kuala Lumpur Madrid Melbourne Mexico City Mumbai Nairobi
São Paulo Shanghai Singapore Taipei Tokyo Toronto

Oxford is a registered trade mark of Oxford University Press
in the UK and in certain other countries

Published in the United States
by Oxford University Press Inc., New York

First published as a World's Classics paperback 1996
Reissued as an Oxford World's Classics paperback 1998
Reissued 2008

British Library Cataloguing in Publication Data

Data available

Library of Congress Cataloging in Publication Data

Wycherley, William, 1640–1716.
The country wife and other plays / William Wycherley; edited by Peter Dixon.
Includes bibliographical references (p.   ).
Contents: Love in a wood–The gentleman dancing-master–
The country wife–The plain dealer.
I. Dixon, Peter, 1932– . II. Title. III. Series.
PR3771.D59 1996 822′.4—dc20 95–13103

ISBN 978–0–19–955518–5

6

Printed in Great Britain by
Clays Ltd, St Ives plc

CONTENTS

ACKNOWLEDGEMENTS

I AM most grateful to Michael Cordner and Peter Holland for their assistance and encouragement throughout the preparation of this edition, and to Kevin Ewart for his thorough checking of the text. Mike Lilly, Ralph Penny, and Aileen Ribeiro have generously provided expert advice on esoteric matters. Finally, I am deeply indebted to Blanche Litwin for transforming my manuscript of the play texts into elegant typescript.

INTRODUCTION

In the spring of 1660 the English monarchy was restored, in the person of Charles II. In the autumn of that year the public theatre was restored to London, when Charles granted patents to two courtier-dramatists, empowering them to establish theatre companies. Though the decade that followed was not productive of many comic masterpieces, it was a period of vigorous experimentation. By 1670, when William Wycherley, in his late twenties, was ready to begin his dramatic career, there was no lack of models for imitation. (There were also some dire examples of what an apprentice dramatist ought to avoid.)[1] The public had been entertained, and sometimes disappointed, with farces, with intrigue-comedies based on Spanish plots, and with plays involving sexual skirmishings and reconciliations. The satiric 'humours' comedies of Ben Jonson and the witty comedies of John Fletcher were well-represented in the repertoires. And Wycherley himself was particularly well-placed to profit from the leading exponents of seventeenth-century comedy on the Continent. He had spent three or four years in France during his adolescence, and he was probably the 'Mr Wycherly' who accompanied the English ambassador on a diplomatic mission to the court of Spain in the mid-1660s. The nature of his debts to Calderón in his first two plays, and to Molière in his last two, shows that he knew his sources in their original languages, and that he knew them well. Added to the stimulus of competition was the challenge of writing good parts for actors who had already demonstrated their abilities by playing such comic types as the frenchified fop, the hypocritical Puritan, and the inept country gentleman, as well as young and charismatic heroes and heroines. The

---

[1] Internal evidence and the dates of the source-materials suggest that the first three plays, at least, were written shortly before they were produced, though Wycherley repeatedly told the young Alexander Pope that all his plays were composed between the ages of 19 and 32, i.e. between 1660 and 1672. He was perhaps trying to impress the precocious poet with his own precocity. He also insisted that *The Plain Dealer* was his third play, preceding *The Country Wife* (Joseph Spence, *Observations, Anecdotes, and Characters of Books and Men*, ed. James M. Osborn (Oxford, 1966), i. 34). It is possible that an early version of *The Plain Dealer* (c.1673) was rejected by the theatres, and subsequently revised for production after the success of *The Country Wife*: see Robert D. Hume, 'William Wycherley: Text, Life, Interpretation', *Modern Philology*, 78 (1981), 401.

charisma was certainly enhanced by the fact that, for the first time in England, women were taking women's roles.

For his first play, *Love in a Wood, or, St James's Park* (1671) Wycherley chose a complex multiple plot. The choice was at once bold—the conduct of the plot would test his dramatic ingenuity—and cautious: better to err on the side of confusing an audience by an over-involved plot than to risk boring it by a paucity of action. The two characters highest in the social scale, the heiress Christina and her lover Valentine, move in the best circles, though not with the best results: Valentine has discovered a supposed rival in Lord Clerimont, whom he has challenged and wounded in a duel. This plot derives from Calderón's *Mañanas de abril y mayo* (Mornings of April and May), where, however, the duel proves fatal to the lover's antagonist. Wycherley wishes to concentrate on the difficulties which stem from Valentine's jealous nature, rather than on the problems arising from a fatal duel. Such problems might have been accommodated to the secondary plot (also taken from the Calderón play), involving a young rake, Ranger, and his mistress Lydia. But too much seriousness would not have fitted so comfortably with a miscellaneous group of characters somewhat lower in the social scale: a bawd (the aptly-named Mrs Joiner), her friend Mrs Crossbite, who is eager to sell her daughter Lucy's favours, and the family of Alderman Gripe, a lecherous, grasping, hypocritical Puritan. To complicate matters further, a foolish knight, Sir Simon Addleplot, has entered Gripe's service disguised as a clerk; he has designs on both Gripe's widowed sister, Lady Flippant, and his daughter Martha. Lady Flippant is a kind of go-between of the plots, being an acquaintance of both Lydia and the heiress Christina. Her male counterpart is Dapperwit, a would-be wit who attaches himself to Ranger, keeps Lucy Crossbite as his mistress, and ends up matched to Gripe's daughter.

Wycherley's friend, John Dennis, later praised his 'incomparable Vivacity':[2] certainly the action of *Love in a Wood* proceeds at a brisk pace—literally so, because many of its characters are constantly on the move. Lady Flippant travels about London in search of a second husband, while Mrs Joiner is active in visiting her many clients. Ranger, another aptly named character, is always out and about in search of pleasure and female prey. We never see him in his own lodgings; he haunts those of others, both men and women, unless he is busy in St James's Park. That park is the habitat of the predatory

---

[2] *The Critical Works of John Dennis*, ed. E. N. Hooker (Baltimore, 1939–43), i. 158.

male, being the prime site in London for sexual foraging. And it is to the park that Lydia pursues him. Given his natural inconstancy, her suspicion and distrust are equally natural, but produce unfortunate complications, since they lead Ranger to Christina's lodgings. As Lydia very justly suspects Ranger's 'faith' as a lover, so the jealous Valentine suspects, with no justice whatsoever, the fidelity of Christina. Her love for him is as 'true and generous' as he could wish, and her consuming passion ought not to be in doubt: she is 'mad' for him. But he meets her trust with suspicious pessimism, bred out of an unwillingness to believe that he can ever be fortunate. He cannot give her his trust, because he is fearful of trusting in himself.

While the Christina–Valentine and Lydia–Ranger plots turn on the need for trust, and the difficulty of trusting, the remaining intrigues show trust foolishly misplaced or betrayed. Thus Sir Simon Addleplot credulously relies on his so-called ally, Dapperwit, and on the slippery assistance of Mrs Joiner. Gripe also puts his trust in Mrs Joiner and in Lucy Crossbite's appearance of innocence, only to find himself forced to hush up a charge of attempted rape. Dapperwit, confident of his own ingenuity and *savoir-faire*, discovers that he has married a woman six months pregnant.

The verb 'discover', in its several meanings—to find out, to reveal one's identity, to betray oneself—is the key-word of the play, as characters are variously led 'out of the dark' to a discovery and recognition of others' true value, or their own shortcomings and folly. The ways in which such discoveries are made are nicely appropriate to the characters. So Dapperwit, forever racking his brains for witticisms, reveals his presence to Martha and Addleplot by laughing at his own joke. Ranger discovers the identity of the woman he has been talking to in the park only when he loses his self-control, and tries to assert his masculinity by a sexual assault.

If everyone is finally brought out of the dark, there is yet something to be said for being in it. More than one character notes that darkness is a great leveller, eliminating differences of social rank, dress, and looks. The night 'blots out all distinctions', and so gives everyone her or his chance in the sexual game. By removing the fear of recognition and shame, darkness removes inhibitions, facilitates sinful pleasures, and encourages a sense of freedom and irresponsibility among old and young alike. Even Gripe, no great frequenter of pleasure grounds, finds that he can walk in the park at night with his mistress 'because in the dark . . . there is no envy nor scandal'. The hint of licence, of the carnivalesque, particularly associated with St James's Park,

somewhat alleviates the determined self-seeking and squalid mercenariness that prevail elsewhere.

For a first play, the manner of *Love in a Wood* is assured, the
engineering of the plot skilful. The writing is not consistently
dramatic—Dapperwit's catalogue of wits (2.1.242 ff.) is a set-piece
which holds up the action—but much of it is lively and crisp, and
many scenes successfully combine laughter and tension. The entrap-
ment of Gripe (3.2.270 ff.) is a masterly example of low comedy, as
Mrs Joiner plays her hand with consummate cunning. Her role
throughout, with its oily sanctimoniousness and smooth impudence,
is a marvellous part for a comic actress.

Love in a Wood was presented by the King's Company at the
Theatre Royal, Bridges Street. In offering his second play, *The
Gentleman Dancing-Master* (1672), to their rivals, the Duke's Company, Wycherley hoped to capitalize on the talents of the two leading
comedians of that company, Edward Angel and James Nokes. Unfortunately, no cast list for the play has survived, but we can safely assign
to Angel the role of Don Diego (the adopted name of Mr James
Formal, a London merchant engaged in the Spanish trade), and to
Nokes that of Diego's nephew, Nathaniel Parris, self-styled 'Monsieur de Paris'. Having resided in Spain, Mr Formal (or Don Diego)
has uncritically copied Spanish phrases, dress, behaviour, and attitudes. His nephew, after three months in France, is correspondingly
frenchified in language, clothes, and manner. Diego is all pomp and
dogmatism; Monsieur is all flutter and shrugs. Since France and
Spain were conventionally held to be opposites in everything, the
stage is set for comic battles. Uncle and nephew trade jeers and
insults, until Monsieur is reluctantly obliged to change his French
attire to Spanish, so as to be eligible to marry Diego's daughter,
Hippolyta. This is not the end of Monsieur's humiliations. James
Nokes was particularly admired in scenes of distress and discomfiture,
where he could display a ludicrous mixture of 'piteous pusillanimity'
and consternation;[3] to show off his acting skills, and delight the
audience, Wycherley has Monsieur drubbed by Gerrard, his rival for
Hippolyta's hand.

Angel and Nokes were a renowned comic duo, and Wycherley must
have thought he had a winning formula. But the play was not a
success. After an opening run of six nights it was not taken into the

[3] Colley Cibber, *An Apology for the Life of Mr Colley Cibber*, ed. B. R. S. Fone (Ann
Arbor, 1968), 84.

repertoire, nor does it seem to have been revived during its author's lifetime. Not even the brilliance of Nokes and Angel could compensate for the tediously prolonged name-calling and the too-often banal humour. There is justice in Hazlitt's complaint that Wycherley tends to hold on to a joke or situation long after the life has gone out of it.[4]

The audience might also have been disappointed by the simplicity of the play's structure, and the lack of variety in the stage settings. Wycherley had turned again to Calderón, borrowing the main action—Hippolyta's passing off her lover Gerrard as a dancing-master—from *El maestro de danzar*, but this time declining to add very much in the way of subsidiary material. And whereas the frenzied activity of *Love in a Wood* required twelve different locations, in *The Gentleman Dancing-Master* all but one of its seven scenes take place in Diego's house, somewhere in the City of London, where Hippolyta is a virtual prisoner. Diego has decided that his daughter shall marry her cousin, Monsieur de Paris. He is also determined, having a Spanish concern for family honour, that she shall be kept out of temptation's way until the marriage is solemnized. She, for her part, is determined to escape from parental tyranny. She sets out to capture Gerrard, the most eligible bachelor of whom she has heard, but she needs to be sure that he is no rake who will seduce and abandon her, no mercenary fellow who desires only her fortune, and no tepid lover who will not reciprocate her warm feelings. Wycherley succeeds in making her both wary and sexually aroused. In her scenes with Gerrard romantic excitement is tempered by circumspection and calculation. He has literally broken into the house, through the gallery window. He is the knight rescuing the imprisoned lady, Romeo come to his Juliet.[5] But he climbs through the window only because Hippolyta has ingeniously brought herself to his attention. In their dialogues, the signs of innocence—blushes, sighs, bashfulness—and the expressions of youthful ardour and commitment are qualified by a spice of archness and bawdiness in the lovers' language. Tension is maintained by the testing of Gerrard (will he prove a fit partner?), and by putting the relationship under constant external threat: the lovers are always liable to be interrupted, Gerrard's disguise as dancing-master is always on the point of being seen through, and time

---

[4] *Lectures on the English Comic Writers*, in *The Complete Works of William Hazlitt*, ed. P. P. Howe, (London and Toronto, 1930–4), vi. 78–9.

[5] Peter Holland notes the relationship to *Romeo and Juliet* in his edition of Wycherley's plays (Cambridge, 1981), 117.

presses—Don Diego intends to marry his daughter to her cousin within a day or two. Wycherley's handling of this developing relationship more than compensates for *longueurs* elsewhere.

Very unusually, the play begins with a dialogue between two female characters, and it tilts the balance throughout in favour of female intelligence and initiative. Having in effect invited Gerrard into the house, Hippolyta not only invents his dancing-master role, but also makes most of the running in their conversations. His wits are certainly slower than hers: her pretended fear that Gerrard might carry her off, a palpable inducement to him to declare his feelings, is a bait which he is comically slow to take; 'Dull, dull man of the town', she exclaims, aside. In a parallel episode the much more obtuse Monsieur de Paris fails to respond to the maid's less subtle advances. Women are everywhere the pacemakers. Monsieur learns that during his three months abroad prostitutes have taken to hunting out the men, who are now forced to hide ignominiously and keep their addresses secret. It is Flirt, one of this new breed of aggressive prostitute (Don Diego suspects that she and her companion Flounce may be men in disguise), who succeeds in signing up Monsieur as her new keeper at the end of the play. Even Hippolyta's aunt, the literally short-sighted Mrs Caution, is more perceptive than her supposedly vigilant brother Don Diego. The women may not be paragons (Mrs Caution is a prurient prude), but they are much more astute than the men. So the play challenges, albeit mildly, the intellectual supremacy of the male, as it also challenges the authority of parents. Its final words are spoken by Hippolyta, recommending a new priority in matters of the heart:

> When children marry, parents should obey,
> Since love claims more obedience far than they.

The dancing-master ruse, thought up on the spur of the moment, and on behalf of true love, is a very different matter from the scheme devised by the protagonist of *The Country Wife* (1675). Harry Horner, a notorious womanizer, successfully spreads the rumour that a cure for venereal disease has rendered him impotent. There is a faint echo here of the *Eunuchus* of the Roman dramatist Terence, in which a young man gains entry to a girl's room by posing as a eunuch; once inside he proceeds to rape her. If Wycherley did indeed borrow that portion of the *Eunuchus*, he refined and intellectualized it almost beyond recognition. Horner's stratagem is a preposterous practical joke, its audacity increasing the risk of discovery, and therefore the audience's comic anxiety. But the stratagem is also the starting-point of a clinical analysis of current sexual mores. As he tells the quack doctor who has helped disseminate the rumour, Horner has, first, a satirical objective: his disparagement of himself will throw into relief the more common vanity of sexual braggarts, a point which is forcefully taken up in the epilogue. His second objective is more practical: wary husbands and keepers, to whose womenfolk Horner the notorious rake could get no access, will now cheerfully accept the harmless Horner into their homes. Enter on cue Sir Jasper Fidget, preoccupied with political affairs, and his female entourage; he proceeds to do exactly as Horner has predicted. When these visitors have departed, Horner declares the further great advantage of his deception: a lascivious woman, by spontaneously revealing her aversion to his company, will identify herself as his seducible target; however great her pretence of respectability, she evidently 'loves the sport'. Lady Fidget and her sister have already more than hinted at their real feelings, and the full proof of this part of Horner's thesis will soon begin to emerge. Finally, the trick is eminently labour-saving. Sir Jasper hastens to his own undoing, and Horner has only to open his mouth for the luscious fruit to fall into it.

Jack Pinchwife, the ex-rake newly married to a country wife, is quite another sort of husband from Sir Jasper, being jealous, tyranni-cal, and brutal. In ignorance of Horner's allegedly damaged condition, he somewhat implausibly courts disaster by visiting the greatest womanizer in London. Pinchwife, boasting his knowledge of the town, is determined not to be cuckolded, but proves quite as obliging as Sir Jasper. He dismisses his sister Alethea's suggestion that his wife should wear her mask when they visit the shops; wearing a mask ensures secrecy, but stimulates curiosity. Instead he has Margery put on a man's suit. He thus exposes her figure, as well as her face, to Horner's delighted gaze, while the playwright exposes to the audience the shapely legs of Elizabeth Boutell, famous for her breeches roles. Persevering in his foolishness, Pinchwife instructs Margery in the art of letter-writing, so opening a fatal line of communication with Horner, and is finally duped into leading his wife to her admirer's arms and bed.[6]

---

[6] The Pinchwife plot owes much to Molière. From *L'École des femmes* comes the middle-aged man thinking to marry securely by marrying an ignorant country girl. From *L'École des maris* come the substituted love-letter and the passing off of one woman for another.

Men's attitudes towards women, especially towards wives, are palpably inadequate, foolish, selfish, and unjust. Pinchwife is the keeper-turned-husband only because the women he tried to keep threw him over. Sir Jasper considers his wife simply as part of his equipage, a piece of decorative property. In the secondary plot, Sparkish, a mere would-be wit, self-satisfied and vain, is almost as purely indifferent to his fiancée Alethea as Sir Jasper is to his wife. Sparkish's incentives to marriage are financial (Alethea's dowry) and social: an attractive wife will enhance his standing among the wits. He is thus not unlike Sir Jasper. But like the vindictive Pinchwife, as a married man he will also enjoy the satisfaction of exercising power over a chattel. He does not hesitate to bully Alethea: 'let me have an earnest [i.e. foretaste] of your obedience, or—', and his fury, when he believes her false, matches Pinchwife's viciousness.

As Horner's scheme has the elegance of a mathematical proof, so the relationships and personalities in the play abound in parallels and antitheses. Pinchwife and Sir Jasper, alike in each having a wife and sister, and in sharing a cuckold's fate, are opposed in their respectively suspicious and credulous natures. But while Sir Jasper's wife and sister have much in common, including Horner, Pinchwife's sister and wife are opposites: London sophistication combined (unusually) with fidelity on one side, rustic inexperience and sexual eagerness on the other. Margery too modestly describes herself as a 'homely country girl'. She is no peasant; her brother is 'Sir James'. Socially and sexually she is the equal of the two Fidget ladies and their companion, Mistress Squeamish. What Margery lacks is their vocabulary (she does not know the meaning of 'jealousy' or 'ruin'), the discretion which serves to deceive a husband, and the good breeding which serves to clothe naked lust. She has the same desires as the hypocritical Lady Fidget, but her own inimitably direct way of expressing them: 'when I think of my husband I tremble and am in a cold sweat, and have inclinations to vomit, but when I think of my gallant, dear Mr Horner, my hot fit comes, and I am all in a fever indeed.'

For both Margery and Lady Fidget success with Horner depends on risky improvising and subterfuge. Margery's skills are exercised in her own lodgings, where she is ably abetted by Lucy, the resourceful maid. Lady Fidget, however, is actually embracing Horner in his lodgings, on the brink of easy success, when she is thwarted by the inopportune appearance of her husband. With nice irony Sir Jasper, having produced a crisis by his arrival, is made to suggest the way out of it. He reminds his wife that she told him she was going out to buy china. Since china-houses (shops specializing in oriental goods) were favoured places for assignations, a little inventiveness by Lady Fidget and Horner is sufficient to convert the latter's adjoining bedroom into a china-house in every sense. Such impromptu solutions are the stuff of farce. And just as in farce, too, doors and windows, the means of ingress and rapid egress, have important roles, so now the several doors in Horner's lodgings come splendidly into their own. Lady Fidget steps into the bedroom, on the pretext of searching out his china, and locks the door decisively behind her. Horner thereupon disappears through another door, going in to Lady Fidget the 'back way', as her husband innocently observes. And now a new arrival, the lustful Mistress Squeamish, not to be outdone in the search for the precious china, tries, unsuccessfully, another possible route into the bedroom. Meanwhile the Quack, the concealed spectator of lust and cuckoldom, voices his and the audience's incredulity: 'This, indeed, I could not have believed from him [i.e. on Horner's mere word], nor any but my own eyes.' For the Quack, as for us, seeing is indeed believing. And as Mistress Squeamish leaves on her search, another basic principle of farce—the more the funnier—comes into play; we begin to wonder just how many more women are in pursuit of Horner's china. The answer is a genuine *coup de théâtre*: enter Old Lady Squeamish, looking about her and asking 'Where is this . . .?' The audience's reaction, to put it crudely, is, 'Grandma too!' But Old Lady Squeamish, completing her sentence, reveals that she is anxiously seeking not Horner but her errant granddaughter. This joke is on us, a moment of recoil before the scene sweeps to its climax, with the reappearance of a frustrated Mistress Squeamish and, from the bedroom, a triumphant Lady Fidget. She carries a tall, cylindrical vase. She is the sole possessor (for the time being) of Horner's china. As she gloats over her success she will no doubt stroke and fondle the phallic object, while Horner, a little breathless, admits that he has no more china left. In its combination of caustic satire, bawdiness, and high-spirited farce the scene is unsurpassed.

Thanks to his own and the women's dissimulation, the course of Horner's lust runs smoothly, until Margery's naïve truthfulness threatens exposure. The course of true love is not so fortunate. Horner's friend Harcourt falls in love with the affianced Alethea. Since she is inflexibly true to her contract to marry Sparkish, despite the attractiveness of Harcourt, she can be released only when Sparkish, in a jealous rage, rejects her, believing her to be about to marry Horner. The bond between Sparkish and his betrothed is snapped, but since Horner refuses to deny that Alethea has visited him, her honour is compromised. Her good name is as really precious to her as it is a mere useful convenience for Lady Fidget and the 'virtuous gang'. So it is left to Harcourt, with total faith in Alethea's virtue, to step forward as her champion: 'I will not only believe your innocence myself, but make all the world believe it.'

Harcourt's words shine brightly in a naughty world. Wycherley is not the complete cynic that some critics have described. On the other hand, Harcourt is no moral heavyweight. His wooing of Alethea has involved him in some farcical absurdities; the presence of a genuine parson in the last scene of the play reminds us that Harcourt had earlier so disguised himself in order to defeat Sparkish. And Alethea's honour is really secured by Lucy's confession, not by Harcourt's chivalric protestation. Though not utterly cynical, Wycherley is certainly sceptical about our motives and conduct. Even Alethea's final words of advice to her brother—'Women and fortune are truest still to those that trust 'em'—are not quite as final as they seem, being uttered in the presence of the egregiously trusting Sir Jasper and his egregiously unfaithful wife. Evidently there are kinds and degrees of trust, as there are of love and honour.

Since the 1950s *The Country Wife* has been fairly often revived, allowing us to judge the effectiveness of the play where it should be judged—in the theatre. Such is not the case with the other plays. *The Gentleman Dancing-Master* has been performed only on rare occasions this century, while *Love in a Wood* disappeared from view in 1718. Wycherley's last play, *The Plain Dealer* (1676), was revived by the Royal Shakespeare Company in 1988 after a gap of nearly two hundred and fifty years. Even the RSC quailed before the play's inordinate length (half of the third act was omitted), and by cautiously softening its harsh physicality somewhat muffled its impact. To experience *The Plain Dealer* in the theatre ought to be an unsettling affair. The play is deliberately designed to prevent any easy response, so that Wycherley must have been doubly gratified by the first-night reaction. He told John Dennis that the well-bred members of the audience 'appeared Doubtful what Judgment to form' of the play, until a group of aristocrats and men of letters, friends of the author, led the applause.[7]

---

[7] *Critical Works of John Dennis*, ed. Hooker, ii. 277.

Wycherley puzzles and disconcerts us even before the curtain rises. Restoration prologues often tease and mock their audiences, but this prologue, delivered by the Plain Dealer (Captain Manly) of the play's title, handles us very roughly. The speaker knows that we hate plain dealing, which immediately sets him at odds with us. He threatens to display us as we are, which makes us feel uncomfortable. He then deprives us of what refuge we might have taken in the turns of the plot by announcing that the 'fine woman' (Manly's mistress, Olivia) is a 'mercenary jilt', and that Manly's perfect friend (Mr Varnish) will 'break his trust'. So much for dramatic surprise. We had best abandon our normal expectations of theatrical entertainment and attend, painful as it may be, to an unflattering depiction of human nature.

To display us as we are, a satirist will distort and magnify, paradoxically using not photographic realism, but exaggeration and simplification, to make us attend to what is being said. Verisimilitude and consistency of character will have to give way to satirical purpose. So in one and the same scene (2.1) Olivia is both foolishly transparent in her hypocritical 'aversion' to society, and cleverly witty as she practises character-assassination. She is less a rounded character than a tool of the satirist, used by him to demonstrate, first, the absurdities of affectation, and then the fashionable malice that passes for wit and raillery. Even more obvious tools of the satirist are Manly's visitors and self-styled friends. Given his well-known truculence and violent propensities, their persistence in seeking his company is downright masochistic. They stick to him only so that their shortcomings—the insincerity of the obsequious Lord Plausible, the mercenariness of the lawyer, and so on—can be thoroughly shown up. The final episode of Act 3, where a string of Manly's acquaintances is sent packing, has the formal structure of those classical verse-satires which parade before us a series of satirical exempla. Then, in a sort of coda, Manly and Freeman, his second-in-command, discuss where they might dine. The sole purpose of the dialogue is to air once more the topic of flattery, and to utter a lament for the decay of old-fashioned hospitality, quite in the tradition of Elizabethan and Jacobean satire on that theme.

The plain dealer, the agent of satire, is a kind of legislator, judging and passing sentence on his fellows. Conversely, a legislator ought to be a plain dealer, a truth-teller. But the play's third act, set among the courts of justice in Westminster Hall, demonstrates that plain dealing is the last virtue one can expect to find among lawyers. The formula of the satiric parade is used here too; a sequence of legal persons reveal their inadequacies and dubious motives while they are being briefed by the litigious Widow Blackacre. The Widow herself is slenderly linked with the Manly–Olivia plot. She is a relative of Olivia, and Manly is the principal witness in a legal action which she has on hand. More important, she is at the centre of the sub-plot, being sought in marriage by both Lieutenant Freeman and Major Oldfox, a Civil War veteran (as he boasts) who has turned to authorship. A woman 'at law and difference with all the world' is appropriately pursued by representatives of the armed forces. Litigation is in the Widow's blood, is, indeed, her very life-blood. We may not wish to go as far as Voltaire, who thought her 'the most comical Character that was ever brought upon the Stage',[8] but her energy and the intensity of her obsession with the law make her the most powerful 'humours' character in Restoration Comedy, a worthy successor to the monomaniacs of Ben Jonson.

Belligerent and self-opinionated, the Widow has affinities with Manly. Like him, she relishes 'discontent' and is happiest when doing battle. When her son Jerry rashly strikes at her pride by sneering at her 'pettifogging', she is willing to sully her name by declaring him illegitimate, as Manly is prepared to sacrifice his honour to his revenge when he discovers Olivia's falsehood. As in the previous plays, parallels and contrasts meet us at every turn. So Oldfox and the pert, loud-mouthed Mr Novel are described as foils to each other, the one harking back to the past, the other delighting only in what is new. Both Novel and Lord Plausible are vain admirers and eventual dupes of Olivia, though their styles of address have nothing in common. In Act 2 Manly contrasts Novel's 'fashionable impudence' with Plausible's 'languishing affected tone', even while he links them in abuse as 'a pair of musk-cats', as 'so like women that you may think it in me a kind of cowardice to beat you.' This is a scene of insult and violence, in which a character called Manly brands one of his adversaries with manneriness (excessive civility), and both of them with their 'effeminacy', while Olivia sneers at the 'manly roughness' of Manly's voice. Throughout the play moral qualities are set against their antitheses and perversions, a procedure which has strong affinities with Aristotle's discussion of the virtues in his *Nicomachean Ethics*. For Aristotle, each virtue occupies the middle ground between two extremes, between a deficiency of that particular quality and an excess of it. Thus generosity lies between miserliness and prodigality.

---

[8] Voltaire, *Letters Concerning the English Nation* (London, 1733), 185.

Such a diagrammatic presentation would have appealed to Wycherley's rather schematic cast of mind. In *The Plain Dealer*, as we have seen, manliness is opposed to effeminacy, but also to vindictive brutality. The related quality of courage finds its antitheses in cowardice or timidity (as exemplified in Jerry's attitude towards his mother) and in desperate rashness, a suspicion of which hangs over Manly's reported conduct in the sea-fight which has taken place just before the play begins. Plain speaking is the reverse of flattery and hypocrisy, but may slide into churlishness and contradiction for contradiction's sake. Wit is opposed to dull insipidity (the complaint against Major Oldfox) but also to noisy buffoonery, with which Novel mistakenly identifies it.

For all its scrutiny of vices and virtues, *The Plain Dealer* is no morality play, as its protagonist is no disinterested analyst of society's failings. Betrayed by Olivia, Manly reacts with vengeful fury. Obsessed by her ('I cannot live unless I have her'), he plots to enjoy her without revealing his own identity, and so to cuckold her as-yet-unidentified husband. But he is forced to lie in order to keep his obsession a secret, and avoid men's scorn:

> How hard it is to be an hypocrite!
> At least to me, who am but newly so.

Manly is not the only character to soliloquize in blank verse. His devoted Fidelia, having followed him to sea disguised as a cabin-boy, is the unhappy witness of his infatuation with the worthless Olivia. She suffers yet more when Manly employs her as an instrument of his revenge. At the end of her third, anguished soliloquy she not unnaturally 'sits down and weeps'. But worse is to come later in the scene (4.2), when Varnish, Olivia's husband, discovers that the cabin-boy is in fact a young woman. True to his nature, he threatens her with rape.

Earlier in the same scene, however, we have watched Fidelia's near-farcical evasions of the lascivious advances of Olivia—and this is by no means the only instance of a violent swing in the mood of the play. Wycherley deliberately prevents us from assigning it comfortably to a given mode. Are we watching tragicomedy, or farce, or comedy of humours, or dramatic satire? Our judgement is continually jolted and unsettled, kept in a state of bewildered alertness. Nowhere is this more emphatically so than at the end of the play; nowhere more subtly so than in the discussion of *The Country Wife* conducted by Olivia and her circle (2.1.379 ff.). This scene is indebted to Molière's

Critique de l'école des femmes, most obviously in having dramatic characters discuss and defend an earlier play that has fallen under censure. More interestingly, Wycherley borrows the name of Eliza (Olivia's cousin) from Molière, and makes her the most Molièresque character, with her moderation and intelligence, in all his plays. She sensibly declines to follow Olivia in confounding life and art: 'I cannot think the worse of my china for that of the playhouse.' But at the end of the discussion she produces a dizzying confusion of her own as she goes off to see *The Country Wife*, 'which is acted today, or another of the same beastly author's, as you call him'. She is leaving the stage to join the audience who are watching her leave the stage. Perhaps, then, we are in effect watching ourselves?

The final scene, however, forcefully tells us that we are watching characters in a play, characters behaving according to theatrical conventions of romantic feeling. Manly, realizing (at last) that Fidelia is a woman, accepts her devotion and her fortune, and does so in uncharacteristically elegant phrases. Here the departure from Wycherley's principal source, *Le Misanthrope*, is most evident. The misanthropic, inflexible protagonist of Molière's play is betrayed, as Manly is, by a false woman, and declines to make his addresses to another. At the end, a rather ridiculous figure, he intends to remain a man of honour; but he intends to do so, illogically, in some spot remote from mankind. Manly, redeemed by the love and money of a good woman, is reconciled to the world—and if we think this implausible and unrealistic, so does the author. The prologue has already demanded:

> where else, but on stages, do we see
> Truth pleasing, or rewarded honesty?

At the play's end we are indubitably in a world of make-believe, but the happy ending that Wycherley has provided makes a wry comment on life. Truth ought to be pleasing, and honesty ought to receive its just deserts, in the world that we re-enter as we leave the theatre.

The abrupt transition to the mode of romance, then, is not a lurch into inconsistency, but the play's final satiric stratagem, the last device by which it seeks to open our eyes to ourselves. Though some of its elements are clearly not satiric—the pathos of Fidelia, the emotional turmoil of Manly—they contribute to that unsettling of our equilibrium on which the effectiveness of satire depends. In assessing the play we could do worse than follow two of Wycherley's literary friends: *The Plain Dealer*, said Dryden, is 'one of the most bold, most general, and most useful satires which has ever been presented on the English theatre'.[9] John Dennis similarly commended it as 'that excellent Play, which is a most instructive, and a most noble Satire upon the Hypocrisy and Villainy of Mankind'.[10] When they wished to praise its author more compendiously, his contemporaries referred to him as 'Manly Wycherley'. They were not simple-mindedly identifying the protagonist of *The Plain Dealer* with the playwright. It would have been manifestly absurd to do so: Wycherley was certainly very witty, but was, by all accounts, gentle, affable, and courteous. His contemporaries meant that in his works he does not soften harsh truths, does not avoid what is squalid and base, but deals plainly and outspokenly with his fellow men and women. He is a tough-minded satirist, his toughness of attitude matched by a colloquial toughness and forcefulness of language. So George Granville judged his writings 'severe and bold', and described him as an author who 'seems without Mercy' in presenting his true and perfect dissection of humankind.[11] And John Evelyn, in an often-quoted tribute, foresaw that Wycherley's works would never lose their relevance, our natures being what they are:

> As long as Men are false, and Women vain,
> While Gold continues to be Virtues bane,
> In pointed Satyr Wycherley shall Reign.[12]

[9] Dryden, *Of Dramatic Poesy and Other Critical Essays*, ed. George Watson (London, 1962), i. 199.

[10] *Critical Works*, ed. Hooker, i. 157.

[11] 'A Character of Mr Wycherley', in *Letters of Wit, Politicks and Morality* (London, 1701), 255.

[12] Cited in Gerard Langbaine, *An Account of the English Dramatick Poets* (Oxford, 1691), 515.

NOTE ON STAGING

WYCHERLEY'S four comedies were first produced at three different theatres: *Love in a Wood* at the Theatre Royal, Bridges Street, which was destroyed by fire in 1672; *The Gentleman Dancing-Master* at the Dorset Garden Theatre, the new home of the Duke's Company; *The Country Wife* and *The Plain Dealer* at the rebuilt Theatre Royal, opened in 1674. Wycherley's use of the physical resources of these three playhouses was relatively austere; he was content to achieve his effects with a limited number of the basic elements which they had in common.

In front of the proscenium arch extended a deep forestage, its walls containing two doors on either side. (Some theatre historians favour a single door on each side.) Actresses and actors normally entered the playing area through these doors; it is likely that in all interior scenes one of the two doors nearest the audience regularly represented the entrance from/exit to the street. The corresponding door on the opposite side of the stage would normally be assumed to be the way into a bedroom or closet. During scenes located inside a house or lodgings the audience has to ignore the fact that these versatile doors are equipped with knockers, and can therefore be readily transformed into the front doors of London houses for scenes which take place in the street. The doors were hinged upstage, and opened off-stage, so a partly opened door is a convenient place for spying or overhearing. In the scenes in *Love in a Wood* which are set in St James's Park a half-opened door may function as a concealing bush or tree (as in 5.1), while all four doors are used for entrances and exits as though they led into and out of the shaded alleys and walks of the park.

Behind the frame of the proscenium arch were sets of wings, perhaps three in all, and behind them the back-scene or back-shutter. The stage-directions 'Enter at a distance' and 'Enter behind' probably mean that the actor emerges from between the furthest wing and the back-scene. The latter consisted of two flats (canvas stretched over a wooden frame) which slid together from opposite sides of the stage to meet in the centre. The flats ran in a groove between battens fixed to the stage-floor, with guide-rails suspended from the flies to keep them upright. A second (perhaps also a third) groove, immediately behind the first, enabled the back-scene to be quickly changed; as the front pair of shutters was slid away, those for the following scene were already in position. A similar system of grooves and rails allowed for changes of the wings, though a full change of wings and back-shutter would be carried out only when the action moved from an indoor to an outdoor setting, and vice versa, or for a distinctive location—the New Exchange shopping mall in *The Country Wife* (3.2), or Westminster Hall in *The Plain Dealer* (3.1). When one interior scene succeeded another, it is likely that the wings—showing panelled or plastered walls—would remain unchanged. All changes of scenery took place in full view of the audience. The front curtain, suspended just behind the proscenium arch, was raised after the prologue had been spoken, and was not lowered until the end of the epilogue.

On several occasions Wycherley has characters 'discovered' on stage. At the beginning of 4.4 of *The Country Wife* Mrs Pinchwife is revealed at her writing-table. At the beginning of 5.2 of *The Plain Dealer* Manly and Fidelia are sitting at a table in the Cock tavern. Such 'discoveries' were presumably accomplished by means of what we may call a 'forward shutter', with its own groove and rail, positioned perhaps midway between the proscenium arch and the back-scene. So 5.1 of *The Plain Dealer*, set in Eliza's lodgings, would have been played with this forward shutter (representing a standard domestic interior) as its background. Before the scene concludes, a table and chairs have been placed behind the shutter, and Manly and Fidelia have taken their seats. When the forward shutter is drawn back they are revealed against a back-scene representing a tavern interior. After Fidelia's exit Manly can remain at the table while he talks to Freeman. When Varnish enters, however, Manly will come forward to meet and embrace him, and their conversation can proceed on the forestage. We may suppose that most of Wycherley's scenes were played on the forestage, not merely so that the sallies of wit would be clearly heard, and facial expressions clearly seen, but also so that jibes directed at the audience would have maximum effect. Monotony of staging is avoided by using the forward part of the rear stage in discovery scenes, and by employing the full depth of the stage in scenes which depict bustling activity in St James's Park, or the New Exchange, or Westminster Hall.

More than half of the fifteen scenes in *Love in a Wood* take place at night. In the first park scene the fact of darkness is established by Ranger's opening speech, informing the audience that it is midnight; later, boys arrive carrying lighted torches. In all night scenes the chandeliers over the stage probably remained fully lit, but subsidiary lighting, such as candles held on vertical battens in the wings, could have been extinguished or shaded to give a hint of darkness. In exterior night scenes the moon could be depicted on the back-shutter; alternatively, a circle of gauze, inserted into the back-shutter and illuminated from behind, would create a semblance of moonlight. For indoor scenes night-time was indicated simply by a character (often a servant) bringing on a lighted candle, or by a 'discovered' table with a candle upon it. Once the candle is extinguished or removed (as in *The Country Wife*, 5.1; *The Plain Dealer*, 4.2 and 5.3) the characters are assumed to be really in the dark, while their gropings and blunders are, of course, clearly visible to the audience.

For their part, the members of the audience were clearly visible to one another and to the actors, since the auditorium was well-lit, by chandeliers and wall-sconces, throughout the performance. A dramatist could flatter or satirize particular groups of spectators (persons of quality in the boxes, wits and critics in the pit), knowing that their reactions would be observed by others in the audience. The prologues and epilogues to Restoration plays regularly exploit the visibility of the spectators, but Wycherley, more than most of his contemporaries, delights to erase the boundary between actors and audience in the course of the play itself. The discussion of 'stage fools' in *The Country Wife* (3.2.102 ff.) would have been all the sharper for being aimed at an illuminated auditorium, in a relatively small, intimate theatre, where six or seven hundred spectators would have constituted a 'good house'.

NOTE ON THE TEXTS

SOME authors are given to revising their work once it is in print. Wycherley was not. For each of his four plays the first quarto edition, deriving from his own manuscript, is the only authoritative text.

Love in a Wood was published early in 1672 (the year given on the title-page) or possibly late in 1671. It is the least satisfactory of the quartos, with more than its fair share of omissions and errors.

Two features of the first quarto of *The Gentleman Dancing-Master* (1673) call for particular comment:

First, the printer's difficulties with Don Diego's unfamiliar Spanish expressions were finally resolved only in W. C. Ward's edition of Wycherley (Mermaid Series, 1888). I have silently incorporated his emendations.

Secondly, to indicate the pronunciation of the mangled French and corrupted English used by Monsieur de Paris, Q1 sprinkles his speeches, rather too lavishly, with grave accents. I have eliminated the accent wherever the frenchified sound is clear from the spelling alone (e.g. 'indèet', 'vèl', 'wàt'). Where the accent simply tells us that Monsieur is using a French word ('Bòn, bòn'), the modern convention of printing foreign words in italic fulfils the same role. Additionally, however, an accent is employed to mark an exaggerated emphasis on a final syllabic 'e', both in French ('Cousinè') and in English ('tinkè', 'oatè', for 'think' and 'oath'). I have retained the accent only where Monsieur puts the stress unexpectedly at the end of an English word ('togedèr', 'vanitỳ'), elsewhere relying on the actor or reader to lean heavily and ludicrously on all Monsieur's final 'e's—some of which, as in 'amoure', are his own invention. Since it is unfair to make Monsieur even more incorrect to the reader's eye than he is to the spectator's ear, I have modified his French in a few cases where no change of pronunciation is involved; so the quarto's 'les grosse villaines' becomes *les grosses vilaines*.

The first quarto of *The Country Wife* (1675) is a carefully printed text, its errors mainly confined to speech-prefixes. Punctuation is light, but not always unambiguous.

In contrast, the first quarto of *The Plain Dealer* (1677) is notable for a heavy punctuation which contributes to the thrusting forcefulness of the play's satire. Four significant new readings appeared in the second quarto (published late 1677 or early 1678). Arthur Friedman suggested that they were perhaps authorial changes, but they can be satisfactorily accounted for as corrections of mistakes made by the compositor of Q1.

In the present edition readings from errata lists (in the first quartos of *Love in a Wood* and *The Gentleman Dancing-Master*) have been silently accepted, and typographical and other obvious errors (accidental duplication of words, *Exeunt* for *Exit*, and so on) have been silently corrected. Other departures from the texts of the first quartos are recorded in the notes. Where the new reading derives from an early edition and has generally been accepted in later ones, the note records only the faulty reading of Q1, without further comment. More controversial emendations are discussed in the notes, as are the conjectural additions (enclosed in square brackets) to the text of *Love in a Wood*.

Square brackets are also used for editorial modifications of the original scene-locations and stage-directions, except where a character's name replaces a pronoun in Q1, or is added to an *Exit*. I have removed almost all directions of the *Manet Fidelia sola* type, and have dropped *Omnes* after a final *Exeunt*. I have retained the formula *Enter X to Y* only when X evidently approaches Y with particular urgency. Stage-directions in all the quartos sometimes appear earlier, and frequently somewhat later, than the point at which the stage-business occurs; I have repositioned them, drawing attention in the notes to those cases where there is room for conjecture. A change of addressee within a speech, or a shift from speaking 'aside' to speaking 'aloud', is normally indicated by a dash, but I have sometimes added [*Aloud*] or [*To X*] for the sake of clarity. In both stage-directions and speech-prefixes the names of characters have been standardized: 'My Lady Fidget' becomes 'Lady Fidget'. Emended speech-prefixes are placed in square brackets.

The punctuation of the quartos commands respect, since it often helps us to hear how the lines should be spoken—a fractional pause for emphasis at one point, a longer pause to create a balanced cadence at another. Wycherley's commas have therefore been jettisoned only when they might impede or mislead the reader. Markedly emphatic speech is indicated in the quartos sometimes by additional commas, sometimes by the use of initial capital letters ('make you Dance thus': *The Gentleman Dancing-Master*, 5.1.73), or by italics. I have either substituted an equivalent stage-direction, such as 'emphatically', or have commented on the original typography in the notes. On a few occasions I have added italics where the tartness of a stressed pronoun or verb might be overlooked. The dash is a special case, being worked very hard in all the quartos. When it clearly represents hesitancy, or faltering speech, or a meaningful pause, it is here replaced by three dots. But it is also used to signal that appropriate stage-business should be supplied by the actor or envisaged by the reader. When the maid Lucy says to Alethea 'Well—Madam, now have I dress'd you' (*The Country Wife*, 4.1.1), the dash suggests that, even as she speaks, she is making final adjustments to her mistress's clothes. Sometimes the quarto text leaves ample room for unstated business, the dash being pointedly followed by a jump to a new line of type, as when Olivia responds to her husband's enquiry as to why she is alone in the dark:

Blame not my melancholy in your absence—. . . But, my soul, since you went . . . (*The Plain Dealer*, 4.2.132–3)

The gap after 'absence' is waiting to be filled by an exaggeratedly doleful sigh. In such cases I have either inserted a likely stage-direction or suggested a possible piece of business in the notes.

Spelling has been modernized, including the characters' names (Vernish becomes Varnish) and foreign words (*fourmage* becomes *fromage*). The standard forms of proper names are used—Hippolyta and Alethea, instead of the quartos' Hippolita and Alithea—except in the case of place-names, where the spelling may reflect a contemporary or non-standard pronunciation ('Moreclack' for Mortlake), and so contribute to the dramatic effect. In late-seventeenth-century speech 'Master' was probably more common than 'Mister' when addressing an adult male; the written abbreviation 'Mr' might represent either form. Since no ambiguity arises I have left 'Mr' and 'Master' as they appear in the quartos, expanding 'Mr' only when it precedes a common noun ('Master Doctor'). The abbreviation 'Mrs', used for single as well as married women at this time, probably represented the pronunciation 'Mistress', though the word was perhaps beginning to move towards its modern pronunciation when a married woman was being addressed. To avoid confusion I have expanded 'Mrs' to 'Mistress' whenever the woman in question is unmarried ('Mistress Martha' instead of 'Mrs Martha'), or is scornfully re-christened ('Mistress Impertinence').

I owe a very great debt to my editorial predecessors, principally David Cook and John Swannell, Arthur Friedman, Peter Holland,

John Dixon Hunt, James Ogden, James Smith, and Gerald Weales. (Details of their editions are given in the list of abbreviations prefixed to the Explanatory Notes.) I have also profited from George B. Churchill's edition, *The Country Wife and The Plain Dealer* (Boston, 1924), and have learned much from the erudite notes in Montague Summers' *Complete Works of Wycherley* (4 vols.; London, 1924).

SELECT BIBLIOGRAPHY

Katharine Rogers' *William Wycherley*, in the Twayne's English Authors Series (New York, 1972), and Paul F. Vernon's booklet, with the same title, in the Writers and their Work Series (London, 1965, rev. 1970), provide balanced introductions to Wycherley's life and works—his poems and prose maxims, as well as the four comedies.

In his pioneering study, *The First Modern Comedies: The Significance of Etherege, Wycherley and Congreve* (Cambridge, Mass., 1959), Norman N. Holland analyses the patterns of contrast and opposition in the three playwrights: outward appearance against inner nature; polite manners against natural desire. Anne Righter shares his view of the love of Harcourt and Alethea as setting a moral standard in *The Country Wife*; Horner, like Manly, she considers a monomaniac (John Russell Brown and Bernard Harris (eds.), *Restoration Theatre*, Stratford-upon-Avon Studies, 6 (London, 1965), 71–91). Rose Zimbardo sees Wycherley as essentially a satirist; her *Wycherley's Drama: A Link in the Development of English Satire* (New Haven, 1965) is most persuasive on *The Plain Dealer*, but her arguments should be placed beside T. W. Craik's reservations about Wycherley's satire: 'Some Aspects of Satire in Wycherley's Plays', *English Studies*, 41 (1960), 168–79.

In *Wild Civility: The English Comic Spirit on the Restoration Stage* (Bloomington, Ind., 1970) Virginia Ogden Birdsall responds to the spiritedness of Wycherley's plays. James Thompson's *Language in Wycherley's Plays: Seventeenth-Century Language Theory and Drama* (Tuscaloosa, Ala., 1984) scrutinizes the key-words in the plays, while Robert Markley's *Two-Edg'd Weapons: Style and Ideology in the Comedies of Etherege, Wycherley and Congreve* (Oxford, 1988) takes a hard line with Harcourt, Alethea, and Manly (a self-righteous bully). An astute reading of the plays which keeps a firm eye on their stage-presence is W. R. Chadwick's *The Four Plays of William Wycherley: A Study in the Development of a Dramatist* (The Hague, 1975).

Contemporary attitudes to marriage and the status of women are surveyed by P. F. Vernon ('Marriage of Convenience and the Moral Code of Restoration Comedy', *Essays in Criticism*, 12 (1962), 370–87), and by Peter Malekin in ch. 14 of *Liberty and Love: English Literature and Society, 1640–88* (London, 1981): both authors pay particular attention to *The Country Wife*. N. J. Rigaud makes a subtle study of gender relations in 'La Femme chez Wycherley, prisonnière du regard d'autrui', *Caliban*, 17 (1980), 45–56.

John Wilcox considers what Wycherley owes to Molière in ch. 5 of *The Relation of Molière to Restoration Comedy* (New York, 1938).

Love in a Wood and *The Gentleman Dancing-Master*

Good criticism is to be found in the books by Vernon, Birdsall, Holland, and Chadwick. In 'Wycherley's First Comedy and its Spanish Source', *Comparative Literature*, 18 (1966), 132–44, P. F. Vernon argues that the virtues of *Love in a Wood* more than outweigh its weaknesses.

The Country Wife

Some of the critical approaches to this play are usefully brought to the test of audience response by John T. Harwood in *Critics, Values, and Restoration Comedy* (Carbondale, Ill., 1982). A complementary account, by Judith Milhous and Robert D. Hume, in their *Producible Interpretation: Eight English Plays, 1675–1707* (Carbondale, Ill., 1985) welcomes the openness of the text, suggesting that the play can plausibly be read and performed as social satire, or libertine comedy, or farce. R. Edgley sees *The Country Wife* as a critique of folly, with wit and intelligence triumphing over stupidity ('The Object of Literary Criticism', *Essays in Criticism*, 14 (1964), 221–36). Exponents of the libertine-sex-comedy approach include Maximillian E. Novak ('Margery Pinchwife's "London Disease": Restoration Comedy and the Libertine Offensive of the 1670s', *Studies in the Literary Imagination*, 10 (1977), 1–23), and David M. Vieth: 'Wycherley's *The Country Wife*: An Anatomy of Masculinity', *Papers on Language and Literature*, 2 (1966), 335–50. In ch. 3 of *Between Men: English Literature and Male Homosocial Desire* (New York, 1985), Eve Kosofsky Sedgwick offers a provocative reading which makes cuckoldry, rather than sexual enjoyment, the mainspring of the action.

To respond to the play as farce is necessarily to consider its effectiveness on stage. C. D. Cecil's 'Libertine and Précieux Elements in Restoration Comedy', *Essays in Criticism*, 9 (1959), 239–53, examines the theatrical potential of the 'china scene'; Peter Malekin discusses 'Wycherley's Dramatic Skills and the Interpretation of *The Country Wife*', in *Durham University Journal*, 61 (1969), 32–40, and Michael Neill demonstrates the significance of the play's visual effects in 'Horned Beasts and China Oranges: Reading the Signs in *The Country Wife*', *Eighteenth-Century Life*, 12 (1988), 3–17. In chapter 7 of his *Restoration Theatre Production* (London, 1984) Jocelyn Powell guides us through the play in performance. Its theatrical allusions are explored in Harold Love's 'The Theatrical Geography of *The Country Wife*', *Southern Review* (Adelaide), 16 (1983), 404–15.

The Plain Dealer

The relationship between this play and Molière's *Le Misanthrope* is studied by A. M. Friedson in 'Wycherley and Molière: Satirical Point of View in *The Plain Dealer*', *Modern Philology*, 64 (1967), 189–97. For Friedson, Manly is the focus of the play's satire, not its butt. For Alexander Chorney, on the other hand, Manly is a strongly satirized figure, the traditional type of the Blunt Man ('Wycherley's Manly Reinterpreted,' in *Essays Critical and Historical Dedicated to Lily B. Campbell* (Berkeley, 1950), 161–9), while for Eric Rothstein and Frances M. Kavenik (*The Designs of Carolean Comedy* (Carbondale, Ill., 1988), 190–201) Manly is hero and rake.

Milhous and Hume (*Producible Interpretation*: see section on *The Country Wife* above) sensibly prompt us to consider which interpretations of *The Plain Dealer* are realizable in the theatre. The context of Restoration performance practice is most richly invoked in Peter Holland's *The Ornament of Action: Text and Performance in Restoration Comedy* (Cambridge, 1979); he shows how the play constantly subverts the audience's expectations. Ian Donaldson (' "Tables Turned": *The Plain Dealer*', *Essays in Criticism*, 17 (1967), 304–21, reprinted as ch. 5 of *The World Upside-Down: Comedy from Jonson to Fielding* (Oxford, 1970)) had earlier explored the play's 'strong feeling of contradictoriness'; more recently Laura Morrow has argued that *The Plain Dealer* 'recommends a course of action while demonstrating the impossibility of successfully pursuing it' ('Phenomenological Psychology and Comic Form in *The Plain Dealer*', *Restoration and Eighteenth-Century Theatre Research*, 2nd ser., 3 (1988), 1–10). The most positive readings of the play thus accept its complications and contradictions as central to its meaning—a position exemplified in Derek Hughes's '*The Plain-Dealer*: A Reappraisal', *Modern Language Quarterly*, 43 (1982), 315–36.

B. Eugene McCarthy has written the standard life—*William Wycherley: A Biography* (Athens, Ohio, 1979)—and has compiled a valuable bibliography, *William Wycherley: A Reference Guide* (Boston, 1985); it includes reviews of productions and is therefore an essential source for the stage-history of the plays.

A CHRONOLOGY OF
WILLIAM WYCHERLEY

Dates in parenthesis after the titles of the plays are those of the first recorded performances, which may (or may not) be the premières.

1641 Born, (?) 28 March, probably at Manor Farm, Whitchurch, Hampshire. Educated at home (London and Whitchurch), and at school in Shrewsbury.

1655(?) Sent to France to further his education. Introduced to courtly circle of the Marquise de Montausier, near Angoulême. Converted to Catholicism.

1659 Returns to England. Enters Inner Temple, to study law.

1660 Registers as a student at Bodleian Library, Oxford, and rejoins Church of England. Re-enters Inner Temple on 10 November.

1662 With Earl of Arran's regiment of guards in Ireland. (?) Organizes Christmas Revels at Inner Temple.

1664 (?) To Madrid in January with the English ambassador.

1665 Takes part in naval battle of Harwich (2nd Dutch War), 3 June.

1669 *Hero and Leander* (burlesque poem) published.

1671 *Love in a Wood* produced, probably in March, at the Theatre Royal, Bridges Street; published 1672. Brief affair with Duchess of Cleveland. Admitted to circle of court wits, including Duke of Buckingham.

1672 *The Gentleman Dancing-Master*, Dorset Garden Theatre (6 February); published 1673. In June is commissioned captain-lieutenant in Duke of Buckingham's regiment of foot.

1673 On active service (3rd Dutch War); stationed in Isle of Wight.

1674 Receives captain's commission in February, and leaves army.

1675 *The Country Wife*, Drury Lane Theatre (12 January); published later in year.

1676 *The Plain Dealer*, Drury Lane Theatre (11 December), published 1677.

1678 Liaison (? May) with Countess of Drogheda. Severe illness (fever? encephalitis?), causing loss of memory. The king sends him to Montpellier in the autumn to recuperate.

1679 Returns to England in spring. Offered post of tutor to the Duke of Richmond (the king's illegitimate son), with handsome salary. ? 29 September marries the recently widowed Countess of Drogheda. Loses the king's favour and the tutorship. Beginning of prolonged lawsuits over his wife's debts and (later) her first husband's will.

1682   Seeks to regain court favour with poetic *Epistles to the King and Duke* (of York).

1685   Death of Charles II, 6 February; accession of James II. Death of Wycherley's wife, ? June. Imprisoned for debt in July. Reconverts to Catholicism. *The Plain Dealer* performed 14 December at court to draw the king's attention to its author's plight.

1686   Released from prison in April; the king grants him a pension.

1688   Loses pension on accession of William III.

1696   Advertisement for proposed publication of volume of poems leads to lawsuit and brief imprisonment.

1697   Death of father, 5 May; some easing of financial problems.

1704   *Miscellany Poems* published; not a success.

1705(?) Meets Alexander Pope, who later undertakes to revise his poems.

1715   Failing health during the winter. His cousin Thomas Shrimpton, to obtain the estate, pushes him into marriage 20 December with Elizabeth Jackson, Shrimpton's mistress. Dies, 31 December.

1716   Buried in St Paul's, Covent Garden, 5 January.

LOVE IN A WOOD,°
or,
St James's Park

Excludit sanos Helicone poetas
Democritus.°

Horace

[DEDICATORY EPISTLE]
To her Grace the Duchess of Cleveland.°

Madam,

All authors whatever in their dedications are poets. But I am now to write to a lady who stands as little in need of flattery as her beauty of art—otherwise I should prove as ill a poet to her in my dedication, as to my reader in my play. I can do your Grace no honour, nor make you more admirers than you have already; yet I can do myself the honour to let the world know I am the greatest you have. You will pardon me, madam, for you know 'tis very hard for a new author (and poet too) to govern his ambition. For poets, let them pass in the world never so much for modest, honest men, but begin praise to others which concludes in themselves,° and are like rooks, who lend people money but to win it back again, and so leave them in debt to 'em for nothing. They offer laurel and incense to their heroes, but wear it themselves, and perfume themselves. This is true, madam, upon the honest word of an author who never yet writ dedication. Yet though I cannot lie like them, I am as vain as they, and cannot but publicly give your Grace my humble acknowledgements for the favours I have received from you. This, I say, is the poet's gratitude, which in plain English is only pride and ambition, and that the world might know your Grace did me the honour to see my play twice together°—yet perhaps my enviers of your favour will suggest 'twas in Lent,° and therefore for your mortification. Then, as a jealous author, I am concerned not to have your Grace's favours lessened, or rather my reputation, and to let them know you were pleased, after that, to command a copy from me of this play—the way, without beauty and wit, to win a poor poet's heart. 'Tis a sign your Grace understands nothing better than obliging all the world after the best and most proper manner. But, madam, to be obliging to that excess as you are (pardon me, if I tell you out of my extreme concern, and service for your Grace) is a dangerous quality, and may be very incommode to you. For civility makes poets as troublesome as charity makes beggars, and your Grace will be hereafter as much pestered with such scurvy offerings as this—poems, panegyrics, and the like—as you are now with petitions.° And, madam, take it from me, no man with papers in's hand is more dreadful than a poet—no, not a lawyer with his declarations. Your Grace sure did not well consider what you did, in sending for my play. You little thought I would have had the confidence to send you a dedication too; but, madam, you find I am as unreasonable, and have as little conscience, as if I had driven the poetic trade longer than I have, and ne'er consider you had enough 40 of the play. But having suffered now so severely, I beseech your Grace have a care for the future; take my counsel and be (if you can possible°) as proud and ill-natured as other people of quality, since your quiet is so much concerned, and since you have more reason than any to value yourself. For you have that perfection of beauty 45 (without thinking it so) which others of your sex but think they have; that generosity in your actions which others of your quality have only in their promises;° that spirit, wit, and judgement, and all other qualifications, which fit heroes to command, and would make any but your Grace proud. I begin now, elevated by my subject, to write with 50 the emotion and fury of a poet, yet the integrity of an historian, and I could never be weary—nay, sure this were my only way to make my readers never weary too, though they were a more impatient generation of people than they are. In fine, speaking thus of your Grace I should please all the world but you. Therefore I must once observe, 55 and obey you against my will, and say no more than that I am, madam,

Your Grace's most obliged and most humble servant,
William Wycherley.

THE PERSONS

Mr Ranger ⎫		*Mr Hart*
Mr Vincent ⎬ (young gentlemen of the town)		*Mr Bell*
Mr Valentine ⎭		*Mr Kynaston*
Alderman Gripe (seemingly precise, but a covetous, lecherous old usurer of the City)		*Mr Lacy* 5
Sir Simon Addleplot (a coxcomb, always in pursuit of women of great fortunes)		*Mr Wintersell*
Mr Dapperwit (a brisk, conceited, half-witted fellow of the town)		*Mr Mohun*
Christina (Valentine's mistress)		*Mrs Boutell* 10
Lydia (Ranger's mistress)		*Mrs Betty Cox*
My Lady Flippant (Gripe's sister, an affected widow, in distress for° a husband, though still declaiming against marriage)		*Mrs Knepp*
Mistress Martha (Gripe's daughter)		*Mrs Farlowe* 15
Mrs Joiner (a matchmaker, or precise City bawd)		*Mrs Corey*
Mrs Crossbite (an old cheating jilt, and bawd to her daughter)		*Mrs Rutter*
Miss Lucy (her daughter)		*Mrs Betty Slade*
Isabel (Christina's woman)		*Mrs James* 20
Leonore (servant to Lydia)		*Mrs Cartwright*

Mrs Crossbite's Landlord and his Prentice;° servants, waiters, and other attendants

THE SCENE

London   25

4

Prologue°

Custom, which bids the thief from cart harangue°
All those that come to make and see him hang,
Wills the damned poet (though he knows he's gone)°
To greet you ere his execution.
    Not having fear of critic 'fore his eyes,°   5
But still rejecting wholesome good advice,
He e'en is come to suffer here today
For counterfeiting (as you judge) a play,°
Which is against dread Phoebus highest treason.
Damned, damning judges, therefore you have reason—   10
You he does mean, who for the selfsame fault
That damning privilege of yours have bought;
So the huge bankers, when they needs must fail,
Send the small brothers of their trade to jail;
Whilst they, by breaking, gentlemen are made,   15
Then, more than any, scorn poor men o'th' trade.
You hardened renegado poets, who
Treat rhyming brother worse than Turk would do,°
But vent your heathenish rage, hang, draw and quarter:°
His muse will die today a fleering martyr,°   20
Since for bald jest, dull libel or lampoon
There are who suffer persecution
With the undaunted briskness of buffoon,
And strict professors live of raillery,
Defying porter's lodge or pillory.°   25
For those who yet write on, our poet's fate
Should as co-sufferers commiserate;
But he in vain their pity now would crave,
Who for themselves (alas) no pity have,
And their own gasping credit will not save.°   30
And those, much less, our criminal would spare,
Who ne'er in rhyme transgress—if such there are.°
Well then, who nothing hopes needs nothing fear;
And he, before your cruel votes shall do it,
By his despair declares himself no poet.   35

1.1

Gripe's house, in the evening
Enter Lady Flippant,° Mrs Joiner

LADY FLIPPANT Not a husband to be had for money! Come come, I might have been a better housewife for myself (as the world goes now) if I had dealt for an heir with his guardian, uncle, or mother-in-law; and you are no better than a chouse, a cheat.

MRS JOINER I a cheat, madam!　　　　　　　　　　　　　　　　　5

LADY FLIPPANT I am out of my money, and my patience too.

MRS JOINER Do not run out of your patience whatever you do; 'tis a necessary virtue° for a widow without a jointure, in truly.°

LADY FLIPPANT Vile woman! Though my fortune be something wasted, my person's in good repair. If I had not depended on you,　10 I had had a husband before this time. When I gave you the last five pound, did not you promise I should be married by Christmas?

MRS JOINER And had kept my promise if you had co-operated.

LADY FLIPPANT Co-operated! What should I have done? 'Tis well known no woman breathing could use more industry to get her a　15 husband than I have. Has not my husband's scutcheon walked as much ground as the citizens' signs since the fire,° that no quarter of the town might be ignorant of the Widow Flippant?

MRS JOINER 'Tis well known, madam, indeed.

LADY FLIPPANT Have I not owned myself (against my stomach) the　20 relict of a citizen, to credit my fortune?°

MRS JOINER 'Tis confessed, madam. ·

LADY FLIPPANT Have I not constantly kept Covent Garden Church,° St Martin's,° the playhouses, Hyde Park, Mulberry Garden, and all other the public marts where widows and maids　25 are exposed?

MRS JOINER Far be it from me to think you have an aversion to a husband. But why, madam, have you refused so many good offers?

LADY FLIPPANT Good offers, Mrs Joiner? I'll be sworn I never had　30 an offer since my late husband's. If I had had an offer, Mrs Joiner . . . there's the thing, Mrs Joiner.

MRS JOINER Then your frequent and public detestation of marriage is thought real; and if you have had no offer . . . there's the thing, madam.　　　　　　　　　　　　　　　　　　　　　　　35

6

LADY FLIPPANT I cannot deny but I always rail against marriage, which is the widow's way to it, certainly.

MRS JOINER 'Tis the desperate way of the desperate widows, in truly.

LADY FLIPPANT Would you have us as tractable as the wenches that   40
eat oatmeal,° and fooled like them too?

MRS JOINER If nobody were wiser than I, I should think, since the widow wants the natural allurement which the virgin has, you ought to give men all other encouragements, in truly.

LADY FLIPPANT Therefore, on the contrary, because the widow's   45
fortune (whether supposed, or real) is her chiefest bait, the more chary she seems of it, and the more she withdraws it, the more eagerly the busy gaping fry will bite. With us widows, husbands are got like bishoprics, by saying no;° and I tell you, a young heir is as shy of a widow as of a rook, to my knowledge.   50

MRS JOINER I can allege nothing against your practice, but your ill success; and indeed you must use another method with Sir Simon Addleplot.

LADY FLIPPANT Will he be at your house at the hour?

MRS JOINER He'll be there by ten. 'Tis now nine. I warrant you he   55
will not fail.

LADY FLIPPANT I'll warrant you then, I will not fail, for 'tis more than time I were sped.°

MRS JOINER Mr Dapperwit has not been too busy with you? I hope your experience has taught you to prevent a mischance.   60

LADY FLIPPANT No, no, my mischance (as you call it) is greater than that. I have but three months to reckon, ere I lie down with my port° and equipage, and must be delivered of a woman, a footman, and a coachman. For my coach must down,° unless I can get Sir Simon to draw with me.   65

MRS JOINER (aside) He will pair with you exactly, if you knew all.

LADY FLIPPANT Ah, Mrs Joiner, nothing grieves me like putting down my coach. For the fine clothes, the fine lodgings, let 'em go. For a lodging is as unnecessary a thing to a widow that has   70
a coach, as a hat to a man that has a good peruke; for as you see about town, she is most properly at home in her coach. She eats, and drinks, and sleeps in her coach, and for her visits—she receives them in the playhouse.

MRS JOINER Ay, ay, let the men keep lodgings (as you say, madam),   75
if they will.

7

[*Enter unobserved*] *Gripe, and Sir Simon Addleplot following him as his man* [*Jonas*] *in the habit of a clerk,° at one door, and Martha at the other*

LADY FLIPPANT Do you think, if things had been with me as they have been,° I would ever have housed with this counterfashion brother of mine (who hates a vest as much as a surplice°), to have my patches assaulted every day, at dinner my freedom censured, and my visitants shut out of doors? Poor Mr Dapperwit cannot be admitted.   80

MRS JOINER He knows him too well to keep his acquaintance.

LADY FLIPPANT He is a censorious rigid fop, and knows nothing.

GRIPE (*behind*) So, so—   85

MRS JOINER (*aside*) Is he here? (*to Lady Flippant*) Nay, with your pardon, madam, I must contradict you there. He is a prying° Commonwealth's man, an implacable magistrate, a sturdy pillar of his cause, and—(*to Gripe*) But, oh me, is your worship so near then? If I had thought you had heard me—   90

GRIPE Why, why, Mrs Joiner, I have said as much of myself ere now, and without vanity, I profess.

MRS JOINER I know your virtue is proof against vainglory, but the truth to your face looks like flattery in your worship's servant.

GRIPE No, no, say what you will of me in that kind; far be it from   95
me to suspect you of flattery.

MRS JOINER In truly, your worship knows yourself, and knows me, for I am none of those—

LADY FLIPPANT (*aside*) Now they are in.°—Mrs Joiner, I'll go before to your house. You'll be sure to come after me?   100

MRS JOINER Immediately.

    Exit Lady Flippant

But as I was saying, I am none of those—

GRIPE No, Mrs Joiner, you cannot sew pillows under folks' elbows; you cannot hold a candle to the devil; you cannot tickle a trout to take him;° you—   105

MRS JOINER Lord, how well you do know me indeed. And you shall see I know your worship as well: you cannot backslide from your principles; you cannot be terrified by the laws, nor bribed to allegiance by office or preferment;° you—

GRIPE Hold, hold, my praise must not interrupt yours.   110

MRS JOINER With your worship's pardon (in truly) I must on.

GRIPE I am full of your praise, and it will run over.

MRS JOINER Nay, sweet sir, you are—

GRIPE Nay, sweet Mrs Joiner, you are—

MRS JOINER Nay, good your worship, you are—   115
    [Gripe] stops her mouth with his handkerchief

GRIPE I say you are—

MRS JOINER I must not be rude with your worship.

GRIPE You are a nursing mother to the saints.° Through you they
    gather together, through you they fructify and increase,° and
    through you the child cries from out of the hand-basket.°   120

MRS JOINER Through you virgins are married, or provided for as
    well; through you the reprobate's wife is made a saint, and through
    you the widow is not disconsolate, nor misses her husband.

GRIPE Through you—

MRS JOINER Indeed, you will put me to the blush.   125

GRIPE Blushes are badges of imperfection;° saints have no shame.
    You are the flower of matrons, Mrs Joiner.

MRS JOINER You are the pink of courteous aldermen.

GRIPE You are the muffler° of secrecy.

MRS JOINER You are the headband° of justice.   130

GRIPE Thank you, sweet Mrs Joiner; do you think so indeed? You
    are . . . you are the bonfire of devotion.

MRS JOINER You are the bellows of zeal.

GRIPE You are the cupboard of charity.

MRS JOINER You are the fob of liberality.   135

GRIPE You are the rivet of sanctified love or wedlock.

MRS JOINER You are the picklock and dark-lantern of policy, and, in
    a word, a conventicle of virtues.

GRIPE Your servant, your servant, sweet Mrs Joiner; you have
    stopped my mouth.   140

MRS JOINER Your servant, your servant, sweet alderman; I have
    nothing to say.

SIR SIMON The half pullet will be cold, sir.

GRIPE Mrs Joiner, you shall sup with me.

MRS JOINER Indeed I am engaged to supper with some of your   145
    man's friends, and I came on purpose to get leave for him too.

GRIPE I cannot deny you anything. But I have forgot to tell you what
    a kind of fellow my sister's Dapperwit is: before a full table of the
    coffee-house sages he had the impudence to hold an argument
    against me in the defence of vests and protections,° and therefore 150
    I forbid° him my house. Besides, when he came I was forced to

lock up my daughter for fear of him—nay, I think the poor child herself was afraid of him. Come hither, child; were you not afraid of Dapperwit?

MARTHA Yes indeed, sir, he is a terrible man. (*Aside*) Yet I durst   155
meet with him in the Piazzo at midnight.°

GRIPE He shall never come into my doors again.

MARTHA Shall Mr Dapperwit never come hither again, then?

GRIPE No, child.

MARTHA I am afraid he will.   160

GRIPE I warrant thee.

MARTHA (*aside*) I warrant you then, I'll go to him. [*Aloud*] I am glad of that, for I hate him as much as a bishop.

GRIPE Thou art no child of mine, if thou dost not hate bishops and wits.° Well, Mrs Joiner, I'll keep you no longer. [*To Sir Simon*   165
Addleplot] Jonas, wait on Mrs Joiner.

MRS JOINER Good night to your worship.

GRIPE But stay, stay, Mrs Joiner; have you spoken with the Widow Crossbite about her little daughter, as I desired?

MRS JOINER I will tomorrow early; it shall be the first thing I'll do,   170
after my prayers.

GRIPE If Dapperwit should contaminate her—I cannot rest till I have redeemed her from the jaws of that lion. Good night.

MRS JOINER Good gentleman. [*Curtsies*]
        Exeunt Gripe and Martha

SIR SIMON Ha ha ha, Mrs Joiner.   175

MRS JOINER What's the matter, Sir Simon?

SIR SIMON Ha ha ha—let us make haste to your house, or I shall burst, faith and troth, to see what fools you and I make of these people.

MRS JOINER I will not rob you of any of the credit. I am but a feeble   180
instrument; you are the engineer.°

SIR SIMON Remember what you say now, when things succeed, and do not tell me then, I must thank your wit for all.

MRS JOINER No, in truly, Sir Simon.

SIR SIMON Nay, I'm sure Dapperwit and I have been partners in   185
many an intrigue, and he uses to serve me so.

MRS JOINER He is an ill man to intrigue with, as you call it.

SIR SIMON Ay, so are all your wits. A pox, if a man's understanding be not so public as theirs, he cannot do a wise action but they go away with the honour of it, if he be of their acquaintance.   190

MRS JOINER Why do you keep such acquaintance then?

SIR SIMON There is a proverb, Mrs Joiner: you may know him by
his company.

MRS JOINER No, no. To be thought a man of parts, you should
always keep company with a man of less wit than yourself.   195

SIR SIMON That's the hardest thing in the world for me to do, faith
and troth.

MRS JOINER What, to find a man of less wit than yourself? Pardon
my raillery, Sir Simon.

SIR SIMON No, no, I cannot keep company with a fool. I wonder how   200
men of parts can do't—there's something in't.°

MRS JOINER If you could, all your wise actions would be your own,
and your money would be your own too.

SIR SIMON Nay, faith and troth, that's true, for your wits are
plaguily given to borrow; they'll borrow of their wench, coachman,   205
or linkboy their hire. Mrs Joiner, Dapperwit has that trick with a
vengeance.

MRS JOINER Why will you keep company with him then, I say? For
to be plain with you, you have followed him so long, that you are
thought but his cully. For every wit has his cully, as every squire   210
his led-captain.

SIR SIMON I his cully? I his cully, Mrs Joiner? Lord, that I should
be thought a cully to any wit breathing!

MRS JOINER Nay, do not take it so to heart, for the best wits of the
town are but cullies themselves.   215

SIR SIMON To whom, to whom, to whom, Mrs Joiner?

MRS JOINER To seamstresses,° and bawds.

SIR SIMON To your knowledge, Mrs Joiner. [*Aside*] There I was with
her.

MRS JOINER To tailors and vintners, but especially to the French   220
houses.°

SIR SIMON But Dapperwit is a cully to none of them, for he ticks.

MRS JOINER I care not, but I wish you were a cully to none but
me—that's all the hurt I wish you.

SIR SIMON Thank you, Mrs Joiner. Well, I will throw off Dapper-   225
wit's acquaintance when I am married, and will only be a cully to
my wife; and that's no more than the wisest husband of 'em all is.

MRS JOINER Then you think you shall carry Mistress Martha?

SIR SIMON Your hundred guineas are as good as in your lap.

MRS JOINER But I am afraid this double plot of yours should fail.   230
You would sooner succeed if you only designed upon Mistress
Martha, or only upon my Lady Flippant.

SIR SIMON Nay then, you are no woman of intrigue, faith and troth.
'Tis good to have two strings to one bow.° If Mistress Martha be
coy, I tell the widow I put on my disguise for her. But if Mistress   235
Martha be kind to Jonas, Sir Simon Addleplot will be false to the
widow, which is no more than widows are used to, for a promise
to a widow is as seldom kept as a vow made at sea°—as Dapperwit
says.

MRS JOINER I am afraid they should discover you.   240

SIR SIMON You have nothing to fear; you have your twenty guineas
in your pocket for helping me into my service, and if I get into
Mistress Martha's quarters you have a hundred more; if into the
widow's, fifty, happy-go-lucky. Will her ladyship be at your house
at the hour?   245

MRS JOINER Yes.

SIR SIMON Then you shall see, when I am Sir Simon Addleplot and
myself, I'll look like myself. Now I am Jonas, I look like an ass.°
You never thought Sir Simon Addleplot could have looked so like
an ass by his ingenuity.   250

MRS JOINER Pardon me,° Sir Simon.

SIR SIMON Nay, do not flatter, faith and troth.

MRS JOINER Come, let us go; 'tis time.

SIR SIMON I will carry the widow to the French house.

MRS JOINER If she will go.   255

SIR SIMON If she will go? Why, did you ever know a widow refuse
a treat? No more than a lawyer a fee, faith and troth. Yet I know
too,
> No treat, sweet words, good mien, but sly intrigue—
> *That* must, at length, the jilting widow feague.   260
> *Exeunt*

1.2

The French House; a table [and chairs], wine, and candles

Enter Vincent, Ranger,° Dapperwit

DAPPERWIT Pray, Mr Ranger, let's have no drinking tonight.

VINCENT Pray, Mr Ranger, let's have no Dapperwit tonight.

RANGER Nay, nay, Vincent.

VINCENT A pox, I hate his impertinent chat more than he does the
honest burgundy.   5

DAPPERWIT But why should you force wine upon us? We are not all of your gusto.

VINCENT But why should you force your chewed jests, your damned ends of your mouldy lampoons and last year's sonnets upon us? We are not all of your gusto.

DAPPERWIT The wine makes me sick, let me perish.

VINCENT Thy rhymes make me spew.

RANGER At repartee already! Come Vincent, I know you would rather have him pledge you.—Here, Dapperwit.

Gives him the glass

But why are you so eager to have him drink always?

VINCENT Because he is so eager to talk always, and there is no other way to silence him.

[Enter] Waiter

WAITER Here is a gentleman desires to speak with Mr Vincent.

VINCENT I come.

Exit Vincent [with Waiter]

DAPPERWIT He may drink because he is obliged to the bottle for all the wit and courage he has. 'Tis not free and natural, like yours.

RANGER He has more courage than wit, but wants neither.

DAPPERWIT As a pump gone dry; if you pour no water down, you will get none out, so—

RANGER Nay, I bar similes too, tonight.

DAPPERWIT Why, is not the thought new? Don't you apprehend it?

RANGER Yes, yes, but—

DAPPERWIT Well, well, will you comply with his sottishness too, and hate brisk things in complaisance to the ignorant dull age? I believe shortly 'twill be as hard to find a patient friend to communicate one's wit to, as a faithful friend to communicate one's secret to. Wit has as few true judges as painting, I see.

RANGER All people pretend to be judges of both.

DAPPERWIT Ay, they pretend. But set you aside, and two more—

RANGER But why has Vincent neither courage nor wit?

DAPPERWIT He has no courage because he beat his wench for giving me *les douces yeux*° once; and no wit, because he does not comprehend my thoughts. And he is a son of a whore for his ignorance. I take ignorance worse from any man than the lie,° because it is as much as to say I am no wit.

Vincent returns

You need not take any notice though, to him, of what I say.

VINCENT Ranger, there is a woman below in a coach, would speak with you.

RANGER With me?   45

Exit Ranger

DAPPERWIT This Ranger, Mr Vincent, is as false to his friend as his wench.

VINCENT You have no reason to say so, but because he is absent.

DAPPERWIT 'Tis disobliging to tell a man of his faults to his face.°
If he had but your grave parts, and manly wit, I should adore him.   50
But a pox, he is a mere buffoon, a jack-pudding, let me perish.

VINCENT You are an ungrateful fellow. I have heard him maintain
you had wit, which was more than e'er you could do for yourself.
I thought you had owned him your Maecenas.

DAPPERWIT A pox, he cannot but esteem me; 'tis for his honour.   55
But I cannot but be just for all that, without favour or affection—
yet I confess I love him so well that I wish he had but the
hundredth part of your courage.

VINCENT He has had the courage to save you from many a beating,
to my knowledge.   60

DAPPERWIT Come, come, I wish the man well, and next to you,
better than any man; and I am sorry to say it, he has not
courage° to snuff a candle with his fingers. When he is drunk,
indeed, he dares get a clap, or so—and swear at a constable.

VINCENT Detracting fop, when did you see him desert his friend?   65

DAPPERWIT You have a rough kind of raillery, Mr Vincent; but
since you will have it (though I love the man heartily, I say), he
deserted me once in breaking of windows,° for fear of the
constable—

Ranger returns

But you need not take notice to him, of what I tell you; I hate to 70
put a man to the blush.

RANGER I have had just now a visit from my mistress, who is as
jealous of me as a wife of her husband when she lies in—my cousin
Lydia; you have heard me speak of her.

VINCENT But she is more troublesome than a wife that lies in,   75
because she follows you to your haunts. Why do you allow her that
privilege before her time?

RANGER Faith, I may allow her any privilege, and be too hard for her
yet. How do you think I have cheated her tonight? Women are poor
credulous creatures, easily deceived.   80

VINCENT We are poor credulous creatures when we think 'em so.

RANGER Intending a ramble to St James's Park tonight, upon
some probable hopes of some fresh game I have in chase, I
appointed her° to stay at home, with a promise to come to her
within this hour, that she might not foil the scent, and prevent my   85
sport.

VINCENT She'll be even with you when you are married, I warrant
you. In the mean time, here's her health, Dapperwit.

RANGER Now had he rather be at the window, writing her anagram
in the glass with his diamond, or biting his nails in the corner for   90
a fine thought to come and divert us with at the table.

DAPPERWIT No, a pox, I have no wit tonight; I am as barren and
hidebound as one of your damned scribbling poets, who are sots in
company for all their wit, as a miser poor for all his money. How
do you like the thought?   95

VINCENT Drink, drink!

DAPPERWIT Well, I can drink this, because I shall be reprieved
presently.

VINCENT Who will be so civil to us?

DAPPERWIT Sir Simon Addleplot; I have bespoke him a supper here,   100
for he treats tonight a new rich mistress.

RANGER That spark who has his fruitless designs upon the bedridden
rich widow, down to the sucking heiress in her pissing-clout? He
was once the sport, but now the public grievance, of all the fortunes
in town, for he watches them like a younger brother° that is afraid   105
to be mumped of his snip, and they cannot steal a marriage, nor
stay their stomachs, but he must know it.

DAPPERWIT He has now pitched his nets for Gripe's daughter, the
rich scrivener, and serves him as a clerk to get admission to her,
which the watchful fop, her father, denies to all others.   110

RANGER I thought you had been nibbling at her once, under pretence
of love to her aunt?

DAPPERWIT I confess I have the same design yet, and Addleplot is
but my agent whilst he thinks me his; he brings me letters
constantly from her, and carries mine back.   115

VINCENT Still betraying your best friends.

DAPPERWIT I cannot in honour but betray him, let me perish. The
poor young wench is taken with my person, and would scratch
through four walls to come to me.

VINCENT 'Tis a sign she is kept up close indeed.°   120

DAPPERWIT Betray him! I'll not be a traitor to love for any man.

[*Enter*] *Sir Simon Addleplot, with the Waiter*

15

SIR SIMON [*to Waiter*] Know 'em? You are a saucy jack-straw to
    question me, faith and troth. I know everybody, and everybody
    knows me.

ALL Sir Simon, Sir Simon, Sir Simon.   125

RANGER And you are a welcome man to everybody.

SIR SIMON Now, son of a whore, do I know the gentlemen?—A dog,
    he would have had a shilling of me before he would let me come
    to you.

RANGER The rogue has been bred at court, sure. Get you out, sirrah.   130
        [*Exit Waiter*]

SIR SIMON He has been bred at a French house, where they are more
    unreasonable.

VINCENT Here's to you, Sir Simon.

SIR SIMON I cannot drink, for I have a mistress within, though I
    would not have the people of the house to know it.   135

RANGER You need not be ashamed of your mistresses, for they are
    commonly rich.

SIR SIMON And because she is rich I would conceal her, for I never
    had a rich mistress yet, but one or other got her from me presently,
    faith and troth.   140

RANGER But this is an ill place to conceal a mistress in; every waiter
    is an intelligencer to your rivals.

SIR SIMON I have a trick for that: I let no waiters come into the
    room; I'll lay the cloth myself rather.

RANGER But who is your mistress?   145

SIR SIMON Your servant, your servant,° Mr Ranger.

VINCENT Come, will you pledge me?

SIR SIMON No, I'll spare your wine, if you will spare me Dapperwit's
    company; I came for that.

VINCENT You do us a double favour, to take him and leave the wine. 150

SIR SIMON Come, come, Dapperwit.

RANGER (*aside* [*to Dapperwit*]) Do not go unless he will suffer us to
    see his mistress too.

SIR SIMON Come, come, man.

DAPPERWIT Would you have me so incivil as to leave my company?   155
    They'll take it ill.

SIR SIMON I cannot find her talk° without thee.—Pray, gentlemen,
    persuade Mr Dapperwit to go with me.

RANGER We will not hinder him of better company.

DAPPERWIT Yours is too good to be left rudely.   160

SIR SIMON Nay, gentlemen, I would desire your company too, if you knew the lady.

DAPPERWIT They know her as well as I—you say I know her not.

SIR SIMON (*aside* [*to Dapperwit*]) You are not everybody.°

RANGER Perhaps we do know the lady, Sir Simon.   165

SIR SIMON You do not, you do not. None of you ever saw her in your lives. But if you could be secret, and civil . . .

RANGER We have drunk yet but our [two] bottles° apiece.

SIR SIMON But will you be civil, Mr Vincent?

RANGER He dares not look a woman in the face under three bottles.   170

SIR SIMON Come along then. But can you be civil, gentlemen? Will you be civil, gentlemen? Pray be civil if you can, and you shall see her.

> *Exit Sir Simon Addleplot* [*and*] *returns with Lady Flippant and Mrs Joiner*

DAPPERWIT (*aside*) How! Has he got this jilt here?

RANGER (*aside*) The Widow Flippant!   175

VINCENT (*aside*) Is this the woman we never saw?

LADY FLIPPANT (*aside*) Does he bring us into company, and Dapperwit one? Though I had married the fool, I thought to have reserved the wit, as well as other ladies.°

SIR SIMON Nay, look as long as you will, madam, you will find them   180
civil gentlemen and good company.

LADY FLIPPANT I am not in doubt of their civility, but yours.

MRS JOINER ([*whispering to her from*] *behind*) You'll never leave snubbing your servants. Did you not promise to use him kindly?

LADY FLIPPANT (*aside* [*to her*]) 'Tis true.—We wanted no good   185
company, Sir Simon, as long as we had yours.

SIR SIMON But they wanted good company, therefore I forced them to accept of yours.

LADY FLIPPANT They will not think the company good they were forced into, certainly.   190

SIR SIMON [*aside*] A pox, I must be using the words in fashion° though I never have any luck with 'em.—Mrs Joiner, help me off.

MRS JOINER I suppose, madam, he means the gentlemen wanted not inclination to your company, but confidence to desire so great an honour; therefore he forced 'em.   195

DAPPERWIT What makes this bawd here? Sure, mistress, you bawds should be like the small cards:° though at first you make up the pack, yet when the play begins you should be put out as useless.

MRS JOINER Well, well, gibing companion, you would have the
   pimps kept in only? You would so?   200

VINCENT What, they are quarrelling?

RANGER Pimp and bawd agree nowadays like doctor and apothecary.°

SIR SIMON [to Lady Flippant] Try, madam, if they are not civil
   gentlemen; talk with 'em, while I go lay the cloth—no waiter comes   205
   here. (Aside) My mother used to tell me I should avoid all occasions
   of talking before my mistress, because silence is a sign of love as
   well as prudence.
       Sir Simon Addleplot laying the cloth

LADY FLIPPANT Methinks you look a little yellow on't, Mr Dapperwit. I hope you do not censure me because you find me pass-   210
   ing away a night with this fool; he is not a man to be jealous of,
   sure.

DAPPERWIT You are not a lady to be jealous of, sure.

LADY FLIPPANT No, certainly; but why do you look as if you were
   jealous, then?   215

DAPPERWIT If I had met you in Whetstone's Park° with a drunken
   footsoldier, I should not have been jealous of you.

LADY FLIPPANT Fie, fie, now you are jealous certainly, for people
   always, when they grow jealous, grow rude. But I can pardon it,
   since it proceeds from love, certainly.   220

DAPPERWIT (aside) I am out of all hopes to be rid of this eternal old
   acquaintance. When I jeer her, she thinks herself praised; now I
   call her whore in plain English, she thinks I am jealous.

LADY FLIPPANT Sweet Mr Dapperwit, be not so censorious. I speak
   for your sake, not my own, for jealousy is a great torment—but my   225
   honour cannot suffer, certainly.

DAPPERWIT No, certainly, but the greatest torment I have is your
   love.

LADY FLIPPANT Alas, sweet Mr Dapperwit, indeed love is a torment, but 'tis a sweet torment.° But jealousy is a bitter torment. I   230
   do not go about to cure you of the torment of my love.

DAPPERWIT 'Tis a sign so.°

LADY FLIPPANT Come, come, look up, man. Is that a rival to contest
   with you?

DAPPERWIT I will contest with no rival, not with my old rival your   235
   coachman,° but they have heartily my resignation.° And to do you
   a favour (but myself a greater) I will help tie the knot you are
   fumbling for now, betwixt your cully here, and you.

LADY FLIPPANT Go, go, I take that kind of jealousy worst of
all—to suspect I would be debauched to beastly matrimony! But
who are those gentlemen, pray?°—Are they men of fortunes, Mrs
Joiner?

MRS JOINER I believe so.

LADY FLIPPANT Do you believe so, indeed? (*Advancing towards
Ranger and Vincent*) Gentlemen—

RANGER If the civility we owe to ladies had not controlled our envy
to Mr Dapperwit, we had interrupted ere this your private
conversation.

LADY FLIPPANT Your interruption, sir, had been most civil and
obliging, for our discourse was of marriage.

RANGER That is a subject, madam, as grateful as common.

LADY FLIPPANT Oh fie, fie, are you of that opinion too? I cannot
suffer any to talk of it in my company.

RANGER Are you married then, madam?

LADY FLIPPANT No, certainly.

RANGER I am sure so much beauty cannot despair of it.

LADY FLIPPANT Despair of it!

RANGER Only those that are married, or cannot be married, hate to
hear of marriage.

LADY FLIPPANT Yet you must know, sir, my aversion to marriage
is such, that you nor no man breathing shall ever persuade me to
it.

RANGER Cursed be the man should do so rude a thing as to persuade
you to anything against your inclination; I would not do it for the
world, madam.

LADY FLIPPANT Come, come; though you seem to be a civil
gentleman, I think you no better than your neighbours. I do not
know a man of you all, that will not thrust a woman up into a
corner, and then talk an hour to her impertinently of marriage.

RANGER You would find me another man in a corner, I assure you,
madam, for you should not have a word of marriage from me,
whatsoever you might find in my actions of it. I hate talking as
much as you.

LADY FLIPPANT I hate it extremely.

RANGER I am your man then, madam, for I find just the same fault
with your sex as you do with ours; I ne'er could have to do with a
woman in my life, but still she would be impertinently talking of
marriage to me.

LADY FLIPPANT (*aside [to Mrs Joiner]*) Observe that, Mrs Joiner.

DAPPERWIT Pray, Mr Ranger, let's go. I had rather drink with Mr   280
Vincent than stay here with you. Besides, 'tis park-time.°

RANGER (*to Dapperwit*) I come. [*To Lady Flippant*] Since you are a
lady that hate marriage, I'll do you the service to withdraw the
company, for those that hate marriage hate loss of time.

LADY FLIPPANT Will you go then, sir? But before you go, sir, pray   285
tell me, is your aversion to marriage real?

RANGER As real as yours.

LADY FLIPPANT (*aside*) If it were no more real than mine . . .

RANGER Your servant, madam.

> [*Lady Flippant*] *plucks him back*

LADY FLIPPANT But do you hate marriage, certainly?   290

RANGER Certainly.

LADY FLIPPANT Come, I cannot believe it; you dissemble it, only
because I pretend° it.

RANGER Do you but pretend it then, madam?

LADY FLIPPANT (*aside*) I shall discover myself.—I mean, because I   295
hold against it, you do the same in complaisance. For I have heard
say, cunning men think to bring the coy and untractable women to
tameness, as they do some mad people, by humouring their
frenzies.

RANGER I am none of those cunning men, yet have too much wit to   300
entertain the presumption of designing upon you.

LADY FLIPPANT 'Twere no such presumption, neither.

DAPPERWIT [*apart to Ranger*] Come away; 'sdeath, don't you see
your danger?

RANGER [*apart to Dapperwit*] Those aims are for Sir Simon°—Good   305
night, madam.

LADY FLIPPANT Will you needs go then?—The gentlemen are
a-going, Sir Simon; will you let 'em?

SIR SIMON Nay, madam, if you cannot keep 'em, how should I?

LADY FLIPPANT [*to Ranger*] Stay, sir. Because you hate marriage I'll   310
sing you a new song° against it.

> *She sings*

> *A spouse I do hate,*
> *For either she's false or she's jealous;*
> *But give us a mate*
> *Who nothing will ask us, or tell us.*   315

> *She stands on no terms,*
> *Nor chaffers (by way of indenture)*

> *Her love for your farms,*
> *But takes her kind man at a venture.*

> *If all prove not right,*   320
> *Without an act°, process, or warning,*
> *From wife for a night*
> *You may be divorced in the morning.*

> *When parents are slaves,*
> *Their brats cannot be any other;*   325
> *Great wits and great braves*
> *Have always a punk to their mother.*

Though it be the fashion for women of quality to sing any song whatever, because the words are not distinguished, yet I should have blushed to have done it now, but for you, sir.   330

RANGER The song is edifying, the voice admirable, and once more—I am your servant, madam.

LADY FLIPPANT What, will you go too, Mr Dapperwit?

SIR SIMON Pray, Mr Dapperwit, do not you go too.

DAPPERWIT I am engaged.   335

SIR SIMON Well, if we cannot have their company, we will not have their room.° Ours is a private back room. They have paid their reckoning; let's go thither again.

LADY FLIPPANT But pray, sweet Mr Dapperwit, do not go. Keep him, Sir Simon!   340

SIR SIMON I cannot keep him.

> *Exeunt Vincent, Ranger, Dapperwit*
> It is impossible (the world is so),
> One cannot keep one's friend and mistress too.
> *Exeunt*

2.1

St James's Park, at night°

Enter Ranger, Vincent, Dapperwit

RANGER Hang me if I am not pleased extremely with this new-fashioned caterwauling, this midnight coursing in the park.

VINCENT A man may come after supper with his three bottles in his head, reel himself sober, without reproof from his mother, aunt, or grave relation.   5

RANGER May bring his bashful wench, and not have her put out of countenance by the impudent honest women of the town.

DAPPERWIT And a man of wit may have the better of the dumb show of well-trimmed vest or fair peruke: no man's now is whitest.°   10

RANGER And now no woman's modest, or proud, for her blushes are hid, and the rubies on her lips are dyed°, and all sleepy and glimmering° eyes have lost their attraction.

VINCENT And now a man may carry a bottle under his arm, instead of his hat, and no observing spruce fop will miss° the [disordered]°   15
cravat that lies on one's shoulder, or count the pimples on one's face.

DAPPERWIT And now the brisk repartee ruins the complaisant cringe, or wise grimace. Something 'twas,° we men of virtue always loved the night.   20

RANGER Oh blessed season.

VINCENT For good-fellows.

RANGER For lovers.

DAPPERWIT And for the muses.

RANGER When I was a boy I loved the night so well, I had a strong   25
vocation to be a bellman's apprentice.

VINCENT I a drawer.

DAPPERWIT And I to attend the waits of Westminster,° let me perish.

RANGER But why do we not do the duty of this and such other   30
places—walk, censure, and speak ill of all we meet?

DAPPERWIT 'Tis no fault of mine, let me perish.

VINCENT Fie, fie, satirical gentlemen, this is not your time; you cannot distinguish a friend from a fop.

DAPPERWIT No matter, no matter; they will deserve amongst 'em   35
the worst we can say.
        People walking slowly over the stage
RANGER Who comes here, Dapperwit?
DAPPERWIT By the toss of his head, training of his feet, and his
elbows playing at bo-peep° behind his back, it should be my Lord
Easy.   40
RANGER And who the woman?
DAPPERWIT My Lord What-d'ye-call's daughter, that had a child
by—
VINCENT Dapperwit, hold your tongue!
RANGER How are you concerned?   45
VINCENT Her brother's an honest fellow, and will drink his glass.
RANGER Prithee, Vincent—Dapperwit did not hinder drinking to-
night, though he spoke° against it; why then should you interrupt
his sport? Now let him talk of anybody.
VINCENT So he will, till you cut his throat.   50
RANGER Why should you in all occasions thwart him, contemn him,
and maliciously look grave at his jests only?
VINCENT Why does he always rail against my friends then, and my
best friend—a beer-glass?°
RANGER Dapperwit, be your own advocate. My game, I think, is   55
before me there!
        Exit Ranger
DAPPERWIT This Ranger, I think, has all the ill qualities of all your
town fops, leaving his company for a spruce lord, or a wench.
VINCENT Nay, if you must rail at your own best friends, I may
forgive you railing at mine.   60
        [*Enter*] *Lydia and Lady Flippant, walking over the stage*
LYDIA (*aside*) False Ranger, shall I find thee here?
VINCENT (*to Dapperwit*) Those are women, are they not?
DAPPERWIT (*aside*) The least° seems to be my Lucy, sure.
VINCENT Faith, I think I dare speak to a woman in the dark; let's
try.   65
DAPPERWIT They are persons of quality of my acquaintance—hold.
VINCENT Nay, if they are persons of quality of your acquaintance, I
may be the bolder with 'em.
        Lydia and Lady Flippant go off; Vincent and Dapperwit
        follow them. Lydia and Lady Flippant re-enter
LYDIA I['m] come° hither to make a discovery tonight.

LADY FLIPPANT Of my love to you, certainly, for nobody but you   70
could have debauched me to the park, certainly. I would not return
another night, if it were to redeem my dear husband from his
grave.

LYDIA I believe you; but to get another, widow . . .?

LADY FLIPPANT Another husband? Another husband? Foh!   75

LYDIA There does not pass a night here, but many a match is made.

LADY FLIPPANT That a woman of honour should have the word
'match' in her mouth! But I hope, madam, the fellows do not make
honourable love here, do they? I abominate honourable love, upon
my honour.   80

LYDIA If they should make honourable love here, I know you would
prevent 'em.

> *Vincent and Dapperwit re-enter, and walk slowly towards*
> *them*

But here come two men will inform you what they do.

LADY FLIPPANT Do they come? Are they men, certainly?

LYDIA Prepare for an assault; they'll put you to't.°   85

LADY FLIPPANT Will they put us to't, certainly? I was never put
to't yet; if they should put us to't, I should drop down, down,
certainly.

LYDIA I believe, truly, you would not have power to run away.

LADY FLIPPANT Therefore I will not stay the push.° They come,   90
they come, oh the fellows come!

> *Lady Flippant runs away, Lydia follows, and Vincent and*
> *Dapperwit after them. Lady Flippant re-enters at t'other door*
> *alone*

LADY FLIPPANT So I am got off clear. I did not run from the men,
but my companion. For all their brags, men have hardly courage
to set upon us, when our number is equal. Now they shall see I
defy 'em, for we women have always most courage when we are   95
alone. But a pox, [*looking about*] the lazy rogues come not, or they
are drunk and cannot run. Oh drink, abominable drink! Instead of
inflaming love, it quenches it, and for one lover it encourages, it
makes a thousand impotent. Curse on all wine, even Rhenish wine
and sugar°—   100

> *Enter Sir Simon Addleplot, muffled in a cloak [and masked]*

But Fortune will not see me want; here comes a single bully—I
wish he may stand,
For now anights the jostling nymph is bolder°
Than modern satyr with his cloak o'er shoulder.

(*She puts on her mask*) Well met, sir.   105

SIR SIMON How shall I know that, forsooth?° Who are you? Do you
know me?

LADY FLIPPANT Who are you? Don't you know me?°

SIR SIMON Not I, faith and troth.

LADY FLIPPANT I am glad on't, for no man e'er liked a woman the   110
better for having known her before.

SIR SIMON Ay, but then one can't be so free with a new acquaintance
as with an old one; she may deny one the civility.

LADY FLIPPANT Not till you ask her.

SIR SIMON But I am afraid to be denied.   115

LADY FLIPPANT Let me tell you, sir, you cannot disoblige us women
more, than in distrusting us.

SIR SIMON Pish, what should one ask for,° when you know one's
meaning? But shall I deal freely with you?

LADY FLIPPANT I love, of my life, men should deal freely with me;   120
there are so few men will deal freely with one—

SIR SIMON Are you not a fireship? A punk, madam?

LADY FLIPPANT Well, sir, I love raillery.

SIR SIMON Faith and troth, I do not rally, I deal freely.

LADY FLIPPANT This is the time and place for freedom, sir.   125

SIR SIMON Are you handsome?

LADY FLIPPANT Joan's as good as my lady in the dark,° certainly.
But men that deal freely, never ask questions, certainly.

SIR SIMON How then! I thought, to deal freely, and put a woman to
the question,° had been all one.   130

LADY FLIPPANT But let me tell you, those that deal freely indeed,
take a woman by—

SIR SIMON What, what, what, what?

LADY FLIPPANT By the hand, and lead her aside.

SIR SIMON Now I understand you; come along then.   135

Enter torches and music at a distance°

LADY FLIPPANT What unmannerly rascals are those, that bring light
into the park? 'Twill not be taken well from 'em by the women,
certainly. (*Aside*) Still disappointed—

SIR SIMON Oh the fiddles, the fiddles! I sent for them hither to
oblige the women, not offend 'em, for I intend to serenade the   140
whole park tonight. But my frolic is not without an intrigue, faith
and troth; for I know the fiddles will call the whole herd of
vizard-masks together, and then shall I discover if a strayed
mistress of mine be not amongst 'em, whom I treated tonight at

the French house; but as soon as the jilt had eat up my meat, and   145
drank her two bottles, she run° away from me, and left me alone.

LADY FLIPPANT (*aside*) How! Is it he? Addleplot! That I could not
know him by his 'faith and troth'!

SIR SIMON Now, I would understand her tricks, because I intend to
marry her, and should be glad to know what I must trust to.   150

LADY FLIPPANT (*aside*) So thou shalt, but not yet.

SIR SIMON Though I can give a great guess already; for if I have any
intrigue or sense in me, she is as arrant a jilt as ever pulled pillow
from under husband's head,° faith and troth. Moreover she is
bow-legged, hopper-hipped, and, betwixt pomatum and Spanish   155
red, has a complexion like a Holland cheese,° and no more teeth
left, than such as give a *haut-goût* to her breath; but she is rich,
faith and troth.

LADY FLIPPANT (*aside*) Oh rascal! He has heard somebody else say
all this of me; but I must not discover myself, lest I should be   160
disappointed of my revenge—for I will marry him.

    The torches and music approaching. Exit Lady Flippant

SIR SIMON What, gone? Come then, strike up, my lads.

    Enter men and women in vizards, and dance; Sir Simon
    Addleplot for the most part standing still in a cloak and
    vizard, but sometimes going about, peeping and examining the
    women's clothes. The dance ended, exeunt dancers, torches,
    music, and Sir Simon Addleplot. Enter Lady Flippant,
    Lydia; after them Vincent, Dapperwit

LADY FLIPPANT (*to Lydia*) Nay, if you stay any longer, I must leave
you again.

VINCENT We have overtaken them at last again; these are they.   165

    Lady Flippant going off

They separate too, and that's but a challenge to us.

DAPPERWIT Let me perish, ladies—

LYDIA Nay, good madam, let's unite, now here's the common enemy
upon us.

VINCENT Damn me, ladies—   170

DAPPERWIT Hold; a pox, you are too rough.—Let me perish,
ladies—

LYDIA Not for want of breath, gentlemen; we'll stay rather.

DAPPERWIT For want of your favour, rather, sweet ladies.

LADY FLIPPANT [*aside*] That's Dapperwit, false villain. But he must   175
not know I am here; if I should, I should lose his thrice agreeable

company, and he would run from me as fast as from the bailiffs.
[*To Lydia*] What! You will not talk with 'em, I hope?

LYDIA Yes, but I will.

LADY FLIPPANT Then you are a park-woman, certainly, and you   180
will take it kindly if I leave you.

LYDIA (*apart* [*to Lady Flippant*]) No, you must not leave me.

LADY FLIPPANT Then you must leave them.

LYDIA I'll see if they are worse company than you, first.

LADY FLIPPANT Monstrous impudence; will you not come?   185
    Pulls Lydia

VINCENT Nay, madam, I never suffer any violence to be used to a
woman, but what I do myself. She must stay, and you must not
go.

LADY FLIPPANT Unhand me, you rude fellow.

VINCENT Nay, now I am sure you will stay and be kind; for coyness   190
in a woman is as little sign of true modesty, as huffing in a man is
of true courage.

DAPPERWIT Use her gently, and speak soft things to her.

LYDIA (*aside*) Now do I guess I know my coxcomb. [*To Dapperwit*]
Sir, I am extremely glad I am fallen into the hands of a gentleman   195
that can speak soft things; and this is so fine a night to hear soft
things in—morning, I should have said.

DAPPERWIT It will not be morning, dear madam, till you pull off
your mask. (*Aside*) That, I think, was brisk!

LYDIA Indeed, dear sir, my face would frighten back the sun.   200

DAPPERWIT With glories more radiant than his own. (*Aside*) I keep
up with her, I think.

LYDIA But why would you put me to the trouble of lighting the
world, when I thought to have gone to sleep?

DAPPERWIT You only can do it, dear madam, let me perish.   205

LYDIA But why would you (of all men) practise treason against your
friend Phoebus, and depose him for a mere stranger?

DAPPERWIT (*aside*) I think she knows me.

LYDIA But he does not do you justice,° I believe, and you are so
positively cocksure of your wit, you would refer to a mere stranger   210
your plea to the bay-tree.°

DAPPERWIT (*aside*) She jeers me, let me perish.

VINCENT Dapperwit, a little of your aid, for my lady's invincibly
dumb.

DAPPERWIT (*aside*) Would mine had been so too.   215

VINCENT I have used as many arguments to make her speak, as are requisite to make other women hold their tongues.

DAPPERWIT Well, I am ready to change sides. Yet before I go, madam, since the moon consents now I should see your face, let me desire you to pull off your mask, which to a handsome lady is a favour, I'm sure.   220

LYDIA Truly, sir, I must not be long in debt to you the obligation.° Pray, let me hear you recite some of your verses, which to a wit is a favour, I'm sure.

DAPPERWIT Madam, it belongs to your sex to be obliged first. Pull   225 off your mask, and I'll pull out my paper. (*Aside*) Brisk again of my side.

LYDIA 'Twould be in vain, for you would want a candle now.

DAPPERWIT (*aside*) I dare not make use again of 'the lustre of her face'.—I'll wait upon you home then, madam.   230

LYDIA Faith no, I believe it will not be much to our advantages to bring my face, or your poetry, to light, for I hope you have yet a pretty good opinion of my face, and so have I of your wit. But if you are for proving your wit, why do not you write a play?

DAPPERWIT Because 'tis now no more reputation to write a play,   235 than it is honour to be a knight. Your true wit despises the title of poet, as much as your true gentleman the title of knight;° for as a man may be a knight and no gentleman, so a man may be a poet and no wit, let me perish.

LYDIA Pray, sir, how are you dignified or distinguished amongst the   240 rates of wits? And how many rates are there?

DAPPERWIT There are as many degrees of wits as of lawyers. As there is first your solicitor, then your attorney, then your pleading-counsel, then your chamber-counsel, and then your judge; so there is first your court-wit, your coffee-wit, your poll-wit or politic-wit,° your   245 chamber-wit or scribble-wit, and last of all your judge-wit or critic.

LYDIA But are there as many wits as lawyers? Lord, what will become of us? What employment can they have? How are they known?

DAPPERWIT First, your court-wit is a fashionable, insinuating, flat-   250 tering, cringing, grimacing fellow, and has wit enough to solicit a suit of love; and if he fail, he has malice enough to ruin the woman with a dull lampoon. But he rails still at the man that is absent, for you must know, all wits rail; and his wit properly lies in combing perukes,° matching ribbons,° and being severe (as they call it) upon   255 other people's clothes.

LYDIA Now, what is the coffee-wit?

DAPPERWIT He is a lying, censorious, gossiping, quibbling wretch, and sets people together by the ears° over that sober drink, coffee. He is a wit as he is a commentator upon the *Gazette*, and he rails 260 at the pirates of Algiers,° the Grand Signior of Constantinople, and the Christian Grand Signior.°

LYDIA What kind of man is your poll-wit?

DAPPERWIT He is a fidgeting, busy, dogmatical, hot-headed fop that speaks always in sentences and proverbs (as others in similitudes), 265 and he rails perpetually against the present government. His wit lies in projects and monopolies, and penning speeches for young parliament men.

LYDIA But what is your chamber-wit or scribble-wit?

DAPPERWIT He is a poring, melancholy, modest sot, ashamed of the 270 world. He searches all the records of wit, to compile a breviate of them for the use of players, printers, booksellers, and sometimes cooks and tobacco-men.° He employs his railing against the ignorance of the age, and all that have more money than he.

LYDIA Now your last. 275

DAPPERWIT Your judge-wit, or critic, is all these together, and yet has the wit to be none of them. He can think, speak, write as well as all the rest, but scorns (himself a judge) to be judged by posterity. He rails at all the other classes of wits, and his wit lies in damning all but himself. He is your true wit. 280

LYDIA Then I suspect you are of his form.°

DAPPERWIT I cannot deny it, madam.

VINCENT Dapperwit, you have been all this time on the wrong side, for you love to talk all, and here's a lady would not have hindered you. 285

DAPPERWIT (*aside*) A pox, I have been talking too long indeed here; for wit is lost upon a silly weak woman, as well as courage.

VINCENT I have used all common means to move a woman's tongue and mask. I called her ugly, old, and 'old acquaintance', and yet she would not disprove me. But here comes Ranger; let him try 290 what he can do, for since my mistress is dogged, I'll go sleep alone.
    Exit Vincent. Ranger enters

LYDIA (*aside*) Ranger! 'Tis he indeed. I am sorry he is here, but glad I discovered him before I went. Yet he must not discover me, lest I should be prevented hereafter in finding him out—false Ranger. [*To Lady Flippant*] Nay, if they bring fresh force upon us, madam, 295 'tis time to quit the field.

Exeunt Lydia, Lady Flippant

RANGER What, play with your quarry till it fly from you!

DAPPERWIT You frightened it away.

RANGER Ha! Is not one of those ladies in mourning?

DAPPERWIT All women are so by this light.   300

RANGER But you might easily discern it; don't you know her?

DAPPERWIT No.

RANGER Did you talk with her?

DAPPERWIT Yes, she's one of your brisk, silly baggages.

RANGER 'Tis she, 'tis she; I was afraid I saw her before. Let us follow   305
'em—prithee make haste. (*Aside*) 'Tis Lydia.

> *Exeunt Ranger and Dapperwit. Lydia, Lady Flippant return at*
> *the other door, Ranger, Dapperwit following them at a distance*

LYDIA They follow us yet, I fear.

LADY FLIPPANT You do not fear it, certainly; otherwise you would
not have encouraged them.

LYDIA For heaven's sake, madam, waive your quarrel a little; and let   310
us pass by your coach, and so on foot to your acquaintance in the
Old Pall Mall; for I would not be discovered by the man that came
up last to us.

> *Exeunt*

2.2

Christina's lodging

Enter Christina, Isabel

ISABEL For heaven's sake undress yourself, madam. They'll not
return tonight; all people have left the park an hour ago.

CHRISTINA What is't o'clock?

ISABEL 'Tis past one.

CHRISTINA It cannot be.   5

ISABEL I thought that time had only stolen from happy lovers; the
disconsolate have nothing to do but to tell the clock.°

CHRISTINA I can only keep account with my misfortunes.°

ISABEL I am glad they are not innumerable.

CHRISTINA And truly, my undergoing so often your impertinency is   10
not the least of them.

ISABEL I am then more glad, madam, for then they cannot be great,
and it is in my power, it seems, to make you in part happy, if I

could but hold this villainous tongue of mine—but then let the
people of the town hold their tongues if they will, for I cannot but   15
tell you what they say.

CHRISTINA What do they say?

ISABEL Faith, madam, I am afraid to tell you, now I think on't.

CHRISTINA Is it so ill?

ISABEL Oh, such base, unworthy things.   20

CHRISTINA Do they say I was really Clerimont's wench, as he
boasted? And that the ground of the quarrel betwixt Valentine and
him, was not Valentine's vindication of my honour, but Clerimont's jealousy of him?

ISABEL Worse, worse a thousand times; such villainous things, to the   25
utter ruin of your reputation!

CHRISTINA What are they?

ISABEL Faith, madam, you'll be angry; 'tis the old trick of lovers to
hate their informers, after they have made 'em such.

CHRISTINA I will not be angry.   30

ISABEL They say then, since Mr Valentine's flying into France,° you
are grown mad, have put yourself into mourning, live in a dark
room, where you'll see nobody, nor take any rest day or night, but
rave and talk to yourself perpetually.

CHRISTINA Now, what else?   35

ISABEL But the surest sign of your madness is, they say, because you
are desperately resolved (in case my Lord Clerimont should die of
his wounds) to transport your self and fortune into France, to Mr
Valentine, a man that has not a groat to return you in exchange.

CHRISTINA All this hitherto, is true. Now to the rest.   40

ISABEL Indeed, madam, I have no more to tell you. I was sorry, I'm
sure, to hear so much of any lady of mine.

CHRISTINA Insupportable insolence!

ISABEL (aside) This is some revenge for my want of sleep tonight.
        [A] knocking at the door
    So, I hope my old second° is come; 'tis seasonable relief.   45
        Exit Isabel

CHRISTINA Unhappy Valentine, couldst thou but see how soon thy
absence and misfortunes have disbanded all thy friends, and turned
thy slaves all renegades, thou sure wouldst prize my only faithful
heart.
        Enter Lady Flippant, Lydia, Isabel, to her

LADY FLIPPANT Hail, faithful shepherdess!° But truly, I had not   50
kept my word with you in coming back tonight, if it had not been

for this lady, who has her intrigues too with the fellows, as well as you.

LYDIA Madam, under my Lady Flippant's protection I am confident to beg yours, being just now pursued out of the park by a 55 relation of mine, by whom it imports me extremely not to be discovered.

[A] *knocking at the door*

But I fear he is now at the door. (*To Isabel*, [*who is*] *going out*) Let me desire you to deny me to him courageously,° for he will hardly believe he can be mistaken in me. 60

[*Exit Isabel*]

CHRISTINA In such an occasion, where impudence is requisite, she will serve you as faithfully as you can wish, madam.

LADY FLIPPANT Come, come, madam, do not upbraid her with her assurance, a qualification that only fits her for a lady's service. A fine woman of the town can be no more without a woman that can 65 make an excuse with an assurance, than she can be without a glass, certainly.

CHRISTINA She needs no advocate.

LADY FLIPPANT How can anyone alone manage an amorous in- trigue? Though the birds are tame, somebody must help draw 70 the net. If 'twere not for a woman that could make an excuse with assurance, how should we wheedle, jilt, trace, discover, countermine, undermine, and blow up the stinking fellows?— which is all the pleasure I receive, or design by them; for I never admitted a man to my conversation, but for his punishment, 75 certainly.

CHRISTINA Nobody will doubt that, certainly.

Isabel returns

ISABEL Madam, the gentleman will not be mistaken. He says you are here, he saw you come in. He is your relation, his name's Ranger, and is come to wait upon you home. I had much ado to keep him 80 from coming up.

LYDIA (*to Christina*) Madam, for heaven's sake help me; 'tis yet in your power—if but while I retire into your dining-room you will please to personate me, and own yourself for her he pursued out of the park. You are in mourning too, and your stature so much 85 mine, it will not contradict you.

CHRISTINA I am sorry, madam, I must dispute any command of yours. I have made a resolution to see the face of no man, till an unfortunate friend of mine, now out of the kingdom, return.

LYDIA By that friend, and by the hopes you have to see him, let me   90
conjure you to keep me from the sight of mine now. Dear madam,
let your charity prevail over your superstition.°

ISABEL He comes, he comes, madam.
Ranger enters; Lydia [and Lady Flippant]° withdraw and
stand unseen at the door

RANGER [*aside*] Ha! This is no Lydia.

CHRISTINA What unworthy defamer has encouraged you to offer me   95
this insolence?

RANGER (*aside*) She is liker Lydia in her style, than her face. I see I
am mistaken, but to tell her I followed her for another, were an
affront rather than an excuse. She's a glorious creature.

CHRISTINA Tell me, sir, whence had you reason for this your rude   100
pursuit of me into my lodging, my chamber? Why should you
follow me?

RANGER Faith, madam, because you run away from me.

CHRISTINA That was no sign of an acquaintance.

RANGER You'll pardon me, madam.   105

CHRISTINA Then it seems you mistook me for another, and the night
is your excuse, which blots out all distinctions. But now you are
satisfied in your mistake, I hope you will go seek out your woman
in another place.

RANGER Madam, I allow not the excuse you make for me. If I have   110
offended, I will rather be condemned for my love, than pardoned
for my insensibility.

LYDIA (*behind*) How's that?

CHRISTINA What do you say?

RANGER Though the night had been darker, my heart would not   115
have suffered me to follow anyone but you; he has been too long
acquainted with you to mistake you.

LYDIA (*behind*) What means this tenderness? He mistook me for her,
sure!

CHRISTINA What says the gentleman? Did you know me then, sir?   120

RANGER (*aside*) Not I, the devil take me; but I must on now.—Could
you imagine, madam, by the innumerable crowd of your admirers,
you had left any man free in the town, or ignorant of the power of
your beauty?

CHRISTINA I never saw your face before, that I remember.   125

RANGER Ah madam! You would never regard your humblest slave; I
was till now a modest lover.

LYDIA (*behind*) Falsest of men.

CHRISTINA My woman said you came to seek a relation here, not a mistress.   130

RANGER I must confess, madam, I thought you would sooner disprove my dissembled error, than admit my visit; and I was resolved to see you.

LYDIA (*behind*) 'Tis clear.

RANGER Indeed, when I followed you first out of the park, I was   135
afraid you might have been a certain relation of mine, for your statures and habits are the same; but when you entered here, I was with joy convinced. Besides, I would not for the world have given her troublesome love so much encouragement, to have disturbed my future addresses to you; for the foolish woman does perpetually   140
torment me to make our relation nearer—but never more in vain than since I have seen you, madam.

LYDIA (*behind*) How shall I suffer this? 'Tis clear he disappointed me tonight for her, and made me stay at home that I might not disappoint him of her company in the park.   145

CHRISTINA I am amazed! But let me tell you, sir, if the lady were here, I would satisfy her the sight of me should never frustrate her ambitious designs upon her cruel kinsman.

LYDIA (*behind*) I wish you *could* satisfy me.

RANGER If she were here, she would satisfy you she were not capable   150
of the honour to be taken for you (though in the dark). Faith, my cousin is but a tolerable woman to a man that had not seen you.

CHRISTINA Sure, to my plague, this is the first time you ever saw me?

RANGER Sure, to the plague of my poor heart, 'tis not the hundredth   155
time I have seen you. For since the time I saw you first, you have not been at the park, playhouse, Exchange, or other public place, but I saw you—for it was my business to watch and follow you.

CHRISTINA Pray, when did you see me last at the park, playhouse, or Exchange?   160

RANGER Some two days, three days, or a week ago.

CHRISTINA I have not been this month out of this chamber.

LYDIA (*behind*) That is to delude me.

CHRISTINA I knew you were mistaken.

RANGER You'll pardon a lover's memory, madam. (*Aside*) A pox, I   165
have hanged myself in my own line. One would think my perpetual ill luck in lying should break me of the quality; but like a losing gamester, I am still for pushing on, till none will trust me.

CHRISTINA Come, sir, you run out of one error into a greater; you   170
would excuse the rudeness of your mistake, and intrusion at this
hour into my lodgings, with your gallantry to me—more unseasonable and offensive.

RANGER Nay, I am in love I see, for I blush, and have not a word to
say for myself.   175

CHRISTINA But, sir, if you will needs play the gallant, pray leave my
house before morning, lest you should be seen go hence, to the
scandal of my honour.

[RANGER (*aside*) If I leave this house before morning, 'twill be to the
scandal of *my* honour.]°   180

CHRISTINA Rather than that should be, I'll call up the house and
neighbours to bear witness I bid you begone.

RANGER Since you take a night-visit so ill, madam, I will never wait
upon you again—but by day. I go, that I may hope to return; and,
for once, I will wish you a good night without me.   185

CHRISTINA Good night, for as long as I live.

    Exit Ranger

LYDIA (*behind*) And good night to my love, I'm sure.

    [*Lydia and Lady Flippant come forward*]

CHRISTINA Though I have done you an inconsiderable service, I
assure you, madam, you are not a little obliged to me. (*Aside*)
Pardon me, dear Valentine.   190

LYDIA I know not yet whether I am more obliged than injured.
When I do, I assure you, madam, I shall not be insensible of either.

CHRISTINA I fear, madam, you are as liable to mistakes as your
kinsman.

LYDIA I fear I am more subject to 'em. It may be for want of sleep,   195
therefore I'll go home.

CHRISTINA My Lady Flippant, good night.

LADY FLIPPANT Good night, or rather good morrow, faithful
shepherdess.

CHRISTINA I'll wait of you down.   200

LYDIA Your coach stays yet, I hope.

LADY FLIPPANT Certainly.

    Exeunt

2.3

The street

Enter Ranger, Dapperwit

DAPPERWIT I was a faithful sentinel; nobody came out, let me perish.

RANGER No, no, I hunted upon a wrong scent; I thought I had followed a woman, but found her an angel.

DAPPERWIT What is her name?   5

RANGER That you must tell me. What very fine woman is there, lies hereabouts?

DAPPERWIT Faith, I know not any. She is, I warrant you, some fine woman of a term's standing° or so in the town; such as seldom appear in public but in their balconies, where they stand so constantly, one   10
would think they had hired no other part of the house.

RANGER And look like the pictures which painters expose to draw in customers. But I must know who she is. Vincent's lodging is hard by; I'll go and enquire of him, and lie with him tonight. But if he will not let me, I'll lie with you, for my lodging is too far off—   15

DAPPERWIT Then I will go before, and expect you at mine.

Exeunt

2.4

Vincent's lodging

Enter Vincent, Valentine in a riding habit, as newly from a journey

VINCENT Your mistress, dear Valentine, will not be more glad to see you. But my wonder is no less than my joy, that you would return ere you were informed Clerimont were out of danger. His surgeons themselves have not been assured of his recovery till within these two days.   5

VALENTINE I feared my mistress, not my life. My life I could trust again with my old enemy Fortune; but not longer my mistress in the hands of my greater enemies, her relations.

VINCENT Your fear was in the wrong place then, for though my Lord Clerimont live, he and his relations may put you in more danger   10
of your life,° than your mistress's relations can of losing her.

VALENTINE Would any could secure me her, I would myself secure my life—for I should value it then.

VINCENT Come, come, her relations can do you no hurt. I dare swear, if her mother should but say your hat did not cock° 15 handsomely, she would never ask her blessing° again.

VALENTINE Prithee leave thy fooling, and tell me if, since my departure, she has given evidences of her love, to clear those doubts I went away with; for as absence is the bane of common and bastard love, 'tis the vindication of that which is true and generous. 20

VINCENT Nay, if you could ever doubt her love, you deserve to doubt on; for there is no punishment great enough for jealousy, but jealousy.

VALENTINE You may remember I told you, before my flight, I had quarrelled with the defamer of my mistress, but thought I had 25 killed my rival.

VINCENT But pray give me now the answer, which the suddenness of your flight denied me: how could Clerimont hope to subdue her heart by the assault of her honour?

VALENTINE Pish, it might be the stratagem of a rival, to make me 30 desist.

VINCENT For shame! If 'twere not rather to vindicate her than satisfy you, I would not tell you how like a Penelope she has behaved herself in your absence.

VALENTINE Let me know. 35

VINCENT Then know, the next day you went, she put herself into mourning and—

VALENTINE That might be for Clerimont, thinking him dead, as all the world besides thought.

VINCENT Still turning the dagger's point on yourself. Hear me out. 40 I say she put herself into mourning for you; locked up herself in her chamber this month for you; shut out her barking relations for you; has not seen the sun, or face of man, since she saw you; thinks and talks of nothing but you; sends to me daily to hear of you; and in short (I think) is mad for you. All this I can swear, for I am to 45 her so near a neighbour, and so inquisitive a friend for you—

    [*Enter*] *Servant*

SERVANT Mr Ranger, sir, is coming up.

    [*Exit Servant*]

[VALENTINE] What brings him now?

VINCENT He comes to lie with me.°

VALENTINE Who, Ranger? 50

37

VINCENT Yes; pray retire a little, till I send him off, unless you have a mind to have your arrival published tomorrow in the coffee-houses.

Valentine retires to the door behind. [*Enter Ranger*]

RANGER What, not yet a-bed? Your man is laying you to sleep with usquebaugh or brandy, is he not so?   55

VINCENT What, punk will not be troubled with you tonight, therefore I am—is it not so?

RANGER I have been turned out of doors indeed just now by a woman—but such a woman, Vincent—

VINCENT Yes, yes, your women are always 'such women'!   60

RANGER A neighbour of yours, and I'm sure the finest you have.

VINCENT Prithee do not asperse my neighbourhood with your acquaintance; 'twould bring a scandal upon an alley.

RANGER Nay, I do not know her; therefore I come to you.

VINCENT 'Twas no wonder she turned you out of doors then; and if   65
she had known you, 'twould have been a wonder she had let you stay. But where does she live?

RANGER Five doors off, on the right hand.

VINCENT Pish, pish—

RANGER What's the matter?   70

VINCENT Does she° live there, do you say?

RANGER Yes, I observed them exactly, that my account from you might be as exact. Do you know who lives there?

VINCENT Yes, so well that I know you are mistaken.

RANGER Is she not a young lady, scarce eighteen, of extraordinary   75
beauty, her stature next to low, and in mourning?

VALENTINE (*behind*) What is this?

VINCENT She is; but if you saw her, you broke in at window.

RANGER I chased her home from the park, indeed, taking her for another lady, who had some claim to my heart till she showed a   80
better title to't.

VINCENT Ha ha ha.

VALENTINE (*behind*) Was she at park then? And have I a new rival?

VINCENT From the park did you follow her, do you say? I knew you were mistaken.   85

RANGER I tell you I am not.

VINCENT If you are sure it was that house, it might be perhaps her woman, stolen to the park unknown to her lady.

RANGER My acquaintance does usually begin with the maid first—but now 'twas with the mistress, I assure you.   90

VINCENT The mistress! I tell you, she has not been out of her doors
since Valentine's flight; she is his mistress, the great heiress
Christina.

RANGER I tell you then again: I followed that Christina from the park
home, where I talked with her half an hour, and intend to see her   95
tomorrow again.

VALENTINE (*behind*) Would she talk with him too?

VINCENT It cannot be.

RANGER Christina, do you call her? Faith I am sorry she is an heiress,
lest it should bring the scandal of interest, and design of lucre,   100
upon my love.

VINCENT No, no, her face and virtues will free you from that
censure. But however, 'tis not fairly done to rival your friend
Valentine in his absence; and when he is present, you know 'twill
be dangerous, by my Lord Clerimont's example. Faith, if you have   105
seen her, I would not advise you to attempt it again.

RANGER You may be merry, sir; you are not in love. Your advice I
came not for, nor will I for your assistance.° Good night.

     Exit Ranger. [*Valentine comes forward*]

VALENTINE Here's your Penelope, the woman that had not seen the
sun, nor face of man, since my departure—for it seems she goes   110
out in the night, when the sun is absent and faces are not
distinguished.

VINCENT Why, do you believe him?

VALENTINE Should I believe you?

VINCENT 'Twere more for your interest, and you would be less   115
deceived. If you believe him, you must doubt the chastity of all the
fine women in town, and five miles about.

VALENTINE His reports of them, will little invalidate his testimony
with me.

VINCENT He spares not the innocents in bibs and aprons. I'll secure   120
you: he has made (at best) some gross mistake concerning Christina, which tomorrow will discover. In the mean time, let us go
sleep.

VALENTINE I will not hinder you because I cannot enjoy it myself.

       Hunger, revenge, to sleep are petty foes,   125
      But only death the jealous eyes can close

     Exeunt

3.1

Mrs Crossbite's house
Enter Mrs Joiner, Mrs Crossbite°

MRS JOINER Good morrow, gossip.

MRS CROSSBITE Good morrow; but why up so early, good gossip?

MRS JOINER My care and passionate concern for you, and yours, would not let me rest, in truly.

MRS CROSSBITE For me and mine? 5

MRS JOINER You know, we have known one another long. I think it be some nine and thirty years since you were married.

MRS CROSSBITE Nine and thirty years old, mistress? I'd have you to know, I am no far-born child; and if the register had not been burned in the last great fire, alas!—but my face needs no register, 10 sure. Nine and thirty years old, said you, mistress?

MRS JOINER I said you had been so long married; but, indeed, you bear your years as well as any she in Pepper Alley.°

MRS CROSSBITE Nine and thirty, mistress.

MRS JOINER This it is; a woman nowadays had rather you should 15 find her faulty with a man, I warrant you, than discover her age, I warrant you.

MRS CROSSBITE Marry, and 'tis the greater secret far. Tell a miser he is rich, and a woman she is old—you will get no money of him, nor kindness of her. To tell me I was nine and thirty! I say no 20 more; 'twas unneighbourly done of you, mistress.

MRS JOINER My memory confesses my age, it seems, as much as my face, for I thought—

MRS CROSSBITE Pray talk nor think no more of anyone's age; but say—what brought you hither so early? 25

MRS JOINER How does my sweet god-daughter, poor wretch?

MRS CROSSBITE Well, very well.

MRS JOINER Ah, sweet creature; alas, alas, I am sorry for her.

MRS CROSSBITE Why, what has she done to deserve your sorrow, or my reprehension? 30

Lucy comes to the door

LUCY (*behind*) What, are they talking of me?

MRS JOINER In short, she was seen going into the meeting-house of the wicked, otherwise called the playhouse, hand in hand with that vile fellow Dapperwit.

MRS CROSSBITE Mr Dapperwit! Let me tell you, if 'twere not for   35
Master Dapperwit we might have lived all this vacation° upon
green cheese, tripe, and ox-cheek. If he had it, we should not
want it.° But poor gentleman, it often goes hard with him, for he's
a wit.

MRS JOINER So then, you are the dog to be fed while the house is   40
broken up.° I say beware—the sweet bits you swallow will make
your daughter's belly swell, mistress; and after all your junkets
there will be a bone for you to pick,° mistress.

MRS CROSSBITE Sure, Master Dapperwit is no such manner of
man?   45

MRS JOINER He is a wit, you say, and what are wits but contemners
of matrons, seducers or defamers of married women, and de-
flowerers of helpless virgins, even in the streets, upon the very
bulks? Affronters of midnight magistracy,° and breakers of windows, in a word.   50

MRS CROSSBITE But he is a little-wit, a modest-wit, and they do no
such outrageous things as your great wits do.

MRS JOINER Nay, I dare say he will not say himself he is a little-wit,
if you ask him.

LUCY (aside) Nay, I cannot hear this with patience.—With your   55
pardon, mother, you are as much mistaken as my godmother in Mr
Dapperwit; for he is as great a wit as any, and in what he speaks
or writes, as happy as any. I can assure you, he contemns all your
tearing wits, in comparison of himself.

MRS JOINER Alas, poor young wretch, I cannot blame thee so much   60
as thy mother, for thou art not thyself; his bewitching madrigals
have charmed thee into some heathenish . . . imp with a hard
name.°

LUCY 'Nymph', you mean, godmother.

MRS JOINER But you, gossip, know what's what. Yesterday, as I told   65
you, a fine old alderman of the City, seeing your daughter in so ill
hands as Dapperwit's, was zealously, and in pure charity,° bent
upon her redemption, and has sent me to tell you he will take her
into his care, and relieve your necessities, if you think good.

MRS CROSSBITE Will he relieve all our necessities?   70

MRS JOINER All.

MRS CROSSBITE Mine, as well as my daughter's?

MRS JOINER Yes.

MRS CROSSBITE Well fare his heart. D'ye hear, daughter, Mrs Joiner
has satisfied me clearly. Dapperwit is a vile fellow, and (in   75

short) you must put an end to that scandalous familiarity between you.

LUCY Leave sweet Mr Dapperwit! Oh furious ingratitude! Was not he the man that gave me my first farandine gown, put me out of worsted stockings and plain handkerchiefs, taught me to dress, talk, and move well. 80

MRS CROSSBITE He has taught you to talk indeed. But, hussy, I will not have my pleasure disputed.

MRS JOINER Nay, indeed you are too tart with her, poor sweet soul. 85

LUCY He taught me to rehearse too, would have brought me into the playhouse,° where I might have had as good luck as others. I might have had good clothes, plate, jewels, and things so well about me that my neighbours, the little gentlemen's wives, of fifteen hundred or two thousand pound a year, should have 90 retired into the country, sick with envy of my prosperity and greatness.

MRS JOINER If you follow your mother's counsel, you are like to enjoy all you talk of sooner than by Dapperwit's assistance—a poor wretch that goes on tick for the paper he writes his lampoons on, 95 and the very ale and coffee that inspires him, as they say.

MRS CROSSBITE I am credibly informed so, indeed, Madam Joiner.

MRS JOINER Well, I have discharged my conscience. Good morrow to you both.

Exeunt

3.2

Mrs Crossbite's dining-room

Enter Dapperwit, Ranger

DAPPERWIT This is the cabinet in which I hide my jewel: a small house, in an obscure, little, retired street too.

RANGER Vulgarly, an alley.

DAPPERWIT Nay, I hid my mistress with as much care as a spark of the town does his money from his dun, after a good hand at play; 5 and nothing but you could have wrought upon me for a sight of her, let me perish.

RANGER My obligation to you is great; do not lessen it, by delays of the favour you promised.

DAPPERWIT But do not censure my honour,° for if you had not been   10
in a desperate condition—For as one nail must beat out another,
one poison expel another, one fire draw out another,° one fit of
drinking cure the sickness of another—so the surfeit you took last
night of Christina's eyes, shall be cured by Lucy's this morning.
Or as—   15

RANGER Nay, I bar more similitudes.

DAPPERWIT What, in my mistress's lodging? That were as hard as
to bar a young parson in the pulpit, the fifth of November, railing
at the church of Rome;° or as hard as to put you to bed to Lucy,
and defend you touching her; or as—   20

RANGER Or as hard as to make you hold your tongue. [*Looking about*]
I shall not see your mistress, I see?

DAPPERWIT Miss Lucy! Miss Lucy!

    Knocks at the door, and returns
The devil take me, if good men (I say no more) have not been upon
their knees to me, to see her, and you at last must obtain it.   25

RANGER I do not believe you.

DAPPERWIT 'Tis such a she; she is beautiful without affectation,
amorous without impertinency, airy and brisk without impudence,
frolic without rudeness, and in a word, the justest creature
breathing, to her assignation.°   30

RANGER You praise her as if you had a mind to part with her; and
yet you resolve, I see, to keep her to yourself.

DAPPERWIT Keep her! Poor creature, she cannot leave me; and rather
than leave her, I would leave writing lampoons or sonnets, almost.

RANGER Well, I'll leave you with her then.   35

DAPPERWIT What, you will go without seeing her?

RANGER Rather than stay without seeing her.

DAPPERWIT Yes, yes, you shall see her. But let me perish if I have
not been offered a hundred guineas for a sight of her, by—;° I say
no more.   40

RANGER (*aside*) I understand you now. [*To him*] If the favour be to be
purchased, then I'll bid all I have about me for't. [*Takes out money*]

DAPPERWIT Fie, fie, Mr Ranger, you are pleasant i' faith. Do you
think I would sell the sight of my rarity?—like those gentlemen
who hang out flags at Charing Cross,° or like—   45

RANGER Nay, then I'm gone again.

DAPPERWIT What, you take it ill I refuse your money? Rather than
that should be, give us it. But take notice I will borrow it—now I
think on't, Lucy wants a gown, and some knacks.

RANGER Here.   50

DAPPERWIT But I must pay it you again. I will not take it, unless
you engage your honour I shall pay it you again.

RANGER You must pardon me; I will not engage my honour for such
a trifle. Go fetch her out.

DAPPERWIT Well, she's a ravishing creature—such eyes, and lips,   55
Mr Ranger.

RANGER Prithee go.

DAPPERWIT Such neck and breasts, Mr Ranger.

RANGER Again, prithee go.

DAPPERWIT Such feet, legs, and thighs, Mr Ranger.   60

RANGER Prithee let me see 'em.

DAPPERWIT And a mouth no bigger than your ring. I need say no
more.

RANGER Would thou wert never to speak again.

DAPPERWIT And then so neat, so sweet a creature in bed, that to my   65
knowledge she does not change her sheets in half a year.

RANGER I thank you for that allay to my impatience.

DAPPERWIT (*knocking at the door*) Miss Lucy, Miss Lucy, Miss!

RANGER Will she not open?

DAPPERWIT I am afraid my pretty miss is not stirring, and therefore 70
will not admit us.

[RANGER I am afraid your pretty miss *is* stirring, and therefore will
not admit us.]°

DAPPERWIT Fie, fie, a quibble next your stomach° in a morning!
What if she should hear us? Would you lose a mistress for a   75
quibble? That's more than I could do, let me perish.

RANGER Is she not gone her walk to Lamb's Conduit?°

DAPPERWIT She is within, I hear her.

RANGER But she will not hear you; she's as deaf as if you were a dun
or a constable.   80

DAPPERWIT Pish, give her but leave to gape, rub her eyes, and put
on her day-pinner, the long patch under the left eye, awaken the
roses on her cheeks with some Spanish wool, and warrant her breath
with some lemon peel—the door flies off of the hinges, and she into
my arms. She knows there is as much artifice to keep a victory as   85
to gain it, and 'tis a sign she values the conquest of my heart.

RANGER I thought her beauty had not stood in need of art.

DAPPERWIT Beauty's a coward still, without the help of art, and may
have the fortune of a conquest, but cannot keep it. Beauty and art
can no more be asunder than love and honour.   90

RANGER Or to speak more like yourself, wit and judgement.

DAPPERWIT Don't you hear the door wag yet?

RANGER Not a whit.

DAPPERWIT Miss, miss, 'tis your slave that calls. Come, all this
tricking for him!—Lend me your comb, Mr Ranger.   95

RANGER No, I am to be preferred° today; you are to set me off. You
are in possession; I will not lend you arms to keep me out.

DAPPERWIT A pox, don't let me be ungrateful. If she has smugged
herself up for me, let me prune and flounce my peruke a little for
her. There's ne'er a young fellow in the town but will do as much   100
for a mere stranger in the playhouse.

RANGER A wit's wig has the privilege of being uncombed in the very
playhouse, or in the presence,—°

DAPPERWIT But not in the presence of his mistress; 'tis a greater
neglect of her than himself. Pray lend me your comb.   105

RANGER I would not have men of wit and courage make use of every
fop's mean arts, to keep or gain a mistress.

DAPPERWIT But don't you see every day, though a man have ne'er
so much wit and courage, his mistress will revolt to those fops that
wear, and comb, perukes well? I'll break off the bargain, and will   110
not receive you my partner.°

RANGER (combs his peruke) Therefore, you see, I am setting up for
myself.

DAPPERWIT She comes, she comes; pray, your comb.

        Snatches Ranger's comb. Enter Mrs Crossbite to them

MRS CROSSBITE 'Bargain'! What, are you offering us to sale?   115

DAPPERWIT A pox, is't she? Here, take your comb again then.

        Returns the comb

MRS CROSSBITE Would you sell us? 'Tis like you, i'fads.

DAPPERWIT Sell thee? Where should we find a chapman? Go,
prithee mother, call out my dear Miss Lucy.

MRS CROSSBITE Your Miss Lucy! I do not wonder you have the   120
conscience to bargain for us behind our backs, since you have the
impudence to claim a propriety in us, to my face.

RANGER How's this, Dapperwit?

DAPPERWIT Come, come, this gentleman will not think the worse of
a woman, for my acquaintance with her. He has seen me bring your   125
daughter to the lure,° with a China orange, from one side of the
playhouse to the other.

MRS CROSSBITE I would have the gentleman and you to know, my
daughter is a girl of reputation, though she has been seen in your

company; but is now so sensible of her past danger that she is   130
resolved never more to venture her pitcher to the well,° as they say.

DAPPERWIT How's that, widow! I wonder at your new confidence.

MRS CROSSBITE I wonder at your old impudence, that where you
have had so frequent repulses, you should provoke another, and
bring your friend here to witness your disgrace.   135

DAPPERWIT Hark you, widow, a little.

MRS CROSSBITE What, you have mortgaged my daughter to that
gentleman, and now would offer me a snip to join in the security!°

DAPPERWIT (*aside*) She overheard me talk of a bargain; 'twas   140
unlucky.—Your wrath is grounded upon a mistake. Miss Lucy
herself shall be judge; call her out, pray.

MRS CROSSBITE She shall not, she will not come to you.

DAPPERWIT Till I hear it from her own mouth, I cannot believe it.

MRS CROSSBITE You shall hear her say't through the door.   145

DAPPERWIT I shall doubt it, unless she say° it to my face.

MRS CROSSBITE Shall we be troubled with you no more then?

DAPPERWIT If she command my death, I cannot disobey her.

MRS CROSSBITE Come out, child.

    [*Enter*] Lucy, *holding down her head*

DAPPERWIT Your servant, dearest miss; can you have—   150

MRS CROSSBITE Let me ask her.

DAPPERWIT No, I'll ask her.

RANGER I'll throw up cross or pile who shall ask her.

DAPPERWIT [*apart to Lucy*] Can you have the heart to say you will
never more break a cheese-cake with me at New Spring Garden,   155
the Neat House, or Chelsea? Never more sit in my lap at a new
play; never more wear a suit of knots of my choice; and last of all,
never more pass away an afternoon with me again in the green
garret, in—° Do not forget the green garret.

LUCY I wish I had never seen the green garret. Demn the green   160
garret!

DAPPERWIT Demn the green garret? You are strangely altered.

LUCY 'Tis you are altered.

DAPPERWIT You have refused Colby's Mulberry Garden, and the
French houses, for the green garret; and a little something in the   165
green garret pleased you more than the best treat the other places
could yield. And can you of a sudden quit the green garret?

LUCY Since you have a design to pawn me for the rent,° 'tis time to
remove my goods.

DAPPERWIT Thou art extremely mistaken. 170

LUCY Besides, I have heard such strange things of you this morning . . .

DAPPERWIT What things?

LUCY I blush to speak 'em.

DAPPERWIT I know my innocence, therefore take my charge as a 175
favour.° What have I done?

LUCY Then know, vile wit, my mother has confessed just now, thou
wert false to me, to her too certain knowledge, and hast forced even
her to be false to me too.

DAPPERWIT Faults in drink, Lucy, when we are not ourselves, 180
should not condemn us.

LUCY And now to let me out to hire like hackney! I tell you my
own dear mother shall bargain for me no more. There are as little
as I can bargain for themselves nowadays, as well as properer
women. 185

MRS CROSSBITE Whispering all this while! Beware of his snares
again; come away, child.

DAPPERWIT Sweet, dear, Miss—

LUCY Bargain for me! You have reckoned without your hostess,° as
they say. Bargain for me! Bargain for me! 190
Exit Lucy

DAPPERWIT I must return then, to treat with you.

MRS CROSSBITE Treat me no treatings, but take a word for all: you
shall no more dishonour my daughter, nor molest my lodgings, as
you have done at all hours.

DAPPERWIT Do you intend to change 'em then, to Bridewell, or 195
Long's powdering-tub?°

MRS CROSSBITE No, to a bailiff's house, and then you'll be so civil,
I presume, as not to trouble us.

RANGER Here, will you have my comb again, Dapperwit?

DAPPERWIT A pox, I think women take inconstancy from me, worse 200
than from any man breathing.

MRS CROSSBITE Pray, sir, forget me before you write your next
lampoon.
*Exit Mrs Crossbite. [Enter] Sir Simon Addleplot, in the dress
of a clerk, to Ranger and Dapperwit*

SIR SIMON Have I found you? Have I found you in your by-walks,
faith and troth? I am almost out of breath in following you. 205
Gentlemen, when they get into an alley, walk so fast—as if they
had more earnest business there than in the broad streets.

47

DAPPERWIT (*aside*) How came this sot hither? Fortune has sent him
to ease my choler.—You impudent rascal, who are you that dare
intrude thus on us?   210
    Strikes him

SIR SIMON (*softly*) Don't you know me, Dapperwit? Sure you know
me.

DAPPERWIT Wilt thou dishonour me with thy acquaintance too?
Thou rascally, insolent, pen-and-ink man.
    Strikes him again

SIR SIMON Oh! Oh! (*Speaks softly*) Sure, you know me; pray know   215
me.

DAPPERWIT By thy saucy familiarity, thou shouldst be a marker at a
tennis-court, a barber, or a slave that fills coffee.°
    [*Strikes him again*]

SIR SIMON Oh! Oh!

DAPPERWIT What art thou?   220
    Kicks him

SIR SIMON [*aside*] Nay, I must not discover myself to Ranger, for a
kick or two.—Oh pray hold, sir.
    Delivers him a letter
By that you will know me.

DAPPERWIT How! Sir Simon!

SIR SIMON Mum, mum, make no excuses, man; I would not Ranger   225
should have known me for five hundred—kicks.

DAPPERWIT Your disguise is so natural, I protest, it will excuse me.

SIR SIMON I know that; prithee make no excuses, I say—no ceremony between thee and I, man. Read the letter.

DAPPERWIT What, you have not opened it?   230

SIR SIMON Prithee don't be angry; the seal is a little cracked, for I
could not help kissing Mistress Martha's letter. The word is: 'now
or never.' Her father, she finds, will be abroad all this day, and she
longs to see your friend Sir Simon Addleplot (faith, 'tis a pretty
jest)—while I am with her, and praising myself to her, at no   235
ordinary rate. Let thee and I alone, at an intrigue.

DAPPERWIT Tell her, I will not fail to meet her, at the place and
time. Have a care of your charge, and manage your business like
yourself, for yourself.

SIR SIMON I warrant you.   240

DAPPERWIT (*aside*) The gaining Gripe's daughter will make me
support the loss of this young jilt here.

RANGER What fellow's that?

48

DAPPERWIT A servant to a friend of mine.

RANGER Methinks he something resembles our acquaintance Sir   245
Simon, but it is no compliment to tell him so—for that knight is
the most egregious coxcomb that ever played with lady's fan.

SIR SIMON (*aside*) So! Thanks to my disguise, I know my enemies.

RANGER The most incorrigible ass, beyond the reproof of a kicking
rival, or a frowning mistress. But if it be possible, thou dost use   250
him worse than his mistress or rival can; thou dost make such a
cully of him.

SIR SIMON (*aside*) Does he think so too?

DAPPERWIT Go, friend, go about your business.

Exit Sir Simon Addleplot

A pox, you would spoil all, just in the critical time of projection—   255
he brings me here a summons from his mistress, to meet her in the
evening. Will you come to my wedding?

RANGER Don't speak so loud, you'll break poor Lucy's heart. Poor
creature, she cannot leave you, and rather than leave her, you
should leave writing of lampoons, or sonnets—almost.   260

DAPPERWIT Come, let her go, ungrateful baggage. But now you talk
of sonnets—I am no living wit, if her love has not cost me two
thousand couplets at least.

RANGER But what would you give now for a new satire against
women, ready-made? 'Twould be as convenient to buy satires   265
against women, ready-made, as it is to buy cravats ready-tied.

DAPPERWIT Or as—

RANGER Hey, come away, come away, Mr Or-as—

Exeunt Ranger and Dapperwit. Enter Mrs Joiner, Gripe

GRIPE Peace, plenty, and pastime be within these walls.°

MRS JOINER 'Tis a small house, you see, and mean furniture, for no   270
gallants are suffered to come hither. She might have had, ere
now, as good lodgings as any in town—her Moreclack hangings,°
great glasses, cabinets, China embroidered beds,° Persia carpets,
gold plate, and the like, if she would have put herself forward. But
your worship may please to make 'em remove to a place fit to   275
receive one of your worship's quality; for this is a little scandalous,
in truly.

GRIPE No, no, I like it well enough; I am not dainty. Besides,
privacy, privacy, Mrs Joiner; I love privacy, in opposition to the
wicked, who hate it.° (*Looks about*)   280

MRS JOINER What do you look for, sir?

GRIPE Walls have ears, walls have ears. But besides, I look for a private place to retire to, in time of need. Oh, here's one convenient.

> *Turns up a hanging, and discovers the slender provisions of the family°*

MRS JOINER But you see, poor innocent souls, to what use they put   285
it—not to hide gallants.

GRIPE Temperance is the nurse of chastity.

MRS JOINER But your worship may please to mend their fare, and
when you come, may make them entertain you better than (you see)
they do themselves.   290

GRIPE No, I am not dainty, as I told you. I abominate entertainments. No entertainments, pray, Mrs Joiner.

MRS JOINER (*aside*) No?

GRIPE There can be no entertainment to me more luscious and
savoury than the communion with that little gentlewoman. Will   295
you call her out? I fast till I see her.

MRS JOINER But in truly, your worship, we should have brought a
bottle or two of Rhenish, and some Naples biscuit, to have
entertained the young gentlewoman; 'tis the mode for lovers to
treat their mistresses.   300

GRIPE Modes! I tell you, Mrs Joiner, I hate modes and forms.°

MRS JOINER You must send for something to entertain her with.

GRIPE Again, entertaining! We will be to each other a feast.

MRS JOINER I shall be ashamed, in truly, your worship. Besides, the
young gentlewoman will despise you.   305

GRIPE I shall content her, I warrant you. Leave it to me.

MRS JOINER (*aside*) I am sure you will not content me, if you will
not content her. 'Tis as impossible for a man to love and be a miser,
as to love and be wise,° as they say.

GRIPE While you talk of treats, you starve my eyes. I long to see the   310
fair one. Fetch her hither.

MRS JOINER I am ashamed she should find me so abominable a liar.
I have so praised you to her, and, above all your virtues, your
liberality—which is so great a virtue that it often excuses youth,
beauty, courage, wit, or anything.   315

GRIPE Pish, pish, 'tis the virtue of fools; every fool can have it.

MRS JOINER And will your worship want it then? I told her—

GRIPE Why would you tell her anything of me? You know I am a
modest man. But come, if you will have me as extravagant as the
wicked—take that, and fetch us a treat, as you call it.   320

MRS JOINER Upon my life, a groat; what will this purchase?

GRIPE Two black-pots of ale and a cake, at the next cellar. Come, the wine has arsenic in't.°

MRS JOINER (*aside*) Well, I am mistaken, and my hopes are abused; I never knew any man so mortified a miser that he would deny his lechery anything. I must be even with thee, then, another way.

    Mrs Joiner goes out

GRIPE These useful old women are more exorbitant and craving in their desires, than the young ones in theirs. These prodigals in white perukes spoil 'em both; and that's the reason, when the squires come under my clutches, I make 'em pay for their folly and mine—and 'tis but conscience. Oh, here comes the fair one at last.

    Enter Mrs Joiner leading in Lucy, who hangs backward as she enters

LUCY Oh Lord, there's a man, godmother!

MRS JOINER Come in, child; thou art so bashful—

LUCY My mother is from home too; I dare not.

MRS JOINER If she were here, she'd teach you better manners.

LUCY I'm afraid she'd be angry.

MRS JOINER To see you so much an ass. Come along, I say.

GRIPE Nay, speak to her gently; if you won't, I will.

LUCY Thank you, sir.

GRIPE Pretty innocent—there is, I see, one left yet of her age. What hap have I! Sweet little gentlewoman, come and sit down by me.

LUCY I am better bred, I hope, sir.

GRIPE You must sit down by me.

LUCY I'd rather stand, if you please.

GRIPE To please me, you must sit, sweetest.

LUCY Not before my godmother, sure.

GRIPE Wonderment of innocence!

MRS JOINER A poor bashful girl, sir; I'm sorry she is not better taught.

GRIPE I am glad she is not taught. I'll teach her myself.

LUCY Are you a dancing-master then, sir? But if I should be dull, and not move as you would have me, you would not beat me, sir, I hope?

GRIPE Beat thee, honeysuckle? I'll use thee thus,

    Kisses her

and thus, and thus. Ah, Mrs Joiner, prithee go fetch our treat now.

MRS JOINER A treat of a groat! I will not wag.

GRIPE Why don't you go? Here, take more money, and fetch what 360
you will. Take here, half a crown.

MRS JOINER What will half a crown do?

GRIPE Take a crown then—an angel—a piece.° Begone.

MRS JOINER [aside] A treat only will not serve my turn. [To Gripe]
I must buy the poor wretch there some toys. 365

GRIPE What toys? What? Speak quickly.

MRS JOINER Pendants, necklaces, fans, ribbons, points, laces, stockings, gloves—

GRIPE Hold, hold, before it comes to a gown.

MRS JOINER Well remembered, sir; indeed, she wants a gown, for 370
she has but that one to her back. For your own sake you should
give her a new gown; for variety of dresses rouses desire, and makes
an old mistress seem every day a new one.

GRIPE For that reason she shall have no new gown; for I am naturally
constant, and as I am still the same, I love she should be still the 375
same. But here, take half a piece for the other things.

MRS JOINER Half a piece!

GRIPE Prithee begone—take t'other piece then. Two pieces, three
pieces, five. Here, 'tis all I have.

MRS JOINER I must have the broad-seal ring° too, or I stir not. 380

GRIPE Insatiable woman! Will you have that too? Prithee spare me
that, 'twas my grandfather's.

          [Mrs Joiner takes the ring]

MRS JOINER (aside) That's false, he had ne'er a coat. So now I go.
This is but a violent fit, and will not hold.

LUCY Oh, whither do you go, godmother? Will you leave me alone? 385

MRS JOINER The gentleman will not hurt you. You may venture
yourself with him alone.

LUCY I think I may, grandmother.

          Exit Mrs Joiner. [Gripe follows her to the door]

What, will you lock me in, sir? Don't lock me in, sir.

GRIPE (fumbling at the door, locks it) 'Tis a private lesson I must teach 390
you, fair.

LUCY I don't see your fiddle, sir; where is your little kit?°

GRIPE I'll show it thee presently, sweetest.

          Setting a chair against the door

Necessity, mother of invention. Come, my dearest.

          Takes her in his arms

LUCY What do you mean, sir? Don't hurt me sir, will you? Oh, oh,   395
you will kill me! (*Cries out*) Murder, murder, oh, oh! Help, help,
oh—

> *The door broke open, enter Mrs Crossbite, and two men in*
> *aprons: her Landlord and his Prentice*

MRS CROSSBITE What, murder my daughter, villain?

LUCY I wish he had murdered me. Oh, oh!

MRS CROSSBITE What has he done?   400

LUCY Why would you go out, and leave me alone? Unfortunate
woman that I am.

GRIPE (*aside*) How now, what will this end in?

MRS CROSSBITE Who brought him in?

LUCY That witch, that treacherous false woman my godmother, who   405
has betrayed me, sold me to his lust; oh, oh!

MRS CROSSBITE Have you ravished my daughter then, you old goat?
Ravished my daughter? Ravished my daughter? Speak, villain.

GRIPE By yea and by nay,° no such matter.

MRS CROSSBITE A canting rogue, too. Take notice, landlord, he has   410
ravished my daughter. You see her all in tears and distraction. And
see there (*pointing to the chair*) the wicked engine of the filthy
execution. [*To the Prentice*] Jeremy, call up my neighbours, and the
constable.—False villain, thou shalt die° for't.

GRIPE Hold, hold! (*Aside*) Nay, I am caught.   415

MRS CROSSBITE [*to the Prentice*] Go, go, make haste.

LUCY Oh, oh!

MRS CROSSBITE Poor wretch!—Go quickly.

GRIPE Hold, hold. [*To Lucy*] Thou young spawn of the old serpent!°
Wicked, as° I thought thee innocent! Wilt thou say I would have   420
ravished thee?

LUCY I will swear you did ravish me.

GRIPE I thought so, treacherous Eve. (*Aside*)° Then I am gone; I
must shift as well as I can.

LUCY Oh, oh!   425

MRS CROSSBITE Will none° of you call up the neighbours, and the
authority of the alley?

GRIPE Hold, I'll give you twenty mark° among you, to let me go.

MRS CROSSBITE Villain, nothing shall buy thy life.

LANDLORD But stay, Mrs Crossbite, let me talk with you.   430

> [*Landlord and Mrs Crossbite whisper together*]

LUCY Oh, oh!

LANDLORD Come, sir, I am your friend. In a word, I have appeased her, and she shall be contented with a little sum. ❋

GRIPE What is it? What is it?

LANDLORD But five hundred pound.   435

GRIPE But five hundred pound! Hang me then, hang me rather.

LANDLORD You will say I have been your friend.

PRENTICE [*looking out at the door*] The constable and neighbours are coming.

GRIPE How, how!   440

    Kneels to Mrs Crossbite

Will you not take a hundred? Pray use conscience in your ways.

MRS CROSSBITE I scorn your money; I will not take a thousand.

GRIPE (*aside*) My enemies are many, and I shall be a scandal to the faithful, as a laughing-stock to the wicked.—Go, prepare your engines for my persecution. I'll give you the best security I can. 445

LANDLORD The instruments are drawing° in the other room, if you please to go thither.

MRS CROSSBITE Indeed, now I consider—a portion will do my daughter more good than his death. That would but publish her shame; money will cover it. *Probatum est*, as they say. [*To Gripe*] 450
Let me tell you, sir, 'tis a charitable thing to give a young maid a portion.

    Exeunt

3.3

Lydia's lodging

Enter Lydia, Lady Flippant

LYDIA 'Tis as hard for a woman to conceal her indignation from her apostate lover, as to conceal her love from her faithful servant.

LADY FLIPPANT Or almost as hard as it is for the prating fellows, nowadays, to conceal the favours of obliging ladies.

LYDIA If Ranger should come up (I saw him just now in the street), 5
the discovery of my anger to him now, would be as mean as the discovery of my love to him before.

LADY FLIPPANT Though I did so mean a thing as to love a fellow, I would not do so mean a thing as to confess it, certainly, by my trouble to part with him. If I confessed love, it should be before 10
they left me.

LYDIA So you would deserve to be left, before you were. But could you ever do so mean a thing as to confess love to any?

LADY FLIPPANT Yes—but I never did so mean a thing as really to love any!   15

LYDIA You had once a husband.

LADY FLIPPANT Fie, madam, do you think me so ill-bred, as to love a husband?

LYDIA You had a widow's heart before you were a widow, I see.

LADY FLIPPANT I should rather make an adventure of° my honour   20
with a gallant, for a gown, a new coach, a necklace, than clap my husband's cheeks for them, or sit in his lap. I should be as ashamed to be caught in such a posture with a husband, as a brisk well-bred [fellow]° of the town would be, to be caught on his knees at prayers—unless to his mistress.   25

    [*Enter*] *Ranger, Dapperwit* [*and Leonore,*° *showing them in*]

LYDIA Mr Ranger, 'twas obligingly done of you.

RANGER Indeed, cousin, I had kept my promise with you last night, but this gentleman knows—

LYDIA You mistake me, but you shall not lessen any favour you do me. You are going to excuse your not coming to me last night,   30
when I take it as a particular obligation, that though you threatened me with a visit, upon consideration you were so civil as not to trouble me.

DAPPERWIT (*aside*) This is an unlucky morning with me; here's my eternal persecution, the Widow Flippant.   35

LADY FLIPPANT What, Mr Dapperwit!

    [*Lady Flippant and Dapperwit converse apart*]

RANGER Indeed, cousin, besides my business, another cause I did not wait on you was my apprehension you were gone to the park, notwithstanding your promise to the contrary.

LYDIA Therefore you went to the park, to visit me there, notwith-   40
standing your promise to the contrary.

RANGER Who, I at the park? When I had promised to wait upon you at your lodging? But were you at the park, madam?

LYDIA Who, I at the park? When I had promised to wait for you at home? I was no more at the park than you were. Were you at the   45
park?

RANGER The park had been a dismal desert to me, notwithstanding all the good company in't, if I had wanted yours.

LYDIA (*aside*) Because it has been the constant endeavour of men to keep women ignorant, they think us so; but 'tis that increases our   50 inquisitiveness, and makes us know them ignorant as false. He is as impudent a dissembler as the Widow Flippant, who is making her importunate addresses in vain, for aught I see.

Lady Flippant driving Dapperwit from one side of the stage to the other

LADY FLIPPANT Dear Mr Dapperwit, merciful Mr Dapperwit.

DAPPERWIT Unmerciful Lady Flippant.   55

LADY FLIPPANT Will you be satisfied?

DAPPERWIT Won't you be satisfied?

LADY FLIPPANT (*aside to Dapperwit*) That a wit should be jealous! That a wit should be jealous! There's never a brisk young fellow in the town (though no wit, heaven knows) but thinks too well of   60
himself to think ill of his wife or mistress. Now, that a wit should lessen his opinion of himself, for shame!

DAPPERWIT (*softly, apart to Ranger*) I promised to bring you off, but I find it enough to shift for myself!

LYDIA What, out of breath, madam?   65

LADY FLIPPANT I have been defending our cause, madam. I have beat him out of the pit.° I do so mumble these prating, censorious fellows they call wits, when I meet with them.

DAPPERWIT [*apart to Ranger*] Her ladyship, indeed, is the only thing in petticoats I dread. 'Twas well for me there was company in the   70
room, for I dare no more venture myself with her alone, than a cully that has been bit dares venture himself in a tavern with an old rook.

LADY FLIPPANT I am the revenger of our sex, certainly.

DAPPERWIT And the most insatiable one I ever knew, madam; I dare   75
not stand your fury longer.—Mr Ranger, I will go before and make a new appointment with your friends that expect you at dinner at the French house. 'Tis fit business still wait on love.°

RANGER Do so—but now I think on't, Sir Thomas goes out of town this afternoon, and I shall not see him here again these three   80
months.

LYDIA [*to Dapperwit*] Nay, pray take him with you, sir.

LADY FLIPPANT No sir, you shall not take the gentleman from his mistress. (*Aside* [*to Dapperwit*]) Do not go yet, sweet Mr Dapperwit.   85

LYDIA Take him with you, sir. I suppose his business may be there to borrow, or win, money, and I ought not to be his hindrance; for when he has none, he has his desperate designs upon that little I have—for want of money makes as devout lovers as Christians.

DAPPERWIT I hope, madam, he offers you no less security than his 90
liberty.°

LYDIA His liberty! As poor a pawn to take up money on,° as honour.
He is like the desperate bankrupts of this age, who, if they can get
people's fortunes into their hands, care not though they spend
them in jail, all their lives. 95

LADY FLIPPANT And the poor crediting ladies, when they have
parted with their money, must be contented with a pitiful composition, or starve for all them.

RANGER But widows are commonly so wise as to be sure their men
are solvable before they trust 'em. 100

LADY FLIPPANT Can you blame 'em? I declare, I will trust no
man—pray do not take it ill, gentlemen. Quacks in their bills, and
poets in the titles of their plays, do not more disappoint us than
gallants with their promises. But I trust none.

DAPPERWIT Nay, she's a very jew in that particular. To my know- 105
ledge, she'll know her man, over and over again, before she trust
him.

RANGER Well, my dearest cousin, good morrow. When I stay from
you so long again, blame me to purpose, and be extremely angry;
for nothing can make me amends for the loss of your company, but 110
your reprehension of my absence. I'll take such a chiding as kindly
as Russian wives do beating.°

LYDIA If you were my husband, I could not take your absence more
kindly than I do.

RANGER And if you were my wife, I would trust you as much out of 115
my sight as I could, to show my opinion of your virtue.

LADY FLIPPANT A well-bred gentleman, I warrant. Will you go
then, cruel Mr Dapperwit? [*Following him to the door*]
Exeunt Ranger and Dapperwit

LYDIA (*apart* [*to Leonore*]) Have I not dissembled well, Leonore?

LEONORE But, madam, to what purpose? Why do you not put him 120
to his trial, and see what he can say for himself?

LYDIA I am afraid lest my proofs, and his guilt, should make him
desperate, and so contemn that pardon which he could not hope
for.

LEONORE 'Tis unjust to condemn him before you hear him. 125

LYDIA I will reprieve him till I have more evidence.

LEONORE How will you get it?

LYDIA I will write him a letter in Christina's name, desiring to meet
him, when I shall soon discover if his love to her be of a longer

standing than since last night; and if it be not, I will not longer   130
trust him with the vanity to think she gave him the occasion to
follow her home from the park—so will at once disabuse him and
myself.

LEONORE What care the jealous take, in making sure of ills which
they, but in imagination, cannot undergo!   135

LYDIA Misfortunes are least dreadful when most near;
   'Tis less to undergo the ill, than fear.

 Exeunt

4.1

Gripe's house

Enter Mrs Joiner, and Gripe in a blue gown° and night-cap

MRS JOINER What, not well, your worship? This it is; you will be laying out yourself beyond your strength. You have taken a surfeit of the little gentlewoman, I find. Indeed, you should not have been so immoderate in your embraces; your worship is something in years, in truly.   5

GRIPE Graceless, perfidious woman, what makest thou here? Art thou not afraid to be used like an informer, since thou hast made me pay thee for betraying me?

MRS JOINER Betray your worship! What do you mean? I an informer! I scorn your words.   10

GRIPE Woman, I say again thou art as treacherous as an informer, and more unreasonable, for he lets us have something for our money, before he disturbs us.°

MRS JOINER Your money, I'm sure, was laid out faithfully; and I went away because I would not disturb you.   15

GRIPE I had not grudged you the money I gave you—but the five hundred pound! The five hundred pound, inconscionable, false woman! The five hundred pound! You cheated, trepanned, robbed me of the five hundred pound.

MRS JOINER I cheat you! I rob you! Well, remember what you   20
say; you shall answer it before Mr Doublecap,° and the best of—

GRIPE Oh, impudent woman, speak softly!

MRS JOINER I will not speak softly, for innocence is loud, as well as barefaced. Is this your return, after you have made me a mere   25
drudge to your filthy lusts?

GRIPE Speak softly; my sister, daughter, and servants will hear.

MRS JOINER I would have witnesses, to take notice that you blast my good name, which was as white as a tulip, and as sweet as the head of your cane,° before you wrought me to the carrying on the work   30
of your fleshly carnal seekings.

GRIPE Softly, softly; they are coming in.

Enter Lady Flippant and Martha

LADY FLIPPANT What's the matter, brother?

GRIPE Nothing, nothing, sister—only the godly woman is fallen into
a fit of zeal against the enormous transgressions of the age. Go, go;   35
you do not love to hear vanity reproved. Pray begone.

MRS JOINER Pray stay, madam, that you may know—

GRIPE (aside to Mrs Joiner) Hold, hold; here are five guineas for thee;
pray say nothing.—Sister, pray begone, I say.

Exeunt Lady Flippant and Martha

Would you prejudice your own reputation, to injure mine?   40

MRS JOINER Would you prejudice your own soul to wrong my
repute, in truly?

She seems to weep

GRIPE Pray have me in excuse.° Indeed, I thought you had a share
of the five hundred pound, because you took away my seal ring,
which they made me send together with a note to my cash-keeper   45
for five hundred pound. Besides, I thought none but you knew it
was my wonted token to send for money by.

MRS JOINER 'Twas unlucky I should forget it, and leave it on the
table. But oh, the harlotry! Did she make that use of it then? 'Twas
no wonder you did not stay till I came back.   50

GRIPE I stayed till the money released me.

MRS JOINER Have they the money then? Five hundred pound?

GRIPE Too certain.

MRS JOINER They told me not a word of it. And have you no way
to retrieve it?   55

GRIPE Not any.

MRS JOINER (aside) I am glad of it. [Aloud] Is there no law but
against saints?°

GRIPE I will not, for five hundred pound, publish my transgression
myself, lest I should be thought to glory in't—though I must   60
confess, 'twould tempt a man to conform to public praying and
sinning, since 'tis so chargeable to pray, and sin, in private.

MRS JOINER But are you resolved to give off, a loser?°

GRIPE How shall I help it?

MRS JOINER Nay, I'll see you shall have what the young jade has,   65
for your money. I'll make 'em use some conscience, however. Take
a man's money for nothing!

GRIPE Thou say'st honestly indeed. And shall I have my penny-
worths out of the little gentlewoman, for all this?

MRS JOINER I'll be engaged body for body for her, and you shall take   70
the forfeiture on me else.

GRIPE No, no, I'll rather take your word, Mrs Joiner.

MRS JOINER Go in and dress yourself smug, and leave the rest to me.
GRIPE No man breathing would give off, a loser, as she says.
 Exeunt

4.2

[Another room in Gripe's house]°

Sir Simon Addleplot, sitting at a desk writing as a clerk,
Lady Flippant jogging him

SIR SIMON 'Tis a lord's mortgage, and therefore requires the more
haste. Pray do not jog me, madam.

LADY FLIPPANT (*aside*) Dull rascal.

SIR SIMON They cannot stay for money, as other folks. If you will
not let me make an end on't, I shall lose my expedition fee. 5

LADY FLIPPANT (*aside*) There are some clerks would have understood me before this.

SIR SIMON Nay, pray be quiet, madam. If you squeeze me so to the
wall, I cannot write.

LADY FLIPPANT (*aside*) 'Tis much for the honour of the gentlemen 10
of this age, that we persons of quality are forced to descend to the
importuning of a clerk, a butler, coachman, or footman, while the
rogues are as dull of apprehension, too, as an unfledged country
squire amongst his mother's maids.
 Jogs him again

SIR SIMON Again! Let me tell you, madam, familiarity breeds 15
contempt. You'll never leave, till you have made me saucy.

LADY FLIPPANT I would I could see that.

SIR SIMON I vow and swear then, get you gone—or I'll add a black
patch or two to those on your face. (*Aside*) I shall have no time to
get Mistress Martha out, for her. 20

LADY FLIPPANT Will you, sir, will you?
 Jogs him again

SIR SIMON (*aside*) I must have a plot for her, she is a coy° woman.—I
vow and swear, if you pass this crevice,° I'll kiss you, in plain
English.

LADY FLIPPANT I would I could see that. Do you defy me? 25
 Steps to him. He kisses her

SIR SIMON (*aside*) How's this! I vow and swear, she kisses as tamely
as Mistress Ticklish, and with her mouth open too.

LADY FLIPPANT I thought you would have been ashamed, to have done so to your master's own sister.

SIR SIMON I hope you'll be quiet now, madam?   30

LADY FLIPPANT Nay, I'll be revenged of you, sure.

SIR SIMON If you come again, I shall do more to you than that. (*Aside*) I'll pursue my plot, and try if she be honest.

LADY FLIPPANT You'll° do more to me than that! Nay, if you'll do more to me than that—   35

> *She throws down his ink, and runs out; he follows her. Enter Mrs Joiner*

MRS JOINER I must visit my young clients in the mean time.

> *Sir Simon Addleplot returns, holding up his hands*

What's the matter, Sir Simon?

SIR SIMON Lord, who would have thought it?

MRS JOINER What ail you,° Sir Simon?

SIR SIMON I have made such a discovery, Mrs Joiner.   40

MRS JOINER What is't?

SIR SIMON Such an one that makes me at once glad and sorry: I am sorry my Lady Flippant is naught, but I'm glad I know it—thanks still to my disguise.

MRS JOINER Fie, fie.   45

SIR SIMON Nay, this hand can tell—

MRS JOINER But how?

SIR SIMON She threw down my ink-glass, and ran away into the next room. I followed her, and, in revenge, threw her down upon the bed. But in short, all that I could do to her, would not make her   50
squeak.

MRS JOINER She was out of breath, man, she was out of breath.

SIR SIMON Ah, Mrs Joiner, say no more, say no more of that.

> *Enter Lady Flippant*

LADY FLIPPANT You rude, unmannerly rascal.

MRS JOINER You see she complains now.   55

SIR SIMON (*apart [to her]*) I know why, Mrs Joiner, I know why.

LADY FLIPPANT I'll have you turned out of the house; you are not fit for my brother's service.

SIR SIMON (*aside*) Not for yours, you mean, madam.

LADY FLIPPANT I'll go and acquaint my brother—   60

MRS JOINER [*apart to her*] Hold, hold, madam, speak not so loud. 'Tis Sir Simon Addleplot, your lover, who has taken this disguise on purpose to be near you, and to watch and supplant his rivals.

LADY FLIPPANT [*aside*] What a beast was I, I could not discover it!   65
(*Aside to Mrs Joiner*) You have undone me; why would you not tell
me sooner of it?

MRS JOINER I thought he had been discernible enough.

LADY FLIPPANT I protest I knew him not—for I must confess to
you, my eyes are none of the best since I have used the last new   70
wash of mercury water.° What will he think of me?

MRS JOINER Let me alone with him. [*To Sir Simon*] Come, come,
did you think you could disguise yourself from my Lady's knowledge? She knew you, man, or else you had ne'er had those
liberties. Alas, poor lady, she cannot resist you.   75

LADY FLIPPANT 'Tis my weakness.

SIR SIMON How's this? But here comes my master.

        Enter Gripe and Martha

GRIPE Come, Mrs Joiner, are you ready to go?

MRS JOINER I am ever ready when your worship commands.

LADY FLIPPANT Brother, if you go to t'other end of the town, you'll   80
set me down near the playhouse.

GRIPE The playhouse! Do you think I will be seen near the playhouse?

LADY FLIPPANT You shall set me down in Lincoln's Inn Fields
then,° for I have earnest business there. (*Apart [to Sir Simon
Addleplot]*) When I come home again, I'll laugh at you soundly, Sir   85
Simon.

SIR SIMON (*aside*) Has Joiner betrayed me then? 'Tis time to look to
my hits.°

GRIPE Martha, be sure you stay within, now. If you go out, you shall
never come into my doors again.   90

MARTHA No, I will not, sir. I'll ne'er come into your doors again, if
once I should go out.

GRIPE 'Tis well said, girl.

        Exeunt Gripe, Mrs Joiner, Lady Flippant

SIR SIMON 'Twas prettily said. I understand you; they are dull, and
have no intrigue in 'em. But dear, sweet Mistress Martha, 'tis time   95
we were gone. You have stole away your scarves and hood from
your maid, I hope.

MARTHA Nay, I am ready, but—

SIR SIMON Come, come, Sir Simon Addleplot, poor gentleman, is an
impatient man, to my knowledge.   100

MARTHA Well, my venture is great, I'm sure, for a man I know not.
But pray, Jonas, do not deceive me. Is he so fine a gentleman as
you say he is?

SIR SIMON Pish, pish, he is the . . . gentleman° of the town, faith and
troth.   105

MARTHA But may I take your word, Jonas?

SIR SIMON 'Tis not my word, 'tis the word of all the town.

MARTHA Excuse me, Jonas, for that—I never heard any speak well
of him but Mr Dapperwit, and you.

SIR SIMON That's because he has been a rival to all men, and a   110
gallant to all ladies. Rivals, and deserted mistresses, never speak
well of a man.

MARTHA Has he been so general in his amours? His kindness is not
to be valued then.

SIR SIMON The more by you, because 'tis for you he deserts all the   115
rest, faith and troth.

MARTHA You plead better for him than he could for himself, I
believe, for indeed they say he is no better than an idiot.

SIR SIMON Then believe me, madam, for nobody knows him better
than I—he has as much wit, courage, and as good a mien to the   120
full as I have. He an idiot!

MARTHA The common gull—so perspicuous a fop, the women find
him out, for none of 'em will marry him.

SIR SIMON You may see now, how he and you are abused; for that
he is not married is a sign of his wit, and for being perspicuous,   125
'tis false—he is as mysterious as a new parliament man, or a young
statesman newly taken from a coffee-house or tennis-court.

MARTHA But is it a sign of his wit because he is not married?

SIR SIMON Yes, yes, your women of the town ravish your fops.
There's not one about the town, unmarried, that has anything.°   130

MARTHA It may be, then, he has spent his estate.

SIR SIMON (aside) How unluckily guessed! [Aloud] If he had, he has
a head can retrieve it again.

MARTHA Besides, they say he has had the modish distemper.°

SIR SIMON He can cure it with the best French chirurgeon° in town.   135

MARTHA Has his practice on himself been so much?°

SIR SIMON Come, come.
            Fame, like deserted jilt, does still belie men;
            Who doubts her man must be advised by Hymen,
            For he knows, best of any, how to try men.   140
        Exeunt

4.3

The Old Pall Mall

Enter Ranger and Dapperwit

RANGER Now the Lucies have renounced us, hey for the Christinas. She cannot use me worse than your honourable mistress did you.

DAPPERWIT A pox, some young heir or another has promised her marriage. There are so many fools in the world, 'tis impossible for a man of wit to keep his wench from being a lady, let me perish. 5

RANGER But have you no other acquaintance that sticks to her vocation in spite of temptations of honour or filthy lucre? I declare, I make honourable love merely out of necessity—as your rooks play on the square, rather than not play at all.

[Enter] Leonore, masked, with a letter in her hand

DAPPERWIT Come, the devil will not lose a gamester—here's ready 10 money for you; push freely.

RANGER (*to her*) Thou'rt as well met as if by assignation.

LEONORE And you are as well met as if you were the man I looked for.

RANGER Kind rogue! 15

LEONORE Sweet sir.

RANGER Come, I am thy prisoner, without more words; show but thy warrant.

Goes to pull off her mask

LEONORE You mistake, sir; here is my pass.

Gives him the letter

RANGER A letter, and directed to me. (*Reads*) 20
'I cannot put up the injuries and affronts you did me last night,'
—a challenge, upon my life, and by such a messenger— 'therefore conjure you by your honour, at eight o'clock precisely, this evening, to send your man to St James's Gate to wait for me with a chair, to conduct me to what place you shall think most fit, for 25 the giving of satisfaction to the injured

Christina.'

Christina! I am amazed! What is't o'clock, Dapperwit?

DAPPERWIT It wants not half an hour of eight.

RANGER (*to Leonore*) Go then back, my pretty herald, and tell my 30 fair enemy, the service she designs my man is only fit for my friend here, of whose faith and honour she may be secure of. He shall

immediately go wait for her at St James's Gate, whilst I go to
prepare a place for our rencounter, and myself to die at her feet.

Exit Leonore

Dapperwit, dear Dapperwit!   35

DAPPERWIT   What lucky surprisal's this?

RANGER   Prithee ask no questions, till I have more leisure, and less
astonishment. I know you will not deny to be an instrument in my
happiness.

DAPPERWIT   No, let me perish, I take as much pleasure to bring   40
lovers together as an old woman, that,° as a bankrupt gamester
loves to look on, though he has no advantage by the play; or as a
bully that fights not himself, yet takes pleasure to set people
together by the ears, or as—

RANGER   'Sdeath, is this a time for similitudes?   45

DAPPERWIT   You have made me miscarry of a good thought now, let
me perish.

RANGER   Go presently to St James's Gate, where you are to expect
the coming of a lady ('tis Christina) accompanied by that woman
you saw even now. She will permit you to put her into a chair, and   50
then conduct her to my lodging, while I go before to remove some
spies, and prepare it for her reception.

DAPPERWIT   Your lodging? Had you not better carry her to Vincent's?—'tis hard by, and there a vizard-mask has as free egress,
and regress,° as at the playhouse.   55

RANGER   Faith, though it be not very prudent, yet she shall come
thither, in my vindication—for he would not believe I had seen her
last night.

DAPPERWIT   To have a fine woman, and not tell on't, as you say, Mr
Ranger . . .   60

RANGER   Go, and bring her to Vincent's lodging; there I'll expect
you.

*Exeunt Ranger and Dapperwit severally. Enter Christina,
Isabel*

ISABEL   This is the door,° madam; here Mr Vincent lodges.

CHRISTINA   'Tis no matter, we will pass it by, lest the people
of our lodging should watch us. But if he should not be here   65
now . . .

ISABEL   Who, Mr Valentine, madam? I warrant you, my intelligencer
dares not fail me.

CHRISTINA   Did he come last night, said he?

ISABEL   Last night, late.   70

CHRISTINA And not see me yet—nay, not send to me! 'Tis false, he is not come! I wish he were not—I know not which I should take more unkindly from him: exposing his life to his revengeful enemies, or being almost four and twenty hours so near me, and not let me know't.   75

ISABEL A lover's dangers are the only secrets kept from his mistress. He came not to you, because he would not purchase his happiness with your fear and apprehensions.

CHRISTINA Nay, he is come, I see, since you are come about again of his side.   80

ISABEL Will you go in, madam, and disprove me if you can? 'Tis better than standing in the street.

CHRISTINA We'll go a little farther first, and return.

Exeunt

4.4

Vincent's lodging

Enter Vincent and Valentine

VINCENT I told you I had sent my man to Christina's this morning, to enquire of her maid (who seldom denies him a secret) if her lady had been at the park last night; which she peremptorily answered to the contrary, and assured him she had not stirred out since your departure.   5

VALENTINE Will not chambermaids lie, Vincent?

VINCENT Will not Ranger lie, Valentine?

VALENTINE The circumstances of his story proved it true.

VINCENT Do you think so old a master in the faculty° as he, will want the varnish of probability for his lies?   10

VALENTINE Do you think a woman, having the advantage of her sex, and education under such a mistress, will want impudence to disavow a truth that might be prejudicial to that mistress?

VINCENT But if both testimonies are fallible, why will you needs believe his? We are apter to believe the things we would have, than   15
those we would not.

VALENTINE My ill luck has taught me to credit my misfortunes, and doubt my happiness.

VINCENT But Fortune we know inconstant.

VALENTINE And all of her sex.   20

VINCENT Will you judge of Fortune by your experience, and not do
your mistress the same justice? Go see her, and satisfy yourself
and her; for if she be innocent, consider how culpable you are, not
only in your censures of her, but in not seeing her since your
coming.   25

VALENTINE If she be innocent, I should be afraid to surprise her, for
her sake. If false, I should be afraid to surprise her, for my own.

VINCENT To be jealous, and not inquisitive, is as hard as to love
extremely and not be something jealous.°

VALENTINE Inquisitiveness as seldom cures jealousy, as drinking in   30
a fever quenches the thirst.

VINCENT If she were at the park last night, 'tis probable she'll not
miss this.° Go watch her house, see who goes out, who in, while I
in the mean time search out Ranger, who (I'll pawn my life) upon
more discourse shall avow his mistake. Here he is; go in. How   35
luckily is he come!

>   *Enter Ranger; Valentine retires to the door behind,*
>   *overhearing them*

Ranger, you have prevented me; I was going to look you out,
between the scenes° at the playhouses, the coffee-house, tennis-
court, or Gifford's.

RANGER Do you want a pretence to go to a bawdyhouse? But I have   40
other visits to make.

VINCENT I forget—I should rather have sought you in Christina's
lodgings, ha ha ha!

RANGER Well, well, I am just come to tell you that Christina—

VINCENT Proves not, by daylight, the kind lady you followed last   45
night out of the park.

RANGER I have better news for you, to my thinking.

VINCENT What is't?

RANGER Not that I have been in Christina's lodging this morning—
but that she'll be presently here in your lodging with me.   50

VALENTINE (*behind*) How!

VINCENT (*drawing back to the door, where Valentine stands, and
speaking softly to him*) You see now, his report was a jest, a mere
jest. (*To Ranger*) Well, must my lodging be your vaulting-school
still? Thou hast appointed a wench to come hither, I find.   55

RANGER A wench! You seemed to have more reverence for Christina
last night.

VINCENT Now you talk of Christina, prithee tell me what was the
meaning of thy last night's romance of Christina.

RANGER You shall know the meaning of all when Christina comes;   60
she'll be here presently.

VINCENT Who will? Christina?

RANGER Yes, Christina.

VINCENT Ha ha ha.

RANGER Incredulous envy! Thou art as envious as an impotent lecher   65
at a wedding.

VINCENT Thou art either mad, or as vain as a Frenchman newly
returned home from a campaign,° or obliging° England.

RANGER Thou art as envious as a rival. But if thou art mine, there's
that will make you desist.   70

    Gives him the letter

And if you are not my rival, entrusting you with such a secret will,
I know, oblige you to keep it and assist me against all other
interests.

VINCENT Do you think I take your secret as an obligation? Don't I
know lovers, travellers, and poets will give money to be heard? But   75
what's the paper? A lampoon upon Christina, hatched last night
betwixt Squire Dapperwit and you, because her maid used you
scurvily?

RANGER No, 'tis only a letter from her, to show my company was
not so disgustful to her last night but that she desires it again today.   80

VALENTINE (*behind*) A letter from her!

VINCENT A letter from Christina . . . (*Reads*) Ha ha ha.

RANGER Nay, 'tis pleasant.

VINCENT You mistake; I laugh at you, not the letter.

RANGER I am like the winning gamester—so pleased with my luck I   85
will not quarrel with any who calls me a fool° for't.

VINCENT Is this the style of a woman of honour?

RANGER It may be, for aught *you* know. I'm sure, 'tis well if your
female correspondents can read.

VINCENT I must confess, I have none of the little letters, half name or   90
title, like your Spanish epistles dedicatory.° But that a man so frequent
in honourable intrigues as you are, should not know the summons of
an impudent common woman from that of a person of honour!

RANGER Christina is so much a person of honour, she'll own what
she has writ when she comes.   95

VINCENT But will she come hither indeed?

RANGER Immediately. You'll excuse my liberty with you. I could not
conceal such a happiness from such a friend as you, lest you should
have taken it unkindly.

VINCENT Faith, you have obliged me indeed; for you, and others,   100
would often have made me believe your honourable intrigues, but
never did me the honour to convince me of 'em before.

RANGER You are merry, I find, yet.

VINCENT When you are happy, I cannot be otherwise.

RANGER (*aside*) But I lose time. I should lay a little parson° in   105
ambush, that lives hard by, in case Christina should be impatient
to be revenged of her friends,° as it often happens with a
discontented heiress. Women, like old soldiers, more nimbly
execute than they resolve. (*Going out*)

VINCENT What now, you will not disappoint a woman of Christina's   110
quality?

RANGER I'll be here before she comes, I warrant you.

     Exit Ranger

VINCENT I do believe you truly.—What think you, Valentine?

VALENTINE [*coming forward*] I think, since she has the courage to
challenge him, she'll have the honour of being first in the field.   115

VINCENT Fie, your opinion of her must be as bad, as Ranger's of
himself is good, to think she would write to him. I long till his
bona-roba comes, that you may be both disabused.

VALENTINE And I have not patience to stay her coming, lest you
should be disabused.   120

     Enter Christina, [masked,] and Isabel

VINCENT Here she is, i'faith; I'm glad she's come.

VALENTINE And I'm sorry. But I will to my post again, lest she
should say she came to me.

     [*Valentine retires.*] *Christina pulls off her mask*

VINCENT (*aside*) By heavens, Christina herself! 'Tis she!

VALENTINE (*behind*) 'Tis she. Cursed be these eyes, more cursed   125
than when they first betrayed me to that false, bewitching face.

CHRISTINA You may wonder, sir, to see me here—

VINCENT I must confess I do.

CHRISTINA But the confidence your friend has in you, is the cause
of mine. And yet some blushes it does cost me, to come to seek a   130
man.

VALENTINE (*behind*) Modest creature.

VINCENT (*aside*) How am I deceived!

CHRISTINA Where is he, sir? Why does he not appear, to keep me in
countenance?° Pray call him, sir; 'tis something hard if he should   135
know I'm here.

VINCENT I hardly can, myself, believe you are here, madam.

CHRISTINA If my visit be troublesome, or unseasonable, 'tis your
friend's fault—I designed it not to you, sir. Pray call him out, that
he may excuse it, and take it on himself, together with my shame.   140

VINCENT (*aside*) How impatient she is!

CHRISTINA Or do you delay the happiness I ask, to make it more
welcome? I have stayed too long for it already, and cannot more
desire it. Dear sir, call him out. Where is he? Above, or here
within? I'll snatch the favour which you will not give.   145

    Goes to the door, and discovers Valentine

What, do you hide yourself for shame?

VALENTINE I must confess I do.

CHRISTINA To see me come hither—

VALENTINE I acknowledge it.

CHRISTINA —before you came to me.   150

    Valentine offers to go out

But whither do you go? Come, I can forgive you.

VALENTINE But I cannot forgive you.

CHRISTINA Whither do you go? You need not forge a quarrel, to
prevent mine to you. Nor need you try if I would follow you. You
know I will—I have, you see.   155

VALENTINE (*aside*) That impudence should look so like innocence!

CHRISTINA Whither would you go? Why would you go?

VALENTINE To call your servant to you.

CHRISTINA She is here; what would you with her?

VALENTINE I mean your lover, the man you came to meet.   160

CHRISTINA Oh heavens! What lover? What man? I came to seek no
man but you, whom I had too long lost.

VALENTINE You could not know that I was here.

CHRISTINA (*points to Isabel*) Ask her; 'twas she that told me.

VALENTINE How could she know?   165

CHRISTINA That you shall know hereafter.

VALENTINE No, you thought me too far out of the way to disturb
your assignation—and I assure you, madam, 'twas my ill fortune,
not my design. And that it may appear so, I do withdraw (as in all
good breeding and civility I am obliged), for sure your wished-for   170
lover's coming.

CHRISTINA What do you mean? Are you a-weary of that title?

VALENTINE I am ashamed of it, since it grows common. (*Going out*)

CHRISTINA Nay, you will not, shall not go.

VALENTINE My stay might give him jealousy, and so do you injury,   175
and him the greatest in the world. Heavens forbid! I would not

make a man jealous. For though you call a thousand vows, and
oaths, and tears to witness (as you safely may) that you have not
the least of love for me—yet if he ever knew how I have loved you,
sure he would not, could not, believe you.   180

CHRISTINA I do confess, your riddle is too hard for me to solve;
therefore you are obliged to do't yourself.

VALENTINE I wish it were capable of any other interpretation than
what you know already.

CHRISTINA Is this that generous, good Valentine? Who has disguised   185
him so?
    She weeps

VINCENT Nay, I must withhold you then.
    Stops Valentine going out
Methinks she should be innocent. Her tongue and eyes, together
with that flood that swells 'em, do vindicate her heart.

VALENTINE They show but their long practice of dissimulation.   190
(*Going out*)

VINCENT Come back—I hear Ranger coming up. Stay but till he
comes.

VALENTINE Do you think I have the patience of an alderman?°

VINCENT You may go out this way, when you will, by the backstairs.   195
But stay a little, till—Oh, here he comes.
    Ranger enters; Christina puts on her mask

VALENTINE My revenge will now detain me.
    Valentine retires again

RANGER (*aside*) What, come already? Where is Dapperwit? [*To
Christina*] The blessing's double that comes quickly.° I did not yet
expect you here, otherwise I had not done myself the injury to be   200
absent. But I hope, madam, I have not made you stay long for me.

CHRISTINA I have not stayed at all for you.

RANGER I am glad of it, madam.

CHRISTINA ([*aside*] *to Isabel*) Is not this that troublesome stranger
who last night followed the lady into my lodgings? 'Tis he.   205
(*Removing from him to t'other side*)

RANGER (*aside*) Why does she remove so disdainfully from me?—I
find you take it ill I was not at your coming here, madam.

CHRISTINA Indeed I do not; you are mistaken, sir.

RANGER Confirm me by a smile then, madam; remove that cloud,   210
which makes me apprehend foul weather.
    Goes to take off her mask

Mr Vincent, pray retire; 'tis you keep on the lady's mask, and no displeasure which she has for me. Yet, madam, you need not distrust his honour, or his faith.—But do not keep the lady under constraint; pray leave us a little, Master Vincent.   215

CHRISTINA You must not leave us, sir. Would you leave me with a stranger?

VALENTINE (*behind*) How's that!

RANGER (*aside*) I've done amiss, I find, to bring her hither. (*Apart to Christina*) Madam, I understand you—   220

CHRISTINA Sir, I do not understand you.

RANGER You would not be known to Mr Vincent.

CHRISTINA 'Tis your acquaintance I would avoid.

RANGER (*aside*) Dull brute that I was, to bring her hither. (*Softly, to her*) I have found my error, madam; give me but a new appoint-   225
ment, where I may meet you by and by, and straight I will withdraw, as if I knew you not.

CHRISTINA Why, do you know me?

RANGER (*aside*) I must not own it.—No, madam, but—(*Offers to whisper*)   230

CHRISTINA Whispering, sir, argues an old acquaintance; but I have not the vanity to be thought of yours, and resolve you shall never have the disparagement of mine.—Mr Vincent, pray let us go in here.

RANGER [*aside*] How's this! I am undone, I see. But if I let her go   235
thus, I shall be an eternal laughing-stock to Vincent.

VINCENT Do you not know him, madam? I thought you had come hither on purpose to meet him.

CHRISTINA To meet him!

VINCENT By your own appointment.   240

CHRISTINA What strange infatuation does delude you all? You know he said he did not know me.

VINCENT You writ to him; he has your letter.

CHRISTINA [*to Ranger*] Then you know my name, sure? Yet you confessed but now, you knew me not.   245

RANGER I must confess, your anger has disguised you more than your mask; for I thought to have met a kinder Christina here.

CHRISTINA Heavens! How could he know me in this place? He watched me hither, sure—or is there any other of my name? That you may no longer mistake me for your Christina, I'll pull off that   250
which soothes your error. (*Pulls off her mask*)

RANGER Take but t'other vizard off too—I mean your anger—and I'll swear you are the same and only Christina which I wished, and thought, to meet here.

CHRISTINA How could you think to meet me here?   255

RANGER By virtue of this your commission,

Gives her the letter

which now, I see, was meant a real challenge—for you look as if you would fight with me.

CHRISTINA The paper is a stranger to me; I never writ it. You are abused.   260

VINCENT Christina is a person of honour, and will own what she has written, Ranger.

RANGER (*aside*) So, the comedy begins. I shall be laughed at sufficiently, if I do not justify myself. I must set my impudence to hers; she is resolved to deny all, I see, and I have lost all hope of   265
her.

VINCENT Come, faith, Ranger—

RANGER You will deny too, madam, that I followed you last night from the park to your lodging, where I stayed with you till morning. You never saw me before, I warrant?   270

CHRISTINA That you rudely intruded, last night, into my lodging, I cannot deny. But I wonder you have the confidence to brag of it; sure you will not of your reception?

RANGER I never was so ill-bred as to brag of my reception in a lady's chamber—not a word of that, madam.   275

VALENTINE [*behind*] How! If he lies, I revenge her; if it be true, I revenge myself.

Valentine draws his sword, which Vincent seeing, thrusts him back and shuts the door upon him before he is discovered by Ranger. Enter Lydia and Leonore, [both masked], stopping at the door

LYDIA [*aside*] What do I see! Christina with him! A counter-plot to mine, to make me, and it, ridiculous. 'Tis true, I find, they have been long acquainted, and I long abused. But since she intends a   280
triumph, in spite as well as shame (not emulation) I retire. She deserves no envy, who will be shortly in my condition. His natural inconstancy will prove my best revenge on her—on both.

Exeunt Lydia with Leonore. [Enter] Dapperwit

DAPPERWIT [*to Ranger*] Christina's going away again—what's the matter?   285

RANGER What do you mean?

DAPPERWIT I scarce had paid the chair-men, and was coming up after her, but I met her on the stairs, in as much haste as if she had been frightened.

RANGER Who do you talk of?   290

DAPPERWIT Christina, whom I took up in a chair, just now, at St James's Gate.

RANGER Thou art mad—here she is, this is Christina.

DAPPERWIT I must confess I did not see her face—but I am sure the lady is gone that I brought just now.   295

RANGER I tell you, again, this is she. Did you bring two?

CHRISTINA I came in no chair, had no guide but my woman there.

VINCENT When did you bring your lady, Dapperwit?

DAPPERWIT Even now, just now.

VINCENT This lady has been here half an hour.   300

RANGER He knows not what he says. He is mad—you are all so; I am so too.

VINCENT 'Tis the best excuse you can make for yourself, and by owning your mistake you'll show you are come to yourself. I myself saw your woman at the door, who but looked in and then   305 immediately went down again, as your friend Dapperwit too affirms.

CHRISTINA [to Ranger] You had best follow her that looked for you; and I'll go seek out him I came to see. Mr Vincent, pray let me in here.   310

RANGER 'Tis very fine, wondrous fine!

Christina goes out a little, and returns

CHRISTINA Oh, he is gone! Mr Vincent, follow him. He were yet more severe to me, in endangering his life, than in his censures of me. You know the power of his enemies is great as their malice; just heaven, preserve him from them, and me from this ill, or   315 unlucky, man.

Exeunt Christina, Isabel, and Vincent

RANGER 'Tis well. Nay, certainly, I shall never be master of my senses more. But why dost thou help to distract me too?

DAPPERWIT My astonishment was as great as yours, to see her go away again. I would have stayed her if I could.   320

RANGER Yet again—talking of a woman you met going out, when I talk of Christina.

DAPPERWIT I talk of Christina too.

RANGER She went out just now; the woman you found me with was she.   325

DAPPERWIT That was not the Christina I brought just now.

RANGER [*emphatically*] You brought her almost half an hour ago. 'Sdeath, will you give me the lie?

DAPPERWIT A lady disappointed by her gallant the night before her journey, could not be more touchy with her maid, or husband, than you are with me now, after your disappointment. But if you thank me so, I'll go serve myself hereafter. For aught I know, I have disappointed Mistress Martha for you, and may lose thirty thousand pound by the bargain. Farewell; a raving lover is fit for solitude. 330

335

Exit Dapperwit

RANGER Lydia, triumph! I now am thine again. Of intrigues, honourable or dishonourable, and all sorts of rambling, I take my leave. When we are giddy, 'tis time to stand still. Why should we be so fond of the by-paths of love, where we are still waylaid with surprises, trepans, dangers, and murdering disappointments? 340

> Just as at blind-man's-buff, we run at all,
> Whilst those that lead us laugh to see us fall;
> And when we think we hold the lady fast,
> We find it but her scarf, or veil, at last.

Exit

5.1

St James's Park [at night]

Enter Sir Simon Addleplot, leading Martha, [and meeting]
Dapperwit

SIR SIMON At length, you see, I have freed the captive lady for
her longing knight. Mr Dapperwit, who brings off a plot cleverly
now?

DAPPERWIT I wish our poets were half so good at it. Mistress
Martha, a thousand welcomes.   5

Dapperwit kisses and embraces Martha

SIR SIMON Hold, hold, sir; your joy is a little too familiar, faith and
troth.

DAPPERWIT Will you not let me salute Mistress Martha?

MARTHA What, Jonas, do you think I do not know good breeding?
Must I be taught by you?   10

SIR SIMON I would have kept the maidenhead of your lips for your
sweet knight, Mistress Martha, that's all. I dare swear you never
kissed any man before, but your father.

MARTHA My sweet knight, if he will be a knight of mine, must be
contented with what he finds, as well as other knights.   15

SIR SIMON So smart already, faith and troth!

MARTHA Dear Mr Dapperwit, I am overjoyed to see you. But I thank
honest Jonas for't.

[She hugs Dapperwit]

SIR SIMON (*aside*) How she hugs him!

MARTHA Poor Mr Dapperwit, I thought I should never have seen   20
you again. But I thank honest Jonas there!

She hugs Dapperwit

SIR SIMON Do not thank me, Mistress Martha, any more than I
thank you.

MARTHA I would not be ungrateful, Jonas.

SIR SIMON Then reserve your kindness only for your worthy, noble, 25
brave, heroic knight—who loves you only, and only deserves your
kindness.

MARTHA I will show my kindness to my worthy, brave, heroic
knight, in being kind to his friend, his dear friend, who helped him
to me.   30

Hugs Dapperwit again

SIR SIMON But Mistress Martha, he is not to help him always. Though he helps him to be married, he is not to help him when he is married.

MARTHA What, Mr Dapperwit, will you love my worthy knight less after marriage than before? That were against the custom—for 35 marriage gets a man friends, instead of losing those he has.

DAPPERWIT I will ever be his servant, and yours. Dear madam, do not doubt me.

MARTHA I do not, sweet, dear Mr Dapperwit. But I should not have seen you these two days, if it had not been for honest Jonas 40 there.

    She kisses Dapperwit

SIR SIMON (*apart to Dapperwit*) For shame, though she be young and foolish, do not you wrong me to my face.

DAPPERWIT Would you have me so ill-bred as to repulse her innocent kindness? (*Aside*) What a thing it is to want wit! 45

SIR SIMON (*aside*) A pox, I must make haste to discover myself, or I shall discover what I would not discover. But if I should discover myself in this habit, 'twould not be to my advantage. But I'll go put on my own clothes, and look like a knight. (*To her*) Well, Mistress Martha, I'll go seek out your knight; are you not impatient 50 to see him?

MARTHA Wives must be obedient; let him take his own time.

SIR SIMON Can you trust yourself a turn or two with Master Dapperwit?

MARTHA Yes, yes, Jonas, as long as you will. 55

SIR SIMON (*aside*) But I would not trust you with him, if I could help it.
    So married wight° sees what he dares not blame,
    And cannot budge for fear, nor stay for shame.
    Exit Sir Simon Addleplot

DAPPERWIT I am glad he is gone, that I may laugh. 'Tis such a 60 miracle of fops, that his conversation should be pleasant to me, even when it hindered me of yours.

MARTHA Indeed, I'm glad he is gone, too, as pleasant as he is.

DAPPERWIT I know why, I know why, sweet Mistress Martha. I warrant you, you had rather have the parson's company than his! 65 Now you are out of your father's house, 'tis time to leave being a hypocrite.

MARTHA Well, for the jest's sake, to disappoint my knight I would not care if I disappointed myself of a ladyship.

DAPPERWIT Come, I will not keep you on the tenters; I know you   70
have a mind to make sure of me. I have a little chaplain—I wish
he were a bishop, or one of the friars,° to perfect our revenge upon
that zealous jew, your father.

MARTHA Do not speak ill of my father; he has been your friend, I'm
sure.   75

DAPPERWIT My friend!

MARTHA His hard usage of me conspired with your good mien and
wit, and to avoid slavery under him, I stoop to your yoke.

DAPPERWIT I will be obliged to your father for nothing but a
portion, nor to you for your love—'twas due to° my merit.   80

MARTHA You show yourself Sir Simon's original;° if 'twere not for
that vanity—

DAPPERWIT I should be no wit. 'Tis the badge of my calling; for
you can no more find a man of wit without vanity, than a fine
woman without affectation. But let us go, before the knight comes   85
again.

MARTHA Let us go before my father comes; he soon will have the
intelligence.

DAPPERWIT Stay, let me think a little. (*Pauses*)

MARTHA What are you thinking of? You should have thought,   90
before this time—or I should have thought, rather.

DAPPERWIT Peace, peace.

MARTHA What are you thinking of?

DAPPERWIT I am thinking what a wit without vanity is like. He is
like—   95

MARTHA You do not think we are in a public place, and may be
surprised and prevented by my father's scouts?

DAPPERWIT What, would have have me lose my thought?

MARTHA You would rather lose your mistress, it seems.

DAPPERWIT He is like—I think I'm a sot tonight, let me perish.   100

MARTHA Nay, if you are so in love with your thought—(*Offers to go*)

DAPPERWIT Are you so impatient to be my wife? He is like—he is
like—a picture without shadows, or, or—a face without patches—
or a diamond without a foil; these are new thoughts now, these are
new.   105

MARTHA You are wedded already to your thoughts, I see; good night.

DAPPERWIT Madam, do not take it ill.

For loss of happy thought there's no amends;
For his new jest, true wit will lose old friends.
That's new again, the thought's new.   110

Exeunt Martha and Dapperwit. Enter Gripe, leading Lucy;
Mrs Joiner, Mrs Crossbite following

GRIPE Mrs Joiner, I can conform to this mode° of public walking by
moonlight, because one is not known.

LUCY Why, are you ashamed of your company?

GRIPE No, pretty one; because in the dark, or as it were the dark,°
there is no envy nor scandal. I would neither lose you, nor my   115
reputation.

MRS JOINER Your reputation! Indeed, your worship, 'tis well known
there are as grave men as your worship—nay, men in office
too—that adjourn their cares and businesses to come and unbend
themselves at night here, with a little vizard-mask.   120

GRIPE I do believe it, I do believe it, Mrs Joiner.

LUCY Ay, godmother, and carries and treats her at Mulberry Garden.

MRS CROSSBITE Nay, does not only treat her, but gives her his whole
gleanings of that day.

GRIPE They may, they may, Mrs Crossbite; they take above six in   125
the hundred.°

MRS CROSSBITE Nay, there are those of so much worth, and honour,
and love, that they'll take it from their wives and children to give
it to their misses. Now your worship has no wife, and but one
child.   130

GRIPE (*aside*) Still for my edification.

MRS JOINER That's true indeed, for I know a great lady that cannot
follow her husband abroad to his haunts, because her farandine is
so ragged and greasy, whilst his mistress is as fine as fippence° in
her embroidered satins.   135

GRIPE Politicly done of him, indeed; if the truth were known, he is
a statesman by that, umph!

MRS CROSSBITE Truly, your women of quality are very troublesome
to their husbands. I have heard 'em complain they will allow them
no separate maintenance,° though the honourable jilts themselves   140
will not marry without it.

MRS JOINER Come, come, mistress; sometimes 'tis the craft of those
gentlemen to complain of their wives' expenses, to excuse their own
narrowness to their misses. But your daughter has a gallant can
make no excuse.   145

GRIPE [*aside*] So, Mrs Joiner—my friend Mrs Joiner!

MRS CROSSBITE I hope, indeed, he'll give my daughter no cause to
dun him; for, poor wretch, she is as modest as her mother.

GRIPE I profess I believe it.

LUCY But I have the boldness to ask him for a treat. Come, gallant,   150
we must walk towards the Mulberry Garden.

GRIPE [aside] So!—I am afraid, little mistress, the rooms are all taken
up by this time.

MRS JOINER (aside to Gripe) Will you shame yourself again?

LUCY If the rooms be full, we'll have an arbour.   155

GRIPE At this time of night! Besides, the waiters will ne'er come near
you.

LUCY They will be observant of good customers, as we shall be.
Come along.

GRIPE Indeed and verily, little mistress, I would go, but that I should   160
be forsworn if I did.

MRS JOINER That's so pitiful an excuse—

GRIPE In truth, I have forsworn the place ever since I was pawned
there for a reckoning.°

LUCY You have broken many an oath for the Good Old Cause, and   165
will you boggle at one for your poor little miss? Come along.

      [Enter] Lady Flippant behind

LADY FLIPPANT [aside] Unfortunate lady that I am! I have left the
herd on purpose to be chased, and have wandered this hour here;
but the park affords not so much as a satyr for me (and that's
strange); no burgundy man, or drunken scourer will reel my way.   170
The rag-women and cinder-women have better luck than I—but
who are these? If this mongrel light° does not deceive me, 'tis my
brother—'tis he; there's Joiner too, and two other women. I'll
follow 'em. It must be he, for this world hath nothing like him; I
know not what the devil may be in the other.   175

      Exeunt Gripe, Lucy, Mrs Joiner, and Mrs Crossbite; [Lady
      Flippant following them]. Enter Sir Simon Addleplot in fine
      clothes, Dapperwit and Martha (unseen by him) at the door

SIR SIMON Well, after all my seeking, I can find those I would not
find.° I'm sure 'twas old Gripe, and Joiner with him, and the
widow followed. He would not have been here but to have sought
his daughter, sure. But vigilant Dapperwit has spied him too, and
has, no doubt, secured her from him.   180

DAPPERWIT (behind) And you.

SIR SIMON The rogue is as good at hiding, as I am at stealing, a
mistress. 'Tis a vain, conceited fellow, yet I think 'tis an honest
fellow. But again, he is a damnable, whoring fellow—and what

opportunity this air and darkness may incline 'em to, heaven   185
knows! For I have heard the rogue say himself, a lady will no more
show her modesty in the dark, than a Spaniard his courage.

DAPPERWIT Ha ha ha!

SIR SIMON Nay, if you are there, my true friend, I'll forgive your
hearkening—if you'll forgive my censures? I speak to you, dear   190
Madam Martha, dear, dear—behold your worthy knight.

MARTHA That's far from neighbours.°

SIR SIMON Is come to reap the fruit of all his labours.

MARTHA I cannot see the knight; well, but° I'm sure I hear Jonas.

SIR SIMON I am no Jonas, Mistress Martha.   195

MARTHA The night is not so dark, nor the peruke so big, but I can
discern Jonas.

SIR SIMON Faith and troth, I am the very Sir Simon Addleplot that
is to marry you—the same Dapperwit solicited you for. Ask him
else.° My name is not Jonas.   200

MARTHA You think my youth and simplicity capable of this cheat.
But let me tell you, Jonas, 'tis not your borrowed clothes, and title,
shall make me marry my father's man.

SIR SIMON Borrowed title! I'll be sworn I bought it of my laundress,°
who was a court laundress. But, indeed, my clothes I have not paid   205
for,° therefore in that sense they are borrowed.

MARTHA Prithee, Jonas, let the jest end, or I shall be presently in
earnest.°

SIR SIMON Pray be in earnest, and let us go. The parson and supper
stay for us, and I am a knight in earnest.°   210

MARTHA You a knight, insolent, saucy fool?

SIR SIMON The devil take me, Mistress Martha, if I am not a knight
now—a knight baronet too. A man ought, I see, to carry his patent
in his pocket when he goes to be married—'tis more necessary than
a licence. [*Emphatically*] I am a knight indeed and indeed now,   215
Mistress Martha.

MARTHA Indeed, and indeed, the trick will not pass, Jonas.

SIR SIMON Poor wretch, she's afraid she shall not be a lady. Come,
come, discover the intrigue, Dapperwit—

MARTHA You need not discover the intrigue, 'tis apparent already.   220
Unworthy Mr Dapperwit, after my confidence reposed in you,
could you be so little generous as to betray me to my father's man?
But I'll be even with you.

SIR SIMON Do not accuse him, poor man, before you hear him. Tell
her the intrigue, man.   225

DAPPERWIT A pox, she will not believe us.

SIR SIMON Will you not excuse yourself? But I must not let it rest
so. Know then, Mistress Martha—

MARTHA Come, I forgive thee before thy confession, Jonas. You
never had had the confidence to have designed this cheat upon me,   230
but from Mr Dapperwit's encouragement; 'twas his plot.

SIR SIMON Nay, do not do me that wrong, madam.

MARTHA But since he has trepanned me out of my father's house, he
is like to keep me as long as I live. And so good night, Jonas.

SIR SIMON Hold, hold, what d'y' mean both? Prithee tell her I am   235
Sir Simon, and no Jonas.

DAPPERWIT A pox, she will not believe us, I tell you.

SIR SIMON I have provided a parson, and supper, at Mulberry
Garden, and invited all my friends I could meet in the park.

DAPPERWIT Nay, rather than they shall be disappointed, there shall   240
be a bride and bridegroom to entertain 'em: Mistress Martha and
I'll go thither presently.

SIR SIMON Why, shall she be your bride?

DAPPERWIT You see she will have it so.

SIR SIMON Will you make Dapperwit your husband?   245

MARTHA Rather than my father's man.

SIR SIMON Oh the devil!

MARTHA Nay, come along, Jonas; you shall make one at the wedding,
since you helped contrive it.

SIR SIMON Will you cheat yourself, for fear of being cheated?   250

MARTHA I am desperate now.

SIR SIMON Wilt thou let her do so ill a thing, Dapperwit, as to marry
thee? Open her eyes, prithee, and tell her I am a true knight.

DAPPERWIT 'Twould be in vain, by my life; you have carried
yourself so like a natural° clerk—and so adieu, good Jonas.   255
        Exeunt Martha and Dapperwit

SIR SIMON What, ruined by my own plot, like an old Cavalier!° Yet
like him, too, I will plot on still, a plot of prevention.° So, I have
it—Her father was here even now, I'm sure. Well—I'll go tell her
father of her, that I will,
And punish so her folly, and his treachery;   260
Revenge is sweet, and makes amends for lechery.
        Exit Sir Simon Addleplot. Enter Lydia and Leonore

LYDIA I wish I had not come hither tonight, Leonore.

LEONORE Why did you, madam, if the place be so disagreeable to
you?

LYDIA We cannot help visiting the place often, where we have lost   265
anything we value; I lost Ranger here last night.

LEONORE You thought you had lost him before, a great while ago;
and therefore you ought to be the less troubled.

LYDIA But 'twas here I missed him first, I'm sure.

LEONORE Come, madam, let not the loss vex you; he is not worth   270
the looking after.

LYDIA I cannot but vex me yet, if I lost him by my own fault.

LEONORE You had but too much care to keep him.

LYDIA It often happens, indeed, that too much care is as bad as
negligence. But I had rather be robbed, than lose what I have   275
carelessly.

LEONORE But I believe you would hang the thief if you could.

LYDIA Not if I could have my own again.

LEONORE I see you would be too merciful.

LYDIA I wish I were tried.   280

LEONORE But, madam, if you please, we will waive the discourse; for
people seldom (I suppose) talk with pleasure of their real losses.

LYDIA 'Tis better than to ruminate on them. Mine, I'm sure, will not
out of my head, nor heart.

LEONORE Grief is so far from retrieving a loss, that it makes it   285
greater. But the way to lessen it is by a comparison with others'
losses. Here are ladies, in the park, of your acquaintance, I doubt
not can compare with you; pray, madam, let us walk and find 'em
out.

LYDIA 'Tis the resentment, you say, makes the loss great or little—   290
and then, I'm sure, there is none like mine. However, go on.

Exeunt Lydia and Leonore. Enter Vincent and Valentine

VINCENT I am glad I have found you, for now I am prepared to lead
you out of the dark, and all your trouble—I have good news.

VALENTINE You are as unmerciful as the physician, who with new
arts keeps his miserable patient alive and in hopes, when he knows   295
the disease is incurable.

VINCENT And you, like the melancholy patient, mistrust and hate
your physician because he will not comply with your despair. But
I'll cure your jealousy now.

VALENTINE You know all diseases grow worse by relapses.   300

VINCENT Trust me once more.

VALENTINE Well, you may try your experiments upon me.

VINCENT Just as I shut the door upon you, the woman Ranger
expected came upstairs; but finding another woman in discourse

with him, went down again—I suppose as jealous of him, as you of   305
Christina.

VALENTINE How does it appear she came to Ranger?

VINCENT Thus: Dapperwit came up after, who had brought her, just
then, in a chair from St James's, by Ranger's appointment; and it
is certain your Christina came to you.   310

VALENTINE How can that be? For she knew not I was in the
kingdom.

VINCENT My man confesses, when I sent him to enquire of her
woman about her lady's being here in the park last night, he told
her you were come, and she, it seems, told her mistress.   315

VALENTINE (aside) That might be . . . [Aloud] But did not Christina
confess Ranger was in her lodging last night?

VINCENT By intrusion, which she had more particularly informed me
of, if her apprehensions of your danger had not posted me after
you—she not having yet (as I suppose) heard of Clerimont's   320
recovery. I left her, poor creature, at home, distracted with a
thousand fears for your life and love.

VALENTINE Her love, I'm sure, has cost me more fears than my life.
Yet that little danger is not past (as you think) till the great one be
over.   325

VINCENT Open but your eyes and the fantastic goblin's vanished,
and all your idle fears will turn to shame; for jealousy is the basest
cowardice.

VALENTINE I had rather, indeed, blush for myself than her.

VINCENT I'm sure you will have more reason—But is not that   330
Ranger there?

> Ranger enters, followed by Christina and Isabel; after them
> Lydia and Leonore

VALENTINE I think it is.

VINCENT I suppose his friend Dapperwit is not far off. I will examine
them both before you, and not leave you so much as the shadow
of a doubt. Ranger's astonishment, at my lodging, confessed his   335
mistake.

VALENTINE His astonishment might proceed from Christina's unex-
pected strangeness to him.

VINCENT He shall satisfy you now himself to the contrary, I warrant
you; have but patience.   340

VALENTINE I had rather, indeed, he should satisfy my doubts than
my revenge; therefore I can have patience.

VINCENT But what women are those that follow him?

VALENTINE Stay a little.

RANGER [*aside*] Lydia, Lydia . . . poor Lydia.   345

LYDIA (*to Leonore*) If she be my rival, 'tis some comfort yet, to see her follow him—rather than he her.

LEONORE But if you follow them a little longer, for your comfort, you shall see them go hand in hand.

CHRISTINA (*to Ranger*) Sir, sir!   350

LEONORE She calls to him already.

LYDIA But he does not hear, you see. Let us go a little nearer.

VINCENT Sure, it is Ranger!

VALENTINE As sure as the woman that follows him closest, is Christina.   355

VINCENT For shame, talk not of Christina. I left her just now at home, surrounded with so many fears and griefs she could not stir.

VALENTINE She is come, it may be, to divert them here in the park. I'm sure 'tis she.   360

VINCENT When the moon, at this instant, scarce affords light enough to distinguish a man from a tree, how can you know her?

VALENTINE How can you know Ranger, then?

VINCENT I heard him speak.

VALENTINE So you may her too. I'll secure you, if you will draw but 365
a little nearer. She came, doubtless, to no other end but to speak with him. Observe—

CHRISTINA (*to Ranger*) Sir, I have followed you hitherto. But now I must desire you to follow me out of the company, for I would not be overheard, nor disturbed.   370

RANGER [*aside*] Ha! Is not this Christina's voice? It is, I am sure; I cannot be deceived now.—Dear madam!

VINCENT (*apart to Valentine*) It is she indeed.

VALENTINE Is it so?

CHRISTINA (*to Ranger*) Come, sir—   375

VALENTINE (*aside*) Nay, I'll follow you too, though not invited.

LYDIA (*aside*) I must not, cannot, stay behind.

> *They all go off together in a huddle, hastily. Christina,*
> *Isabel, and Valentine return on the other side*

CHRISTINA Come along, sir.

VALENTINE (*aside*) So, I must stick to her when all is done. Her new servant has lost her in the crowd; she has gone too fast for him. So 380
much my revenge is swifter than his love. Now shall I not only have the deserted lover's revenge, of disappointing her of her new

man, but an opportunity, infallibly, at once to discover her
falseness, and confront her impudence.

CHRISTINA Pray come along, sir, I am in haste.   385

VALENTINE (aside) So eager, indeed! I wish that cloud may yet
withhold the moon, that this false woman may not discover me
before I do her.

CHRISTINA Here no-one can hear us, and I'm sure we cannot see one
another.   390

VALENTINE (aside) 'Sdeath, what have I giddily run myself upon?
'Tis rather a trial of myself than her—I cannot undergo it.

CHRISTINA Come nearer, sir.

VALENTINE (aside) Hell and vengeance! I cannot suffer it, I cannot.

CHRISTINA Come, come; yet nearer. Pray come nearer.   395

VALENTINE [aside] It is impossible; I cannot hold. I must discover
myself, rather than her infamy.

CHRISTINA (speaks, walking slowly) You are conscious, it seems, of
the wrong you have done me, and are ashamed, though in the dark.

VALENTINE (aside) How's this!   400

CHRISTINA I'm glad to find it so; for all my business with you is to
show you your late mistakes, and force a confession from you of
those unmannerly injuries you have done me.

VALENTINE (aside) What! I think she's honest—or does she know
me? Sure she cannot.   405

CHRISTINA First, your intrusion, last night, into my lodging, which
I suppose has begot your other gross mistakes.

VALENTINE (aside) No, she takes me for Ranger, I see again.

CHRISTINA You are to know then (since needs you must), it was not
me you followed last night to my lodging from the park, but some   410
kinswoman of yours, it seems, whose fear of being discovered by
you prevailed with me to personate her, while she withdrew, our
habits and our statures being much alike—which I did with as
much difficulty as she used importunity to make me. And all this
my Lady Flippant can witness, who was then with your cousin.   415

VALENTINE (aside) I am glad to hear this!

CHRISTINA Now, what your claim to me, at Mr Vincent's lodging,
meant—the letter and promises you unworthily, or erroneously,
laid to my charge—you must explain to me and others, or—

VALENTINE (aside) How's this! I hope I shall discover no guilt but   420
my own. She would not speak in threats to a lover!

CHRISTINA Was it because you found me in Mr Vincent's lodgings,
you took a liberty to use me like one of your common visitants?

But know, I came no more to Mr Vincent than to you. Yet, I
confess, my visit was intended to a man—a brave man, till you   425
made him use a woman ill; worthy the love of a princess, till you
made him censure mine; good as angels, till you made him unjust.
Why—in the name of honour—would you do't?

VALENTINE (*aside*) How happily am I disappointed! Poor, injured
Christina.   430

CHRISTINA He would have sought me out first, if you had not made
him fly from me. Our mutual love, confirmed by a contract,° made
our hearts inseparable, till you rudely, if not maliciously, thrust in
upon us, and broke the close and happy knot. I had lost him before
for a month; now for ever.   435

        She weeps

VALENTINE (*aside*) My joy and pity makes me as mute as my
shame—yet I must discover myself.

CHRISTINA Your silence is a confession of your guilt.

VALENTINE (*aside*) I own it.

CHRISTINA But that will not serve my turn; for straight you must go 440
clear yourself, and me, to him you have injured in me—if he has
not made too much haste from me to be found again. You must, I
say, for he is a man that will have satisfaction, and in satisfying
him, you do me.

VALENTINE Then he is satisfied.   445

CHRISTINA How! Is it you? Then I am not satisfied.

VALENTINE Will you be worse than your word?

CHRISTINA I gave it not to you.

VALENTINE Come, dear Christina; the jealous, like the drunkard, has
his punishment with his offence.   450

        [*Enter*] *Vincent*

VINCENT [*calling*] Valentine, Mr Valentine!

VALENTINE Vincent!

VINCENT Where have you been all this while?

        *Valentine holds Christina by the hand, who seems to struggle
        to get from him*

VALENTINE Here, with my injured Christina.

VINCENT She's behind, with Ranger, who is forced to speak all the   455
tender things himself, for she affords him not a word.

VALENTINE Pish, pish, Vincent, who is blind now? Who deceived
now?

VINCENT You are, for I'm sure Christina is with him. Come back
and see.   460

Vincent, Valentine, and Christina go out at one door, and
return at the other. [Enter Ranger and Lydia, with Leonore
following]

RANGER (*to Lydia*) Still mocked, still abused! Did you not bid me
follow you where we might not be disturbed nor overheard? And
now not allow me a word!

VINCENT (*apart to Valentine*) Did you hear him?

VALENTINE (*apart to Vincent*) Yes, yes, peace! 465

RANGER Disowning your letter, and me, at Vincent's lodging, declaring you came to meet another there, and not me, with a great deal
of such affronting unkindness, might be reasonable enough, because you would not entrust Vincent with our love; but now, when
nobody sees us, nor hears us, why this unseasonable shyness? 470

LYDIA (*aside*) It seems she did not expect him there, but had
appointed to meet another. I wish it were so.

RANGER I have not patience. Do you design thus to revenge my
intrusion into your lodging last night? Sure, if you had then been
displeased with my company, you would not have invited yourself 475
to't again by a letter? Or is this a punishment for bringing you to
a house so near your own, where it seems you were known too? I
do confess, it was a fault. But make me suffer any penance but your
silence, because it is the certain mark of a mistress's lasting
displeasure . . . 480

LYDIA (*aside*) My cue is not yet come.

RANGER Not yet a word? You did not use me so unkindly last
night, when you chid me out of your house, and with indignation
bid me begone. Now you bid me follow you, and yet will have
nothing to say to me. And I am more deceived this day and night 485
than I was last night, when, I must confess, I followed you for
another—

LYDIA (*aside*) I'm glad to hear that.

RANGER One that would have used me better, whose love I have
ungratefully abused for yours, yet from no other reason but my 490
natural inconstancy—(*Aside*) Poor Lydia, Lydia . . .

LYDIA (*aside*) He muttered my name, sure, and with a sigh.

RANGER But as last night, by following (as I thought) her, I found
you, so this night, by following you in vain I do resolve, if I can
find her again, to keep her for ever. 495

LYDIA (*aside*) Now I am obliged and brought in debt to his inconstancy. Faith, now cannot I hold out any longer; I must discover
myself.

RANGER But, madam, because I intend to see you no more, I'll take
my leave of you for good and all. Since you will not speak, I'll try   500
if you will squeak.
> *Goes to throw her down; she squeaks*

LYDIA Mr Ranger, Mr Ranger!

VINCENT Fie, fie, you need not ravish Christina, sure, that loves you
so.

RANGER [*aside*] Is it she? Lydia all this while! How am I gulled—and   505
Vincent in the plot too?

LYDIA Now, false Ranger.

RANGER Now, false Christina too. You thought I did not know you
now, because I offered you such an unusual civility.

LYDIA You knew me! I warrant you knew, too, that I was the   510
Christina you followed out of the park last night; that I was the
Christina that writ the letter too.

RANGER Certainly; therefore I would have taken my revenge, you
see, for your tricks.

VALENTINE (*to Christina*) Is not this the same woman that took   515
refuge in your house last night, madam?

CHRISTINA The very same.

VALENTINE What, Mr Ranger, we have chopped and changed and
hid our Christinas so long, and often, that at last we have drawn°
each of us our own!   520

RANGER Mr Valentine in England! The truth on't is, you have
juggled together and drawn without my knowledge. But since she
will have it so, she shall wear me for good and all now.
> *Goes to take Lydia by the hand*

LYDIA Come not near me.

RANGER Nay, you need not be afraid I would ravish you, now I know   525
you.

LYDIA (*apart to Leonore; Ranger listens*) And yet, Leonore, I think 'tis
but justice to pardon the fault I made him commit?

RANGER You consider it right, cousin; for indeed you are but
merciful to yourself in it.   530

LYDIA Yet, if I would be rigorous, though I made the blot, your
oversight has lost the game.°

RANGER But 'twas rash woman's play, cousin, and ought not to be
played again, let me tell you.
> [*Enter*] *Dapperwit*

DAPPERWIT Who's there? Who's there?   535

RANGER Dapperwit.

DAPPERWIT Mr Ranger, I am glad I have met with you—for I have left my bride, just now, in the house at Mulberry Garden, to come and pick up some of my friends in the park here, to sup with us. 540

RANGER Your bride! Are you married then? Where is your bride?

DAPPERWIT Here at Mulberry Garden, I say, where you, these ladies and gentlemen, shall all be welcome, if you will afford me the honour of your company.

RANGER With all our hearts. But who have you married—Lucy? 545

DAPPERWIT What, do you think I would marry a wench? I have married an heiress worth thirty thousand pound, let me perish.

VINCENT An heiress worth thirty thousand pound!

DAPPERWIT Mr Vincent, your servant; you here too? 550

RANGER Nay, we are more of your acquaintance here, I think. Go, we'll follow you; for if you have not dismissed your parson, perhaps we may make him more work.

Exeunt

5.2

The dining-room in Mulberry Garden House

Enter Sir Simon Addleplot, Gripe, [Lady Flippant,] Martha, Mrs Joiner, Mrs Crossbite, Lucy

SIR SIMON 'Tis as I told you, sir, you see.

GRIPE Oh graceless babe, married to a wit! An idle, loitering, slandering, foul-mouthed, beggarly wit! Oh that my child should ever live to marry a wit!

MRS JOINER Indeed, your worship had better seen her fairly buried, as they say. 5

MRS CROSSBITE If my daughter there should have done so, I would not have gi'n her a groat.

GRIPE Marry a wit!

SIR SIMON (*aside to Mrs Joiner*) Mrs Joiner, do not let me lose the widow too; for if you do, (betwixt friends) I and my small annuity are both blown up; it will follow my estate.° 10

MRS JOINER (*aside [to Sir Simon Addleplot]*) I warrant you.

LADY FLIPPANT (*aside to Mrs Joiner*) Let us make sure of Sir Simon tonight, or— 15

MRS JOINER You need not fear it. (*Aside*) Like the lawyers, while
my clients endeavour to cheat one another, I in justice cheat 'em
both.

GRIPE Marry a wit!

> *Enter Dapperwit, Ranger, and Lydia, Valentine, Christina,*
> *and Vincent. Dapperwit stops 'em, and they stand all behind*

DAPPERWIT (*aside*) What, is he here? Lucy, and her mother?   20

GRIPE Tell me how thou cam'st to marry a wit?

MARTHA Pray, be not angry, sir, and I'll give you a good reason.

GRIPE Reason for marrying a wit!

MARTHA Indeed, I found myself six months gone with child, and saw
no hopes of your getting me a husband—or else I had not married   25
a wit, sir.

MRS JOINER (*aside*) Then you were the wit.

GRIPE Had you that reason? Nay, then—(*Holding up his hands*)

DAPPERWIT (*aside*) How's that!

RANGER (*aside* [*to Dapperwit*]) Who would have thought, Dapperwit,   30
you would have married a wench?

DAPPERWIT (*to Ranger*) Well, thirty thousand pound will make me
amends. I have known my betters wink and fall on for five or six.
(*To Gripe and the rest*) What, you are come, sir, to give me joy?
You, Mistress Lucy, you, and you? Well, unbid guests are doubly   35
welcome.° (*To Sir Simon Addleplot*) Sir Simon, I made bold to
invite these ladies and gentlemen; for you must know, Mr Ranger,
this worthy Sir Simon does not only give me my wedding-supper
but my mistress too, and is (as it were) my father.

SIR SIMON Then I am as it were a grandfather to your new wife's   40
Hans-in-kelder—to which you are but as it were a father. There's
for you again, sir! Ha, ha!

RANGER Ha ha ha!

DAPPERWIT (*to Vincent*)° Fools sometimes say unhappy things,° if
we would mind 'em, but ... [*Turns to Gripe*] What, melancholy at   45
your daughter's wedding, sir?

GRIPE (*aside*) How deplorable is my condition!

DAPPERWIT Nay, if you will rob me of my wench, sir, can you blame
me for robbing you of your daughter? I cannot be without a
woman.   50

GRIPE (*aside*) My daughter, my reputation, and my money gone—but
the last is dearest to me. Yet at once I may retrieve that, and be
revenged for the loss of the other—and all this by marrying Lucy
here. I shall get my five hundred pound again, and get heirs to

exclude my daughter and frustrate Dapperwit. Besides, 'tis agreed 55
on all hands, 'tis cheaper keeping a wife than a wench.

DAPPERWIT If you are so melancholy, sir, we will have the fiddles
and a dance to divert you. Come.

    A dance

GRIPE Indeed, you have put me so upon a merry pin, that I resolve
to marry too. 60

LADY FLIPPANT Nay, if my brother come to marrying once, I may
too. I swore I would when he did, little thinking—

SIR SIMON I take you at your word, madam.

LADY FLIPPANT Well, but if I had thought you would have been so
quick with me— 65

GRIPE Where is your parson?

DAPPERWIT What, you would not revenge yourself upon the parson?

GRIPE No, I would have the parson revenge me upon you; he should
marry me. 70

DAPPERWIT I am glad you are so frolic, sir. But who would you
marry?

GRIPE (*pointing to Lucy*) This innocent lady.

DAPPERWIT That innocent lady?

GRIPE Nay, I am impatient. Mrs Joiner, pray fetch him up, if he be 75
yet in the house.

DAPPERWIT We were not married here. But you cannot be in
earnest.

GRIPE You'll find it so. Since you have robbed me of my housekeeper, I must get another. 80

DAPPERWIT Why, she was my wench.

GRIPE I'll make her honest then.

MRS CROSSBITE [*to Gripe*] Upon my repute he never saw her before.
But will your worship marry my daughter then?

GRIPE I promise her, and you, before all this good company, 85
tomorrow I will make her my wife.

DAPPERWIT How!

RANGER (*to Valentine*) Our ladies, sir, I suppose expect the same
promise from us.

VALENTINE They may be sure of us without a promise; but let us (if 90
we can) obtain theirs, to be sure of them.°

DAPPERWIT (*to Gripe*) But will you marry her tomorrow?

GRIPE I will, verily.

DAPPERWIT I am undone then, ruined, let me perish.

SIR SIMON No, you may hire a little room in Covent Garden and set   95
    up a coffee-house; you and your wife will be sure of the wits'
    custom.

DAPPERWIT Abused by him I have abused!
    Fortune our foe° we cannot over-wit,
    By none but thee our projects are crossbit.   100

VALENTINE Come, dear madam; what, yet angry? Jealousy sure is
    much more pardonable before marriage than after it; but tomorrow,
    by the help of the parson, you will put me out of all my fears.

CHRISTINA I am afraid then you would give me my revenge, and
    make me jealous of you; and I had rather suspect your faith, than   105
    you should mine.

RANGER Cousin Lydia, I had rather suspect your faith too, than you
    should mine. Therefore let us e'en marry tomorrow, that I may
    have my turn of watching, dogging, standing under the window, at
    the door, behind the hanging, or—   110

LYDIA But if I could be desperate now, and give you up my
    liberty—could you find in your heart to quit all other engagements,
    and voluntarily turn yourself over to one woman, and she a wife
    too? Could you away with° the insupportable bondage of matri-
    mony?   115

RANGER You talk of matrimony as irreverently as my Lady Flippant.
    The bondage of matrimony? No—
            The end of marriage now is liberty,
            And two are bound—to set each other free.
    Exeunt°

Epilogue

Spoken by Dapperwit

Now, my brisk brothers of the pit, you'll say
I'm come to speak a good word for the play.
But, gallants, let me perish if I do,
For I have wit, and judgement, just like you;
Wit never partial, judgement free and bold,   5
For fear or friendship never bought or sold,
Nor by good nature e'er to be cajoled.
Good nature in a critic were a crime,
Like mercy in a judge, and renders him
Guilty of all those faults he does forgive.   10
Besides, if thief from gallows you reprieve,
He'll cut your throat; so poet saved from shame,
In damned lampoon will murder your good name.
 Yet in true spite to him, and to his play,
Good faith, you should not rail at 'em today;   15
But to be more his foe, seem most his friend,
And so, maliciously, the play commend,
That he may be betrayed to writing on,
And poet let him be—to be undone.

THE GENTLEMAN
DANCING-MASTER

non satis est risu diducere rictum
auditoris; et est quaedam tamen hic quoque virtus.°

Horace

THE PERSONS°

Mr Gerrard ⎱	(young gentlemen of the town,
Mr Martin ⎰	and friends)
Mr Parris, or Monsieur de Paris	(a vain coxcomb and rich City heir, newly returned from France, and mightily affected with the French language and fashions) 5
Mr James Formal, or Don Diego	(an old, rich Spanish merchant,° newly returned home, as much affected with the habit and customs of Spain, and uncle to Monsieur de Paris) 10
Mistress Hippolyta	(Formal's daughter)
Mrs Caution	(Formal's sister, an impertinent, precise old woman) 15
Prue	(Hippolyta's maid)
Mistress Flirt ⎱	(two common women of the
Mistress Flounce ⎰	town)
A Little Blackamoor	(lackey to Formal)

A Parson, a French Scullion, [a Musical Gentlewoman], servants, 20
Waiter, and attendants

THE SCENE

London

98

Prologue

To the City

Newly after the removal of the Duke's Company from Lincoln's Inn
Fields to their new theatre near Salisbury Court°

Our author (like us) finding 'twould scarce do
At t'other end o'th'town, is come to you;°
And since 'tis his last trial, has that wit
To throw himself on a substantial pit,°
Where needy wit or critic dare not come,   5
Lest neighbour i' the cloak, with looks so grum,
Should prove a dun;
Where punk in visor dare not rant and tear
To put us out, since Bridewell is so near.
In short, we shall be heard, he understood;   10
If not, shall be admired, and that's as good—
For you to senseless plays have still been kind,
Nay, where no sense was, you a jest would find;
And never was it heard of, that the City
Did ever take occasion to be witty   15
Upon dull poet, or stiff player's action,
But still with claps opposed the hissing faction.
But if you hissed, 'twas at the pit, not stage,
So, with the poet, damned the damning age,
And still (we know) are ready to engage   20
Against the flouting, ticking gentry, who°
Citizen, player, poet would undo—
The poet? No, unless by commendation,
For on the Change wits have no reputation;
And rather than be branded for a wit,   25
He with you able men would credit get.

1.1

Don Diego's house, in the evening

Enter Hippolyta° and Prue, her maid

HIPPOLYTA To confine a woman just in her rambling age! Take away her liberty at the very time she should use it! Oh barbarous aunt! Oh unnatural father! To shut up a poor girl at fourteen,° and hinder her budding! All things are ripened by the sun. To shut up a poor girl at fourteen!   5

PRUE 'Tis true, miss, two poor young creatures as we are!

HIPPOLYTA Not suffered to see a play in a twelvemonth!

PRUE Nor to go to Ponchinello° nor Paradise!°

HIPPOLYTA Nor to take a ramble to the park° nor Mulberry Gar'n!°   10

PRUE Nor to Tatnam Court nor Islington!°

HIPPOLYTA Nor to eat a sillabub in New Spring Gar'n with a cousin!

PRUE Nor to drink a pint of wine with a friend at the Prince in the Sun!°   15

HIPPOLYTA Nor to hear a fiddle in good company!

PRUE Nor to hear the organs and tongs° at the Gun in Moorfields!°

HIPPOLYTA Nay, not suffered to go to church, because the men are sometimes there! Little did I think I should ever have longed to go   20
to church.

PRUE Or I either, but between two maids.°

HIPPOLYTA Not see a man!

PRUE Nor come near a man!

HIPPOLYTA Nor hear of a man!   25

PRUE No, miss; but to be denied a man, and to have no use at all of a man!

HIPPOLYTA Hold, hold. Your resentment is as much greater than mine, as your experience has been greater. But all this while, what do we make of my cousin, my husband elect (as my aunt   30
says)? We have had his company these three days. Is he no man?

PRUE No faith, he's but a *monsieur*.° But you'll resolve yourself that question within these three days, for by that time he'll be your husband, if your father come tonight—   35

HIPPOLYTA Or if I provide not myself with another in the mean
time! For fathers seldom choose well, and I will no more take my
father's choice in a husband, than I would in a gown or a suit of
knots. So that if that cousin of mine were not an ill-contrived, ugly,
freakish fool—in being my father's choice, I should hate him.   40
Besides, he has almost made me out of love with mirth and good
humour, for he debases it as much as a jack-pudding, and civility
and good breeding more than a City dancing-master.

PRUE What, won't you marry him then, madam?

HIPPOLYTA Wouldst thou have me marry a fool? An idiot?   45

PRUE Lord, 'tis a sign you have been kept up indeed, and know little
of the world, to refuse a man for a husband only because he's a
fool. Methinks he's a pretty, apish kind of a gentleman, like other
gentlemen, and handsome enough to lie with in the dark, when
husbands take their privileges; and for the day-times, you may take   50
the privilege of a wife.

HIPPOLYTA Excellent governess, you do understand the world, I see.

PRUE Then you should be guided by me.

HIPPOLYTA Art thou in earnest then, damned jade? Wouldst thou
have me marry him? Well—there are more poor young women   55
undone and married to filthy fellows, by the treachery and evil
counsel of chambermaids, than by the obstinacy and covetousness
of parents.

PRUE Does not your father come on purpose out of Spain to marry
you to him? Can you release yourself from your aunt or father any   60
other way? Have you a mind to be shut up as long as you live? For
my part, though you can hold out upon the lime from the walls
here, salt, old shoes, and oatmeal,° I cannot live so. I must confess
my patience is worn out—

HIPPOLYTA Alas, alas, poor Prue! Your stomach lies another way. I   65
will take pity of you, and get me a husband very suddenly, who
may have a servant at your service. But rather than marry my
cousin, I will be a nun in the new Protestant nunnery° they talk of,
where (they say) there will be no hopes of coming near a man.

PRUE But you can marry nobody but your cousin, miss. Your father   70
you expect tonight, and be certain his Spanish policy and wari-
ness, which has kept you up so close ever since you came from
Hackney School,° will make sure of you within a day or two at
farthest—

HIPPOLYTA Then 'tis time to think how to prevent him. Stay—   75

PRUE In vain, vain miss!

HIPPOLYTA If we knew but any man, any man, though he were but
a little handsomer than the devil, so that he were a gentleman . . .

PRUE What if you did know any man? If you had an opportunity,
could you have confidence to speak to a man first? But if you could,   80
how could you come to him, or he to you? Nay, how could you
send to him? For though you could write, which your father in his
Spanish prudence would never permit you to learn, who should
carry the letter? But we need not be concerned for that, since we
know not to whom to send it.   85

HIPPOLYTA Stay! . . . It must be so . . . I'll try, however—
Enter Monsieur de Paris

MONSIEUR *Serviteur, serviteur, la cousine*. I come to give the *bon soir*,
as the French say.

HIPPOLYTA Oh cousin, *you* know him—the fine gentleman they talk
of so much in town.   90

PRUE [*apart to Hippolyta*] What, will you talk to him of any man else?

MONSIEUR I know all the *beau monde, cousine*.

HIPPOLYTA Mister . . .

MONSIEUR Monsieur Tailleur, Monsieur Esmit, Monsieur—

HIPPOLYTA These are Frenchmen.   95

MONSIEUR *Non, non*; vould you have me say Mr Tailor, Mr Smith?
Fie, fie, *tête non*!

HIPPOLYTA But don't you know the brave gentleman they talk of so
much in town?

MONSIEUR Who, Monsieur Gerrard?   100

HIPPOLYTA What kind of man is that Mr Gerrard? And then I'll tell
you.

MONSIEUR [*shrugging affectedly*] Why . . . he is truly a pretty man, a
pretty man . . . a pretty so-so . . . kind of man, for an Englishman.

HIPPOLYTA How! A pretty man?   105

MONSIEUR Why, he is conveniently° tall . . . but—

HIPPOLYTA But what?

MONSIEUR And not ill-shaped . . . but—

HIPPOLYTA But what?

MONSIEUR And handsome, as 'tis thought . . . but—   110

HIPPOLYTA But what are your exceptions to him?

MONSIEUR I can't tell you, because they are innumerable, innumerable, *mon foi*.°

HIPPOLYTA Has he wit?

MONSIEUR Ay, ay, they say he's witty, brave, and *de belle humeur*,°   115
and well-bred with all that . . . but—

HIPPOLYTA But what? He wants judgement?

MONSIEUR *Non, non*, they say he has good sense and judgement, but it is according to the account Englis', for . . .

HIPPOLYTA For what?   120

MONSIEUR For, *jarni* . . . if I think it°—

HIPPOLYTA Why?

MONSIEUR Why? Why, his tailor lives within Ludgate,° his *valet de chambre* is no Frenchman, and he has been seen at noonday to go into an English eating-house.°   125

HIPPOLYTA Say you so, cousin?

MONSIEUR Then for being well-bred, you shall judge: first, he can't dance a step, nor sing a French song, nor swear a French oate, nor use the polite French word in his conversation; and, in fine, can't play at *hombre*, but speaks base good Englis' with the *commune*   130
homebred pronunciation, and in fine, to say no more, he ne'er carries a snuff-box° about with him.

HIPPOLYTA Indeed!

MONSIEUR And yet this man has been abroad as much as any man, and does not make the least show of it, but a little in his mien, not 135
at all in his *discours, jarni*—he never talks so much as of St Peter's church, and Rome, the Escorial, or Madrid, nay not so much as of Henry IV of Pont Neuf, Paris, and the new Louvre, nor of the *Grand Roi*.°

HIPPOLYTA 'Tis for his commendation, if he does not talk of his   140
travels.

MONSIEUR Auh, auh, *cousine*, he is conscious himself of his wants, because he is very envious, for he cannot endure me—

HIPPOLYTA (*aside*) He shall be my man then, for that. [*Apart to Prue*] Ay, ay, 'tis the same, Prue.—No, I know he can't endure you,   145
cousin.

MONSIEUR How do you know it, who never stir out? *Tête non!*

HIPPOLYTA Well, dear cousin, if you will promise me never to tell my aunt, I'll tell you.

MONSIEUR I won't, I won't, *jarni*.   150

HIPPOLYTA Nor to be concerned yourself so as to make a quarrel of it.

MONSIEUR *Non, non.*

HIPPOLYTA Upon the word of a gentleman?

MONSIEUR *Foi de chevalier*,° I will not quarrel.   155

PRUE Lord, miss! I wonder you won't believe him without more ado!

HIPPOLYTA Then he has the hatred of a rival for you.

MONSIEUR *Mal à peste!*

HIPPOLYTA You know my chamber is backward, and has a door into
the gallery, which looks into the back yard of a tavern, whence Mr 160
Gerrard once spying me at the window, has often since attempted
to come in at that window, by the help of the leads of a low
building adjoining; and indeed 'twas as much as my maid and I
could do to keep him out—

MONSIEUR Auh, *le coquin!* 165

HIPPOLYTA But nothing is stronger than aversion; for I hate him
perfectly, even as much as I love you.

PRUE (*aside*) I believe so, faith—but what design have we now on
foot?

HIPPOLYTA This discovery is an argument, sure, of my love to 170
you—

MONSIEUR Ay, ay; say no more, cousin, I doubt not your *amoure* for
me, because I doubt not your judgement. But what's to be done
with this *fanfaron*? I know where he eats tonight. I'll go find him
out, *ventrebleu*. 175

HIPPOLYTA Oh, my dear cousin, you will not make a quarrel of it?
I thought what your promise would come to!

MONSIEUR Would you have a man of honour—

HIPPOLYTA Keep his promise?

MONSIEUR And lose his mistress? That were not for my honour, *ma* 180
foi.

HIPPOLYTA Cousin, though you do me the injury to think I could
be false, do not do your self the injury to think anyone could be
false to you. Will you be afraid of losing your mistress? To show
such a fear to your rival, were for his honour, and not for yours, 185
sure.

MONSIEUR Nay, cousin, I'd have you know I was never afraid of
losing my mistress in earnest. Let me see the man can get my
mistress from me, *jarni*. But he that loves must seem a little jealous.

HIPPOLYTA Not to his rival; those that have jealousy hide it from 190
their rivals.

MONSIEUR But there are some who say jealousy is no more to be hid
than a cough. But it should never be discovered in me, if I had it,
because it is not French, it is not French at all, *ventrebleu!*

HIPPOLYTA No, you should rally your rival, and rather make a jest 195
of your quarrel to him; and that I suppose is French too?

MONSIEUR 'Tis so, 'tis so, cousin, 'tis the veritable French method.
For your Englis', for want of wit, drive everything to a serious

grum quarrel, and then would make a jest on't, when 'tis too late,
when they can't laugh, *jarni!*

HIPPOLYTA Yes, yes, I would have you rally him soundly; do not
spare him a jot. But shall you see him tonight?

MONSIEUR Ay, ay.

HIPPOLYTA Yes, pray be sure to see him for the jest's sake.

MONSIEUR I will, for I love a jeste as well as any *bel esprit* of 'em all,
da.

HIPPOLYTA Ay, and rally him soundly. Be sure you rally him
soundly, and tell him just thus: that the lady he has so long courted
from the great window of the Ship Tavern,° is to be your wife
tomorrow, unless he come at his wonted hour of six in the morning
to her window to forbid the banns, for 'tis the first and last time
of asking. And if he come not, let him for ever hereafter stay away
and hold his tongue.

MONSIEUR Ha ha ha, a ver' good jeste, *têtebleu*.

HIPPOLYTA And if the fool should come again, I would tell him his
own,° I warrant you, cousin. My gentleman should be satisfied for
good and all; I'd secure him.

MONSIEUR *Bon, bon.*

PRUE (*aside*) Well, well, young mistress, you were not at Hackney
School for nothing, I see; nor taken away for nothing. A woman
may soon be too old, but is never too young, to shift for herself!

MONSIEUR Ha ah ah, cousin, dou art a merry grig, *ma foi*. I long to
be with Gerrard, and I am the best at improving a jeste. I shall
have such divertisement tonight, *têtebleu*.

HIPPOLYTA He'll deny maybe, at first, that he never courted any
such lady.

MONSIEUR Nay, I am sure he'll be ashamed of it. I shall make him
look so sillily, *tête non*. I long to find him out. *Adieu, adieu, la
cousine*.

HIPPOLYTA Shall you be sure to find him?

MONSIEUR *Indubitablement*. I'll search the town over but I'll find
him, ha ha ha.

> *Exit Monsieur, and returns*

But I'm afrait, *cousine*, if I should tell him you are to be my wife
tomorrow, he would not come. Now I am for having him come for
the jest's sake, *ventre*—

HIPPOLYTA So am I, cousin, for having him come too—for the jest's
sake.

MONSIEUR Well, well, leave it to me! Ha ha ha.

Enter Mrs Caution

MRS CAUTION What's all this giggling here?

MONSIEUR Hey, do you tinke we'll tell you? No, fait', I warrant you,   240
tête non. Ha ha ha!

HIPPOLYTA My cousin is overjoyed, I suppose, that my father is to
come tonight.

MRS CAUTION I am afraid he will not come tonight—but you'll stay
and see, nephew?   245

MONSIEUR *Non, non*; I am to sup at t'other end of the town tonight.
La la la la, ra ra ra—
Exit Monsieur, singing

MRS CAUTION I wish the French levity of this young man may agree
with your father's Spanish gravity.

HIPPOLYTA Just as your crabbed old age and my youth agree.°   250

MRS CAUTION Well, malapert, I know you hate me, because I have
been the guardian of your reputation. But your husband may thank
me one day.

HIPPOLYTA If he be not a fool, he would rather be obliged to me for
my virtue than to you, since at long run he must, whether he will   255
or no.

MRS CAUTION So, so!

HIPPOLYTA Nay, now I think on't, I'd have you to know, the poor
man (whosoe'er he is) will have little cause to thank you.

MRS CAUTION No?   260

HIPPOLYTA No; for I never lived so wicked a life as I have done this
twelvemonth, since I have not seen a man.

MRS CAUTION How! How! If you have not seen a man, how could
you be wicked? How could you do any ill?

HIPPOLYTA No, I have done no ill—but I have paid it with   265
thinking.

MRS CAUTION Oh that's no hurt—to think is no hurt. The ancient,
grave, and godly cannot help thoughts.

HIPPOLYTA I warrant you have had 'em yourself, aunt.

MRS CAUTION Yes, yes! When I cannot sleep.   270

HIPPOLYTA Ha ha—I believe it. But know, I have had those
thoughts sleeping and waking—for I have dreamt of a man.

MRS CAUTION No matter, no matter, so that it was but a dream. I
have dreamt myself; for you must know, widows are mightily given
to dream, insomuch that a dream is waggishly called the widow's   275
comfort.

HIPPOLYTA But I did not only dream. (*Sighs*) Ah—

MRS CAUTION How, how! Did you more than dream? Speak, young
harlotry. Confess! Did you do more than dream? How could you
do more than dream in this house? Speak! Confess!   280

HIPPOLYTA Well, I will then. Indeed, aunt, I did not only dream,
but I was pleased with my dream when I waked.

MRS CAUTION Oh, is that all? Nay, if a dream only will please
you, you are a modest young woman still; but have a care of a
vision.°   285

HIPPOLYTA Ay—but to be delighted, when we wake, with a naughty
dream is a sin, aunt; and I am so very scrupulous that I would as
soon consent to a naughty man as to a naughty dream.

MRS CAUTION I do believe you.

HIPPOLYTA I am for going into the Throng of Temptations.°   290

MRS CAUTION There I believe you again.

HIPPOLYTA And making myself so familiar with them that I would
not be concerned for 'em a whit.

MRS CAUTION There I do not believe you.

HIPPOLYTA And would take all the innocent liberty of the town, to 295
tattle to your men under a vizard in the playhouses, and meet 'em
at night in masquerade.

MRS CAUTION There I do believe you again; I know you would be
masquerading. But worse would come on't, as it has done to others
who have been in a masquerade, and are now virgins but in   300
masquerade,° and will not be their own women again as long as
they live. The children of this age must be wise children indeed, if
they know their fathers,° since their mothers themselves cannot
inform 'em. Oh the fatal liberty of this masquerading age! When I
was a young woman—   305

HIPPOLYTA Come, come, do not blaspheme this masquerading age,
like an ill-bred City dame whose husband is half broke by living in
Coven' Garden, or who has been turned out of the Temple or
Lincoln's Inn upon a masquerading night.° By what I've heard, 'tis
a pleasant, well-bred, complacent, free, frolic, good-natured, pretty 310
age; and if you do not like it, leave it to us that do.

MRS CAUTION Lord, how impudently you talk, niece! I'm sure I
remember when I was a maid—

HIPPOLYTA Can you remember it, reverend aunt?

MRS CAUTION Yes, modest niece, that a raw young thing, though 315
almost at woman's estate (that was then at thirty or thirty-five years
of age), would not so much as have looked upon a man.

HIPPOLYTA Above her father's butler or coachman.

MRS CAUTION Still taking me up!° Well, thou art a mad girl, and so
good night. We may go to bed, for I suppose now your father will   320
not come tonight.

HIPPOLYTA I am sorry for it, for I long to see him.

Exit Mrs Caution

(*Aside*) But I lie; I had rather see Gerrard here, and yet I know not
how I shall like him. If he has wit he will come, and if he has none
he would not be welcome.   325

Exeunt

1.2

*The French house. [Chairs and] a table, bottles, [glasses] and
candles*

Enter Gerrard, Martin, and Monsieur; [they sit at the table]

MONSIEUR 'Tis ver' *véritable, jarni*, what the French say of you
English: you use the debauch so much, it cannot have with you the
French operation—you are never *enjoyé*.° But come, let us for once
be *enfinement* galliard,° and sing a French sonnet. (*Sings*) 'La
boutelle, la boutelle, glouglou.'°   5

MARTIN (*to Gerrard*) What a melodious fop it is!

MONSIEUR Auh, you have no complaisance.

GERRARD No, we can't sing, but we'll drink to you the lady's health,
whom (you say) I have so long courted at her window.

MONSIEUR Ay, there is your complaisance; all your English com-   10
plaisance is pledging complaisance, *ventre*. (*Takes the glass*) But if I
do you reason here, will you do me reason to a little French *chanson
à boire*? I shall begin to you. (*Sings*) 'La boutelle, la boutelle.'

MARTIN (*to Gerrard*) I had rather keep company with a set of
wide-mouthed, drunken cathedral choristers.   15

GERRARD [*to Monsieur*] Come, sir, drink, and he shall do you reason
to your French song, since you stand upon't. [*To Martin*] Sing him
'Arthur of Bradley', or 'I am the Duke of Norfolk'.°

MONSIEUR Auh, *têtebleu*, an English catch! Fie, fie, *ventre!*

GERRARD He can sing no damned French song.   20

MONSIEUR Nor can I drink the damned Englis' wine.

Sets down the glass

GERRARD Yes—to that lady's health, who has commanded me to wait
upon her tomorrow at her window, which looks (you say) into the

inward yard of the Ship Tavern, near the end of What-d'e-call-'t
Street.   25

MONSIEUR Ay, ay; do you not know her? Not you, *vert et bleu*.

GERRARD But pray repeat again what she said.

MONSIEUR Why, she said she is to be married tomorrow to a person
of honour, a brave gentleman that shall be nameless, and so and so
forth. (*Aside*) Little does he think who 'tis.   30

GERRARD And what else?

MONSIEUR That if you make not your appearance before her window tomorrow at your wonted hour of six in the morning, to
forbid the banns, you must for ever hereafter stay away and
hold your tongue, for 'tis the first and last time of asking, ha ha   35
ha!

GERRARD (*aside*) 'Tis all a riddle to me. I should be unwilling to be
fooled by this coxcomb.

MONSIEUR (*aside*) I won't tell him all she said, lest he should not go.
I would fain have him go, for the jest's sake—ha ha ha.   40

GERRARD Her name is (you say) Hippolyta, daughter to a rich
Spanish merchant?

MONSIEUR Ay, ay, you don't know her, not you; *à d'autres, à
d'autres, ma foi*—ha ha ha!

GERRARD Well, I will be an easy fool for once.   45

MARTIN By all means go.

MONSIEUR Ay, ay, by all means go—ha ha ha.

GERRARD (*aside*) To be caught in a fool's trap . . . I'll venture it.
[*Aloud*] Come, 'tis her health.
    Drinks to him

MONSIEUR And to your good reception, *têtebleu*, ha ha ha.   50

GERRARD Well, Monsieur, I'll say this for thee, thou hast made the
best use of three months at Paris as ever English squire did.

MONSIEUR Considering I was in a damn' Englis' *pension* too.

MARTIN Yet you have conversed with some French, I see—footmen,
I suppose, at the fencing-school; I judge it by your oaths.   55

MONSIEUR French footmen! Well, well, I had rather have the
conversation of a French footman than of an English esquire—
there's for you, *da*.

MARTIN I beg your pardon, Monsieur; I did not think the French
footmen had been so much your friends.   60

GERRARD Yes, yes, I warrant they have obliged° him at Paris much
more than any of their masters did. Well, there shall be no more
said against the French footmen.

MONSIEUR *Non, de grâce.* You are alway turning the nation *français*
into *ridicule*, dat nation so *accomplie*, dat nation which you imitate,   65
so dat in the conclusion you butte turn yourself into *ridicule*, *ma
foi*. If you are for de raillery, abuse the Dutch°—why not abuse the
Dutch, *les grosses vilaines*, panders, insolents? But here in your
England, *ma foi*, you have more *honneur*, respecte and estimation
for de Dushe swabber° who come to cheat your nation, dan for de   70
Franch footman, who come to oblige your nation.

MARTIN Our nation! Then you disown it for yours, it seems?

MONSIEUR Well, wat of dat? Are you the *disobligé°* by datè?

GERRARD No, Monsieur, far from it. You could not oblige us, nor
your country, any other way than by disowning it.   75

MONSIEUR It is de *brutale* country, which abuse de France, an'
reverencè de Dushe. [*Emphatically*] I vill maintain, sustain, and
justify dat one little Franch footman have more *honneur*, courage,
and generosity, more good blood in his veine, an' mush more good
manners an' civility dan all de State General togedèr, *jarni*. Dey are   80
only wise and valiant wen day are drunke.

GERRARD That is—always.

MONSIEUR But dey are never honeste wen dey are drunke.° Dey are
de only rogue in de varlde who are not honeste wen dey are drunk,
ma foi.   85

GERRARD I find you are well acquainted with them, Monsieur.

MONSIEUR Ay, ay, I have made the toure of Holland, but it was *en
poste*, dere was no staying for me, *tête non*, for de gentleman can no
more live dere dan de toad in Irland,° *ma foi*. For I did not see on'
chevalier° in de whole cuntree. Alway, [*emphatically*] you know, de   90
rebel° hate de *gens de* quality. Besides, I had make sufficient
observation of the *canaille barbare* de first nighte of my arrival at
Amsterdame. I did visit, you must know, one of de principal of de
Stat General, to whom I had recommendation from England, and
did find his Excellence weighing soap, *jarni*—ha ha ha.   95

GERRARD Weighing soap!

MONSIEUR Weighing soape, *ma foi*, for he was a wholesale chandeleer,° and his lady was taking the tale of chandels° wid her own
witer hands,° *ma foi*, and de young lady,° his Excellence daughters,
stringing° harring, stringing harring, *jarni*.   100

GERRARD So-o-o! And° what were his sons doing?

MONSIEUR Auh, his son (for he had but one) was making de toure
of France, *Espagne*, Italy, an' Germany in a coach and six—or
rader, now I think on't, gone of an embassy hider to dere master,

Cromwell, whom dey did love and fear because he was something   105
de greater rebel.° Butte now I talk of de rebelle, none but de rebel
can love de rebelle—and so mush for you and your friend the
Dushe. I'll say no more, and pray do you say no more of my friend
de Franch, not so mush as of my friend the Franch footman, *da*.

GERRARD No, no. But, Monsieur, now give me leave to admire thee,   110
that in three months at Paris you could renounce your language,
drinking, and your country (for which we are not angry with you,
as I said), and come home so perfect a Frenchman that the draymen
of your father's own brew-house would be ready to knock thee in
the head.   115

MONSIEUR Vel, vel, my father was a merchant of his own beer, as
the *noblesse* of France of their own wine. But I can forgive you that
raillery, that bob, since you say I have the *aire français*. But have I
the *aire français*?

GERRARD As much as any French footman of 'em all.   120

MONSIEUR And do I speak agreeable ill Englis' enough?

GERRARD Very ill.

MONSIEUR *Véritablement?*

GERRARD *Véritablement.*

MONSIEUR For you must know, 'tis as ill breeding now to speak good   125
Englis' as to write good Englis', good sense, or a good hand.

GERRARD But indeed, methinks you are not slovenly enough for a
Frenchman.

MONSIEUR Slovenly! You mean negligent?

GERRARD No, I mean slovenly.   130

MONSIEUR Then I will be more slovenly.

GERRARD You know, to be a perfect Frenchman you must never be
silent, never sit still, and never be clean.

MARTIN But you have forgot one main qualification of a true
Frenchman: he should never be sound, that is, be very pocky too.   135

MONSIEUR Oh, if dat be all, I am very pocky—pocky enough, *jarni*.
That is the only French qualification° may be had without going
to Paris, *mon foi*.

        Enter a Waiter

WAITER [*to Gerrard*] Here are a couple of ladies coming up to you,
sir.   140

GERRARD To us? Did you appoint any to come hither, Martin?

MARTIN Not I.

GERRARD Nor you, Monsieur?

MONSIEUR Nor I.

GERRARD Sirrah, tell your master, if he cannot protect us from the   145
constable, and these midnight coursers, 'tis not a house for us.

MARTIN Tell 'em you have nobody in the house, and shut the doors.

WAITER They'll not be satisfied with that. They'll break open the
door—they searched last night all over the house for my Lord Fisk
and Sir Jeffrey Jaunty, who were fain to hide themselves in the bar   150
under my mistress's chair and petticoats.

MONSIEUR Wat, do the women hunt out the men so now?

MARTIN Ay, ay, things are altered since you went to Paris. There's
hardly a young man in town dares be known of his lodging for
'em.   155

GERRARD Bailiffs, pursuivants, or a City constable are modest people
in comparison of them.

MARTIN And we are not so much afraid to be taken up by the watch
as by the tearing midnight ramblers or huzza-women.

MONSIEUR *Jarni!* Ha ha ha.   160

GERRARD Where are they? I hope they are gone again?

WAITER No, sir, they are below at the stair-foot, only swearing at
their coachman.

GERRARD Come, you rogue, they are in fee with you waiters, and no
gentleman can come hither but they have the intelligence straight.   165

WAITER Intelligence from us, sir! They should never come here if we
could help it. I am sure we wish 'em choked when we see them
come in; for they bring such good stomachs from St James's Park,
or rambling about in the streets, that we poor waiters have not a
bit left. 'Tis well if we can keep our money in our pockets for   170
'em—I am sure I have paid seventeen and sixpence in half-crowns
for coach hire at several times for a little damned tearing lady, and
when I asked her for it again one morning in her chamber, she bid
me pay myself,° for she had no money. But I wanted the courage
of a gentleman—besides, the lord that kept her was a good   175
customer to our house, and my friend; and I made a conscience of
wronging him.

GERRARD A man of honour!

MONSIEUR *Vert et bleu*, pleasènt, pleasènt, *mon foi*.

GERRARD Go, go, sirrah, shut the door; I hear 'em coming up.   180

WAITER Indeed I dare not—they'll kick me downstairs if I should.

GERRARD Go, you rascal, I say.

> *The Waiter shuts the door; 'tis thrust open again. Enter*
> *Flounce and Flirt° in vizards, striking the Waiter, and come*
> *up to the table*

(*Aside*) Flounce and Flirt, upon my life.—Ladies, I am sorry you
have no volunteers in your service; this is mere pressing, and argues
a great necessity you have for men.   185

FLOUNCE You need not be afraid, sir; we will use no violence to you,
you are not fit for our service. We know you!

FLIRT The hot service° you have been in formerly, makes you unfit
for ours now. Besides, you begin to be something too old for us.
We are for the brisk huzzas of seventeen or eighteen.   190

GERRARD Nay, faith, I am not too old yet. But an old acquaintance
will make any man old. Besides, to tell you the truth, you are come
a little too early for me, for I am not drunk yet. But there [*pointing*]
are your brisk young men who are always drunk, and perhaps have
the happiness not to know you.   195

FLOUNCE The happiness not to know us!

FLIRT The happiness not to know us!

GERRARD Be not angry, ladies. 'Tis rather happiness to have pleasure
to come, than to have it past, and therefore these gentlemen are
happy in not knowing you.   200

MARTIN I'd have you to know, I do know the ladies too, and I will
not lose the honour of the ladies' acquaintance for anything.

FLOUNCE Not for the pleasure of beginning an acquaintance with us,
as Mr Gerrard says? But it is the general vanity of you town-fops
to lay claim to all good acquaintance and persons of honour. You   205
cannot let a woman pass in the Mall at midnight, but, damn you,
you know her straight, you know her. But you would be damned
before you would say so much for one in a mercer's shop.°

GERRARD [*indicating Martin*] He has spoken it in a French house,
where he has very good credit, and I dare swear you may make him   210
eat his words.°

MONSIEUR (*peeping under her scarf*) She does want a gown indeet.
She is in her dishabiliè;° this dishabiliè is a great mode in
England—the women love the dishabiliè as well as the men, *ma foi*.

FLIRT Well, if we should stay and sup with you, I warrant you would   215
be bragging of it tomorrow, amongst your comrades, that you had
the company of two women of quality at the French house, and
name us.

MARTIN (*aside*) Pleasant jilts!

GERRARD No, upon our honours, we would not brag of your   220
company.

FLOUNCE Upon your honours?

MARTIN No, faith.

FLOUNCE Come, we will venture to sit down then. Yet I know the
vanity of you men; you could not contain yourselves from brag-   225
ging.

GERRARD No, no! You women nowadays have found out the pleasure
of bragging, and will allow it the men no longer.

MARTIN Therefore indeed we dare not stay to sup with you, for you
would be sure to tell on't.   230

GERRARD And we are young men who stand upon our reputations.

FLOUNCE You are very pleasant, gentlemen.

MARTIN For my part I am to be married shortly, and know 'twould
quickly come to my mistress's ear.

GERRARD And for my part I must go visit tomorrow morning,   235
betimes, a new City mistress, and you know they are as inquisitive
as precise in the City.

FLIRT Come, come! Pray leave this fooling. Sit down again, and let
us bespeak supper.

GERRARD No, faith, I dare not.   240

MARTIN Besides, we have supped.

FLOUNCE No matter, we only desire you should look on, while we
eat, and put the glass about, or so.

   Gerrard and Martin offer to go out

FLIRT Pray, stay.

GERRARD Upon my life I dare not.   245

FLOUNCE Upon our honours, we will not tell, if you are in earnest.

GERRARD Pshaw, pshaw—I know the vanity of you women; you
could not contain yourselves from bragging.

MONSIEUR *Ma foi*, is it certain! Ha ha ha! Hark you, madam; can't
you fare well, but you must cry roast meat?°   250
You'll spoil your trade by bragging of your gains;
The silent sow, *madame*, does eat most grains.°
Da.

FLIRT Your servant, Monsieur Fop.

FLOUNCE Nay, faith, do not go; we will no more tell—   255

MONSIEUR Than you would of a clape, if you had it; dat's the only
secret you can keep, *jarni*.

MARTIN I am glad we are rid of these jilts.

GERRARD And we have taken a very ridiculous occasion.

MONSIEUR Wat! Must we leave the lady then? Dis is damn' civility   260
Englis', *mon foi*.

FLIRT Nay, sir, you have too much of the French air to have so little
honour and good breeding.

Pulling him back

MONSIEUR D'e tinke° so then, sweet madam? I have mush of de French air? 265

FLIRT More than any Frenchman breathing.

MONSIEUR Auh, you are the *curtoise° dame, morbleu.* I shall stay then, if you think so.—Monsieur Gerrard, you will be certain to see the lady tomorrow? Pray not forget, ha ha ha.

GERRARD No, no, sir. 270

MARTIN You will go then?

GERRARD I will go on a fool's errand for once.

Exeunt Gerrard and Martin

FLOUNCE What will you eat, sir?

MONSIEUR Wat you please, *madame.*

FLOUNCE D'e hear, waiter? Then, some young partridge. 275

WAITER What else, madam?

FLIRT Some ruffs.

WAITER What else, madam?

FLOUNCE Some young pheasants.

WAITER What else, madam? 280

FLIRT Some young rabbits; I love rabbits.

WAITER What else, madam?

FLOUNCE Stay . . .

MONSIEUR (*aside*) Dis Englis' waiter wit his 'Wat else, madam?' will ruin me, *tête non.* 285

WAITER What else, madam?

MONSIEUR 'What else, madam?' again! Call up the French waiter.

WAITER What else, madam?

MONSIEUR Again! Call up the French waiter or *cuisinier, mort-tête-ventre, vite, vite.* 290

Exit Waiter.

Auh, madam, the stupidity of the Englis' waiter; I hate the Englis' waiter, *mon foi.*

FLIRT Be not in passion, dear Monsieur.

MONSIEUR I kiss your hand *obligeant,* madam.

Enter a French Scullion

Chère Pierrot, *serviteur, serviteur.* 295

Kisses the Scullion

Or ça, à manger.°

SCULLION *En voulez-vous* de cram schiquin?°

FLOUNCE Yes.

SCULLION De partrish, de *faisan,* de *cailles?*

MONSIEUR [*aside*] This *bougre* vil ruine me too, but he speak wit datè   300
bel aire and grâce, I cannot bid him hold his tongue, *ventre.—C'est
assez*, Pierrot, *va-t-en*.
     Exit Scullion, and returns
SCULLION And de littel plate *de*—
MONSIEUR *Jarni, va-t-en*.
     Exit Scullion, and returns
SCULLION And de littel plate *de*—   305
MONSIEUR *De grâce*, go dy way.
     Exit Scullion, and returns
SCULLION And de little *de*—
MONSIEUR *De fromage, de Brie; va-t-en*, go go.
FLOUNCE What's that—cheese that stinks?
MONSIEUR Ay, ay, be sure it stinke *extrêmente*,° Pierrot; *va-t-en*—but   310
stay till I drink dy health. Here's to dat pretty fellow's health,
madam.
FLIRT Must we drink the scullion's health?
MONSIEUR Auh, you will not be *disobligeant*, madam; he is the
cuisinier for a king, nay for a cardinal or French abbot. (*Drinks*)   315
     [*Exit Scullion*]
FLOUNCE But how shall we divertise ourselves till supper be
ready?
FLIRT Can we have better divertisement than this gentleman?
FLOUNCE But I think we had better carry the gentleman home with
us, and because it is already late, sup at home, and divertise the   320
gentleman at cards till it be ready. [*Calling offstage*] D'e hear,
waiter? Let it be brought when 'tis ready to my lodging hard by in
Mustard Alley,° at the sign of the Crooked Billet.°
MONSIEUR At the Crook Billet!
FLIRT Come, sir, come.   325
MONSIEUR *Morbleu*, I have take the vow, since my last clap, never to
go again to the *bordel*.
FLOUNCE What is the '*bordel*'?
MONSIEUR How call you the name of your house?
FLIRT The Crooked Billet.   330
MONSIEUR No, no, the—the bawdy-house, *vert et bleu*.
FLOUNCE How! Our lodging! We'd have you to know—
MONSIEUR Auh, *morbleu*, I would *not* know it, de Crooke Billet;
ha ha.
FLIRT Come, sir.   335
MONSIEUR Besides, if I go wit you to the *bordel*, you will tell, *morbleu*.

FLOUNCE Fie, fie, come along.

MONSIEUR Beside, I am to be married within these two days; if you
should tell now—

FLIRT Come, come along; we will not tell.   340

MONSIEUR But will you promise then to have the care of my honour?
Pray, good madam, have de care of my *honneur*; pray have de care
of my *honneur*. Will you have care of my *honneur*? Pray have de
care of my *honneur*, and do not tell, if you can help it.
    Kneels to 'em
Pray, dear madam, do not tell.   345

FLIRT I would not tell, for fear of losing you. My love for you will
make me secret.

MONSIEUR Why, do you love me?

FLIRT Indeed, I cannot help telling you now what my modesty ought
to conceal, but my eyes would disclose it too. I have a passion for   350
you, sir.

MONSIEUR A passion for me!

FLIRT An extreme passion, dear sir; you are so French, so mightily
French, so agreeable French. But I'll tell you more of my heart at
home. Come along.   355

MONSIEUR But is your *passion* sincere?

FLIRT The truest in the world.

MONSIEUR Well then, I'll venture my body wit thee for one night.

FLIRT For one night? Don't you believe that! And so you would
leave me tomorrow? But I love you so, I cannot part with you; you   360
must keep me for good and all, if you will have me. I can't leave
you, for my heart.

MONSIEUR How! 'Keep'! *Jarni*, de whore Englis' have notinge but
keepe, keep in dere mouths nowadays, *tête non*. Formerly 'twas
enough to keepe de shild, *ma foi*.   365

FLIRT Nay I will be kept, else . . . But come, we'll talk on't at home.

MONSIEUR Umh, so so; ver' vel, de *amoure* of de whore does alway
end in 'keep,' ha, 'keep,' *ma foi*, 'keep,' ha!
       The punk that entertains you wit her passion,
       Is like kind host who makes the invitation,   370
       At your own cost, to his *fort bon*° collation.
    Exeunt

2.1

Don Diego's house, in the morning

Enter Don Diego in the Spanish habit,° Mrs Caution

DON DIEGO Have you had a Spanish care of the honour of my
family—that is to say, have you kept up my daughter close in my
absence, as I directed?

MRS CAUTION I have, sir; but it was as much as I could do.

DON DIEGO I knew that; for 'twas as much as I could do, to keep up   5
her mother—I that have been in Spain, look you.

MRS CAUTION Nay, 'tis a hard task tò keep up an Englishwoman.

DON DIEGO As hard as it is for those who are not kept up, to be
honest, look you—*con licentia*, sister.

MRS CAUTION How now, brother! I am sure my husband never kept   10
me up.

DON DIEGO I knew that; therefore I cried '*con licentia*', sister, as the
Spaniards have it.

MRS CAUTION But you Spaniards are too censorious, brother.

DON DIEGO You Englishwomen, sister, give us too much cause (look   15
you); but you are sure my daughter has not seen a man since my
departure?

MRS CAUTION No, not so much as a churchman.

DON DIEGO As a churchman, *voto*! I thank you for that. Not a
churchman! Not a churchman!   20

MRS CAUTION No, not so much as a churchman. But of any, one
would think one might trust a churchman.

DON DIEGO No, we are bold enough in trusting them with our souls.
I'll never trust 'em with the body of my daughter, look you, *guarda*.
You see what comes of trusting churchmen here in England, and   25
'tis because the women govern the families, that chaplains are so
much in fashion. Trust a churchman! Trust a coward with your
honour, a fool with your secret, a gamester with your purse, as soon
as a priest with your wife or daughter, look you, *guarda*. I am no
fool, look you.   30

MRS CAUTION Nay, I know you are a wise man, brother.

DON DIEGO Why, sister, I have been fifteen years in Spain for it,°
at several times, look you. Now in Spain he is wise enough that is
grave, politic enough that says little, and honourable enough that

is jealous. And though I say it that should not say it, I am as grave, 35
grum, and jealous as any Spaniard breathing.

MRS CAUTION I know you are, brother.

DON DIEGO And I will be a Spaniard in everything still, and will not
conform, not I, to their ill-favoured English customs, for I will
wear my Spanish habit still, I will stroke my Spanish whiskers° 40
still, and I will eat my Spanish *olio* still; and my daughter shall go
a maid to her husband's bed, let the English custom be what 'twill.
I would fain see any finical, cunning, insinuating *monsieur* of the
age debauch or steal away my daughter. But well, has she seen my
cousin? How long has he been in England? 45

MRS CAUTION These three days.

DON DIEGO And she has seen him, has she? I was contented he
should see her, intending him for her husband—but she has seen
nobody else, upon your certain knowledge?

MRS CAUTION No, no, alas! How should she? 'Tis impossible she 50
should.

DON DIEGO Where is her chamber? Pray let me see her.

MRS CAUTION You'll find her, poor creature, asleep, I warrant you—or
if awake, thinking no hurt, nor of your coming this morning.

DON DIEGO Let us go to her; I long to see her, poor innocent wretch. 55

Exeunt

2.2°

[Hippolyta's chamber. A table, with a violin upon it]

Enter Hippolyta, Gerrard, and Prue at a distance

GERRARD Am I not come upon your own summons, madam?
And yet receive me so?

HIPPOLYTA My summons, sir? No, I assure you. And if you do not
like your reception, I cannot help it—for I am not used to receive
men, I'd have you to know. 5

GERRARD (*aside*) She is beautiful beyond all things I ever saw.

HIPPOLYTA (*aside*) I like him extremely.

GERRARD Come, fairest, why do you frown?

HIPPOLYTA Because I am angry.

GERRARD I am come on purpose to please you then; do not receive 10
me so unkindly.

HIPPOLYTA I tell you, I do not use to receive men. There has not been a man in the house before, but my cousin, this twelvemonth, I'd have you to know.

GERRARD Then you ought to bid me the more welcome, I'd have you to know. 15

HIPPOLYTA What, do you mock me too? I know I am but a home-bred, simple girl; but I thought you gallants of the town had been better bred than to mock a poor girl in her father's own house. I have heard indeed 'tis a part of good breeding to mock people 20 behind their backs, but not to their faces.

GERRARD (aside) Pretty creature! She has not only the beauty but the innocency of an angel.—Mock you, dear miss! No, I only repeated the words because they were yours, sweet miss; what we like, we imitate. 25

HIPPOLYTA 'Dear miss'! 'Sweet miss'! How came you and I so well acquainted? This is one of your confident tricks too, as I have been told; you'll be acquainted with a woman in the time you can help her over a bench° in the playhouse, or to her coach. But I need not wonder at your confidence, since you could come in at the great 30 gallery window just now. But pray, who shall pay for the glass you have broken?

GERRARD Pretty creature! Your father might have made the window bigger then, since he has so fine a daughter, and will not allow people to come in at the door to her. 35

HIPPOLYTA (aside) A pleasant man! Well, 'tis harder playing the hypocrite with him, I see, than with my aunt or father; and if dissimulation were not very natural to a woman, I'm sure I could not use it at this time. But the mask of simplicity and innocency is as useful to an intriguing woman, as the mask of religion to a 40 statesman, they say.

GERRARD Why do you look away, dearest miss?

HIPPOLYTA Because you quarrelled with me just now for frowning upon you, and I cannot help it, if I look upon you.

GERRARD Oh let me see that face at any rate. 45

HIPPOLYTA Would you have me frown upon you? For I shall be sure to do't.

GERRARD Come, I'll stand fair. You have done your worst to my heart already.

HIPPOLYTA (aside) Now I dare not look upon him, lest I should not 50 be able to keep my word.

GERRARD Come, I am ready. (*Aside*) And yet I am afraid of her frowns.—Come, look, I—ah—am° ready, I—ah—am ready.

HIPPOLYTA (*aside*) But I am not ready.

GERRARD Turn, dear miss. Come, I—ah—am ready.   55

HIPPOLYTA Are you ready? Then I'll look.
    Turns upon him
    (*Aside*) No, faith, I can't frown upon him, if I should be hanged.

GERRARD Dear miss, I thank you; that look has no terror in't.

HIPPOLYTA [*Aside*] No, I cannot frown (for my heart). [*To him*] For blushing°—I don't use to look upon men, you must know.   60

GERRARD (*aside*) If it were possible anything could, those blushes would add to her beauty. Well, bashfulness is the only out-of-fashion thing that is agreeable.

HIPPOLYTA (*aside*) I—a—ah—like this man strangely—I was going to say loved him. Courage then, Hippolyta, make use of the only   65
opportunity thou canst have to enfranchise thyself. Women formerly (they say) never knew how to make use of their time till it was past; but let it not be said so of a young woman of this age. My damned aunt will be stirring presently. Well then, courage, I say, Hippolyta; thou art full fourteen years old; shift for thyself.   70

GERRARD (*aside*) So, I have looked upon her so long, till I am grown bashful too. Love and modesty come together like money and covetousness, and the more we have, the less we can show it. I dare not look her in the face now, nor speak a word.

HIPPOLYTA What, sir, methinks *you* look away now.   75

GERRARD Because you would not look upon me, miss.

HIPPOLYTA Nay, I hope you can't look me in the face, since you have done so rude a thing as to come in at the window upon me. Come, come, when once we women find the men bashful, then we take heart—now I can look upon you as long as you will. Let's see   80
if you can frown upon me now!

GERRARD Lovely innocency! No, you may swear I can't frown upon you, miss.

HIPPOLYTA So, I knew you were ashamed of what you have done. Well, since you are ashamed, and because you did not come of your   85
own head,° but were sent by my cousin, you say—

GERRARD (*aside*) Which I wonder at.

HIPPOLYTA For all these reasons I do forgive you.

GERRARD In token of your forgiveness then, dearest miss, let me have the honour to kiss your hand.   90

HIPPOLYTA Nay, there 'tis you men are like our little shock-dogs; if we don't keep you off from us, but use you a little kindly, you grow so fiddling,° and so troublesome, there is no enduring you.

GERRARD Oh, dear miss, if I am like your shock-dog, let it be in his   95
privileges.

HIPPOLYTA Why, I'd have you know he does not lie with me.

GERRARD 'Twas well guessed, miss, for one so innocent.

HIPPOLYTA No, I always kick him off from the bed, and never will let him come near it; for of late indeed (I do not know what's the   100
reason) I don't much care for my shock-dog nor my babies.

GERRARD Oh then, miss, I may have hopes—for after the shock-dog and the babies, 'tis the man's turn to be beloved.

HIPPOLYTA Why, could you be so good-natured as to come after my shock-dog in my love? It may be indeed, rather than after one of   105
your brother men.

GERRARD Ha ha ha! [*Aside*] Poor creature, a wonder of innocency.

HIPPOLYTA But I see you are humble, because you would kiss my hand.

GERRARD No, I am ambitious therefore.   110

HIPPOLYTA (*aside*) Well, all this fooling but loses time; I must make better use of it.—I could let you kiss my hand, but then I'm afraid you would take hold of me, and carry me away.

GERRARD Indeed I would not.

HIPPOLYTA Come! I know you would.   115

GERRARD Truly I would not.

HIPPOLYTA You would, you would, I know you would.

GERRARD I'll swear I won't, by—

HIPPOLYTA Nay, don't swear, for you'll be the apter to do it then. (*Aside*) I would not have him forswear it neither. He does not like   120
me, sure, well enough to carry me away.

GERRARD Dear miss, let me kiss your hand.

HIPPOLYTA I am sure you would carry me away, if I should.

GERRARD Be not afraid of it.

HIPPOLYTA (*aside*) Nay, I am afraid of the contrary. Either he   125
dislikes me, and therefore will not be troubled with me, or (what is as bad) he loves me and is dull, or fearful to displease me.

GERRARD Trust me, sweetest, I can use no violence to you.

HIPPOLYTA Nay, I am sure you would carry me away. What should you come in at the window for, if you did not mean to steal   130
me?

GERRARD If I should endeavour it, you might cry out, and I should
be prevented.

HIPPOLYTA (*aside*) Dull, dull man of the town, are all like thee? He
is as dull as a country squire at questions and commands.° [*To him*] 135
No, if I should cry out never so loud, this is quite at the farther
end of the house, and there nobody could hear me.

GERRARD I will not give you the occasion, dearest.

HIPPOLYTA (*aside*) Well, I will quicken thy sense, if it be possible.
[*To him*] Nay, I know you come to steal me away—because I am an 140
heiress, and have twelve hundred pound a year, lately left me by my
mother's brother, which my father cannot meddle with, and which
is the chiefest reason (I suppose) why he keeps me up so close.

GERRARD (*aside*) Ha!

HIPPOLYTA [*aside*] So—this has made him consider. Oh money, 145
powerful money! How the ugly, old, crooked, straight, handsome,
young women are beholding to thee!

GERRARD [*aside*] Twelve hundred pound a year . . .

HIPPOLYTA Besides, I have been told my fortune, and the woman
said I should be stolen away, because she says 'tis the fate of 150
heiresses to be stolen away.

GERRARD (*aside*) Twelve hundred pound a° year . . .

HIPPOLYTA Nay more, she described the man to me, that was to do
it, and he was as like you as could be! Have you any brothers?

GERRARD Not any! 'Twas I, I warrant you, sweetest. 155

HIPPOLYTA [*aside*] So, he understands himself now.

GERRARD Well, madam, since 'twas foretold you, what do you think
on't? 'Tis in vain, you know, to resist Fate.°

HIPPOLYTA I do know (indeed) they say 'tis to no purpose. Besides,
the woman that told me my fortune, or you, have bewitched me, 160
I—ah—think. (*Sighs*)

GERRARD My soul, my life, 'tis you have charms powerful as
numberless, especially those of your innocency irresistible, and do
surprise the wariest heart—such mine was, while I could call it
mine; but now 'tis yours for ever. 165

HIPPOLYTA Well, well, get you gone then; I'll keep it safe for your
sake.

GERRARD Nay, you must go with me, sweetest.

HIPPOLYTA Well, I see you will part with the jewel—but you'll have
the keeping of the cabinet to which you commit it. 170

GERRARD Come, come, my dearest, let us begone. Fortune, as well
as women, must be taken in the humour.

Prue [runs] hastily [forward] to stop 'em. Enter Don Diego
and Mrs Caution immediately after

PRUE Oh miss, miss! Your father, it seems, is just now arrived, and
here is coming in upon you.

HIPPOLYTA My father!   175

DON DIEGO My daughter! And a man!

MRS CAUTION A man! A man in the house!

GERRARD Ha! What mean these? A Spaniard!

HIPPOLYTA [*Aside*] What shall I do? Stay—[*Apart to Gerrard*] Nay,
pray stir not from me, but lead me about as if you led me a courante.   180
[*He*] *leads her about*

DON DIEGO Is this your government, sister, and this your innocent
charge that has not seen the face of a man this twelvemonth? *En*
hora mala!

MRS CAUTION Oh sure it is not a man; it cannot be a man! (*Puts on*
her spectacles)   185

DON DIEGO 'It cannot be a man'! If he be not a man he's a devil—he
has her lovingly by the hand too, *valgame el cielo!*

HIPPOLYTA [*apart to Gerrard*] Do not seem to mind them, but dance
on, or lead me about still.

GERRARD (*apart to Hippolyta*) What d'e mean by't?   190

DON DIEGO Hey! They are frolic, a-dancing.

MRS CAUTION Indeed, they are dancing, I think. Why, niece—

DON DIEGO Nay, hold a little. I'll make 'em dance in the devil's
name, but it shall not be *la gaillarda.*°
Draws his sword; Mrs Caution holds him

MRS CAUTION Oh niece! Why, niece!   195

GERRARD (*apart to Hippolyta*) Do you hear her? What do you mean?

HIPPOLYTA Take no notice of them, but walk about still, and sing a
little, sing a courante.

GERRARD I can't sing—but I'll hum, if you will.

DON DIEGO Are you so merry? Well, I'll be with you, *en hora mala.*   200

MRS CAUTION Oh niece, niece; why, niece, oh—

DON DIEGO Why, daughter, my dainty daughter, my shame, my
ruin, my plague—
Struggling, gets from Mrs Caution, goes towards 'em with his
sword drawn

HIPPOLYTA Mind him not, but dance and sing on.

GERRARD A pretty time to dance and sing indeed, when I have a   205
Spaniard with naked Toledo at my tail. No, pray excuse me, miss,
from fooling any longer.

HIPPOLYTA (*turning about*) Oh my father, my father! Poor father!
You are welcome; pray give me your blessing.°

DON DIEGO My blessing, *en hora mala!*   210

HIPPOLYTA What, am I not your daughter, sir?

DON DIEGO My daughter?—*mi mal, mi muertè.*°

HIPPOLYTA My name's Hippolyta, sir; I don't own your Spanish
names. But pray, father, why do you frighten one so? You know I
don't love to see a sword. What do you mean to do with that ugly   215
thing out?

DON DIEGO I'll show you. *Traidor, ladrón de mi honra,*° thou diest.
Runs at Gerrard

GERRARD Not if I can help it, good don. But by the names you give
me, I find you mistake your man.° I suppose some Spaniard has
affronted you. (*Draws*)   220

DON DIEGO None but thee, *ladrón,* and thou diest for't.
[*They*] *fight*

MRS CAUTION Oh, oh, oh—help, help, help!

HIPPOLYTA Oh! What, will you kill my poor dancing-master?
(*Kneels* [*to Don Diego*])

DON DIEGO A dancing-master! He's a fencing-master rather, I think.   225
But is he your dancing-master? Umph . . .

GERRARD (*aside*) So much wit and innocency were never together
before.

DON DIEGO (*pausing*) Is he a dancing-master?

MRS CAUTION Is he a dancing-master? He does not look like a   230
dancing-master.

HIPPOLYTA Pish—you don't know a dancing-master; you have not
seen one these threescore years, I warrant.

MRS CAUTION No matter; but he does not look like a dancing-
master.   235

DON DIEGO Nay, nay, dancing-masters look like gentlemen enough,
sister. But he's no dancing-master, by drawing his sword so briskly.
Those tripping outsides of gentlemen are like gentlemen enough in
everything but in drawing a sword; and since he is a gentleman, he
shall die by mine.   240
[*They*] *fight again.*

HIPPOLYTA Oh, hold, hold!

MRS CAUTION Hold, hold! Pray, brother, let's talk with him a little
first. I warrant you I shall trap him, and if he confesses, you may
kill him. For those that confess, they say, ought to be hanged.°
Let's see . . .   245

GERRARD (*aside*) Poor Hippolyta, I wish I had not had this occasion
of admiring thy wit. I have increased my love, whilst I have lost
my hopes—the common fate of poor lovers.

MRS CAUTION Come, you are guilty, by that hanging down of your
head. Speak; are you a dancing-master? Speak, speak; a dancing-   250
master?

GERRARD Yes, forsooth,° I am a dancing-master, ay, ay.

DON DIEGO How does't° appear?

HIPPOLYTA Why, there is his fiddle, there upon the table, father.

MRS CAUTION No, busybody, but it is not—that is my nephew's   255
fiddle.

HIPPOLYTA Why, he lent it to my cousin; I tell you it is his.

MRS CAUTION Nay, it may be indeed; he might lend it him, for
aught I know.

DON DIEGO Ay, ay, but ask him, sister—if he be a dancing-master,   260
where?

MRS CAUTION Pray, brother, let me alone with him; I know what to
ask him, sure!

DON DIEGO What, will you be wiser than I? Nay then, stand
away.—Come, if you are a dancing-master, where's your school?   265
Adonde, adonde?

MRS CAUTION Why, he'll say, maybe, he has ne'er a one.

DON DIEGO Who asked you, nimble-chaps? So you have put an
excuse in his head.

GERRARD Indeed, sir, 'tis no excuse; I have no school.   270

MRS CAUTION Well! But who sent you? How came you hither?

GERRARD (*aside*) There I am puzzled indeed.

MRS CAUTION How came you hither, I say? How—

GERRARD Why, how, how, how should I come hither?

DON DIEGO Ay, how should he come hither? Upon his legs.   275

MRS CAUTION So, so now you have put an excuse in his head too;
that you have, so you have. But stay—

DON DIEGO Nay, with your favour, mistress, I'll ask him now.

MRS CAUTION I'facks, but you shan't; I'll ask him, and ask you no
favour, that I will.   280

DON DIEGO I'fackins, but you shan't ask him, if you go thereto, look
you, you prattle-box you; I'll ask him.

MRS CAUTION I will ask him, I say. Come—

DON DIEGO Where—

MRS CAUTION What—   285

DON DIEGO Mine's a shrewd question.

MRS CAUTION Mine's as shrewd as yours.

DON DIEGO Nay then, we shall have it. Come, answer me; where's your lodging? Come, come, sir.

MRS CAUTION A shrewd question, indeed. At the Surgeon's Arms, I warrant, in—For 'tis springtime,° you know.   290

DON DIEGO Must you make lies for him?

MRS CAUTION But come, sir, what's your name? Answer me to that, come.

DON DIEGO His name? Why, 'tis an easy matter to tell you a false name, I hope.   295

MRS CAUTION So, must you teach him to cheat us?

DON DIEGO Why did you say my questions were not shrewd questions then?

MRS CAUTION And why would you not let me ask him the question then? Brother, brother, ever while you live, for all your Spanish wisdom, let an old woman make discoveries. The young fellows cannot cheat us in anything, I'd have you to know. Set your old woman still to grope out an intrigue, because (you know) the mother found her daughter in the oven.° A word to the wise,° brother.   300   305

DON DIEGO Come, come, leave this tattling. He has dishonoured my family, debauched my daughter—and what if he could excuse himself? The Spanish proverb says 'Excuses neither satisfy creditors nor the injured'. The wounds of honour must have blood and wounds, *Santiago para mi*.°   310

    Kisses the cross of his sword, and runs at Gerrard

HIPPOLYTA Oh hold, dear father, and I'll confess all.

GERRARD (*aside*) She will not, sure, after all?

HIPPOLYTA My cousin sent him, because, as he said, he would have me recover my dancing a little, before our wedding, having made a vow he would never marry a wife who could not dance a courante. I am sure I was unwilling, but he would have him come, saying I was to be his wife as soon as you came, and therefore expected obedience from me.   315

DON DIEGO Indeed the venture is most his, and the shame would be most his. For I know here in England 'tis not the custom for the father to be much concerned what the daughter does—but I will be a Spaniard still.   320

HIPPOLYTA [*to Mrs Caution*] Did not you hear him say last night he would send me one this morning?   325

MRS CAUTION No, not I, sure. If I had, he had never come here.

HIPPOLYTA Indeed, aunt, you grow old, I see; your memory fails you very much.—Did not you hear him, Prue, say he would send him to me?

PRUE Yes, I'll be sworn did I.   330

HIPPOLYTA Look you there, aunt.

MRS CAUTION I wonder I should not remember it.

DON DIEGO Come, come, you are a doting old fool.

MRS CAUTION So, so, the fault will be mine now. But pray, mistress, how did he come in? I am sure I had the keys of the doors, which,   335
till your father came in, were not opened today.

HIPPOLYTA He came in just after my father, I suppose.

MRS CAUTION [to Don Diego] It might be, indeed, while the porters brought in the things, and I was talking with you.

DON DIEGO Oh might he so, forsooth! You are a brave *govern-*   340
ante, look you; you a *duenna*, *voto*, and not know who comes in and out!

MRS CAUTION So, 'twas my fault, I know.

DON DIEGO Your maid was in the room with you, was she not, child?

HIPPOLYTA Yes, indeed and indeed, father, all the while.   345

DON DIEGO Well, child, I am satisfied then. But I hope he does not use the dancing-master's tricks of squeezing your hands, setting your legs and feet by handling your thighs and seeing your legs.°

HIPPOLYTA No indeed, father—I'd give him a box on the ear if he should.   350

DON DIEGO Poor innocent! Well, I am contented you should learn to dance. Since for aught I know you shall be married tomorrow, or the next day at furthest, by that time you may recover a courante—a saraband, I would say; and since your cousin too will have a dancing wife, it shall be so, and I'll see you dance myself.   355
You shall be my charge these two days, and then I dare venture you in the hand of any dancing-master, even a saucy French dancing-master, look you.

MRS CAUTION Well, have a care though, for this man is not dressed like a dancing-master.   360

DON DIEGO Go, go, you dote; are they not (for the most part) better dressed and prouder than many a good gentleman? You would be wiser than I, would you? *Cuerno!*

MRS CAUTION Well, I say only look to't, look to't.

DON DIEGO Hey, hey! Come friend, to your business. Teach her her   365
lesson over again; let's see.

HIPPOLYTA Come, master.

DON DIEGO Come, come, let's see your English method; I understand something of dancing myself. Come.

HIPPOLYTA Come, master.   370

GERRARD (*apart to Hippolyta*) I shall betray you yet, dearest miss, for
I know not a step—I could never dance.

HIPPOLYTA No!

DON DIEGO Come, come, child.

HIPPOLYTA Indeed, I'm ashamed, father.   375

DON DIEGO You must not be ashamed, child; you'll never dance well
if you are ashamed.

HIPPOLYTA Indeed I can't help it, father.

DON DIEGO Come, come, I say; go to't.

HIPPOLYTA Indeed I can't, father, before you. 'Tis my first lesson,   380
and I shall do it so ill. Pray, good father, go into the next room for
this once, and the next time my master comes, you shall see I shall
be confident enough.

DON DIEGO Poor, foolish, innocent creature! Well, well, I will, child.
Who but a Spanish kind of a father could have so innocent a   385
daughter in England? Well, I would fain see anyone steal or
debauch my daughter from me.

HIPPOLYTA Nay, won't you go, father?

DON DIEGO Yes, yes, I go, child—we will all go, but your maid. You
can dance before your maid?   390

HIPPOLYTA Yes, yes, father; a maid at most times with her mistress
is nobody.

Exeunt Don Diego and Mrs Caution

GERRARD He peeps yet at the door.

HIPPOLYTA Nay, father, you peep. Indeed you must not see me;
when we have done you shall come in.   395

She pulls the door to

PRUE [*apart to Hippolyta*] Indeed, little mistress, like the young
kitten (you see) you played with your prey till you had almost lost
it!

HIPPOLYTA 'Tis true. A good old mouser like you had taken it
up° and run away with it presently.   400

GERRARD (*going to embrace her*) Let me adore you, dearest miss, and
give you—

HIPPOLYTA No, no embracing, good master; that ought to be the
last lesson you are to teach me, I have heard.

GERRARD Though an after-game° be the more tedious and danger-   405
ous, 'tis won, miss, with the more honour and pleasure—for all that

I repent we were put to't. The coming in of your father, as he did, was the most unlucky thing that ever befell me.

HIPPOLYTA What, then you think I would have gone with you?

GERRARD Yes, and will go with me yet, I hope. Courage, miss; we   410
have yet an opportunity, and the gallery window is yet open.

HIPPOLYTA No, no; if I went, I would go for good and all. But now
my father will soon come in again, and may quickly overtake us.
Besides, now I think on't, you are a stranger to me. I know not
where you live, nor whither you might carry me. For aught I know,   415
you might be a spirit,° and carry me to Barbados.

GERRARD No, dear miss, I would carry you to court, the playhouses,
and Hyde Park—

HIPPOLYTA Nay, I know 'tis the trick of all you that spirit women
away, to speak 'em mighty fair at first. But when you have got 'em   420
in your clutches, you carry 'em into Yorkshire, Wales, or Cornwall,
which is as bad as to Barbados, and rather than be served so, I
would be a prisoner in London still, as I am.

GERRARD [aside] I see the air of this town, without the pleasures of
it, is enough to infect women with an aversion for the country.—   425
Well, miss, since it seems you have some diffidence in me, give me
leave to visit you as your dancing-master, now you have honoured
me with the character, and under that, I may have your father's
permission to see you, till you may better know me and my heart,
and have a better opportunity to reward it.   430

HIPPOLYTA I am afraid, to know your heart would require a great
deal of time, and my father intends to marry me very suddenly to
my cousin who sent you hither.

GERRARD Pray, sweet miss, then let us make the better use of our
time, if it be short. But how shall we do with that cousin of yours   435
in the mean time? We must needs charm him.

HIPPOLYTA Leave that to me!

GERRARD But what's worse—how shall I be able to act a dancing-
master, who ever wanted inclination and patience to learn myself?

HIPPOLYTA A dancing-school in half an hour will furnish you with   440
terms of the art. Besides, Love (as I have heard say) supplies his
scholars with all sorts of capacities they have need of, in spite of
nature—but what has Love to do with you?

GERRARD Love indeed has made a grave, gouty statesman fight
duels, the soldier fly from his colours, a pedant a fine gentleman—   445
nay, and the very lawyer a poet; and therefore may make me a
dancing-master.

HIPPOLYTA If he were your master.

GERRARD I'm sure, dearest miss, there is nothing else which I cannot
do for you already, and therefore may hope to succeed in that.   450
    Enter Don Diego

DON DIEGO Come, have you done?

HIPPOLYTA Oh! my father again.

DON DIEGO Come, now let us see you dance.

HIPPOLYTA Indeed I am not perfect yet; pray excuse me till the next
time my master comes. But when must he come again, father?   455

DON DIEGO Let me see, friend; you must needs come after dinner
again, and then at night again, and so three times tomorrow too. If
she be not married tomorrow (which I am to consider of), she will
dance a courante in twice or thrice teaching more, will she not? For
'tis but a twelvemonth since she came from Hackney School.   460

GERRARD We will lose no time, I warrant you, sir, if she be to be
married tomorrow.

DON DIEGO Truly, I think she may be married tomorrow, therefore
I would not have you lose any time, look you.

GERRARD You need not caution me, I warrant you, sir.—Sweet   465
scholar, your humble servant; I will not fail you immediately after
dinner.

DON DIEGO No, no, pray do not, and I will not fail to satisfy you
very well, look you.

HIPPOLYTA He does not doubt his reward, father, for his pains. If   470
you should not, I would make that good to him.

DON DIEGO Come, let us go in to your aunt; I must talk with you
both together, child.

HIPPOLYTA I follow you, sir.
    Exeunt Gerrard, Don Diego

PRUE Here's the gentlewoman o'th'next house come to see you,   475
mistress.
    [*Enter Gentlewoman*]

HIPPOLYTA (*aside*) She's come as if she came expressly to sing the
new song° she sang last night. I must hear it, for 'tis to my purpose
now.—Madam, your servant. I dreamt all night of the song you
sang last—the new song against delays in love. Pray, let's hear it   480
again.

[GENTLEWOMAN] (*sings*)
    Since we poor slavish women know
        Our men we cannot pick and choose,
    To him we like, why say we 'No',

> And both our time and lover lose?   485
> With feigned repulses and delays,
>   A lover's appetite we pall;
> And if too long the gallant stays,
>   His stomach's gone for good and all.
>
> Or our impatient, am'rous guest,   490
>   Unknown to us, away may steal,
> And rather than stay for a feast,
>   Take up with some coarse ready meal.
> When opportunity is kind,
>   Let prudent woman be so too;   495
> And if the man be to your mind,
>   Till needs you must, ne'er let him go.
>
> The match soon made is happy still,
>   For only love has there to do;
> Let no-one marry 'gainst her will,   500
>   But stand off, when her parents woo,
> And only to their suits be coy;
>   For she whom jointure can obtain
> To let a fop her bed enjoy,
>   Is but a lawful wench° for gain.   505

[*Prue*] *steps to the door*°

PRUE   Your father calls for you, miss.

HIPPOLYTA   I come, I come. I must be obedient as long as I am with
him. (*Pausing*)

> Our parents who restrain our liberty,
> But take the course to make us sooner free;   510
> Though all we gain be but new slavery,°
> We leave our fathers, and to husbands fly.

Exeunt

3.1

Don Diego's house

Enter Monsieur, Hippolyta, and Prue

MONSIEUR *Serviteur, serviteur, la* cousin; your maid told me she
watched at the stair-foot for my coming, because you had a mind
to speak wit me before I saw your fadèr, it seem.

HIPPOLYTA I would so indeed, cousin.

MONSIEUR *Or ça, or ça*, I know your affair: it is to tell me wat   5
recreation you 'adde with Monsieur Gerrard. But did he come? I
was afrait he would not come.

HIPPOLYTA Yes, yes, he did come.

MONSIEUR Ha ha ha! And were you not *infiniment* divertisè and
pleasè? Confess.   10

HIPPOLYTA I was indeed, cousin, I was very well pleased.

MONSIEUR I do tinke so. I did tinke to come and be divertisè myself
this morning with the sight of his reception. But I did rencounter
last night wit damn' company dat keep me up so late I could not
rise in de morning. *Mal à peste de putains!*°   15

HIPPOLYTA Indeed we wanted you here mightily, cousin.

MONSIEUR To 'elpe you to laugh. For if I 'adde been here, I had
made such recreation wid dat coxcomb Gerrard!

HIPPOLYTA Indeed, cousin? You need not have any subject or
property° to make one laugh, you are so pleasant yourself, and   20
when you are but alone, you would make one burst.

MONSIEUR Am I so happy, cousin, then, in the *bon* quality of making
people laugh?

HIPPOLYTA Mighty happy, cousin.

MONSIEUR *De grâce.*   25

HIPPOLYTA Indeed!

MONSIEUR Nay, *sans* vanitỳ, I observe wheresoe'er I come I make
everybody merry, *sans* vanitỳ, *da*.

HIPPOLYTA I do believe you do.

MONSIEUR Nay, as I *marche* in de street I can make de dull *apprenti*   30
laugh and sneer.

HIPPOLYTA (*aside*) This fool, I see, is as apt as an ill poet to
mistake the contempt and scorn of people for applause and admiration.

MONSIEUR Ah, cousin, you see wat it is to have been in France.   35
Before I went into France I could get nobody to laugh at me, *ma foi*.

HIPPOLYTA No? Truly, cousin, I think you deserved it before, but you are improved indeed by going into France.

MONSIEUR Ay, ay, the Franch education make us *propre à tout*.   40
Beside, cousin, you must know, to play the fool is the science in France, and I didde go to the Italian Academy° at Paris thrice a week to learn to play de fool of Signior Scaramouchè,° who is the most excellent *personnage* in the world for dat noble science. Angel° is a damn' English fool to him.   45

HIPPOLYTA Methinks now, Angel is a very good fool.

MONSIEUR Nauh, nauh, Nokes is a better fool; but indeed the Englis' are not fit to be fools. Here are ver' few good fools. 'Tis true, you have many a young cavalier who go over into France to learn to be the buffoon; but for all dat, dey return but *mauvais* buffoon, *jarni*.   50

HIPPOLYTA I'm sure, cousin, you have lost no time there.

MONSIEUR Auh, *le brave* Scaramouchè!

HIPPOLYTA But is it a science in France, cousin? And is there an academy for fooling? Sure none go to it but players?

MONSIEUR Dey are comedians dat are de *matrès*,° but all the *beau*   55
monde go to learn, as they do here of Angel and Nokes—for if you did go abroad into company, you would find the best almost of de nation conning in all places the lessons which dey have learnt of the fools dere *matrès*, Nokes and Angel.

HIPPOLYTA Indeed!   60

MONSIEUR Yes, yes, dey are the *gens de* quality that practise dat science most, and the most *ambitieux*; for fools and buffoons have been always most welcome to courts, and desired in all companies. Auh, to be de fool, de buffoon, is to be de great *personnage*.

HIPPOLYTA Fools have fortune,° they say indeed.   65

MONSIEUR So say old *Sénèque*.°

HIPPOLYTA Well, cousin (not to make you proud), you are the greatest fool in England, I am sure.

MONSIEUR *Non, non, de grâce, non*; Nokes de comedian is a pretty man, a pretty man for a comedian, *da!*   70

HIPPOLYTA You are modest, cousin. But lest my father should come in presently (which he will do as soon as he knows you are here), I must give you a caution, which 'tis fit you should have before you see him.

MONSIEUR Well—vel,° cousin, vat is dat?   75

134

HIPPOLYTA You must know then (as commonly the conclusion of all mirth is sad°), after I had a good while pleased myself in jesting and leading the poor gentleman you sent into a fool's paradise, and almost made him believe I would go away with him, my father, coming home this morning, came in upon us, and caught him with me. 80

MONSIEUR *Mal à peste!*

HIPPOLYTA And drew his sword upon him, and would have killed him—for you know my father's Spanish fierceness and jealousy.

MONSIEUR But how did he come off then, *tête non*? 85

HIPPOLYTA In short, I was fain to bring him off by saying he was my dancing-master.

MONSIEUR Ha ha ha, ver' good jeste.

HIPPOLYTA I was unwilling to have the poor man killed (you know) for our foolish frolic with him. But then, upon my aunt's and father's enquiry, how he came in, and who sent him, I was forced to say you did, desiring I should be able to dance a courante before our wedding. 90

MONSIEUR A ver' good jest, *da*, still bettre as bettre.

HIPPOLYTA Now all that I am to desire of you, is to own you sent him, that I may not be caught in a lie. 95

MONSIEUR Yes, yes, a ver' good jest—Gerrard, a mastre *de* dance, ha ha ha.

HIPPOLYTA Nay, the jest is like to be better yet, for my father himself has obliged him now to come and teach me. So that now he must take the dancing-master upon him, and come three or four times to me before our wedding, lest my father, if he should come no more, should be suspicious I had told him a lie. And (for aught I know) if he should know or but guess he were not a dancing-master, in his Spanish strictness and punctilios of honour he might kill me, as the shame and stain of his honour and family, which he talks of so much. Now you know the jealous cruel fathers in Spain serve their poor innocent daughters often so, and he is more than a Spaniard. 100 105

MONSIEUR *Non, non,* fear noting; I warrant you he shall come as often as you will to the house, and your father shall never know who he is till we are married—but then I'll tell him all, for the jest's sake. 110

HIPPOLYTA But will you keep my counsel, dear cousin, till we are married? 115

MONSIEUR Poor dear fool, I warrant thee, *mon foi*.

HIPPOLYTA Nay, what a fool am I indeed, for you would not have
  me killed. You love me too well, sure, to be an instrument of my
  death—
      Enter Don Diego walking gravely, a little Blackamoor behind
      him, [and] Mrs Caution
  But here comes my father; remember.   120

MONSIEUR I would no more tell him of it, than I would tell you if I
  had been with a wench, *jarni*. (*Aside*) She's afraid to be killed, poor
  wretch, and he's a capricious, jealous fop enough to do't. But here
  he comes. [*To Hippolyta*] I'll keep thy counsel, I warrant thee, my
  dear soul, *mon petit cœur*.   125

HIPPOLYTA Peace, peace, my father's coming this way.

MONSIEUR Ay, but by his march he won't be near enough to hear us
  this half-hour, ha ha ha.
      Don Diego walks leisurely round Monsieur, surveying him
      and shrugging up his shoulders, whilst Monsieur makes legs
      and faces

DON DIEGO (*aside [to Mrs Caution]*) Is that thing my cousin, sister?

MRS CAUTION 'Tis he, sir.   130

DON DIEGO Cousin, I'm sorry to see you.

MONSIEUR Is that a Spanish compliment?

DON DIEGO So much disguised, cousin!

MONSIEUR (*aside*) Oh, is it out at last, *ventre*? [*To him*]—*Serviteur,*
  serviteur, à monsieur mon oncle, and I am glad to see you here within   135
  doors, most Spanish *oncle*, ha ha ha. But I should be sorry to see
  you in the streets, *tête non*.

DON DIEGO Why, soh? Would you be ashamed of me, ha? *Voto a*
  Santiago! Would you? Hauh—

MONSIEUR Ay, it may be you would be ashamed yourself, *mon-*   140
  sieur mon oncle, of the great train you would get to wait upon
  your Spanish hose,° puh! The boys would follow you, and hoot at
  you, *vert et bleu*—pardone my Franch *franchise, monsieur mon*
  oncle.

HIPPOLYTA (*apart to Prue*) We shall have sport anon, betwixt these   145
  two contraries.°

DON DIEGO Dost thou call me *monsieur, voto a Santiago*?

MONSIEUR No, I did not call you Monsieur Voto a Santiago, sir; I
  know you are my uncle, Mr James Formal,° *da!*

DON DIEGO But I can hardly know you are my cousin, Mr Nathaniel   150
  Parris. But call me Sir Don Diego henceforward, look you, and no
  monsieur. Call me *monsieur—guarda!*

MONSIEUR I confess my error, sir, for none but a blind man would call you *monsieur*, ha ha ha! But pray do not call me nedèr° Parris, but 'de Paris', 'de Paris' (*si vous plaît*), Monsieur de Paris! Call me *monsieur*, and welcome, *da*. 155

DON DIEGO Monsieur de Pantaloons then, *voto*.

MONSIEUR Monsieur de Pantaloons! A pretty name, a pretty name, *ma foi, da—bien trové,*° 'de Pantaloons'. How much bettre dan your de la Fountaines, de la Rivières, de la Roches, and all the *de*'s in 160 France, *da*. Well, but have you not the admiration for my pantaloon, Don Diego *mon oncle*?

DON DIEGO I am astonished at them, *verdaderamente*; they are wonderfully ridiculous.

MONSIEUR Ridicule,° ridicule! Ah, 'tis well you are my uncle, *da*. 165 Ridicule! Ah, is dere anyting in de universe so *gentil* as de pantaloons? Anyting so *ravissaunt* as de pantaloons? Auh, I could kneel down and varship a pair of *gentil* pantaloons! Vat, vat, you would have me have de admiration for dis outward skin of your thigh, which you call Spanish hose? Fie, fie, fie—ha ha ha. 170

DON DIEGO Dost thou deride my Spanish hose, young man, hauh?

MONSIEUR In comparison of pantaloon I do undervalue 'em indeet, Don Diègue *mon oncle*, ha ha ha.

DON DIEGO Thou art then a *gabacho de malo gusto,*° look you.

MONSIEUR You may call me vat you vil, *oncle* Don Diègue, but I 175 must needs say your Spanish hose are scurvy hose, ugly hose, lousy hose, and stinking hose.

DON DIEGO Do not provoke me, *borracho*. (*Puts his hand to his sword*)

MONSIEUR Indeet, for 'lousy', I recant dat epithet, for dere is scarce room in 'em for dat little animal, ha ha ha. But for 'stinking' hose, 180 dat epithet may stand—for how can dey choose but stink, since dey are so *furieusemente* close to your Spanish tail, *da*.

HIPPOLYTA (*aside*) Ha ha—ridiculous!

DON DIEGO (*seems to draw*) Do not provoke me, I say, *en hora mala*.

MONSIEUR Nay, *oncle*, I am sorry you are in de *passion*; but I must 185 live and die for de pantaloon against de Spanish hose, *da*.

DON DIEGO You are a rash young man, and while you wear pantaloons you are beneath my passion, *voto*. Auh, they make thee look and waddle (with all those gewgaw ribbons) like a great, old, fat, slovenly water-dog. 190

MONSIEUR And your Spanish hose, and your nose in the air, make you look like a great, grizzled, long, Irish greyhound reaching a crust off from a high shelf, ha ha ha.

DON DIEGO *Bueno, bueno.*

MRS CAUTION [*to Monsieur*] What, have you a mind to ruin yourself,   195
and break off the match?

MONSIEUR Pshaw, wat do you telle me of de matche? D'e tinke I will
not vindicate pantaloons, *morbleu?*

DON DIEGO (*aside*) Well, he is a lost young man, I see, and
desperately far gone in the epidemic malady of our nation, the   200
affectation of the worst of French vanities. But I must be wiser than
him, as I am a Spaniard (look you, Don Diego), and endeavour to
reclaim him by art and fair means (look you, Don Diego); if not,
he shall never marry my daughter (look you, Don Diego), though
he be my own sister's son, and has two thousand five hundred   205
seventy-three pound sterling, twelve shillings and twopence a year
penny-rent, *seguramente.*—Come, young man, since you are so
obstinate, we will refer our difference to arbitration; your mistress
my daughter shall be umpire betwixt us, concerning Spanish hose
and pantaloons.   210

MONSIEUR Pantaloons and Spanish hose, *si vous plaît.*

DON DIEGO Your mistress is the fittest judge of your dress, sure?

MONSIEUR I know ver' vel dat most of the *jeunesse* of Englandt will
not change the riband upon de cravat° widout the consultation of
dere *matress,*° but I am no *anglais, da,* nor shall I make de   215
reference of my dress to any in the universe, *da.* I, judged by any
in England! *Tête non!* I would not be judged by an English
looking-glass, *jarni.*

DON DIEGO Be not *positivo,* young man.

MRS CAUTION Nay, pray refer it, cousin, pray do.   220

MONSIEUR *Non, non,* your servant, your servant, aunt.

DON DIEGO But pray be not so positive.—Come hither, daughter,
tell me which is best.

HIPPOLYTA Indeed, father, you have kept me in universal ignorance;
I know nothing.   225

MONSIEUR And do you tink I shall refer an affair of dat consequence
to a poor young ting who have not see the varld, *da?* I am wiser
than so, *voto.*°

DON DIEGO Well, in short, if you will not be wiser, and leave off
your French dress, stammering, and tricks, look you, you shall be   230
a fool and go without my° daughter, *voto.*

MONSIEUR How, must I leave off my *gentil* Franch accoutrements,
and speak base Englis' too, or not marry my cousin, *mon oncle* Don
Diego? Do not break off the match, do not; for know I will not

leave off my pantaloon and Franch pronunciation for ne'er a cousin   235
in Englandt, *da*.

DON DIEGO I tell you again, he that marries my daughter shall at
least look like a wise man, for he shall wear the Spanish habit; I am
a Spanish *positivo*.

MONSIEUR Ver' vel, ver' vel! And I am a Franch *positivo*.   240

DON DIEGO Then I am *definitivo*; and if you do not go immediately
into your chamber, and put on a Spanish habit I have brought over
on purpose for your wedding clothes, and put off all these French
fopperies and *vanidades*, with all your grimaces, '*agréables*', '*ador-
ables*', '*ma fois*', and '*jarnis*', I swear you shall never marry my   245
daughter (and by an oath by Spaniard never broken), by my
whiskers and snuff-box.°

MONSIEUR Oh hold; do not swear, uncle, for I love your daughter
furieusement.

DON DIEGO If you love her, you'll obey me.   250

MONSIEUR Auh, wat vil become of me? But have the consideration;
must I leave off all the Franch *beautés*, *grâces*, and *embellissements*,
bote of my person and language?

> *Exeunt Hippolyta, Mrs Caution, and Prue laughing,*
> [*followed by the Blackamoor*°]

DON DIEGO I will have it so.

MONSIEUR I am ruinne den, undonne. Have some consideration for   255
me, for dere is not the least ribbon of my garniture but is as dear
to me as your daughter, *jarni*.

DON DIEGO Then you do not deserve her, and for that reason I will
be satisfied you love her better, or you shall not have her, for I am
positivo.   260

MONSIEUR Vil you breake mine 'arte? Pray have de consideration for
me.

DON DIEGO I say again, you shall be dressed before night from top
to toe in the Spanish habit, or you shall never marry my daughter,
look you.   265

MONSIEUR If you will not have de consideration for me, have de
consideration for your daughter. For she have de passionate *amour*
for me, and like me in dis habite bettre dan in yours, *da*.

DON DIEGO What I have said I have said, and I am *uno positivo*.

MONSIEUR Will you not so mush as allow me one little Franch   270
oate?

DON DIEGO No, you shall look like a Spaniard, but speak and swear
like an Englishman, look you.

MONSIEUR *Hélas, hélas*, den I shall take my leave, *mort, tête, ventre,*
jarni, têtebleu, ventrebleu, ma foi, certes.   275

DON DIEGO (*calls at the door*) Pedro, Sanchez,° wait upon this
cavaliero into his chamber with those things I ordered you to take
out of the trunks. [*To Monsieur*] I would have you a little
accustomed to your clothes before your wedding; for if you comply
with me, you shall marry my daughter tomorrow, look you.   280

MONSIEUR *Adieu* then, dear pantaloon! Dear *belte*! Dear sword!°
Dear *perruque*, and dear *chapeau retroussé*,° and dear shoe *garni!°*
Adieu, adieu, adieu; hélas, hélas, hélas. Will you have yet no pity?

DON DIEGO I am a Spanish *positivo*, look you.

MONSIEUR And more cruel than de Spanish *Inquisitiono*, to compel   285
a man to a habit against his conscience, *hélas, hélas, hélas*.

        Exit Monsieur. Enter Prue and Gerrard

PRUE Here is the dancing-master. Shall I call my mistress, sir?

DON DIEGO Yes.

        Exit Prue

Oh, you are as punctual as a Spaniard. I love your punctual men.
Nay, I think 'tis before your time something.   290

GERRARD Nay, I am resolved your daughter, sir, shall lose no time
by my fault.

DON DIEGO So, so, 'tis well.

GERRARD I were a very unworthy man if I should not be punctual
with her, sir.   295

DON DIEGO You speak honestly, very honestly, friend—and, I
believe, a very honest man, though a dancing-master.

GERRARD I am very glad you think me so, sir.

DON DIEGO What, you are but a young man; are you married yet?

GERRARD No, sir, but I hope I shall, sir, very suddenly, if things hit   300
right.

DON DIEGO What, the old folks her friends are wary, and cannot
agree with you so soon as the daughter can?

GERRARD Yes, sir, the father hinders it a little at present. But the
daughter (I hope) is resolved, and then we shall do well enough.   305

DON DIEGO What! You do not steal her, according to the laudable
custom of some of your brother dancing-masters?

GERRARD No, no, sir. Steal her, sir! Steal her! You are pleased to be
merry, sir, ha ha ha! (*Aside*) I cannot but laugh at that question.

DON DIEGO No, sir—methinks *you* are pleased to be merry. But you   310
say the father does not consent?

GERRARD Not yet, sir; but 'twill be no matter whether he does or no.

DON DIEGO Was she one of your scholars? If she were, 'tis a hundred to ten but you steal her.

GERRARD (*aside*) I shall not be able to hold laughing. (*Laughs*) 315

DON DIEGO Nay, nay, I find by your laughing you steal her; she was your scholar, was she not?

GERRARD Yes, sir, she was the first I ever had, and may be the last too. For she has a fortune (if I can get her) will keep me from teaching to dance any more. 320

DON DIEGO So, so, then she is your scholar still, it seems, and she has a good portion. I am glad on't—nay, I knew you stole her.

GERRARD (*aside*) My laughing may give him suspicions, yet I cannot hold.

DON DIEGO What, you laugh, I warrant, to think how the young 325
baggage and you will mump the poor old father. But if all her dependence for a fortune be upon the father, he may chance to mump you both, and spoil the jest.

GERRARD I hope it will not be in his power, sir, ha ha ha. (*Aside*) I shall laugh too much anon.—Pray, sir, be pleased to call for your 330
daughter; I am impatient till she comes. For time was never more precious with me and with her too. It ought to be so, sure, since you say she is to be married tomorrow.

DON DIEGO She ought to bestir her, as you say indeed. (*Calls at the door*) Wuh, daughter, daughter, Prue, Hippolyta! Come away, 335
child; why do you stay so long?

Enter Hippolyta, Prue, and Mrs Caution

HIPPOLYTA Your servant, master! Indeed I am ashamed you have stayed for me.

GERRARD Oh good madam, 'tis my duty; I know you came as soon 340
as you could.

HIPPOLYTA I knew my father was with you, therefore I did not make altogether so much haste as I might. But if you had been alone, nothing should have kept me from you; I would not have been so rude as to have made you stay a minute for me, I warrant you. 345

DON DIEGO Come, fiddle-faddle, what a deal of ceremony there is betwixt your dancing-master and you, *cuerno!*

HIPPOLYTA Lord, sir, I hope you'll allow me to show my respect to my master, for I have a great respect for my master.

GERRARD And I am very proud of my scholar, and am a very great 350
honourer of my scholar.

DON DIEGO Come, come, friend, about your business, and honour the king.° (*To Mrs Caution*) Your dancing-masters and barbers are such finical, smooth-tongued, tattling fellows, and if you set 'em once a-talking they'll ne'er ha' done, no more than when you set 'em a-fiddling.° Indeed, all that deal with fiddles are given to impertinency.°   355

MRS CAUTION Well, well! This is an impertinent fellow, without being a dancing-master. He's no more a dancing-master than I am a maid.

DON DIEGO What, will you still be wiser than I, *voto*? [*To Gerrard*]   360
Come, come, about with my daughter, man.

PRUE So he would, I warrant you, if your worship would let him alone.

DON DIEGO How now, Mistress Nimble-Chaps!

GERRARD (*aside to Hippolyta*) Well, though I have got a little canting   365
at the dancing-school since I was here, yet I do all so bunglingly, he'll discover me.

HIPPOLYTA [*aside to Gerrard*] Try. [*Aloud*] Come, take my hand, master.

MRS CAUTION Look you, brother, the impudent harlotry gives him   370
her hand.

DON DIEGO Can he dance with her without holding her by the hand?

HIPPOLYTA Here, take my hand, master.

GERRARD (*aside to her*) I wish it were for good and all.

HIPPOLYTA You dancing-masters are always so hasty, so nimble.   375

DON DIEGO *Voto a Santiago*, not that I can see! About, about with her, man.

GERRARD Indeed, sir, I cannot about with her as I would do, unless you will please to go out a little, sir; for I see she is bashful still before you, sir.   380

DON DIEGO Hey, hey, more fooling yet. Come, come, about with her.

HIPPOLYTA Nay, indeed, father, I am ashamed and cannot help it.

DON DIEGO But you shall help it, for I will not stir. Move her, I say.
Begin, hussy; move when he'll have you.   385

PRUE (*aside*) I cannot but laugh at that, ha ha ha.

GERRARD (*apart to Hippolyta*) Come then, madam, since it must be so, let us try—but I shall discover all. [*Aloud*] One, two, and coupee.

MRS CAUTION Nay, d'e see how he squeezes her hand, brother? Oh,   390
the lewd villain!

DON DIEGO Come, move, I say, and mind her not.

GERRARD One, two, three, four, and turn round.

MRS CAUTION D'e see again? He took her by the bare arm.

DON DIEGO Come, move on; she's mad.   395

GERRARD One, two, and a coupee.

DON DIEGO Come.

[GERRARD]° One, two; turn out your toes.

MRS CAUTION There, there! He pinched her by the thigh; will you
    suffer it?   400

GERRARD One, two, three, and fall back.

DON DIEGO Fall back, fall back, back; some of you are forward
    enough to fall° back.

GERRARD Back, madam.

DON DIEGO Fall back when he bids you, hussy.   405

MRS CAUTION How, how! Fall back, fall back? Marry, but she shall
    not fall back when he bids her.

DON DIEGO I say she shall. Hussy, come.

GERRARD She will, she will, I warrant you, sir, if you won't be angry
    with her.   410

MRS CAUTION Do you know what he means by that now? You, a
    Spaniard!°

DON DIEGO How's that! I not a Spaniard? Say such a word again.

GERRARD Come forward, madam, three steps again.

MRS CAUTION See, see, she squeezes his hand now! Oh, the   415
    debauched harlotry!

DON DIEGO So, so, mind her not. She moves forward pretty
    well—but you must move as well backward as forward, or you'll
    never do anything to purpose.

MRS CAUTION Do you know what you say, brother, yourself now?   420
    Are you at your beastliness before your young daughter?

PRUE Ha ha ha!

DON DIEGO How now, mistress, are you so merry? [To Mrs Caution]
    Is this your staid maid, as you call her, sister impertinent?

GERRARD (aside to Hippolyta) I have not much to say to you, miss,   425
    but I shall not have an opportunity to do it, unless we can get your
    father out.

DON DIEGO Come, about again with her.

MRS CAUTION Look you, there she squeezes his hand hard again.

HIPPOLYTA Indeed and indeed, father, my aunt puts me quite out;   430
    I cannot dance while she looks on, for my heart. She makes me
    ashamed and afraid together.

GERRARD Indeed, if you would please to take her out, sir, I am sure
    I should make my scholar do better than when you are present,

sir. Pray, sir, be pleased for this time to take her away. For the   435
next time, I hope I shall order it so, we shall trouble neither of
you.

MRS CAUTION No, no, brother, stir not; they have a mind to be left
alone. Come, there's a beastly trick in't. He's no dancing-master, I
tell you.   440

GERRARD (*aside to Hippolyta*) Damned jade, she'll discover us.

DON DIEGO What, will you teach me? Nay then, I will go out, and
you shall go out too, look you.

MRS CAUTION I will not go out, look you.

DON DIEGO Come, come, thou art a censorious, wicked woman, and   445
you shall disturb them no longer.

MRS CAUTION What, will you bawd for your daughter?

DON DIEGO Ay, ay; come, go out, out, out.

MRS CAUTION I will not go out, I will not go out; my conscience will
not suffer me—for I know by experience what will follow.   450

GERRARD I warrant you, sir, we'll make good use of our time when
you are gone.

MRS CAUTION Do you hear him again? Don't you know what he
means?

Exit Don Diego, thrusting Mrs Caution out

HIPPOLYTA 'Tis very well; you are a fine gentleman, to abuse my   455
poor father so.

GERRARD 'Tis but by your example, miss.

HIPPOLYTA Well, I am his daughter, and may make the bolder with
him, I hope.

GERRARD And I am his son-in-law that shall be, and therefore may   460
claim my privilege too of making bold with him, I hope.

HIPPOLYTA Methinks you should be contented in making bold with
his daughter—for you have made very bold with her, sure.

GERRARD I hope I shall make bolder with her yet.

HIPPOLYTA I do not doubt your confidence, for you are a dancing-   465
master.

GERRARD Why, miss, I hope you would not have me a fine, senseless,
whining,° modest lover? For modesty in a man is as ill as the want
of it in a woman.

HIPPOLYTA I thank you for that, sir; now you have made bold with   470
me indeed. But if I am such a confident piece, I am sure you made
me so. If you had not had the confidence to come in at the window,
I had not had the confidence to look upon a man. I am sure I could
not look upon a man before.

GERRARD But that, I humbly conceive, sweet miss, was your father's   475
fault, because you had not a man to look upon. But, dearest miss,
I do not think you confident; you are only innocent. For that which
would be called confidence, nay impudence, in a woman of years,
is called innocency in one of your age; and the more impudent you
appear, the more innocent you are thought.   480

HIPPOLYTA Say you so? Has youth such privileges? I do not wonder,
then, most women seem impudent, since it is to be thought
younger than they are, it seems. But indeed, master, you are as
great an encourager of impudence, I see, as if you were a
dancing-master in good earnest.   485

GERRARD Yes, yes, a young thing may do anything, may leap out of
the window, and go away with her dancing-master, if she please.

HIPPOLYTA So, so, the use follows the doctrine° very suddenly.

GERRARD Well, dearest, pray let us make the use we should of it, lest
your father should make too bold with us, and come in before we   490
would have him.

HIPPOLYTA Indeed, old relations are apt to take that ill-bred freedom of pressing into young company at unseasonable hours.

GERRARD Come, dear miss, let me tell you how I have designed
matters—for in talking of anything else we lose time and oppor-   495
tunity. People abroad indeed say the English women are the worst
in the world in using an opportunity; they love tittle-tattle and
ceremony.

HIPPOLYTA 'Tis because (I warrant) opportunities are not so scarce
here as abroad; they have more here than they can use. But let   500
people abroad say what they will of English women, because they
do not know 'em; but what say people at home?

GERRARD Pretty innocent, ha ha ha. Well, I say you will not make
use of your opportunity.

HIPPOLYTA I say you have no reason to say so yet.   505

GERRARD Well then, anon at nine of the clock at night I'll try you;
for I have already bespoke a parson, and have taken up the three
back rooms of the tavern, which front upon the gallery window,
that nobody may see us escape, and I have appointed (precisely
betwixt eight and nine of the clock when it is dark) a coach and six   510
to wait at the tavern door for us.

HIPPOLYTA A coach and six, a coach and six, do you say? Nay then
I see you are resolved to carry me away, for a coach and six, though
there were not a man but the coachman° with it, would carry away
any young girl of my age in England. A coach and six!   515

GERRARD Then you will be sure to be ready to go with me.

HIPPOLYTA What young woman of the town could ever say no to a coach and six, unless it were going into the country. A coach and six—'tis not in the power of fourteen-year-old to resist it.

GERRARD You will be sure to be ready?   520

HIPPOLYTA You are sure 'tis a coach and six?

GERRARD I warrant you, miss.

HIPPOLYTA I warrant you then, they'll carry us merrily away. A coach and six!

GERRARD But have you charmed your cousin the *monsieur* (as you   525
said you would), that he in the mean time say nothing to prevent us?

HIPPOLYTA I warrant you.

    Enter to 'em Don Diego, and Mrs Caution pressing in

MRS CAUTION I *will* come in.

DON DIEGO Well, I hope by this time you have given her full   530
instructions, you have told her what and how to do, you have done all.

GERRARD We have just done, indeed, sir.

HIPPOLYTA Ay, sir, we have just done, sir.

MRS CAUTION And I fear just undone, sir.   535

GERRARD (*aside to Hippolyta*) D'e hear that damned witch?

DON DIEGO Come, leave your censorious prating. Thou hast been a false right woman thyself in thy youth, I warrant you.

MRS CAUTION I right! I right! I scorn your words; I'd have you to know, and 'tis well known—I right! No, 'tis your dainty minx, that   540
gill-flirt your daughter here, that is right. Do you see how her handkerchief is ruffled, and what a heat she's in?

DON DIEGO She has been dancing.

MRS CAUTION Ay, ay, Adam and Eve's dance, or the beginning of the world. D'e see how she pants?   545

DON DIEGO She has not been used to motion.

MRS CAUTION Motion, motion! Motion, d'e call it? No, indeed; I kept her from motion till now. Motion, with a vengeance!

DON DIEGO You put the poor bashful girl to the blush, you see; hold your peace.   550

MRS CAUTION 'Tis her guilt, not her modesty, marry.

DON DIEGO Come, come, mind her not, child.—Come, master, let me see her dance now the whole dance roundly together.° Come, sing to her.

GERRARD (*aside to Hippolyta*) Faith, we shall be discovered after 555
all—you know I cannot sing a note, miss.

DON DIEGO Come, come, man.

HIPPOLYTA Indeed, father, my master's in haste now; pray let it
alone till anon at night, when you say he is to come again, and then
you shall see me dance it to the violin. Pray stay till then, father. 560

DON DIEGO I will not be put off so. Come, begin.

HIPPOLYTA Pray, father.

DON DIEGO Come, sing to her; come, begin.

GERRARD Pray, sir, excuse me till anon; I am in some haste.

DON DIEGO I say begin; I will not excuse you. Come, take her by 565
the hand, and about with her.

MRS CAUTION I say he shall not take her by the hand. He shall touch
her no more. While I am here there shall be no more squeezing,
and tickling her palm. Good Mr Dancing-Master, stand off.

Thrusts Gerrard away

DON DIEGO Get you out, Mistress Impertinence.—Take her by the 570
hand, I say.

MRS CAUTION Stand off, I say. He shall not touch her; he has
touched her too much already.

DON DIEGO If patience were not a Spanish virtue, I would lay it
aside now. I say, let 'em dance. 575

MRS CAUTION I say they shall not dance.

HIPPOLYTA Pray, father, since you see my aunt's obstinacy, let us
alone till anon, when you may keep her out.

DON DIEGO Well then, friend, do not fail to come.

HIPPOLYTA [*aside*] Nay, if he fail me at last . . . 580

DON DIEGO Be sure you come, for she's to be married tomorrow—
do you know it?

GERRARD Yes, yes, sir.—Sweet scholar, your humble servant till
night, and think in the mean time of the instructions I have given
you, that you may be the readier when I come. 585

DON DIEGO Ay, girl, be sure you do.—And do you be sure to come.

MRS CAUTION You need not be so concerned; he'll be sure to come,
I warrant you. But if I could help it, he should never set foot again
in the house.

DON DIEGO You would frighten the poor dancing-master from the 590
house.—But be sure you come, for all her.

GERRARD Yes, sir. (*Aside*) But this jade will pay me when I am gone.
[*He moves to the door*]

MRS CAUTION Hold, hold, sir; I must let you out—and I wish I could keep you out. He a dancing-master! He's a chouse, a cheat, a mere cheat, and that you'll find. 595

DON DIEGO I find any man a cheat! I cheated by any man! I scorn your words. I that have so much Spanish care, circumspection, and prudence, cheated by a man! Do you think I, who have been in Spain, look you, and have kept up my daughter a twelvemonth, for fear of being cheated of her, look you—I cheated of her! 600

MRS CAUTION Well, say no more.

Exeunt Don Diego, Hippolyta, Mrs Caution and Prue

GERRARD (*aside* [*as they go out*]) Well, old Formality, if you had not kept up your daughter, I am sure I had never cheated you of her.

[*Aloud*] The wary fool is by his care betrayed,
As cuckolds by their jealousy are made. 605

Exit

4.1

[Don Diego's house. A table, with a violin upon it]

Enter Monsieur, without a peruke, with a Spanish hat, a Spanish doublet, stockings, and shoes, but in pantaloons, a waist-belt and a Spanish dagger in't, and a cravat about his neck. Enter Hippolyta and Prue behind, laughing

MONSIEUR To see wat a fool love do make of one, *jarni!* *[Surveying himself]* It do metamorphose de brave man into de beast, de sotte, de animal.

HIPPOLYTA Ha ha ha.

MONSIEUR Nay, you may laugh. 'Tis ver' vel, I am become as   5
ridicule for you as can be, *morbleu.* I have deform myself into an ugly Spaniard.

HIPPOLYTA Why, do you call this disguising yourself like a Spaniard, while you wear pantaloons still, and the cravat?

MONSIEUR But is here not the double° doublet, and the Spanish   10
dagger *aussi?*

HIPPOLYTA But 'tis as long as the French sword, and worn like it. But where's your Spanish beard, the thing of most consequence?

MONSIEUR *Jarni*, do you tink beards are as easy to be had as in de   15
playhouses? *Non.* But if here be no the ugly, long Spanish beard, here are, I am certain, the ugly, long Spanish ear.°

HIPPOLYTA That's very true, ha ha ha.

MONSIEUR Auh, de ingrate dat de woman is! When we poor men are your gallants, you laugh at us yourselves, and wen we are your   20
husband, you make all the warld laugh at us, *jarni.* Love, damn' love, it make the man more ridicule than poverty, poetry, or a new title of *honneur*,° *jarni.*

Enter Don Diego and Mrs Caution

DON DIEGO What, at your '*jarnis*' still, *voto?*

MONSIEUR Why, *oncle*, you are at your '*votos*' still.   25

DON DIEGO Nay, I'll allow you to be at your '*votos*' too, but not to make the incongruous match of Spanish doublet and French pantaloons.

MONSIEUR Nay, pray dear *oncle*, let me unite France and Spain. *(Holding his hat before his pantaloons)* 'Tis the mode of France now,°   30
jarni—voto.

DON DIEGO Well, I see I must pronounce. I told you, if you were not dressed in the Spanish habit tonight, you should not marry my daughter tomorrow, look you.

MONSIEUR Well, am I not *habillé* in de Spanish habit? My doublet, ear, and hat, leg and feet are Spanish, that dey are. 35

DON DIEGO I told you I was a Spanish *positivo, voto*.

MONSIEUR Vil you not spare my pantaloon, begar? I will give you one little finger to excuse my pantaloon, *da!*

DON DIEGO I have said, look you. 40

MONSIEUR Auh, *chères* pantaloons!—Speak for my pantaloons, cousin; my poor pantaloons are as dear to me as de scarf to de countree *capitaine*,° or de new-made officer. Therefore have de compassion for my pantaloons, Don Diego, *mon oncle*; *hélas, hélas, hélas*. 45

    Kneels to Don Diego

DON DIEGO I have said, look you, your dress must be Spanish, and your language English; I am *uno positivo*.

MONSIEUR And must speak base good English too? Ah *la pitié, hélas!*

DON DIEGO It must be done, and I will see this great change ere it be dark, *voto*. Your time is not long; look to't, look you. 50

MONSIEUR *Hélas, hélas, hélas*, dat *Espagne* should conquer *la France* in England, *hélas, hélas, hélas!*

    Exit Monsieur

DON DIEGO You see what pains I take to make him the more agreeable to you, daughter.

HIPPOLYTA But indeed and indeed, father, you wash the blackamoor white° in endeavouring to make a Spaniard of a *monsieur*—nay, an English *monsieur*° too. Consider that, father. For when once they have taken the French ply° (as they call it) they are never to be made so much as Englishmen again, I have heard say. 55

DON DIEGO What, I warrant you are like the rest of the young silly baggages of England, that like nothing but what is French. You would not have him reformed; you would have a *monsieur* to your husband, would you, *cuerno?* 60

HIPPOLYTA No indeed, father, I would not have a *monsieur* to my husband, not I indeed, and I am sure you'll never make my cousin otherwise. 65

DON DIEGO I warrant you.

HIPPOLYTA You can't, you can't indeed, father. And you have sworn, you know, he shall never have me if he does not leave off his monsieurship. Now as I told you, 'tis as hard for him to 70 cease being a *monsieur*, as 'tis for you to break a Spanish oath—so that I am not in any great danger of having a *monsieur* to my husband.

DON DIEGO Well, but you shall have him for your husband, look you. 75

HIPPOLYTA Then you will break your Spanish oath.

DON DIEGO No, I will break him of his French tricks, and you shall have him for your husband, *cuerno*.

HIPPOLYTA Indeed and indeed, father, I shall not have him.

DON DIEGO Indeed you shall, daughter. 80

HIPPOLYTA Well, you shall see, father.

MRS CAUTION No, I warrant you, she will not have him, she'll have her dancing-master rather. I know her meaning; I understand her.

DON DIEGO Thou malicious, foolish woman—you understand her! 85
But I do understand her. She says I will not break my oath, nor he his French customs, so through our difference she thinks she shall not have him—but she shall.

HIPPOLYTA But I shan't.

MRS CAUTION I know she will not have him, because she hates him. 90

DON DIEGO I tell you, if she does hate him, 'tis a sign she will have him for her husband; for 'tis not one of a thousand that marries the man she loves, look you. Besides, 'tis all one whether she loves him now or not; for as soon as she's married she'd be sure to hate him. That's the reason we wise Spaniards are jealous, and only expecte, 95
nay will be sure our wives shall fear us, look you.

HIPPOLYTA Pray, good father and aunt, do not dispute about nothing, for I am sure he will never be my husband to hate.

MRS CAUTION I am of your opinion indeed. I understand you. I can see as far as another. 100

DON DIEGO You! You cannot see so much as through your spectacles. But I understand her; 'tis her mere desire to marriage makes her say she shall not have him; for your poor young things, when they are once in the teens, think they shall never be married.

HIPPOLYTA Well, father, think you what you will, but I know what 105
I think.

Enter Monsieur in the Spanish habit entire, only with a
cravat, and followed by the little Blackamoor with a golilla
in his hand

DON DIEGO Come, did not I tell you you should have him? Look you there, he has complied with me, and is a perfect Spaniard.

MONSIEUR Ay, ay, I am ugly rogue enough now, sure, for my cousin. But 'tis your father's fault, cousin, that you ha'n't the handsomest 110 best-dressed man in the nation, a man *bien mise*.

DON DIEGO Yet again at your French? And a cravat on still, *voto a Santiago*. Off, off with it.

MONSIEUR Nay, I will ever hereafter speak clownish good English; do but spare me my cravat.` 115

DON DIEGO I am *uno positivo*, look you.

MONSIEUR Let me not put on that Spanish yoke, but spare me my cravat—for I love cravat *furieusement*.

DON DIEGO Again at your '*furieusements*'!

MONSIEUR Indeed, I have forgot myself; but have some mercy. 120 (*Kneels*)

DON DIEGO Off, off, off with it, I say. Come; refuse the *ornamento principal* of the Spanish habit?

> *Takes him by the cravat, pulls it off, and the Blackamoor
> puts on the golilla*

MONSIEUR Will you have no mercy, no pity, alas, alas, alas! Oh I had rather put on the English pillory than this Spanish *golilla* [*pulls it* 125 *off*], for 'twill be all a case, I'm sure—for when I go abroad I shall soon have a crowd of boys about me, peppering me with rotten eggs and turnips, *hélas, hélas*.

> *Don Diego puts on the golilla*

DON DIEGO '*Hélas*' again?

MONSIEUR Alas, alas, alas. 130

HIPPOLYTA } [*together*] { I shall die, ha ha ha.
PRUE } { I shall burst, ha ha ha.

MONSIEUR Ay, ay, you see what I am come to for your sake, cousin.—And uncle, pray take notice how ridiculous I am grown to my cousin, that loves me above all the world! She can no more 135 forbear laughing at me, I vow and swear, than if I were as arrant a Spaniard as yourself.

DON DIEGO Be a Spaniard like me, and ne'er think people laugh at you. There was never a Spaniard that thought anyone laughed at him. [*To Hippolyta*] But, what, do you laugh at a *golilla*, 140 baggage?—Come, sirrah black, now do you teach him to walk with the *verdadero gesto, gracia*, and *gravedad* of a true Castilian.°

MONSIEUR Must I have my dancing-master too? Come, little master then, lead on. 145

The Blackamoor struts about the stage; Monsieur follows him,
imitating awkwardly all he does

DON DIEGO *Malo, malo*, with your hat on your poll as if it hung
upon a pin. The French and English wear their hats as if their
horns° would not suffer 'em to come over their foreheads, *voto*.

MONSIEUR 'Tis true; there are some well-bred gentlemen have so
much reverence for their *perruques*, that they would refuse to be   150
grandees of your Spain,° for fear of putting on their hats, I vow
and swear.

DON DIEGO Come, black, teach him now to make a Spanish leg.
  [*The Blackamoor demonstrates a deep bow*]

MONSIEUR Ha ha ha, your Spanish leg is an English curtsy, I vow
and swear, ha ha ha.   155

DON DIEGO Well, the hood does not make the monk; the ass was an
ass still, though he had the lion's skin on.° This will be a light
French fool, in spite of the grave Spanish habit, look you.—But,
black, do what you can; make the most of him; walk him about.

Prue goes to the door, and returns

PRUE Here are the people, sir, you sent to speak with about   160
provisions for the wedding.—And here are your clothes brought
home too, mistress.

DON DIEGO Well, I come.—Black, do what you can with him; walk
him about.

MONSIEUR Indeed, uncle, if I were as you, I would not have the   165
grave Spanish habit so travestied. I shall disgrace it and my little
black master too, I vow and swear.

DON DIEGO Learn, learn of him, improve yourself by him. [*To the*
Blackamoor] And do you walk him, walk him about soundly.—
Come, sister and daughter, I must have your judgements, though   170
I shall not need 'em, look you.—Walk him, see you walk him.

Exeunt Don Diego, Hippolyta, and Mrs Caution

MONSIEUR *Jarni*, he does not only make a Spaniard of me, but a
Spanish jennet, in giving me to his lackey to walk. But come along,
little master.

The Blackamoor instructs Monsieur on one side of the stage,
Prue standing on the other

PRUE (*aside*) Oh, the unfortunate condition of us poor chamber-   175
maids, who have all the carking and caring, the watching and sitting
up, the trouble and danger of our mistresses' intrigues, whilst they
go away with all the pleasure! And if they can get their man in a

corner, 'tis well enough; they ne'er think of the poor watchful chambermaid who sits knocking her heels in the cold, for want of   180
better exercise, in some melancholy lobby or entry, when she could employ her time every whit as well as her mistress, for all her quality, if she were but put to't.

BLACKAMOOR Hold up your head, hold up your head, sir. A stooping Spaniard, *malo!*   185

MONSIEUR True, a Spaniard scorns to look upon the ground.

PRUE (*aside*) We can shift for our mistresses, and not for ourselves. Mine has got a handsome, proper young man, and is just going to make the most of him, whilst I must be left in the lurch here with a couple of ugly little blackamoor boys in bonnets,° and an old,   190
withered Spanish eunuch—not a servant else in the house; nor have I hopes of any comfortable society at all.

BLACKAMOOR Now let me see you make your visit-leg. Thus. [*Bows ceremoniously*]

MONSIEUR Auh, *tête non*, ha ha ha.   195

BLACKAMOOR What, a Spaniard, and laugh aloud! No, if you laugh—thus [*laughs silently*]; only so. Now, your salutation in the street as you pass by your acquaintance, look you—thus. If to a woman, thus, putting your hat upon your heart. If to a man, thus, with a nod, so.   200

   Monsieur imitating the Blackamoor

But frown a little more, frown. But if to a woman you would be very ceremonious to,° thus. So—your neck nearer your shoulder, so. Now, if you would speak contemptibly of any man or thing, do ·thus with your hand°—so—and shrug up your shoulders, till they hide your ears. Now walk again.   205

   The Blackamoor and Monsieur walk off the stage

PRUE All my hopes are in that coxcomb there. I must take up with my mistress's leavings, though we chambermaids are wont to be beforehand with them. But he is the dullest, modestest fool, for a frenchified fool, as ever I saw—for nobody could be more coming to him than I have been (though I say it), and yet I am ne'er the   210
nearer. I have stolen away his handkerchief, and told him of it, and yet he would never so much as struggle with me to get it° again. I have pulled off his peruke, untied his ribbons, and have been very bold with him; yet he would never be so with me. Nay, I have pinched him, punched him, and tickled him, and yet he would   215
never do the like for me.

   The Blackamoor and Monsieur return

BLACKAMOOR Nay, thus, thus, sir.

PRUE [*aside*] And to make my person more acceptable to him, I have
used art, as they say—for every night since he came I have worn
the forehead-piece of beeswax and hogs'-grease, and every morning   220
washed with buttermilk and wild tansy, and have put on every day
for his only sake my Sundays' Bow-dye stockings, and have
new-chalked my shoes, and's constantly as the morning came. Nay,
I have taken an occasion to garter my stockings before him, as if
unawares of him—for a good leg and foot, with good shoes and   225
stockings, are very provoking, as they say. But the devil a bit would
he be provoked. But I must think of a way.

BLACKAMOOR Thus, thus.

MONSIEUR What, so? Well, well, I have lessons enow for this time.
Little master, I will have no more, lest the multiplicity of 'em make   230
me forget 'em, *da*.—Prue, art thou there, and so pensive? What art
thou thinking of?

PRUE Indeed I am ashamed to tell your worship.

MONSIEUR What, ashamed! Wert thou thinking, then, of my beastliness? Ha ha ha.   235

PRUE Nay, then I am forced to tell your worship in my own
vindication.

MONSIEUR Come then.

PRUE But indeed, your worship . . . I'm ashamed, that I am, though
it was nothing but of a dream I had of your sweet worship last   240
night.

MONSIEUR Of my sweet worship! I warrant it was a sweet dream
then; what was it? Ha ha ha.

PRUE Nay, indeed, I have told your worship enough already; you
may guess the rest.   245

MONSIEUR I cannot guess, ha ha ha. What should it be? Prithee, let's
know the rest.

PRUE Would you have me so impudent?

MONSIEUR Impudent! Ha ha ha; nay prithee, tell me, for I can't
guess, *da*.   250

PRUE Nay, 'tis always so. For want of the men's guessing, the poor
women are forced to be impudent. But I am still ashamed.

MONSIEUR I will know it; speak.

PRUE Why then, methoughts last night you came up into my
chamber in your shirt, when I was in bed—and that you might   255
easily do, for I have ne'er a lock to my door. Now, I warrant, I am
as red as my petticoat.

MONSIEUR No, thou'rt as yellow as e'er thou wert.

PRUE Yellow, sir!

MONSIEUR Ay, ay; but let's hear the dream out.   260

PRUE Why, can't you guess the rest, now?

MONSIEUR No, not I, I vow and swear. Come, let's hear.

PRUE But can't you guess, in earnest?

MONSIEUR Not I, the devil eat me.

PRUE Not guess yet? Why then, methoughts you came to bed to me!   265
Now am I as red as my petticoat again.

MONSIEUR Ha ha ha! Well, and what then? Ha ha ha.

PRUE Nay, now I know by your worship's laughing, you guess what
you did. I'm sure I cried out, and waked all in tears, with these
words in my mouth: 'You have undone me, you have undone me!   270
Your worship has undone me!'

MONSIEUR Ha ha ha! But you waked and found it was but a
dream.

PRUE Indeed, it was so lively, I know not whether 'twas a dream or
no. But if you were not there, I'll undertake you may come when   275
you will, and do anything to me you will—I sleep so fast.

MONSIEUR No, no, I don't believe that.

PRUE Indeed you may, your worship—

MONSIEUR It cannot be.

PRUE (aside) Insensible beast! He will not understand me yet, and one   280
would think I speak plain enough.

MONSIEUR Well—but, Prue, what art thou thinking of?

PRUE Of the dream, whether it were a dream or no.

MONSIEUR 'Twas a dream, I warrant thee.

PRUE Was it? I am hugeous glad it was a dream.   285

MONSIEUR Ay, ay, it was a dream. [Aside] And I am hugeous glad it
was a dream too.

PRUE But now I have told your worship my door hath neither lock
nor latch to it—if you should be so naughty as to come one night,
and prove the dream true . . . I am so afraid on't.   290

MONSIEUR Ne'er fear it; dreams go by the contraries.°

PRUE Then by that I should come into your worship's chamber, and
come to bed to your worship. Now am I as red as my petticoat
again, I warrant.

MONSIEUR No, thou art no redder than a brick unburnt,° Prue.   295

PRUE But if I should do such a trick in my sleep, your worship would
not censure a poor harmless maid, I hope—for I am apt to walk in
my sleep.

MONSIEUR Well then, Prue, because thou shalt not shame thyself (poor wench), I'll be sure to lock my door every night fast.   300

PRUE [aside] So, so, this way I find will not do. I must come roundly and downright to the business, like other women, or—

    Enter Gerrard

MONSIEUR Oh, the dancing-master!

PRUE [to Monsieur] Dear sir, I have something to say to you in your ear, which I am ashamed to speak aloud.   305

MONSIEUR Another time, another time, Prue; but now go call your mistress to her dancing-master. Go, go.

PRUE Nay, pray hear me, sir, first.

MONSIEUR Another time, another time, Prue; prithee begone.

PRUE Nay, I beseech your worship hear me.   310

MONSIEUR No, prithee begone.

PRUE [aside] Nay, I am e'en well enough served for not speaking my mind when I had an opportunity. Well, I must be playing the modest woman, forsooth! A woman's hypocrisy in this case does only deceive herself.   315

    Exit Prue

MONSIEUR Oh, the brave dancing-master, the fine dancing-master! Your servant, your servant.

GERRARD Your servant, sir; I protest I did not know you at first. (*Aside*) I am afraid this fool should spoil all, notwithstanding Hippolyta's care and management. Yet I ought to trust her—but a   320
secret is more safe with a treacherous knave than a talkative fool.

MONSIEUR Come, sir, you must know a little brother dancing-master of yours—walking-master, I should have said, for he teaches me to walk and make legs by the by. [*Indicating the Blackamoor*] Pray know him, sir; salute him, sir—you Christian dancing-masters are   325
so proud.

GERRARD But, Monsieur, what strange metamorphosis is this? You look like a Spaniard, and talk like an Englishman again, which I thought had been impossible.

MONSIEUR Nothing impossible to love.° I must do't, or lose my   330
mistress, your pretty scholar, for 'tis I am to have her. You may remember I told you she was to be married to a great man, a man of honour and quality.

GERRARD But does she enjoin you to this severe penance? Such I am sure it is to you.   335

MONSIEUR (*draws him aside*) No, no, 'tis by the compulsion of the starched fop her father, who is so arrant a Spaniard he would kill you, and his daughter, if he knew who you were—therefore have a special care to dissemble well.

GERRARD I warrant you.   340

MONSIEUR Dear Gerrard—[*To the Blackamoor*] Go, little master, and call my cousin; tell her, her dancing-master is here.

    Exit the Blackamoor

I say, dear Gerrard, faith I'm obliged to you for the trouble you have had. When I sent you, I intended a jest indeed, but did not think it would have been so dangerous a jest—therefore pray   345
forgive me.

GERRARD I do, do heartily forgive you.

MONSIEUR But can you forgive me for sending you at first, like a fool as I was? 'Twas ill done of me. Can you forgive me?

GERRARD Yes, yes, I do forgive you.   350

MONSIEUR Well, thou art a generous man, I vow and swear, to come and take upon you this trouble, danger, and shame, to be thought a paltry dancing-master, and all this to preserve a lady's honour and life, who intended to abuse you. But I take the obligation upon me.°

GERRARD Pish, pish, you are not obliged to me at all.   355

MONSIEUR Faith, but I am strangely obliged to you.

GERRARD Faith, but you are not.

MONSIEUR I vow and swear but I am.

GERRARD I swear you are not.

MONSIEUR Nay, thou art so generous a dancing-master, ha ha ha.   360

    Enter Don Diego, Hippolyta, Mrs Caution, and Prue

DON DIEGO You shall not come in, sister.

MRS CAUTION I will come in.

DON DIEGO You will not be civil.

MRS CAUTION I'm sure they will not be civil if I do not come in. I must, I will.   365

DON DIEGO Well, honest friend, you are very punctual, which is a rare virtue in a dancing-master. I take notice of it, and will remember it; I will, look you.

MONSIEUR (*aside*) So, silly, damned, politic, Spanish uncle, ha ha ha.

GERRARD My fine scholar, sir, there, shall never have reason (as I   370
told you, sir) to say I am not a punctual man, for I am more her servant than to any scholar I ever had.

MONSIEUR (*aside*) Well said, i'faith; thou dost make a pretty fool of him, I vow and swear. But I wonder people can be made such fools of, ha ha ha.   375

HIPPOLYTA Well, master, I thank you, and I hope I shall be a grateful kind scholar to you.

MONSIEUR (*aside*) Ha ha ha! Cunning little jilt, what a fool she makes of him too. I wonder people can be made such fools of, I vow and swear, ha ha ha.   380

HIPPOLYTA Indeed it shall go hard but I'll° be a grateful kind scholar to you.

MRS CAUTION As kind as ever your mother was to your father, I warrant.

DON DIEGO How! Again with your senseless suspicions!   385

MONSIEUR Pish, pish, aunt! (*Aside*) Ha ha ha, she's a fool another way. She thinks she loves him, ha ha ha. Lord, that people should be such fools!

MRS CAUTION Come, come, I cannot but speak. I tell you, beware in time—for he is no dancing-master, but some debauched person   390 who will mump you of your daughter.

DON DIEGO Will you be wiser than I, still? Mump me of my daughter! I would I could see anyone mump me of my daughter.

MRS CAUTION [*to Monsieur*] And mump you of your mistress too, young Spaniard.   395

MONSIEUR (*to Mrs Caution*) Ha ha ha, will you be wiser than I too, *voto*? Mump me of my mistress! I would I could see anyone mump me of my mistress. (*Aside to Gerrard and Hippolyta*) I am afraid this damned old aunt should discover us, I vow and swear. Be careful therefore, and resolute.   400

MRS CAUTION He, he does not go about his business like a dancing-master. He'll ne'er teach her to dance, but he'll teach her no goodness soon enough, I warrant. He a dancing-master!

MONSIEUR Ay, the devil eat me if he be not the best dancing-master in England now. (*Aside to Gerrard and Hippolyta*) Was not that well   405 said, cousin? Was it not? For he's a gentleman dancing-master, you know.

DON DIEGO You know him, cousin, very well, cousin? You sent him to my daughter?

MONSIEUR Yes, yes, uncle, [I] know him.° (*Aside* [*to Gerrard and*   410 *Hippolyta*]) We'll ne'er be discovered, I warrant, ha ha ha.

MRS CAUTION But will you be made a fool of, too?

MONSIEUR Ay, ay, aunt, ne'er trouble yourself.

DON DIEGO Come, friend, about your business; about with my daughter.   415

HIPPOLYTA Nay, pray father, be pleased to go out a little, and let us but practise a while, and then you shall see me dance the whole dance to the violin.

DON DIEGO Tittle-tattle, more fooling still! Did not you say, when your master was here last, I should see you dance to the violin when   420 he came again?

HIPPOLYTA So I did, father; but let me practise a little first before, that I may be perfect. Besides, my aunt is here, and she will put me out; you know I cannot dance before her.

DON DIEGO Fiddle-faddle.   425

MONSIEUR (*aside*) They're afraid to be discovered by Gerrard's bungling, I see.—Come, come, uncle, turn out; let 'em practise.

DON DIEGO I won't, *voto a Santiago*. What a fooling's here!

MONSIEUR Come, come, let 'em practise. Turn out, turn out, uncle.   430

DON DIEGO Why, can't she practise it before me?

MONSIEUR Come, dancers and singers are sometimes humoursome. Besides, 'twill be more grateful to you, to see it danced all at once to the violin. Come, turn out, turn out, I say.

DON DIEGO What a fooling's here still amongst you, *voto*!   435

MONSIEUR So, there he is with you,° *voto*. Turn out, turn out; I vow and swear you shall turn out.

    Takes him by the shoulder

DON DIEGO Well, shall I see her dance it to the violin at last?

GERRARD Yes, yes, sir; what do you think I teach her for?

MONSIEUR Go, go, turn out.   440

    Exit Don Diego

And you too, aunt.

MRS CAUTION Seriously, nephew, I shall not budge; royally, I shall not.

MONSIEUR Royally, you must, aunt; come.

MRS CAUTION Pray hear me, nephew.   445

MONSIEUR I will not hear you.

MRS CAUTION 'Tis for your sake I stay; I must not suffer you to be wronged.

MONSIEUR Come, no wheedling, aunt; come away.

MRS CAUTION That slippery fellow will do't.   450

MONSIEUR Let him do't.

MRS CAUTION Indeed he will do't, royally he will.

MONSIEUR Well, let him do't, royally.

MRS CAUTION He will wrong you.

MONSIEUR Well, let him, I say. I have a mind to be wronged.   455
What's that to you? I *will* be wronged, if you go thereto, I vow and
swear.

MRS CAUTION You shall not be wronged.

MONSIEUR I will.

MRS CAUTION You shall not.   460

  Don Diego returns

DON DIEGO What's the matter? Won't she be ruled? Come, come
away, you shall not disturb 'em.

MRS CAUTION ([*as*] *Don Diego and Monsieur thrust* [*her*] *out*) D'e see
how they laugh at you both? Well, go to, the troth-telling Trojan
gentlewoman of old° was ne'er believed till the town was taken,   465
rummaged, and ransacked. Even, even so—

MONSIEUR Ha ha ha! Turn out.

  [*Exeunt*] *Mrs Caution* [*and Don Diego*]

Lord, that people should be such arrant cuddens, ha ha ha. But I
may stay, may I not?

HIPPOLYTA No, no, I'd have you go out and hold the door, cousin,   470
or else my father will come in again before his time.

MONSIEUR I will, I will then, sweet cousin—'twas well thought on.
That was well thought on indeed, for me to hold the door.

HIPPOLYTA But be sure you keep him out, cousin, till we knock.

MONSIEUR I warrant you, cousin. Lord, that people should be made   475
such fools of, ha ha ha.

  Exit Monsieur

GERRARD So, so, to make him hold the door, while I steal his
mistress, is not unpleasant.

HIPPOLYTA Ay, but would you do so ill a thing, so treacherous a
thing? Faith, 'tis not well.   480

GERRARD Faith, I can't help it, since 'tis for your sake. Come,
sweetest, is not this our way into the gallery?

HIPPOLYTA Yes, but it goes against my conscience to be accessory
to so ill a thing. You say you do it for my sake?

GERRARD Alas, poor miss! 'Tis not against your conscience, but   485
against your modesty, you think, to do it frankly.

HIPPOLYTA Nay, if it be against my modesty too, I can't do it
indeed.

GERRARD Come, come, miss, let us make haste; all's ready.

HIPPOLYTA Nay, faith, I can't satisfy my scruple.   490

GERRARD Come, dearest, this is not a time for scruples nor modesty;
modesty between lovers is as impertinent as ceremony between

friends, and modesty is now as unseasonable as on the wedding
night. Come away, my dearest.

HIPPOLYTA Whither?   495

GERRARD Nay, sure, we have lost too much time already. Is that a
proper question now? If you would know, come along, for I have
all ready.

HIPPOLYTA But I am not ready.

GERRARD Truly, miss, we shall have your father come in upon us,   500
and prevent us again, as he did in the morning.

HIPPOLYTA 'Twas well for me he did—for on my conscience, if he
had not come in, I had gone clear away with you when I was in the
humour.

GERRARD Come, dearest, you would frighten me as if you were not   505
yet° in the same humour. Come, come away, the coach and six is
ready.

HIPPOLYTA 'Tis too late to take the air, and I am not ready.

GERRARD You were ready in the morning.

HIPPOLYTA Ay, so I was.   510

GERRARD Come, come, miss; indeed the jest begins to be none.

HIPPOLYTA What, I warrant you think me in jest then?

GERRARD In jest, certainly—but it begins to be troublesome.

HIPPOLYTA But, sir, you could believe I was in earnest in the
morning, when I but seemed to be ready to go with you; and why   515
won't you believe me now, when I declare to the contrary? I take
it unkindly, that the longer I am acquainted with you, you should
have the less confidence in me.

GERRARD For heaven's sake, miss, lose no more time thus; your
father will come in upon us, as he did—   520

HIPPOLYTA Let him, if he will.

GERRARD He'll hinder our design.

HIPPOLYTA No, he will not, for mine is to stay here now.

GERRARD Are you in earnest?

HIPPOLYTA You'll find it so.   525

GERRARD How! Why, you confessed but now you would have gone
with me in the morning.

HIPPOLYTA I was in the humour then.

GERRARD And I hope you are in the same still; you cannot change
so soon.   530

HIPPOLYTA Why, is it not a whole day ago?

GERRARD What, are you not a day in the same humour?

HIPPOLYTA Lord! That you, who know the town (they say), should think any woman could be a whole day together in an humour! Ha ha ha.   535

GERRARD Hey! This begins to be pleasant. What, won't you go with me then, after all?

HIPPOLYTA No indeed, sir; I desire to be excused.

GERRARD Then you have abused me all this while?

HIPPOLYTA It may be so.   540

GERRARD Could all that so natural innocency be dissembled? Faith, it could not, dearest miss.

HIPPOLYTA Faith, it was, dear master.

GERRARD Was it, faith?

HIPPOLYTA Methinks you might believe me without an oath. You   545
saw I could dissemble with my father; why should you think I could not with you?

GERRARD So young a wheedle?

HIPPOLYTA Ay, a mere damned jade I am.

GERRARD And I have been abused, you say?   550

HIPPOLYTA 'Tis well you can believe it at last.

GERRARD And I must never hope for you?

HIPPOLYTA Would you have me abuse you again?

GERRARD Then you will not go with me?

HIPPOLYTA No—but for your comfort, your loss will not be great;   555
and that you may not resent it, for once I'll be ingenuous and disabuse you: I am no heiress, as I told you, to twelve hundred pound a year. I was only a lying jade then; now you will part with me willingly, I doubt not.

GERRARD (sighs) I wish I could.   560

HIPPOLYTA Come, now I find 'tis your turn to dissemble. But men use to dissemble for money—will you dissemble for nothing?

GERRARD 'Tis too late for me to dissemble.

HIPPOLYTA Don't you dissemble, faith?

GERRARD Nay, this is too cruel.   565

HIPPOLYTA What, would you take me without the twelve hundred pound a year? Would you be such a fool as to steal a woman with nothing?

GERRARD I'll convince you, for you *shall* go with me—and since you are twelve hundred pound a year the lighter, you'll be the easier   570
carried away.

He takes her in his arms; she struggles

PRUE What, he takes her away against her will; I find I must knock
for my master then.
>   *She knocks. Enter Don Diego and Mrs Caution*

HIPPOLYTA My father, my father is here.

GERRARD Prevented again!   575
>   *Gerrard sets her down again*

DON DIEGO What, you have done (I hope) now, friend, for good and
all?

GERRARD Yes, yes, we have done for good and all indeed.

DON DIEGO How now! You seem to be out of humour, friend.

GERRARD Yes, so I am; I can't help it.   580

MRS CAUTION He's a dissembler in his very throat, brother.

HIPPOLYTA (*aside to Gerrard*) Pray do not carry things so as to
discover yourself, if it be but for my sake, good master.

GERRARD (*aside*) She is grown impudent.

MRS CAUTION See, see, they whisper, brother. To steal a kiss under   585
a whisper—oh, the harlotry!

DON DIEGO What's the matter, friend?

HIPPOLYTA (*to Gerrard*) I say for my sake be in humour, and do not
discover yourself, but be as patient as a dancing-master still.

DON DIEGO What, she is whispering to him indeed! What's the   590
matter? I will know it, friend, look you.

GERRARD Will you know it?

DON DIEGO Yes, I will know it.

GERRARD Why, if you will know it, then she would not do as I
would have her, and whispered me to desire me not to discover it   595
to you.

DON DIEGO What, hussy, would you not do as he'd have you? I'll
make you do as he'd have you.

GERRARD I wish you would.

MRS CAUTION 'Tis a lie; she'll do all he'll have her do, and more   600
too, to my knowledge.

DON DIEGO Come, tell me what 'twas then she would not do.—
Come, do it, hussy, or . . .—Come, take her by the hand, friend;
come, begin. Let's see if she will not do anything now I am here.

HIPPOLYTA Come, pray be in humour, master.   605

GERRARD I cannot dissemble like you.

DON DIEGO What, she can't dissemble already, can she?

MRS CAUTION Yes but she can—but 'tis with you she dissembles.
For they are not fallen out, as we think, for I'll be sworn I saw her
just now give him the languishing eye, as they call it, that is, the   610

whiting's eye, of old called the sheep's eye. I'll be sworn I saw it
with these two eyes, that I did.

HIPPOLYTA (*aside to Gerrard*) You'll betray us; have a care, good
master.

[DON DIEGO (*to Mrs Caution*)] Hold your peace, I say, silly woman.°   615
[*To Gerrard*] But does she dissemble already? How do you mean?

GERRARD She pretends she can't do what she should do, and that she
is not in humour, the common excuse of women for not doing what
they should do.

DON DIEGO Come, I'll put her in humour. Dance, I say. Come,   620
about with her, master.

GERRARD (*aside*) I am in a pretty humour to dance! ([*Apart*] *to
Hippolyta*) I cannot fool any longer, since you have fooled me.

HIPPOLYTA [*apart to Gerrard*] You would not be so ungenerous as
to betray the woman that hated you; I do not do that yet. For   625
heaven's sake, for this once be more obedient to my desires than
your passion.

DON DIEGO What, is she humoursome still? But methinks you look
yourself as if you were in an ill humour. But about with her.

GERRARD I am in no good dancing humour, indeed.   630

    Enter Monsieur

MONSIEUR Well, how goes the dancing forward? [*Aside*] What, my
aunt here, to disturb 'em again!

DON DIEGO Come, come.

    Gerrard leads her about

MRS CAUTION I say stand off. Thou shalt not come near. Avoid,
Satan,° as they say.   635

DON DIEGO Nay then, we shall have it. Nephew, hold her a little,
that she may not disturb 'em. [*To Gerrard*] Come, now away with
her.

GERRARD One, two, and a coupee. (*Aside*) Fooled and abused!

    Monsieur holding Mrs Caution

MRS CAUTION Wilt thou lay violent hands upon thy own natural   640
aunt, wretch?

DON DIEGO Come, about with her.

GERRARD One, two, three, four, and turn round. (*Aside*) By such a
piece of innocency!

MRS CAUTION Dost thou see, fool, how he squeezes her hand?   645

MONSIEUR That won't do, aunt.

HIPPOLYTA Pray, master, have patience, and let's mind our business.

DON DIEGO Why, did you anger him then, hussy, look you?

MRS CAUTION Do you see how she smiles in his face, and squeezes   650
his hand now?

MONSIEUR Your servant, aunt; that won't do, I say.

HIPPOLYTA Have patience, master.

GERRARD (*aside*) I am become her sport. [*Aloud*] One, two, three.
Death, hell, and the devil!

DON DIEGO Ay, they are three indeed; but pray have patience.   655

MRS CAUTION Do you see how she leers upon him and clings to
him? Can you suffer it?

MONSIEUR Ay, ay.

GERRARD One, two, and a slur. Can you be so unconcerned after all?

DON DIEGO What, is she unconcerned? Hussy, mind your business.   660

GERRARD One, two, three, and turn round. One, two, fall back—hell
and damnation.

DON DIEGO Ay, people fall back indeed into hell and damnation,
heaven knows.

GERRARD One, two, three, and your honour. I can fool no longer.   665

MRS CAUTION Nor will I be withheld any longer, like a poor hen in
her pen, while the kite is carrying away her chicken before her face.

DON DIEGO [*to Gerrard*] What, have you done? Well then, let's see
her dance it now to the violin.

MONSIEUR Ay, ay, let's see her dance it to the violin.   670

GERRARD Another time, another time.

DON DIEGO Don't you believe that, friend. These dancing-masters
make no bones° of breaking their words. Did not you promise, just
now, I should see her dance it to the violin, and that I will too,
before I stir.   675

GERRARD Let Monsieur play then, while I dance with her; she can't
dance alone.

MONSIEUR I can't play at all, I'm but a learner. But if you'll play,
I'll dance with her.

GERRARD I can't play neither.   680

DON DIEGO What, a dancing-master, and not play!

MRS CAUTION Ay, you see what a dancing-master he is. 'Tis as I
told you, I warrant. A dancing-master, and not play upon the
fiddle!

DON DIEGO How!   685

HIPPOLYTA (*apart to Gerrard*) Oh, you have betrayed us all! If you
confess that, you undo us for ever.

GERRARD [*apart to Hippolyta*] I cannot play. What would you have
me say?

MONSIEUR [*apart to Gerrard*] I vow and swear, we are all undone if 690
you cannot play.

DON DIEGO What, are you a dancing-master, and cannot play? Umph!

HIPPOLYTA He is only out of humour, sir.

> *She offers Gerrard the violin*

Here, master, I know you will play for me yet—for he has an
excellent hand. 695

MONSIEUR Ay, that he has—(*aside*) at giving a box on the ear.

DON DIEGO Why does he not play, then?

> [*Hippolyta*] *gives Gerrard the violin*

HIPPOLYTA Here, master; pray play for my sake.

GERRARD [*apart to Hippolyta*] What would you have me do with it?
I cannot play a stroke. 700

HIPPOLYTA (*apart to Gerrard*) No? Stay then—seem to tune it, and
break the strings.

GERRARD Come then. (*Aside*) Next to the devil's the invention of
women. They'll no more want an excuse to cheat a father with,
than an opportunity to abuse a husband. 705

> *Winds up the strings till they break, and throws the violin on
> the ground*

[*Aloud*] But what do you give me such a damned fiddle with rotten
strings for?

DON DIEGO Hey-day, the dancing-master is frantic.

MONSIEUR [*aside*] Ha ha ha, that people should be made such fools
of. 710

MRS CAUTION He broke the strings on purpose, because he could
not play. You are blind, brother.

DON DIEGO What, will you see farther than I, look you?

HIPPOLYTA But pray, master, why in such haste?

GERRARD Because you have done with me. 715

DON DIEGO But don't you intend to come tomorrow again?

GERRARD Your daughter does not desire it.

DON DIEGO No matter; I do. I must be your paymaster, I'm sure. I
would have you come betimes too, not only to make her perfect,
but (since you have so good a hand upon the violin) to play your 720
part with half a dozen of musicians more, whom I would have you
bring with you. For we will have a very merry wedding, though a
very private one. You'll be sure to come?

GERRARD Your daughter does not desire it.

DON DIEGO Come, come, baggage, you shall desire it of him; he is 725
your master.

HIPPOLYTA My father will have me desire it of you, it seems.

GERRARD But you'll make a fool of me again, if I should come, would
    you not?

HIPPOLYTA If I should tell you so, you'd be sure not to come.   730

DON DIEGO Come, come, she shall not make a fool of you, upon my
    word. I'll secure you; she shall do what you'll have her.

MONSIEUR (*aside*) Ha ha ha! So, so, silly don.

GERRARD But, madam, will you have me come?

HIPPOLYTA I'd have you to know, for my part, I care not whether   735
    you come or no. There are other dancing-masters to be had. It is
    my father's request to you. All that I have to say to you is a little
    good advice, which (because I will not shame you) I'll give you in
    private. (*Whispers Gerrard*)

MRS CAUTION What, will you let her whisper with him too?   740

DON DIEGO Nay, if you find fault with it, they *shall* whisper.
    Though I did not like it before, I'll ha' nobody wiser than myself.
    But do you think, if 'twere any hurt, she would whisper it to him
    before us?

MRS CAUTION If it be no hurt, why does she not speak aloud?   745

DON DIEGO Because she says she will not put the man out of
    countenance.

MRS CAUTION Hey-day, put a dancing-master out of countenance!

DON DIEGO You say he is no dancing-master.

MRS CAUTION Yes, for his impudence he may be a dancing-master.   750

DON DIEGO Well, well, let her whisper before me as much as she
    will tonight, since she is to be married tomorrow—especially since
    her husband that shall be stands by consenting too.

MONSIEUR Ay, ay, let 'em whisper (as you say) as much as they will
    before we marry. (*Aside*) She's making more sport with him, I   755
    warrant—but I wonder how people can be fooled so, ha ha ha.

DON DIEGO Well, a penny for the secret, daughter.

HIPPOLYTA Indeed, father, you shall have it for nothing tomorrow.

DON DIEGO Well, friend, you will not fail to come?

GERRARD No, no, sir. (*Aside*) Yet I am a fool, if I do.   760

DON DIEGO And be sure you bring the fiddlers with you, as I bid
    you.

HIPPOLYTA Yes, be sure you bring the fiddlers with you, as I bid
    you.

MRS CAUTION So, so, he'll fiddle your daughter out of the house.   765
    Must you have fiddles, with a fiddle-faddle?

MONSIEUR [*aside*] Lord, that people should be made such fools of, ha ha.

> *Exeunt Don Diego, Hippolyta, Monsieur, Mrs Caution, and Prue*

GERRARD Fortune we sooner may than woman trust—
> To her confiding gallant she is just;   770
> But falser woman only him deceives
> Who to her tongue and eyes most credit gives.
> *Exit*

5.1

[Don Diego's house]

Enter Monsieur and the Blackamoor, stalking over the stage;
to them Gerrard

MONSIEUR Good morrow to thee, noble dancing-master, ha ha ha.
Your little black brother here, my master, I see is the more diligent
man of the two. But why do you come so late? What, you begin to
neglect your scholar, do you?—Little black master, *con licentia*,
pray get you out of the room.   5

Exit the Blackamoor

What, out of humour, man? A dancing-master should be like his
fiddle, always in tune. Come, my cousin has made an ass of
thee—what then? I know it.

GERRARD *(aside)* Does he know it?

MONSIEUR But prithee don't be angry; 'twas agreed upon betwixt us 10
(before I sent you) to make a fool of thee, ha ha ha.

GERRARD Was it so?

MONSIEUR I knew you would be apt to entertain vain hopes from the
summons of a lady. But, faith, the design was but to make a fool
of thee, as you find.   15

GERRARD 'Tis very well.

MONSIEUR But indeed I did not think the jest would have lasted so
long, and that my cousin would have made a dancing-master of
you, ha ha ha.

GERRARD *(aside)* The fool has reason, I find, and I am the coxcomb 20
while I thought him so.

MONSIEUR Come, I see you are uneasy, and the jest of being a
dancing-master grows tedious to you. But have a little patience; the
parson is sent for, and when once my cousin and I are married, my
uncle may know who you are.   25

GERRARD *([to himself,] Monsieur listens)* I am certainly abused.

MONSIEUR What do you say?

GERRARD *(aside)* Merely fooled.

MONSIEUR Why, do you doubt it? Ha ha ha.

GERRARD *(aside)* Can it be?   30

MONSIEUR Pish, pish, she told me yesterday, as soon as you were
gone, that she had led you into a fool's paradise, and made you
believe she would go away with you, ha ha ha.

GERRARD Did she so? (*Aside*) I am no longer to doubt it then!

MONSIEUR Ay, ay, she makes a mere fool of thee, I vow and swear.   35
But don't be concerned; there's hardly a man of a thousand but has
been made a fool of by some woman or other. I have been made a
fool of myself, man, by the women—I have, I vow and swear, I
have.

GERRARD Well, you have, I believe it, for you are a coxcomb.   40

MONSIEUR Lord, you need not be so touchy with one! I tell you but
the truth for your good; for though she does, I would not fool you
any longer. But prithee don't be troubled at what can't be helped.°
Women are made on purpose to fool men. When they are children
they fool their fathers, and when they have taken their leaves of   45
their hanging-sleeves they fool their gallants—or dancing-masters,
ha ha ha.

GERRARD Hark you, sir, to be fooled by a woman (you say) is not to
be helped. But I will not be fooled by a fool.

MONSIEUR You show your English breeding now. An English rival   50
is so dull and brutish as not to understand raillery. But what is
spoken in your passion I'll take no notice of, for I am your friend,
and would not have you my rival to make yourself ridiculous.
Come, prithee, prithee, don't be so concerned—for as I was saying,
women first fool their fathers, then their gallants, and then their   55
husbands, so that it will be my turn to be fooled too (for your
comfort). And when they come to be widows they would fool the
devil, I vow and swear. Come, come, dear Gerrard, prithee don't
be out of humour and look so sillily.

GERRARD Prithee do not talk so sillily.   60

MONSIEUR Nay, faith, I am resolved to beat you out of this ill
humour.

GERRARD Faith, I am afraid I shall first beat you into an ill humour.

MONSIEUR Ha ha ha! That thou shouldst be gulled so by a little
gipsy who left off her bib but yesterday! Faith, I can't but laugh at   65
thee.

GERRARD Faith, then I shall make your mirth (as being too violent)
conclude in some little misfortune to you. The fool begins to be
tyrannical.

MONSIEUR Ha ha ha, poor angry dancing-master. Prithee match my   70
Spanish pumps and legs with one of your best and newest
sarabands. Ha ha ha! Come—

GERRARD I will match your Spanish ear thus, sir, and make you
dance° thus.

Strikes and kicks him

MONSIEUR How! Sa sa sa. (*Draws his sword*) Then I'll make you   75
dance thus.

[*Monsieur*] *runs at him, but Gerrard drawing, he retires*

Hold, hold a little. (*Aside*) A desperate, disappointed lover will cut
his own throat; then sure he will make nothing of cutting his rival's
throat.

GERRARD Consideration is an enemy to fighting. If you have a mind   80
to revenge yourself, your sword's in your hand.

MONSIEUR Pray, sir, hold your peace. I'll ne'er take my rival's
counsel, be't what 'twill. I know what you would be at. You are
disappointed of your mistress, and could hang yourself, and
therefore will not fear hanging.° But I am a successful lover, and   85
need neither hang for you nor my mistress. Nay, if I should kill
you, I know I should do you a kindness—therefore e'en live to die
daily with envy of my happiness. But if you will needs die, kill
yourself and be damned for me, I vow and swear.

GERRARD But won't you fight for your mistress?   90

MONSIEUR I tell you, you shall not have the honour to be killed for
her. Besides, I will not be hit in the teeth by her, as long as I live,
with° the great love you had for her. Women speak well of their
dead husbands; what will they do of their dead gallants?

GERRARD But if you will not fight for her, you shall dance for her,   95
since you desired me to teach you to dance too. I'll teach you to
dance thus—

Strikes his sword at his legs; Monsieur leaps

MONSIEUR Nay, if it be for the sake of my mistress, there's nothing
I will refuse to do.

GERRARD Nay, you must dance on.   100

MONSIEUR Ay, ay, for my mistress, and sing too—la la la ra la.

Enter Hippolyta and Prue

HIPPOLYTA What, swords drawn betwixt you two?° What's the
matter?

MONSIEUR (*aside*) Is she here? [*To Gerrard*] Come, put up your
sword. You see this is no place for us. But the devil eat me if you   105
shall not eat my sword, but—

HIPPOLYTA What's the matter, cousin?

MONSIEUR Nothing, nothing, cousin; but your presence is a sanctuary for my greatest enemy, or else—*tête non*.

HIPPOLYTA (*to Gerrard*) What, you have not hurt my cousin, sir, I   110
hope?

GERRARD (*aside*) How she's concerned for him! Nay, then I need not doubt; my fears are true.

MONSIEUR What was that you said, cousin? Hurt me, ha ha ha! Hurt me! If any man hurt me, he must do it basely. He shall ne'er do it 115 when my sword's drawn, sa sa sa.

HIPPOLYTA Because you will ne'er draw your sword, perhaps.

MONSIEUR (*aside*) Scurvily guessed.—You ladies may say anything. But, cousin, pray do not you talk of swords and fighting; meddle with your guitar, and talk of dancing with your dancing-master 120 there, ha ha ha.

HIPPOLYTA But I am afraid you have hurt my master, cousin. He says nothing. Can he draw his breath?

MONSIEUR No, 'tis you have hurt your master, cousin, in the very heart, cousin, and therefore he would hurt me. For love is a disease 125 makes people as malicious as the plague does.°

HIPPOLYTA Indeed, poor master, something does ail you.

MONSIEUR Nay, nay, cousin, faith, don't abuse him any longer. He's an honest gentleman, and has been long of my acquaintance, and a man of tolerable sense (to take him out of his love).° But prithee, 130 cousin, don't drive the jest too far for my sake.

GERRARD He counsels you well, pleasant, cunning, jilting miss, for his sake. For if I am your divertisement, it shall be at his cost, since he's your gallant in favour.

HIPPOLYTA I don't understand you. 135

MONSIEUR (*aside*) But I do, a pox take him, and the custom that so orders it, forsooth: that if a lady abuse or affront a man, presently the gallant must be beaten. Nay, what's more unreasonable—if a woman abuse her husband, the poor cuckold must bear the shame as well as the injury. 140

HIPPOLYTA But what's the matter, master? What was it you said?

GERRARD I say, pleasant, cunning, jilting lady, though you make him a cuckold, it will not be revenge enough for me upon him for marrying you.

HIPPOLYTA How, my surly, huffing, jealous, senseless, saucy master! 145

MONSIEUR Nay, nay, faith, give losers leave to speak,° losers of mistresses especially, ha ha ha. Besides, your anger is too great a favour for him; I scorn to honour him with mine, you see.

HIPPOLYTA I tell you, my saucy master, my cousin shall never be made that monstrous thing you mention, by me. 150

MONSIEUR Thank you, I vow and swear, cousin. No, no, I never thought I should.

GERRARD Sure you marry him by the sage maxim of your sex, which is: 'Wittols° make the best husbands'—that is, cuckolds.

HIPPOLYTA Indeed, master, whatsoever you think, I would sooner   155
choose you for that purpose than him.

MONSIEUR Ha ha ha, there she was with him, i'faith. I thank you for that, cousin, I vow and swear.

HIPPOLYTA Nay, he shall thank me for that too. But how came you two to quarrel? I thought, cousin, you had had more wit   160
than to quarrel, or more kindness for me than to quarrel here. What if my father, hearing the bustle, should have come in? He would soon have discovered our false dancing-master (for passion unmasks every man) and then the result of your quarrel had been my ruin.   165

MONSIEUR Nay, you had both felt his desperate, deadly, daunting dagger—there are your d's for you.

HIPPOLYTA Go, go presently therefore, and hinder my father from coming in, whilst I put my master into a better humour, that we may not be discovered, to the prevention of our wedding, or worse,   170
when he comes. Go, go.

MONSIEUR Well, well, I will, cousin.

HIPPOLYTA Be sure you let him not come in this good while.

MONSIEUR No, no, I warrant you.
      Monsieur goes out and returns
But if he should come before I would have him, I'll come before   175
him, and cough and hawk soundly, that you may not be surprised. Won't that do well, cousin?

HIPPOLYTA Very well. Pray begone.
      Exit Monsieur
Well, master, since I find you are quarrelsome and melancholy, and would have taken me away without a portion—three infallible signs   180
of a true lover—faith, here's my hand now in earnest, to lead me a dance as long as I live.

GERRARD How's this? You surprise me as much as when first I found so much beauty and wit in company with so much innocency. But, dearest, I would be assured of what you say, and yet dare not ask   185
the question. You—ah—do not abuse me again? You—ah—will fool me no more, sure?

HIPPOLYTA Yes, but I will, sure.

GERRARD How! Nay, I was afraid on't.

HIPPOLYTA For I say you are to be my husband, and you say   190
husbands must be wittols, and some strange things to boot.

GERRARD Well, I will take my fortune.

HIPPOLYTA But have a care, rash man.

GERRARD I will venture.

HIPPOLYTA At your peril; remember I wished you to have a care: 195
forewarned, forearmed.

PRUE Indeed now, that's fair; for most men are forearmed before
they are warned.°

HIPPOLYTA Plain dealing is some kind of honesty,° however, and
few women would have said so much. 200

GERRARD None but those who would delight in a husband's jealousy
as the proof of his love and her honour.

HIPPOLYTA Hold, sir, let us have a good understanding betwixt one
another at first, that we may be long friends. I differ from you in
the point, for a husband's jealousy, which cunning men would pass 205
upon their wives for a compliment, is the worst can be made 'em;
for indeed it is a compliment to their beauty, but an affront to their
honour.

GERRARD But, madam—

HIPPOLYTA So that upon the whole matter I conclude: jealousy in a 210
gallant is humble true love, and the height of respect, and only an
undervaluing of himself to overvalue her; but in a husband 'tis
arrant sauciness, cowardice, and ill breeding, and not to be
suffered.

GERRARD I stand corrected, gracious miss. 215

HIPPOLYTA Well! But have you brought the gentlemen fiddlers with
you, as I desired?

GERRARD They are below.

HIPPOLYTA Are they armed well?

GERRARD Yes, they have instruments too that are not of wood. But 220
what will you do with them?

HIPPOLYTA What did you think I intended to do with them? When
I whispered you to bring gentlemen of your acquaintance instead
of fiddlers, as my father desired you to bring—pray, what did you
think I intended? 225

GERRARD Faith, e'en to make fools of the gentlemen fiddlers, as you
had done of your gentleman dancing-master.

HIPPOLYTA I intended 'em for our guard and defence against my
father's Spanish and Guinea force,° when we were to make our
retreat from hence, and to help us to take the keys from my aunt, 230
who has been the watchful porter of this house this twelvemonth.
And this design (if your heart do not fail you) we will put in

execution, as soon as you have given your friends below instructions.

GERRARD   Are you sure your heart will stand right, still? You flinched   235
last night, when I little expected it, I am sure.

HIPPOLYTA   The time last night was not so proper for us as now, for
reasons I will give you. But besides that, I confess I had a mind to
try whether your interest did not sway you more than your love,
whether the twelve hundred pounds a year I told you of, had not   240
made a greater impression in your heart than Hippolyta. But
finding it otherwise—yet hold; perhaps upon consideration you are
grown wiser. Can you yet, as I said, be so desperate, so out of
fashion, as to steal a woman with nothing?

GERRARD   With you I can want nothing, nor can be made by anything   245
more rich or happy.

HIPPOLYTA   Think well again. Can you take me without the twelve
hundred pounds a year—the twelve hundred pounds a year?

GERRARD   Indeed, miss, now you begin to be unkind again, and use
me worse than e'er you did.   250

HIPPOLYTA   Well, though you are so modest a gentleman as to suffer
a wife to be put upon you with nothing, I have more conscience
than to do it. I have the twelve hundred pounds a year, out of my
father's power, which is yours—and I am sorry it is not the Indies
to mend your bargain.   255

GERRARD   Dear miss, you but increase my fears, and not my wealth.
Pray, let us make haste away; I desire but to be secure of you.
Come, what are you thinking of?

HIPPOLYTA   I am thinking, if some little, filching, inquisitive poet
should get my story, and represent it on the stage; what those   260
ladies, who are never precise but at a play, would say of me
now—that I were a confident, coming piece, I warrant, and they
would damn the poor poet for libelling the sex. But sure, though I
give myself and fortune away frankly, without the consent of my
friends, my confidence is less than theirs who stand off only for   265
separate maintenance.

GERRARD   They would be widows before their time, have a husband
and no husband. But let us begone, lest Fortune should recant my
happiness. Now you are fixed, my dearest miss.

> *He kisses her hand. Enter Monsieur, coughing, and Don*
> *Diego*

HIPPOLYTA   Oh, here's my father!   270

DON DIEGO   How now, sir! What, kissing her hand? What means that, friend, ha? Daughter, ha? Do you permit this insolence, ha? *Voto a mi honra!*

GERRARD [*aside*] We are prevented again.

HIPPOLYTA Ha ha ha, you are so full of your Spanish jealousy, father! 275
Why, you must know he's a City dancing-master, and they, forsooth,
think it fine to kiss the hand at the honour before the courante.

MONSIEUR Ay, ay, uncle; don't you know that?

DON DIEGO Go to, go to; you are an easy French fool. There's more
in it than so, look you. 280

MONSIEUR I vow and swear there's nothing more in't, if you'll
believe one. (*Aside to Hippolyta and Gerrard*) Did not I cough and
hawk? A jealous, prudent husband could not cough and hawk
louder at the approach of his wife's chamber in visiting-time, and
yet you would not hear me. He'll make now ado about nothing, and 285
you'll be discovered both.

DON DIEGO Umph, umph, no no; I see it plain. He is no dancing-
master. Now I have found it out, and I think I can see as far into
matters as another. I have found it now, look you.

GERRARD [*apart to Hippolyta*] My fear was prophetical. 290

HIPPOLYTA [*apart to Gerrard*] What shall we do?

      Gerrard offers to go out with her

Nay, pray sir, do not stir yet.

      Enter Mrs Caution

MRS CAUTION What's the matter, brother? What's the matter?

DON DIEGO I have found it out, sister, I have found it out, sister;
this villain here is no dancing-master, but a dishonourer of my 295
house and daughter. I caught him kissing her hand.

MONSIEUR Pish, pish, you are a strange Spanish kind of an uncle,
that you are. A dishonourer of your daughter, because he kissed
her hand? Pray how could he honour her more? He kissed her
hand, you see, while he was making his honour to her. 300

DON DIEGO You are an unthinking, shallow, French fop, *voto.*—But
I tell you, sister, I have thought of it, and have found it out. He is
no dancing-master, sister. Do you remember the whispering last
night? I have found out the meaning of that too, and I tell you,
sister, he's no dancing-master. I have found it out. 305

MRS CAUTION You found it out! Marry come up! Did not I tell you
always, he was no dancing-master?

DON DIEGO You tell me, you silly woman! What then? What of that?
You tell me! D'e think I heeded what you told me? But I tell you
now: I have found it out. 310

MRS CAUTION I say I found it out.

DON DIEGO I say 'tis false, gossip; I found him out.

MRS CAUTION I say I found him out first, say you what you will.

DON DIEGO Sister, mum! Not such a word again, *guarda*. You found   315
him out!

MRS CAUTION [*aside*] Nay, I must submit, or dissemble like other
prudent women, or—

DON DIEGO Come, come, sister, take it from me: he is no dancing-
master.   320

MRS CAUTION [*ironically*] Oh yes, he is a dancing-master.

DON DIEGO What, will you be wiser than I every way? Remember
the whispering, I say.

MRS CAUTION (*aside*) So, he thinks I speak in earnest; then I'll fit
him still.—But what do you talk of their whispering? They would   325
not whisper any ill before us, sure.

DON DIEGO Will you still be an idiot, a dolt, and see nothing?

MONSIEUR [*to Don Diego*] Lord, you'll be wiser than all the world,
will you? Are we not all against you? Pshaw, pshaw, I ne'er saw
such a *donissimo* as you are, I vow and swear.   330

DON DIEGO No, sister, he's no dancing-master—for now I think on't
too, he could not play upon the fiddle.

MRS CAUTION Pish, pish, what dancing-master can play upon a
fiddle without strings?

DON DIEGO Again! I tell you he broke 'em on purpose, because he   335
could not play. I have found it out now, sister.

MRS CAUTION Nay, you see farther than I, brother.

Gerrard offers to lead Hippolyta out

HIPPOLYTA [*apart to Gerrard*] For heaven's sake, stir not yet.

DON DIEGO Besides, if you remember, they were perpetually putting
me out of the room; that was, sister, because they had a mind to   340
be alone. I have found that out, too. Now sister, look you, he is no
dancing-master.

MRS CAUTION But has he not given her lesson often before you?

DON DIEGO Ay, but, sister, he did not go about his business like a
dancing-master. But go, go down to the door; somebody rings.   345

Exit Mrs Caution

MONSIEUR I vow and swear, uncle, he is a dancing-master. Pray be
appeased. Lord, d'e think I'd tell you a lie?

DON DIEGO If it prove to be a lie, and you do not confess it, though
you are my next heir after my daughter, I will disown thee as much

as I do her, for thy folly and treachery to thyself, as well as me.   350
You may have her, but never my estate, look you.

MONSIEUR (*aside*) How! I must look to my hits° then.

DON DIEGO Look to't.

MONSIEUR [*aside*] Then I had best confess all, before he discover all,
which he will soon do.   355

    Enter Parson

Oh, here's the parson too! He won't be in choler, nor brandish
Toledo before the parson, sure? [*Aloud*] Well, uncle, I must confess
(rather than lose your favour) he is no dancing-master.

DON DIEGO No.

GERRARD What, has the fool betrayed us then at last? Nay, then 'tis   360
time to begone. Come away, miss.

    Going out

DON DIEGO Nay, sir, if you pass this way, my Toledo will pass that
way, look you.

    Thrusts at him with his sword; [Gerrard draws]

HIPPOLYTA Oh, hold, Mr Gerrard! Hold, father!

MONSIEUR (*stops his uncle*) I tell you, uncle, he's an honest gentle-   365
man, means no hurt, and came hither but upon a frolic of mine and
your daughter's.

DON DIEGO *Ladrón, traidor!*

MONSIEUR I tell you, all's but a jest, a mere jest, I vow and swear.

DON DIEGO A jest! Jest with my honour, *voto*, ha! No family to   370
dishonour but the grave, wise, noble, honourable, illustrious,
puissant, and right worshipful family of the Formals! Nay, I am
contented to reprieve you, till you know who you have dishonoured, and convict you of the greatness of your crime before you
die. We are descended, look you—   375

MONSIEUR Nay, pray, uncle, hear me.

DON DIEGO I say, we are descended—

MONSIEUR 'Tis no matter for that.

DON DIEGO And my great-great-grandfather° was—

MONSIEUR Well, well, I have something to say, more to the purpose.   380

DON DIEGO My great-great-grandfather, I say, was—

MONSIEUR Well, a pin-maker in—

DON DIEGO But he was a gentleman for all that, fop, for he was a
sergeant to a company of the train-bands, and my great-grandfather
was—   385

MONSIEUR Was his son; what then? Won't you let me clear this
gentleman?

DON DIEGO He was, he was—

MONSIEUR He was a felt-maker, his son a wine-cooper, your father
a vintner, and so you came to be a Canary merchant.°   390

DON DIEGO But we were still gentlemen, for our coat was, as the
heralds say, was—

MONSIEUR Was—your sign was the three tuns, and the field canary.°
Now let me tell you, this honest gentleman—

DON DIEGO [to Gerrard] Now, that you should dare to dishonour this   395
family! By the graves of my ancestors in Great St Ellen's Church—

MONSIEUR Yard.°

DON DIEGO Thou shalt die for't, ladrón.
        Runs at Gerrard

MONSIEUR Hold, hold, uncle! Are you mad?

HIPPOLYTA Oh, oh!   400

MONSIEUR (draws his sword) Nay then, by your own Spanish rules of
honour, though he be my rival I must help him, since I brought
him into danger. (Aside) Sure he will not show his valour upon his
nephew and son-in-law, otherwise I should be afraid of showing
mine.   405
        Opens a door
Here, Mr Gerrard, go in here. Nay, you shall go in, Mr Gerrard.
I'll secure you all—and, parson, do you go in too with 'em, for I
see you are afraid of a sword and the other world, though you talk
of it so familiarly, and make it so fine a place.
        Thrusts Gerrard, Hippolyta, [Prue] and Parson in, then shuts
        [the door] and guards it with his sword

DON DIEGO 'Tu quoque, Brutè.'°   410

MONSIEUR Nay, now, uncle, you must understand reason. What, you
are not only a don, but you are a Don Quixote° too, I vow and
swear.

DON DIEGO Thou spot, splotch of my family and blood! I will have
his blood, look you.   415

MONSIEUR Pray, good Spanish uncle, have but patience to hear me.
Suppose . . . I say, suppose he had done, done, done the feat to
your daughter.

DON DIEGO How! Done the feat, done the feat, done the feat, en hora
mala!   420

MONSIEUR I say, suppose, suppose—

DON DIEGO Suppose—

MONSIEUR I say, suppose he had—for I do but suppose it. Well, I
am ready to marry her, however. Now marriage is as good a solder

for cracked female honour as blood, and can't you suffer the shame 425
but for a quarter of an hour, till the parson has married us? And
then, if there be any shame, it becomes mine. For here in England
the father has nothing to do with the daughter's business, honour,
what-d'e-call-it, when once she's married, d'e see?

DON DIEGO England! What d'e tell me of England? I'll be a Spaniard 430
still, *voto a mi honra*, and I will be revenged. (*Calls at the door*)
Pedro, Juan, Sanchez!

*Enter Mrs Caution, followed by Flirt and Flounce in
vizard-masks*

MRS CAUTION What's the matter, brother?

DON DIEGO Pedro, Sanchez, Juan!—But who are these, sister? Are
they not men in women's clothes? What make they here? 435

MRS CAUTION They are relations, they say, of my cousin's, who
pressed in when I let in the parson. They say my cousin invited
'em to his wedding.

MONSIEUR Two of my relations? [*Aside*] Ha!—they are my cousins
indeed of the other night. A pox take 'em—but that's no curse for 440
'em. A plague take 'em then! But how came they here?

DON DIEGO (*aside*) Now must I have witnesses too of the dishonour
of my family! It were Spanish prudence to dispatch 'em away out
of the house, before I begin my revenge.—What are you? What
make you here? Who would you speak with? 445

FLIRT With Monsieur.

DON DIEGO Here he is.

MONSIEUR [*aside*] Now will these jades discredit me, and spoil my
match, just in the coupling minute.

DON DIEGO Do you know 'em? 450

MONSIEUR Yes, sir, sure, I know 'em. (*Aside to 'em*) Pray, ladies, say
as I say, or you will spoil my wedding, for I am just going to be
married, and if my uncle, or mistress, should know who you are,
it might break off the match.

FLOUNCE We come on purpose to break the match. 455

MONSIEUR How!

FLIRT Why, d'e think to marry, and leave us so in the lurch?

MONSIEUR (*aside*) What do the jades mean?

DON DIEGO Come, who are they? What would they have? If they come
to the wedding—Ladies, I assure you there will be none today here. 460

MONSIEUR They won't trouble you, sir, they are going again.—
Ladies, you hear what my uncle says. I know you won't trouble
him. (*Aside*) I wish I were well rid of 'em.

FLOUNCE (*aside* [*to Monsieur*]) You shall not think to put us off so.

DON DIEGO Who are they? What are their names?   465

FLIRT We are, sir—

MONSIEUR (*aside to 'em*) Nay, for heaven's sake don't tell who you are, for you will undo me, and spoil my match infallibly.

FLOUNCE We care not; 'tis our business to spoil matches.

MONSIEUR You need not, for (I believe) married men are your best   470
customers, for greedy bachelors take up with their wives.

DON DIEGO Come, pray, ladies; if you have no business here, be pleased to retire, for few of us are in humour to be so civil to you as you may deserve.

MONSIEUR Ay, prithee dear jades, get you gone.   475

FLIRT We will not stir.

DON DIEGO Who are they, I say, fool? And why don't they go?

FLOUNCE We are, sir—

MONSIEUR Hold, hold.—They are persons of honour and quality, and—   480

FLIRT We are no persons of honour and quality, sir, we are—

MONSIEUR They are modest ladies, and being in a kind of disguise, will not own their quality.

FLOUNCE We, modest ladies!

MONSIEUR (*aside to 'em*) Why, sometimes you are in the humour to   485
pass for women of honour and quality. Prithee, dear jades, let your modesty and greatness come upon you now.

FLIRT [*to Don Diego*] Come, sir, not to delude you, as he would have us, we are—

MONSIEUR Hold, hold!   490

FLIRT The other night at the French house—

MONSIEUR Hold, I say! [*Aside*] 'Tis even true, as Gerrard says, the women will tell, I see.

FLOUNCE [*aside to Monsieur*] If you would have her silent, stop her mouth with that ring.   495

MONSIEUR Will that do't? Here, here.

> *Takes off his ring and gives it her*

[*Aside*] 'Tis worth one hundred and fifty pounds—but I must not lose my match, I must not lose a trout for a fly.° That men should live to hire women to silence!

> *Enter Gerrard, Hippolyta, Parson, and Prue*

DON DIEGO Oh, are you come again?   500

> *Draws his sword and runs at 'em*

MONSIEUR Oh, hold, hold, uncle!

Monsieur holds him

What, are you mad, Gerrard, to expose yourself to a new danger?
Why would you come out yet?

GERRARD Because our danger now is over, I thank the parson there.
And now we must beg—   505

Gerrard and Hippolyta kneel [before Don Diego]

MONSIEUR Nay, faith, uncle, forgive him now, since he asks you
forgiveness upon his knees, and my poor cousin too.

HIPPOLYTA You are mistaken, cousin. We ask him blessing,° and
you forgiveness.

MONSIEUR How, how, how! What° do you talk of blessing? What,   510
do you ask your father blessing, and he asks me forgiveness? But
why should he ask me forgiveness?

HIPPOLYTA Because he asks my father blessing.

MONSIEUR Pish, pish, I don't understand you, I vow and swear.

HIPPOLYTA The parson will expound to you, cousin.   515

MONSIEUR Hey! What say you to it, parson?

PARSON They are married, sir.

MONSIEUR Married!

MRS CAUTION Married! So, I told you what 'twould come to.

DON DIEGO You told us!   520

MONSIEUR Nay, she is setting up for the reputation of a witch.

DON DIEGO Married! Juan, Sanchez, Pedro! Arm, arm, arm!

MRS CAUTION A witch! A witch!

HIPPOLYTA Nay indeed, father, now we are married you had better
call the fiddles.—Call 'em, Prue, quickly.   525

Exit Prue

MONSIEUR [*to Parson*] Who do you say married, man?

PARSON Was I not sent for on purpose to marry 'em? Why should
you wonder at it?

MONSIEUR No, no, you were to marry me, man, to her. I knew there
was a mistake in't somehow. You were merely mistaken, therefore   530
you must do your business over again for me now.—The parson
was mistaken, uncle, it seems. Ha ha ha.

MRS CAUTION I suppose five or six guineas made him make the
mistake, which will not be rectified now, nephew. They'll marry all
that come near 'em, and for a guinea or two care not what mischief   535
they do, nephew.

DON DIEGO Married! Pedro, Sanchez!

MONSIEUR How! And must she be his wife then for ever and ever?
Have I held the door then for this, like a fool as I was?

MRS CAUTION Yes, indeed.   540

MONSIEUR Have I worn *golilla* here for this? Little breeches for this?

MRS CAUTION Yes, truly.

MONSIEUR And put on the Spanish honour with the habit, in
defending my rival? Nay, then I'll have another turn of honour in
revenge. Come, uncle, I'm of your side now, sa sa sa [*begins to draw*   545
his sword]—but let's stay for our force. Sanchez, Juan, Pedro! Arm,
arm, arm!

> *Enter two Blackamoors and the Spaniard, followed by Prue,*
> *Martin, and five other gentlemen like fiddlers*

DON DIEGO Murder the villain, kill him!

> [*Don Diego, Monsieur, and servants run*] *upon Gerrard.*

MARTIN [*interposing*] Hold, hold, sir.

DON DIEGO How now! Who sent for you, friends?   550

MARTIN We fiddlers, sir, often come unsent for.°

DON DIEGO And you are often kicked downstairs for't too.

MARTIN No, sir, our company was never kicked, I think.

DON DIEGO Fiddlers, and not kicked? Then, to preserve your virgin
honour, get you downstairs quickly—for we are not at present   555
disposed much for mirth, *voto*.

MONSIEUR (*peeping*) A pox, is it you, Martin?—Nay, uncle, then 'tis
in vain—for they won't be kicked downstairs, to my knowledge.
They are gentlemen fiddlers, forsooth. A pox on all gentlemen
fiddlers and gentlemen dancing-masters, say I.   560

DON DIEGO (*pausing*) How! Ha!

MONSIEUR Well, Flirt, now I am a match for thee; now I may keep
you, and there's little difference betwixt keeping a wench and
marriage, only marriage is a little the cheaper. But the other is the
more honourable now, *vert et bleu*—nay, now I may swear a   565
French oath too. Come, come, I am thine; let us strike up the
bargain: thine, according to the honourable institution of keeping.
Come.

FLIRT Nay, hold, sir; two words to the bargain.° First, I have ne'er
a lawyer here to draw articles and settlements.   570

MONSIEUR How! Is the world come to that? A man cannot keep a
wench without articles and settlements? Nay then, 'tis e'en as bad
as marriage indeed, and there's no difference betwixt a wife and a
wench.

FLIRT Only in cohabitation; for the first article shall be against   575
cohabitation. We mistresses suffer no cohabitation.

MONSIEUR Nor wives neither, now.

FLIRT Then separate maintenance, in case you should take a wife, or
I a new friend.

MONSIEUR How! That too? Then you are every whit as bad as a wife.   580

FLIRT Then my house in town, and yours in the country, if you will.

MONSIEUR A mere wife.

FLIRT Then my coach apart, as well as my bed apart.

MONSIEUR As bad as a wife still.

FLIRT But take notice I will have no little, dirty, second-hand chariot   585
new-furbished, but a large, sociable, well-painted coach, nor will I
keep it till it be as well known as myself, and it come to be called
'Flirt coach';° nor will I have such pitiful horses as cannot carry
me every night to the park°—for I will not miss a night in the park,
I'd have you to know.   590

MONSIEUR 'Tis very well; you must have your great, gilt, fine,
painted coaches. I'm sure they are grown so common already
amongst you, that ladies of quality begin to take up with hackneys
again, *jarni*. But what else?

FLIRT Then, that you do not think I will be served by a little dirty   595
boy in a bonnet, but a couple of handsome, lusty, cleanly footmen,
fit to serve ladies of quality, and do their business as they should do.

MONSIEUR What then?

FLIRT Then, that you never grow jealous of them.

MONSIEUR Why, will you make so much of them?   600

FLIRT I delight to be kind to my servants.

MONSIEUR Well, is this all?

FLIRT No. Then, that when you come to my house you never
presume to touch a key, lift up a latch, or thrust a door, without
knocking beforehand. And that you ask no questions if you see a   605
stray piece of plate, cabinet, or looking-glass in my house.

MONSIEUR Just a wife in everything. But what else?

FLIRT Then, that you take no acquaintance with me abroad,° nor
bring me home any,° when you are drunk, whom you will not be
willing to see there when you are sober.   610

MONSIEUR But what allowance? Let's come to the main business, the
money.

FLIRT Stay, let me think . . . First, for advance-money, five hundred
pound for pins.

MONSIEUR A very wife.   615

FLIRT Then you must take the lease of my house, and furnish it as
becomes one of my quality—for don't you think we'll take up with
your old Queen Elizabeth° furniture, as your wives do.

MONSIEUR Indeed, there she is least like a wife, as she says.

FLIRT Then, for housekeeping, servant wages, clothes, and the rest,   620
I'll be contented with a thousand pound a year present maintenance, and but three hundred pound a year separate maintenance for
my life, when our love grows cold. But I am contented with a
thousand pound a year, because for pendants, necklaces, and all
sorts of jewels and such trifles, nay and some plate, I will shift   625
myself as I can—make shifts which you shall not take any notice
of.

MONSIEUR A thousand pound a year! What will wenching come to?
Time was, a man might have fared as well at a much cheaper rate,
and a lady of one's affections, instead of a house, would have been   630
contented with a little chamber three pair of stairs backward, with
a little closet or larder to't; and instead of variety of new gowns and
rich petticoats, with her dishabiliè or flame-colour gown called
Indian,° and slippers of the same, would have been contented for
a twelvemonth;° and instead of visits, and gadding to plays, would   635
have entertained herself at home with *St George for England*,° *The
Knight of the Sun*,° or *The Practice of Piety*;° and instead of
sending° her wine and meat from the French houses, would have
been contented if you had given her (poor wretch) but credit at the
next chandler's and chequered cellar; and then instead of a coach,   640
would have been well satisfied to have gone out and taken the air
for three or four hours in the evening in the balcony, poor soul.
Well, Flirt, however, we'll agree. 'Tis but three hundred pound a
year separate maintenance, you say, when I am weary of thee and
the charge.   645

DON DIEGO [*aside*] Robbed of my honour, my daughter, and my
revenge too! Oh, my dear honour! Nothing vexes me but that the
world should say I had not Spanish policy enough to keep my
daughter from being debauched from me—but methinks my
Spanish policy might help me yet . . . I have it so—I will cheat 'em   650
all, for I will declare I understood the whole plot and contrivance,
and connived at it, finding my cousin a fool and not answering my
expectation. Well—but then, if I approve of the match, I must give
this mock dancing-master my estate, especially since half he would
have in right of my daughter, and in spite of me. Well, I am   655
resolved to turn the cheat upon themselves, and give them my
consent and estate.

MONSIEUR Come, come, ne'er be troubled, uncle; 'twas a combination, you see, of all these heads and your daughter's (you know

what I mean,° uncle), not to be thwarted or governed by all the   660
Spanish policy in Christendom. I'm sure my French policy would
not have governed her; so, since I have scaped her, I am glad I have
scaped her, *jarni*.

MRS CAUTION Come, brother, you are wiser than I, you see; ay ay.

DON DIEGO No, you think you are wiser than I now, in earnest. But   665
know, while I was thought a gull, I gulled you all, and made them
and you think I knew nothing of the contrivance. Confess, did
not you think, verily, that I knew nothing of it, and that I was a
gull?

MRS CAUTION Yes indeed, brother, I did think verily you were a   670
gull.

HIPPOLYTA (*listening*) How's this?

DON DIEGO Alas, alas, all the sputter I made was but to make this
young man my cousin believe, when the thing should be effected,
that it was not with my connivance or consent. But since he is so   675
well satisfied, I own it. For do you think I would ever have suffered
her to marry a *monsieur*, a *monsieur*, *guarda*? Besides, it had been
but a beastly incestuous kind of a match, *voto*!

MRS CAUTION Nay, then I see, brother, you were wiser than I,
indeed.   680

GERRARD (*aside*) So, so.

MRS CAUTION Nay, young man, you have danced a fair dance for
yourself, royally, and now you may go jig it together till you are
both weary. [*To Hippolyta*] And though you were so eager to have
him, Mistress Minx, you'll soon have your bellyful of him, let me   685
tell you, mistress.

PRUE Ha ha!

MONSIEUR How, uncle! What was't you said? Nay, if I had your
Spanish policy against me, it was no wonder I missed of my aim,
mon foi.   690

DON DIEGO [*to Gerrard*] I was resolved, too, my daughter should not
marry a coward, therefore made the more ado to try you, sir; but
I find you are a brisk man of honour, firm, stiff, Spanish honour.
And that you may see I deceived you all along, and you not
me—ay, and am able to deceive you still, for, I know, now you   695
think that I will give you little or nothing with my daughter (like
other fathers), since you have married her without my consent; but,
I say, I'll deceive you now, for you shall have the most part of my
estate in present, and the rest at my death. There's for you! I think
I have deceived you now, look you.   700

GERRARD No indeed, sir, you have not deceived me, for I never
   suspected your love to your daughter, nor your generosity.

DON DIEGO How, sir! Have a care of saying I have not deceived you,
   lest I deceive you another way, *guarda!*—Pray, gentlemen, do not
   think any man could deceive me, look you, that any man could steal   705
   my daughter, look you, without my connivance.
   The less we speak, the more we think,
   And he sees most that seems to wink.

HIPPOLYTA So, so. Now I could give you my blessing, father; now
   you are a good complaisant father, indeed.   710
       When children marry, parents should obey,
       Since love claims more obedience far than they.
      Exeunt

Epilogue
Spoken by Flirt

The ladies first I am to compliment,
Whom (if he could) the poet would content,
But to their pleasure then they must consent.
Most spoil their sport still by their modesty,
And when they should be pleased, cry out 'O fie!'   5
And the least smutty jest will ne'er pass by.
But City damsel ne'er had confidence
At smutty play to take the least offence,
But mercy shows—to show her innocence.
　　Yet lest the merchants' daughters should today   10
Be scandalized, not at our harmless play,
But our Hippolyta, since she's like one
Of us bold flirts of t'other end o'th' town,
Our poet, sending to you (though unknown)
His best respects by me, does frankly own   15
The character to be unnatural:
Hippolyta is not like you at all.
You, while your lovers court you, still look grum,
And, far from wooing, when they woo, cry 'Mum';
And if some of you e'er were stol'n away,   20
Your portion's fault 'twas only (I dare say).
　　Thus much for him the poet bid me speak;
Now to the men I my own mind will break.
You good men o'th' Exchange, on whom alone
We must depend, when sparks to sea are gone,°   25
Into the pit already you are come—°
'Tis but a step more to our tiring-room,
Where none of us but will be wondrous sweet
Upon an able love of Lumber Street.°
You we had rather see between our scenes°   30
Than spendthrift fops with better clothes and miens;
Instead of laced coats, belts, and pantaloons,
Your velvet jumps, gold chains, and grave fur gowns;°
Instead of periwigs, and broad cocked hats,°
Your satin caps, small cuffs, and vast cravats.°   35

For you are fair and square in all your dealings;
You never cheat your doxies with gilt shillings;°
You ne'er will break our windows—then you are°
Fit to make love, while our huzzas make war.
And since all gentlemen must pack to sea,   40
Our gallants and our judges you must be.
We, therefore, and our poet, do submit
To all the camlet cloaks now i'the pit.°

THE COUNTRY WIFE

Indignor quicquam reprehendi, non quia crasse
compositum illepideve putetur, sed quia nuper;
nec veniam antiquis, sed honorem et praemia posci.°

Horace

THE PERSONS

Mr Horner   *Mr Hart*
Mr Harcourt   *Mr Kynaston*
Mr Dorilant   *Mr Lydall*
Mr Pinchwife   *Mr Mohun*
Mr Sparkish [betrothed to Alethea]   *Mr Haines*   5
Sir Jasper Fidget   *Mr Cartwright*

Mrs Margery Pinchwife   *Mrs Boutell*
Mistress Alethea [Mrs Pinchwife's sister,   *Mrs James*
  betrothed to Sparkish]
My Lady Fidget   *Mrs Knepp*   10
Mistress Dainty Fidget [Sir Jasper's sister]   *Mrs Corbett*
Mistress Squeamish [a relative of the Fidgets]   *Mrs Wyatt*
Old Lady Squeamish [her grandmother]   *Mrs Rutter*

A Boy [Horner's servant]
A Quack°   *Mr Shatterell*   15
Lucy [Alethea's maid]   *Mrs Corey*
[Clasp (a bookseller)]
[A parson], waiters, servants, and attendants

THE SCENE

London

Prologue
Spoken by Mr Hart

Poets, like cudgelled bullies, never do
At first, or second blow, submit to you,
But will provoke you still, and ne'er have done
Till you are weary first, with laying on.
The late so baffled scribbler of this day,°   5
Though he stands trembling, bids me boldly say
What we before most plays are used to do—
For poets, out of fear, first draw on you,
In a fierce prologue the still pit defy,
And ere you speak, like Kastril give the lie.°   10
But though our Bayses' battles oft I've fought,°
And with bruised knuckles their dear conquests bought—
Nay, never yet feared odds upon the stage—
In prologue dare not hector with the age,
But would take quarter from your saving hands,   15
Though Bays (within) all yielding countermands,°
Says you confed'rate wits no quarter give,
Therefore his play shan't ask your leave to live.
Well, let the vain rash fop, by huffing so,
Think to obtain the better terms of you;   20
But we the actors humbly will submit,
Now, and at any time, to a full pit—
Nay, often we anticipate your rage,
And murder poets for you, on our stage.
We set no guards upon our tiring-room,°   25
But when with flying colours there you come,
We patiently, you see, give up to you
Our poets, virgins, nay our matrons too.

1.1

Horner's lodging

Enter Horner,° and Quack following him at a distance

HORNER (*aside*) A quack is as fit for° a pimp as a midwife for a bawd; they are still but in their way both° helpers of nature.—Well, my dear doctor, hast thou done what I desired?

QUACK I have undone you for ever with the women, and reported you throughout the whole town as bad as an eunuch, with as much 5 trouble as if I had made you one in earnest.

HORNER But have you told all the midwives you know, the orange-wenches° at the playhouses, the City husbands, and old fumbling keepers of this end of the town?°—for they'll be the readiest to report it.

QUACK I have told all the chambermaids, waiting-women, tire-women,° and old women of my acquaintance—nay, and whispered 10 it as a secret to 'em, and to the whisperers of Whitehall, so that you need not doubt 'twill spread, and you will be as odious to the handsome young women, as—

HORNER As the smallpox. Well— 15

QUACK And to the married women of this end of the town, as—

HORNER As the great ones°—nay, as their own husbands.

QUACK And to the City dames, as Aniseed Robin° of filthy and contemptible memory; and they will frighten their children with your name, especially their females. 20

HORNER And cry, 'Horner's coming, to carry you away!' I am only afraid 'twill not be believed. You told 'em 'twas by an English-French disaster, and an English-French chirurgeon,° who has given me at once not only a cure, but an antidote for the future against that damned malady, and that worse distemper, love, and all other 25 women's evils?

QUACK Your late journey into France has made it the more credible, and your being here a fortnight before you appeared in public, looks as if you apprehended the shame—which I wonder you do not. Well, I have been hired by young gallants to belie 'em 30 t'other way; but you are the first would be thought a man unfit for women.

HORNER Dear Master Doctor, let vain rogues be contented only to be thought abler men than they are; generally 'tis all the pleasure they have. But mine lies another way. 35

QUACK You take, methinks, a very preposterous way to it, and as ridiculous as if we operators in physic should put forth bills to disparage our medicaments, with hopes to gain customers.

HORNER Doctor, there are quacks in love, as well as physic, who get but the fewer and worse patients for their boasting. A good name   40
is seldom got by giving it one's self, and women, no more than honour, are compassed by bragging. Come, come, doctor, the wisest lawyer never discovers the merits of his cause till the trial; the wealthiest man conceals his riches, and the cunning gamester his play. Shy husbands and keepers, like old rooks, are not to be   45
cheated but by a new unpractised trick. False friendship will pass now no more than false dice upon 'em—no, not in the City.°

    Enter Boy

BOY There are two ladies and a gentleman coming up.

    [*Exit Boy*]

HORNER A pox! Some unbelieving sisters of my former acquaintance, who, I am afraid, expect their sense should be satisfied of the   50
falsity of the report.

    Enter Sir Jasper° *Fidget, Lady Fidget, and Dainty*° *Fidget*

No—this formal fool, and women!

QUACK His wife and sister.

SIR JASPER My coach breaking just now before your door sir, I look upon as an occasional reprimand to me sir, for not kissing your   55
hands sir, since your coming out of France sir. And so my disaster sir, has been my good fortune sir; and this is my wife, and sister sir.°

HORNER What then, sir?

SIR JASPER My lady, and sister, sir.—Wife, this is Master Horner.   60

LADY FIDGET Master Horner, husband!

SIR JASPER My lady, my Lady Fidget, sir.

HORNER So, sir.

SIR JASPER Won't you be acquainted with her sir? (*Aside*) So the report is true, I find, by his coldness or aversion to the sex. But I'll   65
play the wag with him.—Pray salute my wife, my lady, sir.

HORNER I will kiss no man's wife, sir, for him, sir. I have taken my eternal leave, sir, of the sex already, sir.

SIR JASPER (*aside*) Ha ha ha! I'll plague him yet.—Not know my wife, sir?   70

HORNER I do know your wife, sir, she's a woman, sir, and consequently a monster, sir, a greater monster than a husband, sir.

SIR JASPER A husband! How, sir?

HORNER So, sir. (*Makes horns*)° But I make no more cuckolds, sir.

SIR JASPER Ha ha ha! Mercury,° Mercury! 75

LADY FIDGET Pray, Sir Jasper, let us begone from this rude fellow.

DAINTY FIDGET Who, by his breeding, would think he had ever been in France?

LADY FIDGET Foh, he's but too much a French fellow, such as hate women of quality and virtue for their love to their husbands, Sir 80
Jasper. A woman is hated by 'em as much for loving her husband, as for loving their money. But pray, let's begone.

HORNER You do well, madam, for I have nothing that you came for. I have brought over not so much as a bawdy picture, new postures,° nor the second part of the *École des filles*,° nor— 85

QUACK (*apart to Horner*) Hold, for shame, sir. What d'y' mean? You'll ruin yourself for ever with the sex!

SIR JASPER Ha ha ha! He hates women perfectly, I find.

DAINTY FIDGET What pity 'tis he should.

LADY FIDGET Ay, he's a base, rude fellow for't. But affection 90
makes not a woman more odious to them than virtue.

HORNER Because your virtue is your greatest affectation, madam.

LADY FIDGET How, you saucy fellow! Would you wrong my honour?

HORNER If I could.

LADY FIDGET How d'y' mean, sir? 95

SIR JASPER Ha ha ha! No, he can't wrong your ladyship's honour, upon my honour. He, poor man—hark you in your ear—a mere eunuch.

LADY FIDGET Oh filthy French beast! Foh, foh! Why do we stay? Let's begone—I can't endure the sight of him. 100

SIR JASPER Stay but till the chairs come; they'll be here presently.

LADY FIDGET No, no.

SIR JASPER Nor can I stay longer. [*Consults his watch*] 'Tis, let me see . . . a quarter and a half quarter of a minute past eleven. The Council° will be sat; I must away. Business must be preferred 105
always before love and ceremony with the wise, Mr Horner.

HORNER And the impotent, Sir Jasper.

SIR JASPER Ay, ay, the impotent,° Master Horner. Ha ha ha!

LADY FIDGET What, leave us with a filthy man alone in his lodgings? 110

SIR JASPER He's an innocent man now, you know. Pray stay; I'll hasten the chairs to you.—Mr Horner, your servant; I should be glad to see you at my house. Pray, come and dine with me, and play at cards with my wife after dinner; you are fit for women at

that game—yet, ha ha! (*Aside*) 'Tis as much a husband's prudence   115
to provide innocent diversion for a wife, as to hinder her unlawful
pleasures; and he had better employ her, than let her employ
herself.—Farewell.

HORNER Your servant, Sir Jasper.

    Exit Sir Jasper

LADY FIDGET I will not stay with him, foh!   120

HORNER Nay, madam, I beseech you stay, if it be but to see I can
be as civil to ladies yet, as they would desire.

LADY FIDGET No, no! Foh, you cannot be civil to ladies.

DAINTY FIDGET You, as civil as ladies would desire!

LADY FIDGET No, no, no; foh, foh, foh!   125

    Exeunt Lady Fidget and Dainty Fidget

QUACK Now I think I, or you yourself rather, have done your
business with the women.°

HORNER Thou art an ass. Don't you see already, upon the report and
my carriage, this grave man of business leaves his wife in my
lodgings, invites me to his house and wife, who before would not   130
be acquainted with me out of jealousy.

QUACK Nay, by this means you may be the more acquainted with the
husbands, but the less with the wives.

HORNER Let me alone. If I can but abuse the husbands, I'll soon
disabuse the wives. Stay, I'll reckon you up the advantages I am   135
like to have by my stratagem: first, I shall be rid of all my old
acquaintances, the most insatiable sorts of duns that invade our
lodgings in a morning; and next to the pleasure of making a new
mistress, is that of being rid of an old one; and of all old debts, love
(when it comes to be so) is paid the most unwillingly.°   140

QUACK Well, you may be so rid of your old acquaintances—but how
will you get any new ones?

HORNER Doctor, thou wilt never make a good chemist, thou art so
incredulous and impatient. Ask but all the young fellows of the
town, if they do not lose more time, like huntsmen, in starting the   145
game than in running it down. One knows not where to find 'em,
who will, or will not. Women of quality are so civil, you can hardly
distinguish love from good breeding, and a man is often mistaken.
But now I can be sure, she that shows an aversion to me, loves the
sport, as those women that are gone, whom I warrant to be right.   150
And then the next thing is, your women of honour, as you call 'em,
are only chary of their reputations, not their persons, and 'tis
scandal they would avoid, not men. Now may I have, by the

reputation of an eunuch, the privileges of one, and be seen in a lady's chamber in a morning, as early as her husband; kiss virgins   155
before their parents, or lovers; and may be, in short, the *passe-partout* of the town. Now, doctor—

QUACK Nay, now you shall be the doctor; and your process is so new, that we do not know but it may succeed.

HORNER Not so new neither;° *probatum est*, doctor.   160

QUACK Well, I wish you luck and many patients, whilst I go to mine.
Exit Quack. Enter Harcourt and Dorilant to Horner

HARCOURT Come, your appearance at the play yesterday has, I hope, hardened you for the future against the women's contempt, and the men's raillery; and now you'll abroad as you were wont.

HORNER Did I not bear it bravely?   165

DORILANT With a most theatrical impudence; nay, more than the orange-wenches show there, or a drunken vizard-mask, or a great-bellied actress°—nay, or the most impudent of creatures, an ill poet; or what is yet more impudent, a second-hand critic.

HORNER But what say the ladies? Have they no pity?   170

HARCOURT What ladies? The vizard-masks, you know, never pity a man when all's gone, though in their service.

DORILANT And for the women in the boxes, you'd never pity them, when 'twas in your power.

HARCOURT They say 'tis pity but° all that deal with common women   175
should be served so.

DORILANT Nay, I dare swear they won't admit you to play at cards with them, go to plays with 'em, or do the little duties which other shadows of men are wont to do for 'em.

HORNER Who do you call shadows of men?   180

DORILANT Half-men.

HORNER What, boys?

DORILANT Ay, your old boys, old *beaux garçons*, who like super-annuated stallions are suffered to run, feed, and whinny with the mares as long as they live, though they can do nothing else.   185

HORNER Well, a pox on love and wenching; women serve but to keep a man from better company. Though I can't enjoy them, I shall you the more. Good fellowship and friendship are lasting, rational, and manly pleasures.

HARCOURT For all that, give me some of those pleasures you call   190
effeminate, too; they help to relish one another.

HORNER They disturb one another.

HARCOURT No, mistresses are like books; if you pore upon them too

much, they doze you, and make you unfit for company; but if used
discreetly, you are the fitter for conversation by 'em.   195

DORILANT A mistress should be like a little country° retreat near the
town, not to dwell in constantly, but only for a night and away—to
taste the town better when a man returns.

HORNER I tell you, 'tis as hard to be a good fellow, a good friend,
and a lover of women, as 'tis to be a good fellow, a good friend,   200
and a lover of money. You cannot follow both; then choose your
side. Wine gives you liberty, love takes it away.

DORILANT Gad, he's in the right ont't.

HORNER Wine gives you joy; love, grief and tortures, besides the
chirurgeon's. Wine makes us witty; love, only sots. Wine makes us   205
sleep; love breaks it.

DORILANT By the world, he has reason, Harcourt.

HORNER Wine makes—

DORILANT Ay, wine makes us—makes us princes; love makes us
beggars, poor rogues, egad—and wine°—   210

HORNER So, there's one converted. No, no; love and wine, oil and
vinegar.

HARCOURT I grant it; love will still be uppermost.

HORNER Come, for my part I will have only those glorious, manly
pleasures of being very drunk, and very slovenly.   215

  Enter Boy

BOY Mr Sparkish° is below, sir.

  [*Exit Boy*]

HARCOURT What, my dear friend! A rogue that is fond of me only,
I think, for abusing him.

DORILANT No, he can no more think the men laugh at him, than
that women jilt him, his opinion of himself is so good.   220

HORNER Well, there's another pleasure by drinking, I thought not
of—I shall lose his acquaintance, because he cannot drink.° And
you know 'tis a very hard thing to be rid of him, for he's one of
those nauseous offerers at wit, who, like the worst fiddlers, run
themselves into all companies.°   225

HARCOURT One that by being in the company of men of sense would
pass for one.

HORNER And may so to the short-sighted world, as a false jewel
amongst true ones is not discerned at a distance. His company is as
troublesome to us as a cuckold's, when you have a mind to his wife's.   230

HARCOURT No, the rogue will not let us enjoy one another, but
ravishes our conversation, though he signifies no more to't,° than

Sir Martin Mar-all's gaping, and awkward thrumming upon the
lute, does to his man's voice and music.°

DORILANT And to pass for a wit in town, shows himself a fool every   235
night to us that are guilty of the plot.°

HORNER Such wits as he, are, to a company of reasonable men, like
rooks to the gamesters, who only fill a room at the table, but are so
far from contributing to the play, that they only serve to spoil the
fancy of those that do.   240

DORILANT Nay, they are used like rooks too: snubbed, checked, and
abused; yet the rogues will hang on.

HORNER A pox on 'em, and all that force Nature, and would be still
what she forbids 'em. Affectation is her greatest monster.

HARCOURT Most men are the contraries to that they would seem.   245
Your bully, you see, is a coward with a long sword; the little,
humbly fawning physician, with his ebony cane,° is he that destroys
men.

DORILANT The usurer, a poor rogue possessed of mouldy bonds, and
mortgages; and we they call spendthrifts are only wealthy, who lay   250
out his money upon daily new purchases of pleasure.

HORNER Ay, your arrantest cheat is your trustee, or executor; your
jealous man, the greatest cuckold; your churchman, the greatest
atheist; and your noisy pert rogue of a wit, the greatest fop, dullest
ass, and worst company—as you shall see; for here he comes.   255

Enter Sparkish to them

SPARKISH How is't, sparks, how is't? Well, faith, Harry, I must rally
thee a little, ha ha ha, upon the report in town of thee, ha ha ha—I
can't hold i'faith; shall I speak?

HORNER Yes, but you'll be so bitter then.

SPARKISH Honest Dick and Frank here shall answer for me; I will   260
not be extreme bitter, by the universe.

HARCOURT We will be bound in ten thousand pound bond, he shall
not be bitter at all.

DORILANT Nor sharp, nor sweet.

HORNER What, not downright insipid?   265

SPARKISH Nay then, since you are so brisk, and provoke me, take
what follows. You must know, I was discoursing and rallying with
some ladies yesterday, and they happened to talk of the fine new
signs in town.

HORNER Very fine ladies, I believe.°   270

SPARKISH Said I, 'I know where the best new sign is.' 'Where?' says
one of the ladies. 'In Covent Garden,' I replied. Said another, 'In

what street?' 'In Russell Street,' answered I. 'Lord,' says another,
'I'm sure there was ne'er a fine new sign there yesterday.' 'Yes, but
there was,' said I again, 'and it came out of France, and has been   275
there a fortnight.'

DORILANT A pox, I can hear no more, prithee.

HORNER No, hear him out; let him tune his crowd a while.

HARCOURT The worst music, the greatest preparation.

SPARKISH Nay, faith, I'll make you laugh. 'It cannot be,' says a third   280
lady. 'Yes, yes,' quoth I again. Says a fourth lady—

HORNER Look to't, we'll have no more ladies.

SPARKISH No?—Then mark, mark now. Said I to the fourth, 'Did
you never see Mr Horner? He lodges in Russell Street, and he's a
sign of a man, you know, since he came out of France.' He ha he!   285

HORNER But the devil take me, if thine be the sign of a jest.

SPARKISH With that they all fell a-laughing, till they bepissed
themselves. What, but it does not move you, methinks? Well, I°
see one had as good go to law without a witness, as break a jest
without a laugher on one's side. Come, come, sparks, but where do   290
we dine? I have left at Whitehall an earl, to dine with you.

DORILANT Why, I thought thou hadst loved a man with a title better
than a suit with a French trimming to't.

HARCOURT Go to him again.°

SPARKISH No sir, a wit to me is the greatest title in the world.   295

HORNER But go dine with your earl, sir; he may be exceptious. We
are your friends, and will not take it ill to be left, I do assure you.

HARCOURT Nay, faith, he shall go to him.

SPARKISH Nay, pray, gentlemen.

DORILANT We'll thrust you out if you won't. What, disappoint   300
anybody for us?

SPARKISH Nay, dear gentlemen, hear me.

HORNER No, no, sir, by no means. Pray go, sir.

SPARKISH Why, dear rogues—

DORILANT No, no.   305

    They all thrust him out of the room

ALL Ha ha ha!

    Sparkish returns

SPARKISH But, sparks, pray hear me. What, d'ye think I'll eat then
with gay shallow fops, and silent coxcombs? I think wit as necessary
at dinner as a glass of good wine, and that's the reason I never have
any stomach when I eat alone. Come, but where do we dine?   310

HORNER Even where you will.

SPARKISH At Chateline's.

DORILANT Yes, if you will.

SPARKISH Or at the Cock.

DORILANT Yes, if you please.   315

SPARKISH Or at the Dog and Partridge.°

HORNER Ay, if you have a° mind to't, for we shall dine at neither.

SPARKISH Pshaw, with your fooling we shall lose the new play—and
I would no more miss seeing a new play the first day, than I would
miss sitting in the wits' row.° Therefore I'll go fetch my mistress,   320
and away.

    Exit Sparkish. Enter Pinchwife°

HORNER Who have we here? Pinchwife?

PINCHWIFE Gentlemen, your humble servant.

HORNER Well, Jack, by the long absence from the town, the grumness of thy countenance, and the slovenliness of thy habit, I should   325
give thee joy, should I not, of marriage?

PINCHWIFE (*aside*) Death, does he know I'm married too? I thought
to have concealed it from him at least. [*Aloud*] My long stay in
the country will excuse my dress, and I have a suit of law that
brings me up to town—*that* puts me out of humour. Besides, I   330
must give Sparkish tomorrow five thousand pound° to lie with my
sister.

HORNER Nay, you country gentlemen, rather than not purchase, will
buy anything; and he is a cracked title,° if we may quibble. Well,
but am I to give thee joy? I heard thou wert married.   335

PINCHWIFE What then?

HORNER Why, the next thing that is to be heard is—thou'rt a
cuckold.

PINCHWIFE (*aside*) Insupportable name.

HORNER But I did not expect marriage from such a whoremaster as   340
you, one that knew the town so much, and women so well.

PINCHWIFE Why, I have married no London wife.

HORNER Pshaw, that's all one; that grave circumspection in marrying
a country wife, is like refusing a deceitful, pampered Smithfield
jade,° to go and be cheated by a friend in the country.   345

PINCHWIFE (*aside*) A pox on him and his simile! [*Aloud*] At least we
are a little surer of the breed there, know what her keeping has
been, whether foiled or unsound.

HORNER Come, come, I have known a clap gotten in Wales;° and
there are cousins,° justices' clerks,° and chaplains in the country—I   350
won't say coachmen.° But she's handsome and young?

PINCHWIFE (*aside*) I'll answer as I should do.—No, no, she has no beauty but her youth; no attraction but her modesty; wholesome, homely, and housewifely, that's all.

DORILANT [*apart to Harcourt*] He talks as like a grazier° as he looks.   355

PINCHWIFE She's too awkward, ill-favoured, and silly to bring to town.

[HORNER]° Then methinks you should bring her, to be taught breeding.°

PINCHWIFE To be taught—? No, sir, I thank you; good wives, and   360
private soldiers, should be ignorant. (*Aside*) I'll keep her from your instructions, I warrant you.

HARCOURT (*aside* [*to Dorilant*]) The rogue is as jealous as if his wife were not ignorant.

HORNER Why, if she be ill-favoured, there will be less danger here   365
for you than by leaving her in the country; we have such variety of dainties that we are seldom hungry.

DORILANT But they have always coarse, constant, swingeing stomachs in the country.

HARCOURT Foul feeders indeed.   370

DORILANT And your hospitality is great there.

HARCOURT Open house, every man's welcome.

PINCHWIFE So, so, gentlemen.

HORNER But prithee, why wouldst thou marry her? If she be ugly, ill-bred, and silly, she must be rich then.   375

PINCHWIFE As rich as if she brought me twenty thousand pound out of this town; for she'll be as sure not to spend her moderate portion, as a London baggage would be to spend hers, let it be what it would. So 'tis all one. Then because she's ugly, she's the likelier to be my own; and being ill-bred, she'll hate conversation; and   380
since silly and innocent, will not know the difference betwixt a man of one-and-twenty, and one of forty—

HORNER Nine, to my knowledge. But if she be silly, she'll expect as much from a man of forty-nine, as from him of one-and-twenty. But methinks wit is more necessary than beauty, and I think no   385
young woman ugly that has it, and no handsome woman agreeable without it.

PINCHWIFE 'Tis my maxim: he's a fool that marries, but he's a greater that does not marry a fool. What is wit in a wife good for, but to make a man a cuckold?   390

HORNER Yes, to keep it from his knowledge.

PINCHWIFE A fool cannot contrive to make her husband a cuckold.

HORNER No, but she'll club with a man that can; and what is worse, if she cannot make her husband a cuckold, she'll make him jealous, and pass for one—and then 'tis all one.   395

PINCHWIFE Well, well, I'll take care, for one; my wife shall make me no cuckold, though she had your help, Mr Horner. I understand the town, sir.

DORILANT (*aside [to Harcourt]*) His help!

HARCOURT (*aside [to Dorilant]*) He's come newly to town, it seems,   400 and has not heard how things are with him.

HORNER But tell me, has marriage cured thee of whoring, which it seldom does?

HARCOURT 'Tis more than age can do.

HORNER No, the word is, 'I'll marry and live honest'; but a marriage   405 vow is like a penitent gamester's oath, and entering into bonds and penalties to stint himself to such a particular small sum at play for the future, which makes him but the more eager; and not being able to hold out, loses his money again, and his forfeit to boot.

DORILANT Ay, ay, a gamester will be a gamester, whilst his money   410 lasts; and a whoremaster, whilst his vigour.

HARCOURT Nay, I have known 'em, when they are broke,° and can lose no more, keep a-fumbling with the box in their hands, to fool with only, and hinder other gamesters.

DORILANT That had wherewithal to make lusty stakes.   415

PINCHWIFE Well, gentlemen, you may laugh at me, but you shall never lie with my wife; I know the town.

HORNER But prithee, was not the way you were in better? Is not keeping better than marriage?

PINCHWIFE A pox on't, the jades would jilt me; I could never keep   420 a whore to myself.

HORNER So then, you only married to keep a whore to yourself. Well, but let me tell you, women (as you say) are like soldiers, made constant and loyal by good pay, rather than by oaths and covenants. Therefore I'd advise my friends to keep rather than   425 marry—since, too, I find by your example it does not serve one's turn, for I saw you yesterday in the eighteen-penny place° with a pretty country wench.

PINCHWIFE (*aside*) How the devil! Did he see my wife then? I sat there that she might not be seen. But she shall never go to a play   430 again.

HORNER What, dost thou blush, at nine-and-forty, for having been seen with a wench?

DORILANT No, faith, I warrant 'twas his wife, which he seated there
out of sight—for he's a cunning rogue, and understands the town.   435

HARCOURT He blushes; then 'twas his wife—for men are now more
ashamed to be seen with them in public, than with a wench.

PINCHWIFE (*aside*) Hell and damnation! I'm undone, since Horner
has seen her, and they know 'twas she.

HORNER But prithee, was it thy wife? She was exceedingly pretty; I   440
was in love with her at that distance.

PINCHWIFE You are like never to be nearer to her. Your servant,
gentlemen. (*Offers to go*)

HORNER Nay, prithee stay.

PINCHWIFE I cannot; I will not.   445

HORNER Come, you shall dine with us.

PINCHWIFE I have dined already.

HORNER Come, I know thou hast not. I'll treat thee, dear rogue; thou
sha't spend none of thy Hampshire° money today.

PINCHWIFE (*aside*) Treat me! So, he uses me already like his   450
cuckold.

HORNER Nay, you shall not go.

PINCHWIFE I must, I have business at home.
Exit Pinchwife

HARCOURT To beat his wife. He's as jealous of her as a Cheapside°
husband of a Covent Garden wife.°   455

HORNER Why, 'tis as hard to find an old whoremaster without
jealousy and the gout, as a young one without fear or the pox.
As gout in age, from pox in youth proceeds,
So, wenching past, then jealousy succeeds—
The worst disease that love and wenching breeds.   460
Exeunt

2.1

[Pinchwife's lodging]

[Enter] Mrs Pinchwife and Alethea;° Pinchwife peeping behind at the door

MRS PINCHWIFE Pray, sister, where are the best fields and woods to walk in, in London?

ALETHEA A pretty question! Why, sister, Mulberry Garden, and St James's Park; and for close walks, the New Exchange.

MRS PINCHWIFE Pray, sister, tell me why my husband looks so grum here in town?° And keeps me up so close, and will not let me go a-walking, nor let me wear my best gown yesterday?°

ALETHEA Oh, he's jealous, sister.

MRS PINCHWIFE Jealous? What's that?

ALETHEA He's afraid you should love another man.

MRS PINCHWIFE How should he be afraid of my loving another man, when he will not let me see any but himself.

ALETHEA Did he not carry you yesterday to a play?

MRS PINCHWIFE Ay, but we sat amongst ugly people; he would not let me come near the gentry, who sat under us, so that I could not see 'em. He told me, none but naughty women sat there, whom they toused and moused—but I would have ventured, for all that.

ALETHEA But how did you like the play?

MRS PINCHWIFE Indeed I was aweary of the play—but I liked hugeously the actors; they are the goodliest, proper'st men, sister.

ALETHEA Oh, but you must not like the actors, sister!

MRS PINCHWIFE Ay, how should I help it, sister? Pray, sister, when my husband comes in, will you ask leave for me to go a-walking?

ALETHEA *(aside)* A-walking, ha ha! Lord, a country gentlewoman's leisure is the drudgery of a foot-post, and she requires as much airing as her husband's horses.

Enter Pinchwife

But here comes your husband; I'll ask, though I'm sure he'll not grant it.

MRS PINCHWIFE He says he won't let me go abroad, for fear of catching the pox.

ALETHEA Fie! 'The smallpox' you should say.

MRS PINCHWIFE Oh my dear, dear bud,° welcome home. Why dost thou look so froppish? Who has nangered thee? 35

PINCHWIFE You're a fool.

Mrs Pinchwife goes aside, and cries

ALETHEA Faith, so she is, for crying for no fault—poor, tender creature!

PINCHWIFE What, you would have her as impudent as yourself, as arrant a gill-flirt, a gadder, a magpie, and—to say all—a mere 40
notorious town-woman?

ALETHEA Brother, you are my only censurer; and the honour of your family shall sooner suffer in your wife there, than in me, though I take the innocent liberty of the town.

PINCHWIFE Hark you, mistress, do not talk so before my wife. The 45
innocent liberty of the town!

ALETHEA Why, pray, who boasts of any intrigue with me? What lampoon has made my name notorious? What ill women frequent my lodgings? I keep no company with any women of scandalous reputations. 50

PINCHWIFE No, you keep the men of scandalous reputations company.

ALETHEA Where? Would you not have me civil? Answer 'em in a box at the plays? In the drawing-room at Whitehall? In St James's Park, Mulberry Garden, or—

PINCHWIFE Hold, hold; do not teach my wife where the men are to 55
be found. I believe she's the worse for your town documents already. I bid you keep her in ignorance, as I do.

MRS PINCHWIFE Indeed, be not angry with her, bud; she will tell me nothing of the town, though I ask her a thousand times a day.

PINCHWIFE Then you are very inquisitive to know, I find? 60

MRS PINCHWIFE Not I indeed, dear; I hate London. Our place-house in the country is worth a thousand of 't; would I were there again.

PINCHWIFE So you shall, I warrant. But were you not talking of plays, and players, when I came in? [*To Alethea*] You are her 65
encourager in such discourses.

MRS PINCHWIFE No indeed, dear; she chid me just now for liking the player-men.

PINCHWIFE (*aside*) Nay, if she be so innocent as to own to me her liking them, there is no hurt in't.—Come, my poor rogue; but thou 70
lik'st none better than me?

MRS PINCHWIFE Yes, indeed, but I do; the player men are finer folks.

PINCHWIFE But you love none better than me?

MRS PINCHWIFE You are mine own dear bud, and I know you; I 75
hate a stranger.

PINCHWIFE Ay, my dear, you must love me only, and not be like the
naughty town-women, who only hate their husbands, and love
every man else—love plays, visits, fine coaches, fine clothes, fiddles,
balls, treats, and so lead a wicked town-life. 80

MRS PINCHWIFE Nay, if to enjoy all these things be a town-life,
London is not so bad a place, dear.

PINCHWIFE How! If you love me, you must hate London.

ALETHEA [aside] The fool has forbid me discovering to her the
pleasures of the town, and he is now setting her agog upon them 85
himself.

MRS PINCHWIFE But, husband, do the town-women love the player-
men too?

PINCHWIFE Yes, I warrant you.

MRS PINCHWIFE [smiling dreamily] Ay, I warrant you. 90

PINCHWIFE Why, you do not, I hope?

MRS PINCHWIFE No, no, bud. But why have we no player-men in
the country?

PINCHWIFE Ha! Mistress Minx, ask me no more to go to a play.

MRS PINCHWIFE Nay, why, love? I did not care for going; but when 95
you forbid me, you make me (as 'twere) desire it.

ALETHEA (aside) So 'twill be in other things, I warrant.

MRS PINCHWIFE Pray, let me go to a play, dear.

PINCHWIFE Hold your peace; I won't.

MRS PINCHWIFE Why, love? 100

PINCHWIFE Why? I'll tell you.

ALETHEA (aside) Nay, if he tell her, she'll give him more cause to
forbid her that place.

MRS PINCHWIFE Pray, why, dear?

PINCHWIFE First, you like the actors, and the gallants may like you. 105

MRS PINCHWIFE What, a homely country girl? No, bud, nobody will
like me.

PINCHWIFE I tell you, yes, they may.

MRS PINCHWIFE No, no, you jest—I won't believe you; I will go.

PINCHWIFE I tell you then, that one of the lewdest fellows in town, 110
who saw you there, told me he was in love with you.

MRS PINCHWIFE Indeed! Who, who, pray who was't?

PINCHWIFE (aside) I've gone too far, and slipped before I was aware.
How overjoyed she is!

MRS PINCHWIFE Was it any Hampshire gallant, any of our neigh-   115
bours? I promise you, I am beholding to him.

PINCHWIFE I promise you, you lie—for he would but ruin you, as
he has done hundreds. He has no other love for women but
that; such as he, look upon women like basilisks, but to destroy
'em.   120

MRS PINCHWIFE Ay, but if he loves me, why should he ruin me?
Answer me to that. Methinks he should not; I would do him no
harm.

ALETHEA Ha ha ha!

PINCHWIFE 'Tis very well—but I'll keep him from doing you any   125
harm, or me either.

    Enter Sparkish and Harcourt

But here comes company; get you in, get you in.

MRS PINCHWIFE But pray, husband, is he a pretty gentleman that
loves me?

PINCHWIFE In, baggage, in.   130

    Thrusts her in; shuts the door

[*Aside*] What, all the lewd libertines of the town brought to my
lodging by this easy coxcomb! 'Sdeath, I'll not suffer it.

SPARKISH Here, Harcourt, do you approve my choice? [*To Alethea*]
Dear little rogue, I told you I'd bring you acquainted with all my
friends, the wits, and—   135

    Harcourt salutes her

PINCHWIFE [*aside*] Ay, they shall know her, as well as you yourself
will, I warrant you.

SPARKISH This is one of those, my pretty rogue, that are to dance at
your wedding tomorrow; and him you must bid welcome ever, to
what you and I have.   140

PINCHWIFE (*aside*) Monstrous!

SPARKISH Harcourt, how dost thou like her, faith?—Nay, dear, do
not look down; I should hate to have a wife of mine out of
countenance at anything.

PINCHWIFE [*aside*] Wonderful!   145

SPARKISH Tell me, I say, Harcourt, how dost thou like her? Thou
hast stared upon her enough to resolve me.

HARCOURT So infinitely well, that I could wish I had a mistress too,
that might differ from her in nothing—but her love and engagement to you.   150

ALETHEA Sir, Master Sparkish has often told me that his acquaintance were all wits and railleurs; and now I find it.

SPARKISH No, by the universe, madam, he does not rally now; you may believe him. I do assure you, he is the honestest, worthiest, true-hearted gentleman—a man of such perfect honour, he would   155
say nothing to a lady he does not mean.

PINCHWIFE [*aside*] Praising another man to his mistress!

HARCOURT Sir, you are so beyond expectation obliging, that—

SPARKISH Nay, egad, I am sure you do admire her extremely; I see't in your eyes.—He does admire you, madam.—By the world, don't   160
you?

HARCOURT Yes, above the world, or the most glorious part of it, her whole sex—and till now I never thought I should have envied you, or any man about to marry; but you have the best excuse for marriage I ever knew.   165

ALETHEA Nay, now, sir, I'm satisfied you are of the society of the wits and railleurs, since you cannot spare your friend, even when he is but too civil to you. But the surest sign is, since you are an enemy to marriage—for that, I hear, you hate as much as business or bad wine.   170

HARCOURT Truly, madam, I never was an enemy to marriage till now, because marriage was never an enemy to me before.

ALETHEA But why, sir, is marriage an enemy to you now? Because it robs you of your friend here? For you look upon a friend married, as one gone into a monastery, that is, dead to the   175
world.

HARCOURT 'Tis, indeed, because you marry him. I see, madam, you can guess my meaning. I do confess heartily and openly, I wish it were in my power to break the match; by heavens I would.

SPARKISH Poor Frank!   180

ALETHEA Would you be so unkind to me?

HARCOURT No, no, 'tis not because I would be unkind to you.

SPARKISH Poor Frank! No, gad, 'tis only his kindness to me.

PINCHWIFE (*aside*) Great kindness to you, indeed. Insensible fop, let a man make love to his wife to his face!   185

SPARKISH Come, dear Frank, for all my wife there that shall be, thou shalt enjoy me sometimes, dear rogue. By my honour, we men of wit condole for our deceased brother in marriage, as much as for one dead in earnest. I think that was prettily said of me, ha, Harcourt? But come, Frank, be not melancholy for me.   190

HARCOURT No, I assure you I am not melancholy for you.

SPARKISH Prithee, Frank, dost think my wife that shall be, there, a fine person?

HARCOURT I could gaze upon her till I became as blind as you are.

SPARKISH How! As I am! How?   195

HARCOURT Because you are a lover, and true lovers are blind, stock-blind.°

SPARKISH True, true. But, by the world, she has wit too, as well as beauty. Go, go with her into a corner, and try if she has wit; talk to her anything—she's bashful before me.   200

HARCOURT Indeed, if a woman wants wit in a corner, she has it nowhere.

ALETHEA (*aside to Sparkish*) Sir, you dispose of me a little before your time—

SPARKISH Nay, nay, madam, let me have an earnest of your obedi-   205
ence, or—Go, go, madam.

Harcourt courts Alethea aside

PINCHWIFE How, sir! If you are not concerned for the honour of a wife, I am for that of a sister—he shall not debauch her. Be a pander to your own wife! Bring men to her, let 'em make love before your face, thrust 'em into a corner together, then leave 'em   210
in private! Is this your town wit and conduct?

SPARKISH Ha ha ha! A silly wise rogue would make one laugh more than a stark fool, ha ha! I shall burst. Nay, you shall not disturb 'em; I'll vex thee, by the world.

Struggles with Pinchwife to keep him from Harcourt and Alethea

ALETHEA The writings are drawn, sir, settlements made; 'tis too late,   215
sir, and past all revocation.

HARCOURT Then so is my death.

ALETHEA I would not be unjust to him.

HARCOURT Then why to me so?

ALETHEA I have no obligation to you.   220

HARCOURT My love.

ALETHEA I had his before.

HARCOURT You never had it; he wants, you see, jealousy, the only infallible sign of it.°

ALETHEA Love proceeds from esteem. He cannot distrust my virtue.   225
Besides, he loves me, or he would not marry me.

HARCOURT Marrying you is no more sign of his love than bribing your woman, that he may marry you, is a sign of his generosity. Marriage is rather a sign of interest, than love; and he that marries a fortune, covets a mistress, not loves her. But if you take marriage   230
for a sign of love, take it from me immediately.

ALETHEA No, now you have put a scruple in my head.° But in short, sir, to end our dispute, I must marry him; my reputation would suffer in the world else.

HARCOURT No, if you do marry him—with your pardon, madam— 235 your reputation suffers in the world, and you would be thought in necessity for a cloak.°

ALETHEA Nay, now you are rude, sir.—Mr Sparkish, pray come hither; your friend here is very troublesome, and very loving.

HARCOURT (*aside to Alethea*) Hold, hold— 240

PINCHWIFE D'ye hear that?

SPARKISH Why, d'ye think I'll seem to be jealous, like a country bumpkin?

PINCHWIFE No, rather be a cuckold, like a credulous cit.

HARCOURT Madam, you would not have been so little generous as 245 to have told him?

ALETHEA Yes, since you could be so little generous as to wrong him.

HARCOURT Wrong him! No man can do't, he's beneath an injury—a bubble, a coward, a senseless idiot, a wretch so contemptible to all the world but you, that— 250

ALETHEA Hold, do not rail at him, for since he is like to be my husband, I am resolved to like him. Nay, I think I am obliged to tell him you are not his friend.—Master Sparkish, Master Sparkish!

SPARKISH What, what? Now, dear rogue, has not she wit?

HARCOURT (*speaks surlily*) Not so much as I thought, and hoped, she 255 had.

ALETHEA Mr Sparkish, do you bring people to rail at you?

HARCOURT Madam—

SPARKISH How! No, but if he does rail at me, 'tis but in jest, I warrant—what we wits do for one another, and never take any 260 notice of it.

ALETHEA He spoke so scurrilously of you, I had no patience to hear him. Besides, he has been making love to me.

HARCOURT (*aside*) True,° damned, tell-tale woman.

SPARKISH Pshaw, to show his parts; we wits rail and make love often, 265 but to show our parts. As we have no affections, so we have no malice; we—

ALETHEA He said you were a wretch, below an injury.

SPARKISH Pshaw.

HARCOURT [*aside*] Damned, senseless, impudent, virtuous jade! 270 Well, since she won't let me have her, she'll do as good: she'll make me hate her.

ALETHEA A common bubble.

SPARKISH Pshaw.

ALETHEA A coward.   275

SPARKISH Pshaw, pshaw.

ALETHEA A senseless, drivelling idiot.

SPARKISH How, did he disparage my parts? Nay, then my honour's
    concerned. I can't put up that, sir, by the world. [*Apart to
    Pinchwife*] Brother, help me to kill him. (*Aside*) I may draw now,   280
    since we have the odds of him. 'Tis a good occasion too, before my
    mistress. (*Offers to draw*)

ALETHEA Hold, hold.

SPARKISH What, what?°

ALETHEA [*aside*] I must not let 'em kill the gentleman, neither, for   285
    his kindness to me. I am so far from hating him, that I wish
    my gallant had his person and understanding. Nay, if my
    honour° . . .

SPARKISH I'll be thy death.

ALETHEA Hold, hold! Indeed, to tell the truth, the gentleman said,   290
    after all,° that what he spoke was but out of friendship to you.

SPARKISH How! Say I am—I am a fool, that is, no wit, out of
    friendship to me?

ALETHEA Yes, to try whether I was concerned enough for you, and
    made love to me only to be satisfied of my virtue, for your sake.   295

HARCOURT (*aside*) Kind, however!

SPARKISH Nay, if it were so, my dear rogue, I ask thee pardon. But
    why would not you tell me so, faith?

HARCOURT Because I did not think on't, faith.

SPARKISH Come; Horner does not come. Harcourt, let's begone to   300
    the new play.—Come, madam.

ALETHEA I will not go, if you intend to leave me alone in the box,
    and run into the pit, as you use to do.

SPARKISH Pshaw, I'll leave Harcourt with you in the box, to
    entertain you, and that's as good. If I sat in the box, I should be   305
    thought no judge but of trimmings.°—Come away, Harcourt; lead
    her down.

    Exeunt Sparkish, Harcourt, and Alethea

PINCHWIFE Well, go thy ways for the flower of the true town fops,
    such as spend their estates before they come to 'em, and are
    cuckolds before they're married. But let me go look to my own   310
    freehold—How!

    Enter Lady Fidget, Dainty Fidget, and Mistress Squeamish°

LADY FIDGET Your servant, sir. Where is your lady? We are come
to wait upon her to the new play.

PINCHWIFE New play!

LADY FIDGET And my husband will wait upon you presently.   315

PINCHWIFE (*aside*) Damn your civility.—Madam, by no means; I
will not see Sir Jasper here, till I have waited upon him at home.
Nor shall my wife see you, till she has waited upon your ladyship
at your lodgings.

LADY FIDGET Now we are here, sir—   320

PINCHWIFE No, madam.

DAINTY FIDGET Pray, let us see her.

MISTRESS SQUEAMISH We will not stir, till we see her.

PINCHWIFE (*aside*) A pox on you all.
      Goes to the door, and returns
She has locked the door, and is gone abroad.   325

LADY FIDGET No, you have locked the door, and she's within.

DAINTY FIDGET They told us below, she was here.

PINCHWIFE (*aside*) Will nothing do? [*Aloud*] Well, it must out then.
To tell you the truth, ladies, which I was afraid to let you know
before, lest it might endanger your lives, my wife has just now the   330
smallpox come out upon her—do not be frightened; but pray
begone, ladies. You shall not stay here in danger of your lives. Pray,
get you gone, ladies.

LADY FIDGET No, no, we have all had 'em.

MISTRESS SQUEAMISH Alack, alack!   335

DAINTY FIDGET Come, come, we must see how it goes with her; I
understand the disease.

LADY FIDGET Come.

PINCHWIFE (*aside*) Well, there is no being too hard for women at
their own weapon, lying; therefore I'll quit the field.   340
      Exit Pinchwife

MISTRESS SQUEAMISH Here's an example of jealousy.

LADY FIDGET Indeed, as the world goes, I wonder there are no more
jealous, since wives are so neglected.

DAINTY FIDGET Pshaw, as the world goes, to what end should they
be jealous?°   345

LADY FIDGET Foh, 'tis a nasty world.

MISTRESS SQUEAMISH That men of parts, great acquaintance, and
quality should take up with, and spend themselves and fortunes in
keeping, little playhouse creatures°—foh!

LADY FIDGET Nay, that women of understanding, great acquaint-   350
ance, and good quality should fall a-keeping too of little creatures—foh!

MISTRESS SQUEAMISH Why, 'tis the men of quality's fault; they
never visit women of honour, and reputation, as they used to do,
and have not so much as common civility for ladies of our rank,   355
but use us with the same indifferency, and ill-breeding, as if we
were all married to 'em.

LADY FIDGET She says true; 'tis an arrant shame women of quality
should be so slighted. Methinks birth, birth should go for something; I have known men admired, courted, and followed for their   360
titles only.

MISTRESS SQUEAMISH Ay, one would think men of honour should
not love, no more than marry, out of their own rank.

DAINTY FIDGET Fie, fie upon 'em; they are come to think cross-
breeding for themselves best, as well as for their dogs and horses.   365

LADY FIDGET They are dogs and horses for't.

MISTRESS SQUEAMISH One would think, if not for love, for vanity a
little.

DAINTY FIDGET Nay, they do satisfy their vanity upon us sometimes, and are kind to us in their report—tell all the world they lie   370
with us.

LADY FIDGET Damned rascals, that we should be only wronged by
'em! To report a man has had a person, when he has not had a
person, is the greatest wrong in the whole world, that can be done
to a person.   375

MISTRESS SQUEAMISH Well, 'tis an arrant shame noble persons
should be so wronged and neglected.

LADY FIDGET But still 'tis an arranter shame for a noble person to
neglect her own honour, and defame her own noble person, with
little inconsiderable fellows—foh!   380

DAINTY FIDGET I suppose the crime against our honour is the same
with a man of quality as with another.

LADY FIDGET How! No sure, the man of quality is likest one's
husband, and therefore the fault should be the less.

DAINTY FIDGET But then the pleasure should be the less.   385

LADY FIDGET Fie, fie, fie, for shame, sister; whither shall we ramble?
Be continent in your discourse, or I shall hate you.

DAINTY FIDGET Besides, an intrigue is so much the more notorious
for the man's quality.

MISTRESS SQUEAMISH 'Tis true, nobody takes notice of a private   390
man, and therefore with him 'tis more secret; and the crime's the
less, when 'tis not known.

LADY FIDGET You say true. I'faith, I think you are in the right on't.
'Tis not an injury to a husband, till it be an injury to our honours;
so that a woman of honour loses no honour with a private person;   395
and to say truth—

DAINTY FIDGET (*apart to Mistress Squeamish*) So the 'little fellow' is
grown a 'private person' with her.

LADY FIDGET But still my dear, dear honour—

    Enter Sir Jasper Fidget, Horner, Dorilant

SIR JASPER Ay, my dear, dear of honour,° thou hast still so much   400
honour in thy mouth—

HORNER (*aside*) That she has none elsewhere.

LADY FIDGET Oh, what d'ye mean, to bring in these upon us?

DAINTY FIDGET Foh, these are as bad as wits.

MISTRESS SQUEAMISH Foh!   405

LADY FIDGET Let us leave the room.

SIR JASPER Stay, stay; faith, to tell you the naked truth—

LADY FIDGET Fie, Sir Jasper, do not use that word 'naked'.

SIR JASPER Well, well; in short, I have business at Whitehall, and
cannot go to the play with you, therefore would have you go—   410

LADY FIDGET With those two to a play?

SIR JASPER No, not with t'other, but with Mr Horner; there can be
no more scandal to go with him, than with Mr Tattle, or Master
Limberham.°

LADY FIDGET With that nasty fellow! No, no.   415

SIR JASPER Nay, prithee dear, hear me. (*Whispers to Lady Fidget*)°

    Horner, Dorilant drawing near Mistress Squeamish and
    Dainty Fidget

HORNER Ladies!

DAINTY FIDGET Stand off.

MISTRESS SQUEAMISH Do not approach us.

DAINTY FIDGET You herd with the wits; you are obscenity all over.   420

MISTRESS SQUEAMISH And I would as soon look upon a picture of
Adam and Eve without fig-leaves, as any of you, if I could help it;
therefore keep off, and do not make us sick.

DORILANT What a devil are these?

HORNER Why, these are pretenders to honour, as critics to wit, only   425
by censuring others; and as every raw, peevish, out-of-humoured,
affected, dull, tea-drinking, arithmetical fop sets up for a wit by

railing at men of sense, so these for honour by railing at the court, and ladies of as great honour as quality.

SIR JASPER Come, Mr Horner, I must desire you to go with these ladies to the play, sir. 430

HORNER I, sir!

SIR JASPER Ay, ay, come, sir.

HORNER I must beg your pardon, sir, and theirs; I will not be seen in women's company in public again, for the world. 435

SIR JASPER Ha ha; strange aversion!

MISTRESS SQUEAMISH No, he's for women's company in private.

SIR JASPER He—poor man—he! Ha ha ha!

DAINTY FIDGET 'Tis a greater shame amongst lewd fellows to be seen in virtuous women's company, than for the women to be seen 440 with them.

HORNER Indeed, madam, the time was I only hated virtuous women; but now I hate the other too—I beg your pardon, ladies.

LADY FIDGET You are very obliging, sir, because we would not be troubled with you. 445

SIR JASPER In sober sadness,° he shall go.

DORILANT Nay, if he won't, I am ready to wait upon the ladies—and I think I am the fitter man.

SIR JASPER You, sir? No, I thank you for that. Master Horner is a privileged man amongst the virtuous ladies; 'twill be a great while 450 before you are so. He he he! He's my wife's gallant, he he he! No, pray withdraw, sir, for (as I take it) the virtuous ladies have no business with you.

DORILANT And I am sure he can have none with them. 'Tis strange a man can't come amongst virtuous women now, but upon the 455 same terms as men are admitted into the Great Turk's° seraglio; but heavens keep me from being an ombre player° with 'em. But where is Pinchwife?

Exit Dorilant

SIR JASPER Come, come, man. What, avoid the sweet society of womankind? That sweet, soft, gentle, tame, noble creature woman, 460 made for man's companion—

HORNER So is that soft, gentle, tame, and more noble creature a spaniel, and has all their tricks—can fawn, lie down, suffer beating and fawn the more; barks at your friends, when they come to see you; makes your bed hard, gives you fleas, and the mange 465 sometimes. And all the difference is, the spaniel's the more faithful animal, and fawns but upon one master.

SIR JASPER He he he!

MISTRESS SQUEAMISH Oh, the rude beast!

DAINTY FIDGET Insolent brute!   470

LADY FIDGET Brute! Stinking, mortified, rotten French wether,° to
dare—

SIR JASPER Hold, an't please your ladyship.—For shame, Master
Horner; your mother was a woman. (*Aside*) Now shall I never
reconcile 'em. [*Apart to Lady Fidget*] Hark you, madam, take my   475
advice in your anger. You know you often want one to make up
your drolling° pack of ombre players; and you may cheat him
easily, for he's an ill gamester, and consequently loves play.
Besides, you know you have but two old civil gentlemen (with
stinking breaths too) to wait upon you abroad. Take in the third   480
into your service; the other° are but crazy. And a lady should have
a supernumerary gentleman-usher, as a supernumerary coach-
horse, lest sometimes you should be forced to stay at home.

LADY FIDGET But are you sure he loves play, and has money?

SIR JASPER He loves play as much as you, and has money as much   485
as I.

LADY FIDGET Then I am contented to make him pay for his
scurrility; money makes up in a measure all other wants in men.
(*Aside*) Those whom we cannot make hold for gallants, we make
fine.°   490

SIR JASPER (*aside*) So, so; now to mollify, to wheedle him.—Master
Horner, will you never keep civil company? Methinks 'tis time
now, since you are only fit for them. Come, come, man, you must
e'en fall to visiting our wives, eating at our tables, drinking tea
with our virtuous relations after dinner, dealing cards to 'em,   495
reading plays and gazettes to 'em, picking fleas out of their shocks
for 'em, collecting receipts, new songs, women, pages, and footmen
for 'em.

HORNER I hope they'll afford me better employment, sir.

SIR JASPER He he he! 'Tis fit you know your work before you come   500
into your place. And since you are unprovided of a lady to flatter,
and a good house to eat at, pray frequent mine, and call my wife
'mistress', and she shall call you 'gallant', according to the custom.

HORNER Who, I?

SIR JASPER Faith, thou sha't for my sake; come for my sake only.   505

HORNER For your sake. [*Bows*]

SIR JASPER [*to Lady Fidget, drawing Horner towards her*] Come,
come, here's a gamester for you. Let him be a little familiar

sometimes—nay, what if a little rude; gamesters may be rude with
ladies, you know.   510

LADY FIDGET Yes, losing gamesters have a privilege with women.

HORNER I always thought the contrary, that the winning gamester
had most privilege with women, for when you have lost your
money to a man, you'll lose anything you have—all you have, they
say, and he may use you as he pleases.   515

SIR JASPER He he he! Well, win or lose, you shall have your liberty
with her.

LADY FIDGET As he behaves himself; and for your sake I'll give him
admittance and freedom.

HORNER All sorts of freedom, madam?   520

SIR JASPER Ay, ay, ay, all sorts of freedom thou canst take—and so,
go to her, begin thy new employment; wheedle her, jest with her,
and be better acquainted one with another.

HORNER (aside) I think I know her already—therefore may venture
with her, my secret for hers.   525

    Horner and Lady Fidget whisper

SIR JASPER Sister, cuz, I have provided an innocent play-fellow for
you there.

DAINTY FIDGET Who, he?

MISTRESS SQUEAMISH There's a playfellow indeed.

SIR JASPER Yes, sure; what, he is good enough to play at cards,   530
blind-man's-buff, or the fool with, sometimes.

MISTRESS SQUEAMISH Foh, we'll have no such playfellows.

DAINTY FIDGET No, sir, you shan't choose playfellows for us, we
thank you.

SIR JASPER Nay, pray hear me. (Whispering to them)°   535

LADY FIDGET [apart to Horner] But, poor gentleman, could you be
so generous? So truly a man of honour, as for the sakes of us
women of honour, to cause yourself to be reported no man? No
man! And to suffer yourself the greatest shame that could fall upon
a man, that none might fall upon us women by your conversation.   540
But indeed, sir, as perfectly, perfectly the same man as before your
going into France, sir? As perfectly, perfectly, sir?

HORNER As perfectly, perfectly, madam. Nay, I scorn you should
take my word; I desire to be tried only, madam.

LADY FIDGET Well, that's spoken again like a man of honour; all   545
men of honour desire to come to the test. But indeed, generally you
men report such things of yourselves, one does not know how, or
whom, to believe; and it is come to that pass, we dare not take your

words, no more than your tailors,° without some staid servant of
yours be bound with you. But I have so strong a faith in your   550
honour, dear, dear, noble sir, that I'd forfeit mine for yours at any
time, dear sir.

HORNER No, madam, you should not need to forfeit it for me; I have
given you security already to save you harmless,° my late reputation being so well known in the world, madam.   555

LADY FIDGET But if upon any future falling out, or upon a suspicion
of my taking the trust out of your hands, to employ some other,
you yourself should betray your trust, dear sir—I mean (if you'll
give me leave to speak obscenely°) you might tell, dear sir.

HORNER If I did, nobody would believe me; the reputation of   560
impotency is as hardly recovered again in the world as that of
cowardice, dear madam.

LADY FIDGET Nay then, as one may say, you may do your worst,
dear, dear sir.

SIR JASPER Come, is your ladyship reconciled to him yet? Have you   565
agreed on matters?—for I must begone to Whitehall.

LADY FIDGET Why, indeed, Sir Jasper, Master Horner is a thousand, thousand times a better man than I thought him.—Cousin
Squeamish, sister Dainty, I can name him now; truly, not long ago
(you know) I thought his very name obscenity, and I would as soon   570
have lain with him, as have named him.

SIR JASPER Very likely, poor madam.

DAINTY FIDGET I believe it.

MISTRESS SQUEAMISH No doubt on't.

SIR JASPER Well, well, that your ladyship is as virtuous as any she,   575
I know; and him all the town knows—he he he! Therefore, now
you like him, get you gone to your business together. Go, go, to
your business, I say—pleasure, whilst I go to my pleasure—business.

LADY FIDGET Come then, dear gallant.   580

HORNER Come away, my dearest mistress.

SIR JASPER So, so; why, 'tis as I'd have it.
        Exit Sir Jasper Fidget

HORNER And as I'd have it.

LADY FIDGET Who, for his business, from his wife will run,
        Takes the best care to have her business done.   585
        Exeunt

3.1

[Pinchwife's lodging]

[Enter] Alethea° and Mrs Pinchwife [at opposite doors]

ALETHEA Sister, what ails you? You are grown melancholy.

MRS PINCHWIFE Would it not make anyone melancholy, to see you
go every day fluttering about abroad, whilst I must stay at home
like a poor, lonely, sullen bird in a cage?

ALETHEA Ay, sister, but you came young, and just from the nest, to   5
your cage, so that I thought you liked it, and could be as cheerful
in't as others that took their flight themselves early, and are
hopping abroad in the open air.

MRS PINCHWIFE Nay, I confess I was quiet enough, till my husband
told me what pure lives the London ladies live abroad, with their   10
dancing, meetings, and junketings, and dressed every day in their
best gowns—and, I warrant you, play at ninepins° every day of the
week, so they do.

Enter Pinchwife

PINCHWIFE Come, what's here to do? You are putting the town
pleasures in her head, and setting her a-longing.   15

ALETHEA Yes, after ninepins. You suffer none to give her those
longings you mean, but yourself.

PINCHWIFE I tell her of the vanities of the town like a confessor.

ALETHEA A confessor! Just such a confessor as he that by forbid-
ding a silly ostler to grease the horses' teeth,° taught him to   20
do't.

PINCHWIFE Come, Mistress Flippant, good precepts are lost when
bad examples are still before us.° The liberty you take abroad
makes her hanker after it, and out of humour at home, poor wretch!
She desired not to come to London; I would bring her.   25

ALETHEA Very well.

PINCHWIFE She has been this week in town, and never desired, till
this afternoon, to go abroad.

ALETHEA Was she not at a play yesterday?

PINCHWIFE Yes, but she ne'er asked me; I was myself the cause of   30
her going.

ALETHEA Then if she ask you again, you are the cause of her asking,
and not my example.

PINCHWIFE Well, tomorrow night I shall be rid of you; and the next

day, before 'tis light, she and I'll be rid of the town, and my   35
dreadful apprehensions. [*To Mrs Pinchwife*] Come, be not melancholy, for thou sha't go into the country after tomorrow, dearest.

ALETHEA Great comfort.

MRS PINCHWIFE Pish, what d'ye tell me of the country for?

PINCHWIFE How's this! What, pish at the country?   40

MRS PINCHWIFE Let me alone, I am not well.

PINCHWIFE Oh, if that be all—what ails my dearest?

MRS PINCHWIFE Truly, I don't know—but I have not been well
since you told me there was a gallant at the play in love with me.

PINCHWIFE Ha!   45

ALETHEA That's by my example too.

PINCHWIFE Nay, if you are not well, but are so concerned because
a lewd fellow chanced to lie, and say he liked you, you'll make me
sick too.

MRS PINCHWIFE Of what sickness?   50

PINCHWIFE Oh, of that which is worse than the plague—jealousy.

MRS PINCHWIFE Pish, you jeer; I'm sure there's no such disease in
our receipt-book at home.

PINCHWIFE No, thou never met'st with it, poor innocent. (*Aside*)
Well, if thou cuckold me, 'twill be my own fault—for cuckolds and   55
bastards are generally makers of their own fortune.

MRS PINCHWIFE Well, but pray, bud, let's go to a play tonight.

PINCHWIFE 'Tis just done°—she comes from it. But why are you so
eager to see a play?

MRS PINCHWIFE Faith, dear, not that I care one pin for their talk   60
there; but I like to look upon the player-men, and would see, if I
could, the gallant you say loves me—that's all, dear bud.

PINCHWIFE Is that all, dear bud?

ALETHEA This proceeds from my example.

MRS PINCHWIFE But if the play be done, let's go abroad however,   65
dear bud.

PINCHWIFE Come, have a little patience, and thou shalt go into the
country on Friday.

MRS PINCHWIFE Therefore I would see first some sights, to tell my
neighbours of. Nay, I *will* go abroad, that's once.   70

ALETHEA I'm the cause of this desire, too.

PINCHWIFE But now I think on't, who was the cause of Horner's
coming to my lodging today? That was you.

ALETHEA No, you—because you would not let him see your handsome wife out of your lodging.   75

MRS PINCHWIFE Why! Oh Lord! Did the gentleman come hither to
see me indeed?

PINCHWIFE No, no.—You are not cause of that damned question
too, Mistress Alethea? (*Aside*) Well, she's in the right of it; he is in
love with my wife, and comes after her—'tis so. But I'll nip his love   80
in the bud, lest he should follow us into the country, and break his
chariot-wheel near our house, on purpose for an excuse to come
to't. But I think I know the town.

MRS PINCHWIFE Come, pray, bud, let's go abroad before 'tis
late—for I *will* go, that's flat and plain.   85

PINCHWIFE (*aside*) So! The obstinacy already of a town wife, and I
must, whilst she's here, humour her like one.—Sister, how shall we
do, that she may not be seen, or known?

ALETHEA Let her put on her mask.

PINCHWIFE Pshaw, a mask makes people but the more inquisitive,   90
and is as ridiculous a disguise as a stage beard. Her shape, stature,
habit will be known. And if we should meet with Horner, he would
be sure to take acquaintance with us, must wish her joy, kiss her,
talk to her, leer upon her, and the devil and all. No, I'll not use her
to a mask, 'tis dangerous; for masks have made more cuckolds than   95
the best faces that ever were known.

ALETHEA How will you do, then?

MRS PINCHWIFE Nay, shall we go? The Exchange will be shut, and
I have a mind to see that.

PINCHWIFE So—I have it; I'll dress her up in the suit we are to carry   100
down to her brother, little Sir James. Nay, I understand the town
tricks. Come, let's go dress her. A mask! No; a woman masked, like
a covered dish, gives a man curiosity and appetite, when (it may
be) uncovered 'twould turn his stomach. No, no.

ALETHEA Indeed, your comparison is something a greasy one. But I   105
had a gentle gallant used to say, a beauty masked, like the sun in
eclipse, gathers together more gazers than if it shined out.

  Exeunt

3.2

The New Exchange.° [*Among the shops and stalls, that of Clasp, a bookseller*]

Enter Horner, Harcourt, Dorilant

DORILANT Engaged to women, and not sup with us?

HORNER Ay, a pox on 'em all.

HARCOURT You were much a more reasonable man in the morning, and had as noble resolutions against 'em as a widower of a week's liberty.   5

DORILANT Did I ever think to see you keep company with women in vain?

HORNER In vain? No; 'tis, since I can't love 'em, to be revenged on 'em.

HARCOURT Now your sting is gone, you looked, in the box amongst   10
all those women, like a drone in the hive—all upon you; shoved and ill-used by 'em all, and thrust from one side to t'other.

DORILANT Yet he must be buzzing amongst 'em still, like other old, beetle-headed, lickerish drones. Avoid 'em, and hate 'em as they hate you.   15

HORNER Because I do hate 'em, and would hate 'em yet more, I'll frequent 'em. You may see by marriage, nothing makes a man hate a woman more, than her constant conversation. In short, I converse with 'em as you do with rich fools, to laugh at 'em, and use 'em ill.   20

DORILANT But I would no more sup with women, unless I could lie with 'em, than sup with a rich coxcomb, unless I could cheat him.

HORNER Yes,° I have known thee sup with a fool, for his drinking; if he could set out your hand that way only,° you were satisfied; and if he were a wine-swallowing mouth, 'twas enough.   25

HARCOURT Yes, a man drinks often with a fool, as he tosses with a marker, only to keep his hand in ure°—but do the ladies drink?

HORNER Yes, sir, and I shall have the pleasure at least of laying 'em flat with a bottle; and bring as much scandal that way upon 'em, as formerly t'other.   30

HARCOURT Perhaps you may prove as weak a brother amongst 'em that way as t'other.

DORILANT Foh, drinking with women is as unnatural as scolding with 'em; 'tis but° a pleasure of decayed fornicators, and the basest way of quenching love.   35

HARCOURT Nay, 'tis drowning love, instead of quenching it. But leave us for civil women too!

DORILANT Ay, when he can't be the better for 'em. We hardly pardon a man that leaves his friend for a wench—and that's a pretty lawful call. 40

HORNER Faith, I would not leave you for 'em, if they would not drink.

DORILANT Who would disappoint his company at Lewis's,° for a gossiping?

HARCOURT Foh, wine and women: good apart, together as nauseous 45 as sack and sugar.° But hark you, sir, before you go, a little of your advice; an old, maimed general, when unfit for action, is fittest for counsel. I have other designs upon women than eating and drinking with them. I am in love with Sparkish's mistress, whom he is to marry tomorrow. Now, how shall I get her? 50

Enter Sparkish, looking about

HORNER Why, here comes one will help you to her.

HARCOURT He! He, I tell you, is my rival, and will hinder my love.

HORNER No, a foolish rival, and a jealous husband, assist their rival's designs; for they are sure to make their women hate them, which is the first step to their love for another man. 55

HARCOURT But I cannot come near his mistress but in his company.

HORNER Still the better for you, for fools are most easily cheated when they themselves are accessories; and he is to be bubbled of his mistress, as of his money (the common mistress), by keeping him company. 60

SPARKISH Who is that, that is to be bubbled? Faith, let me snack; I han't met with a bubble since Christmas. Gad, I think bubbles are like their brother woodcocks—go out with the cold weather.°

HARCOURT (*apart to Horner*) A pox, he did not hear all, I hope!

SPARKISH Come, you bubbling rogues you, where do we sup?—Oh, 65 Harcourt, my mistress tells me you have been making fierce love to her all the play long, ha ha! But I—

HARCOURT I make love to her?

SPARKISH Nay, I forgive thee; for I think I know thee, and I know her, but I am sure I know myself. 70

HARCOURT Did she tell you so? I see all women are like these of the Exchange, who, to enhance the price of their commodities, report to their fond customers offers which were never made 'em.

HORNER Ay, women are as apt to tell before the intrigue, as men after it, and so show themselves the vainer sex. But hast thou a 75

mistress, Sparkish? 'Tis as hard for me to believe it, as that thou
ever hadst a bubble, as you bragged just now.

SPARKISH Oh, your servant, sir. Are you at your raillery, sir? But we
were some of us beforehand with you today at the play; the wits
were something bold with you, sir—did you not hear us laugh?   80

[HORNER]° Yes, but I thought you had gone to plays to laugh at the
poet's wit, not at your own.

SPARKISH Your servant, sir. No, I thank you. Gad, I go to a play as
to a country treat: I carry my own wine to one, and my own wit to
t'other, or else I'm sure I should not be merry at either. And the   85
reason why we are so often louder than the players, is because we
think we speak more wit, and so become the poet's rivals in his
audience. For to tell you the truth, we hate the silly rogues—nay,
so much that we find fault even with their bawdy upon the stage,
whilst we talk nothing else in the pit as loud.   90

HORNER But why shouldst thou hate the silly poets? Thou hast too
much wit to be one, and they, like whores, are only hated by each
other. And thou dost scorn writing, I'm° sure.

SPARKISH Yes, I'd have you to know, I scorn writing. But women,
women, that make men do all foolish things, make 'em write songs   95
too. Everybody does it. 'Tis even as common with lovers as playing
with fans, and you can no more help rhyming to your Phyllis,° than
drinking to your Phyllis.

HARCOURT Nay, poetry in love is no more to be avoided than
jealousy.°   100

DORILANT But the poets damned your songs, did they?

SPARKISH Damn the poets! They turned 'em into burlesque, as they
call it—that burlesque is a hocus-pocus trick they have got, which
by the virtue of *hictius doctius*, topsy-turvy, they make a wise and
witty man in the world, a fool upon the stage, you know not how.   105
And 'tis therefore I hate 'em too, for I know not but it may be my
own case—for they'll put a man into a play for looking asquint.
Their predecessors were contented to make servingmen, only, their
stage fools, but these rogues must have gentlemen—with a pox to
'em—nay, knights. And indeed you shall hardly see a fool upon the   110
stage but he's a knight;° and to tell you the truth, they have kept
me these six years from being a knight in earnest, for fear of being
knighted in a play, and dubbed a fool.

DORILANT Blame 'em not; they must follow their copy, the age.

HARCOURT But why shouldst thou be afraid of being in a play, who   115
expose yourself every day in the playhouses, and as public places?

HORNER 'Tis but being on the stage, instead of standing on a bench in the pit.

DORILANT Don't you give money to painters to draw you like? And are you afraid of your pictures at length in a playhouse, where all your mistresses may see you? 120

SPARKISH A pox, painters don't draw the smallpox, or pimples, in one's face. Come, damn all silly authors whatever, all books and booksellers, by the world, and all readers, courteous or uncourteous.° 125

HARCOURT But who comes here, Sparkish?

Enter Pinchwife, and his wife in man's clothes, Alethea, Lucy her maid

SPARKISH Oh hide me, there's my mistress too.

Sparkish hides himself behind Harcourt

HARCOURT She sees you.

SPARKISH But I will not see her. 'Tis time to go to Whitehall, and I must not fail the drawing-room. 130

HARCOURT Pray, first carry me and reconcile me to her.

SPARKISH Another time—faith, the king will have supped.°

HARCOURT Not with the worse stomach for thy absence. Thou art one of those fools that think their attendance at the king's meals as necessary as his physicians', when you are more troublesome to him 135 than his doctors or his dogs.°

SPARKISH Pshaw, I know my interest, sir; prithee hide me.

HORNER Your servant, Pinchwife.—What, he knows us not!

PINCHWIFE (*to his wife, aside*) Come along.

MRS PINCHWIFE [*to Clasp*] Pray, have you any ballads? Give me six 140 pennyworth.

CLASP° We have no ballads.

MRS PINCHWIFE Then give me *Covent Garden Drollery*,° and a play or two—oh, here's *Tarugo's Wiles*, and *The Slighted Maiden*;° I'll have them. 145

PINCHWIFE (*apart to her*) No, plays are not for your reading. Come along; will you discover yourself?

HORNER Who is that pretty youth with him, Sparkish?

SPARKISH I believe, his wife's brother, because he's something like her—but I never saw her but once. 150

HORNER Extremely handsome; I have seen a face like it too. Let us follow 'em.

Exeunt Pinchwife, Mrs Pinchwife; Alethea, Lucy; Horner, Dorilant following them

HARCOURT Come, Sparkish, your mistress saw you, and will be angry you go not to her. Besides, I would fain be reconciled to her, which none but you can do, dear friend.   155

SPARKISH Well, that's a better reason, dear friend. I would not go near her now, for hers or my own sake: but I can deny you nothing—for though I have known thee a great while, never go, if I do not love thee as well as a new acquaintance.

HARCOURT I am obliged to you indeed, dear friend; I would be well   160 with her, only to be well with thee still, for these ties to wives usually dissolve all ties to friends. I would be contented she should enjoy you a-nights, but I would have you to myself a-days, as I have had, dear friend.

SPARKISH And thou shalt enjoy me a-days, dear, dear friend, never   165 stir; and I'll be divorced from her, sooner than from thee. Come along—

HARCOURT (aside) So, we are hard put to't, when we make our rival our procurer. But neither she, nor her brother, would let me come near her now. When all's done, a rival is the best cloak to steal to   170 a mistress under, without suspicion; and when we have once got to her as we desire, we throw him off like other cloaks.

> *Exit Sparkish, and Harcourt following him. Re-enter*
> *Pinchwife, Mrs Pinchwife in man's clothes*

PINCHWIFE ([*calling*] *to Alethea*) Sister, if you will not go, we must leave you. (*Aside*) The fool her gallant, and she, will muster up all the young saunterers of this place, and they will leave their dear   175 seamstresses,° to follow us. What a swarm of cuckolds and cuckold-makers are here!—Come, let's begone, Mistress Margery.

MRS PINCHWIFE Don't you believe that; I ha'n't half my bellyful of sights yet.

PINCHWIFE Then walk this way.   180

MRS PINCHWIFE Lord, what a power of brave signs are here! Stay—the Bull's Head, the Ram's Head, and the Stag's Head, dear.

PINCHWIFE Nay, if every husband's proper sign here were visible, they would be all alike.   185

MRS PINCHWIFE What d'ye mean by that, bud?

PINCHWIFE 'Tis no matter, no matter, bud.

MRS PINCHWIFE Pray tell me; nay, I will know.

PINCHWIFE They would be all bulls', stags', and rams' heads.

> *Exeunt Pinchwife, Mrs Pinchwife. Re-enter Sparkish,*
> *Harcourt, Alethea, Lucy at t'other door*

SPARKISH Come, dear madam, for my sake you shall be reconciled 190
to him.

ALETHEA For your sake I hate him.

HARCOURT That's something too cruel, madam, to hate me for his
sake.

SPARKISH Ay indeed, madam, too, too cruel to me, to hate my friend 195
for my sake.

ALETHEA I hate him because he is your enemy—and you ought to
hate him too, for making love to me, if you love me.

SPARKISH That's a good one! I, hate a man for loving you? If he did
love you, 'tis but what he can't help, and 'tis your fault, not his, if 200
he admires you. I, hate a man for being of my opinion? I'll ne'er
do't, by the world.

ALETHEA Is it for your honour, or mine, to suffer a man to make love
to me, who am to marry you tomorrow?

SPARKISH Is it for your honour, or mine, to have me jealous? That 205
he makes love to you is a sign you are handsome; and that I am not
jealous is a sign you are virtuous—that, I think, is for your honour.

ALETHEA But 'tis your honour too I am concerned for.

HARCOURT But why, dearest madam, will you be more concerned for
his honour than he is himself? Let his honour alone for my sake, 210
and his; he, he has no honour—

SPARKISH How's that?

HARCOURT But what my dear friend can guard himself.

SPARKISH Oh ho, that's right again.

HARCOURT Your care of his honour argues his neglect of it, which 215
is no honour to my dear friend here. Therefore, once more, let his
honour go which way it will, dear madam.

SPARKISH Ay, ay; were it for my honour to marry a woman whose
virtue I suspected, and could not trust her in a friend's hands?

ALETHEA Are you not afraid to lose me? 220

HARCOURT He afraid to lose you, madam! No, no—you may see how
the most estimable, and most glorious creature in the world is
valued by him; will you not see it?

SPARKISH Right, honest Frank; I have that noble value for her, that
I cannot be jealous of her. 225

ALETHEA You mistake him; he means you care not for me, nor who
has me.

SPARKISH Lord, madam, I see you are jealous. Will you wrest a poor
man's meaning from his words?

ALETHEA You astonish me, sir, with your want of jealousy. 230

SPARKISH And you make me giddy, madam, with your jealousy, and fears, and virtue, and honour. Gad, I see virtue makes a woman as troublesome as a little reading or learning.

ALETHEA Monstrous!

LUCY (*behind*) Well, to see what easy husbands these women of   235
quality can meet with! A poor chambermaid can never have such ladylike luck. Besides, he's thrown away upon her—she'll make no use of her fortune, her blessing. None to a gentleman for° a pure cuckold, for it requires good breeding to be a cuckold.

ALETHEA I tell you then plainly, he pursues me to marry me.   240

SPARKISH Pshaw!

HARCOURT Come, madam, you see you strive in vain to make him jealous of me. My dear friend is the kindest creature in the world to me.

SPARKISH Poor fellow.   245

HARCOURT But his kindness only is not enough for me, without your favour. Your good opinion, dear madam—'tis that must perfect my happiness. Good gentleman, he believes all I say; would you would do so. Jealous of me! I would not wrong him nor you for the world.

SPARKISH Look you there.   250

Alethea walks carelessly to and fro

Hear him, hear him, and do not walk away so.

HARCOURT I love you, madam, so—

SPARKISH How's that? Nay, now you begin to go too far indeed.

HARCOURT So much, I confess, I say I love you, that I would not have you miserable, and cast yourself away upon so unworthy and   255
inconsiderable a thing as what you see here. (*Clapping his hand on his breast, points at Sparkish*)

SPARKISH No, faith, I believe thou wouldst not. [*To Alethea*] Now his meaning is plain. [*To Harcourt*] But I knew before, thou wouldst not wrong me nor her.   260

HARCOURT No, no, heavens forbid the glory of her sex should fall so low as into the embraces of such a contemptible wretch, the last° of mankind! My dear friend here—I injure him?

Embracing Sparkish

ALETHEA Very well.

SPARKISH No, no, dear friend.—I knew it, madam; you see he will   265
rather wrong himself than me, in giving himself such names.

ALETHEA Do not you understand him yet?

SPARKISH Yes, how modestly he speaks of himself, poor fellow.

ALETHEA Methinks he speaks impudently of yourself, since—before°

yourself too, insomuch that I can no longer suffer his scurrilous   270
abusiveness to you, no more than his love to me. (*Offers to go*)

SPARKISH Nay, nay, madam, pray stay. His love to you? Lord,
madam, has he not spoke yet plain enough?

ALETHEA Yes indeed, I should think so.

SPARKISH Well then, by the world, a man can't speak civilly to a   275
woman now, but presently she says he makes love to her. Nay,
madam, you shall stay, with your pardon, since you have not yet
understood him, till he has made an *éclaircissement* of his love to
you—that is, what kind of love it is. [*To Harcourt*] Answer to thy
catechism: friend, do you love my mistress here?   280

HARCOURT Yes, I wish she would not doubt it.

SPARKISH But how do you love her?

HARCOURT With all my soul.

ALETHEA I thank him; methinks he speaks plain enough now.

SPARKISH (*to Alethea*) You are out still.—But with what kind of love,   285
Harcourt?

HARCOURT With the best and truest love in the world.

SPARKISH Look you there, then—that is, with no matrimonial love,
I'm sure.

ALETHEA How's that? Do you say matrimonial love is not best?   290

SPARKISH Gad, I went too far ere I was aware. But speak for thyself,
Harcourt; you said you would not wrong me, nor her.

HARCOURT No, no, madam, e'en take him for heaven's sake—

SPARKISH Look you there, madam.

HARCOURT Who should in all justice be yours; he that loves you   295
most. (*Claps his hand on his breast*)

ALETHEA Look you there, Mr Sparkish; who's that?

SPARKISH Who should it be? Go on, Harcourt.

HARCOURT Who loves you more than women titles, or Fortune
fools.° (*Points at Sparkish*)   300

SPARKISH Look you there—he means me still, for he points at me.

ALETHEA Ridiculous!

HARCOURT Who can only match your faith and constancy in love.

SPARKISH Ay.

HARCOURT Who knows, if it be possible, how to value so much   305
beauty and virtue.

SPARKISH Ay.

HARCOURT Whose love can no more be equalled in the world, than
that heavenly form of yours.

SPARKISH No.   310

HARCOURT Who could no more suffer a rival than your absence, and yet could no more suspect your virtue than his own constancy in his love to you.

SPARKISH No.

HARCOURT Who, in fine, loves you better than his eyes, that first made him love you.

SPARKISH Ay.—Nay, madam, faith you shan't go, till—

ALETHEA Have a care, lest you make me stay too long—

SPARKISH But till he has saluted you, that I may be assured you are friends,° after his honest advice and declaration.°

Enter Pinchwife, Mrs Pinchwife

Come, pray, madam, be friends with him.

ALETHEA You must pardon me, sir, that I am not yet so obedient to you.

PINCHWIFE What, invite your wife to kiss men? Monstrous! Are you not ashamed? I will never forgive you.

SPARKISH Are you not ashamed, that I should have more confidence in the chastity of your family than you have? You must not teach me. I am a man of honour, sir, though I am frank and free;° I am frank, sir—

PINCHWIFE Very frank, sir, to share your wife with your friends.

SPARKISH He is an humble, menial° friend, such as reconciles the differences of the marriage-bed. You know man and wife do not always agree; I design him for that use, therefore would have him well with my wife.

PINCHWIFE A menial friend! You will get a great many menial friends, by showing your wife as you do.

SPARKISH What then? It may be I have a pleasure in't, as I have to show fine clothes at a playhouse the first day,° and count money before poor rogues.

PINCHWIFE He that shows his wife, or money, will be in danger of having them borrowed sometimes.

SPARKISH I love to be envied, and would not marry a wife that I alone could love. Loving alone is as dull as eating alone. Is it not a frank age? And I am a frank person. And to tell you the truth, it may be I love to have rivals in a wife; they make her seem to a man still but as a kept mistress. And so, good night, for I must to Whitehall. Madam, I hope you are now reconciled to my friend. And so I wish you a good night, madam, and sleep if you can, for tomorrow, you know, I must visit you early with a canonical gentleman.°—Good night, dear Harcourt.

Exit Sparkish

HARCOURT Madam, I hope you will not refuse my visit tomorrow, if it should be earlier, with a canonical gentleman, than Mr Sparkish's.

PINCHWIFE (*coming between Alethea and Harcourt*) This gentle- 355
woman is yet under my care; therefore you must yet forbear your freedom with her, sir.

HARCOURT Must, sir?°

PINCHWIFE Yes, sir, she is my sister.

HARCOURT 'Tis well she is, sir—for I must be her servant, sir. Madam— 360

PINCHWIFE Come away, sister. We had been gone, if it had not been for you—

Enter Horner, Dorilant to them

and so avoided these lewd rakehells who seem to haunt us.

HORNER How now, Pinchwife?

PINCHWIFE Your servant. 365

HORNER What, I see a little time in the country makes a man turn wild and unsociable, and only fit to converse with his horses, dogs, and his herds.

PINCHWIFE I have business, sir, and must mind it. Your business is pleasure; therefore you and I must go different ways. 370

HORNER Well, you may go on, but this pretty young gentleman—

Takes hold of Mrs Pinchwife

HARCOURT The lady—

DORILANT And the maid—

HORNER Shall stay with us, for I suppose their business is the same with ours: pleasure. 375

PINCHWIFE (*aside*) 'Sdeath, he knows her, she carries it so sillily; yet if he does not, I should be more silly to discover it first.

ALETHEA [*to Harcourt*] Pray, let us go, sir.

PINCHWIFE Come, come—

HORNER (*to Mrs Pinchwife*) Had you not rather stay with us?— 380
Prithee, Pinchwife, who is this pretty young gentleman?

PINCHWIFE One to whom I'm a guardian. (*Aside*) I wish I could keep her out of your hands.

HORNER Who is he? I never saw anything so pretty in all my life.

PINCHWIFE Pshaw, do not look upon him so much. He's a poor 385
bashful youth; you'll put him out of countenance.—Come away, brother.

Offers to take her away

HORNER Oh, your brother!

PINCHWIFE Yes, my wife's brother.—Come, come, she'll stay supper for us.   390

HORNER I thought so, for he is very like her I saw you at the play with—whom I told you I was in love with.

MRS PINCHWIFE (*aside*) Oh Jeminy! Is this he that was in love with me? I am glad on't, I vow, for he's a curious fine gentleman, and I love him already too. (*To Pinchwife*) Is this he, bud?   395

PINCHWIFE (*to his wife*) Come away, come away.

HORNER Why, what haste are you in! Why won't you let me talk with him?

PINCHWIFE Because you'll debauch him; he's yet young and innocent, and I would not have him debauched for anything in the world. (*Aside*) How she gazes on him! The devil!   400

HORNER Harcourt, Dorilant, look you here; this is the likeness of that dowdy he told us of, his wife. Did you ever see a lovelier creature? The rogue has reason to be jealous of his wife, since she is like him, for she would make all that see her, in love with her.   405

HARCOURT And as I remember now, she is as like him here as can be.

DORILANT She is indeed very pretty, if she be like him.

HORNER 'Very pretty'? A very pretty commendation! She is a glorious creature, beautiful beyond all things I ever beheld.   410

PINCHWIFE So, so.

HARCOURT More beautiful than a poet's first mistress of imagination.

HORNER Or another man's last mistress of flesh and blood.

MRS PINCHWIFE Nay, now you jeer, sir. Pray don't jeer me—   415

PINCHWIFE Come, come. (*Aside*) By heavens, she'll discover herself.

HORNER [*to Mrs Pinchwife*] I speak of your sister, sir.

PINCHWIFE Ay, but saying she was handsome, if like him, made him blush. (*Aside*) I am upon a rack!

HORNER Methinks he is so handsome, he should not be a man.   420

PINCHWIFE [*aside*] Oh, there 'tis out; he has discovered her. I am not able to suffer any longer. (*To his wife*) Come, come away, I say.

HORNER Nay, by your leave, sir, he shall not go yet. ([*Apart*] *to them*) Harcourt, Dorilant, let us torment this jealous rogue a little.

HARCOURT, DORILANT How?   425

HORNER I'll show you.

PINCHWIFE Come, pray let him go. I cannot stay fooling any longer—I tell you his sister stays supper for us.

HORNER Does she? Come then, we'll all go sup with her and thee.

PINCHWIFE No, now I think on't—having stayed so long for us, I   430
warrant she's gone to bed. (*Aside*) I wish she and I were well out
of their hands. [*To his wife*] Come, I must rise early tomorrow;
come.

HORNER Well then, if she be gone to bed, I wish her and you a good
night. But pray, young gentleman, present my humble service to   435
her.

MRS PINCHWIFE Thank you heartily, sir.

PINCHWIFE (*aside*) 'Sdeath, she will discover herself yet, in spite of
me. [*To Horner*] He is something more civil to you, for your
kindness to his sister, than I am, it seems.   440

HORNER Tell her, dear, sweet little gentleman, for all your brother
there, that you have revived the love I had for her at first sight in
the playhouse.

MRS PINCHWIFE But did you love her indeed, and indeed?

PINCHWIFE (*aside*) So, so.—Away, I say.   445

HORNER Nay, stay. Yes, indeed, and indeed; pray do you tell her so,
and give her this kiss from me. (*Kisses her*)

PINCHWIFE (*aside*) Oh heavens! What do I suffer! Now 'tis too plain
he knows her, and yet—

HORNER And this, and this. (*Kisses her again*)   450

MRS PINCHWIFE What do you kiss me for? I am no woman.

PINCHWIFE (*aside*) So, there 'tis out.—Come, I cannot, nor will stay
any longer.

HORNER Nay, they shall send your lady a kiss too.—Here, Harcourt,
Dorilant, will you not?   455

   They kiss her

PINCHWIFE (*aside*) How! Do I suffer this? Was I not accusing
another just now for this° rascally patience, in permitting his wife
to be kissed before his face? Ten thousand ulcers gnaw away their
lips!—Come, come.

HORNER Good night, dear little gentleman. [*To Alethea*] Madam,   460
good night.—Farewell, Pinchwife. (*Apart to Harcourt and Dorilant*)
Did not I tell you I would raise his jealous gall?

   Exeunt Horner, Harcourt, and Dorilant

PINCHWIFE So, they are gone at last; stay, let me see first if the coach
be at this door.

   Exit Pinchwife. Horner, Harcourt, Dorilant return

HORNER What, not gone yet? Will you be sure to do as I desired you,   465
sweet sir?

MRS PINCHWIFE 'Sweet sir'—but what will you give me then?

HORNER Anything; come away into the next walk.

Exit Horner, hauling away Mrs Pinchwife

ALETHEA Hold, hold—what d'ye do?

LUCY Stay, stay, hold—   470

HARCOURT Hold, madam, hold; let him present him. He'll come presently. Nay, I will never let you go, till you answer my question.

Alethea, Lucy struggling with Harcourt and Dorilant

LUCY For God's sake, sir, I must follow 'em.

DORILANT No, I have something to present you with too; you shan't   475
follow them.

Pinchwife returns

PINCHWIFE Where—? How—? What's become of—? Gone! Whither?

LUCY He's only gone with the gentleman, who will give him something, an't please your worship.

PINCHWIFE Something! Give him something, with a pox! Where are   480
they?

ALETHEA In the next walk only, brother.

PINCHWIFE Only, only! Where, where?

Exit Pinchwife, and returns presently, then goes out again

HARCOURT What's the matter with him? Why so much concerned?
But, dearest madam—   485

ALETHEA Pray let me go, sir; I have said and suffered enough already.

HARCOURT Then you will not look upon, nor pity, my sufferings?

ALETHEA To look upon 'em, when I cannot help 'em, were cruelty, not pity; therefore I will never see you more.   490

HARCOURT Let me then, madam, have my privilege of a banished lover: complaining or railing, and giving you but a farewell reason why, if you cannot condescend to marry me, you should not take that wretch my rival.

ALETHEA He only, not you, since my honour is engaged so far to   495
him, can give me a reason why I should not marry him. But if he be true, and what I think him to me, I must be so to him. Your servant, sir.

HARCOURT Have women only constancy when 'tis a vice, and, like Fortune, only true to fools?   500

DORILANT (*to Lucy, who struggles to get from him*) Thou sha't not stir, thou robust creature. You see I can deal with you; therefore you should stay the rather, and be kind.

Enter Pinchwife

PINCHWIFE Gone, gone, not to be found—quite gone. Ten thousand
plagues go with 'em. Which way went they?   505

ALETHEA But into t'other walk, brother.

LUCY Their business will be done presently, sure, an't please your
worship. It can't be long in doing, I'm sure on't.

ALETHEA Are they not there?

PINCHWIFE No—you know where they are, you infamous wretch,   510
eternal shame of your family, which you do not dishonour enough
yourself, you think, but you must help her to do it too, thou legion°
of bawds.

ALETHEA Good brother!

PINCHWIFE Damned, damned sister!   515

ALETHEA Look you here, she's coming.

*Enter Mrs Pinchwife in man's clothes, running, with her hat
under her arm full of oranges and dried fruit,° Horner
following*

MRS PINCHWIFE Oh dear bud, look you here what I have got—see.

PINCHWIFE (*aside, rubbing his forehead*) And what I have got here,
too, which you can't see.

MRS PINCHWIFE The fine gentleman has given me better things yet.   520

PINCHWIFE Has he so? (*Aside*) Out of breath, and coloured! I must
hold yet.

HORNER I have only given your little brother an orange, sir.

PINCHWIFE (*to Horner*) Thank you, sir. (*Aside*) You have only
squeezed my orange,° I suppose, and given it me again. Yet I must   525
have a City patience.° (*To his wife*) Come, come away—

MRS PINCHWIFE Stay till I have put up my fine things, bud.

Enter Sir Jasper Fidget

SIR JASPER Oh, Master Horner, come, come, the ladies stay for you;
your mistress—my wife—wonders you make not more haste to her.

HORNER I have stayed this half-hour for you here, and 'tis your fault   530
I am not now with your wife.

SIR JASPER But pray, don't let her know so much; the truth on't is, I
was advancing a certain project to his Majesty, about—I'll tell you—

HORNER No, let's go and hear it at your house. [*To Mrs Pinchwife*]
Good night, sweet little gentleman. One kiss more. (*Kisses her*)   535
You'll remember me now, I hope.°

DORILANT What, Sir Jasper, will you separate friends? He promised
to sup with us—and if you take him to your house, you'll be in
danger of our company too.

SIR JASPER Alas, gentlemen, my house is not fit for you; there are   540
  none but civil women there, which are not for your turn. He, you
  know, can bear with the society of civil women, now, ha ha ha!
  Besides, he's one of my family—he's—heh heh heh!

DORILANT What is he?

SIR JASPER Faith, my eunuch, since you'll have it, heh heh heh!   545
  Exeunt Sir Jasper Fidget and Horner

DORILANT I rather wish thou wert his, or my, cuckold. Harcourt,
  what a good cuckold is lost there, for want of a man to make him
  one. Thee and I cannot have Horner's privilege, who can make use
  of it.

HARCOURT Ay, to poor Horner 'tis like coming to an estate at   550
  threescore, when a man can't be the better for 't.

PINCHWIFE Come.

MRS PINCHWIFE Presently, bud.

DORILANT Come, let us go too. (*To Alethea*) Madam, your servant.
  (*To Lucy*) Good night, strapper°—   555

HARCOURT Madam, though you will not let me have a good day, or
  night, I wish you one—but dare not name the other half of my
  wish.

ALETHEA Good night, sir, for ever.

MRS PINCHWIFE I don't know where to put this; here, dear bud, you   560
  shall eat it. [*Offers him an orange*] Nay, you shall have part of the
  fine gentleman's good things, or treat as you call it, when we come
  home.

PINCHWIFE Indeed I deserve it, since I furnished the best part of it.
  (*Strikes away the orange*)   565
      The gallant treats, presents, and gives the ball—
      But 'tis the absent cuckold pays for all.
  [*Exeunt*]

4.1

In Pinchwife's house, in the morning

[Enter] Lucy, [and] Alethea dressed in new clothes

LUCY Well—°madam, now have I dressed you, and set you out with
so many ornaments, and spent upon you ounces of essence and
pulvilio; and all this for no other purpose but as people adorn and
perfume a corpse for a stinking, second-hand grave°—such, or as
bad, I think Master Sparkish's bed.   5

ALETHEA Hold your peace.

LUCY Nay, madam, I will ask you the reason why you would banish
poor Master Harcourt for ever from your sight. How could you be
so hard-hearted?

ALETHEA 'Twas because I was not hard-hearted.   10

LUCY No, no—'twas stark love and kindness, I warrant.

ALETHEA It was so; I would see him no more, because I love
him.

LUCY Hey-day! A very pretty reason.

ALETHEA You do not understand me.   15

LUCY I wish you may yourself.

ALETHEA I was engaged to marry, you see, another man, whom my
justice will not suffer me to deceive, or injure.

LUCY Can there be a greater cheat or wrong done to a man, than to
give him your person without your heart? I should make a   20
conscience of it.

ALETHEA I'll retrieve it for him after I am married awhile.

LUCY The woman that marries to love better, will be as much
mistaken as the wencher that marries to live better. No, madam;
marrying to increase love is like gaming to become rich—alas, you   25
only lose what little stock you had before.

ALETHEA I find, by your rhetoric, you have been bribed to betray
me.

LUCY Only by his merit, that has bribed your heart (you see) against
your word and rigid honour. But what a devil is this honour? 'Tis   30
sure a disease in the head, like the megrim, or falling-sickness, that
always hurries people away to do themselves mischief. Men lose
their lives by it; women what's dearer to 'em, their love, the life of
life.

ALETHEA Come, pray talk you no more of honour, nor Master   35
Harcourt. I wish the other would come, to secure my fidelity to
him, and his right in me.

LUCY You will marry him, then?

ALETHEA Certainly. I have given him already my word, and will my
hand too, to make it good when he comes.   40

LUCY Well, I wish I may never stick pin more, if he be not an arrant
natural to° t'other fine gentleman.

ALETHEA I own he wants the wit of Harcourt, which I will dispense
withal for another want he has, which is want of jealousy, which
men of wit seldom want.   45

LUCY Lord, madam, what should you do with a fool to your
husband? You intend to be honest, don't you? Then that husbandly
virtue, credulity, is thrown away upon you.

ALETHEA He only that could suspect my virtue should have cause to
do it; 'tis Sparkish's confidence in my truth that obliges me to be   50
so faithful to him.

LUCY You are not sure his opinion may last.

ALETHEA I am satisfied 'tis impossible for him to be jealous, after the
proofs I have had of him. Jealousy in a husband—heaven defend
me from it; it begets a thousand plagues to a poor woman: the loss   55
of her honour, her quiet, and her—

LUCY And her pleasure.

ALETHEA What d'ye mean, impertinent?

LUCY Liberty is a great pleasure, madam.

ALETHEA I say loss of her honour, her quiet, nay, her life sometimes;   60
and what's as bad almost, the loss of this town—that is, she is sent
into the country, which is the last ill usage of a husband to a wife,
I think.

LUCY (aside) Oh, does the wind lie there?—Then of necessity,
madam, you think a man must carry his wife into the country, if   65
he be wise. The country is as terrible, I find, to our young English
ladies, as a monastery to those abroad. And on my virginity, I think
they would rather marry a London jailer than a high sheriff° of a
county, since neither can stir from his employment. Formerly,
women of wit married fools for a great estate, a fine seat, or the   70
like; but now 'tis for a pretty seat only in Lincoln's Inn Fields, St
James's Fields, or the Pall Mall.°

Enter to them Sparkish, and Harcourt dressed like a parson

SPARKISH Madam, your humble servant; a happy day to you, and to
us all.

HARCOURT Amen.

ALETHEA Who have we here?

SPARKISH My chaplain, faith. Oh madam, poor Harcourt remembers his humble service to you, and in obedience to your last commands, refrains coming into your sight.

ALETHEA Is not that he?   80

SPARKISH No, fie, no; but to show that he ne'er intended to hinder our match, has sent his brother here to join our hands. When I get me a wife, I must get her a chaplain, according to the custom. This is his brother, and my chaplain.

ALETHEA His brother?   85

LUCY (*aside*) And your chaplain, to preach in your pulpit, then.

ALETHEA His brother!

SPARKISH Nay, I knew you would not believe it.—I told you, sir, she would take you for your brother Frank.

ALETHEA Believe it!   90

LUCY (*aside*) His brother! Ha ha he! He has a trick left still, it seems.

SPARKISH Come, my dearest, pray let us go to church before the canonical hour is past.°

ALETHEA For shame, you are abused still.

SPARKISH By the world, 'tis strange now, you are so incredulous.   95

ALETHEA 'Tis strange you are so credulous.

SPARKISH Dearest of my life, hear me. I tell you this is Ned Harcourt of Cambridge, by the world; you see he has a sneaking° college look. 'Tis true he's something like his brother Frank, and they differ from each other no more than in their age, for they were   100 twins.

LUCY Ha ha he!

ALETHEA Your servant, sir; I cannot be so deceived, though you are. But come, let's hear—how do you know what you affirm so confidently?   105

SPARKISH Why, I'll tell you all. Frank Harcourt coming to me this morning, to wish me joy and present his service to you, I asked him if he could help me to a parson; whereupon he told me he had a brother in town who was in orders, and he went straight away and sent him you see there to me.   110

ALETHEA Yes, Frank goes and puts on a black coat, then tells you he is Ned—that's all you have for't.°

SPARKISH Pshaw, pshaw, I tell you by the same token,° the midwife put her garter about Frank's neck, to know 'em asunder, they were so like.   115

ALETHEA Frank tells you this too?

SPARKISH Ay, and Ned there too—nay, they are both in a story.°

ALETHEA So, so; very foolish.

SPARKISH Lord, if you won't believe one, you had best try him by
your chambermaid there; for chambermaids must needs know   120
chaplains from other men, they are so used to 'em.

LUCY Let's see. Nay, I'll be sworn he has the canonical smirk, and
the filthy, clammy palm° of a chaplain.

ALETHEA Well, most reverend doctor, pray let us make an end of this
fooling.   125

HARCOURT With all my soul, divine, heavenly creature, when you
please.

ALETHEA He speaks like a chaplain indeed!

SPARKISH Why, was there not 'soul', 'divine', 'heavenly', in what he
said?   130

ALETHEA Once more, most impertinent black-coat, cease your persecution, and let us have a conclusion of this ridiculous love.

HARCOURT (aside) I had forgot; I must suit my style to my coat, or
I wear it in vain.

ALETHEA I have no more patience left; let us make once an end of   135
this troublesome love, I say.

HARCOURT So be it, seraphic lady, when your honour shall think it
meet and convenient so to do.°

SPARKISH Gad, I'm sure none but a chaplain could speak so, I
think.   140

ALETHEA Let me tell you, sir, this dull trick will not serve your turn;
though you delay our marriage, you shall not hinder it.

HARCOURT Far be it from me, munificent patroness, to delay your
marriage. I desire nothing more than to marry you presently, which
I might do, if you yourself would; for my noble, good-natured, and   145
thrice generous patron here would not hinder it.

SPARKISH No, poor man, not I, faith.

HARCOURT And now, madam, let me tell you plainly, nobody else
shall marry you, by heavens; I'll die first, for I'm sure I should die
after it.   150

LUCY [aside] How his love has made him forget his function!—as I
have seen it in real parsons.

ALETHEA That was spoken like a chaplain too! Now you understand
him, I hope.

SPARKISH Poor man, he takes it heinously to be refused. I can't   155
blame him, 'tis putting an indignity upon him not to be suffered.

But you'll pardon me, madam, it shan't be; he shall marry us. Come away, pray madam; 'tis late.°

LUCY [*aside*] Ha ha he, more ado!

ALETHEA Invincible stupidity! I tell you he would marry me as your   160
rival, not as your chaplain.

SPARKISH Come, come, madam. (*Pulling her away*)

LUCY Ay, pray° madam, do not refuse this reverend divine the honour and satisfaction of marrying you—for I dare say he has set his heart upon't, good doctor.   165

ALETHEA [*to Harcourt*] What can you hope, or design, by this?

HARCOURT [*aside*] I could answer her, a reprieve for a day only, often revokes a hasty doom. At worst, if she will not take mercy on me, and let me marry her, I have at least the lover's second pleasure, hindering my rival's enjoyment, though but for a time.   170

SPARKISH Come madam, 'tis e'en twelve o'clock, and my mother charged me never to be married out of the canonical hours. Come, come. Lord, here's such a deal of modesty, I warrant, the first day.

LUCY Yes, an't please your worship, married women show all their modesty the first day, because married men show all their love the   175
first day.

Exeunt

4.2

[In Pinchwife's house:] a bedchamber, [with table and chair,] where appear Pinchwife, Mrs Pinchwife

PINCHWIFE Come, tell me, I say.

MRS PINCHWIFE Lord, ha'n't I told it an hundred times over?

PINCHWIFE (*aside*) I would try if, in the repetition of the ungrateful tale, I could find her altering it in the least circumstance; for if her story be false, she is so too.—Come, how was't, baggage?   5

MRS PINCHWIFE Lord, what pleasure you take to hear it, sure!

PINCHWIFE No, you take more in telling it, I find—but speak: how was't?

MRS PINCHWIFE He carried me up into the house next to° the Exchange.   10

PINCHWIFE So—and you two were only in the room?

MRS PINCHWIFE Yes, for he sent away a youth that was there, for some dried fruit, and China oranges.

PINCHWIFE Did he so? Damn him for it, and for—

MRS PINCHWIFE But presently came up the gentlewoman of the   15
house.

PINCHWIFE Oh, 'twas well she did—but what did he do whilst the
fruit came?

MRS PINCHWIFE He kissed me an hundred times, and told me he
fancied he kissed my fine sister (meaning me, you know) whom he   20
said he loved with all his soul, and bid me be sure to tell her so,
and to desire her to be at her window by eleven of the clock this
morning, and he would walk under it at that time.

PINCHWIFE (aside) And he was as good as his word, very punctual—
a pox reward him for't.   25

MRS PINCHWIFE Well, and he said, if you were not within he would
come up to her, meaning me you know, bud, still.

PINCHWIFE (aside) So—he knew her certainly; but for this confession I am obliged to her simplicity.—But what, you stood very still
when he kissed you?   30

MRS PINCHWIFE Yes, I warrant you; would you have had me
discovered myself?

PINCHWIFE But you told me he did some beastliness to you, as you
called it. What was't?

MRS PINCHWIFE Why, he put . . .   35

PINCHWIFE What?

MRS PINCHWIFE Why, he put the tip of his tongue between my lips,
and so muzzled me—and I said I'd bite it.

PINCHWIFE An eternal canker seize it, for a dog.

MRS PINCHWIFE Nay, you need not be so angry with him neither,   40
for to say truth, he has the sweetest breath I ever knew.

PINCHWIFE The devil! You were satisfied with it, then, and would
do it again?

MRS PINCHWIFE Not unless he should force me.

PINCHWIFE Force you, changeling! I tell you no woman can be   45
forced.

MRS PINCHWIFE Yes, but she may, sure, by such a one as he, for
he's a proper, goodly, strong man; 'tis hard, let me tell you, to resist
him.

PINCHWIFE [aside] So, 'tis plain she loves him, yet she has not love   50
enough to make her conceal it from me. But the sight of him
will increase her aversion for me, and love for him, and that
love instruct her how to deceive me, and satisfy him, all idiot as

she is. Love, 'twas he gave women first their craft, their art of
deluding. Out of Nature's hands they came plain, open, silly,   55
and fit for slaves, as she and heaven intended 'em; but damned
Love—Well, I must strangle that little monster,° whilst I can
deal with him.—Go fetch pen, ink, and paper out of the next
room.

MRS PINCHWIFE Yes bud.   60

        Exit Mrs Pinchwife

PINCHWIFE Why should women have more invention in love than
    men? It can only be because they have more desires, more soliciting
    passions, more lust, and more of the devil.

        Mrs Pinchwife returns

    Come, minx, sit down and write.

MRS PINCHWIFE Ay, dear bud, but I can't do't very well.   65

PINCHWIFE I wish you could not at all.

MRS PINCHWIFE But what should I write for?

PINCHWIFE I'll have you write a letter to your lover.

MRS PINCHWIFE Oh Lord, to the fine gentleman a letter!

PINCHWIFE Yes, to the fine gentleman.   70

MRS PINCHWIFE Lord, you do but jeer; sure you jest.

PINCHWIFE I am not so merry; come, write as I bid you.

MRS PINCHWIFE What, do you think I am a fool?

PINCHWIFE [*aside*] She's afraid I would not dictate any love to him,
    therefore she's unwilling.—But you had best begin.   75

MRS PINCHWIFE Indeed, and indeed, but I won't, so I won't.

PINCHWIFE Why?

MRS PINCHWIFE Because he's in town; you may send for him if you
    will.

PINCHWIFE Very well; you would have him brought to you. Is it   80
    come to this? I say take the pen and write, or you'll provoke
    me.

MRS PINCHWIFE Lord, what d'ye make a fool of me for? Don't I
    know that letters are never writ but from the country to London,
    and from London into the country? Now, he's in town, and I am   85
    in town too; therefore I can't write to him, you know.

PINCHWIFE (*aside*) So, I am glad it is no worse; she is innocent
    enough yet.—Yes, you may, when your husband bids you, write
    letters to people that are in town.

MRS PINCHWIFE Oh, may I so? Then I'm satisfied.°   90

PINCHWIFE Come begin. (*Dictates*) 'Sir'—

MRS PINCHWIFE Shan't I say 'Dear Sir'? You know one says always something more than bare 'Sir'.°

PINCHWIFE Write as I bid you, or I will write 'Whore' with this penknife in your face.   95

MRS PINCHWIFE Nay, good bud. (*She writes*) 'Sir' . . .

PINCHWIFE 'Though I suffered last night your nauseous, loathed kisses and embraces'—write.

MRS PINCHWIFE Nay, why should I say so? You know I told you he had a sweet breath.   100

PINCHWIFE Write.

MRS PINCHWIFE Let me but put out 'loathed'.

PINCHWIFE Write, I say.

MRS PINCHWIFE Well then . . . (*Writes*)

PINCHWIFE Let's see; what have you writ? (*Takes the paper, and*   105
reads) 'Though I suffered last night your kisses and embraces'—
thou impudent creature, where is 'nauseous' and 'loathed'?

MRS PINCHWIFE I can't abide to write such filthy words.

PINCHWIFE Once more, write as I'd have you, and question it not, or I will spoil thy writing with this (*holds up the penknife*); I will   110
stab out those eyes that cause my mischief.

MRS PINCHWIFE O Lord, I will. [*Writes*]

PINCHWIFE So . . . So . . . Let's see now. (*Reads*) 'Though I suffered last night your nauseous, loathed kisses and embraces'; go on—'yet I would not have you presume that you shall ever repeat them.' So . . .   115
    She writes

MRS PINCHWIFE I have writ it.

PINCHWIFE On, then. 'I then concealed myself from your knowledge, to avoid your insolencies.'
    She writes

MRS PINCHWIFE So . . .

PINCHWIFE 'The same reason, now I am out of your hands—'   120
    She writes

MRS PINCHWIFE So . . .

PINCHWIFE 'Makes me own to you my unfortunate, though innocent frolic, of being in man's clothes—'
    She writes

MRS PINCHWIFE So . . .

PINCHWIFE 'That you may for evermore cease to pursue her who   125
hates and detests you—'
    She writes on

MRS PINCHWIFE (*Sighs*) So—h.

PINCHWIFE What, do you sigh? 'Detests you, as much as she loves her husband and her honour.'

MRS PINCHWIFE I vow, husband, he'll ne'er believe I should write   130
such a letter.

PINCHWIFE What, he'd expect a kinder from you? Come now, your name only.

MRS PINCHWIFE What, shan't I say 'Your most faithful, humble servant till death'?   135

PINCHWIFE No, tormenting fiend. (*Aside*) Her style, I find, would be very soft.—Come, wrap it up now, whilst I go fetch wax and a candle; and write on the back side 'For Mr Horner'.

Exit Pinchwife

MRS PINCHWIFE 'For Mr Horner'—so. I am glad he has told me his name. Dear Mr Horner—but why should I send thee such a letter,   140
that will vex thee, and make thee angry with me? Well, I will not send it . . . Ay, but then my husband will kill me—for I see plainly, he won't let me love Mr Horner. But what care I for my husband? I won't, so I won't, send poor Mr Horner such a letter—but then my husband . . . But oh, what if I writ at bottom 'My husband   145
made me write it'? Ay, but then my husband would see't. Can one have no shift? Ah, a London woman would have had a hundred presently. Stay—what if I should write a letter, and wrap it up like this, and write upon't too? Ay, but then my husband would see't. I don't know what to do—but yet i'vads I'll try, so I will—for I   ·150
will not send this letter to poor Mr Horner, come what will on't.

She writes, and repeats what she hath writ

'Dear, sweet Mr Horner,'—so—
'My husband would have me send you a base, rude, unmannerly letter, but I won't'—so—'and would have me forbid you loving me, but I won't'—so—'and would have me say to you, I hate you, poor   155
Mr Horner, but I won't tell a lie for him'°—there—'for I'm sure if you and I were in the country at cards together'—so—'I could not help treading on your toe under the table'—so—'or rubbing knees with you, and staring in your face, till you saw me'—very well—'and then looking down, and blushing for an hour   160
together,'—so—'but I must make haste before my husband come; and now he has taught me to write letters, you shall have longer ones from me, who am,

Dear, dear, poor dear Mr Horner,
Your most humble friend, and servant to command till death,   165
Margery Pinchwife.'

Stay—I must give him a hint at bottom°—so . . . Now wrap it up just like t'other—so. Now write 'For Mr Horner'—But oh, now what shall I do with it? For here comes my husband.

    Enter Pinchwife

PINCHWIFE (*aside*) I have been detained by a sparkish coxcomb, who   170
pretended a visit to me; but I fear 'twas to my wife.—What, have you done?

MRS PINCHWIFE Ay, ay bud, just now.

PINCHWIFE Let's see't. What d'ye tremble for? What, you would not have it go?   175

MRS PINCHWIFE Here. (*Aside*, [*keeping the second letter out of sight*]) No, I must not give him that.

    He opens and reads the first letter

So, I had been served if I had given him this.°

PINCHWIFE Come, where's the wax and seal?

MRS PINCHWIFE (*aside*) Lord, what shall I do now? Nay then, I have   180
it—[*Aloud*] Pray, let me see't. Lord, you think me so errand a fool I cannot seal a letter? I will do't, so I will.

    Snatches the letter from him, changes it for the other, seals it,
    and delivers it to him

PINCHWIFE Nay, I believe you will learn that, and other things too, which I would not have you.

MRS PINCHWIFE So, han't I done it curiously? (*Aside*) I think I have;   185
there's my letter going to Mr Horner—since he'll needs have me send letters to folks.

PINCHWIFE 'Tis very well; but I warrant you would not have it go now?

MRS PINCHWIFE Yes indeed, but I would, bud, now.   190

PINCHWIFE Well, you are a good girl then. Come, let me lock you up in your chamber till I come back. And be sure you come not within three strides of the window, when I am gone—for I have a spy in the street.

    Exit Mrs Pinchwife; Pinchwife locks the door

At least 'tis fit she think so. If we do not cheat women, they'll cheat   195
us; and fraud may be justly used with secret enemies, of which a wife is the most dangerous. And he that has a handsome one to keep, and a frontier town,° must provide against treachery rather than open force. Now I have secured all within, I'll deal with the foe without (*holds up the letter*) with false intelligence.   200

    Exit

4.3

Horner's lodgings

[*Enter*] *Quack and Horner*

QUACK Well sir, how fadges the new design? Have you not the luck of all your brother projectors, to deceive only yourself at last?

HORNER No, good domine doctor, I deceive you, it seems, and others too; for the grave matrons and old rigid husbands think me as unfit for love as they are; but their wives, sisters, and daughters know   5
(some of 'em) better things already.

QUACK Already!

HORNER Already, I say. Last night I was drunk with half a dozen of your civil persons, as you call 'em, and people of honour, and so was made free of their society and dressing-rooms for ever   10
hereafter, and am already come to the privileges of sleeping upon their pallets,° warming smocks, tying shoes and garters, and the like, doctor—already, already, doctor.

QUACK You have made use of your time, sir.

HORNER I tell thee, I am now no more interruption to 'em, when   15
they sing or talk bawdy, than a little squab° French page who speaks no English.

QUACK But do civil persons, and women of honour, drink and sing bawdy songs?

HORNER Oh, amongst friends, amongst friends; for your bigots in   20
honour are just like those in religion: they fear the eye of the world more than the eye of heaven, and think there is no virtue but railing at vice, and no sin but giving° scandal. They rail at a poor, little, kept player,° and keep themselves some young, modest, pulpit comedian° to be privy to their sins in their closets, not to tell 'em   25
of them in their chapels.

QUACK Nay, the truth on't is, priests amongst the women, now, have quite got the better of us lay confessors, physicians.

HORNER And they are rather their patients; but—

Enter Lady Fidget, looking about her

Now we talk of women of honour, here comes one. Step behind the   30
screen° there, and but observe if I have not particular privileges with the women of reputation already, doctor, already.

[*Quack conceals himself*]

LADY FIDGET Well, Horner, am not I a woman of honour? You see I'm as good as my word.

HORNER And you shall see, madam, I'll not be behindhand with you   35
in honour—and I'll be as good as my word too, if you please but
to withdraw into the next room.

LADY FIDGET But first, my dear sir, you must promise to have a care
of my dear honour.

HORNER If you talk a word more of your honour, you'll make me   40
incapable to wrong it. To talk of honour in the mysteries of love,
is like talking of heaven, or the Deity, in an operation of witchcraft,
just when you are employing the devil: it makes the charm
impotent.

LADY FIDGET Nay, fie, let us not be smutty. But you talk of   45
mysteries and bewitching to me—I don't understand you.°

HORNER I tell you, madam, the word 'money' in a mistress's mouth,
at such a nick of time, is not a more disheartening sound to a
younger brother,° than that of 'honour' to an eager lover like
myself.   50

LADY FIDGET But you can't blame a lady of my reputation to be
chary.

HORNER Chary! I have been chary of it already, by the report I have
caused of myself.

LADY FIDGET Ay, but if you should ever let other women know that   55
dear secret, it would come out. Nay, you must have a great care of
your conduct, for my acquaintance are so censorious (oh, 'tis a
wicked, censorious world, Mr Horner), I say are so censorious and
detracting, that perhaps they'll talk to the prejudice of my honour,
though you should not let them know the dear secret.   60

HORNER Nay, madam, rather than they shall prejudice your honour,
I'll prejudice theirs—and to serve you, I'll lie with 'em all, make
the secret their own, and then they'll keep it. I am a Machiavel in
love, madam.

LADY FIDGET Oh no, sir, not that way.   65

HORNER Nay, the devil take me, if censorious women are to be
silenced any other way.

LADY FIDGET A secret is better kept, I hope, by a single person than
a multitude; therefore pray do not trust anybody else with it, dear,
dear Mr Horner. (*Embracing him*)   70
    Enter Sir Jasper Fidget

SIR JASPER How now!

LADY FIDGET (*aside*) Oh, my husband! Prevented—and (what's
almost as bad) found with my arms about another man: that
will appear too much. What shall I say?—Sir Jasper, come hither;

I am trying if Mr Horner were ticklish, and he's as ticklish as can   75
be. I love to torment the confounded toad. Let you and I tickle
him.

SIR JASPER No, your ladyship will tickle him better without me, I
suppose. But is this your buying china?° I thought you had been
at the china-house.   80

HORNER (*aside*) China-house—that's my cue; I must take it. [*To Sir
Jasper*] A pox, can't you keep your impertinent wives at home?
Some men are troubled with the husbands, but I with the wives.
But I'd have you to know, since I cannot be your journeyman by
night, I will not be your drudge by day, to squire your wife about,   85
and be your man of straw, or scarecrow only, to pies and jays° that
would be nibbling at your forbidden fruit.° I shall be shortly the
hackney gentleman-usher of the town.

SIR JASPER (*aside*) Heh heh heh! Poor fellow, he's in the right on't,
faith; to squire women about for other folks, is as ungrateful an   90
employment as to tell money for other folks. [*Aloud*] Heh heh heh!
Ben't angry, Horner—

LADY FIDGET No, 'tis I have more reason to be angry, who am left
by you to go abroad indecently alone; or, what is more indecent, to
pin myself upon such ill-bred people of your acquaintance as this   95
is.

SIR JASPER Nay, prithee what has he done?

LADY FIDGET Nay, he has done nothing.

SIR JASPER But what d'ye take ill, if he has done nothing?

LADY FIDGET Ha ha ha! Faith, I can't but laugh however. Why, d'ye   100
think,° the unmannerly toad would not come down to me to the
coach; I was fain to come up to fetch him, or go without him,
which I was resolved not to do; for he knows china very well, and
has himself very good, but will not let me see it, lest I should beg
some. But I will find it out, [*moving to the door*] and have what I   105
came for yet.

HORNER (*apart to Lady Fidget*) Lock the door, madam.

> *Exit Lady Fidget, and locks the door, followed by Horner to
> the door*

So, she has got into my chamber, and locked me out. Oh, the
impertinency of womankind! Well, Sir Jasper, plain dealing is a
jewel:° if ever you suffer your wife to trouble me again here, she   110
shall carry you home a pair of horns, by my Lord Mayor she shall.
Though I cannot furnish you myself, you are sure, yet I'll find a
way.

SIR JASPER (*aside*) Ha ha he! At my first coming in, and finding her
arms about him, tickling him it seems, I was half jealous; but now   115
I see my folly. [*Aloud*] Heh heh heh! Poor Horner.

HORNER Nay, though you laugh now, 'twill be my turn ere long. Oh
women, more impertinent, more cunning, and more mischievous
than their monkeys, and to me almost as ugly. [*Listening at the door*]
Now is she throwing my things about, and rifling all I have, but   120
I'll get in to her the back way, and so rifle her for it—

SIR JASPER Ha ha ha! Poor angry Horner.

HORNER Stay here a little; I'll ferret her out to you presently, I
warrant.

> *Exit Horner at t'other door*

SIR JASPER (*calls through the door to his wife*) Wife, my Lady Fidget,   125
wife, he is coming in to you the back way.

LADY FIDGET (*answers from within*) Let him come, and welcome,
which way he will.

SIR JASPER He'll catch you, and use you roughly, and be too strong
for you.   130

LADY FIDGET Don't you trouble yourself; let him if he can.

QUACK (*behind*) This, indeed, I could not have believed from him,
nor any but my own eyes.

> *Enter Mistress Squeamish*

MISTRESS SQUEAMISH Where's this woman-hater, this toad, this
ugly, greasy, dirty sloven?   135

SIR JASPER [*aside*] So, the women all will have him ugly; methinks
he is a comely person, but his wants make his form contemptible
to 'em. And 'tis e'en as my wife said yesterday, talking of him, that
a proper, handsome eunuch was as ridiculous a thing as a gigantic
coward.   140

MISTRESS SQUEAMISH Sir Jasper, your servant; where is the odious
beast?

SIR JASPER He's within, in his chamber, with my wife; she's playing
the wag with him.

MISTRESS SQUEAMISH Is she so? And he's a clownish beast, he'll   145
give her no quarter; he'll play the wag with her again, let me tell
you. Come, let's go help her—what, the door's locked!

SIR JASPER Ay, my wife locked it—

MISTRESS SQUEAMISH Did she so? Let us break it open then.

SIR JASPER No, no, he'll do her no hurt.   150

MISTRESS SQUEAMISH No . . . (*Aside*) But is there no other way to
get in to 'em? Whither goes this? I will disturb 'em.

Exit Mistress Squeamish at another door. Enter Old Lady Squeamish

OLD LADY SQUEAMISH Where is this harlotry, this impudent baggage, this rambling tomrig?—Oh, Sir Jasper, I'm glad to see you here; did you not see my vild grandchild come in hither just now?   155

SIR JASPER Yes.

OLD LADY SQUEAMISH Ay, but where is she, then? Where is she? Lord, Sir Jasper, I have e'en rattled myself to pieces in pursuit of her. But can you tell what she makes here? They say below, no woman lodges here.   160

SIR JASPER No.

OLD LADY SQUEAMISH No? What does she here, then? Say, if it be not a woman's lodging, what makes she here? But are you sure no woman lodges here?   165

SIR JASPER No, nor no man neither; this is Mr Horner's lodging.

OLD LADY SQUEAMISH Is it so? Are you sure?

SIR JASPER Yes, yes.

OLD LADY SQUEAMISH So then, there's no hurt in't, I hope. But where is he?   170

SIR JASPER He's in the next room with my wife.

OLD LADY SQUEAMISH Nay, if you trust him with your wife, I may with my Biddy.° They say he's a merry, harmless man now, e'en as harmless a man as ever came out of Italy with a good voice,° and as pretty, harmless company for a lady as a snake without his teeth.   175

SIR JASPER Ay, ay, poor man.

Enter Mistress Squeamish

MISTRESS SQUEAMISH I can't find 'em—Oh, are you here, grandmother? I followed, you must know, my Lady Fidget hither; 'tis the prettiest lodging, and I have been staring on the prettiest pictures.°   180

Enter Lady Fidget, with a piece of china in her hand, and Horner following

LADY FIDGET And I have been toiling and moiling° for the prettiest piece of china, my dear.

HORNER Nay, she has been too hard for me, do what I could.

MISTRESS SQUEAMISH Oh Lord, I'll have some china too, good Mr Horner—don't think to give other people china, and me none. Come in with me too.   185

HORNER Upon my honour, I have none left now.

MISTRESS SQUEAMISH Nay, nay, I have known you deny your china
before now; but you shan't put me off so. Come—   190

HORNER This lady had the last there.

LADY FIDGET Yes indeed, madam; to my certain knowledge he has
no more left.

MISTRESS SQUEAMISH Oh, but it may be he may have some you
could not find.   195

LADY FIDGET What, d'y' think if he had had any left, I would not
have had it too? For we women of quality never think we have
china enough.

HORNER Do not take it ill; I cannot make china for you all, but I will
have a rolwagen for you too, another time.   200

MISTRESS SQUEAMISH Thank you, dear toad.

LADY FIDGET (to Horner aside) What do you mean by that promise?

HORNER (apart to Lady Fidget) Alas, she has an innocent, literal
understanding.

OLD LADY SQUEAMISH Poor Mr Horner, he has enough to do to   205
please you all, I see.

HORNER Ay madam, you see how they use me.

OLD LADY SQUEAMISH Poor gentleman, I pity you.

HORNER I thank you, madam; I could never find pity but from such
reverend ladies as you are; the young ones will never spare a man.   210

MISTRESS SQUEAMISH Come, come, beast, and go dine with us, for
we shall want a man at ombre after dinner.

HORNER [to Old Lady Squeamish] That's all their use of me, madam,
you see.

MISTRESS SQUEAMISH Come, sloven, I'll lead you to be sure of you.   215
       Pulls him by the cravat

OLD LADY SQUEAMISH Alas, poor man, how she tugs him. Kiss, kiss
her, that's the way to make such nice women quiet.

HORNER No, madam, that remedy is worse than the torment;° they
know I dare suffer anything rather than do it.

OLD LADY SQUEAMISH Prithee kiss her, and I'll give you her picture   220
in little,° that you admired so last night; prithee do.

HORNER Well, nothing but that could bribe me. I love a woman only
in effigy and good painting, as much as I hate them—I'll do't, for
I could adore the devil well painted.
       Kisses Mistress Squeamish

MISTRESS SQUEAMISH Foh, you filthy toad; nay, now I've done   225
jesting.

OLD LADY SQUEAMISH Ha ha ha, I told you so.

MISTRESS SQUEAMISH Foh, a kiss of his—

SIR JASPER Has no more hurt in't, than one of my spaniel's.

MISTRESS SQUEAMISH Nor no more good neither.   230

QUACK (*behind*) I will now believe anything he tells me.

> *Enter Pinchwife*

LADY FIDGET Oh Lord, here's a man, Sir Jasper—my mask, my mask; I would not be seen here for the world.

SIR JASPER What, not when I am with you?

LADY FIDGET No, no, my honour—let's begone.   235

MISTRESS SQUEAMISH Oh, grandmother, let us begone; make haste, make haste, I know not how he may censure us.

LADY FIDGET Be found in the lodging of anything like a man! Away.

> *Exeunt Sir Jasper Fidget, Lady Fidget, Old Lady*
> *Squeamish, Mistress Squeamish*

QUACK (*behind*) What's here, another cuckold? He looks like one, and none else sure have any business with him.   240

HORNER Well, what brings my dear friend hither?

PINCHWIFE Your impertinency.

HORNER My impertinency? Why, you gentlemen that have got handsome wives think you have a privilege of saying anything to your friends, and are as brutish as if you were our creditors.   245

PINCHWIFE No, sir, I'll ne'er trust you any way.

HORNER But why not, dear Jack? Why diffide in me thou know'st so well?

PINCHWIFE Because I do know you so well.

HORNER Ha'n't I been always thy friend, honest Jack? Always ready   250
to serve thee, in love, or battle, before thou wert married, and am so still.

PINCHWIFE I believe so; you would be my second now indeed.

HORNER Well then, dear Jack, why so unkind, so grum, so strange to me? Come, prithee kiss me,° dear rogue. Gad, I was always, I   255
say, and am still as much thy servant as—

PINCHWIFE As I am yours, sir. What, you would send a kiss to my wife, is that it?

HORNER So there 'tis—a man can't show his friendship to a married man, but presently he talks of his wife to you. Prithee let thy wife   260
alone, and let thee and I be all one as we were wont.° What, thou art as shy of my kindness as a Lombard Street alderman of a courtier's civility at Locket's.°

PINCHWIFE But you are over-kind to me, as kind as if I were your cuckold already. Yet I must confess you ought to be kind and civil   265 to me, since I am so kind, so civil to you as to bring you this; look you there, sir.

Delivers him a letter

HORNER What is't?

PINCHWIFE Only a love-letter, sir.

HORNER From whom? How, this is from your wife! (*Reads*) H'm . . .   270
and h'm . . .

PINCHWIFE Even from my wife, sir; am I not wondrous kind and civil to you now, too? (*Aside*) But you'll not think her so.

HORNER (*aside*) Ha, is this a trick of his, or hers?

PINCHWIFE The gentleman's surprised, I find. What, you expected   275
a kinder letter?

HORNER No faith, not I; how could I?

PINCHWIFE Yes, yes, I'm sure you did; a man so well made as you are must needs be disappointed, if the women declare not their passion at first sight or opportunity.   280

HORNER [*aside*] But what should this mean? Stay, the postscript: (*Reads*) 'Be sure you love me whatsoever my husband says to the contrary, and let him not see this, lest he should come home, and pinch me, or kill my squirrel.'° It seems he knows not what the letter contains.   285

PINCHWIFE Come, ne'er wonder at it so much.

HORNER Faith, I can't help it.

PINCHWIFE Now I think I have deserved your infinite friendship and kindness, and have showed myself sufficiently an obliging, kind friend and husband—am I not so, to bring a letter from my wife   290
to her gallant?

HORNER Ay, the devil take me, art thou°—the most obliging, kind friend and husband in the world, ha ha!

PINCHWIFE Well, you may be merry, sir, but in short I must tell you, sir, my honour will suffer no jesting.   295

HORNER What dost thou mean?

PINCHWIFE Does the letter want a comment? Then know, sir, though I have been so civil a husband as to bring you a letter from my wife, to let you kiss and court her to my face, I will not be a cuckold, sir, I will not.   300

HORNER Thou art mad with jealousy. I never saw thy wife in my life, but at the play yesterday, and I know not if it were she or no. I court her, kiss her!

PINCHWIFE I will not be a cuckold, I say; there will be danger in making me a cuckold.   305

HORNER Why, wert thou not well cured of thy last clap?

PINCHWIFE I wear a sword.

HORNER It should be taken from thee, lest thou shouldst do thyself a mischief with it. Thou art mad, man.

PINCHWIFE As mad as I am, and as merry as you are, I must have more reason° from you ere we part. I say again, though you kissed and courted last night my wife in man's clothes, as she confesses in her letter—

HORNER (aside) Ha!

PINCHWIFE Both she and I say you must not design it again, for you have mistaken your woman, as you have done your man.°

HORNER (aside) Oh—I understand something now. [Aloud] Was that thy wife? Why wouldst thou not tell me 'twas she? Faith, my freedom with her was your fault, not mine.

PINCHWIFE (aside) Faith, so 'twas.

HORNER Fie, I'd never do't to a woman before her husband's face, sure.

PINCHWIFE But I had rather you should do't to my wife before my face than behind my back—and that you shall never do.

HORNER No—you will hinder me.°

PINCHWIFE If I would not hinder you, you see by her letter, she would.

HORNER Well, I must e'en acquiesce then, and be contented with what she writes.

PINCHWIFE I'll assure you, 'twas voluntarily writ; I had no hand in't, you may believe me.

HORNER I do believe thee, faith.

PINCHWIFE And believe her too, for she's an innocent creature, has no dissembling in her. And so fare you well, sir.

HORNER Pray, however, present my humble service to her, and tell her I will obey her letter to a tittle, and fulfil her desires, be what they will, or with what difficulty soever I do't; and you shall be no more jealous of me, I warrant her, and you.°

PINCHWIFE Well then, fare you well, and play with any man's honour but mine, kiss any man's wife but mine, and welcome.

          Exit Pinchwife

HORNER Ha ha ha!—Doctor!

QUACK [coming forward] It seems he has not heard the report of you, or does not believe it.

HORNER Ha ha! Now doctor, what think you?

QUACK Pray, let's see the letter. (Reads the letter) H'm . . . 'for . . . dear . . . love you° . . .'

HORNER I wonder how she could contrive it! What say'st thou to't? 'Tis an original.

QUACK So are your cuckolds too, originals—for they are like no other common cuckolds, and I will henceforth believe it not impossible for you to cuckold the Grand Signior° amidst his guards of   350 eunuchs—*that* I say!°

HORNER And I say, for the letter, 'tis the first love-letter that ever was without flames, darts, fates, destinies, lying, and dissembling in't.

Enter Sparkish, pulling in Pinchwife. [Quack withdraws]

SPARKISH Come back; you are a pretty brother-in-law—neither go   355 to church nor to dinner with your sister bride!

PINCHWIFE My sister denies her marriage, and you see is gone away from you dissatisfied.

SPARKISH Pshaw, upon a foolish scruple that our parson was not in lawful orders, and did not say all the Common Prayer;° but 'tis her   360 modesty only, I believe. But let women be never so modest the first day, they'll be sure to come to themselves by night, and I shall have enough of her then. In the mean time, Harry Horner, you must dine with me; I keep my wedding at my aunt's in the Piazza.

HORNER Thy wedding?° What stale maid has lived to despair of a   365 husband, or what young one of a gallant?

SPARKISH Oh, your servant, sir. This gentleman's sister, then—no stale maid.

HORNER I'm sorry for't.

PINCHWIFE (*aside*) How comes he so concerned for her?   370

SPARKISH You sorry for't? Why, do you know any ill by her?°

HORNER No, I know none but by thee. 'Tis for her sake, not yours, and another man's sake that might have hoped, I thought—

SPARKISH Another man, another man? What is his name?

HORNER Nay, since 'tis past he shall be nameless. (*Aside*) Poor   375 Harcourt, I am sorry thou hast missed her.

PINCHWIFE (*aside*) He seems to be much troubled at the match.

SPARKISH Prithee tell me.—Nay, you shan't go, brother.

PINCHWIFE I must, of necessity, but I'll come to you to dinner.

Exit Pinchwife

SPARKISH But Harry—what, have I a rival in my wife already? But   380 with all my heart, for he may be of use to me hereafter, for though my hunger is now my sauce, and I can fall on heartily without, but the time will come when a rival will be as good sauce for a married man to a wife, as an orange to veal.

HORNER Oh, thou damned rogue, thou hast set my teeth on edge 385
with thy orange.

SPARKISH Then let's to dinner—there I was with you again. Come.

HORNER But who dines with thee?

SPARKISH My friends and relations; my brother Pinchwife, you see,
of your acquaintance. 390

HORNER And his wife.

SPARKISH No, gad, he'll ne'er let her come amongst us good fellows;
your stingy country coxcomb keeps his wife from his friends, as he
does his little firkin of ale for his own drinking, and a gentleman
can't get a smack on't; but his servants, when his back is turned, 395
broach it at their pleasures, and dust it away, ha ha ha! Gad, I am
witty, I think, considering I was married today, by the world. But
come—

HORNER No, I will not dine with you, unless you can fetch her too.

SPARKISH Pshaw, what pleasure canst thou have with women now, 400
Harry?

HORNER My eyes are not gone; I love a good prospect yet, and will
not dine with you unless she does too. Go fetch her therefore, but
do not tell her husband 'tis for my sake.

SPARKISH Well, I'll go try what I can do. In the mean time, come 405
away to my aunt's lodging, 'tis in the way to Pinchwife's.

[*Exit Sparkish. Quack comes forward*]

HORNER The poor woman has called for aid, and stretched forth her
hand, doctor. I cannot but help her over the pale, out of the briars.°

Exeunt

4.4

Pinchwife's house. A table, pen, ink, and paper [and a chair]

Mrs Pinchwife alone, [seated and] leaning on her elbow

MRS PINCHWIFE Well, 'tis e'en so; I have got the London disease
they call love; I am sick of my husband, and for my gallant. I have
heard this distemper called a fever, but methinks 'tis liker an ague,
for when I think of my husband I tremble and am in a cold sweat,
and have inclinations to vomit, but when I think of my gallant, dear 5
Mr Horner, my hot fit comes, and I am all in a fever indeed, and
as in other fevers, my own chamber is tedious to me, and I would
fain be removed to his, and then methinks I should be well. Ah,

poor Mr Horner! Well, I cannot, will not stay here, therefore I'll
make an end of my letter to him, which shall be a finer letter than   10
my last, because I have studied it like anything. Oh, sick, sick!
(*Takes the pen and writes*)

> *Enter Pinchwife, who, seeing her writing, steals softly behind
> her, and, looking over her shoulder, snatches the paper from
> her*

PINCHWIFE What, writing more letters?
MRS PINCHWIFE Oh Lord, bud, why d'ye fright me so?
PINCHWIFE How's this?   15

> *She offers to run out*

Nay, you shall not stir, madam.

> *He stops her, and reads*

'Dear, dear, dear Mr Horner,'—very well; I have taught you to
write letters to good purpose—but let's see't. 'First I am to beg
your pardon for my boldness in writing to you, which I'd have you
to know I would not have done, had not you said first you loved   20
me so extremely, which if you do, you will never suffer me to lie
in the arms of another man, whom I loathe, nauseate, and
detest,'—Now you can write these filthy words. But what follows?
'therefore I hope you will speedily find some way to free me from
this unfortunate match, which was never, I assure you, of my   25
choice, but I'm afraid 'tis already too far gone; however, if you love
me, as I do you, you will try what you can do, but you must help
me away before tomorrow, or else alas I shall be for ever out of
your reach, for I can defer no longer our—' (*The letter concludes*)
'Our'—what is to follow 'our'? Speak, what? Our 'journey into the   30
country,' I suppose. Oh, woman, damned woman! And Love,
damned Love, their old tempter—for this is one of his miracles. In
a moment he can make those blind that could see, and those see
that were blind; those dumb that could speak, and those prattle
who were dumb before—nay, what is more than all, make these   35
dough-baked, senseless, indocile animals, women, too hard for us,
their politic lords and rulers, in a moment. But make an end of
your letter, and then I'll make an end of you thus, and all my
plagues together.

> *Draws his sword*

MRS PINCHWIFE Oh Lord, oh Lord, you are such a passionate man,   40
bud.

> [*Covers her face with her handkerchief.*] *Enter Sparkish*

SPARKISH How now, what's here to do?

PINCHWIFE This fool here now!

SPARKISH What, drawn upon your wife? You should never do that
but at night in the dark, when you can't hurt her. This is my   45
sister-in-law, is it not?
       Pulls aside her handkerchief
Ay faith, e'en our country Margery; one may know her. Come, she
and you must go dine with me; dinner's ready, come. But where's
my wife? Is she not come home yet? Where is she?

PINCHWIFE Making you a cuckold; 'tis that they all do, as soon as   50
they can.

SPARKISH What, the wedding day? No, a wife that designs to make
a cully of her husband will be sure to let him win the first stake of
love,° by the world. But come, they stay dinner for us. Come, I'll
lead down our Margery.   55

[PINCHWIFE]° No—sir! Go; we'll follow you.

SPARKISH I will not wag without you.

PINCHWIFE [*aside*] This coxcomb is a sensible torment to me, amidst
the greatest in the world.

SPARKISH Come, come, Madam Margery.   60

PINCHWIFE No, I'll lead her my way.
       Leads her to t'other door, and locks her in, and returns
What, would you treat your friends with mine, for want of your
own wife? (*Aside*) I am contented my rage should take breath.

SPARKISH [*aside*] I told Horner this.

PINCHWIFE Come now.   65

SPARKISH Lord, how shy you are of your wife. But let me tell you,
brother, we men of wit have amongst us a saying, that cuckolding
(like the smallpox) comes with a fear;° and you may keep your wife
as much as you will out of danger of infection, but if her
constitution incline her to't, she'll have it sooner or later, by the   70
world, say they.

PINCHWIFE (*aside*) What a thing is a cuckold, that every fool can
make him ridiculous!—Well, sir; but let me advise you (now you
are come to be concerned°), because you suspect the danger, not to
neglect the means to prevent it, especially when the greatest share   75
of the malady will light upon your own head; for,
       Hows'e'er the kind wife's belly comes to swell,
       The husband breeds for her,° and first is ill.
   [*Exeunt*]

5.1

Pinchwife's house. A table and candle [and a chair]

Enter Pinchwife and Mrs Pinchwife

PINCHWIFE Come, take the pen and make an end of the letter, just
as you intended. If you are false in a tittle I shall soon perceive it,
and punish you with this as you deserve. (*Lays his hand on his
sword*) Write what was to follow. Let's see: 'You must make
haste and help me away before tomorrow, or else I shall be for ever   5
out of your reach, for I can defer no longer our—' What follows
'our'?

MRS PINCHWIFE Must all out then, bud? (*Takes the pen and writes*)
Look you there, then.

PINCHWIFE Let's see. 'For I can defer no longer our—wedding,   10
Your slighted Alethea.' What's the meaning of this? My sister's
name to't? Speak, unriddle.

MRS PINCHWIFE Yes, indeed, bud.

PINCHWIFE But why her name to't? Speak—speak, I say.

MRS PINCHWIFE Ay, but you'll tell her then again. If you would not   15
tell her again . . .

PINCHWIFE I will not. I am stunned, my head turns round. Speak.

MRS PINCHWIFE Won't you tell her indeed, and indeed?

PINCHWIFE No. Speak, I say.

MRS PINCHWIFE She'll be angry with me, but I had rather she   20
should be angry with me than you, bud. And to tell you the truth,
'twas she made me write the letter, and taught me what I should
write.

PINCHWIFE [*aside*] Ha, I thought the style was somewhat better than
her own. [*Aloud*] But how could she come to you to teach you,   25
since I had locked you up alone?

MRS PINCHWIFE Oh, through the keyhole, bud.

PINCHWIFE But why should she make you write a letter for her to
him, since she can write herself?

MRS PINCHWIFE Why, she said because—For I was unwilling to do   30
it.

PINCHWIFE Because what? Because—

MRS PINCHWIFE Because lest Mr Horner should be cruel, and refuse
her, or vain afterwards and show the letter, she might disown it,
the hand not being hers.   35

PINCHWIFE (*aside*) How's this? Ha—then I think I shall come to
myself again. This changeling could not invent this lie; but if she
could, why should she? She might think° I should soon discover it.
Stay—now I think on't too, Horner said he was sorry she had
married Sparkish, and her disowning her marriage to me, makes   40
me think she has evaded it for Horner's sake. Yet why should she
take this course? But men in love are fools; women may well be so.
[*Aloud*] But hark you, madam, your sister went out in the morning,
and I have not seen her within since.

MRS PINCHWIFE Alack-a-day, she has been crying all day above, it   45
seems, in a corner.

PINCHWIFE Where is she? Let me speak with her.

MRS PINCHWIFE (*aside*) Oh Lord, then he'll discover all.—Pray
hold, bud; what, d'y' mean to discover me? She'll know I have told
you then. Pray bud, let me talk with her first—   50

PINCHWIFE I must speak with her to know whether Horner ever
made her any promise; and whether she be married to Sparkish or
no.

MRS PINCHWIFE Pray dear bud, don't, till I have spoken with her,
and told her that I have told you all, for she'll kill me else.   55

PINCHWIFE Go then, and bid her come out to me.

MRS PINCHWIFE Yes, yes, bud.

PINCHWIFE [*aside*] Let me see . . .

MRS PINCHWIFE [*aside*] I'll go; but she is not within to come to
him. I have just got time to know of Lucy, her maid, who first set   60
me on work, what lie I shall tell next, for I am e'en at my wit's
end.

    Exit Mrs Pinchwife

PINCHWIFE Well, I resolve it: Horner shall have her. I'd rather give
him my sister than lend him my wife, and such an alliance will
prevent his pretensions to my wife, sure—I'll make him of kin to   65
her, and then he won't care for her.

    Mrs Pinchwife returns

MRS PINCHWIFE Oh Lord, bud, I told you what anger you would
make me with my sister.

PINCHWIFE Won't she come hither?

MRS PINCHWIFE No, no, alack-a-day, she's ashamed to look you in   70
the face, and she says if you go in to her, she'll run away
downstairs, and shamefully go herself to Mr Horner, who has
promised her marriage, she says, and she will have no other, so she
won't!

PINCHWIFE Did he so? Promise her marriage? Then she shall have 75
   no other. Go tell her so, and if she will come and discourse with
   me a little concerning the means, I will about it immediately. Go.
      [*He puts the letter in his pocket.*] *Exit Mrs Pinchwife*
   His estate is equal to Sparkish's, and his extraction as much better
   than his as his parts are; but my chief reason is, I'd rather be of kin
   to him by the name of brother-in-law than that of cuckold. 80
      Enter Mrs Pinchwife
   Well, what says she now?
MRS PINCHWIFE Why, she says she would only have you lead her to
   Horner's lodging, with whom she first will discourse the matter
   before she talk with you, which yet° she cannot do—for alack, poor
   creature, she says she can't so much as look you in the face; 85
   therefore she'll come to you in a mask, and you must excuse her if
   she make you no answer to any question of yours, till you have
   brought her to Mr Horner, and if you will not chide her, nor
   question her, she'll come out to you immediately.
PINCHWIFE Let her come. I will not speak a word to her, nor require 90
   a word from her.
MRS PINCHWIFE Oh, I forgot; besides, she says, she cannot look you
   in the face, though through a mask, therefore would desire you to
   put out the candle.
PINCHWIFE I agree to all. Let her make haste. 95
      Puts out the candle
   There, 'tis out.
      Exit Mrs Pinchwife
   My case is something better; I'd rather fight with Horner for not
   lying with my sister, than for lying with my wife, and of the two I
   had rather find my sister too forward than my wife. I expected no
   other from her free education, as she calls it, and her passion for 100
   the town. Well, wife and sister are names which make us expect
   love and duty, pleasure and comfort, but we find 'em plagues and
   torments, and are equally, though differently, troublesome to their
   keeper; for we have as much ado to get people to lie with our
   sisters, as to keep 'em from lying with our wives. 105
      Enter Mrs Pinchwife, masked and in hoods and scarves, and
      a night-gown and petticoat of Alethea's, in the dark
   What, are you come, sister? Let us go then—but first let me lock
   up my wife. Mistress Margery, where are you?
MRS PINCHWIFE Here, bud.
PINCHWIFE Come hither, that I may lock you up.°

Mrs Pinchwife gives him her hand, but when he lets her go,
she steals softly on t'other side of him

Get you in.   110

Locks the door

Come sister, where are you now?

[Mrs Pinchwife] is led away by him for° his sister Alethea

5.2

Horner's lodging

[Enter] Quack, Horner

QUACK What, all alone! Not so much as one of your cuckolds here,
nor one of their wives! They use to take their turns with you, as if
they were to watch you.

HORNER Yes, it often happens that a cuckold is but his wife's spy,
and is more upon family duty when he is with her gallant abroad,   5
hindering his pleasure, than when he is at home with her, playing
the gallant. But the hardest duty a married woman imposes upon
a lover, is keeping her husband company always.

QUACK And his fondness wearies you almost as soon as hers.

HORNER A pox, keeping a cuckold company after you have had his   10
wife, is as tiresome as the company of a country squire to a witty
fellow of the town, when he has got all his money.

QUACK And as at first a man makes a friend of the husband to get
the wife, so at last you are fain to fall out with the wife to be rid
of the husband.   15

HORNER Ay, most cuckold-makers are true courtiers; when once a
poor man has cracked his credit for 'em,° they can't abide to come
near him.

QUACK But at first, to draw him in, are so sweet, so kind, so dear,
just as you are to Pinchwife. But what becomes of that intrigue   20
with his wife?

HORNER A pox, he's as surly as an alderman that has been bit, and
since he's so coy, his wife's kindness is in vain, for she's a silly
innocent.

QUACK Did she not send you a letter by him?   25

HORNER Yes, but that's a riddle I have not yet solved. Allow the
poor creature to be willing; she is silly too, and he keeps her up so
close—

265

QUACK Yes, so close that he makes her but the more willing, and
adds but revenge to her love, which two, when met, seldom fail of 30
satisfying each other one way or other.

HORNER What, here's the man we are talking of, I think.
*Enter Pinchwife leading in his wife, masked, muffled, and in
her sister's gown*
Pshaw!°

QUACK Bringing his wife to you is the next thing to bringing a
love-letter from her. 35

HORNER What means this?

PINCHWIFE The last time, you know sir, I brought you a love-letter.
Now you see a mistress, I think you'll say I am a civil man to you.

HORNER Ay, the devil take me, will I say thou art the civillest man
I ever met with—and I have known some. I fancy I understand thee 40
now, better than I did the letter. But hark thee in thy ear—

PINCHWIFE What?

HORNER Nothing but the usual question, man: is she sound, on thy
word?

PINCHWIFE What! You take her for a wench, and me for a pimp? 45

HORNER Pshaw, 'wench' and 'pimp'—paw words. I know thou art
an honest fellow, and hast a great acquaintance among the ladies,
and perhaps hast made love for me, rather than let me make love
to thy wife.

PINCHWIFE Come sir; in short, I am for no fooling. 50

HORNER Nor I neither, therefore prithee let's see her face presently.
Make her show, man. Art thou sure I don't know her?

PINCHWIFE I am sure you do know her.

HORNER A pox, why dost thou bring her to me then?

PINCHWIFE Because she's a relation of mine— 55

HORNER Is she, faith, man? Then thou art still more civil and
obliging, dear rogue.

PINCHWIFE Who desired me to bring her to you.

HORNER Then *she* is obliging, dear rogue.

PINCHWIFE You'll make her welcome for my sake, I hope? 60

HORNER I hope she is handsome enough to make herself welcome.
Prithee let her unmask.

PINCHWIFE Do you speak to her; she would never be ruled by
me.

HORNER Madam— 65
Mrs Pinchwife whispers to Horner
She says she must speak with me in private. Withdraw, prithee.

PINCHWIFE (*aside*) She's unwilling, it seems, I should know all her undecent conduct in this business.—Well then, I'll leave you together, and hope when I am gone you'll agree. If not, you and I shan't agree, sir.   70
    [*Lays his hand on his sword*]

HORNER [*aside*] What means the fool?—If she and I agree, 'tis no matter what you and I do.
    Whispers to Mrs Pinchwife

PINCHWIFE In the mean time I'll fetch a parson, and find out Sparkish and disabuse him. [*To Mrs Pinchwife*] You would have me fetch a parson, would you not?   75
    She makes signs with her hand for him to begone
Well then. [*Aside*] Now, I think, I am rid of her, and shall have no more trouble with her. Our sisters and daughters, like usurers' money, are safest when put out; but our wives, like their writings, never safe but in our closets, under lock and key.
    Exit Pinchwife. Enter Boy

BOY Sir Jasper Fidget, sir, is coming up.   80
    [*Exit Boy*]

HORNER [*to Quack*] Here's the trouble of a cuckold, now, we are talking of.° A pox on him, has he not enough to do to hinder his wife's sport, but he must other women's too?—Step in here, madam.
    Exit Mrs Pinchwife. Enter Sir Jasper Fidget

SIR JASPER My best and dearest friend!   85

HORNER [*aside to Quack*] The old style, doctor. [*To Sir Jasper*] Well, be short, for I am busy. What would your impertinent wife have now?

SIR JASPER Well guessed, i'faith, for I do come from her.

HORNER To invite me to supper. Tell her I can't come; go.   90

SIR JASPER Nay, now you are out, faith, for my lady and the whole knot° of the virtuous gang°, as they call themselves, are resolved upon a frolic of coming to you tonight in a masquerade, and are all dressed already.

HORNER I shan't be at home.   95

SIR JASPER Lord, how churlish he is to women! Nay, prithee don't disappoint 'em, they'll think 'tis my fault; prithee don't. I'll send in the banquet and the fiddles. But make no noise on't, for the poor virtuous rogues would not have it known for the world that they go a-masquerading, and they would come to no man's ball but   100
yours.

HORNER Well, well, get you gone. And tell 'em, if they come 'twill
be at the peril of their honour and yours.

SIR JASPER Heh heh heh! We'll trust you for that. Farewell.

Exit Sir Jasper Fidget

HORNER Doctor, anon you too shall be my guest,   105
        But now I'm going to a private feast.

[*Exeunt severally*]

5.3

The Piazza of Covent Garden

[*Enter*] *Sparkish, Pinchwife*

SPARKISH (*with the letter° in his hand*) But who would have thought
a woman could have been false to me? By the world, I could not
have thought it.

PINCHWIFE You were for giving and taking liberty; she has taken it
only, sir, now you find in that letter. You are a frank person, and   5
so is she, you see there.

SPARKISH Nay, if this be her hand—for I never saw it.

PINCHWIFE [*taking the letter from Sparkish*] 'Tis no matter whether
that be her hand or no; I am sure this hand, at her desire, led her
to Mr Horner, with whom I left her just now, to go fetch a parson   10
to 'em, at their desire too, to deprive you of her for ever—for it
seems yours was but a mock marriage.

SPARKISH Indeed, she would needs have it that 'twas Harcourt
himself, in a parson's habit, that married us; but I'm sure he told
me 'twas his brother Ned.   15

PINCHWIFE Oh, there 'tis out; and you were deceived, not she, for
you are such a frank person! But I must begone. You'll find her at
Mr Horner's; go, and believe your eyes.

Exit Pinchwife

SPARKISH Nay, I'll to her, and call her as many crocodiles, sirens,
harpies, and other heathenish names, as a poet would do a mistress   20
who had refused to hear his suit—nay more, his verses on her. But
stay, is not that she, following a torch at t'other end of the Piazza,
and from Horner's certainly? 'Tis so.

Enter Alethea, following a torch, and Lucy behind

You are well met, madam, though you don't think so. What,
you have made a short visit to Mr Horner, but I suppose   25

you'll return to him presently, by that time° the parson can be with
him.

ALETHEA Mr Horner, and the parson, sir?

SPARKISH Come, madam, no more dissembling, no more jilting, for
I am no more a frank person.   30

ALETHEA How's this?

LUCY (*aside*) So, 'twill work, I see.

SPARKISH Could you find out no easy country fool to abuse? None
but me, a gentleman of wit and pleasure about the town?° But it
was your pride to be too hard for a man of parts, unworthy, false   35
woman, false as a friend that lends a man money to lose, false as
dice, who undo those that trust all they have to 'em.

LUCY (*aside*) He has been a great bubble by° his similes, as they say.

ALETHEA You have been too merry, sir, at your wedding-dinner, sure.

SPARKISH What, d'y' mock me too?   40

ALETHEA Or you have been deluded.

SPARKISH By you.

ALETHEA Let me understand you.

SPARKISH Have you the confidence—I should call it something else,
since you know your guilt—to stand my just reproaches? You did   45
not write an impudent letter to Mr Horner?—who I find now has
clubbed with you in deluding me with his aversion for women, that
I might not (forsooth) suspect him for my rival.

LUCY (*aside* [*to Alethea*]) D'y' think the gentleman can be jealous
now, madam?   50

ALETHEA I write a letter to Mr Horner!

SPARKISH Nay madam, do not deny it; your brother showed it me
just now, and told me likewise he left you at Horner's lodging, to
fetch a parson to marry you to him. And I wish you joy, madam,
joy, joy, and to him too, much joy, and to myself more joy—for   55
not marrying you.

ALETHEA (*aside*) So, I find my brother would break off the match;
and I can consent to't, since I see this gentleman can be made
jealous.—Oh, Lucy, by his rude usage and jealousy he makes me
almost afraid I am married to him—art thou sure 'twas Harcourt   60
himself, and no parson, that married us?

SPARKISH No, madam, I thank you; I suppose that was a contrivance
too of Mr Horner's and yours, to make Harcourt play the parson.
But I would, as little as you, have him one now, no, not for the
world—for shall I tell you another truth? I never had any passion   65
for you—till now, for now I hate you. 'Tis true, I might have

married your portion, as other men of parts of the town do
sometimes—and so, your servant. And to show my unconcerned-
ness, I'll come to your wedding, and resign you with as much joy
as I would a stale wench to a new cully, nay, with as much joy as   70
I would after the first night, if I had been married to you. There's
for you; and so, your servant, servant.°

    Exit Sparkish

ALETHEA How was I deceived in a man!

LUCY You'll believe, then, a fool may be made jealous now? For that
easiness in him that suffers him to be led by a wife, will likewise   75
permit him to be persuaded against her by others.

ALETHEA But marry Mr Horner! My brother does not intend it,
sure. If I thought he did, I would take thy advice, and Mr Harcourt
for my husband. And now I wish that if there be any over-
wise woman of the town who, like me, would marry a fool for   80
fortune, liberty, or title: first, that her husband may love play, and
be a cully to all the town but her, and suffer none but Fortune to
be mistress of his purse; then if for liberty, that he may send her
into the country under the conduct of some housewifely mother-
in-law; and if for title, may the world give 'em none but that of   85
cuckold.

LUCY And for her greater curse, madam, may he not deserve it.

ALETHEA Away, impertinent. Is not this my old Lady Lanterloo's?

LUCY Yes, madam—(*aside*) and here I hope we shall find Mr
Harcourt.   90

    Exeunt

5.4

Horner's lodging. [Chairs,] a table, banquet, and bottles°

[Enter] Horner [on one side of the stage], Lady Fidget,
Dainty Fidget, Mistress Squeamish [on the other]

HORNER (*aside*) A pox, they are come too soon—before I have sent
back my new—° mistress. All I have now to do, is to lock her in,
that they may not see her.

LADY FIDGET That we may be sure of our welcome, we have
brought our entertainment with us, and are resolved to treat thee,   5
dear toad.

DAINTY FIDGET And that we may be merry to purpose, have left Sir
Jasper and my old Lady Squeamish quarrelling at home at backgammon.

MISTRESS SQUEAMISH Therefore let us make use of our time, lest 10
they should chance to interrupt us.

LADY FIDGET Let us sit then.

HORNER First, that you may be private, let me lock this door, and
that, and I'll wait upon you presently.

LADY FIDGET No sir, shut 'em only, and your lips for ever, for we 15
must trust you as much as our women.

HORNER You know all vanity's killed in me; I have no occasion for
talking.

LADY FIDGET Now ladies, supposing we had drank each of us our
two bottles: let us speak the truth of our hearts. 20

DAINTY FIDGET and MISTRESS SQUEAMISH Agreed.

LADY FIDGET By this brimmer, for truth is nowhere else to be
found°—(*Aside to Horner*) Not in thy heart, false man.

HORNER (*aside to Lady Fidget*) You have found me a true man, I'm
sure. 25

LADY FIDGET (*aside to Horner*) Not every way. [*Aloud*] But let us sit
and be merry. (*Sings*)

> Why should our damned tyrants oblige us to live
> On the pittance of pleasure which they only give?
>   We must not rejoice 30
>   With wine and with noise;
> In vain we must wake in a dull bed alone,
> Whilst to our warm rival, the bottle, they're gone.
>   Then lay aside charms,
>   And take up these arms. ([*She points to*] *the glasses*) 35
>
> 'Tis wine only gives 'em their courage and wit;
> Because we live sober, to men we submit.
>   If for beauties you'd pass,
>   Take a lick of the glass;
> 'Twill mend your complexions, and when they are gone, 40
> The best red we have, is the red of the grape.
>   Then sisters, lay't on,
>   And damn a good shape.° [*She holds up the brimmer*]

DAINTY FIDGET Dear brimmer! Well, in token of our openness and
plain dealing, let us throw our masks over our heads. 45

HORNER [*aside*] So 'twill come to the glasses anon.

MISTRESS SQUEAMISH Lovely brimmer! Let me enjoy him first.

LADY FIDGET No, I never part with a gallant till I've tried him. Dear brimmer, that mak'st our husbands short-sighted. [*Drinks*]°

DAINTY FIDGET And our bashful gallants bold. [*Drinks*]   50

MISTRESS SQUEAMISH And, for want of a gallant, the butler lovely in our eyes. [*Drinks*] Drink, eunuch.

LADY FIDGET Drink, thou representative of a husband. Damn a husband.

            [*Horner drinks*]

DAINTY FIDGET And, as it were° a husband, an old keeper.   55

MISTRESS SQUEAMISH And an old grandmother.

HORNER And an English bawd, and a French chirurgeon.°

LADY FIDGET Ay, we have all reason to curse 'em.

HORNER For my sake, ladies.

LADY FIDGET No, for our own; for the first spoils all young gallants'   60
industry—

DAINTY FIDGET And the other's art makes 'em bold only with common women.

MISTRESS SQUEAMISH And rather run the hazard of the vile distemper amongst them, than of a denial amongst us.   65

DAINTY FIDGET The filthy toads choose mistresses now, as they do stuffs, for having been fancied and worn by others.

MISTRESS SQUEAMISH For being common and cheap.

LADY FIDGET Whilst women of quality, like the richest stuffs, lie untumbled and unasked for.   70

HORNER Ay, neat,° and cheap, and new, often they think best.

DAINTY FIDGET No sir, the beasts will be known by a mistress longer than by a suit.

MISTRESS SQUEAMISH And 'tis not for cheapness neither.

LADY FIDGET No, for the vain fops will take up druggets, and   75
embroider 'em. But I wonder at the depraved appetites of witty men; they use to be out of the common road, and hate imitation. Pray tell me, beast, when you were a man, why you rather chose to club with a multitude in a common house,° for an entertainment, than to be the only guest at a good table.   80

HORNER Why, faith, ceremony and expectation are unsufferable to those that are sharp bent. People always eat with the best stomach at an ordinary, where every man is snatching for the best bit.

LADY FIDGET Though he get a cut over the fingers. But I have   85 heard, people eat most heartily of another man's meat, that is, what they do not pay for.

HORNER When they are sure of their welcome and freedom; for ceremony in love and eating is as ridiculous as in fighting—falling on briskly is all should be done in those occasions. 90

LADY FIDGET Well then, let me tell you, sir, there is nowhere more freedom than in our houses, and we take freedom from a young person as a sign of good breeding, and a person may be as free as he pleases with us, as frolic, as gamesome, as wild as he will.

HORNER Ha'n't I heard you all declaim against wild men? 95

LADY FIDGET Yes, but for all that, we think wildness in a man as desirable a quality as in a duck, or rabbit.° A tame man, foh!

HORNER I know not, but your reputations frightened me, as much as your faces invited me.

LADY FIDGET Our reputation? Lord! Why should you not think that 100 we women make use of our reputation, as you men of yours, only to deceive the world with less suspicion? Our virtue is like the statesman's religion, the Quaker's word, the gamester's oath, and the great man's honour: but to cheat those that trust us.

MISTRESS SQUEAMISH And that demureness, coyness, and modesty 105 that you see in our faces in the boxes at plays, is as much a sign of a kind woman, as a vizard-mask in the pit.

DAINTY FIDGET For I assure you, women are least masked when they have the velvet vizard on.

LADY FIDGET You would have found us modest women in our 110 denials only.

MISTRESS SQUEAMISH Our bashfulness is only the reflection of the men's.

DAINTY FIDGET We blush when they are shamefaced.

HORNER I beg your pardon, ladies, I was deceived in you devilishly. 115 But why that mighty pretence to honour?

LADY FIDGET We have told you. But sometimes 'twas for the same reason you men pretend business often: to avoid ill company, to enjoy the better and more privately those you love.

HORNER But why would you ne'er give a friend a wink, then? 120

LADY FIDGET Faith, your reputation frightened us as much as ours did you—you were so notoriously lewd.

HORNER And you so seemingly honest.

LADY FIDGET Was that all that deterred you?

HORNER And so expensive—you allow freedom, you say?°— 125

LADY FIDGET Ay, ay.

HORNER That I was afraid of losing my little money, as well as my
little time, both which my other pleasures required.

LADY FIDGET Money, foh! You talk like a little fellow now. Do such
as we expect money?   130

HORNER I beg your pardon, madam. I must confess I have heard that
great ladies, like great merchants, set but the higher prices upon
what they have, because they are not in necessity of taking the first
offer.

DAINTY FIDGET Such as we, make sale of our hearts?   135

MISTRESS SQUEAMISH We bribed for our love? Foh!

HORNER With your pardon, ladies; I know, like great men in offices,
you seem to exact flattery and attendance only from your followers;
but you have receivers° about you, and such fees to pay, a man is
afraid to pass your grants.° Besides, we must let you win at cards,   140
or we lose your hearts.° And if you make an assignation, 'tis at a
goldsmith's, jeweller's, or china-house, where, for your honour you
deposit to him, he must pawn his to the punctual cit, and so paying
for what you take up, pays for what he takes up.°

DAINTY FIDGET Would you not have us assured of our gallants'   145
love?

MISTRESS SQUEAMISH For love is better known by liberality than by
jealousy.

LADY FIDGET For one may be dissembled, the other not. (*Aside*) But
my jealousy can be no longer dissembled, and they are telling-ripe.° 150
[*Aloud*] Come, here's to our gallants in waiting, whom we must
name; and I'll begin. This is my false rogue. (*Claps him on the back*)

MISTRESS SQUEAMISH How!

HORNER [*aside*] So all will out now!

MISTRESS SQUEAMISH (*aside to Horner*) Did you not tell me, 'twas   155
for my sake only you reported yourself no man?

DAINTY FIDGET (*aside to Horner*) Oh wretch! Did you not swear to
me, 'twas for my love and honour you passed for that thing you
do?

HORNER So, so.   160

LADY FIDGET Come, speak, ladies. This is my false villain.

MISTRESS SQUEAMISH And mine too.

DAINTY FIDGET And mine.

HORNER Well then, you are all three my false rogues too, and there's
an end on't.   165

LADY FIDGET Well then, there's no remedy. Sister sharers, let us not
fall out, but have a care of our honour; though we get no presents,

no jewels of him, we are savers of our honour, the jewel of most
value and use, which shines yet to the world unsuspected, though
it be counterfeit.   170
HORNER Nay, and is e'en as good as if it were true, provided the
world think so. For honour, like beauty now, only depends on the
opinion of others.
LADY FIDGET Well, Harry Common,° I hope you can be true to
three. Swear—but 'tis no purpose to require your oath, for you are   175
as often forsworn as you swear to new women.
HORNER Come, faith, madam, let us e'en pardon one another. For
all the difference I find betwixt we men, and you women: we
forswear ourselves at the beginning of an amour, you—as long as
it lasts.   180
  Enter Sir Jasper Fidget, and Old Lady Squeamish
SIR JASPER Oh, my Lady Fidget, was this your cunning, to come
to Mr Horner without me? But you have been nowhere else, I
hope?
LADY FIDGET No, Sir Jasper.
OLD LADY SQUEAMISH And you came straight hither, Biddy?   185
MISTRESS SQUEAMISH Yes indeed, lady grandmother.
SIR JASPER 'Tis well, 'tis well; I knew when once they were
throughly acquainted with poor Horner, they'd ne'er be from him.
[*To Old Lady Squeamish*] You may let her masquerade it with my
wife, and Horner, and I warrant her reputation safe.   190
  Enter Boy
BOY Oh sir, here's the gentleman come, whom you bid me not suffer
to come up without giving you notice—with a lady too, and other
gentlemen.
HORNER Do you all go in there, whilst I send 'em away—
  Exeunt Sir Jasper Fidget, Old Lady Squeamish, Lady
  Fidget, Dainty Fidget, Mistress Squeamish
And, boy, do you desire 'em to stay below till I come, which shall   195
be immediately.
BOY Yes, sir.
  Exit Boy. Exit Horner at t'other door, and returns with Mrs
  Pinchwife
HORNER You would not take my advice to begone home, before your
husband came back. He'll now discover all. Yet pray, my dearest,
be persuaded to go home, and leave the rest to my management.   200
I'll let you down the back way.
MRS PINCHWIFE I don't know the way home, so I don't.

HORNER My man shall wait upon you.

MRS PINCHWIFE No. Don't you believe that I'll go at all. What, are
you weary of me already?   205

HORNER No, my life, 'tis that I may love you long; 'tis to secure my
love, and your reputation with your husband—he'll never receive
you again else.

MRS PINCHWIFE What care I? D'ye think to frighten me with
that? I don't intend to go to him again. You shall be my husband   210
now.

HORNER I cannot be your husband, dearest, since you are married to
him.

MRS PINCHWIFE Oh, would you make me believe that? Don't I see
every day at London here, women leave their first husbands, and   215
go and live with other men as their wives. Pish! Pshaw! You'd make
me angry, but that I love you so mainly.

HORNER So, they are coming up—in again, in; I hear 'em.
       Exit Mrs Pinchwife
Well, a silly mistress is like a weak place:° soon got, soon lost; a
man has scarce time for plunder. She betrays her husband first to   220
her gallant, and then her gallant to her husband.
       *Enter Pinchwife, Alethea, Harcourt, Sparkish, Lucy, and a
       parson*

PINCHWIFE Come, madam, 'tis not the sudden change of your dress,
the confidence of your asseverations, and your false witness
there [*pointing to Lucy*], shall persuade me I did not bring you
hither just now. Here's *my* witness, who cannot deny it, since   225
you must be confronted.—Mr Horner, did not I bring this lady to
you just now?

HORNER (*aside*) Now must I wrong one woman for another's sake—
but that's no new thing with me, for in these cases I am still on the
criminal's side, against the innocent.   230

ALETHEA Pray speak, sir.

HORNER (*aside*) It must be so. I must be impudent, and try my luck;
impudence uses to be too hard for truth.

PINCHWIFE What, you are studying an evasion, or excuse for her?
Speak, sir.   235

HORNER No, faith, I am something backward only to speak° in
women's affairs or disputes.

PINCHWIFE She bids you speak.

ALETHEA Ay, pray sir, do; pray, satisfy him.

HORNER Then, truly, you did bring that lady to me just now.   240

PINCHWIFE Oh ho!—

ALETHEA How, sir!—

HARCOURT How, Horner!

ALETHEA What mean you, sir? I always took you for a man of honour. 245

HORNER (*aside*) Ay, so much a man of honour that I must save my mistress, I thank you, come what will on't.

SPARKISH So, if I had had her, she'd have made me believe the moon had been made of a Christmas pie.°

LUCY (*aside*) Now could I speak, if I durst, and solve the riddle, who 250 am the author of it.

ALETHEA Oh unfortunate woman! A combination against my honour, [*turning to Harcourt*] which most concerns me now because you share in my disgrace, sir, and it is your censure, which I must now suffer, that troubles me, not theirs. 255

HARCOURT Madam, then have no trouble. You shall now see 'tis possible for me to love too, without being jealous. I will not only believe your innocence myself, but make all the world believe it. (*Apart to Horner*) Horner, I must now be concerned for this lady's honour. 260

HORNER And I must be concerned for a lady's honour too.

HARCOURT This lady has her honour, and I will protect it.

HORNER My lady has not her honour, but has given it me to keep, and I will preserve it.

HARCOURT I understand you not. 265

HORNER I would not have you.

MRS PINCHWIFE (*peeping in behind*) What's the matter with 'em all?

PINCHWIFE Come, come, Mr Horner, no more disputing. Here's the parson; I brought him not in vain.

[HARCOURT]° No, sir; I'll employ him, if this lady please. 270

PINCHWIFE How! What d'ye mean?

SPARKISH Ay, what does he mean?

HORNER Why, I have resigned your sister to him; he has my consent.

PINCHWIFE But he has not mine, sir. A woman's injured honour, no more than a man's, can be repaired or satisfied by any but him that 275 first wronged it; and you shall marry her presently, or—(*Lays his hand on his sword*)

> *Enter Mrs Pinchwife*

MRS PINCHWIFE [*aside*] Oh Lord, they'll kill poor Mr Horner! Besides, he shan't marry her, whilst I stand by and look on; I'll not lose my second husband so. 280

PINCHWIFE What do I see?

ALETHEA My sister in my clothes!

SPARKISH Ha!

MRS PINCHWIFE Nay, pray now don't quarrel about finding work   285
for the parson. He shall marry me to Mr Horner, (*to Pinchwife*) for
now, I believe, you have enough of me.

HORNER [*aside*] Damned, damned, loving changeling!

MRS PINCHWIFE Pray sister, pardon me for telling so many lies of
you.

HARCOURT I suppose the riddle is plain now.   290

LUCY No, that must be my work.
    *Kneels to Pinchwife, who stands doggedly, with his hat over
    his eyes*
Good sir, hear me.

PINCHWIFE I will never hear woman again, but make 'em all silent,
thus—(*Offers to draw upon his wife*)

HORNER No, that must not be.   295

PINCHWIFE You, then, shall go first; 'tis all one to me.
    Offers to draw on Horner; stopped by Harcourt

HARCOURT Hold!
    *Enter Sir Jasper Fidget, Lady Fidget, Old Lady Squeamish,
    Dainty Fidget, Mistress Squeamish*

SIR JASPER What's the matter, what's the matter? Pray what's the
matter, sir? I beseech you, communicate, sir.

PINCHWIFE Why, my wife has communicated, sir, as your wife may   300
have done too, sir, if she knows him, sir.

SIR JASPER Pshaw! With him? Ha ha he!

PINCHWIFE D'ye mock me, sir? A cuckold is a kind of a wild beast;
have a care, sir!

SIR JASPER No, sure, you mock me, sir. He cuckold you? It can't be,   305
ha ha he! Why, I'll tell you, sir—(*Offers to whisper*)

PINCHWIFE I tell you again, he has whored my wife, and yours too,
if he knows her, and all the women he comes near. 'Tis not his
dissembling, his hypocrisy, can wheedle me.

SIR JASPER How! Does he dissemble? Is he a hypocrite? Nay   310
then—How!—Wife, sister, is he an hypocrite?

OLD LADY SQUEAMISH An hypocrite, a dissembler? Speak, young
harlotry; speak. How!

SIR JASPER Nay, then—Oh, my head too! Oh thou libidinous lady!

OLD LADY SQUEAMISH Oh thou harloting harlotry, hast thou done't   315
then?

SIR JASPER Speak, good Horner; art thou a dissembler, a rogue? Hast thou—?

HORNER Soh!°

LUCY (*apart to Horner*) I'll fetch you off, and her too, if she° will but   320
hold her tongue.

HORNER (*apart to Lucy*) Canst thou? I'll give thee—

LUCY (*to Pinchwife*) Pray have but patience to hear me, sir, who am the unfortunate cause of all this confusion. Your wife is innocent, I only culpable. For I put her upon telling you all these lies   325
concerning my mistress, in order to the breaking off the match between Mr Sparkish and her, to make way for Mr Harcourt.

SPARKISH Did you so, eternal rotten tooth? Then it seems my mistress was not false to me; I was only deceived by you. [*To Pinchwife*] Brother that should have been—now, man of con-   330
duct,° who is a frank person now, to bring your wife to her lover, ha?

LUCY I assure you, sir, she came not to Mr Horner out of love, for she loves him no more—

MRS PINCHWIFE Hold! I told lies for you, but you shall tell none for   335
me, for I do love Mr Horner with all my soul, and nobody shall say me nay. Pray, don't you go to make poor Mr Horner believe to the contrary; 'tis spitefully done of you, I'm sure.

HORNER (*aside to Mrs Pinchwife*) Peace, dear idiot.

MRS PINCHWIFE Nay, I will not peace.   340

PINCHWIFE Not till I make you.

Enter Dorilant, Quack

DORILANT Horner, your servant. I am the doctor's guest; he must excuse our intrusion.

QUACK But what's the matter, gentlemen? For heaven's sake, what's the matter?   345

HORNER Oh, 'tis well you are come! 'Tis a censorious world° we live in; you may have brought me a reprieve, or else I had died for a crime I never committed, and these innocent ladies had suffered with me. Therefore, pray satisfy these worthy, honourable, jealous gentlemen, that—(*Whispers*)   350

QUACK Oh, I understand you. Is that all?—Sir Jasper, by heavens, and upon the word of a physician, sir—(*Whispers to Sir Jasper*)

SIR JASPER Nay, I do believe you, truly.—Pardon me, my virtuous lady, and dear of honour.

OLD LADY SQUEAMISH What, then all's right again?   355

SIR JASPER Ay, ay, and now let us satisfy him too.

They whisper with Pinchwife

PINCHWIFE An eunuch? Pray, no fooling with me.

QUACK I'll bring half the chirurgeons in town to swear it.

PINCHWIFE They? They'll swear a man that bled to death through his wounds died of an apoplexy.°   360

QUACK Pray, hear me sir. Why, all the town has heard the report of him.

PINCHWIFE But does all the town believe it?

QUACK Pray, enquire a little, and first, of all these.

PINCHWIFE I'm sure when I left the town he was the lewdest fellow   365
in't.

QUACK I tell you, sir, he has been in France since. Pray ask but these ladies and gentlemen, your friend Mr Dorilant.—Gentlemen and ladies, ha'n't you all heard the late sad report of poor Mr Horner?

LADY FIDGET

DAINTY FIDGET

MISTRESS SQUEAMISH } Ay, ay, ay.   370

OLD LADY SQUEAMISH

DORILANT Why, thou jealous fool, dost thou doubt it? He's an arrant French capon.

MRS PINCHWIFE 'Tis false, sir; you shall not disparage poor Mr Horner, for to my certain knowledge—

LUCY Oh, hold!   375

MISTRESS SQUEAMISH (*aside to Lucy*) Stop her mouth!

LADY FIDGET (*to Pinchwife*) Upon my honour, sir, 'tis as true—

DAINTY FIDGET D'y' think we would have been seen in his company—?

MISTRESS SQUEAMISH Trust our unspotted reputations with him!   380

LADY FIDGET (*aside to Horner*) This you get, and we too, by trusting your secret to a fool—

HORNER Peace, madam. (*Aside to Quack*) Well, doctor, is not this a good design, that carries a man on unsuspected, and brings him off safe?   385

PINCHWIFE (*aside*) Well, if this were true; but my wife . . .

Dorilant whispers with Mrs Pinchwife°

ALETHEA Come, brother, your wife is yet innocent, you see. But have a care of too strong an imagination, lest like an over-concerned, timorous gamester, by fancying an unlucky cast, it should come. Women and Fortune are truest still to those that trust 'em.   390

LUCY And any wild thing grows but the more fierce and hungry for being kept up, and more dangerous to the keeper.

ALETHEA There's doctrine for all husbands, Mr Harcourt.

HARCOURT I edify, madam, so much, that I am impatient till I am one.   395

DORILANT And I edify so much by example, I will never be one.

SPARKISH And because I will not disparage my parts, I'll ne'er be one.

HORNER And I, alas, can't be one.

PINCHWIFE But I must be one—against my will, to a country wife,   400
with a country murrain to me.

MRS PINCHWIFE (*aside*) And I must be a country wife still too, I
find, for I can't (like a city one) be rid of my musty husband, and
do what I list.

HORNER Now, sir, I must pronounce your wife innocent, though I   405
blush whilst I do it, and I am the only man by her now exposed to
shame, which I will straight drown in wine, as you shall your
suspicion; and the ladies' troubles we'll divert with a ballet.—Doctor, where are your maskers?°

LUCY [*to Pinchwife*] Indeed, she's innocent, sir, I am her witness; and   410
her end of coming out was but to see her sister's wedding, and what
she has said to your face of her love to Mr Horner was but the
usual innocent revenge on a husband's jealousy—was it not,
madam? Speak.

MRS PINCHWIFE (*aside to Lucy and Horner*) Since you'll have me tell   415
more lies . . . —Yes indeed, bud.

PINCHWIFE For my own sake fain I would all believe;
    Cuckolds, like lovers, should themselves deceive.
    But—(*Sighs*)
    His honour is least safe (too late I find)   420
    Who trusts it with a foolish wife or friend.
    A dance of cuckolds°

HORNER Vain fops but court, and dress, and keep a pother,
    To pass for women's men with one another.
    But he who aims by women to be prized,
    First by the men (you see) must be despised.°   425

Epilogue

Spoken by Mrs Knepp°

Now you, the vigorous, who daily here
O'er vizard-mask in public domineer,
And what you'd do to her if in place where—°
Nay, have the confidence to cry 'Come out,'°
Yet when she says 'Lead on,' you are not stout,   5
But to your well-dressed brother straight turn round,
And cry, 'Pox on her, Ned, she can't be sound!'
Then slink away, a fresh one to engage,
With so much seeming heat and loving rage,
You'd frighten listening actress on the stage;   10
Till she at last has seen you huffing come,
And talk of keeping in the tiring-room,
Yet cannot be provoked to lead her home.
Next, you Falstaffs of fifty, who beset
Your buckram maidenheads, which your friends get;°   15
And whilst to them you of achievements boast,
They share the booty, and laugh at your cost.
In fine, you essenced boys, both old and young,
Who would be thought so eager, brisk, and strong,
Yet do the ladies, not their husbands, wrong,   20
Whose purses for your manhood make excuse,
And keep your Flanders mares for show, not use;°
Encouraged by our woman's man today,
A Horner's part may vainly think to play,
And may intrigues so bashfully disown   25
That they may doubted be by few or none;
May kiss the cards at piquet, ombre, loo—°
And so be thought to kiss the lady too.
But, gallants, have a care, faith, what you do;
The world, which to no man his due will give,   30
You, by experience, know you can deceive,
And men may still believe you vigorous;
But then, we women—there's no coz'ning us.

THE PLAIN DEALER°

Ridiculum acri
Fortius et melius magnas plerumque secat res.°

Horace

[DEDICATORY EPISTLE]
To my Lady B——°

Madam,

Though I never had the honour to receive a favour° from you, nay, or be known to you, I take the confidence of an author to write to you a *Billet-doux* Dedicatory—which is no new thing, for by most dedications it appears that authors, though they praise their patrons from top to toe, and seem to turn 'em inside out, know 'em as little 5 as sometimes their patrons their books, though they read 'em out;° and if the poetical daubers did not write the name of the man or woman on top of the picture, 'twere impossible to guess whose it were. But you, madam, without the help of a poet, have made yourself known and famous in the world, and, because you do not want it, are 10 therefore most worthy of an Epistle Dedicatory. And this play claims naturally your protection, since it has lost its reputation with the ladies of stricter lives in the playhouse; and (you know) when men's endeavours are discountenanced and refused by the nice, coy women of honour, they come to you—to you, the great and noble° patroness 15 of rejected and bashful men (of which number I profess myself to be one, though a poet, a dedicating poet), to you, I say, madam, who have as discerning a judgement, in what's obscene or not, as any quick-sighted civil person of 'em all, and can make as much of a double-meaning saying as the best of 'em; yet would not, as some do, 20 make nonsense of a poet's jest rather than not make it bawdy—by which they show they as little value wit in a play, as in a lover, provided they can bring t'other thing about. Their sense indeed lies all one way, and therefore are only for that in a poet which is moving, as they say. But what do they mean by that word 'moving'? Well, I 25 must not put 'em to the blush, since I find I can do't. In short, madam, you would not be one of those who ravish a poet's innocent words, and make 'em guilty of their own naughtiness (as 'tis termed) in spite of his teeth.° Nay, nothing is secure from the power of their imaginations—no, not their husbands, whom they cuckold with 30 themselves, by thinking of other men, and so make the lawful matrimonial embraces adultery, wrong husbands and poets in thought and word, to keep their own reputations. But your ladyship's justice, I know, would think a woman's arraigning and damning a poet for

her own obscenity, like her crying out a rape, and hanging° a man for   35
giving her pleasure, only that she might be thought not to consent
to't, and so, to vindicate her honour, forfeits her modesty. But you,
madam, have too much modesty to pretend to't, though you have as
much to say for your modesty as many a nicer she—for you never
were seen at this play, no, not the first day;° and 'tis no matter what   40
people's lives have been, they are unquestionably modest who frequent not this play. For, as Mr Bays says of his,° that it is the only
touchstone of men's wit and understanding, mine is (it seems) the
only touchstone of women's virtue and modesty. But hold: that
'touchstone'° is equivocal, and, by the strength of a lady's imagin-   45
ation, may become something that is not civil; but your ladyship, I
know, scorns to misapply a touchstone. And, madam, though you
have not seen this play, I hope (like other nice ladies) you will the
rather read it. Yet, lest the chambermaid or page should not be
trusted, and their indulgence could gain no further admittance for it   50
than to their ladies' lobbies or outward rooms, take it into your care
and protection, for by your recommendation and procurement° it may
have the honour to get into their closets: for what they renounce in
public often entertains 'em there, with your help especially. In fine,
madam, for these and many other reasons, you are the fittest patroness   55
or judge of this play, for you show no partiality to this or that author.
For from some, many ladies will take a broad jest as cheerfully as from
the watermen,° and sit at some downright filthy plays (as they call
'em) as well satisfied, and as still, as a poet could wish 'em elsewhere.
Therefore it must be the doubtful obscenity of my plays alone they   60
take exceptions at, because it is too bashful for 'em—and indeed most
women hate men for attempting to halves° on their chastity; and
bawdy, I find, like satire, should be home, not to have it taken notice
of. But now I mention satire, some there are who say 'tis the plain
dealing of the play, not the obscenity; 'tis taking off the ladies' masks,   65
not offering at their petticoats, which offends 'em. And generally they
are not the handsomest, or most innocent, who are the most angry at
being discovered:

> Nihil est audacius illis
> Deprehensis; iram atque animos a crimine sumunt.°   70

Pardon, madam, the quotation, for a dedication can no more be
without ends of Latin, than flattery; and 'tis no matter whom it is writ
to, for an author can as easily (I hope) suppose people to have more
understanding and languages than they have, as well as more virtues.

But why the devil should any of the few modest and handsome be   75
alarmed? (For some there are who as well as any deserve those
attributes, yet refrain not from seeing this play, nor think it any
addition to their virtue to set up for it in a playhouse, lest there it
should look too much like acting.) But why, I say, should any at all
of the truly virtuous be concerned, if those who are not so are   80
distinguished from 'em? For by that mask of modesty which women
wear promiscuously in public, they are all alike, and you can no more
know a kept wench from a woman of honour by her looks than by
her dress. For those who are of quality without honour (if any such
there are), they have their quality to set off their false modesty, as well   85
as their false jewels, and you must no more suspect their countenances
for counterfeit than their pendants, though, as the plain dealer
Montaigne says, 'Elles envoient leur conscience au bordel, et tiennent
leur contenance en règle.'° But those who act as they look, ought not
to be scandalized at the reprehension of others' faults, lest they tax   90
themselves with 'em, and by too delicate and quick an apprehension
not only make that obscene which I meant innocent, but that satire
on all, which was intended only on those who deserved it. But,
madam, I beg your pardon for this digression to civil women and
ladies of honour, since you and I shall never be the better for 'em; for   95
a comic poet, and a lady of your profession, make most of the other
sort, and the stage and your houses, like our plantations, are
propagated by the least nice women;° and as with the ministers of
justice, the vices of the age are our best business. But now I mention
public persons, I can no longer defer doing you the justice of a   100
dedication, and telling you your own,° who are, of all public-spirited
people, the most necessary, most communicative,° most generous and
hospitable. Your house has been the house of the people, your sleep
still disturbed for the public, and when you arose 'twas that others
might lie down, and you waked that others might rest. The good   105
you have done is unspeakable. How many young unexperienced
heirs have you kept from rash foolish marriages, and from being jilted
for their lives° by the worst sort of jilts, wives? How many unbe-
witched° widowers' children have you preserved from the tyranny of
stepmothers? How many old dotards from cuckoldage, and keeping   110
other men's wenches and children? How many adulteries and unnatural sins have you prevented? In fine, you have been a constant scourge
to the old lecher, and often a terror to the young. You have made
concupiscence its own punishment, and extinguished lust with
lust, like blowing up of houses to stop the fire.° 'Nimirum propter   115

continentiam, incontinentia necessaria est, incendium ignibus extinguitur.'°

There's Latin for you again, madam. I protest to you, as I am an author, I cannot help it—nay, I can hardly keep myself from quoting Aristotle and Horace, and talking to you of the rules of writing (like the French authors°), to show you and my readers I understand 'em, in my epistle, lest neither of you should find it out by the play. And according to the rules of dedications, 'tis no matter whether you understand or no, what I quote or say to you of writing, for an author can as easily make anyone a judge or critic, in an epistle, as an hero in his play. But, madam, that this may prove to the end a true Epistle Dedicatory, I'd have you know 'tis not without a design upon you, which is in the behalf of the fraternity of Parnassus,° that songs and sonnets may go° at your houses, and in your liberties,° for guineas° and half-guineas; and that wit, at least with you, as of old, may be the price of beauty, and so you will prove a true encourager of poetry, for love is a better help to it than wine, and poets, like painters, draw better after the life than by fancy. Nay, in justice, madam, I think a poet ought to be as free of your houses as of the playhouses,° since he contributes to the support of both, and is as necessary to such as you, as a ballad-singer to the pickpurse, in convening the cullies at the theatres, to be picked up and carried to supper and bed at your houses. And, madam, the reason of this motion of mine is because poor poets can get no favour in the tiring-rooms, for they are no keepers, you know; and folly and money, the old enemies of wit, are even too hard for it on its own dunghill.° And for other ladies, a poet can least go to the price of them. Besides, his wit, which ought to recommend him to 'em, is as much an obstruction to his love as to his wealth or preferment, for most women nowadays apprehend wit in a lover, as much as in a husband; they hate a man that knows 'em, they must have a blind easy fool, whom they can lead by the nose,° and as the Scythian women of old, must baffle a man, and put out his eyes, ere they will lie with him,° and then too, like thieves, when they have plundered and stripped a man, leave him. But if there should be one of an hundred of those ladies, generous enough to give herself to a man that has more wit than money, all things considered he would think it cheaper coming to you for a mistress, though you made him pay his guinea; as a man in a journey, out of good husbandry, had better pay for what he has in an inn, than lie on free cost at a gentleman's house.°

In fine, madam, like a faithful dedicator, I hope I have done myself right in the first place, then you and your profession, which in the wisest and most religious government of the world, is honoured with the public allowance,° and in those that are thought the most uncivilised and barbarous, is protected and supported by the ministers 160 of justice. And of you, madam, I ought to say no more here, for your virtues deserve a poem rather than an epistle, or a volume entire to give the world your memoirs, or life at large, and which (upon the word of an author that has a mind to make an end of his dedication) I promise to do, when I write the annals of our British love (which 165 shall be dedicated to the ladies concerned, if they will not think them something too obscene too), when your life, compared with many that are thought innocent, I doubt not may vindicate you, and me, to the world, for the confidence I have taken in this address to you, which then may be thought neither impertinent nor immodest. And what- 170 soever your amorous misfortunes have been, none can charge you with that heinous, and worst of women's crimes, hypocrisy—nay, in spite of misfortunes or age, you are the same woman still, though most of your sex grow magdalens at fifty, and, as a solid French author has it, 175

> Après le plaisir vient la peine,
> Après la peine, la vertue.°

But sure an old sinner's continency is much like a gamester's forswearing play when he has lost all his money; and modesty is a kind of a youthful dress which, as it makes a young woman more 180 amiable, makes an old one more nauseous. A bashful old woman is like an hopeful old man, and the affected chastity of antiquated beauties is rather a reproach than an honour to 'em, for it shows the men's virtue only, not theirs. But you, in fine, madam, are no more an hypocrite than I am when I praise you, therefore I doubt not will 185 be thought (even by yours and the play's enemies, the nicest ladies) to be the fittest patroness for, madam,

> Your ladyship's most obedient, faithful,
>> humble servant, and
>>> The Plain Dealer. 190

THE PERSONS

Manly (of an honest, surly, nice humour; supposed *Mr Hart*
    first, in the time of the Dutch War,° to have
    procured the command of a ship, out of honour,
    not interest, and choosing a sea life only to avoid
    the world)   5
Freeman (Manly's lieutenant, a gentleman well *Mr Kynaston*
    educated, but of a broken fortune; a complier
    with the age)
Varnish (Manly's bosom, and only, friend)   *Mr Griffin*
Novel (a pert, railing coxcomb, and an admirer of *Mr Clark*   10
    novelties; makes love to Olivia)
Major Oldfox (an old, impertinent fop, given to *Mr Cartwright*
    scribbling; makes love to the Widow Blackacre)
My Lord Plausible (a ceremonious, supple, com- *Mr Haines*
    mending coxcomb, in love with Olivia)   15
Jerry Blackacre (a true raw squire, under age, and *Mr Carlton*
    his mother's government; bred to the law)

Olivia (Manly's mistress)   *Mrs Marshall*
Fidelia (in love with Manly, and followed him to *Mrs Boutell*
    sea in man's clothes)   20
Eliza (cousin to Olivia)   *Mrs Knepp*
Letice° (Olivia's woman)   *Mrs Knight*
The Widow Blackacre (a petulant, litigious widow, *Mrs Corey*
    always in law, and mother to Squire Jerry; [a
    relative of Olivia])   25

Lawyers, Knights of the Post, Bailiffs, an Alderman, a Bookseller's
    Prentice, a Footboy, Sailors, Waiters, [a Servant, a constable], and
    attendants

THE SCENE

London

Prologue

Spoken by the Plain Dealer

I the Plain Dealer am to act today,°
And my rough part begins before the play.
First, you who scribble, yet hate all that write,
And keep each other company in spite,
As rivals in your common mistress, fame,   5
And with faint praises one another damn—°
'Tis a good play (we know) you can't forgive,
But grudge yourselves the pleasure you receive.
Our scribbler therefore bluntly bid me say
He would not have the wits pleased here today.   10
Next, you, the fine loud gentlemen o'th'pit,
Who damn all plays, yet, if y'ave any wit,
'Tis but what here you sponge and daily get;
Poets, like friends to whom you are in debt,
You hate: and so rooks laugh, to see undone   15
Those pushing gamesters whom they live upon.
Well, you are sparks, and still will be i'th'fashion:
Rail then at plays, to hide your obligation.
Now, you shrewd judges who the boxes sway,
Leading the ladies' hearts, and sense, astray,   20
And, for their sakes, see all, and hear no play,
Correct your cravats, foretops, lock behind,
The dress and breeding of the play ne'er mind;
Plain dealing is, you'll say, quite out of fashion;
You'll hate it here, as in a dedication.   25
And your fair neighbours, in a limning poet°
No more than in a painter will allow it.
Pictures too like, the ladies will not please:
They must be drawn too, here, like goddesses,°
You, as at Lely's too, would truncheon wield,°   30
And look like heroes, in a painted field;
But the coarse dauber of the coming scenes,
To follow life, and nature, only means—
Displays you as you are; makes his fine woman
A mercenary jilt, and true to no man.   35
His men of wit and pleasure of the age,°

290

Are as dull rogues as ever cumbered stage.
He draws a friend, only to custom just,°
And makes him naturally break his trust.
I, only, act a part like none of you;   40
And yet, you'll say, it is a fool's part too:
An honest man, who, like you, never winks
At faults, but, unlike you, speaks what he thinks;
The only fool who ne'er found patron yet,
For truth is now a fault, as well as wit.   45
And where else, but on stages, do we see
Truth pleasing, or rewarded honesty?—
Which our bold poet does this day in me.
If not to th'honest, be to th'prosp'rous kind:
Some friends at court let the Plain Dealer find.°   50

1.1

Captain Manly's lodging

*Enter Captain Manly, surlily, and Lord Plausible° following
him, and two Sailors behind*

MANLY Tell not me (my good Lord Plausible) of your decorums,
supercilious forms, and slavish ceremonies, your little tricks
which you, the spaniels of the world, do daily over and over, for
and to one another—not out of love or duty, but your servile
fear.   5

LORD PLAUSIBLE Nay, i'faith, i'faith, you are too passionate, and I
must humbly beg your pardon and leave to tell you they are the
arts, and rules, the prudent of the world walk by.

MANLY Let 'em. But I'll have no leading-strings; I can walk alone. I
hate a harness, and will not tug on in a faction, kissing my leader   10
behind,° that another slave may do the like to me.

LORD PLAUSIBLE What, will you be singular then? Like nobody?
Follow, love, and esteem nobody?

MANLY Rather than be general, like you—follow everybody, court
and kiss everybody, though, perhaps at the same time, you hate   15
everybody.

LORD PLAUSIBLE Why, seriously, with your pardon, my dear
friend—

MANLY With your pardon, my no-friend; I will not, as you do,
whisper my hatred, or my scorn, call a man fool or knave by signs,   20
or mouths over his shoulder, whilst you have him in your arms; for
such as you, like common whores and pickpockets, are only
dangerous to those you embrace.

LORD PLAUSIBLE Such as I! Heavens defend me! Upon my hon-
our—   25

MANLY Upon your title, my lord, if you'd have me believe you.

LORD PLAUSIBLE Well then, as I am a person of honour, I never
attempted to abuse or lessen any person, in my life.

MANLY What, you were afraid?

LORD PLAUSIBLE No. But seriously, I hate to do a rude thing. No,   30
faith, I speak well of all mankind.

MANLY I thought so. But know that speaking well of all mankind is
the worst kind of detraction, for it takes away the reputation of the
few good men in the world, by making all alike. Now I speak ill of

most men, because they deserve it—I, that can do a rude thing,   35
rather than an unjust thing.

LORD PLAUSIBLE Well, tell not me, my dear friend, what people
deserve; I ne'er mind that. I, like an author in a dedication, never
speak well of a man for his sake, but my own. I will not disparage
any man, to disparage myself; for to speak ill of people behind their   40
backs is not like a person of honour; and truly, to speak ill of 'em
to their faces, is not like a complaisant person. But if I did say, or
do, an ill thing to anybody, it should be sure to be behind their
backs, out of pure good manners.

MANLY Very well. But I, that am an unmannerly sea-fellow, if I ever   45
speak well of people (which is very seldom indeed) it should be sure
to be behind their backs, and if I would say or do ill to any, it
should be to their faces. I would jostle a proud, strutting, overlooking coxcomb, at the head of his sycophants, rather than put out my
tongue at him when he were past me; would frown in the arrogant,   50
big, dull face of an overgrown knave of business, rather than vent
my spleen against him when his back were turned; would give
fawning slaves the lie, whilst they embrace or commend me;
cowards, whilst they brag; call a rascal by no other title, though his
father had left him a duke's; laugh at fools aloud, before their   55
mistresses; and must desire people to leave me, when their visits
grow at last as troublesome, as they were at first impertinent.

LORD PLAUSIBLE I would not have my visits troublesome.

MANLY The only way to be sure not to have 'em troublesome, is to
make 'em when people are not at home; for your visits, like other   60
good turns, are most obliging when made, or done, to a man in his
absence. A pox, why should anyone, because he has nothing to do,
go and disturb another man's business?

LORD PLAUSIBLE I beg your pardon, my dear friend. What, you
have business?   65

MANLY If you have any, I would not detain your lordship.

LORD PLAUSIBLE Detain me, dear sir! I can never have enough of
your company.

MANLY I'm afraid I should be tiresome. I know not what you think.°

LORD PLAUSIBLE Well, dear sir, I see you would have me gone.   70

MANLY (aside) But I see you won't.

LORD PLAUSIBLE Your most faithful—

MANLY God be w'ye, my lord.

LORD PLAUSIBLE Your most humble—

MANLY Farewell.   75

LORD PLAUSIBLE And eternally—

MANLY And eternally ceremony—(*Aside*) Then the devil take thee eternally.

LORD PLAUSIBLE You shall use no ceremony, by my life.

MANLY I do not intend it.   80

LORD PLAUSIBLE Why do you stir then?

MANLY Only to see you out of doors, that I may shut 'em against more welcomes.

LORD PLAUSIBLE Nay, faith, that shan't pass upon your most faithful, humble servant.   85

MANLY (*aside*) Nor this any more upon me.
          [*Pushing Lord Plausible to the door*]

LORD PLAUSIBLE Well, you are too strong for me.

MANLY (*aside*) I'd sooner be visited by the plague, for that only would keep a man from visits, and his doors shut.
          Exit Manly, thrusting out Lord Plausible. Manent Sailors

FIRST SAILOR Here's a finical fellow, Jack! What a brave fairweather   90
captain of a ship he would make!

SECOND SAILOR He a captain of a ship! It must be when she's in the dock, then; for he looks like one of those that get the king's commissions for hulls,° to sell a king's ship when a brave fellow has fought her almost to a longboat.°   95

FIRST SAILOR On my conscience then, Jack, that's the reason our bully tar sunk our ship: not only that the Dutch might not have her, but that the courtiers, who laugh at wooden legs, might not make her prize.

SECOND SAILOR A pox of his sinking, Tom; we have made a base,   100
broken, short voyage of it.

FIRST SAILOR Ay, your brisk dealers in honour always make quick returns with their ship to the dock, and their men to the hospitals. 'Tis, let me see, just a month since we set out of the river, and the wind was almost as cross to us as the Dutch.   105

SECOND SAILOR Well, I forgive him sinking my own poor truck, if he would but have given me time and leave to have saved black Kate of Wapping's small venture.

FIRST SAILOR Faith, I forgive him, since, as the purser told me, he sunk the value of five or six thousand pound of his own, with which   110
he was to settle himself somewhere in the Indies, for our merry lieutenant was to succeed him in his commission for the ship back, for he was resolved never to return again for England.

SECOND SAILOR So it seemed, by his fighting.

FIRST SAILOR No, but he was aweary of this side of the world here,   115
they say.

SECOND SAILOR Ay, or else he would not have bid so fair for a
passage into t'other.

FIRST SAILOR Jack, thou think'st thyself in the forecastle, thou'rt so
waggish. But I tell you then, he had a mind to go live and bask   120
himself on the sunny side of the globe.

SECOND SAILOR What, out of any discontent?° For he's always as
dogged as an old tarpaulin when hindered of a voyage by a young
pantaloon captain.°

FIRST SAILOR 'Tis true, I never saw him pleased but in the fight,   125
and then he looked like one of us, coming from the pay-table, with
a new lining to our hats° under our arms—

SECOND SAILOR A pox, he's like the Bay of Biscay, rough and angry,
let the wind blow where 'twill.

FIRST SAILOR Nay, there's no more dealing with him, than with the   130
land in a storm: no near!°

SECOND SAILOR 'Tis a hurry-durry blade. Dost thou remember,
after we had tugged hard the old leaky longboat, to save his life,
when I welcomed him ashore he gave me a box on the ear, and
called me fawning water-dog?   135

Enter Manly and Freeman°

FIRST SAILOR Hold thy peace, Jack, and stand by; the foul weather's
coming.

MANLY You rascals, dogs, how could this tame thing get through
you?

FIRST SAILOR Faith, to tell your honour the truth, we were at   140
hob° in the hall, and whilst my brother and I were quarrelling
about a cast, he slunk by us.

SECOND SAILOR He's a sneaking fellow, I warrant for't.

MANLY Have more care for the future, you slaves. Go, and with
drawn cutlasses stand at the stair-foot, and keep all that ask for me   145
from coming up. Suppose you were guarding the scuttle to the
powder-room. Let none enter here, at your and their peril.

FIRST SAILOR No, for the danger would be the same: you would
blow them and us up, if we should.

SECOND SAILOR Must no-one come to you, sir?   150

MANLY No man, sir.

FIRST SAILOR No man, sir; but a woman then, an't like your honour—

MANLY No woman neither, you impertinent dog. Would you be
pimping? A sea-pimp is the strangest monster she has.

SECOND SAILOR Indeed, an't like your honour, 'twill be hard for us   155
to deny a woman anything, since we are so newly come on shore.

FIRST SAILOR We'll let no old woman come up, though it were our
trusting landlady at Wapping.

MANLY Would you be witty, you brandy casks you? You become a
jest as ill as you do a horse.° Begone, you dogs, I hear a noise on   160
the stairs.

    Exeunt Sailors

FREEMAN Faith, I am sorry you would let the fop go; I intended to
have had some sport with him.

MANLY Sport with him! A pox then, why did you not stay? You
should have enjoyed your coxcomb, and had him to yourself, for   165
me.

FREEMAN No, I should not have cared for him without you, neither;
for the pleasure which fops afford is like that of drinking, only good
when 'tis shared; and a fool, like a bottle, which would make you
merry in company, will make you dull alone. But how the devil   170
could you turn a man of his quality downstairs? You use a lord with
very little ceremony, it seems.

MANLY A lord! What, thou art one of those who esteem men only
by the marks and value Fortune has set upon 'em, and never
consider intrinsic worth. But counterfeit honour will not be current   175
with me; I weigh the man, not his title. 'Tis not the king's stamp
can make the metal better or heavier. Your lord is a leaden shilling,
which you may bend every way, and debases the stamp he bears,
instead of being raised by't.

    Enter Sailors

Here again, you slaves?   180

FIRST SAILOR Only to receive further instructions, an't like your
honour. What if a man should bring you money; should we turn
him back?

MANLY All men, I say. Must I be pestered with you too? You dogs,
away.   185

SECOND SAILOR Nay, I know one man your honour would not have
us hinder coming to you, I'm sure.

MANLY Who's that? Speak quickly, slaves.

SECOND SAILOR Why, a man that should bring you a challenge; for
though you refuse money, I'm sure you love fighting too well to   190
refuse that.

MANLY Rogue, rascal, dog.

    Kicks the Sailors out

FREEMAN Nay, let the poor rogues have their forecastle jests; they cannot help 'em in a fight, scarce when a ship's sinking.

MANLY Damn their untimely jests; a servant's jest is more sauciness than his counsel. 195

FREEMAN But what, will you see nobody? Not your friends?

MANLY Friends! I have but one, and he, I hear, is not in town—nay, can have but one friend, for a true heart admits but of one friendship, as of one love; but in having that friend I have a 200 thousand, for he has the courage of men in despair, yet the diffidency and caution of cowards; the secrecy of the revengeful, and the constancy of martyrs: one fit to advise, to keep a secret, to fight and die for his friend. Such I think him, for I have trusted him with my mistress in my absence; and the trust of beauty is sure 205 the greatest we can show.

FREEMAN Well, but all your good thoughts are not for him alone (I hope)? Pray, what d'ye think of me for a friend?

MANLY Of thee? Why, thou art a latitudinarian° in friendship, that is, no friend. Thou dost side with all mankind, but wilt suffer for 210 none. Thou art indeed like your Lord Plausible, the pink of courtesy, therefore hast no friendship; for ceremony, and great professing, renders friendship as much suspected as it does religion.

FREEMAN And no professing, no ceremony at all in friendship, were as unnatural and as undecent as in religion. And there is hardly 215 such a thing as an honest hypocrite, who professes himself to be worse than he is, unless it be yourself—for though I could never get you to say you were my friend, I know you'll prove so.

MANLY I must confess, I am so much your friend, I would not deceive you; therefore must tell you (not only because my heart is 220 taken up, but according to your rules of friendship) I cannot be your friend.

FREEMAN Why, pray?

MANLY Because he that is (you'll say) a true friend to a man, is a friend to all his friends; but you must pardon me—I cannot wish 225 well to pimps, flatterers, detractors, and cowards, stiff, nodding knaves, and supple, pliant, kissing fools. Now, all these I have seen you use like the dearest friends in the world.

FREEMAN Ha ha ha—What, you observed me, I warrant, in the galleries at Whitehall, doing the business of the place! Pshaw, court 230 professions, like court promises, go for nothing, man. But, faith, could you think I was a friend to all those I hugged, kissed, flattered, bowed to? Ha ha—

MANLY You told 'em so, and swore it too; I heard you.

FREEMAN Ay, but when their backs were turned, did I not tell you   235
they were rogues, villains, rascals, whom I despised and hated?

MANLY Very fine! But what reason had I to believe you spoke your
heart to me, since you professed deceiving so many?

FREEMAN Why, don't you know, good captain, that telling truth is a
quality as prejudicial, to a man that would thrive in the world, as   240
square play to a cheat, or true love to a whore? Would you have a
man speak truth to his ruin? You are severer than the law, which
requires no man to swear against himself. You would have me
speak truth against myself, I warrant, and tell my promising friend,
the courtier, he has a bad memory?   245

MANLY Yes.

FREEMAN And so make him remember to forget my business. And I
should tell the great lawyer too, that he takes oftener fees to hold
his tongue, than to speak?

MANLY No doubt on't.   250

FREEMAN Ay, and have him hang, or ruin me, when he should come
to be a judge, and I before him. And you would have me tell the
new officer, who bought his employment° lately, that he is a
coward.

MANLY Ay.   255

FREEMAN And so get myself cashiered, not him, he having the better
friends, though I the better sword. And I should tell the scribbler
of honour, that heraldry were a prettier and fitter study, for so fine
a gentleman, than poetry?

MANLY Certainly.   260

FREEMAN And so find myself mauled in his next hired° lampoon.
And you would have me tell the holy lady, too, she lies with her
chaplain?

MANLY No doubt on't.

FREEMAN And so draw the clergy upon my back, and want a good   265
table to dine at sometimes. And by the same reason too, I should
tell you that the world thinks you a madman, a brutal—and have
you cut my throat, or worse, hate me! What other good success of
all my plain dealing could I have, than what I've mentioned?

MANLY Why, first, your promising courtier would keep his word,   270
out of fear of more reproaches; or at least would give you no more
vain hopes. Your lawyer would serve you more faithfully, for he,
having no honour but his interest, is truest still to him he knows
suspects him. The new officer would provoke thee to make him a

coward, and so be cashiered, that thou, or some other honest   275
fellow, who had more courage than money, might get his place.
The noble sonneteer would trouble thee no more with his madrigals; the praying lady would leave off railing at wenching before
thee, and not turn away her chambermaid for her own known
frailty with thee; and I, instead of hating thee, should love thee for   280
thy plain dealing, and in lieu of being mortified, am proud that the
world and I think not well of one another.

FREEMAN Well, doctors differ.° You are for plain dealing, I find; but
against your particular notions, I have the practice of the whole
world. Observe but any morning what people do when they get   285
together on the Exchange, in Westminster Hall, or the galleries in
Whitehall.°

MANLY I must confess, there they seem to rehearse Bays's grand
dance.° Here you see a bishop bowing low to a gaudy atheist; a
judge, to a door-keeper;° a great lord, to a fishmonger, or a   290
scrivener with a jack-chain° about his neck; a lawyer, to a serjeant
at arms; a velvet physician, to a threadbare chemist, and a supple
gentleman-usher, to a surly beefeater; and so tread round in a
preposterous huddle of ceremony to each other, whilst they can
hardly hold their solemn false countenances.   295

FREEMAN Well, they understand the world.

MANLY Which I do not, I confess.

FREEMAN But, sir, pray believe the friendship I promise you real,
whatsoever I have professed to others. Try me, at least.

MANLY Why, what would you do for me?   300

FREEMAN I would fight for you.

MANLY That you would do for your own honour. But what else?

FREEMAN I would lend you money, if I had it.

MANLY To borrow more of me another time. That were but putting
your money to interest; a usurer would be as good a friend. But   305
what other piece of friendship?

FREEMAN I would speak well of you to your enemies.

MANLY To encourage others to be your friends, by a show of
gratitude. But what else?

FREEMAN Nay, I would not hear you ill spoken of behind your back,   310
by my friend.

MANLY Nay, then thou'rt a friend indeed. But it were unreasonable
to expect it from thee, as the world goes now, when new friends,
like new mistresses, are got by disparaging old ones.

    Enter Fidelia° [*in man's clothes*]

But here comes another, will say as much at least. Dost not thou   315
love me devilishly too, my little volunteer,° as well as he or any
man can?

FIDELIA Better than any man can love you, my dear captain.

MANLY Look you there; I told you so.

FIDELIA As well as you do truth, or honour, sir; as well.   320

MANLY Nay, good young gentleman, enough, for shame! Thou hast
been a page, by thy flattering and lying, to one of those praying
ladies, who love flattery so well they are jealous of it, and wert
turned away for saying the same things to the old housekeeper for
sweetmeats, as you did to your lady; for thou flatterest everything   325
and everybody alike.

FIDELIA You, dear sir, should not suspect the truth of what I say of
you, though to you. Fame, the old liar,° is believed, when she
speaks wonders of you. You cannot be flattered, sir, your merit is
unspeakable.   330

MANLY Hold, hold, sir, or I shall suspect worse of you—that you
have been a cushion-bearer° to some state hypocrite, and turned
away by the chaplains for out-flattering their probation sermons°
for a benefice.

FIDELIA Suspect me for anything, sir, but the want of love, faith, and   335
duty to you, the bravest, worthiest of mankind. Believe me, I could
die for you, sir.

MANLY Nay, there you lie, sir. Did I not see thee more afraid in the
fight than the chaplain of the ship, or the purser that bought his
place?°   340

FIDELIA Can he be said to be afraid, that ventures to sea with you?

MANLY Fie, fie, no more; I shall hate thy flattery worse than thy
cowardice, nay, than thy bragging.

FIDELIA Well, I own then I was afraid, mightily afraid. Yet for you
I would be afraid again, an hundred times afraid. Dying is ceasing   345
to be afraid, and that I could do, sure, for you, and you'll believe
me one day. (*Weeps*)

FREEMAN Poor youth! Believe his eyes, if not his tongue: he seems
to speak truth with them.

MANLY What, does he cry? A pox on't, a maudlin flatterer is as   350
nauseously troublesome as a maudlin drunkard. No more, you little
milksop. Do not cry; I'll never make thee afraid again. For of all
men, if I had occasion, thou shouldst not be my second, and when
I go to sea again, thou shalt venture thy life no more with me.

FIDELIA Why, will you leave me behind then? (*Aside*) If you would   355
preserve my life, I'm sure you should not.

MANLY Leave thee behind! Ay, ay, thou art a hopeful youth for the
shore only. Here thou wilt live to be cherished by Fortune, and the
great ones—for thou mayst easily come to out-flatter a dull poet,
out-lie a coffee-house or gazette writer,° out-swear a knight of the   360
post, out-watch a pimp, out-fawn a rook, out-promise a lover,
out-rail a wit, and out-brag a sea captain. All this thou canst do,
because thou'rt a coward, a thing I hate. Therefore thou'lt do better
with the world than with me; and these are the good courses you
must take in the world. There's good advice, at least, at parting.   365
Go, and be happy with't.

FIDELIA Parting, sir! Oh let me not hear that dismal word.

MANLY If my words frighten thee, begone the sooner. For, to be
plain with thee, cowardice and I cannot dwell together.

FIDELIA And cruelty and courage never dwelt together, sure, sir. Do   370
not turn me off to shame and misery, for I am helpless, and
friendless.

MANLY Friendless! There are half-a-score friends for thee then.
        Offers her gold
I leave myself no more. They'll help thee a little. Begone, go; I
must be cruel to thee (if thou call'st it so) out of pity.   375

FIDELIA If you would be cruelly pitiful, sir, let it be with your sword,
not gold.
        Exit Fidelia. Enter First Sailor

FIRST SAILOR We have, with much ado, turned away two gentlemen,
who told us forty times over, their names were Mr Novel and
Major Oldfox.   380

MANLY Well, to your post again.
        Exit First Sailor
But how come those puppies coupled always together?

FREEMAN Oh, the coxcombs keep each other company, to show each
other, as Novel calls it; or, as Oldfox says, like two knives, to whet
one another.°   385

MANLY And set other people's teeth on edge.
        Enter Second Sailor

SECOND SAILOR Here is a woman, an't like your honour, scolds and
bustles with us to come in, as much as a seaman's widow at the
Navy Office.° Her name is Mrs Blackacre.°

MANLY That fiend too!   390

FREEMAN The Widow Blackacre, is it not? That litigious she-pettifogger, who is at law and difference with all the world; but I wish I could make her agree with me in the church—they say she has fifteen hundred pounds a year jointure, and the care of her son, that is, the destruction of his estate.   395

MANLY Her lawyers, attornies, and solicitors have fifteen hundred pound a year, whilst she is contented to be poor, to make other people so. For she is as vexatious as her father was, the great attorney, nay, as a dozen Norfolk° attornies, and as implacable an adversary as a wife suing for alimony, or a parson for his tithes; and   400
she loves an Easter term,° or any term, not as other country ladies do, to come up to be fine, cuckold their husbands, and take their pleasure—for she has no pleasure, but in vexing others, and is usually clothed and daggled like a bawd in disguise, pursued through alleys by serjeants. When she is in town she lodges in one   405
of the Inns of Chancery,° where she breeds her son, and is herself his tutoress in law-French. And for her country abode, though she has no estate there, she chooses Norfolk. But bid her come in, with a pox to her. She is Olivia's kinswoman, and may make me amends for her visit by some discourse of that dear woman.   410

> *Exit Second Sailor. Enter Widow Blackacre, with a mantle°*
> *and a green bag, and several papers in the other hand; Jerry*
> *Blackacre her son, in a gown, laden with green bags,*
> *following her*

WIDOW BLACKACRE I never had so much to-do with a judge's door-keeper, as with yours, but—

MANLY But the incomparable Olivia, how does she since I went?

WIDOW BLACKACRE Since you went, my suit—

MANLY Olivia, I say, is she well?   415

WIDOW BLACKACRE My suit, if you had not returned—

MANLY Damn your suit, how does your cousin Olivia?

WIDOW BLACKACRE My suit, I say, had been quite lost; but now—

MANLY But now, where is Olivia? In town? For—

WIDOW BLACKACRE For tomorrow we are to have a hearing.   420

MANLY Would you'd let me have a hearing today.

WIDOW BLACKACRE But why won't you hear me?

MANLY I am no judge, and you talk of nothing but suits. But, pray tell me, when did you see Olivia?

WIDOW BLACKACRE I am no visitor, but a woman of business; or,   425
if I ever visit, 'tis only the Chancery Lane ladies, ladies towards the law,° and not any of your lazy good-for-nothing flirts, who cannot

read law-French, though a gallant writ it. But, as I was telling you, my suit—

MANLY Damn these impertinent, vexatious people of business, of all 430
sexes. They are still troubling the world with the tedious recitals of their lawsuits; and one can no more stop their mouths, than a wit's, when he talks of himself, or an intelligencer's, when he talks of other people.

WIDOW BLACKACRE And a pox of all vexatious, impertinent lovers. 435
They are still perplexing the world with the tedious narrations of their love-suits, and discourses of their mistresses: you are as troublesome to a poor widow of business, as a young, coxcombly, rhyming lover.

MANLY And thou art as troublesome to me, as a rook to a losing 440
gamester, or a young putter of cases to his mistress and seamstress,° who has love in her head for another.

WIDOW BLACKACRE Nay, since you talk of putting of cases, and will not hear me speak, hear our Jerry a little. Let him put our case to you, for the trial's tomorrow; and since you are my chief witness, 445
I would have your memory refreshed, and your judgement informed, that you may not give your evidence improperly. Speak out, child.

JERRY Yes, forsooth. Hem, hem! John-a-Stiles°—

MANLY You may talk, young lawyer, but I shall no more mind you 450
than a hungry judge does a cause, after the clock has struck one.°

FREEMAN [to Jerry] Nay, you'll find him as peevish too.

WIDOW BLACKACRE No matter. Jerry, go on. [To Freeman] Do you observe it then, sir, for I think I have seen you in a gown once. Lord, I could hear our Jerry put cases all day long! Mark him, sir. 455

JERRY John-a-Stiles—no—There are first: Fitz, Pere, and Ayle—no, no, Ayle, Pere, and Fitz. Ayle is seized in fee of Blackacre; John-a-Stiles disseises Ayle; Ayle makes claim, and the disseisor dies; then the Ayle—no, the Fitz—

WIDOW BLACKACRE No, the Pere, sirrah. 460

JERRY Oh, the Pere; ay, the Pere, sir, and the Fitz—no, the Ayle—no, the Pere and the Fitz, sir, and—

MANLY Damn Pere, Mere, and Fitz, sir.

WIDOW BLACKACRE No, you are out, child. Hear me, captain, then. There are Ayle, Pere, and Fitz. Ayle is seised in fee of Blackacre, 465
and being so seised, John-a-Stiles disseises the Ayle, Ayle makes claim, and the disseisor dies; and then the Pere re-enters, (To Jerry) the Pere, sirrah, the Pere.—And the Fitz enters upon the Pere, and

the Ayle brings his writ of disseisin, in the *post*, and the Pere brings
his writ of disseisin, in the *per*,° and— 470

MANLY Canst thou hear this stuff, Freeman? I could as soon suffer
a whole noise of flatterers at a great man's levee in a morning. But
thou hast servile complaisancy enough to listen to a quibbling
statesman in disgrace—nay, and be beforehand with him, in
laughing at his dull no-jest. But I—(*Offering to go out*) 475

WIDOW BLACKACRE Nay, sir, hold. Where's the subpoena, Jerry? I
must serve you, sir. You are required, by this, to give your
testimony—

MANLY I'll be forsworn, to be revenged on thee.
            Exit Manly, throwing away the subpoena

WIDOW BLACKACRE Get you gone, for a lawless companion. Come, 480
Jerry, I had almost forgot we were to meet at the Master's° at three.
Let us mind our business still, child.

JERRY Ay, forsooth, e'en so let's.

FREEMAN Nay, madam, now I would beg you to hear me a little—a
little of my business. 485

WIDOW BLACKACRE I have business of my own calls me away, sir.

FREEMAN My business would prove yours too, dear madam.

WIDOW BLACKACRE Yours would be some sweet business, I warrant. What, 'tis no Westminster Hall business? Would you have my
advice? 490

FREEMAN No, faith, 'tis a little Westminster Abbey business. I would
have your consent.

WIDOW BLACKACRE Oh fie, fie, sir—to me such discourse, before
my dear minor there!

JERRY Ay, ay, mother, he would be taking livery and seisin of your 495
jointure, by digging the turf;° but I'll watch your waters,° bully,
i'fac. Come away, mother.
            *Exit Jerry, hauling away his mother. Enter to Freeman,
            Fidelia*

FIDELIA Dear sir, you have pity; beget but some in our captain for
me.

FREEMAN Where is he? 500

FIDELIA Within—swearing, as much as he did in the great storm,
and cursing you, and sometimes sinks into calms, and sighs, and
talks of his Olivia.

FREEMAN He would never trust me to see her. Is she handsome?

FIDELIA No, if you'll take my word. But I am not a proper judge. 505

FREEMAN What is she?

FIDELIA A gentlewoman, I suppose, but of as mean a fortune as
beauty. But her relations would not suffer her to go with him to
the Indies; and his aversion to this side of the world, together with
the late opportunity of commanding the convoy, would not let him   510
stay here longer, though to enjoy her.

FREEMAN He loves her mightily then.

FIDELIA Yes, so well, that the remainder of his fortune (I hear about
five or six thousand pounds) he has left her, in case he had died by
the way,° or before she could prevail with her friends to follow   515
him, which he expected she should do; and has left behind him his
great bosom friend to be her convoy to him.

FREEMAN What charms has she for him, if she be not handsome?

FIDELIA He fancies her, I suppose, the only woman of truth and
sincerity in the world.   520

FREEMAN No common beauty, I confess.

FIDELIA Or else sure he would not have trusted her with so great a
share of his fortune, in his absence—I suppose (since his late loss)
all he has.

FREEMAN Why, has he left it in her own custody?   525

FIDELIA I am told so.

FREEMAN Then he has showed love to her indeed, in leaving her,
like an old husband that dies as soon as he has made his wife a good
jointure. But I'll go in to him, and speak for you, and know more
from him of his Olivia.   530

    Exit Freeman

FIDELIA His Olivia indeed, his happy Olivia,
  Yet she was left behind, when I was with him—
  But she was ne'er out of his mind or heart.
  She has told him she loved him; I have showed it,
  And durst not tell him so, till I had done,   535
  Under this habit, such convincing acts
  Of loving friendship for him, that through it
  He first might find out both my sex and love;
  And, when I'd had him from his fair Olivia,
  And this bright world of artful beauties here,   540
  Might then have hoped he would have looked on me
  Amongst the sooty Indians; and I could,
  To choose, there live his wife, where wives are forced
  To live no longer, when their husbands die—
  Nay, what's yet worse, to share 'em whilst they live   545
  With many rival wives. But here he comes,

And I must yet keep out of his sight, not
To lose it for ever.
   Exit Fidelia. Enter Manly and Freeman

FREEMAN But pray, what strange charms has she that could make
you love?   550

MANLY Strange charms indeed! She has beauty enough to call in
question her wit or virtue, and her form would make a starved
hermit a ravisher. Yet her virtue, and conduct, would preserve her
from the subtle lust of a pampered prelate. She is so perfect a
beauty that art could not better it, nor affectation deform it—yet   555
all this is nothing. Her tongue, as well as face, ne'er knew artifice;
nor ever did her words or looks contradict her heart. She is all
truth, and hates the lying, masking, daubing world, as I do; for
which I love her, and for which I think she dislikes not me. For
she has often shut out of her conversation, for mine, the gaudy   560
fluttering parrots of the town, apes, and echoes of men only, and
refused their commonplace pert chat, flattery, and submissions, to
be entertained with my sullen bluntness, and honest love. And, last
of all, swore to me, since her parents would not suffer her to go
with me, she would stay behind for no other man, but follow me   565
without their leave, if not to be obtained. Which oath—

FREEMAN Did you think she would keep?

MANLY Yes: for she is not (I tell you) like other women, but can keep
her promise, though she has sworn to keep it. But, that she might
the better keep it, I left her the value of five or six thousand pound;   570
for women's wants are generally their most importunate solicitors
to love, or marriage.

FREEMAN And money summons lovers more than beauty, and
augments but their importunity and their number; so makes it the
harder for a woman to deny 'em. For my part, I am for the French   575
maxim:° if you would have your female subjects loyal, keep 'em
poor. But, in short, that your mistress may not marry, you have
given her a portion.

MANLY She had given me her heart first, and I am satisfied with the
security; I can never doubt her truth and constancy.   580

FREEMAN It seems you do, since you are fain to bribe it with money.
But how come you to be so diffident of the man that says he loves
you, and not doubt the woman that says it?

MANLY I should (I confess) doubt the love of any other woman but
her, as I do the friendship of any other man but him I have trusted.   585
But I have such proofs of their faith as cannot deceive me.

FREEMAN Cannot!

MANLY Not but I know that, generally, no man can be a great
enemy, but under the name of friend; and if you are a cuckold, it
is your friend only that makes you so—for your enemy is not   590
admitted to your house. If you are cheated in your fortune, 'tis your
friend that does it, for your enemy is not made your trustee. If your
honour, or good name be injured, 'tis your friend that does it still,
because your enemy is not believed against you. Therefore I rather
choose to go where honest, downright barbarity is professed; where   595
men devour one another like generous hungry lions and tigers, not
like crocodiles; where they think the devil white, of our complexion, and I am already so far an Indian. But, if your weak faith
doubts this miracle of a woman, come along with me, and believe,
and thou wilt find her so handsome, that thou, who art so much   600
my friend, wilt have a mind to lie with her, and so will not fail to
discover what her faith and thine is to me.

　　　When we're in love, the great adversity,
　　　Our friends and mistresses at once we try.
　[*Exeunt*]

2.1

Olivia's lodging

Enter Olivia, Eliza, Letice

OLIVIA Ah, cousin, what a world 'tis we live in! I am so weary of it.

ELIZA Truly, cousin, I can find no fault with it, but that we cannot always live in't; for I can never be weary of it.

OLIVIA Oh hideous! You cannot be in earnest, sure, when you say you like the filthy world. 5

ELIZA You cannot be in earnest, sure, when you say you dislike it.

OLIVIA You are a very censorious creature, I find.

ELIZA I must confess I think we women as often discover where we love, by railing, as men when they lie, by their swearing. And the world is but a constant keeping gallant, whom we fail not to quarrel 10 with, when anything crosses us, yet cannot part with't for our hearts.

LETICE A gallant indeed, madam, whom ladies first make jealous, and then quarrel with it for being so; for if, by her indiscretion, a lady be talked of for a man,° she cries presently, ''Tis a censorious 15 world.' If, by her vanity, the intrigue be found out, ''Tis a prying, malicious world.' If, by her over-fondness, the gallant proves unconstant, ''Tis a false world.' And if, by her niggardliness, the chambermaid tells,° ''Tis a perfidious world'—but that, I'm sure, your ladyship cannot say of the world yet, as bad as 'tis. 20

OLIVIA But I may say, ''Tis a very impertinent world.' Hold your peace.—And, cousin, if the world be a gallant, 'tis such an one as is my aversion.° Pray name it no more.

ELIZA But is it possible the world, which has such variety of charms for other women, can have none for you? Let's see . . . First, what 25 d'ye think of dressing, and fine clothes?

OLIVIA Dressing! Fie, fie, 'tis my aversion. [*To Letice*] But come hither, you dowdy, methinks you might have opened this *tour* better. Oh hideous! I cannot suffer it! [*To Eliza*] D'ye see how't sits?

ELIZA Well enough, cousin, if dressing be your aversion. 30

OLIVIA 'Tis so. And for variety of rich clothes, they are more my aversion.

LETICE Ay, 'tis because your ladyship wears 'em too long. For indeed a gown, like a gallant, grows one's aversion by having too much of it. 35

OLIVIA Insatiable creature! I'll be sworn I have had this not above
three days, cousin, and within this month have made some six
more.

ELIZA Then your aversion to 'em is not altogether so great.

OLIVIA Alas! 'Tis for my woman only I wear 'em, cousin.   40

LETICE If it be for me only, madam, pray do not wear 'em.

ELIZA But what d'ye think of visits—balls—

OLIVIA Oh, I detest 'em.

ELIZA Of plays?

OLIVIA I abominate 'em—filthy, obscene, hideous things!   45

ELIZA What say you to masquerading in the winter, and Hyde Park
in the summer?

OLIVIA Insipid pleasures I taste not.

ELIZA Nay, if you are for more solid pleasure, what think you of a
rich, young husband?   50

OLIVIA Oh horrid! Marriage! What a pleasure you have found out! I
nauseate it of all things.

LETICE But what does your ladyship think then of a liberal, handsome, young lover?

OLIVIA A handsome young fellow, you impudent! Begone; out of my   55
sight. Name a handsome young fellow to me! Foh, a hideous
handsome young fellow I abominate. (*Spits*)

ELIZA Indeed! But let's see . . . Will nothing please you? What d'ye
think of the court?

OLIVIA How! The court! The court, cousin! My aversion, my   60
aversion, my aversion of all aversions.

ELIZA How! The court! Where—

OLIVIA Where sincerity is a quality as out of fashion, and as un-
prosperous, as bashfulness. I could not laugh at a quibble, though
it were a fat privy councillor's; nor praise a lord's ill verses, though I   65
were myself the subject; nor an old lady's young looks, though I were
her woman; nor sit to a vain young simile-maker, though he
flattered me. In short, I could not gloat upon a man when he comes
into a room, and laugh at him when he goes out. I cannot rail at
the absent, to flatter the standers-by; I—   70

ELIZA Well, but railing now is so common, that 'tis no more malice,
but the fashion; and the absent think they are no more the worse
for being railed at, than the present think they are the better for
being flattered. And for the court—

OLIVIA Nay, do not defend the court, for you'll make me rail at it,   75
like a trusting citizen's widow.°

ELIZA Or like a Holborn° lady, who could not get into the last ball,
or was out of countenance in the drawing-room the last Sunday of
her appearance there. For none rail at the court but those who
cannot get into it, or else who are ridiculous when they are there.   80
And I shall suspect you were laughed at, when you were last there,
or would be a maid of honour.

OLIVIA I a maid of honour! To be a maid of honour were yet of all
things my aversion.

ELIZA In what sense am I to understand you? But, in fine, by the   85
word 'aversion' I'm sure you dissemble—for I never knew woman
yet that used it, who did not. Come, our tongues belie our hearts,
more than our pocket-glasses do our faces. But methinks we ought
to leave off dissembling, since 'tis grown of no use to us; for all
wise observers understand us nowadays as they do dreams, alman-   90
acs, and Dutch gazettes: by the contrary.° And a man no more
believes a woman, when she says she has an aversion for him, than
when she says she'll cry out.

OLIVIA Oh filthy, hideous! Peace, cousin, or your discourse will be
my aversion—and you may believe me.   95

ELIZA Yes; for if anything be a woman's aversion, 'tis plain dealing
from another woman. And perhaps that's your quarrel to the world;
for that will talk, as your woman says.

OLIVIA Talk not of me, sure; for what men do I converse with? What
visits do I admit?   100

    Enter Boy

BOY Here's the gentleman to wait upon you, madam.

OLIVIA On me! You little, unthinking fop, d'ye know what you
say?

BOY Yes, madam, 'tis the gentleman that comes every day to you,
who—   105

OLIVIA Hold your peace, you heedless little animal, and get you
gone.—This country boy, cousin, takes my dancing-master, tailor,
or the spruce milliner, for visitors.

    Exit Boy

LETICE No, madam, 'tis Mr Novel, I'm sure, by his talking so loud.
I know his voice too, madam.   110

OLIVIA You know nothing, you buffle-headed, stupid creature you.
You would make my cousin believe I receive visits. But if it be
Mr—what did you call him?

LETICE Mr Novel, madam, he that—

OLIVIA Hold you peace, I'll hear no more of him. But if it be your   115

Mr—(I can't think of his name again), I suppose he has followed
my cousin hither.

ELIZA No, cousin, I will not rob you of the honour of the visit: 'tis
to you, cousin, for I know him not.

OLIVIA Nor did I ever hear of him before, upon my honour, cousin.   120
Besides, ha'n't I told you, that visits, and the business of visits—
flattery and detraction—are my aversion? D'ye think, then, I would
admit such a coxcomb as he is?—who, rather than not rail, will rail
at the dead, whom none speak ill of;° and rather than not flatter,
will flatter the poets of the age, whom none will flatter; who affects   125
novelty as much as the fashion, and is as fantastical as changeable,
and as well known as the fashion; who likes nothing but what is
new—nay, would choose to have his friend, or his title, a new one.
In fine, he is my aversion.

ELIZA I find you do know him, cousin; at least, have heard of him.   130

OLIVIA Yes, now I remember, I have heard of him.

ELIZA Well; but since he is such a coxcomb, for heaven's sake let him
not come up.—Tell him, Mistress Letice, your lady is not within.

OLIVIA No, Lettice, tell him my cousin is here, and that he may
come up. [To Eliza] For notwithstanding I detest the sight of him,   135
you may like his conversation, and though I would use him
scurvily, I will not be rude to you in my own lodging. Since he has
followed you hither, let him come up, I say.

ELIZA Very fine! Pray let him go to the devil, I say, for me: I know
him not, nor desire it. Send him away, Mistress Letice.   140

OLIVIA Upon my word, she shan't. I must disobey your commands,
to comply with your desires. Call him up, Letice.

ELIZA Nay, I'll swear she shall not stir on that errand.
        Holds Letice

OLIVIA Well then, I'll call him myself for you, since you will have it
so. (*Calls out at the door*) Mr Novel, sir, sir!   145
        Enter Novel

NOVEL Madam, I beg your pardon; perhaps you were busy—I did
not think you had company with you.

ELIZA (*aside [to Olivia]*) Yet he comes to me, cousin!

OLIVIA Chairs there!
        [*Servants bring in chairs;*] *Olivia, Eliza, and Novel sit.*
        [*Exeunt Letice and Servants*]°

NOVEL Well, but madam, d'ye know whence I come now?   150

OLIVIA From some melancholy place, I warrant, sir, since they have
lost your good company.

ELIZA So.

NOVEL From a place where they have treated me, at dinner, with so
much civility and kindness, a pox on 'em, that I could hardly get   155
away to you, dear madam.

OLIVIA You have a way with you so new, and obliging, sir.

ELIZA (*apart to Olivia*) You hate flattery, cousin!

NOVEL Nay faith, madam, d'ye think my way new? Then *you* are
obliging, madam. I must confess, I hate imitation, to do anything   160
like other people: all that know me, do me the honour to say I am
an original, faith. But as I was saying, madam, I have been treated
today with all the ceremony and kindness imaginable, at my Lady
Autumn's. But the nauseous old woman at the upper end of her
table—   165

OLIVIA Revives the old Grecian custom of serving in a death's head
with their banquets.°

NOVEL Ha ha! Fine, just, i'faith—nay, and new. 'Tis like eating with
the ghost in *The Libertine*;° she would frighten a man from her
dinner, with her hollow invitations, and spoil one's stomach—   170

OLIVIA To meat, or women. I detest her hollow cherry cheeks; she
looks like an old coach new painted: affecting an unseemly smugness, whilst she is ready to drop in pieces.

ELIZA (*apart to Olivia*) You hate detraction I see, cousin!

NOVEL But the silly old fury, whilst she affects to look like a woman   175
of this age, talks—

OLIVIA Like one of the last—and as passionately as an old courtier
who has outlived his office.

NOVEL Yes, madam, but pray let me give you her character. Then,
she never counts her age by the years, but—   180

OLIVIA By the masques she has lived to see.

NOVEL Nay then, madam, I see you think a little harmless railing too
great a pleasure for any but yourself, and therefore I've done.

OLIVIA Nay, faith, you shall tell me who you had there at dinner.

NOVEL If you would hear me, madam.   185

OLIVIA Most patiently. Speak, sir.

NOVEL Then, we had her daughter—

OLIVIA Ay, her daughter, the very disgrace to good clothes, which
she always wears but to heighten her deformity, not mend it; for
she is still most splendidly, gallantly ugly, and looks like an ill piece   190
of daubing in a rich frame.

NOVEL So! But have you done with her, madam? And can you spare
her to me a little now?

OLIVIA Ay, ay, sir.

NOVEL Then, she is like—   195

OLIVIA She is, you'd say, like a City bride,° the greater fortune, but
not the greater beauty, for her dress.

NOVEL Well; yet have you done, madam? Then, she—

OLIVIA Then she bestows as unfortunately on her face all the graces
in fashion, as the languishing eye, the hanging or pouting lip; but   200
as the fool is never more provoking than when he aims at wit, the
ill-favoured of our sex are never more nauseous than when they
would be beauties, adding to their natural deformity the artificial
ugliness of affectation.

ELIZA So, cousin, I find one may have a collection of all one's   205
acquaintances' pictures as well at your house as at Mr Lely's;° only
the difference is, there we find 'em much handsomer than they are,
and like; here, much uglier, and like. And you are the first of the
profession of picture-drawing I ever knew without flattery.

OLIVIA I draw after the life, do nobody wrong, cousin.   210

ELIZA No, you hate flattery and detraction!

OLIVIA But, Mr Novel, who had you besides at dinner?

NOVEL Nay, the devil take me if I tell you, unless you will allow me
the privilege of railing in my turn. But, now I think on't, the
women ought to be your province, as the men are mine; and you   215
must know, we had him whom—

OLIVIA Him, whom—

NOVEL What! Invading me already? And giving the character, before
you know the man?

ELIZA No, that is not fair, though it be usual.   220

OLIVIA I beg your pardon, Mr Novel; pray, go on.

NOVEL Then, I say, we had that familiar coxcomb, who is at home
wheresoe'er he comes.

OLIVIA Ay, that fool—

NOVEL Nay then, madam, your servant; I'm gone. Taking a fool out   225
of one's mouth is worse than taking the bread out of one's mouth.°

OLIVIA I've done. Your pardon, Mr Novel; pray proceed.

NOVEL I say, the rogue, that he may be the only wit in company, will
let nobody else talk, and—

OLIVIA Ay, those fops who love to talk all themselves, are of all   230
things my aversion.

NOVEL Then you'll let me speak, madam, sure. The rogue, I say, will
force his jest upon you—and I hate a jest that's forced upon a man,
as much as a glass.

ELIZA Why, I hope, sir, he does not expect a man of your temperance   235
in jesting should do him reason?

NOVEL What, interruption from this side too! I must then—
Offers to rise; Olivia holds him

OLIVIA No, sir.—You must know, cousin, that fop he means, though
he talks only to be commended, will not give you leave to do't.

NOVEL But, madam—   240

OLIVIA He a wit! Hang him, he's only an adopter of straggling jests,
and fatherless lampoons, by the credit of which he eats at good
tables, and so, like the barren beggar-woman, lives by borrowed
children.

NOVEL Madam—   245

OLIVIA And never was author of anything, but his news—but that is
still all his own.

NOVEL Madam, pray—

OLIVIA An eternal babbler; and makes no more use of his ears than
a man that sits at a play by his mistress, or in fop-corner.° He's, in   250
fine, a base detracting fellow, and is my aversion. But who else
prithee, Mr Novel, was there with you? Nay, you shan't stir.

NOVEL I beg your pardon, madam, I cannot stay in any place where
I'm not allowed a little Christian liberty of railing.

OLIVIA Nay, prithee, Mr Novel, stay; and, though you should rail at   255
me, I would hear you with patience. Prithee who else was there
with you?

NOVEL Your servant, madam.

OLIVIA Nay, prithee tell us, Mr Novel, prithee do.

NOVEL We had nobody else.   260

OLIVIA Nay, faith I know you had. Come, my Lord Plausible was
there too, who is, cousin, a—

ELIZA You need not tell me what he is, cousin, for I know him to be
a civil, good-natured, harmless gentleman, that speaks well of all
the world, and is always in good humour, and—   265

OLIVIA Hold, cousin, hold. I hate detraction—but I must tell you,
cousin, his civility is cowardice; his good nature, want of wit; and
has neither courage or sense to rail. And for his being always
in humour, 'tis because he is never dissatisfied with himself.
In fine, he is my aversion, and I never admit his visits beyond my   270
hall.

NOVEL No! He visit you! Damn him, cringing, grinning rogue; if I
should see him coming up to you, I would make bold to kick him
down again.

Enter Lord Plausible

Ha!—My dear lord, your most humble servant.   275

Rises and salutes Lord Plausible, and kisses him°

ELIZA (*aside*) So! I find kissing and railing succeed each other with
the angry men, as well as with the angry women; and their quarrels
are like love-quarrels, since absence is the only cause of them—for
as soon as the man appears again, they are over.

LORD PLAUSIBLE Your most faithful, humble servant, generous Mr   280
Novel. [*To Olivia*] And, madam, I am your eternal slave, and kiss
your fair hands; which I had done sooner, according to your
commands, but—

OLIVIA No excuses, my lord.

ELIZA (*apart* [*to Olivia*]) What, you sent for him then, cousin?   285

NOVEL (*aside*) Ha! Invited!

OLIVIA I know you must divide yourself, for your good company is
too general a good to be engrossed by any particular friend.

LORD PLAUSIBLE Oh Lord, madam, my company! Your most
obliged, faithful, humble servant. But I could have brought you   290
good company indeed, for I parted at your door with two of the
worthiest, bravest men—

OLIVIA Who were they, my lord?

NOVEL Who do you call the worthiest, bravest men, pray?

LORD PLAUSIBLE Oh, the wisest, bravest gentlemen! Men of such   295
honour and virtue! Of such good qualities! Ah—

ELIZA (*aside*) This is a coxcomb that speaks ill of all people a different
way, and libels everybody with dull praise, and commonly in the
wrong place; so makes his panegyrics abusive lampoons.

OLIVIA But pray let me know who they were.   300

LORD PLAUSIBLE Ah! Such patterns of heroic virtue! Such—

NOVEL Well, but who the devil were they?

LORD PLAUSIBLE The honour of our nation, the glory of our age.
Ah! I could dwell a twelvemonth on their praise—which indeed I
might spare by telling their names: Sir John Current, and Sir   305
Richard Court-Title.

NOVEL Court-Title! Ha ha!

OLIVIA And Sir John Current! Why will you keep such a wretch
company, my lord?

LORD PLAUSIBLE Oh, madam, seriously you are a little too severe;   310
for he is a man of unquestioned reputation in everything.

OLIVIA Yes, because he endeavours only with the women to pass for
a man of courage, and with the bullies for a wit; with the wits, for

315

a man of business, and with the men of business, for a favourite at court; and at court, for good City security.° 315

NOVEL And for Sir Richard, he—

LORD PLAUSIBLE He loves your choice, picked company, persons that—

OLIVIA He loves a lord indeed; but—

NOVEL Pray, dear madam, let me have but a bold stroke or two at 320 his picture. He loves a lord, as you say, though—

OLIVIA Though he borrowed his money, and ne'er paid him again.

NOVEL And would bespeak a place three days before at the back-end of a lord's coach,° to Hyde Park.

LORD PLAUSIBLE Nay, i'faith, i'faith, you are both too severe. 325

OLIVIA Then, to show yet more his passion for quality, he makes love to that fulsome coachload of honour, my Lady Goodly—for he is always at her lodging.

LORD PLAUSIBLE Because it is the conventicle gallant,° the meeting-house of all the fair ladies, and glorious superfine beauties of the 330 town.

NOVEL Very fine ladies! There's first—

OLIVIA Her honour, as fat as an hostess.

LORD PLAUSIBLE She is something plump indeed, a goodly, comely, graceful person. 335

NOVEL Then there's my Lady Frances . . . what d'ye call 'er? As ugly—

OLIVIA As a citizen's lawfully begotten daughter.

LORD PLAUSIBLE She has wit in abundance; and the handsomest heel, elbow, and tip of an ear, you ever saw. 340

NOVEL Heel, and elbow! Ha ha! And there's my Lady Betty, you know—

OLIVIA As sluttish, and slatternly, as an Irishwoman bred in France.

LORD PLAUSIBLE Ah, all she has hangs with a loose air indeed, and becoming negligence. 345

ELIZA You see all faults with lover's eyes, I find, my lord.

LORD PLAUSIBLE Ah, madam, your most obliged, faithful, humble servant to command! [To Olivia] But you can say nothing, sure, against the superfine Mistress—

OLIVIA I know who you mean. She is as censorious and detracting a 350 jade, as a superannuated sinner.

LORD PLAUSIBLE She has a smart way of raillery, 'tis confessed.

NOVEL And then, for Mistress Gridelin°—

LORD PLAUSIBLE She I'm sure is—

OLIVIA One that never spoke ill of anybody, 'tis confessed; for she is   355
as silent in conversation as a country lover, and no better company
than a clock, or a weather-glass—for if she sounds, 'tis but once an
hour, to put you in mind of the time of day, or to tell you 'twill
be cold or hot, rain or snow.

LORD PLAUSIBLE Ah, poor creature! She's extremely good and   360
modest.

NOVEL And for Mistress Bridlechin, she's—

OLIVIA As proud as a churchman's wife.°

LORD PLAUSIBLE She's a woman of great spirit and honour, and will
not make herself cheap, 'tis true.   365

NOVEL Then Mistress Hoyden, that calls all people by their sur-
names, and is—

OLIVIA As familiar a duck—

NOVEL As an actress in the tiring-room. There I was once beforehand with you, madam!   370

LORD PLAUSIBLE Mistress Hoyden! A poor, affable, good-natured
soul! But the divine Mistress Trifle comes thither too; sure, her
beauty, virtue, and conduct you can say nothing to.

OLIVIA No?

NOVEL No?—Pray let me speak, madam.   375

OLIVIA First, can anyone be called beautiful that squints?

LORD PLAUSIBLE Her eyes languish a little, I own.

NOVEL Languish! Ha ha.

OLIVIA Languish! Then, for her conduct, she was seen at *The
Country Wife*, after the first day.° There's for you, my lord.   380

LORD PLAUSIBLE But, madam, she was not seen to use her fan all
the play long, turn aside her head, or by a conscious blush discover
more guilt than modesty.

OLIVIA Very fine! Then you think a woman modest, that sees the
hideous *Country Wife* without blushing, or publishing her detesta-   385
tion of it?—D'ye hear him, cousin?

ELIZA Yes; and am, I must confess, something of his opinion, and
think that as an over-captious° fool at a play, by endeavouring to
show the author's want of wit, exposes his own to more censure,
so may a lady call her own modesty in question, by publicly   390
cavilling with the poet's; for all those grimaces of honour, and
artificial modesty, disparage a woman's real virtue, as much as the
use of white and red° does the natural complexion; and you
must use very, very little, if you would have it thought your
own.   395

OLIVIA Then you would have a woman of honour with passive looks, ears, and tongue, undergo all the hideous obscenity she hears at nasty plays?

ELIZA Truly, I think a woman betrays her want of modesty, by showing it publicly in a playhouse, as much as a man does his want 400 of courage by a quarrel there; for the truly modest and stout say least, and are least exceptious, especially in public.

OLIVIA Oh hideous! Cousin, this cannot be your opinion—but you are one of those who have the confidence to pardon the filthy play.

ELIZA Why, what is there of ill in't, say you? 405

OLIVIA Oh fie, fie, fie, would you put me to the blush anew? Call all the blood into my face again? But, to satisfy you then: first, the clandestine obscenity in the very name of Horner.°

ELIZA Truly, 'tis so hidden I cannot find it out, I confess.

OLIVIA Oh horrid! Does it not give you the rank conception, or 410 image, of a goat, a town-bull, or a satyr? Nay, what is yet a filthier image than all the rest, that of an eunuch?

ELIZA What then? I can think of a goat, a bull, or satyr, without any hurt.

OLIVIA Ay, but, cousin, one cannot stop there. 415

ELIZA I can, cousin.

OLIVIA Oh no—for when you have those filthy creatures in your head once, the next thing you think, is what they do: as their defiling of honest men's beds and couches, rapes upon sleeping and waking country virgins, under hedges and on haycocks. Nay, 420 further—

ELIZA Nay, no further, cousin; we have enough of your comment on the play, which will make me more ashamed than the play itself.

OLIVIA Oh, believe me, 'tis a filthy play, and you may take my word for a filthy play as soon as another's. But the filthiest thing in that 425 play, or any other play, is—

ELIZA Pray keep it to yourself, if it be so.

OLIVIA No, faith, you shall know it; I'm resolved to make you out of love with the play. I say, the lewdest, filthiest thing, is his china°—nay, I will never forgive the beastly author his china. He 430 has quite taken away the reputation of poor china itself, and sullied the most innocent and pretty furniture of a lady's chamber—insomuch that I was fain to break all my defiled vessels. You see I have none left; nor you, I hope.

ELIZA You'll pardon me; I cannot think the worse of my china, for 435 that of the playhouse.

OLIVIA Why, you will not keep any now, sure? 'Tis now as unfit an ornament for a lady's chamber as the pictures that come from Italy, and other hot countries,° as appears by their nudities, which I always cover, or scratch out, wheresoe'er I find 'em. But china! Out 440
upon't, filthy china, nasty, debauched china!

ELIZA All this will not put me out of conceit° with china, nor the play, which is acted today, or another of the same beastly author's, as you call him, which I'll go see.

OLIVIA You will not, sure! Nay, you shan't venture your reputation 445
by going, and mine by leaving me alone with two men here.
        Pulls her back
Nay, you'll disoblige me for ever, if—

ELIZA I stay! [*Freeing herself*] Your servant.
        Exit Eliza

OLIVIA Well—But my lord, though you justify everybody, you cannot in earnest uphold so beastly a writer, whose ink is so smutty, 450
as one may say.

LORD PLAUSIBLE Faith, I dare swear the poor man did not think to disoblige the ladies, by any amorous, soft, passionate, luscious saying in his play.

OLIVIA Foy, my lord.—But what think you, Mr Novel, of the play? 455
Though I know you are a friend to all that are new.

NOVEL Faith, madam, I must confess the new plays would not be the worse for my advice, but I could never get the silly rogues, the poets, to mind what I say. But I'll tell you what counsel I gave the surly fool you speak of. 460

OLIVIA What was't?

NOVEL Faith, to put his play into rhyme°—for rhyme, you know, often makes mystical nonsense pass with the critics for wit, and a double-meaning saying with the ladies for soft, tender, and moving passion. But, now I talk of passion, I saw your old lover this 465
morning, Captain—(*Whispers*)
        Enter Manly, Freeman, and Fidelia, standing behind

OLIVIA Whom? Nay, you need not whisper.

MANLY We are luckily got hither unobserved—How! In a close conversation with these supple rascals, the outcasts of seamstresses' shops?° 470

FREEMAN Faith, pardon her, captain, that, since she could no longer be entertained with your manly bluntness, and honest love, she takes up with the pert chat and commonplace flattery of these fluttering parrots of the town, apes and echoes of men only.°

MANLY Do not you, sir, play the echo too, mock me, dally with my   475
own words, and show yourself as impertinent as they are.

FREEMAN Nay, captain—

FIDELIA Nay, lieutenant, do not excuse her; methinks she looks very
kindly upon 'em both, and seems to be pleased with what that fool
there says to her.   480

MANLY You lie, sir—and hold your peace, that I may not be
provoked to give you a worse reply.

OLIVIA Manly returned, d'ye say! And is he safe?

NOVEL My lord saw him too. Hark you, my lord.
Whispers to Lord Plausible

MANLY (*aside*) She yet seems concerned for my safety, and perhaps   485
they are admitted now here but for their news of me; for
intelligence indeed is the common passport of nauseous fools, when
they go their round of good tables and houses.

OLIVIA I heard of his fighting only, without particulars, and confess
I always loved his brutal courage, because it made me hope it might   490
rid me of his more brutal love.

MANLY (*apart*) What's that?   .

OLIVIA But is he at last returned, d'ye say, unhurt?

NOVEL Ay faith, without doing his business;° for the rogue has been
these two years pretending to a wooden leg, which he would take   495
from Fortune as kindly as the staff of a marshal of France,° and
rather read his name in a gazette°—

OLIVIA Than in the entail of a good estate.

MANLY (*aside*) So!

NOVEL I have an ambition, I must confess, of losing my heart before   500
such a fair enemy as yourself, madam; but that silly rogues should
be ambitious of losing their arms, and—

OLIVIA Looking like a pair of compasses.

NOVEL But he has no use of his arms but to set 'em akimbo, for he
never pulls off his hat, at least not to me, I'm sure; for you must   505
know, madam, he has a fanatical hatred° to good company: he can't
abide me.

LORD PLAUSIBLE Oh, be not so severe to him, as to say he hates
good company; for I assure you he has a great respect, esteem, and
kindness for me.   510

MANLY [*aside*] That kind, civil rogue has spoken yet ten thousand
times worse of me than t'other.

OLIVIA Well, if he be returned, Mr Novel, then shall I be pestered
again with his boisterous sea-love, have my alcove smell like a

cabin, my chamber perfumed with his tarpaulin brandenburgh, and   515
hear volleys of brandy sighs, enough to make a fog in one's room.
Foh! I hate a lover that smells like Thames Street!°

MANLY (*aside*) I can bear no longer, and need hear no more.
        [*Comes forward*]
    [*To Olivia*] But, since you have these two pulvilio boxes, these
    essence-bottles, this pair of musk-cats° here, I hope I may venture   520
    to come yet nearer you.

OLIVIA Overheard us, then?

NOVEL (*aside*) I hope he heard me not.

LORD PLAUSIBLE Most noble and heroic captain, your most obliged,
    faithful, humble servant.   525

NOVEL Dear tar, thy humble servant.

MANLY Away!
        Thrusts Novel and Lord Plausible on each side
    Madam—

OLIVIA Nay, I think I have fitted you for listening.

MANLY You have fitted me for believing you could not be fickle,   530
    though you were young; could not dissemble love, though 'twas
    your interest; nor be vain, though you were handsome; nor break
    your promise, though to a parting lover; nor abuse your best friend,
    though you had wit. But I take not your contempt of me worse
    than your esteem, or civility, for these things here, though you   535
    know 'em.

NOVEL Things!

LORD PLAUSIBLE Let the captain rally a little.

MANLY Yes, things.
        Coming up to Novel
    Canst thou be angry, thou thing?   540

NOVEL No, since my lord says you speak in raillery; for though your
    sea-raillery be something rough, yet I confess we use one another
    to as bad every day, at Locket's, and never quarrel for the matter.

LORD PLAUSIBLE Nay, noble captain, be not angry with him. A
    word with you, I beseech you.   545
        Whispers to Manly

OLIVIA (*aside*) Well, we women, like the rest of the cheats of the
    world, when our cullies or creditors have found us out and will (or
    can) trust no longer, pay debts and satisfy obligations with a
    quarrel, the kindest present a man can make to his mistress, when
    he can make no more presents. For oftentimes in love, as at cards,   550
    we are forced to play foul, only to give over the game, and use our

lovers like the cards: when we can get no more by 'em, throw 'em
up in a pet, upon the first dispute.

MANLY My lord, all that you have made me know by your whispering, which I knew not before, is that you have a stinking breath: 555
there's a secret, for your secret.

LORD PLAUSIBLE Pshaw! Pshaw!

MANLY But, madam, tell me, pray, what was't, about this spark,
[*pointing at Novel*] could take you? Was it the merit of his
fashionable impudence, the briskness of his noise, the wit of his   560
laugh, his judgement, or fancy, in his garniture? Or was it a
well-trimmed glove, or the scent of it,° that charmed you?

NOVEL Very well, sir. 'Gad, these sea-captains make nothing of
dressing. But let me tell you, sir, a man by his dress, as much as
by anything, shows his wit and judgement, nay, and his courage   565
too.

FREEMAN How his courage, Mr Novel?

NOVEL Why, for example, by red breeches, tucked-up hair or
peruke, a greasy broad belt, and nowadays a short sword.°

MANLY Thy courage will appear more by thy belt than thy sword,°   570
I dare swear.—Then, madam, for this gentle piece of courtesy,
[*pointing at Lord Plausible*] this man of tame honour, what could
you find in him? Was it his languishing, affected tone? His
mannerly look? His secondhand flattery, the refuse of the playhouse
tiring-rooms? Or his slavish obsequiousness, in watching at the   575
door of your box at the playhouse, for your hand to your chair? Or
his jaunty way of playing with your fan? Or was it the gunpowder
spot° on his hand, or the jewel in his ear,° that purchased your
heart?

OLIVIA Good jealous captain, no more of your—   580

LORD PLAUSIBLE No, let him go on, madam, for perhaps he
may make you laugh: and I would contribute to your pleasure any
way.

MANLY Gentle rogue!

OLIVIA No, noble captain, you cannot sure think anything could take   585
me more than that heroic title of yours—'Captain'; for you know
we women love honour inordinately.

NOVEL Ha ha! Faith, she is with thee, bully, for thy raillery.

MANLY (*aside to Novel*) Faith, so shall I be with you, no-bully, for
your grinning.   590

OLIVIA Then, that noble lion-like mien of yours, that soldier-like
weather-beaten complexion, and that manly roughness of your

voice—how can they otherwise than charm us women, who hate effeminacy?

NOVEL Ha ha! Faith, I can't hold from laughing.   595

MANLY (*aside to Novel*) Nor shall I from kicking anon.

OLIVIA And then, that captain-like carelessness in your dress, but especially your scarf—'twas just such another, only a little higher tied, made me in love with my tailor,° as he passed by my window the last training day;° for we women adore a martial man, and you   600
have nothing wanting to make you more one, or more agreeable, but a wooden leg.

LORD PLAUSIBLE Nay, i'faith there your ladyship was a wag, and it was fine, just, and well rallied.

NOVEL Ay, ay, madam, with you ladies too, martial men must needs   605
be very killing.

MANLY Peace, you Bartholomew Fair° buffoons. [*To Olivia*] And be not you vain that these laugh on your side, for they will laugh at their own dull jests. [*To Novel and Lord Plausible*] But no more of 'em, for I will only suffer now this lady to be witty and merry.   610

OLIVIA You would not have your panegyric interrupted. I go on then to your humour. Is there anything more agreeable than the pretty sullenness of that? Than the greatness of your courage?—which most of all appears in your spirit of contradiction, for you dare give all mankind the lie; and your opinion is your only mistress, for you   615
renounce that too, when it becomes another man's.

NOVEL Ha ha! I cannot hold; I must laugh at thee, tar, faith!

LORD PLAUSIBLE And i' faith, dear captain, I beg your pardon, and leave, to laugh at you too, though I protest I mean you no hurt. But when a lady rallies, a stander-by must be complaisant, and do   620
her reason in laughing. Ha ha!

MANLY Why, you impudent, pitiful wretches, you presume sure upon your effeminacy to urge me,° for you are in all things so like women, that you may think it in me a kind of cowardice to beat you.   625

OLIVIA No hectoring, good captain.

MANLY Or, perhaps, you think this lady's presence secures you. But have a care. She has talked herself out of all the respect I had for her; and by using me ill before you, has given me a privilege of using you so before her. But if you would preserve your respect to   630
her,° and not be beaten before her, go, begone immediately.

NOVEL 'Begone'! What?

LORD PLAUSIBLE Nay, worthy, noble, generous captain.

MANLY Begone, I say.

NOVEL 'Begone,' again! To us, 'Begone'!   635

MANLY No chattering, baboons! Instantly begone, or—
       *Manly puts 'em out of the room; Novel struts, Lord Plausible
       cringes*

NOVEL Well, madam, we'll go make the cards ready in your bed-
       chamber;° sure you will not stay long with him.
       Exeunt Lord Plausible, Novel

OLIVIA Turn hither your rage, good Captain° Swagger-Huff, and be
        saucy with your mistress, like a true captain. But be civil to your   640
        rivals and betters, and do not threaten anything but me here—no,
        not so much as my windows,° nor do not think yourself in the
        lodgings of one of your suburb mistresses beyond the Tower.°

MANLY Do not give me cause to think so, for those less infamous
       women part with their lovers, just as you did from me, with   645
       unforced vows of constancy, and floods of willing tears; but the
       same winds bear away their lovers and their vows. And for° their
       grief, if the credulous unexpected fools return, they find new
       comforters, fresh cullies, such as I found here. The mercenary love
       of those women too, suffers shipwreck with their gallants' fortunes;   650
       now you have heard Chance has used me scurvily, therefore you
       do too. Well, persevere in your ingratitude, falsehood, and disdain;
       have constancy in something, and I promise you to be as just to
       your real scorn, as I was to your feigned love: and henceforward
       will despise, contemn, hate, loathe, and detest you, most faithfully.   655
       Enter Letice°

OLIVIA Get the ombre cards ready in the next room, Letice, and—
        Whispers to Letice. [Exit Letice]

FREEMAN Bravely resolved, captain.

FIDELIA And you'll be sure to keep your word, I hope, sir.

MANLY I hope so too.

FIDELIA Do you but hope it, sir? If you are not as good as your word,   660
        'twill be the first time you ever bragged, sure.

MANLY She has restored my reason with my heart.

FREEMAN But, now you talk of restoring, captain, there are other
         things which, next to one's heart, one would not part with—I mean
         your jewels and money, which it seems she has, sir.   665

MANLY What's that to you, sir?

FREEMAN Pardon me; whatsoever is yours, I have a share in't, I'm
         sure, which I will not lose for asking, though you may be too
         generous, or too angry now, to do't yourself.

FIDELIA Nay, then I'll make bold to make my claim too.   670
    Both going towards Olivia

MANLY Hold, you impertinent, officious fops—(*Aside*) How have I
been deceived!

FREEMAN Madam, there are certain appurtenances to a lover's heart,
called jewels, which always go along with it.

FIDELIA And which, with lovers, have no value in themselves, but   675
from the heart they come with; our captain's, madam, it seems you
scorn to keep, and much more will those worthless things without
it, I am confident.

OLIVIA A gentleman, so well made as you are, may be confident—us
easy women could not deny you anything you ask, if 'twere for   680
yourself; but since 'tis for another, I beg your leave to give him my
answer. (*Aside*) An agreeable young fellow this! . . . And would not
be my aversion!—Captain, your young friend here has a very
persuading face, I confess; yet you might have asked me yourself
for those trifles you left with me, which—(*Aside to Manly*) Hark   685
you a little, for I dare trust you with the secret; you are a man of
so much honour, I'm sure. I say then, not expecting your return,
or hoping ever to see you again, I have delivered your jewels to—

MANLY Whom?

OLIVIA My husband.   690

MANLY Your husband!

OLIVIA Ay, my husband; for, since you could leave me, I am lately,
and privately, married to one who is a man of so much honour and
experience in the world, that I dare not ask him for your jewels
again, to restore 'em to you—lest he should conclude you never   695
would have parted with 'em to me on any other score but the
exchange of my honour; which, rather than you'd let me lose, you'd
lose (I'm sure) yourself those trifles of yours.

MANLY Triumphant impudence! But married too!

OLIVIA Oh speak not so loud, my servants know it not. I am married;   700
there's no resisting one's destiny,° or love, you know.

MANLY Why, did you love him too?

OLIVIA Most passionately—nay, love him now, though I have married him, and he me; which mutual love I hope you are too good,
too generous a man to disturb, by any future claim, or visits to me.   705
'Tis true, he is now absent in the country, but returns shortly;
therefore I beg of you, for your own ease and quiet, and my
honour, you will never see me more.

MANLY I wish I never had seen you.

OLIVIA But if you should ever have anything to say to me hereafter,   710
let that young gentleman there be your messenger.

MANLY You would be kinder to him; I find he should be welcome.

OLIVIA Alas, his youth would keep my husband from suspicions, and
his visits from scandal; for we women may have pity for such as   715
he, but no love. And I already think you do not well to spirit him
away to sea, and the sea is already but too rich with the spoils of
the shore.

MANLY True perfect woman! (*Aside*)° If I could say anything more
injurious to her now, I would; for I could out-rail a bilked whore,   720
or a kicked coward. But, now I think on't, that were rather to
discover my love, than hatred; and I must not talk, for something
I must do.

OLIVIA (*aside*) I think I have given him enough of me now, never to
be troubled with him again.   725
    Enter Letice
Well, Letice, are the cards and all ready within? I come then.—
Captain, I beg your pardon. You will not make one at ombre?

MANLY No, madam, but I'll wish you a little good luck before you
go.

OLIVIA No, if you would have me thrive, curse me—for that you'll   730
do heartily, I suppose.

MANLY Then, if you will have it so: may all the curses light upon
you, women ought to fear, and you deserve. First, may the curse
of loving play attend your sordid covetousness, and Fortune cheat
you, by trusting to her, as you have cheated me; the curse of pride,   735
or a good reputation, fall on your lust; the curse of affectation on
your beauty; the curse of your husband's company on your
pleasures; and the curse of your gallant's disappointments° in his
absence; and the curse of scorn, jealousy, or despair, on your love;
and then the curse of loving on.   740

OLIVIA And, to requite all your curses, I will only return you your
last. May the curse of loving me still, fall upon your proud hard
heart, that could be so cruel to me in these horrid curses—but
heaven forgive you.
    Exit Olivia

MANLY Hell, and the devil, reward thee.   745

FREEMAN Well, you see now, mistresses, like friends, are lost by
letting 'em handle your money; and most women are such kind of
witches, who can have no power over a man unless you give 'em

money. But when once they have got any from you, they never
leave you till they have all—therefore I never dare give a woman a   750
farthing.

MANLY Well, there is yet this comfort by losing one's money with
one's mistress: a man is out of danger of getting another, of being
made prize again by love, who, like a pirate, takes you by spreading
false colours; but when once you have run your ship aground, the   755
treacherous picaroon luffs, so by your ruin you save yourself from
slavery at least.°

Enter Boy

BOY Mistress Letice, here's Madam Blackacre come to wait upon her
honour.

[Exeunt Boy and Letice]

MANLY D'ye hear that? Let us begone, before she comes; for   760
henceforward I'll avoid the whole damned sex for ever, and woman
as a sinking ship.

Exeunt Manly and Fidelia

FREEMAN And I'll stay, to revenge on her your quarrel to the
sex; for out of love to her jointure, and hatred to business, I would
marry her, to make an end of her thousand suits,° and my   765
thousand engagements, to the comfort of two unfortunate sorts of
people: my plaintiffs, and her defendants; my creditors, and her
adversaries.

*Enter Widow Blackacre, led in by Major Oldfox,° and Jerry
Blackacre following, laden with green bags*

WIDOW BLACKACRE 'Tis an arrant sea-ruffian, but I am glad I met
with him at last, to serve him again, major, for the last service was   770
not good in law.° Boy, duck, Jerry, where is my paper of
memorandums? Give me, child: so. Where is my cousin Olivia
now, my kind relation?

FREEMAN Here is one that would be your kind relation, madam.

WIDOW BLACKACRE What mean you, sir?   775

FREEMAN Why, faith (to be short) to marry you, widow.

WIDOW BLACKACRE Is not this the wild rude person we saw at
Captain Manly's?

JERRY Ay, forsooth, an't please.

WIDOW BLACKACRE What would you? What are you? Marry me!   780

FREEMAN Ay faith, for I am a younger brother,° and you are a
widow.

WIDOW BLACKACRE You are an impertinent person—and go about
your business!

FREEMAN I have none, but to marry thee, widow.   785

WIDOW BLACKACRE But I have other business, I'd have you to
know.

FREEMAN But you have no business anights, widow; and I'll make
you pleasanter business than any you have: for anights, I assure
you, I am a man of great business, for the business—   790

WIDOW BLACKACRE Go, I'm sure you're an idle fellow.

FREEMAN Try me but, widow, and employ me as you find my
abilities, and industry.

OLDFOX Pray be civil to the lady, Mr—. She's a person of quality, a
person that is no person°—   795

FREEMAN Yes, but she's a person that is a widow. Be you mannerly
to her, because you are to pretend only to be her squire, to arm
her° to her lawyers' chambers; but I will be impudent and bawdy,
for she must love and marry me.

WIDOW BLACKACRE Marry come up, you saucy familiar Jack! You   800
think with us widows 'tis no more than up, and ride. Gad forgive
me, nowadays every idle, young, hectoring, roaring companion,
with a pair of turned red breeches,° and a broad back,° thinks to
carry away any widow of the best degree; but I'd have you to know,
sir, all widows are not got, like places at court, by impudence and   805
importunity only.

OLDFOX No, no, soft, soft; you are a young man, and not fit—

FREEMAN For a widow? Yes sure, old man, the fitter.

OLDFOX Go to, go to; if others had not laid in their claims before
you—   810

FREEMAN Not you, I hope.

OLDFOX Why not I, sir? Sure I am a much more proportionable
match for her than you, sir; I, who am an elder brother, of a
comfortable fortune, and of equal years with her.

WIDOW BLACKACRE How's that? You unmannerly person, I'd have   815
you to know, I was born but in *ann' undec' Caroli prim'*.°

OLDFOX Your pardon, lady, your pardon; be not offended with your
very servant.°—But I say, sir, you are a beggarly younger brother,
twenty years younger than her; without any land or stock, but your
great stock of impudence. Therefore what pretension can you have   820
to her?

FREEMAN You have made it for me. First, because I am a younger
brother.

WIDOW BLACKACRE Why, is that a sufficient plea to a relict? How
appears° it, sir? By what foolish custom?   825

FREEMAN By custom, time out of mind,° only.—Then, sir, because
I have nothing to keep me after her death, I am the likelier to take
care of her life. And for my being twenty years younger than her,
and having a sufficient stock of impudence, I leave it to her whether
they will be valid exceptions to me, in her widow's law or   830
equity.°

OLDFOX Well, she has been so long in Chancery that I'll stand to her
equity and decree between us. Come, lady, pray snap up this young
snap at first,° or we shall be troubled with him. Give him a City
widow's answer—(aside to Widow Blackacre) that is, with all the ill   835
breeding imaginable. [Aloud] Come, madam.

WIDOW BLACKACRE Well then, to make an end of this foolish
wooing, for nothing interrupts business more: first, for you,
major—

OLDFOX You declare in my favour then?   840

FREEMAN What, direct the court? (To Jerry) Come, young lawyer,
thou sha't be a counsel for me.

JERRY Gad, I shall betray your cause then, as well as an older lawyer,
never stir.

WIDOW BLACKACRE First, I say, for you, major, my walking   845
hospital of an ancient foundation, thou bag of mummy, that
wouldst fall asunder if 'twere not for thy cerecloths—

OLDFOX How, lady?

FREEMAN Ha ha!

JERRY Hey, brave mother! Use all suitors thus, for my sake.   850

WIDOW BLACKACRE Thou withered, hobbling, distorted cripple—
nay, thou art a cripple all over; wouldst thou make me the staff of
thy age, the crutch of thy decrepitness? Me—

FREEMAN Well said, widow! Faith, thou wouldst make a man love
thee now, without dissembling.   855

WIDOW BLACKACRE Thou senseless, impertinent, quibbling, drivelling, feeble, paralytic, impotent, fumbling, frigid nincom-
poop.

JERRY Hey, brave mother, for calling of names, i'fac!

WIDOW BLACKACRE Wouldst thou make a caudlemaker, a nurse, of   860
me? Can't you be bedrid, without a bedfellow? Won't your
swanskins, furs, flannels, and the scorched trencher° keep you
warm there? Would you have me your Scotch warming-pan,° with
a pox to you? Me—

OLDFOX Oh heavens!   865

FREEMAN I told you I should be thought the fitter man, major.

JERRY Ay, you old fobus, and you would have been my guardian, would you? To have taken care of my estate, that half of't should never come to me, by letting long leases at peppercorn rents.°

WIDOW BLACKACRE If I would have married an old man, 'tis well   870
known I might have married an earl—nay, what's more, a judge, and been covered the winter nights with the lambskins, which I prefer to the ermines of nobles. And dost thou think I would wrong my poor minor there, for you?

FREEMAN Your minor is a chopping minor, God bless him.   875
    Strokes Jerry on the head

OLDFOX Your minor may be a major of horse or foot, for his bigness; and, it seems, you will have the cheating of your minor to yourself.

WIDOW BLACKACRE [*to Freeman*] Pray, sir, bear witness. Cheat my minor! I'll bring my action of the case° for the slander.

FREEMAN Nay, I would bear false witness for thee now, widow, since   880
you have done me justice, and have thought me the fitter man for you.

WIDOW BLACKACRE Fair and softly, sir; 'tis my minor's case, more than my own; and I must do him justice now on you.

FREEMAN How!   885

OLDFOX So then.

WIDOW BLACKACRE You are first (I warrant) some renegado from the Inns of Court, and the law; and thou'lt come to suffer for't, by the law: that is, be hanged.

JERRY Not about your neck, forsooth, I hope.   890

FREEMAN But, madam—

OLDFOX Hear the court.

WIDOW BLACKACRE Thou art some debauched, drunken, lewd, hectoring, gaming companion, and want'st some widow's old gold to nick upon; but I thank you, sir, that's for my lawyers.   895

FREEMAN Faith, we should ne'er quarrel about that—for guineas° would serve my turn. But, widow—

WIDOW BLACKACRE Thou art a foul-mouthed boaster of thy lust, a mere braggadocio of thy strength for wine and women, and wilt belie thyself more than thou dost women, and art every way a base   900
deceiver of women; and would deceive me too, would you?

FREEMAN Nay faith, widow, this is judging without seeing the evidence.

WIDOW BLACKACRE I say, you are a worn-out whoremaster, at five and twenty, both in body and fortune. And cannot be trusted by   905
the common wenches of the town, lest you should not pay 'em; nor

by the wives of the town, lest you should pay 'em.° So you want
women, and would have me your bawd, to procure 'em for you.

FREEMAN Faith, if you had any good acquaintance, widow, 'twould
be civilly done of thee—for I am just come from sea.   910

WIDOW BLACKACRE I mean, you would have me keep you, that you
might turn keeper; for poor widows are only used like bawds by
you. You go to church with us but to get other women to lie with.
In fine, you are a cheating, chousing spendthrift; and, having sold
your own annuity, would waste my jointure.°   915

JERRY And make havoc of our estate personal,° and all our old gilt
plate; I should soon be picking up all our mortgaged apostle
spoons, bowls, and beakers, out of most of the alehouses betwixt
Hercules' Pillars and the Boatswain in Wapping.° Nay, and you'd
be scouring amongst my trees,° and make 'em knock down one   920
another, like routed reeling watchmen at midnight. Would you so,
bully?

FREEMAN Nay, prithee, widow, hear me.

WIDOW BLACKACRE No, sir, I'd have you to know, thou pitiful,
paltry, lath-backed° fellow, if I would have married a young man,   925
'tis well known I could have had any young heir in Norfolk°—nay,
the hopefull'st young man this day at the King's Bench bar;° I that
am a relict and executrix of known plentiful assets and parts, who
understand myself and the law. And would you have me under
covert-baron again? No, sir, no covert-baron for me.   930

FREEMAN But, dear widow, hear me. I value you only, not your
jointure.

WIDOW BLACKACRE Nay, sir, hold there; I know your love to a
widow is covetousness of her jointure. And a widow, a little
stricken in years, with a good jointure, is like an old mansion house 935
in a good purchase:° never valued, but take one, take t'other. And
perhaps, when you are in possession, you'd neglect it, let it drop
to the ground for want of necessary repairs, or expenses upon't.

FREEMAN No, widow, one would be sure to keep all tight, when one
is to forfeit one's lease by dilapidation.   940

WIDOW BLACKACRE Fie, fie, I neglect my business with this foolish
discourse of love. Jerry, child, let me see the list of the jury: I'm
sure my cousin Olivia has some relations amongst 'em. But where
is she?

FREEMAN Nay, widow, but hear me one word only.   945

WIDOW BLACKACRE Nay, sir, no more, pray; I will no more harken
again to your foolish love motions, than to offers of arbitration.

Exeunt Widow Blackacre and Jerry

FREEMAN Well, I'll follow thee yet; for he that has a pretension at court, or to a widow, must never give over for a little ill usage.

OLDFOX Therefore I'll get her by assiduity, patience, and long-   950
sufferings, which you will not undergo. For you idle young fellows leave off love, when it comes to be business; and industry gets more women than love.

FREEMAN Ay, industry, the fool's and old man's merit; but I'll be industrious too, and make a business on't, and get her by law,   955
wrangling, and contests, and not by sufferings. And, because you are no dangerous rival, I'll give thee counsel, major:

> If you litigious widow e'er would gain,
> Sigh not to her, but by the law complain;
> To her, as to a bawd defendant, sue   960
> With statutes, and make justice pimp for you.

Exeunt

3.1

Westminster Hall.° [*A bookseller's stall, with a Boy in attendance. A crowd of lawyers at the rear of the stage.*]

Enter Manly and Freeman, two Sailors° behind

MANLY I hate this place, worse than a man that has inherited a Chancery suit. I wish I were well out on't again.

FREEMAN Why, you need not be afraid of this place—for a man without money needs no more fear a crowd of lawyers, than a crowd of pickpockets. 5

MANLY This, the reverend of the law would have thought° the palace or residence of justice; but, if it be, she lives here with the state of a Turkish emperor, rarely seen, and besieged, rather than defended, by her numerous black guard° here.

FREEMAN Methinks 'tis like one of their own halls, in Christmas 10 time,° whither, from all parts, fools bring their money, to try by the dice (not the worst judges) whether it shall be their own, or no. But, after a tedious fretting and wrangling, they drop away all their money, on both sides; and finding neither the better, at last go emptily and lovingly away together to the tavern, joining their 15 curses against the young lawyers' box, that sweeps all, like the old ones'.°

MANLY Spoken like a revelling Christmas lawyer.

FREEMAN Yes, I was one, I confess; but was fain to leave the law, out of conscience, and fall to making false musters;° rather chose 20 to cheat the king than his subjects; plunder, rather than take fees.

MANLY Well, a plague and a purse-famine light on the law; and that female limb of it,° who dragged me hither today. But prithee go see if, in that crowd of daggled gowns there, thou canst find her. (*Pointing to* [*the*] *crowd of lawyers at the end of the stage*) 25

Exit Freeman [*followed by the two Sailors*]

How hard it is to be an hypocrite!
At least to me, who am but newly so.
I thought it once a kind of knavery,
Nay cowardice, to hide one's faults; but now
The common frailty, love, becomes my shame. 30
He must not know I love th'ungrateful still,
Lest he contemn me, more than she; for I,
It seems, can undergo a woman's scorn,
But not a man's—

333

Enter to him Fidelia

FIDELIA Sir, good sir, generous captain.   35

MANLY Prithee, kind impertinence, leave me. Why shouldst thou
follow me, flatter my generosity now, since thou know'st I have no
money left? If I had it, I'd give it thee, to buy my quiet.

FIDELIA I never followed yet, sir, reward or fame, but you alone; nor
do I now beg anything but leave to share your miseries. You should   40
not be a niggard of 'em, since, methinks, you have enough to spare.
Let me follow you now, because you hate me, as you have often
said.

MANLY I ever hated a coward's company, I must confess.

FIDELIA Let me follow you, till I am none then; for you, I'm sure,   45
will through such worlds of dangers, that I shall be inured to
'em—nay, I shall be afraid of your anger more than danger, and so
turn valiant out of fear. Dear captain, do not cast me off, till you
have tried me once more. Do not, do not go to sea again without
me.   50

MANLY Thou to sea! To court, thou fool; remember the advice I
gave thee: thou art a handsome spaniel, and canst fawn naturally.
Go, busk about, and run thyself into the next great man's lobby;
first fawn upon the slaves without, and then run into the lady's
bedchamber; thou may'st be admitted, at last, to tumble her bed.   55
Go, seek, I say, and lose me; for I am not able to keep thee. I have
not bread for myself.

FIDELIA Therefore I will not go, because then I may help and serve
you.

MANLY Thou!   60

FIDELIA I warrant you, sir; for, at worst, I could beg or steal for you.

MANLY Nay, more bragging! Dost thou not know there's venturing
your life, in stealing?° Go, prithee, away. Thou art as hard to shake
off as that flattering effeminating mischief, love.

FIDELIA Love, did you name? Why, you are not so miserable as to   65
be yet in love, sure!

MANLY No, no, prithee away, begone, or—(*Aside*) I had almost
discovered my love and shame. Well, if I had? That thing could
not think the worse of me . . . Or if he did? . . . No—yes, he shall
know it, he shall—but then I must never leave him, for they are   70
such secrets that make parasites and pimps lords of their masters;
for any slavery or tyranny is easier than love's. [*To Fidelia*] Come
hither. Since thou art so forward to serve me, hast thou but

resolution enough to endure the torture of a secret? For such, to
some, is insupportable.   75

FIDELIA I would keep it as safe as if your dear precious life depended
on't.

MANLY Damn your dearness. It concerns more than my life—my
honour.

FIDELIA Doubt it not, sir.   80

MANLY And do not discover it, by too much fear of discovering it;
but have a great care you let not Freeman find it out.

FIDELIA I warrant you, sir. I am already all joy, with the hopes of
your commands; and shall be all wings, in the execution of 'em.
Speak quickly, sir.   85

MANLY You said you would beg for me.

FIDELIA I did, sir.

MANLY Then you shall beg for me.

FIDELIA With all my heart, sir.

MANLY That is, pimp for me.   90

FIDELIA How, sir!

MANLY D'ye start? Thinkst thou, thou couldst do me any other
service? Come, no dissembling honour. I know you can do it
handsomely; thou wert made for't. You have lost your time with
me at sea; you must recover it.   95

FIDELIA Do not, sir, beget yourself more reasons for your aversion
to me, and make my obedience to you a fault. I am the unfittest in
the world, to do you such a service.

MANLY Your cunning arguing against it, shows but how fit you are
for it. No more dissembling. Here (I say) you must go use it for   100
me, to Olivia.

FIDELIA To her, sir?

MANLY Go flatter, lie, kneel, promise—anything to get her for me.
I cannot live unless I have her. Didst thou not say thou wouldst
do anything, to save my life? And she said you had a persuading   105
face.

FIDELIA But did not you say, sir, your honour was dearer to you
than your life? And would you have me contribute to the loss of
that, and carry love from you, to the most infamous, most false,
and—   110

MANLY (*sighs, aside*) And most beautiful!

FIDELIA Most ungrateful woman that ever lived; for sure she must
be so, that could desert you so soon, use you so basely, and so lately
too. Do not, do not forget it, sir, and think—

MANLY No, I will not forget it, but think of revenge. I will lie with   115
her, out of revenge. Go, begone, and prevail for me, or never see
me more.

FIDELIA You scorned her last night.

MANLY I know not what I did last night; I dissembled last night.

FIDELIA Heavens!   120

MANLY Begone, I say, and bring me love or compliance back, or
hopes at least, or I'll never see thy face again. By—

FIDELIA Oh do not swear, sir; first hear me.

MANLY I am impatient. Away; you'll find me here till twelve. (*Turns
away*)   125

FIDELIA Sir—

MANLY Not one word, no insinuating argument more, or soothing
persuasion; you'll have need of all your rhetoric with her. Go, strive
to alter her, not me. Begone.

> *Exit Manly at the end of the stage*

FIDELIA Should I discover to him now my sex,   130
And lay before him his strange cruelty,
'Twould but incense it more—No, 'tis not time.
For his love, must I then betray my own?
Were ever Love or Chance, till now, severe?
Or shifting woman posed with such a task?   135
Forced to beg that which kills her, if obtained,
And give away her lover, not to° lose him.

> *Exit Fidelia. Enter Widow Blackacre in the middle of half a
> dozen lawyers, [including Serjeant Ploddon, Quaint, Blunder,
> Petulant, and Splitcause,] whispered to by a fellow in black;
> Jerry, [laden with green bags,] following the crowd*

WIDOW BLACKACRE Offer me a reference,° you saucy companion
you! D'ye know who you speak to? Art thou a solicitor in
Chancery, and offer a reference? A pretty fellow!—Master Serjeant   140
Ploddon,° here's a fellow has the impudence to offer me a
reference.

PLODDON Who's that, has the impudence to offer a reference within
these walls?

WIDOW BLACKACRE Nay, for a splitter of causes° to do't!   145

> [*The fellow in black slips into the crowd*]

PLODDON No, madam, to a lady learned in the law, as you are, the
offer of a reference were to impose upon you.

WIDOW BLACKACRE No, no, never fear me for a reference, Master
Serjeant. But, come, have you not forgot your brief? Are you sure

you shan't make the mistake of—hark you (*whispers*). Go then, go 150
to your Court of Common Pleas, and say one thing over and over
again. You do it so naturally, you'll never be suspected for
protracting time.

PLODDON Come, I know the course of the court, and your business.
Exit Serjeant Ploddon

WIDOW BLACKACRE Let's see, Jerry, where are my minutes?— 155
Come, Mr Quaint,° pray go talk a great deal for me in Chancery.
Let your words be easy, and your sense hard; my cause requires it.
Branch it bravely, and deck my cause with flowers, that the snake
may lie hidden. Go, go, and be sure you remember the decree of
my Lord Chancellor *tricesimo quart'* of the queen.° 160

QUAINT I will, as I see cause, extenuate or examplify matter of fact;°
baffle truth with impudence; answer exceptions with questions,
though never so impertinent; for reasons, give 'em words; for law
and equity, tropes and figures: and so relax and enervate the sinews
of their argument with the oil of my eloquence. But when my lungs 165
can reason no longer, and not being able to say anything more for
our cause, say everything of our adversary—whose reputation,
though never so clear and evident in the eye of the world, yet with
sharp invectives—

WIDOW BLACKACRE [*aside*] Alias Billingsgate.° 170

QUAINT With poignant and sour invectives, I say, I will deface, wipe
out, and obliterate his fair reputation, even as a record with the
juice of lemons; and tell such a story (for the truth on't is, all that
we can do for our client, in Chancery, is telling a story) a fine story,
a long story, such a story— 175

WIDOW BLACKACRE Go, save thy breath for the cause; talk at the
bar, Mr Quaint. You are so copiously fluent, you can weary
anyone's ears, sooner than your own tongue. Go, weary our
adversary's counsel, and the court. Go, thou art a fine-spoken
person. Adad, I shall make thy wife jealous of me, if you can but 180
court the court into a decree for us. Go, get you gone, and
remember—(*Whispers*)
Exit Quaint

Come, Mr Blunder, pray bawl soundly for me at the King's Bench;
bluster, sputter, question, cavil—but be sure your argument be
intricate enough to confound the court; and then you do my 185
business. Talk what you will, but be sure your tongue never stand
still; for your own noise will secure your sense from censure: 'tis
like coughing or hemming when one has got the belly-ache, which

stifles the unmannerly noise. Go, dear rogue, and succeed; and I'll
invite thee, ere it be long, to more soused venison.   190

BLUNDER I'll warrant you, after your verdict, your judgement shall
not be arrested upon ifs and ands.°

   [*Exit Blunder*]

WIDOW BLACKACRE Come, Mr Petulant, let me give you some new
instructions for our cause in the Exchequer.° Are the barons sat?

PETULANT Yes, no; maybe they are, maybe they are not. What know   195
I? What care I?

WIDOW BLACKACRE Hey day! I wish you would but snap up the
counsel on t'other side anon, at the bar, as much; and have a little
more patience with me, that I might instruct you a little better.

PETULANT You instruct me! What is my brief for, mistress?   200

WIDOW BLACKACRE Ay, but you seldom read your brief, but at the
bar—if you do it then.

PETULANT Perhaps I do, perhaps I don't, and perhaps 'tis time
enough. Pray hold yourself contented, mistress.

WIDOW BLACKACRE Nay, if you go thereto, I will not be contented,   205
sir; though you, I see, will lose my cause for want of speaking, I
won't. You shall hear me, and shall be instructed. Let's see your
brief.

PETULANT Send your solicitor to me. Instructed by a woman! I'd
have you to know, I do not wear a bar-gown—   210

WIDOW BLACKACRE By a woman! And I'd have you to know, I am
no common woman, but a woman conversant in the laws of the
land, as well as yourself, though I have no bar-gown.

PETULANT Go to, go to, mistress, you are impertinent, and there's
your brief for you.   215

   Flings her breviate at her

Instruct me!

WIDOW BLACKACRE 'Impertinent' to me, you saucy Jack you! You
return my breviate, but where's my fee? You'll be sure to keep that,
and scan that so well, that if there chance to be but a brass
half-crown° in't, one's sure to hear on't again. Would you would   220
but look on your breviate half so narrowly. But pray give me my
fee too, as well as my brief.

PETULANT Mistress, that's without precedent. When did a counsel
ever return his fee, pray? And you are impertinent, and ignorant,
to demand it.   225

WIDOW BLACKACRE 'Impertinent' again, and 'ignorant'—to me!
Gadsbodikins, you puny upstart in the law, to use me so, you green

bag carrier, you murderer of unfortunate causes; the clerk's ink is scarce off of your fingers, you that newly come from lamp-blacking the judge's shoes, and are not fit to wipe mine. You call me impertinent and ignorant! I would give thee a cuff on the ear, sitting the courts,° if I were ignorant. Marry gep, if it had not been for me, thou hadst been yet but a hearing counsel at the bar.

> *Exit Petulant. Enter Mr Buttongown, crossing the stage in haste*

Mr Buttongown, Mr Buttongown, whither so fast? What, won't you stay till we are heard?

BUTTONGOWN I cannot, Mrs Blackacre, I must be at the Council;° my lord's cause stays there for me.

WIDOW BLACKACRE And mine suffers here.

BUTTONGOWN I cannot help it.

WIDOW BLACKACRE I'm undone.

BUTTONGOWN What's that to me?

WIDOW BLACKACRE Consider the five pound fee,° if not my cause: that was something to you.

BUTTONGOWN Away, away, pray be not so troublesome, mistress; I must begone.

WIDOW BLACKACRE Nay, but consider a little; I am your old client, my lord but a new one; or, let him be what he will, he will hardly be a better client to you than myself. I hope you believe I shall be in law as long as I live?—therefore am no despicable client. Well, but go to your lord; I know you expect he should make you a judge one day; but I hope his promise to you will prove a true lord's promise. But, that he might be sure to fail you, I wish you had his bond for't.

BUTTONGOWN But what, will you yet be thus impertinent, mistress?

WIDOW BLACKACRE Nay, I beseech you, sir, stay; if it be but to tell me my lord's case. Come, in short.

BUTTONGOWN Nay, then—

> *Exit Buttongown*

WIDOW BLACKACRE Well, Jerry; observe, child, and lay it up for hereafter: these are those lawyers who, by being in all causes, are in none. Therefore if you would have 'em for you, let your adversary fee 'em, for he may chance to depend upon 'em; and so, in being against thee, they'll be for thee.

JERRY Ay, mother, they put me in mind of the unconscionable wooers of widows, who undertake briskly their matrimonial

business for their money; but when they have got it once, let who
s' will° drudge for them. Therefore have a care of 'em, forsooth:
there's advice for your advice.

WIDOW BLACKACRE Well said, boy.—Come, Mr Splitcause,° pray
go see when my cause in Chancery comes on; and go speak with   270
Mr Quillet° in the King's Bench, and Mr Quirk° in the Common
Pleas, and see how our matters go there.

    Enter Oldfox

OLDFOX Lady, a good and propitious morning to you; and may all
your causes go as well as if I myself were judge of 'em.

WIDOW BLACKACRE Sir, excuse me, I am busy, and cannot answer   275
compliments in Westminster Hall.—Go, Mr Splitcause, and come
to me again, to that bookseller's; there I'll stay for you, that you
may be sure to find me.

OLDFOX No, sir, come to the other bookseller's; I'll attend your
ladyship thither.   280

    Exit Splitcause

WIDOW BLACKACRE Why to the other?

OLDFOX Because he is my bookseller, lady.

WIDOW BLACKACRE What, to sell you lozenges for your catarrh? Or
medicines for your corns?° What else can a major deal with a
bookseller for?   285

OLDFOX Lady, he prints for me.

WIDOW BLACKACRE Why, are you an author?

OLDFOX Of some few essays; deign you, lady, to peruse 'em.

    [*Drawing her towards the bookseller's stall*]

    (*Aside*) She is a woman of parts, and I must win her by showing
mine.   290

BOOKSELLER'S BOY Will you see Culpeper, mistress? *Aristotle's
Problems? The Complete Midwife?*°

WIDOW BLACKACRE No, let's see Dalton, Hughes, Sheppard, Wingate.°

BOOKSELLER'S BOY We have no law-books.   295

WIDOW BLACKACRE No? You are a pretty bookseller then.

OLDFOX Come, have you e'er a one of my essays left?

BOOKSELLER'S BOY Yes, sir, we have enough, and shall always have
'em.

OLDFOX How so?   300

BOOKSELLER'S BOY Why, they are good, steady, lasting ware.

OLDFOX Nay, I hope they will live. Let's see. Be pleased, madam, to
peruse the poor endeavours of my pen.

Gives her a book.

For I have a pen,° though I say it that—

JERRY Pray let me see *St George for Christendom; or, The Seven*   305
Champions of England.°

WIDOW BLACKACRE No, no, give him *The Young Clerk's Guide.*°
What, we shall have you read yourself into a humour of rambling,
and fighting, and studying military discipline, and wearing red
breeches!   310

OLDFOX Nay, if you talk of military discipline—show him my
treatise of *The Art Military.*

WIDOW BLACKACRE Hold; I would as willingly he should read a
play.

JERRY Oh pray, forsooth mother, let me have a play.   315

WIDOW BLACKACRE No, sirrah, there are young students of the law
enough spoiled already by plays; they would make you in love with
your laundress, or what's worse, some queen of the stage° that was
a laundress—and so turn keeper before you are of age.

Several crossing the stage

But stay, Jerry, is not that Mr What-d'y'-call-him that goes   320
there?—he that offered to sell me a suit in Chancery for five
hundred pound, for a hundred down, and only paying the clerk's
fees.°

JERRY Ay, forsooth, 'tis he.

WIDOW BLACKACRE Then stay here, and have a care of the bags,   325
whilst I follow him—have a care of the bags, I say.

JERRY And do you have a care, forsooth, of the statute against
champerty, I say.

*Exit Widow Blackacre. Enter Freeman [followed by the two
Sailors]*

FREEMAN (*aside*) So, there's a limb of my widow, which was wont to
be inseparable from her: she can't be far. [*To Jerry*] How now, my   330
pretty son-in-law that shall be, where's my widow?

JERRY My mother, but not your widow, will be forthcoming presently.

FREEMAN Your servant, major; what, are you buying furniture for a
little sleeping closet, which you miscall a study? For you do only by   335
your books as by your wenches—bind 'em up neatly, and make 'em
fine, for other people to use 'em; and your bookseller is properly
your upholster, for he furnishes your room, rather than your head.

OLDFOX Well, well, good sea-lieutenant, study you your compass,
that's more than your head can deal with. (*Aside*) I will go find out   340

the widow, to keep her out of his sight, or he'll board her whilst I am treating a peace.

Exit Oldfox

JERRY [*to Bookseller's Boy*] Nay prithee, friend, now, let me have but *The Seven Champions*; you shall trust me no longer than till my mother's Mr Splitcause comes, for I hope he'll lend me where-   345 withal to pay for't.

FREEMAN Lend thee! Here, I'll pay him. Do you want money, squire? I'm sorry a man of your estate should want money.

JERRY Nay, my mother will ne'er let me be at age.° And till then, she says—   350

FREEMAN At age! Why, you are at age already, to have spent an estate, man; there are younger than you, have kept their women these three years, have had half a dozen claps, and lost as many thousand pounds at play.

JERRY Ay, they are happy sparks! Nay, I know some of my school-   355 fellows who, when we were at school, were two years younger than me; but now, I know not how, are grown men before me, and go where they will, and look to themselves.° But my curmudgeonly mother won't allow me wherewithal to be a man of myself° with.

FREEMAN Why, there 'tis; I knew your mother was in the fault. Ask   360 but your schoolfellows what they did, to be men of themselves.

JERRY Why, I know they went to law with their mothers; for they say there's no good to be done upon a widow mother, till one goes to law with her. But mine is as plaguy a lawyer as any's of our Inn.° Then would she marry too, and cut down my trees.° Now I should   365 hate, man, to have my father's wife kissed, and slapped, and t'other thing too (you know what I mean) by another man; and our trees are the purest, tall, even, shady twigs, by my fa'.

FREEMAN Come, squire, let your mother and your trees fall as she pleases, rather than wear this gown, and carry green bags all thy   370 life, and be pointed at for a tony. But you shall be able to deal with her yet the common way; thou shalt make false love to some lawyer's daughter, whose father, upon the hopes of thy marrying her, shall lend thee money, and law, to preserve thy estate and trees—and thy mother is so ugly, nobody will have her, if she   375 cannot cut down thy trees.

JERRY Nay, if I had but anybody to stand by me, I am as stomachful as another.

FREEMAN That will I; I'll not see any hopeful young gentleman abused.   380

BOOKSELLER'S BOY (*aside*) By any but yourself.

JERRY The truth on't is, mine's as arrant a widow-mother, to her poor child, as any's in England: she won't so much as let one have sixpence in one's pocket, to see a motion, or the dancing of the ropes° or— 385

FREEMAN Come, you shan't want money; there's gold for you.

JERRY O Lurd, sir, two guineas! D'ye lend me this? Is there no trick in't? Well, sir, I'll give you my bond, for security.

FREEMAN No, no, thou hast given me thy face for security: anybody would swear thou dost not look like a cheat. You shall have what 390 you will of me; and, if your mother will not be kinder to you, come to me, who will.

JERRY (*aside*) By my fa', he's a curious fine gentleman!—But, will you stand by one?

FREEMAN If you can be resolute. 395

JERRY Can be resolved! Gad, if she gives me but a cross word, I'll leave her tonight, and come to you. But now I have got money, I'll go to Jack of All Trades,° at t'other end of the hall, and buy the neatest, purest things—

FREEMAN [*aside*] And I'll follow the great boy, and my blow at° his 400 mother. Steal away the calf, and the cow will follow you.

Exit Jerry, followed by Freeman [and the two Sailors].
Enter, on the other side, Manly, Widow Blaçkacre, and Oldfox

MANLY Damn your cause; can't you lose it without me?—which you are like enough to do, if it be as you say, an honest one. I will suffer no longer for't.

WIDOW BLACKACRE Nay, captain, I tell you, you are my prime 405 witness, and the cause is just now coming on, Mr Splitcause tells me. Lord, methinks you should take a pleasure in walking here, as half you see now do—for they have no business here, I assure you.

MANLY Yes, but I'll assure you then, their business is to persecute me; but d'ye think I'll stay any longer, to have a rogue, because he 410 knows my name, pluck me aside, and whisper a news-book secret° to me, with a stinking breath? A second come piping angry from the court, and sputter in my face his tedious complaints against it? A third law-coxcomb, because he saw me once at a reader's dinner,° come and put me a long law-case, to make a 415 discovery of his indefatigable dulness, and my wearied patience? A fourth, a most barbarous civil rogue, who will keep a man half an hour in the crowd with a bowed body, and a hat off, acting the

reformed sign of the Salutation Tavern,° to hear his bountiful
professions of service and friendship, whilst he cares not if I were   420
damned, and I am wishing him hanged out of my way? I'd as soon
run the gauntlet, as walk t'other turn.

    Enter to them Jerry, without his bags, but laden with trinkets,
    which he endeavours to hide from his mother; and followed at
    a distance by Freeman [and Second Sailor]

WIDOW BLACKACRE Oh, are you come, sir? But where have you
been, you ass? And how come you thus laden?

JERRY Look here, forsooth mother, now here's a duck, here's a   425
boar-cat, and here's an owl.

    Making a noise with catcalls, and other suchlike instruments

WIDOW BLACKACRE Yes, there is an owl, sir.

OLDFOX He's an ungracious bird,° indeed.

WIDOW BLACKACRE But go, thou trangam, and carry back those
trangams, which thou hast stolen or purloined; for nobody would   430
trust a minor in Westminster Hall, sure.

JERRY Hold yourself contented, forsooth, I have these com-
modities° by a fair bargain and sale; and there stands my witness,
and creditor.

WIDOW BLACKACRE How's that! [*To Freeman*] What, sir, d'ye think   435
to get the mother by giving the child a rattle? [*To Jerry*] But where
are my bags, my writings, you rascal?

JERRY (*aside*) O Law! Where are they indeed?

WIDOW BLACKACRE How, sirrah? Speak, come—

MANLY (*apart to Freeman*) You can tell her, Freeman, I suppose?   440

FREEMAN (*apart to him*) 'Tis true, I made one of your saltwater
sharks steal 'em, whilst he was eagerly choosing his commodities,
as he calls 'em, in order to° my design upon his mother.

WIDOW BLACKACRE Won't you speak? Where were you, I say, you
son of a—an unfortunate woman? Oh, major, I'm undone; they are   445
all that concern my estate, my jointure, my husband's deed of gift,
my evidences for all my suits now depending! What will become
of them?

FREEMAN (*aside*) I'm glad to hear this. [*To her*] They'll be safe, I
warrant you, madam.   450

WIDOW BLACKACRE Oh where? Where? Come, you villain, along
with me, and show me where.

    Exeunt Widow Blackacre, Jerry, Oldfox

MANLY Thou hast taken the right way to get a widow, by making
her great boy rebel; for, when nothing will make a widow marry,

she'll do't to cross her children. But canst thou in earnest marry   455
this harpy, this volume of shrivelled, blurred parchments and law,
this attorney's desk?

FREEMAN Ay, ay, I'll marry, and live honestly: that is, give my
creditors, not her, due benevolence°—pay my debts.

MANLY Thy creditors, you see, are not so barbarous as to put thee   460
in prison, and wilt thou commit thyself to a noisome dungeon for
thy life?—which is the only satisfaction thou canst give thy
creditors, by this match.

FREEMAN Why, is not she rich?

MANLY Ay, but he that marries a widow, for her money, will find   465
himself as much mistaken as the widow that marries a young fellow
for due benevolence, as you call it.

FREEMAN Why, d'ye think I shan't deserve wages? I'll drudge
faithfully.

MANLY I tell thee again, he that is the slave in the mine, has the least   470
propriety in the ore. You may dig, and dig; but, if thou wouldst
have her money, rather get to be her trustee than her husband. For
a true widow will make over her estate to anybody, and cheat
herself, rather than be cheated by her children, or a second
husband.   475

Enter to them Jerry, running in a fright

JERRY Oh Law! I'm undone, I'm undone; my mother will kill me.
You said you'd stand by one.

FREEMAN So I will, my brave squire, I warrant thee.

JERRY Ay, but I dare not stay till she comes; for she's as furious, now
she has lost her writings, as a bitch when she has lost her puppies.   480

MANLY The comparison's handsome!

JERRY Oh, she's here!

Enter Widow Blackacre and Oldfox

FREEMAN (*to [Second] Sailor*) Take him, Jack, and make haste with
him, to your master's lodging; and be sure you keep him up till I
come.   485

Exeunt Jerry and [Second] Sailor

WIDOW BLACKACRE Oh my dear writings! Where's this heathen
rogue, my minor?

FREEMAN Gone to drown or hang himself.

WIDOW BLACKACRE No, I know him too well, he'll ne'er be *felo de
se*° that way; but he may go and choose a guardian° of his own   490
head, and so be *felo de ses biens:*° for he has not yet chosen one.

FREEMAN (*aside*) Say you so? And he shan't want one.

WIDOW BLACKACRE But now I think on't, 'tis you, sir, have put this
cheat upon me. For there is a saying,° 'Take hold of a maid by her
smock, and a widow by her writings, and they cannot get from   495
you.' But I'll play fast and loose with you yet, if there be law; and
my minor and writings are not forthcoming, I'll bring my action of
detinue or trover.° But first, I'll try to find out this guardianless,
graceless villain. Will you jog, major?

MANLY If you have lost your evidence, I hope your causes cannot go   500
on, and I may begone?

WIDOW BLACKACRE Oh no, stay but a making-water while° (as one
may say), and I'll be with you again.

   Exeunt Widow Blackacre and Oldfox

FREEMAN Well, sure I am the first man that ever began a love
intrigue in Westminster Hall.   505

MANLY No, sure; for the love to a widow generally begins here. And
as the widow's cause goes against the heir or executors, the jointure
rivals commence their suit to the widow.

FREEMAN Well, but how, pray, have you passed your time here, since
I was forced to leave you alone? You have had a great deal of   510
patience.

MANLY Is this a place to be alone, or have patience in? But I have
had patience indeed; for I have drawn upon me, since I came, but
three quarrels and two lawsuits.

FREEMAN Nay, faith, you are too curst to be let loose in the world;   515
you should be tied up again, in your sea-kennel, called a ship. But
how could you quarrel here?

MANLY How could I refrain? A lawyer talked peremptorily and
saucily to me, and as good as gave me the lie.

FREEMAN They do it so often to one another at the bar, that they   520
make no bones on't° elsewhere.

MANLY However, I gave him a cuff on the ear; whereupon he jogs
two men, whose backs were turned to us (for they were reading at
a bookseller's) to witness I struck him sitting the courts; which
office they so readily promised that I called 'em rascals and knights   525
of the post. One of 'em presently calls two other absent witnesses,
who were coming towards us at a distance, whilst the other, with
a whisper, desires to know my name, that he might have satisfaction by way of challenge, as t'other by way of writ—but if it were
not° rather to direct his brother's writ, than his own challenge: 530
there you see is one of my quarrels, and two of my lawsuits.

FREEMAN So. And the other two?

MANLY For advising a poet to leave off writing, and turn lawyer, because he is dull, and impudent, and says or writes nothing now, but by precedent.   535

FREEMAN And the third quarrel?

MANLY For giving more sincere advice to a handsome, well-dressed young fellow (who asked it too) not to marry a wench that he loved, and I had lain with.

FREEMAN Nay, if you will be giving your sincere advice to lovers and   540
poets, you will not fail of quarrels.

MANLY Or if I stay in this place—for I see more quarrels crowding upon me. Let's begone, and avoid 'em.
        Enter Novel, at a distance, coming towards them
A plague on him; that sneer is ominous to us. He is coming upon us, and we shall not be rid of him.   545

NOVEL Dear bully, don't look so grum upon me. You told me just now, you had forgiven me a little harmless raillery upon wooden legs last night.

MANLY Yes, yes, pray begone; I am talking of business.

NOVEL Can't I hear it? I love thee, and will be faithful, and always—   550

MANLY Impertinent! 'Tis business that concerns Freeman only.

NOVEL Well, I love Freeman too, and would not divulge his secret. Prithee speak, prithee; I must—

MANLY Prithee let me be rid of thee, I must be rid of thee.

NOVEL Faith, thou canst hardly, I love thee so. Come, I must know   555
the business.

MANLY (*aside*) So, I have it now.—Why, if you needs will know it, he has a quarrel, and his adversary bids him bring two friends with him. Now, I am one—and we are thinking who we shall have for a third.   560
        Several crossing the stage

NOVEL A pox, there goes a fellow owes me an hundred pound, and goes out of town tomorrow: I'll speak with him, and come to you presently.
        Exit Novel

MANLY No, but you won't.

FREEMAN You are dexterously rid of him.   565
        Enter Oldfox

MANLY To what purpose?—since here comes another, as impertinent. I know, by his grin, he is bound hither.

OLDFOX Your servant, worthy, noble captain. Well, I have left the widow, because she carried me from your company. For, faith,

captain, I must needs tell thee, thou art the only officer in England, 570
who was not an Edgehill officer,° that I care for.

MANLY I'm sorry for't.

OLDFOX Why, wouldst thou have me love them?

MANLY Anybody, rather than me.

OLDFOX What, you are modest I see! Therefore too, I love thee. 575

MANLY No, I am not modest, but love to brag myself, and can't
patiently hear you fight over the last Civil War. Therefore go look
out the fellow I saw just now here, that walks with his stockings
and his sword out at heels, and let him tell you the history of that
scar on his cheek, to give you occasion to show yours, got in the 580
field at Bloomsbury,° not that of Edgehill. Go to him; poor fellow,
he is fasting, and has not yet the happiness this morning to stink
of brandy and tobacco. Go, give him some to hear you; I am busy.

OLDFOX Well, egad, I love thee now, boy, for thy surliness. Thou
art no tame captain, I see, that will suffer— 585

MANLY An old fox.

OLDFOX All that shan't make me angry. I consider thou art peevish,
and fretting at some ill success at law. Prithee tell me what ill luck
you have met with here.

MANLY You. 590

OLDFOX Do I look like the picture of ill luck?° Gadsnouns, I love
thee more and more—and shall I tell thee what made me love thee
first?

MANLY Do: that I may be rid of that damned quality, and thee.

OLDFOX 'Twas thy wearing that broadsword° there. 595

MANLY Here, Freeman, let's change. I'll never wear it more.

OLDFOX How! You won't sure! Prithee don't look like one of our
holiday captains° nowadays, with a bodkin by your side, your
martinet rogues.°

MANLY (*aside*) Oh, then there's hopes.—What, d'ye find fault with 600
martinet? Let me tell you, sir, 'tis the best exercise in the world,
the most ready, most easy, most graceful exercise that ever was
used, and the most—

OLDFOX Nay, nay, sir, no more, sir, your servant; if you praise
martinet once, I have done with you, sir. Martinet! Martinet! 605
     Exit Oldfox

FREEMAN Nay, you have made him leave you as willingly as ever he
did an enemy; for he was truly for the king and parliament: for the
parliament, in their list; and for the king, in cheating 'em of their
pay, and never hurting the king's party in the field.°

Enter a Lawyer towards them

MANLY A pox! This way. Here's a lawyer I know, threatening us   610
with another greeting.

LAWYER Sir, sir, your very servant. I was afraid you had forgotten
me.

MANLY I was not afraid you had forgotten me.

LAWYER No, sir, we lawyers have pretty good memories.   615

MANLY You ought to have, by your wits.°

LAWYER Oh, you are a merry gentleman, sir. I remember you were
merry, when I was last in your company.

MANLY I was never merry in thy company, Master Lawyer, sure.

LAWYER Why, I'm sure you joked upon me, and shammed me all   620
night long.

MANLY Shammed! Prithee, what barbarous law-term is that?

LAWYER Shamming! Why, don't you know that? 'Tis all our way of
wit, sir.

MANLY I am glad I do not know it then. Shamming! What does he   625
mean by't, Freeman?

FREEMAN Shamming is telling you an insipid, dull lie, with a dull
face, which the sly wag the author only laughs at himself; and
making himself believe 'tis a good jest, puts the sham only upon
himself.   630

MANLY So, your lawyer's jest, I find, like his practice, has more
knavery than wit in't. I should make the worst shammer in
England; I must always deal ingenuously, as I will with you, Master
Lawyer, and advise you to be seen rather with attornies and
solicitors, than such fellows as I am; they will credit your practice   635
more.

LAWYER No, sir, your company's an honour to me.

MANLY No, faith, go thy ways.° There goes an attorney; leave me
for him. Let it be never said, a lawyer's civility did him hurt.

LAWYER No, worthy honoured sir, I'll not leave you for any   640
attorney, sure.

MANLY Unless he had a fee in his hand.

LAWYER Have you any business here, sir? Try me: I'd serve you
sooner than any attorney breathing.

MANLY Business! (*Aside*) So, I have thought of a sure way. [*Aloud*]   645
Yes, faith, I have a little business.

LAWYER Have you so, sir? In what court, sir? What is't, sir? Tell me
but how I may serve you, and I'll do't, sir, and take it for as great
an honour—

MANLY Faith, 'tis for a poor orphan of a sea-officer of mine, that has   650
  no money; but if it could be followed *in forma pauperis*,° and when
  the legacy's recovered—

LAWYER *Forma pauperis*, sir!

MANLY Ay, sir.

  Several crossing the stage

LAWYER Mr Bumblecase,° Mr Bumblecase, a word with you. [*To*   655
  Manly] Sir, I beg your pardon at present, I have a little business—

MANLY Which is not *in forma pauperis*.

  Exit Lawyer

FREEMAN So, you have now found a way to be rid of people without
  quarrelling.

  Enter Alderman

MANLY But here's a City rogue will stick as hard upon us, as if I   660
  owed him money.

ALDERMAN Captain, noble sir, I am yours heartily, d'ye see. Why
  should you avoid your old friends?

MANLY And why should you follow me? I owe you nothing.

ALDERMAN Out of my hearty respects to you; for there is not a man   665
  in England—

MANLY Thou wouldst save from hanging, with the expense of a
  shilling only.

ALDERMAN Nay, nay, but captain, you are like enough to tell me—

MANLY Truth,° which you won't care to hear. Therefore you had   670
  better go talk with somebody else.

ALDERMAN No, I know nobody can inform me better of some young
  wit, or spendthrift, that has a good dipped seat and estate in
  Middlesex, Hertfordshire, Essex, or Kent: any of these would serve
  my turn. Now, if you knew of such an one, and would but help—   675

MANLY You to finish his ruin.

ALDERMAN I'faith, you should have a snip—

MANLY Of your nose.

  Takes him by the nose

  You thirty in the hundred° rascal, would you make me your squire
  setter,° your bawd for manors?   680

ALDERMAN Oh!

FREEMAN Hold, or here will be your third lawsuit.

ALDERMAN Gad's precious, you hectoring person you, are you wild?
  I meant you no hurt, sir. I begin to think (as things go) land
  security° best, and have, for a convenient mortgage, some ten,   685
  fifteen, or twenty thousand pound by me.

MANLY Then go lay it out upon an hospital, and take a mortgage of
heaven, according to your City custom; for you think, by laying out
a little money, to hook in that too hereafter. Do, I say, and keep
the poor you've made by taking forfeitures, that heaven may not   690
take yours.

ALDERMAN No, to keep the cripples you make this war; this war
spoils our trade.

MANLY Damn your trade, 'tis the better for't.°

ALDERMAN What, will you speak against our trade?   695

MANLY And dare you speak against the war, our trade?

ALDERMAN (aside) Well, he may be a convoy of ships I am concerned
in.—Come, captain, I will have a fair correspondency with you, say
what you will.

MANLY Then prithee begone.   700

ALDERMAN No, faith. Prithee, captain, let's go drink a dish of laced
coffee,° and talk of the times. Come, I'll treat you—nay, you shall
go, for I have no business here.

MANLY But I have.

ALDERMAN To pick up a man to give thee a dinner? Come, I'll do   705
thy business for thee.

MANLY Faith, now I think on't, so you may, as well as any man; for
'tis to pick up a man, to be bound with me to one who expects City
security,° for—

ALDERMAN Nay, then your servant, captain; business must be done.   710

MANLY Ay, if it can. But hark you, alderman, without you—

ALDERMAN Business, sir, I say, must be done—
         Several crossing the stage
and there's an officer of the Treasury I have an affair with—
         Exit Alderman

MANLY You see now what the mighty friendship of the world is;
what all ceremony, embraces, and plentiful professions come to.   715
You are no more to believe a professing friend than a threatening
enemy; and as no man hurts you, that tells you he'll do you a
mischief, no man (you see) is your servant who says he is so. Why
the devil, then, should a man be troubled with the flattery of
knaves, if he be not a fool, or cully; or with the fondness of fools,   720
if he be not a knave, or cheat?

FREEMAN Only for his pleasure; for there is some in laughing at
fools, and disappointing knaves.

MANLY That's a pleasure, I think, would cost you too dear, as well
as marrying your widow to disappoint her; but for my part, I have   725

no pleasure by 'em, but in despising 'em, wheresoe'er I meet 'em; and then, the pleasure of hoping so to be rid of 'em. But now my comfort is, I am not worth a shilling in the world, which all the world shall know; and then I'm sure I shall have none of 'em come near me.   730

FREEMAN A very pretty comfort, which I think you pay too dear for. But is the twenty pound gone since the morning?

MANLY To my boat's crew. Would you have the poor, honest, brave fellows want?

FREEMAN Rather than you, or I.   735

MANLY Why, art thou without money? Thou who art a friend to everybody?

FREEMAN I ventured my last stake upon the squire, to nick him of his mother;° and cannot help you to a dinner, unless you will go dine with my Lord—   740

MANLY No, no, the ordinary is too dear for me, where flattery must pay for my dinner: I am no herald, or poet.°

FREEMAN We'll go then to the bishop's—

MANLY There you must flatter the old philosophy:° I cannot renounce my reason for a dinner.   745

FREEMAN Why, then let's go to your alderman's.

MANLY Hang him, rogue! That were not to dine, for he makes you drunk with lees of sack before dinner, to take away your stomach; and there you must call usury and extortion, God's blessings, or the honest turning of the penny; hear him brag of the leather   750 breeches in which he trotted first to town; and make a greater noise with his money in his parlour, than his cashiers do in his counting-house, without hopes of borrowing a shilling.

FREEMAN Ay, a pox on't, 'tis like dining with the great gamesters; and, when they fall to their common dessert,° see the heaps of gold   755 drawn on all hands, without going to twelve.° Let us go to my Lady Goodly's.

MANLY There, to flatter her looks, you must mistake her grandchildren for her own; praise her cook, that she may rail at him; and feed her dogs, not yourself.   760

FREEMAN What d'ye think of eating with your lawyer then?

MANLY Eat with him! Damn him! To hear him employ his barbarous eloquence in a reading upon the two and thirty good bits in a shoulder of veal;° and be forced yourself to praise the cold bribe pie,° that stinks, and drink law-French wine,° as rough and harsh   765 as his law-French. A pox on him, I'd rather dine in the Temple

Round or walks, with the knights without noses, or the knights of
the post,° who are honester fellows, and better company. But let
us home, and try our fortune; for I'll stay no longer here for your
damned widow.   770

FREEMAN Well, let us go home then; for I must go for my damned
widow, and look after my new damned charge. Three or four
hundred year ago, a man might have dined in this hall.°

MANLY But now the lawyer only here is fed,
       And, bully-like, by quarrels gets his bread.   775
    Exeunt

4.1

Manly's lodging.

Enter Manly and Fidelia

MANLY Well, there's success in thy face; hast thou prevailed? Say.

FIDELIA As I could wish, sir.

MANLY So, I told thee what thou wert fit for, and thou wouldst not believe me. Come, thank me for bringing thee acquainted with thy genius. Well, thou hast mollified her heart for me? 5

FIDELIA No sir, not so; but what's better.

MANLY How! What's better!

FIDELIA I shall harden your heart against her.

MANLY Have a care, sir, my heart is too much in earnest to be fooled with, and my desire at height, and needs no delays to incite it. 10 What, you are too good a pimp already, and know how to endear pleasure by withholding it? But leave off your page's bawdy-house tricks, sir, and tell me: will she be kind?

FIDELIA Kinder than you could wish, sir.

MANLY So then. Well, prithee what said she? 15

FIDELIA She said—

MANLY What? Thou'rt so tedious. Speak comfort to me. What?

FIDELIA That, of all things, you were her aversion.

MANLY How!

FIDELIA That she would sooner take a bedfellow out of an hospital, 20 and diseases, into her arms, than you.

MANLY What?

FIDELIA That she would rather trust her honour with a dissolute, debauched hector—nay worse, with a finical, baffled coward, all over loathsome with affectation of the fine gentleman— 25

MANLY What's all this you say?

FIDELIA Nay, that my offers of your love to her, were more offensive than when parents woo their virgin daughters to the enjoyment of riches only; and that you were, in all circumstances, as nauseous to her as a husband on compulsion. 30

MANLY Hold; I understand you not.

FIDELIA (*aside*) So, 'twill work, I see.

MANLY Did not you tell me—

FIDELIA She called you ten thousand ruffians.

MANLY Hold, I say. 35

FIDELIA Brutes—

MANLY Hold.

FIDELIA Sea-monsters—

MANLY Damn your intelligence. Hear me a little now.

FIDELIA Nay, surly coward she called you too.   40

MANLY Won't you hold yet? Hold, or—

FIDELIA Nay, sir, pardon me; I could not but tell you she had the
    baseness, the injustice, to call you coward, sir, coward, coward, sir.

MANLY Not yet?—°

FIDELIA I've done. Coward, sir.   45

MANLY Did not you say she was kinder than I could wish her?

FIDELIA Yes, sir.

MANLY How then . . .? Oh—I understand you now. At first she
    appeared in rage, and disdain, the truest sign of a coming woman;
    but at last you prevailed, it seems; did you not?   50

FIDELIA Yes, sir.

MANLY So then, let's know that only. Come, prithee, without
    delays—I'll kiss thee° for that news beforehand.

FIDELIA (aside) So; the kiss, I'm sure, is welcome to me, whatsoe'er
    the news will be to you.   55

MANLY Come, speak, my dear volunteer.

FIDELIA (aside) How welcome were that kind word too, if it were not
    for another woman's sake!

MANLY What, won't you speak? You prevailed for me, at last, you say?

FIDELIA No, sir.   60

MANLY No more of your fooling, sir; it will not agree with my
    impatience, or temper.

FIDELIA Then, not to fool you, sir: I spoke to her for you, but
    prevailed for myself. She would not hear me when I spoke in your
    behalf, but bid me say what I would in my own, though she gave   65
    me no occasion, she was so coming. And so was kinder, sir, than
    you could wish; which I was only afraid to let you know, without
    some warning.

MANLY How's this? Young man, you are of a lying age; but I must
    hear you out, and if—   70

FIDELIA I would not abuse you, and cannot wrong her by any report
    of her, she is so wicked.

MANLY How, wicked! Had she the impudence, at the second sight
    of you only—

FIDELIA Impudence, sir! Oh, she has impudence enough to put a   75
    court out of countenance, and debauch a stews.

MANLY Why, what said she?

FIDELIA Her tongue, I confess, was silent; but her speaking eyes
gloated such things, more immodest, and lascivious, than ravishers
can act, or women under a confinement° think.   80

MANLY I know there are whose eyes reflect more obscenity than the
glasses in alcoves; but there are others too who use a little art with
their looks, to make 'em seem more beautiful, not more loving;
which vain young fellows, like you, are apt to interpret in their own
favour, and to the lady's wrong.   85

FIDELIA Seldom, sir. Pray have you a care of gloating eyes; for he
that loves to gaze upon 'em, will find, at last, a thousand fools and
cuckolds in 'em, instead of cupids.

MANLY Very well, sir. But what, you had only eye-kindness from
Olivia?   90

FIDELIA I tell you again, sir, no woman sticks there. Eye-promises of
love they only keep°—nay, they are contracts which make you sure
of 'em. In short, sir, she, seeing me with shame and amazement
dumb, unactive, and resistless, threw her twisting arms about my
neck, and smothered me with a thousand tasteless kisses—believe   95
me, sir, they were so to me.

MANLY Why did you not avoid 'em then?

FIDELIA I fenced with her eager arms, as you did with the grapples
of the enemy's fireship; and nothing but cutting 'em off, could have
freed me.   100

MANLY Damned, damned woman, that could be so false and infamous! And damned, damned heart of mine, that cannot yet be false,
though so infamous! What easy, tame, suffering, trampled things
does that little god of talking cowards make of us! But—

FIDELIA (aside) So! It works, I find, as I expected.   105

MANLY But she was false to me before; she told me so herself, and
yet I could not quite believe it. But she was, so that her second
falseness is a favour to me, not an injury, in revenging me upon the
man that wronged me first of her love. Her love! A whore's, a
witch's love! . . . But, what, did she not kiss well, sir? I'm sure I   110
thought her lips—but I must not think of 'em more—but yet they
are such I could still kiss—grow to—and then tear off with my
teeth, grind 'em into mammocks, and spit 'em into her cuckold's
face.

FIDELIA (aside) Poor man, how uneasy he is! I have hardly the heart   115
to give him so much pain, though withal I give him a cure—and

to myself new life.

MANLY But, what, her kisses sure could not but warm you into
    desire at last, or a compliance with hers, at least?

FIDELIA Nay more, I confess—   120

MANLY What more? Speak.

FIDELIA All you could fear had passed between us, if I could have
    been made to wrong you, sir, in that nature.°

MANLY 'Could have been made'! You lie; you did.

FIDELIA Indeed, sir, 'twas impossible for me. Besides, we were   125
    interrupted by a visit. But, I confess, she would not let me stir till
    I promised to return to her again, within this hour, as soon as it
    should be dark; by which time she would dispose of her visit, and
    her servants, and herself for my reception—which I was fain to
    promise, to get from her.   130

MANLY Ha!

FIDELIA But if ever I go near her again, may you, sir, think me as
    false to you as she is; hate, and renounce me—as you ought to do
    her, and I hope will do now.

MANLY Well, but now I think on't, you shall keep your word with   135
    your lady. What, a young fellow, and fail the first, nay, so tempting
    an assignation!

FIDELIA How, sir!

MANLY I say you shall go to her when 'tis dark, and shall not
    disappoint her.   140

FIDELIA I, sir! I should disappoint her more by going, for—

MANLY How so?

FIDELIA Her impudence, and injustice to you, will make me disap-
    point her love—loathe her.

MANLY Come, you have my leave; and if you disgust her, I'll go with   145
    you, and act love, whilst you shall talk it only.

FIDELIA You, sir! Nay, then I'll never go near her. You act love, sir!
    You must but act it indeed, after all I have said to you. Think of
    your honour, sir; love—

MANLY Well, call it revenge, and that is honourable. I'll be revenged   150
    on her, and thou shalt be my second.

FIDELIA Not in a base action, sir, when you are your own enemy. Oh
    go not near her, sir, for heaven's sake, for your own, think not of
    it.°

MANLY How concerned you are! I thought I should catch you. What,   155
    you are my rival at last, and are in love with her yourself; and have

spoken ill of her, out of your love to her, not me; and therefore
would not have me go to her!

FIDELIA Heaven witness for me, 'tis because I love you only, I would
not have you go to her.   160

MANLY Come, come, the more I think on't, the more I'm satisfied
you do love her. Those kisses, young man, I knew were irresistible;
'tis certain.

FIDELIA There is nothing certain in the world, sir, but my truth, and
your courage.   165

MANLY Your servant, sir. Besides, false and ungrateful as she has
been to me, and though I may believe her hatred to me great as
you report it, yet I cannot think you are so soon, and at that rate,
beloved by her, though you may endeavour it.

FIDELIA Nay, if that be all, and you doubt it still, sir, I will conduct   170
you to her; and, unseen, your ears shall judge of her falseness, and
my truth to you, if that will satisfy you.

MANLY Yes, there is some satisfaction in being quite out of doubt;
because 'tis that alone withholds us from the pleasure of revenge.

FIDELIA Revenge! What revenge can you have, sir? Disdain is best   175
revenged by scorn, and faithless love by loving another, and making
her happy with the other's losings; which, if I might advise—

Enter Freeman

MANLY Not a word more.

FREEMAN What, are you talking of love yet, captain? I thought you
had done with't.   180

MANLY Why, what did you hear me say?

FREEMAN Something imperfectly of love, I think.

MANLY I was only wondering why fools, rascals, and desertless
wretches should still have the better of men of merit, with all
women, as much as with their own common mistress, Fortune!°   185

FREEMAN Because most women, like Fortune, are blind,° seem to do
all things in jest, and take pleasure in extravagant actions. Their
love deserves neither thanks or blame, for they cannot help it: 'tis
all sympathy. Therefore the noisy, the finical, the talkative, the
cowardly and effeminate, have the better of the brave, the reason-   190
able, and man of honour; for they have no more reason in their love
or kindness, than Fortune herself.

MANLY Yes, they have their reason. First, honour in a man they fear
too much to love; and sense in a lover upbraids their want of it;
and they hate anything that disturbs their admiration of them-   195
selves. But they are of that vain number who had rather show their

false generosity, in giving away profusely to worthless flatterers, than in paying just debts; and, in short, all women, like Fortune (as you say) and rewards, are lost by too much meriting.

FIDELIA   All women, sir? Sure there are some, who have no other   200
quarrel to a lover's merit, but that it begets their despair of him.

MANLY   Thou art young enough to be credulous; but we—
Enter First Sailor

FIRST SAILOR   Here are now below, the scolding, daggled gentlewoman, and that Major Old—Old—fop, I think you call him.

FREEMAN   Oldfox. Prithee, bid 'em come up—   205
[*Exit First Sailor*]
with your leave, captain, for now I can talk with her upon the
square, if I shall not disturb you.

MANLY   No, for I'll begone. Come, volunteer.

FREEMAN   Nay, pray stay; the scene between us will not be so tedious
to you as you think. Besides, you shall see how I have rigged   210
my squire out, with the remains of my shipwrecked wardrobe.
He is under your sea-*valet-de-chambre*'s hands, and by this
time dressed, and will be worth your seeing. Stay, and I'll fetch my
fool.

MANLY   No; you know I cannot easily laugh. Besides, my volunteer   215
and I have business abroad.
Exeunt Manly [and] Fidelia on one side, Freeman on t'other.
Enter Oldfox and Widow Blackacre

WIDOW BLACKACRE   What, nobody here! Did not the fellow say he
was within?

OLDFOX   Yes, lady; and he may be perhaps a little busy at present.
But, if you think the time long till he comes, (*unfolding papers*) I'll   220
read you here some of the fruits of my leisure, the overflowings of
my fancy and pen. (*Aside*) To value me right, she must know my
parts. [*To her*] Come.

WIDOW BLACKACRE   No, no; I have reading work enough of my own
in my bag, I thank you.   225

OLDFOX   Ay, law, madam—but here is a poem, in blank verse, which
I think a handsome declaration of one's passion.

WIDOW BLACKACRE   Oh, if you talk of declarations, I'll show you
one of the prettiest penned things, which I mended too myself, you
must know—   230

OLDFOX   Nay, lady, if you have used yourself so much to the reading
of harsh law that you hate smooth poetry, here is a character for
you, of—

WIDOW BLACKACRE A character! Nay, then I'll show you my bill in
Chancery here, that gives you such a character of my adversary,   235
makes him as black—

OLDFOX Pshaw! Away, away, lady. But if you think the character too
long, here is an epigram, not above twenty lines, upon a cruel lady,
who decreed her servant should hang himself, to demonstrate his
passion.   240

WIDOW BLACKACRE Decreed! If you talk of decreeing, I have such
a decree here, drawn by the finest clerk—

OLDFOX Oh lady, lady, all interruption, and no sense between us, as
if we were lawyers at the bar! But I had forgot; Apollo and Littelton°
never lodge in a head together. If you hate verses, I'll give   245
you a cast of my politics in prose: 'tis a letter to a friend in the
country,° which is now the way of all such sober, solid persons as
myself, when they have a mind to publish their disgust to the
times—though perhaps, between you and I, they have no friend
in the country. And sure a politic, serious person may as well   250
have a feigned friend in the country to write to, as well as an idle
poet a feigned mistress to write to. And so here is my *Letter to a
Friend* (or no-friend) *in the Country, Concerning the late Conjunc-
ture of Affairs, in relation to Coffee-houses;*° *or, The Coffee-Man's
Case.*   255

WIDOW BLACKACRE Nay, if your letter have a case in't, 'tis something; but first I'll read you a letter of mine to a friend in the
country, called a letter of attorney.

> *Enter to them Freeman, and Jerry in an old gaudy suit and
> red breeches of Freeman's*

OLDFOX (*aside*) What, interruption still? Oh the plague of interruption! Worse to an author than the plague of critics!   260

WIDOW BLACKACRE What's this I see? Jerry Blackacre, my minor,
in red breeches! What, hast thou left the modest, seemly garb of
gown and cap, for this? And have I lost all my good Inns of
Chancery° breeding upon thee then? And thou wilt go a-breeding
thyself, from our Inn of Chancery and Westminster Hall, at   265
coffee-houses and ordinaries, playhouses, tennis-courts, and
bawdy-houses.

JERRY Ay, ay, what then? Perhaps I will; but what's that to you?
Here's my guardian and tutor now, forsooth, that I am out of your
huckster's hands.°   270

WIDOW BLACKACRE How! Thou hast not chosen him for thy
guardian yet?

JERRY No, but he has chosen me for his charge, and that's all one; and I'll do anything he'll have me, and go all the world over with him—to ordinaries, and bawdy-houses, or anywhere else.   275

WIDOW BLACKACRE To ordinaries and bawdy-houses! Have a care, minor, thou wilt enfeeble there thy estate and body. Do not go to ordinaries and bawdy-houses, good Jerry.

JERRY Why, how come you to know any ill by bawdy-houses? You never had any hurt by 'em, had you, forsooth? Pray hold yourself   280
contented; if I do go where money and wenches are to be had, you may thank yourself; for you used me so unnaturally, you would never let me have a penny to go abroad with, nor so much as come near the garret where your maidens lay—nay, you would not so much as let me play at hot cockles° with 'em, nor have any   285
recreation with 'em, though one should have kissed you behind;° you were so unnatural a mother, so you were.

FREEMAN Ay, a very unnatural mother, faith, squire.

WIDOW BLACKACRE But, Jerry, consider thou art yet but a minor; however, if thou wilt go home with me again, and be a good child,   290
thou shalt see—

FREEMAN Madam, I must have a better care of my heir under age, than so; I would sooner trust him alone with a stale waiting-woman and a parson, than with his widow mother and her lover or lawyer.   295

WIDOW BLACKACRE Why, thou villain, part mother and minor! Rob me of my child and my writings! But thou shalt find there's law—and as in the case of ravishment of guard: Westminster the Second.°

OLDFOX Young gentleman, squire, pray be ruled by your mother,   300
and your friends.

JERRY Yes, I'll be ruled by my friends, therefore not by my mother, so I won't. I'll choose him for my guardian till I am of age—nay, maybe for as long as I live.

WIDOW BLACKACRE Wilt thou so, thou wretch? And when thou'rt   305
of age, thou wilt sign, seal, and deliver too, wilt thou?

JERRY Yes, marry will I, if you go thereto.

WIDOW BLACKACRE Oh do not squeeze wax,° son; rather go to ordinaries, and bawdy-houses, than squeeze wax. If thou dost that, farewell the goodly manor of Blackacre, with all its woods,   310
underwoods, and appurtenances whatever. Oh, oh! (Weeps)

FREEMAN Come, madam, in short, you see I am resolved to have a share in the estate, yours or your son's. If I cannot get you, I'll keep him, who is less coy, you find. But, if you would have your son again, you must take me too. Peace, or war? Love, or law? You see my hostage is in my hand; I'm in possession. 315

WIDOW BLACKACRE Nay, if one of us must be ruined, e'en let it be him. By my body, a good one! Did you ever know yet a widow marry or not marry for the sake of her child? I'd have you to know, sir, I shall be hard enough for you both yet, without marrying you. 320 If Jerry won't be ruled by me—What say you, booby, will you be ruled? Speak.

JERRY Let one alone, can't you?

WIDOW BLACKACRE Wilt thou choose him for guardian, whom I refuse for husband? 325

JERRY Ay, to choose, I thank you.

WIDOW BLACKACRE And are all my hopes frustrated? Shall I never hear thee put cases again to John the butler, or our vicar? Never see thee amble the circuit with the judges;° and hear thee, in our town hall, louder than the crier? 330

JERRY No—for I have taken my leave of lawyering and pettifogging.

WIDOW BLACKACRE Pettifogging! Thou profane villain, hast thou so? Pettifogging! Then you shall take your leave of me, and your estate too; thou shalt be an alien to me and it for ever. Pettifogging!

JERRY Oh, but if you go thereto, mother, we have the deeds 335 and settlements, I thank you. Would you cheat me of my estate, i'fac?

WIDOW BLACKACRE No, no, I will not cheat your little brother Bob—for thou wert not born in wedlock.

FREEMAN How's that! 340

JERRY How! What quirk has she got in her head now?

WIDOW BLACKACRE I say thou canst not, shalt not inherit the Blackacres' estate.

JERRY Why? Why, forsooth? What d'ye mean, if you go thereto?

WIDOW BLACKACRE Thou art but my base child; and, according to 345 the law, canst not inherit it. Nay, thou art not so much as bastard eigne.°

JERRY What, what? Am I then the son of a whore, mother?

WIDOW BLACKACRE The law says—

FREEMAN Madam, we know what the law says; but have a care what 350 you say. Do not let your passion to ruin your son, ruin your reputation.

WIDOW BLACKACRE Hang reputation, sir, am not I a widow? Have no husband, nor intend to have any? Nor would you, I suppose,

362

now have me for a wife. So, I think now I'm revenged on my son   355
and you, without marrying, as I told you.

FREEMAN But consider, madam.

JERRY What, have you no shame left in you, mother?

WIDOW BLACKACRE (*aside to Oldfox*) Wonder not at it, major, 'tis
often the poor pressed widow's case, to give up her honour to save   360
her jointure, and seem to be a light woman, rather than marry: as
some young men, they say, pretend to have the filthy disease, and
lose their credit with most women, to avoid the importunities of
some.

FREEMAN But one word with you, madam.   365

WIDOW BLACKACRE No, no, sir.—Come, major, let us make haste
now to the Prerogative Court.°

OLDFOX But, lady, if what you say be true, will you stigmatize your
reputation on record? And, if it be not true, how will you prove it?

WIDOW BLACKACRE Pshaw! I can prove anything. And for my   370
reputation, know, major, a wise woman will no more value her
reputation in disinheriting a rebellious son of a good estate, than
she would in getting him, to inherit an estate.

Exeunt Widow Blackacre and Oldfox

FREEMAN Madam—We must not let her go so, squire.

JERRY Nay, the devil can't stop her though,° if she has a mind to't.   375
But come, bully guardian, we'll go and advise with three attornies,
two proctors, two solicitors, and a shrewd man of Whitefriars,°
neither attorney, proctor, or solicitor, but as pure a pimp to the law
as any of 'em; and sure all they will be hard enough for her. For I
fear, bully guardian, you are too good a joker to have any law in   380
your head.

FREEMAN Thou'rt in the right on't, squire; I understand no law,
especially that against bastards, since I'm sure the custom is against
that law; and more people get estates by being so, than lose 'em.

Exeunt

4.2

Olivia's lodging; [a table and chair]

Enter Lord Plausible, and Boy with a candle [which he sets down]

LORD PLAUSIBLE Little gentleman, your most obedient, faithful, humble servant. Where, I beseech you, is that divine person, your noble lady?

BOY Gone out, my lord; but commanded me to give you this letter.
    Gives him a letter. Enter Novel

LORD PLAUSIBLE (*aside*) Which he must not observe. (*Puts it up*)   5

NOVEL Hey, boy, where is thy lady?

BOY Gone out, sir; but I must beg a word with you.
    Gives him a letter, and exit

NOVEL [*aside*] For me? So. (*Puts up the letter*)—Servant, servant, my lord. You see the lady knew of your coming, for she is gone out.   10

LORD PLAUSIBLE Sir, I humbly beseech you not to censure the lady's good breeding; she has reason to use more liberty with me, than with any other man.

NOVEL How, viscount, how?

LORD PLAUSIBLE Nay, I humbly beseech you, be not in choler.   15
Where there is most love, there may be most freedom.

NOVEL Nay, then 'tis time to come to an *éclaircissement* with you, and to tell you, you must think no more of this lady's love.

LORD PLAUSIBLE Why, under correction, dear sir?

NOVEL There are reasons, reasons, viscount.   20

LORD PLAUSIBLE What, I beseech you, noble° sir?

NOVEL Prithee, prithee, be not impertinent, my lord; some of you lords are such conceited, well-assured, impertinent rogues—

LORD PLAUSIBLE And you noble wits are so full of shamming, and drolling, one knows not where to have you, seriously.   25

NOVEL Well, you shall find me in bed with this lady,° one of these days.

LORD PLAUSIBLE Nay, I beseech you, spare the lady's honour—for hers and mine will be all one shortly.

NOVEL Prithee, my lord, be not an ass. Dost thou think to get her   30
from me? I have had such encouragements—

LORD PLAUSIBLE I have not been thought unworthy of 'em.

NOVEL What, not like mine! Come to an *éclaircissement*, as I said.

LORD PLAUSIBLE Why, seriously then, she has told me 'viscountess'
sounded prettily.   35

NOVEL And me, that Novel was a name she would sooner change
hers for, than for any title in England.

LORD PLAUSIBLE She has commended the softness and respectful-
ness of my behaviour.

NOVEL She has praised the briskness of my raillery of all things,°   40
man.

LORD PLAUSIBLE The sleepiness of my eyes she liked.

NOVEL Sleepiness! Dulness, dulness. But the fierceness of mine she
adored.

LORD PLAUSIBLE The brightness of my hair she liked.   45

NOVEL The brightness! No, the greasiness, I warrant. But the°
blackness and lustre of mine, she admires.

LORD PLAUSIBLE The gentleness of my smile.

NOVEL The subtlety of my leer.

LORD PLAUSIBLE The clearness of my complexion.   50

NOVEL The redness of my lips.

LORD PLAUSIBLE The whiteness of my teeth.

NOVEL My jaunty way of picking them.

LORD PLAUSIBLE The sweetness of my breath.

NOVEL Ha ha! Nay then she abused you, 'tis plain; for you know   55
what Manly said. The sweetness of your pulvilio she might
mean—but for your breath! Ha ha ha! Your breath is such, man,
that nothing but tobacco can perfume; and your complexion
nothing could mend, but the smallpox.

LORD PLAUSIBLE Well, sir, you may please to be merry; but, to put   60
you out of all doubt, sir, she has received some jewels from me, of
value.

NOVEL And presents from me; besides what I presented her jauntily,
by way of ombre,° of three or four hundred pound value, which
I'm sure are the earnest pence for our love bargain.   65

LORD PLAUSIBLE Nay then, sir, with your favour, and to make an
end of all your hopes—look you there, sir; [*shows the letter*] she has
writ to me—

NOVEL How! How! Well, well, and so she has to me. Look you there.
         Deliver to each other their letters

LORD PLAUSIBLE What's here!   70

NOVEL How's this?

Reads out

'My dear lord,

You'll excuse me for breaking my word with you, since 'twas to oblige, not offend you; for I am only gone abroad but to disappoint Novel, and meet you in the drawing-room—where I expect you, with as much impatience as when I used to suffer Novel's visits, the most impertinent fop that ever affected the name of a wit, therefore not capable, I hope, to give you jealousy. For, for your sake alone (you saw) I renounced an old lover, and will do all the world. Burn the letter, but lay up the kindness of it in your heart, with your

Olivia.'

Very fine! But pray let's see mine.

LORD PLAUSIBLE I understand it not; but sure she cannot think so of me.

[*Novel takes and*] *reads the other letter*

NOVEL Humh! Ha! 'meet . . . for your sake'—umh—'quitted an old lover . . . world . . . burn . . . in your heart, with your Olivia.' Just the same, the names only altered.

LORD PLAUSIBLE Surely there must be some mistake; or somebody has abused her, and us.

NOVEL Yes, you are abused, no doubt on't, my lord; but I'll to Whitehall, and see.

LORD PLAUSIBLE And I, where I shall find you are abused.

NOVEL Where, if it be so, for our comfort we cannot fail of meeting with fellow-sufferers enough. For, as Freeman said of another, she stands in the drawing-room like the glass, ready for all comers to set their gallantry by her; and like the glass too, lets no man go from her unsatisfied with himself.

Exeunt Lord Plausible and Novel. Enter Olivia and Boy

OLIVIA Both here, and just gone?

BOY Yes, madam.

OLIVIA But are you sure neither saw you deliver the other a letter?

BOY Yes, yes, madam, I am very sure.

OLIVIA Go then to the Old Exchange, to Westminster, Holborn, and all the other places I told you of.° I shall not need you these two hours. Begone, and take the candle with you, and be sure you leave word again below: I am gone out, to all that ask.

BOY Yes, madam.

Exit Boy

OLIVIA And my new lover will not ask, I'm sure. He has his lesson, and cannot miss me here, though in the dark—which I have

purposely designed, as a remedy against my blushing gallant's
modesty; for young lovers, like game-cocks,° are made bolder by   110
being kept without light.

Enter her husband Varnish,° as from a journey°

VARNISH (*softly*) Where is she? Darkness everywhere!

OLIVIA What, come before your time? My soul! My life! Your haste
has augmented your kindness;° and let me thank you for it thus,
and thus—   115

Embracing and kissing him

And though (my soul) the little time since you left me, has seemed
an age to my impatience, sure it is yet but seven—

VARNISH How! Who's that you expected after seven?

OLIVIA [*aside*] Ha! My husband returned! And have I been throwing
away so many kind kisses on my husband, and wronged my lover   120
already?

VARNISH Speak, I say; who was't you expected after seven?

OLIVIA (*aside*) What shall I say?—Oh!—[*Aloud*] Why, 'tis but seven
days, is it, dearest, since you went out of town? And I expected you
not so soon.   125

VARNISH No, sure, 'tis but five days since I left you.

OLIVIA Pardon my impatience, dearest, I thought 'em seven at least.

VARNISH Nay then—

OLIVIA But, my life, you shall never stay half so long from me
again—you shan't, indeed, by this kiss, you shan't.   130

VARNISH No, no; but why alone in the dark?

OLIVIA Blame not my melancholy in your absence. [*Sighs*] But, my
soul, since you went, I have strange news to tell you: Manly is
returned.

VARNISH Manly returned! Fortune forbid.   135

OLIVIA Met with the Dutch in the Channel, fought, sunk his ship
and all he carried with him. He was here with me yesterday.

VARNISH And did you own our marriage to him?

OLIVIA I told him I was married, to put an end to his love, and my
trouble; but to whom, is yet a secret kept from him, and all the   140
world. And I have used him so scurvily, his great spirit will ne'er
return, to reason it further with me. I have sent him to sea again,
I warrant.

VARNISH 'Twas bravely done. And sure he will now hate the shore
more than ever, after so great a disappointment. Be you sure only   145
to keep awhile our great secret, till he be gone. In the mean time,
I'll lead the easy honest fool by the nose,° as I used to do; and,

whilst he stays, rail with him at thee—and, when he's gone, laugh
with thee at him. But have you his cabinet of jewels safe? Part not
with a seed pearl to him, to keep him from starving.   150

OLIVIA Nor from hanging.

VARNISH He cannot recover 'em; and, I think, will scorn to beg 'em
again.

OLIVIA But, my life, have you taken the thousand guineas he left in
my name, out of the goldsmith's hands?   155

VARNISH Ay, ay, they are removed to another goldsmith's.

OLIVIA Ay but, my soul, you had best have a care he find not where
the money is; for his present wants (as I'm informed) are such as
will make him inquisitive enough.

VARNISH You say true, and he knows the man too; but I'll remove   160
it tomorrow.

OLIVIA Tomorrow! Oh do not stay till tomorrow—go tonight,
immediately.

VARNISH Now I think on't, you advise well, and I will go presently.

OLIVIA Presently? Instantly—I will not let you stay a jot.   165

VARNISH I will then, though I return not home till twelve.

OLIVIA Nay, though not till morning, with all my heart. Go, dearest,
I am impatient till you are gone.
          Thrusts him out
So, I have at once now brought about those two grateful businesses,
which all prudent women do together: secured money and pleasure;   170
and now all interruptions of the last° are removed. Go, husband,
and come up, friend—just the buckets in the well: the absence of
one brings the other. But I hope, like them too, they will not meet
in the way, jostle, and clash together.
          *Enter Fidelia, and Manly treading softly and staying behind
          at some distance*

(*Softly*) So, are you come? [*Aside*] But not the husband-bucket (I   175
hope) again.—Who's there? My dearest?

FIDELIA My life—

OLIVIA Right, right—where are thy lips? Here, take the dumb and best
welcomes, kisses and embraces; 'tis not a time for idle words. In a duel
of love, as in others, parleying shows basely. Come, we are alone. And 180
now the word is only 'Satisfaction, and defend not thyself.'

MANLY (*aside*) How's this! Wuh, she makes love like a devil in a
play;° and in this darkness, which conceals her angel's face, if I
were apt to be afraid, I should think her a devil.
          Fidelia avoiding Olivia

OLIVIA What, you traverse ground, young gentleman!   185

FIDELIA I take breath only.

MANLY (*aside*) Good heavens! How was I deceived!

OLIVIA Nay, you are a coward. What, are you afraid of the fierceness of my love?

FIDELIA Yes, madam, lest its violence might presage its change; and   190
I must needs be afraid you would leave me quickly, who could desert so brave a gentleman as Manly.

OLIVIA Oh! Name not his name; for in a time of stolen joys, as this is, the filthy name of husband were not a more allaying sound.

MANLY (*aside*) There's some comfort yet.   195

FIDELIA But did you not love him?

OLIVIA Never. How could you think it?

FIDELIA Because he thought it, who is a man of that sense, nice discerning, and diffidency, that I should think it hard to deceive him.   200

OLIVIA No; he that distrusts most the world, trusts most to himself, and is but the more easily deceived, because he thinks he can't be deceived. His cunning is like the coward's sword, by which he is oftener worsted than defended.

FIDELIA Yet, sure, you used no common art to deceive him.   205

OLIVIA I knew he loved his own singular moroseness so well, as to dote upon any copy of it; wherefore I feigned an hatred to the world too, that he might love me in earnest. But, if it had been hard to deceive him, I'm sure 'twere much harder to love him. A dogged, ill-mannered—   210

FIDELIA (*aside to Manly*) D'ye hear her, sir? Pray hear her.

OLIVIA Surly, untractable, snarling brute! He! A masty dog were as fit a thing to make a gallant of.

MANLY (*aside*) Ay, a goat, or monkey, were fitter for thee.

FIDELIA I must confess, for my part (though my rival), I cannot but   215
say, he has a manly handsomeness in's face and mien.

OLIVIA So has a Saracen in the sign.°

FIDELIA Is proper, and well made—

OLIVIA As a drayman.

FIDELIA Has wit—   220

OLIVIA He rails at all mankind.

FIDELIA And undoubted courage—

OLIVIA Like the hangman's: can murder a man when his hands are tied. He has cruelty indeed; which is no more courage than his railing is wit.   225

MANLY (*aside*) Thus women, and men like women, are too hard for
us when they think we do not hear 'em; and reputation, like other
mistresses, is never true to a man in his absence.

FIDELIA He is—

OLIVIA Prithee no more of him. I thought I had satisfied you enough   230
before, that he could never be a rival for you to apprehend; and
you need not be more assured of my aversion to him, but by the
last testimony of my love to you—which I am ready to give you.
Come, my soul, this way—

  Pulls Fidelia

FIDELIA But, madam, what could make you dissemble love to him,   235
when 'twas so hard a thing for you, and flatter his love to you?

OLIVIA That which makes all the world flatter and dissemble: 'twas
his money; I had a real passion for that. Yet I loved not that so
well, as for it,° to take him; for, as soon as I had his money I
hastened his departure: like a wife who, when she has made the   240
most of a dying husband's breath, pulls away the pillow.°

MANLY [*aside*] Damned money! Its master's potent rival still; and,
like a saucy pimp, corrupts itself the mistress it procures for us.

OLIVIA But I did not think with you, my life, to pass my time in
talking. Come hither, come—yet stay, till I have locked a door in   245
the other room, that might chance to let us in some interruption—
which reciting poets, or losing gamesters, fear not more than I at
this time do.

  Exit Olivia

FIDELIA Well, I hope you are now satisfied, sir, and will begone, to
think of your revenge.   250

MANLY No, I am not satisfied, and must stay to be revenged.

FIDELIA How, sir? You'll use no violence to her, I hope, and forfeit
your own life, to take away hers? That were no revenge.

MANLY No, no, you need not fear; my revenge shall only be upon
her honour, not her life.   255

FIDELIA How, sir! Her honour? Oh heavens! Consider, sir, she has
no honour. D'ye call that revenge? Can you think of such a thing?
But reflect, sir, how she hates and loathes you.

MANLY Yes, so much she hates me, that it would be a revenge
sufficient, to make her accessory to my pleasure, and then let her   260
know it.

FIDELIA No, sir, no; to be revenged on her now, were to disappoint
her.° Pray, sir, let us begone.

Pulls Manly

MANLY Hold off. What, you are my rival then; and therefore you
shall stay, and keep the door° for me, whilst I go in for you. But,   265
when I'm gone, if you dare to stir off from this very board, or
breathe the least murmuring accent, I'll cut her throat first, and if
you love her, you will not venture her life—nay, then I'll cut your
throat too; and I know you love your own life at least.

FIDELIA But, sir, good sir—   270

MANLY Not a word more, lest I begin my revenge on her, by killing
you.

FIDELIA But are you sure 'tis revenge that makes you do this? How
can it be?

MANLY Whist!   275

FIDELIA 'Tis a strange revenge indeed.

MANLY If you make me stay, I shall keep my word, and begin with
you. No more.

Exit Manly, at the same door Olivia went

FIDELIA Oh heavens, is there not punishment enough
In loving well (if you will have't a crime),   280
But you must add fresh torments daily to't,
And punish us, like peevish rivals still,
Because we fain would find a heaven here?
But did there never any love like me,
That untried tortures you must find me out?°   285
Others, at worst, you force to kill themselves,
But I must be self-murd'ress of my love,
Yet will not grant me power to end my life,
My cruel life; for when a lover's hopes
Are dead, and gone, life is unmerciful.   290

Sits down and weeps. Enter Manly

MANLY [*aside*] I have thought better on't; I must not discover myself
now, I am without witnesses; for if I barely should publish it, she
would deny it with as much impudence as she would act it again
with this young fellow here.—Where are you?

FIDELIA Here—Oh—Now I suppose we may begone.   295

MANLY I will, but not you. You must stay, and act the second part
of a lover: that is, talk kindness to her.

FIDELIA Not I, sir.

MANLY No disputing, sir; you must. 'Tis necessary to my design, of
coming again tomorrow night.   300

FIDELIA What, can you come again then hither?

MANLY Yes, and you must make the appointment, and an apology
for your leaving her so soon—for I have said not a word to her, but
have kept your counsel, as I expect you should do mine. Do this
faithfully, and I promise you here, you shall run my fortune° still,   305
and we will never part as long as we live. But, if you do not do it,
expect not to live.

FIDELIA 'Tis hard, sir; but such a consideration will make it easier.
You won't forget your promise, sir?

MANLY No, by heavens. But I hear her coming.   310

    Exit Manly. Enter Olivia to Fidelia

OLIVIA Where is my life? Run from me already! You do not love me,
dearest; nay, you are angry with me, for you would not so much as
speak a kind word to me within. What was the reason?

FIDELIA I was transported too much.

OLIVIA That's kind. But come, my soul, what make you here? Let   315
us go in again; we may be surprised in this room, 'tis so near the
stairs.

FIDELIA No, we shall hear the better here, if anybody should come
up.

OLIVIA Nay, I assure you, we shall be secure enough within. Come,   320
come—

FIDELIA I am sick, and troubled with a sudden dizziness; cannot stir
yet.

OLIVIA Come, I have spirits° within.

FIDELIA Oh!—Don't you hear a noise, madam?   325

OLIVIA No, no, there is none. Come, come.

    Pulls her

FIDELIA Indeed there is; and I love you so much, I must have a care
of your honour, if you won't—and go, but to come to you
tomorrow night, if you please.

OLIVIA With all my soul—but you must not go yet. Come, prithee.   330

FIDELIA Oh!—I am now sicker, and am afraid of one of my fits.

OLIVIA What fits?

FIDELIA Of the falling-sickness; and I lie generally an hour in a
trance. Therefore pray consider your honour, for the sake of my
love, and let me go, that I may return to you often.   335

OLIVIA But will you be sure then to come tomorrow night?

FIDELIA Yes.

OLIVIA Swear.

FIDELIA By our past kindness.

OLIVIA Well, go your ways then, if you will, you naughty creature you.   340
  Exit Fidelia
  These young lovers, with their fears and modesty, make themselves
  as bad as old ones to us; and I apprehend their bashfulness, more
  than their tattling.°
  Fidelia returns

FIDELIA Oh, madam, we're undone! There was a gentleman upon the
  stairs, coming up, with a candle—which made me retire. Look you,   345
  here he comes!
  Enter Varnish, and his man with a light

OLIVIA How! My husband! Oh, undone indeed! This way.
  Exit Olivia

VARNISH Ha! You shall not 'scape me so, sir.
  Stops Fidelia

FIDELIA (*aside*) Oh heavens! More fears, plagues, and torments yet
  in store!   350

VARNISH Come, sir, I guess what your business was here—but this
  must be your business now. (*Draws*) Draw!

FIDELIA Sir—

VARNISH No expostulations; I shall not care to hear of 't. Draw.

FIDELIA Good sir—   355

VARNISH How, you rascal! Not courage to draw, yet durst do me
  the greatest injury in the world? Thy cowardice shall not save thy
  life.
  Offers to run at Fidelia

FIDELIA Oh hold, sir, and send but your servant down, and I'll
  satisfy you, sir, I could not injure you, as you imagine.   360

VARNISH [*to Servant*] Leave the light, and begone.
  Exit Servant
  Now quickly, sir, what you've to say, or—

FIDELIA I am a woman, sir, a very unfortunate woman.

VARNISH How! A very handsome woman, I'm sure, then.
  Pulls off her peruke, and feels her breasts
  Here are witnesses of 't too, I confess. (*Aside*) Well, I'm glad to find   365
  the tables turned,° my wife in more danger of cuckolding than I
  was.

FIDELIA Now, sir, I hope you are so much a man of honour, as to
  let me go, now I have satisfied you, sir.

VARNISH When you have satisfied me, madam, I will.   370

FIDELIA I hope, sir, you are too much a gentleman to urge those
  secrets from a woman which concern her honour. You may guess

my misfortune to be love, by my disguise; but a pair of breeches
could not wrong you, sir.

VARNISH I may believe love has changed your outside, which could   375
not wrong me—but why did my wife run away?

FIDELIA I know not, sir; perhaps because she would not be forced to
discover me to you—or to guide me from your suspicions,° that
you might not discover me yourself; which ungentlemanlike curiosity I hope you will cease to have, and let me go.   380

VARNISH Well, madam, if I must not know who you are, 'twill suffice
for me only to know certainly what you are—which you must not
deny me. Come, there is a bed within, the proper rack for lovers;
and if you are a woman, there you can keep no secrets, you'll tell
me there all, unasked. Come.   385

   Pulls her

FIDELIA Oh! What d'ye mean? Help, oh—

VARNISH I'll show you; but 'tis in vain to cry out: no-one dares help
you, for I am lord here.

FIDELIA Tyrant here. But if you are master of this house, which I
have taken for a sanctuary, do not violate it yourself.   390

VARNISH No, I'll preserve you here, and nothing shall hurt you, and
will be as true to you as your disguise; but you must trust me then.
Come, come.

FIDELIA Oh! Oh! Rather than you shall drag me to a death so horrid,
and so shameful, I'll die here a thousand deaths. But you do not   395
look like a ravisher, sir.

VARNISH Nor you like one would put me to't; but if you will—

FIDELIA Oh! Oh! Help, help—

   Enter Servant

VARNISH You saucy rascal, how durst you come in when you heard
a woman squeak? That should have been your cue to shut° the   400
door.

SERVANT I come, sir, to let you know, the alderman coming home
immediately after you were at his house, has sent his cashier with
the money, according to your note.

VARNISH Damn his money! Money never came to any, sure, un-   405
seasonably, till now. Bid him stay.

SERVANT He says, he cannot a moment.

VARNISH Receive it you, then.

SERVANT He says, he must have your receipt for it. He is in haste,
for I hear him coming up, sir.   410

VARNISH Damn him. Help me in here then with this dishonourer of
my family.

FIDELIA Oh, oh!

SERVANT You say she is a woman, sir.

VARNISH No matter, sir—must you prate?   415

FIDELIA Oh heavens! Is there—

They thrust her in, and lock the door

VARNISH Stay there, my prisoner; you have a short reprieve.
        I'll fetch the gold, and that she can't resist;
        For with a full hand 'tis we ravish best.

        Exeunt

5.1

Eliza's lodging

Enter Olivia and Eliza

OLIVIA Ah, cousin, nothing troubles me, but that I have given the malicious world its revenge, and reason now to talk as freely of me, as I used to do of it.

ELIZA Faith, then, let not that trouble you; for, to be plain, cousin, the world cannot talk worse of you than it did before. 5

OLIVIA How, cousin! I'd have you to know, before this *faux pas*, this trip of mine, the world could not talk of me.

ELIZA Only, that you mind other people's actions so much that you take no care of your own, but to hide 'em; that, like a thief, because you know yourself most guilty, you impeach your fellow criminals 10 first, to clear yourself.

OLIVIA Oh wicked world!

ELIZA That you pretend an aversion to all mankind, in public, only that their wives and mistresses may not be jealous, and hinder you of their conversation, in private. 15

OLIVIA Base world!

ELIZA That, abroad, you fasten quarrels upon innocent men, for talking of you, only to bring 'em to ask you pardon at home, and to become dear friends with 'em, who were hardly your acquaintance before. 20

OLIVIA Abominable world!

ELIZA That you condemn the obscenity of modern plays, only that you may not be censured for never missing the most obscene of the old ones.

OLIVIA Damned world! 25

ELIZA That you deface the nudities of pictures, and little statues, only because they are not real.°

OLIVIA Oh fie, fie, fie; hideous, hideous, cousin! The obscenity of their censures makes me blush.

ELIZA The truth of 'em, the naughty world would say now. 30

Enter Letice hastily

LETICE Oh madam, here is that gentleman coming up, who now you say is my master.

OLIVIA Oh! Cousin, whither shall I run? Protect me, or—

Enter Varnish; Olivia runs away, and stands at a distance

376

VARNISH Nay, nay, come—

OLIVIA Oh, sir, forgive me.   35

VARNISH Yes, yes, I can forgive you being alone in the dark with a
woman in man's clothes, but have a care of a man in woman's
clothes.

OLIVIA (*aside*) What does he mean? He dissembles, only to get me
into his power—or has my dear friend made him believe he was a   40
woman? My husband may be deceived by him, but I'm sure I was
not.

VARNISH Come, come, you need not have lain out of your house for
this. But perhaps you were afraid, when I was warm with suspicions, you must have discovered who she was; and prithee, may I   45
not know it?

OLIVIA She was—(*Aside*) I hope he has been deceived; and since my
lover has played the card, I must not renounce.

VARNISH Come, what's the matter with thee? If I must not know
who she is, I'm satisfied without. Come hither.   50

OLIVIA Sure you do know her—she has told you herself, I suppose.

VARNISH No; I might have known her better, but that I was
interrupted, by the goldsmith, you know, and was forced to lock
her into your chamber—to keep her from his sight; but when I
returned, I found she was got away, by tying the window curtains   55
to the balcony, by which she slid down into the street. For you
must know, I jested with her, and made her believe I'd ravish her;
which she apprehended, it seems, in earnest.

OLIVIA Then she got from you?

VARNISH Yes.   60

OLIVIA And is quite gone?

VARNISH Yes.

OLIVIA I'm glad on't—otherwise you had ravished her, sir? But how
durst you go so far, as to make her believe you would ravish her?
Let me understand that, sir. What! There's guilt in your face, you   65
blush too. Nay, then you did ravish her, you did, you base fellow.
What, ravish a woman in the first month of our marriage! 'Tis a
double injury to me, thou base ungrateful man; wrong my bed
already, villain! I could tear out those false eyes, barbarous,
unworthy wretch.   70

ELIZA So, so!

VARNISH Prithee hear, my dear.

OLIVIA I will never hear you, my plague, my torment.

VARNISH I swear—prithee hear me.

OLIVIA I have heard already too many of your false oaths and vows,   75
especially your last in the church. Oh wicked man! And wretched
woman that I was! I wish I had then sunk down into a grave, rather
than to have given you my hand, to be led to your loathsome bed.
Oh—Oh—
Seems to weep

VARNISH So, very fine! Just a marriage quarrel! Which, though it   80
generally begins by the wife's fault, yet, in the conclusion, it
becomes the husband's; and whosoever offends at first, he only is
sure to ask pardon at last. My dear—

OLIVIA My devil—

VARNISH Come, prithee be appeased, and go home; I have bespoken   85
our supper betimes;° for I could not eat, till I found you. Go, I'll
give you all kind of satisfactions—and one which uses to be a
reconciling one: two hundred of those guineas I received last night,
to do what you will with.

OLIVIA What, would you pay me for being your bawd?   90

VARNISH Nay, prithee no more. Go, and I'll thoroughly satisfy you
when I come home; and then, too, we will have a fit of laughter at
Manly, whom I am going to find at the Cock in Bow Street, where
(I hear) he dined. Go, dearest, go home.

ELIZA (*aside*) A very pretty turn, indeed, this!   95

VARNISH Now, cousin, since by my wife I have that honour, and
privilege of calling you so, I have something to beg of you too;
which is, not to take notice of our marriage to any whatever, yet
awhile, for some reasons very important to me; and next, that
you will do my wife the honour to go home with her, and me   100
the favour to use that power you have with her, in our reconcilement.

ELIZA That, I dare promise, sir, will be no hard matter.° Your
servant.
Exit Varnish
Well, cousin, this I confess was reasonable hypocrisy; you were the   105
better for't.

OLIVIA What hypocrisy?

ELIZA Why, this last deceit of your husband was lawful, since in your
own defence.

OLIVIA What deceit? I'd have you to know, I never deceived my   110
husband.

ELIZA You do not understand me, sure. I say this was an honest
come-off, and a good one. But 'twas a sign your gallant had had

enough of your conversation, since he could so dexterously cheat
your husband, in passing for a woman.   115

OLIVIA What d'ye mean, once more, with 'my gallant,' and 'passing
for a woman'?

ELIZA What do *you* mean? You see your husband took him for a
woman.

OLIVIA Whom?   120

ELIZA Hey-day! Why, the man he found you with, for whom last
night you were so much afraid, and who you told me—

OLIVIA Lord, you rave sure!

ELIZA Why, did not you tell me last night—

OLIVIA I know not what I might tell you last night, in a fright. 125

ELIZA Ay, what was that fright for? For a woman? Besides, were you
not afraid to see your husband just now? I warrant, only for having
been found with a woman! Nay, did you not just now, too, own
your false step, or trip, as you called it? Which was with a woman
too! Fie, this fooling is so insipid, 'tis offensive.   130

OLIVIA And fooling with my honour will be more offensive. Did you
not hear my husband say, he found me with a woman in man's
clothes? And d'ye think he does not know a man from a woman?

ELIZA Not so well, I'm sure, as you do. Therefore I'd rather take
your word.   135

OLIVIA What, you grow scurrilous, and are, I find, more censorious
than the world! I must have a care of you, I see.

ELIZA No, you need not fear yet; I'll keep your secret.

OLIVIA My secret! I'd have you to know, I have no need of
confidantes, though you value yourself upon being a good one.   140

ELIZA Oh admirable confidence! You show more in denying your
wickedness, than other people in glorying in't.

OLIVIA 'Confidence', to me! To me, such language! Nay, then I'll
never see your face again. (*Aside*) I'll quarrel with her, that people
may never believe I was in her power, but take for malice all the 145
truth she may speak against me.—Letice, where are you? Let us
begone from this censorious, ill woman.

ELIZA (*aside*) Nay, thou shalt stay a little, to damn thyself quite.—
One word first, pray madam. Can you swear that whom your
husband found you with—   150

OLIVIA Swear! Ay, that whosoever 'twas that stole up, unknown, into
my room, when 'twas dark, I know not whether man or woman, by
heavens, by all that's good—or, may I never more have joys here,
or in the other world; nay, may I eternally—

ELIZA Be damned. So, so, you are damned enough already, by your   155
oaths; and I enough confirmed. And now you may please to begone.
Yet take this advice with you, in this plain-dealing age, to leave off
forswearing yourself; for when people hardly think the better of a
woman for her real modesty, why should you put that great
constraint upon yourself to feign it?   160

OLIVIA Oh hideous, hideous advice! Let us go out of the hearing of
it. She will spoil us, Letice.

> *Exeunt Olivia and Letice at one door, Eliza at t'other*

5.2

> *The Cock in Bow Street. A table [with chairs,] bottles, [and glasses]*
>
> *Manly and Fidelia [seated at the table]*

MANLY How! Saved her honour by making her husband believe you
were a woman! 'Twas well, but hard enough to do, sure.

FIDELIA We were interrupted before he could contradict me.

MANLY But can't you tell me, d'ye say, what kind of man he
was?   5

FIDELIA I was so frightened, I confess, I can give no other account
of him but that he was pretty tall, round-faced, and one I'm sure
I ne'er had seen before.

MANLY But she, you say, made you swear to return tonight?

FIDELIA But I have since sworn never to go near her again; for the   10
husband would murder me, or worse, if he caught me again.

MANLY No, I'll go with you, and defend you tonight, and then I'll
swear too, never to go near her again.

FIDELIA Nay, indeed sir, I will not go, to be accessory to your death
too. Besides, what should you go again, sir, for?   15

MANLY No disputing, or advice, sir. You have reason to know I am
unalterable. Go therefore, presently, and write her a note to
enquire if her assignation with you holds; and if not to be at her
own house, where else? And be importunate to gain admittance to
her tonight. Let your messenger, ere he deliver your letter, enquire   20
first if her husband be gone out. Go, 'tis now almost six of the
clock; I expect you back here before seven, with leave to see her

then. Go, do this dexterously, and expect the performance of my last night's promise, never to part with you.

FIDELIA Ay, sir—but will you be sure to remember that?   25

MANLY Did I ever break my word? Go, no more replies, or doubts.
Exit Fidelia. Enter Freeman
Where hast thou been?

FREEMAN In the next room, with my Lord Plausible and Novel.

MANLY Ay, we came hither because 'twas a private house; but with thee indeed no house can be private, for thou hast that pretty   30 quality of the familiar fops of the town, who, in an eating-house, always keep company with all people in't, but those they came with.

FREEMAN I went into their room but to keep them, and my own fool the squire, out of your room; but you shall be peevish now, because   35 you have no money. But why the devil won't you write to those we were speaking of? Since your modesty, or your spirit, will not suffer you to speak to 'em, to lend you money, why won't you try 'em at last that way?

MANLY Because I know 'em already, and can bear want better than   40 denials—nay, than obligations.

FREEMAN Deny you! They cannot—all of 'em have been your intimate friends.

MANLY No, they have been people only I have obliged particularly.

FREEMAN Very well. Therefore you ought to go to 'em the rather,   45 sure.

MANLY No, no. Those you have obliged most, most certainly avoid you, when you can oblige 'em no longer; and they take your visits like so many duns. Friends, like mistresses, are avoided for obligations past.   50

FREEMAN Pshaw! But most of 'em are your relations, men of great fortune, and honour.

MANLY Yes; but relations have so much honour as to think poverty taints the blood, and disown their wanting kindred; believing, I suppose, that as riches at first makes a gentleman,° the want of 'em   55 degrades him. But, damn 'em, now I'm poor I'll anticipate their contempt, and disown them.

FREEMAN But you have many a female acquaintance whom you have been liberal to, who may have a heart to refund to you a little, if you would ask it: they are not all Olivias.   60

MANLY Damn thee! How couldst thou think of such a thing? I would as soon rob my footman of his wages. Besides, 'twere in vain too;

for a wench is like a box in an ordinary, receives all people's money easily; but there's no getting, nay shaking any out again; and he that fills it, is surest° never to keep the key.   65

FREEMAN Well, but noble captain, would you make me believe that you, who know half the town, have so many friends, and have obliged so many, can't borrow fifty or an hundred pound?

MANLY Why, noble lieutenant, you, who know all the town, and call all you know friends, methinks should not wonder at it, since you   70 find ingratitude too. For how many lords' families (though descended from blacksmiths, or tinkers) hast thou called great, and illustrious? How many ill tables called° good eating? How many noisy coxcombs, wits? How many pert, cocking° cowards, stout? How many tawdry, affected rogues, well-dressed? How many   75 perukes admired? And how many ill verses applauded? And yet canst not borrow a shilling. Dost thou expect I, who always spoke truth, should?

FREEMAN Nay, now you think you have paid me. But hark you, captain, I have heard of a thing called grinning honour,° but never   80 of starving honour.°

MANLY Well, but it has been the fate of some brave men. And if they won't give me a ship again, I can go starve anywhere, with a musket on my shoulder.

FREEMAN Give you a ship! Why, you will not solicit it?   85

MANLY If I have not solicited it by my services, I know no other way.

FREEMAN Your servant, sir. Nay then I'm satisfied;° I must solicit my widow the closer, and run the desperate fortune° of matrimony on shore.

    Exit Freeman. Enter to Manly, Varnish

MANLY How!   90

    Embraces Varnish

Nay, here is a friend indeed; and he that has him in his arms can know no wants.

VARNISH Dear sir! And he that is in your arms is secure from all fears whatever. Nay, our nation is secure by your defeat at sea, and the Dutch that fought against you have proved enemies to them-   95 selves only, in bringing you back to us.

MANLY Fie, fie—this from a friend? And yet from any other 'twere unsufferable. I thought I should never have taken anything ill from you.

VARNISH A friend's privilege is to speak his mind, though it be taken   100 ill.

MANLY But your tongue need not tell me you think too well of me; I have found it from your heart, which spoke in actions—your unalterable heart. But Olivia is false, my friend, which I suppose is no news to you.   105

VARNISH (*aside*) He's in the right on't.

MANLY But couldst thou not keep her true to me?

VARNISH Not for my heart, sir.

MANLY But could you not perceive it at all, before I went? Could she so deceive us both?   110

VARNISH I must confess, the first time I knew it, was three days after your departure, when she received the money you had left in Lombard Street in her name; and her tears did not hinder her, it seems, from counting that. You would trust her with all, like a true generous lover!   115

MANLY And she, like a mean, jilting—

VARNISH Traitorous—

MANLY Base—

VARNISH Damned—

MANLY Covetous—   120

VARNISH Mercenary whore—(*Aside*) I can hardly hold from laughing.

MANLY Ay, a mercenary whore indeed; for she made me pay her, before I lay with her.

VARNISH How!—Why, have you lain with her?   125

MANLY Ay, ay.

VARNISH Nay, she deserves you should report it at least, though you have not.

MANLY Report it! By heaven, 'tis true.

VARNISH How! Sure not.   130

MANLY I do not use to lie, nor you to doubt me.

VARNISH When?

MANLY Last night, about seven or eight of the clock.

VARNISH Ha! (*Aside*) Now I remember, I thought she spake as if she expected some other, rather than me. A confounded whore indeed!   135

MANLY But, what, thou wonder'st at it! Nay, you seem to be angry too.

VARNISH I cannot but be enraged against her, for her usage of you. Damned, infamous, common jade.

MANLY Nay, her cuckold, who first cuckolded me in my money,   140
shall not laugh all himself. We will do him reason, shan't we?

VARNISH Ay, ay.

MANLY But thou dost not, for so great a friend, take pleasure enough
in your friend's revenge, methinks.

VARNISH Yes, yes; I'm glad to know it, since you have lain with her.   145

MANLY Thou canst not tell me who that rascal, her cuckold, is?

VARNISH No.

MANLY She would keep it from you, I suppose.

VARNISH Yes, yes—

MANLY Thou wouldst laugh, if thou knew'st but all the circum-   150
stances of my having her. Come, I'll tell thee.

VARNISH Damn her; I care not to hear any more of her.

MANLY Faith, thou shalt. You must know—

> *Enter Freeman backwards, endeavouring to keep out Novel,*
> *Lord Plausible, Jerry, and Oldfox, who all press in upon him*

FREEMAN I tell you, he has a wench with him, and would be private.

MANLY Damn 'em! A man can't open a bottle, in these eating-   155
houses, but presently you have these impudent, intruding, buzzing
flies and insects in your glass. Well, I'll tell thee all anon. In the
mean time prithee go to her (but not from me°) and try if you can
get her to lend me but an hundred pound of my money, to supply
my present wants—for I suppose there is no recovering any of it   160
by law.

VARNISH Not any. Think not of it. Nor by this way neither.

MANLY Go; try, at least.

VARNISH I'll go; but I can satisy you beforehand, 'twill be to no
purpose. You'll no more find a refunding wench—   165

MANLY Than a refunding lawyer; indeed their fees alike scarce ever
return. However, try her, put it to her.

VARNISH Ay, ay, I'll try her, put it to her home, with a vengeance.

> *Exit Varnish. [Novel, Oldfox, and Lord Plausible advance*
> *towards Manly]*

NOVEL Nay, you shall be our judge, Manly. Come, major, I'll speak
it to your teeth.° If people provoke me to say bitter things to their   170
faces, they must take what follows; though, like my Lord Plausible,
I'd rather do't civilly behind their backs.

MANLY Nay, thou art a dangerous rogue, I've heard, behind a man's
back.

LORD PLAUSIBLE You wrong him sure, noble captain; he would do   175
a man no more harm behind his back, than to his face.

FREEMAN I am of my lord's mind.

MANLY Yes, a fool, like a coward, is the more to be feared behind
a man's back, more than a witty man: for as a coward is more

bloody than a brave man, a fool is more malicious than a man of   180
wit.

NOVEL A fool, tar—a fool! Nay, thou art a brave sea-judge of wit! A
fool! Prithee when did you ever find me want something to say, as
you do often?

MANLY Nay, I confess thou art always talking, roaring, or making a   185
noise; that I'll say for thee.

NOVEL Well, and is talking a sign of a fool?

MANLY Yes, always talking—especially too if it be loud and fast—is
the sign of a fool.

NOVEL Pshaw! Talking is like fencing, the quicker the better; run   190
'em down, run 'em down. No matter for parrying, push on still, sa,
sa, sa! No matter whether you argue in form, push in guard,° or
no.

MANLY Or hit, or no. I think thou always talk'st without thinking,
Novel.   195

NOVEL Ay, ay, studied play's the worse—to follow the allegory,° as
the old pedant says. [*Pointing derisively at Oldfox*]

OLDFOX A young fop!

MANLY I ever thought the man of most wit had been like him of
most money, who has no vanity in showing it everywhere, whilst   200
the beggarly pusher of his fortune has all he has about him still,
only to show.

NOVEL Well, sir, and makes a very pretty show in the world, let me
tell you—nay, a better than your close hunks.° A pox, give me
ready money in play; what care I for a man's reputation? What are   205
we the better for your substantial, thrifty curmudgeon in wit, sir?

OLDFOX Thou art a profuse young rogue indeed.

NOVEL So much for talking, which I think I have proved a mark of
wit; and so is railing, roaring, and making a noise: for railing is
satire, you know, and roaring and making a noise, humour.   210

Enter Fidelia, taking Manly aside, and showing him a paper

FIDELIA The hour is betwixt seven and eight exactly.° 'Tis now half
an hour after six.

MANLY Well, go then to the Piazza, and wait for me; as soon as it is
quite dark, I'll be with you. I must stay here yet awhile, for my friend.

Exit Fidelia

But is railing satire, Novel?   215

FREEMAN And roaring, and making a noise, humour?

NOVEL What, won't you confess there's humour in roaring, and
making a noise?

FREEMAN No.

NOVEL Nor in cutting napkins and hangings?°   220

MANLY No, sure.

NOVEL Dull fops!

OLDFOX Oh rogue, rogue, insipid rogue! Nay, gentlemen, allow him
those things for wit—for his parts lie only that way.

NOVEL Peace, old fool, I wonder not at thee. But that young fellows   225
should be so dull as to say there's no humour in making a noise,
and breaking windows!° I tell you, there's wit and humour too, in
both. And a wit is as well known by his frolic, as by his simile.

OLDFOX Pure rogue! There's your modern wit for you! Wit, and
humour, in breaking of windows! There's mischief, if you will, but   230
no wit, or humour.

NOVEL Prithee, prithee peace, old fool. I tell you, where there is
mischief, there's wit. Don't we esteem the monkey a wit amongst
beasts, only because he's mischievous? And let me tell you, as good
nature is a sign of a fool, being mischievous is a sign of wit.   235

OLDFOX Oh rogue, rogue! Pretend to be a wit, by doing mischief and
railing!

NOVEL Why, thou, old fool, hast no other pretence to the name of a
wit, but by railing at new plays.

OLDFOX Thou, by railing at that facetious, noble way of wit,   240
quibbling.°

NOVEL Thou call'st thy dulness, gravity, and thy dozing, thinking.

OLDFOX You, sir, your dulness, spleen; and you talk much, and say
nothing.

NOVEL Thou read'st much, and understand'st nothing, sir.   245

OLDFOX You laugh loud, and break no jest.

NOVEL You rail, and nobody hangs himself;° and thou hast nothing
of the satyr,° but in thy face.

OLDFOX And you have no jest but your face, sir.

NOVEL Thou art an illiterate pedant.   250

OLDFOX Thou art a fool, with a bad memory.°

MANLY Come, a pox on you both; you have done like wits now, for
you wits, when you quarrel, never give over till you prove one
another fools.

NOVEL And you fools have never any occasion of laughing at us wits,   255
but when we quarrel. Therefore, let us be friends, Oldfox.

MANLY They are such wits as thou art, who make the name of a wit
as scandalous as that of bully, and signify a loud-laughing, talking,
incorrigible coxcomb, as 'bully' a roaring, hardened coward.

FREEMAN And would have his noise and laughter pass for wit, as 260
t'other his huffing and blustering for courage.
Enter Varnish

MANLY Gentlemen, with your leave, here is one I would speak with,
and I have nothing to say to you.
*Puts Freeman, Novel, Lord Plausible, Oldfox, and Jerry out
of the room*

VARNISH I told you 'twas in vain to think of getting money out of
her. She says, if a shilling would do't, she would not save you from 265
starving, or hanging, or what you would think worse, begging or
flattering; and rails so at you, one would not think you had lain
with her—

MANLY Oh friend, never trust, for that matter, a woman's railing, for
she is no less a dissembler in her hatred than her love. And as her 270
fondness of her husband is a sign he's a cuckold, her railing at
another man is a sign she lies with him.

VARNISH (*aside*) He's in the right on't; I know not what to trust to.

MANLY But you did not take any notice of it to her, I hope?

VARNISH (*aside*) So! . . . Sure he is afraid I should have disproved 275
him, by an enquiry of her; all may be well yet.

MANLY What hast thou in thy head that makes thee seem so unquiet?

VARNISH Only this base, impudent woman's falseness; I cannot put
her out of my head.

MANLY Oh my dear friend, be not you too sensible of my wrongs, 280
for then I shall feel 'em too, with more pain, and think 'em
unsufferable. Damn her, her money, and that ill-natured whore too,
Fortune herself. But if thou wouldst ease a little my present
trouble, prithee go borrow me, somewhere else, some money; I can
trouble thee. 285

VARNISH You trouble me indeed, most sensibly, when you command
me anything I cannot do. I have lately lost a great deal of money
at play, more than I can yet pay, so that not only my money, but
my credit too is gone, and know not where to borrow—but could
rob a church for you. (*Aside*) Yet would rather end your wants by 290
cutting your throat.

MANLY Nay, then I doubly feel my poverty, since I'm incapable of
supplying thee.
Embraces Varnish

VARNISH But, methinks, she that granted you the last favour (as they
call it) should not deny you anything— 295
Novel looks in

NOVEL Hey, tarpaulin, have you done?
        And retires again
VARNISH I understand not that point of kindness, I confess.
MANLY No, thou dost not understand it, and I have not time to let
    you know all now, for these fools, you see, will interrupt us. But
    anon, at supper, we'll laugh at leisure together, at Olivia's cuckold,   300
    who took a young fellow, that goes between his wife and me, for a
    woman.
VARNISH Ha!
MANLY Senseless, easy rascal! 'Twas no wonder she chose him for a
    husband. But she thought him, I thank her, fitter than me for that   305
    blind, bearing office.°
VARNISH (*aside*) I could not be deceived in that long woman's hair
    tied up behind, nor those infallible proofs, her pouting, swelling
    breasts—I have handled too many, sure, not to know 'em.
MANLY What, you wonder the fellow could be such a blind coxcomb!   310
VARNISH Yes, yes!
        Novel looks in again
NOVEL Nay, prithee come to us, Manly. Gad, all the fine things one
    says in their company are lost, without thee.
MANLY Away, fop; I'm busy yet.
        Novel retires
    You see we cannot talk here at our ease. Besides, I must begone   315
    immediately, in order to meeting with Olivia again tonight.
VARNISH Tonight! It cannot be, sure—
MANLY I had an appointment just now from her.
VARNISH For what time?
MANLY At half an hour after seven precisely.   320
VARNISH Don't you apprehend the husband?
MANLY He! Snivelling gull! He a thing to be feared! A husband, the
    tamest of creatures!
VARNISH (*aside*) Very fine!
MANLY But, prithee, in the mean time, go try to get me some money.   325
    Though thou art too modest to borrow for thyself, thou canst do
    anything for me, I know. Go—for I must begone to Olivia. Go, and
    meet me here anon.—Freeman, where are you?
        Exit Manly
VARNISH Ay, I'll meet with you, I warrant—but it shall be at
    Olivia's. Sure it cannot be; she denies it so calmly, and with that   330
    honest, modest assurance—it can't be true . . . And he does not use
    to lie—but belying a woman, when she won't be kind, is the only

lie a brave man will least scruple. But then the woman in man's
clothes, whom he calls a man!—Well, but by her breasts I know
her to be a woman . . . But then, again, his appointment from her   335
to meet with him tonight! I am distracted more with doubt than
jealousy. Well, I have no way to disabuse or revenge myself, but
by going home immediately, putting on a riding suit, and pretending to my wife, the same business which carried me out of town
last, requires me again to go post to Oxford tonight. Then, if the   340
appointment he boasts of be true, it's sure to hold, and I shall have
an opportunity either of clearing her, or revenging myself on both.
Perhaps she is his wench, of an old date, and I am his cully, whilst
I think him mine; and he has seemed to make his wench rich only
that I might take her off of his hands. Or if he has but lately lain   345
with her, he must needs discover, by her, my treachery to him,
which I'm sure he will revenge with my death, and which I must
prevent with his, if it were only but for fear of his too just
reproaches; for, I must confess, I never had till now any excuse,
but that of interest, for doing ill to him.   350

> *Exit Varnish. Re-enter Manly and Freeman*

MANLY Come hither; only (I say) be sure you mistake not the time.
You know the house exactly where Olivia lodges: 'tis just hard by.
FREEMAN Yes, yes.
MANLY Well then, bring 'em all, I say, thither, and all you know that
may be then in the house;° for the more witnesses I have of her   355
infamy, the greater will be my revenge. And be sure you come
straight up to her chamber without more ado. Here, take the watch.
You see 'tis above a quarter past seven. Be there in half an hour
exactly.
FREEMAN You need not doubt my diligence, or dexterity. I am an   360
old scourer, and can naturally beat up a wench's quarters that won't
be civil. Shan't we break her windows too?
MANLY No, no. Be punctual only.

> *Exeunt Manly and Freeman. Enter Widow Blackacre, and*
> *two Knights of the Post;° a Waiter with wine*

WIDOW BLACKACRE [*to the Waiter*] Sweetheart, are you sure the
door was shut close, that none of those roisters saw us come in?   365
WAITER [*setting down the wine*] Yes, mistress; and you shall have a
privater room above, instantly.

> *Exit Waiter*

WIDOW BLACKACRE You are safe enough, gentlemen, for I have
been private in this house ere now, upon other occasions, when I

was something younger. Come, gentlemen; in short, I leave my   370
business to your care and fidelity. And so, here's to you.

FIRST KNIGHT We were ungrateful rogues, if we should not be
honest to you; for we have had a great deal of your money.

WIDOW BLACKACRE And you have done me many a good job for't.
And so, here's to you again.   375

SECOND KNIGHT Why, we have been perjured but six times for you.

FIRST KNIGHT Forged but four deeds, with your husband's last deed
of gift.

SECOND KNIGHT And but three wills.

FIRST KNIGHT And counterfeited hands and seals to some six   380
bonds—I think that's all, brother.

WIDOW BLACKACRE Ay, that's all, gentlemen. And so, here's to you
again.

SECOND KNIGHT Nay, 'twould do one's heart good to be forsworn
for you: you have a conscience in your ways, and pay us well.   385

FIRST KNIGHT You are in the right on't, brother. One would be
damned for her, with all one's heart.

SECOND KNIGHT But there are rogues, who make us forsworn for
'em, and when we come to be paid, they'll be forsworn too, and
not pay us our wages, which they promised with oaths sufficient.   390

FIRST KNIGHT Ay, a great lawyer (that shall be nameless) bilked me
too.

WIDOW BLACKACRE That was hard, methinks, that a lawyer should
use gentlemen witnesses no better.

SECOND KNIGHT A lawyer! D'ye wonder a lawyer should do't? I was   395
bilked by a reverend divine, that preaches twice on Sundays, and
prays half an hour still before dinner.

WIDOW BLACKACRE How! A conscientious divine, and not pay
people for damning themselves! Sure then, for all his talking, he
does not believe damnation. But come, to our business.   400

   Pulls out a deed or two

Pray be sure to imitate exactly the flourish at the end of this name.

FIRST KNIGHT Oh, he's the best in England at untangling a flourish,
madam.

WIDOW BLACKACRE And let not the seal be a jot bigger. Observe
well the dash too, at the end of this name.   405

SECOND KNIGHT I warrant you, madam.

WIDOW BLACKACRE Well, these, and many other shifts, poor widows are put to sometimes; for everybody would be riding a

widow,° as they say, and breaking into her jointure. They think
marrying a widow an easy business, like leaping the hedge where   410
another has gone over before;° a widow is a mere gap, a gap with
them.

> *Enter Oldfox, with two Waiters. The Knights of the Post*
> *huddle up the writings*

What, he here! Go then, go, my hearts; you have your instructions.

> *Exeunt Knights of the Post*

OLDFOX Come, madam, to be plain with you, I'll be fobbed off no
longer. (*Aside*) I'll bind her and gag her, but she shall hear me.   415
[*Apart to the Waiters*] Look you, friends, there's the money I
promised you; and now do you what you promised me. Here are
my garters, and here's a gag.—You shall be acquainted with my
parts, lady, you shall.

WIDOW BLACKACRE Acquainted with your parts! A rape, a rape—   420
What, will you ravish me?

> *The Waiters tie her to the chair and gag her, and exeunt*

OLDFOX Yes lady, I will ravish you; but it shall be through the ear,
lady, the ear only, with my well-penned acrostics.°

> *Enter to them Freeman, Jerry, three Bailiffs, a constable° and*
> *his assistants, with the two Knights of the Post [as their*
> *prisoners]*

What, shall I never read my things undisturbed again?

JERRY Oh Law! My mother bound hand and foot, and gaping as if   425
she rose before her time today!°

FREEMAN What means this, Oldfox? [*To Widow Blackacre*] But I'll
release you from him; you shall be no man's prisoner but mine.

> *Freeman unties her*

Bailiffs, execute your writ.

OLDFOX Nay, then I'll begone, for fear of being bail, and paying her   430
debts, without being her husband.

> *Exit Oldfox*

FIRST BAILIFF [*to Widow Blackacre*] We arrest you, in the king's
name, at the suit of Mr Freeman, guardian to Jeremiah Blackacre,
Esquire, in an action of ten thousand pounds.°

WIDOW BLACKACRE How! How! In a choke-bail action!° What, and   435
the pen-and-ink gentlemen taken too! Have you confessed, you
rogues?

FIRST KNIGHT We needed not to confess, for the bailiffs dogged us
hither to the very door, and overheard all that you and we said.

WIDOW BLACKACRE Undone, undone then! No man was ever too   440
hard for me, till now. Oh, Jerry, child, wilt thou vex again the
womb that bore thee?

JERRY Ay, for bearing me before wedlock, as you say. But I'll teach
you to call a Blackacre a bastard, though you were never so much
my mother.   445

WIDOW BLACKACRE (aside) Well, I'm undone. Not one trick left?
No law-meuse imaginable? [To Freeman] Cruel sir, a word with
you, I pray.

FREEMAN In vain, madam; for you have no other way to release
yourself, but by the bonds of matrimony.   450

WIDOW BLACKACRE How, sir, how! That were but to sue out an
habeas corpus, for a removal from one prison to another. Matrimony!

FREEMAN Well, bailiffs, away with her.

WIDOW BLACKACRE Oh stay, sir; can you be so cruel as to bring me   455
under covert-baron again?—and put it out of my power to sue in
my own name. Matrimony, to a woman, is° worse than excom-
munication, in depriving her of the benefit of the law; and I would
rather be deprived of life. But hark you, sir, I am contented you
should hold and enjoy my person by lease or patent, but not by the   460
spiritual patent called a license—that is, to have the privileges of a
husband without the dominion; that is, durante beneplacito.° In
consideration of which, I will, out of my jointure, secure you an
annuity of three hundred pounds a year, and pay your debts; and
that's all you younger brothers desire to marry a widow for, I'm   465
sure.

FREEMAN Well, widow, if—

JERRY What! I hope, bully guardian, you are not making agreements,
without me?

FREEMAN No, no.—First, widow, you must say no more that he is   470
the son of a whore; have a care of that. And then he must have a
settled exhibition° of forty pounds a year, and a nag of assizes,°
kept by you, but not upon the common;° and have free ingress,
egress, and regress° to and from your maids' garret.

WIDOW BLACKACRE Well, I can grant all that too.   475

JERRY Ay, ay, fair words butter no cabbage.° But, guardian, make
her sign, sign and seal—for otherwise, if you knew her as well as
I, you would not trust her word for a farthing.

FREEMAN I warrant thee, squire.—Well, widow, since thou art so
generous, I will be generous too; and if you'll secure me four   480

hundred pound a year, but during your life, and pay my debts—not above a thousand pound—I'll bate you your person, to dispose of as you please.

WIDOW BLACKACRE Have a care, sir, a settlement without a consideration is void in law. You must do something for't.   485

FREEMAN Prithee then let the settlement on me be called alimony, and the consideration our separation. Come, my lawyer, with writings ready drawn, is within, and in haste. Come.

WIDOW BLACKACRE But, what, no other kind of consideration, Mr Freeman? Well, a widow, I see, is a kind of a sinecure, by custom   490
of which the unconscionable incumbent enjoys the profits without any duty, but does that still elsewhere.

Exeunt

5.3

Olivia's lodging

Enter Olivia, with a candle in her hand

OLIVIA So, I am now prepared once more for my timorous young lover's reception. My husband is gone; and go thou out too, thou next interrupter of love.

Puts out the candle

Kind darkness, that frees us lovers from scandal and bashfulness, from the censure of our gallants and the world.   5

Enter Fidelia, followed softly by Manly

So, are you there? Come, my dear punctual lover, there is not such another in the world. Thou hast beauty and youth to please a wife; address and wit to amuse and fool a husband; nay, thou hast all things to be wished in a lover, but your fits°—I hope, my dear, you won't have one tonight; and that you may not, I'll lock the door,   10
though there be no need of it, but to lock out your fits; for my husband is just gone out of town again.

Goes to the door, and locks it

Come, where are you?

MANLY (*aside*) Well, thou hast impudence enough to give me fits too, and make revenge itself impotent, hinder me from making thee yet   15
more infamous, if it can be.

OLIVIA Come, come, my soul, come.

FIDELIA Presently, my dear; we have time enough, sure.

OLIVIA How! Time enough! True lovers can no more think they ever
have time enough, than love enough. You shall stay with me all   20
night—but that is but a lover's moment. Come.

FIDELIA But won't you let me give you and myself the satisfaction
of telling you how I abused your husband last night?

OLIVIA Not when you can give me, and yourself too, the satisfaction
of abusing him again, tonight. Come.   25

FIDELIA Let me but tell you how your husband—

OLIVIA Oh name not his, or Manly's more loathsome name, if you
love me. I forbid° 'em last night; and you know I mentioned my
husband but once, and he came.° No talking, pray; 'twas ominous
to us.   30

A noise at the door

You make me fancy a noise at the door already, but I'm resolved
not to be interrupted. Where are you? Come—for rather than lose
my dear expectation now, though my husband were at the door,
and the bloody ruffian Manly here in the room, with all his awful
insolence, I would give myself to this dear hand, to be led away to   35
heavens of joys, which none but thou canst give.

The noise at the door increases

But what's this noise at the door? So, I told you what talking would
come to.

Olivia listens at the door

Ha!—Oh heavens, my husband's voice!

MANLY (*aside*) Freeman is come too soon.   40

OLIVIA Oh 'tis he!—Then here is the happiest minute° lost, that ever
bashful boy, or trifling woman fooled away! I'm undone! My
husband's reconcilement too was false as my joy—all delusion. But
come this way, here's a back-door.

Exit Olivia, and returns

The officious jade has locked us in, instead of locking others out.   45
But let us then escape your way, by the balcony, and whilst you
pull down the curtains, I'll fetch from my closet what next will best
secure our escape. I have left my key in the door, and 'twill not
suddenly be broke open.

Exit Olivia. A noise, as it were people forcing the door

MANLY Stir not, yet fear nothing.   50

FIDELIA Nothing, but your life, sir.

MANLY We shall now know this happy man she calls husband.

Olivia re-enters [carrying a cabinet and purse]

OLIVIA Oh, where are you? What, idle with fear? Come, I'll tie the curtains, if you will hold. Here, take this cabinet and purse, for it is thine if we escape.   55

> *Manly takes from her the cabinet and purse*

Therefore let us make haste.

> *Exit Olivia*

MANLY 'Tis mine indeed now again, and it shall never escape more from me—to you at least.

> *The door broken open, enter Varnish alone, with a dark lantern and a sword, running at Manly*

VARNISH (*with a low voice*) So, there I'm right,° sure—

MANLY (*softly*) Sword and dark lantern, villain, are some odds, but—   60

> *Manly draws, puts by the thrust, and defends himself, whilst Fidelia runs at Varnish behind°*

VARNISH (*with a low voice*) Odds! I'm sure I find more odds than I expected. What, has my insatiable two seconds at once? But—

> *Whilst they fight, Olivia re-enters, tying two curtains together*

OLIVIA Where are you now?—What, is he entered then, and are they fighting? Oh, do not kill one that can make no defence.

> *Manly throws Varnish down, and disarms him*

How! But I think he has the better on't: here's his scarf; 'tis he.°   65
So, keep him down still; I hope thou hast no hurt, my dearest?

> *Embracing Manly. Enter to them Freeman, Lord Plausible, Novel, Jerry, and the Widow Blackacre, lighted in by the two Sailors with torches*

Ha! What?—Manly! [*Aside*] And have I been thus concerned for *him*—embracing *him*? And has he his jewels again too? What means this? Oh 'tis too sure, as well as my shame!—which I'll go hide for ever.   70

> *Offers to go out; Manly stops her*

MANLY No, my dearest, after so much kindness as has passed between us, I cannot part with you yet.—Freeman, let nobody stir out of the room; for notwithstanding your lights, we are yet in the dark, till this gentleman please to turn his face.

> *Pulls Varnish by the sleeve*

How! Varnish! Art thou the happy man then? Thou! Thou! Speak,   75
I say—but thy guilty silence tells me all. Well, I shall not upbraid thee; for my wonder is striking me as dumb as thy shame has made thee.—But what! My little volunteer hurt, and fainting!

FIDELIA My wound, sir, is but a slight one, in my arm; 'tis only my   80
fear of your danger, sir, not yet well over.

MANLY But what's here? More strange things!
Observing Fidelia's hair untied behind, and without a peruke,
which she lost in the scuffle

What means this long woman's hair?—and face, now all of it
appears, too beautiful for a man; which I still thought woman-
ish indeed! What, you have not deceived me too, my little volunteer?   85

OLIVIA (*aside*) Me she has, I'm sure.

MANLY Speak.
Enter Eliza and Letice

ELIZA What, cousin, I am brought hither by your woman, I suppose,
to be a witness of the second vindication of your honour?

OLIVIA Insulting is not generous. You might spare me—I have you.   90

ELIZA Have a care, cousin, you'll confess anon too much; and I
would not have your secrets.

MANLY (*to Fidelia*) Come, your blushes answer me sufficiently, and
you have been my volunteer in love.

FIDELIA I must confess I needed no compulsion to follow you all   95
the world over; which I attempted in this habit, partly out of
shame to own my love to you, and fear of a greater shame, your
refusal of it; for I knew of your engagement to this lady, and the
constancy of your nature, which nothing could have altered, but
herself.   100

MANLY Dear madam, I desired you to bring me out of confusion,
and you have given me more. I know not what to speak to you, or
how to look upon you. The sense of my rough, hard, and ill usage
of you (though chiefly your own fault) gives me more pain now 'tis
over, than you had when you suffered it. And if my heart, the   105
refusal° of such a woman, (*pointing to Olivia*) were not a sacrifice
to profane your love,° and a greater wrong to you than ever yet I
did you, I would beg of you to receive it, though you used it as she
had done; for though it deserved not from her the treatment she
gave it, it does from you.   110

FIDELIA Then it has had punishment sufficient from her already, and
needs no more from me; and, I must confess, I would not be the
only cause of making you break your last night's oath to me, of
never parting with me—if you do not forget, or repent it.

MANLY Then take for ever my heart, and this with it,   115
Gives her the cabinet

for 'twas given to you before, and my heart was, before, your due. I only beg leave to dispose of these few. [*To Olivia*] Here, madam, I never yet left my wench unpaid.

> *Takes some of the jewels, and offers 'em to Olivia; she strikes*
> *'em down. Lord Plausible and Novel take 'em up*

OLIVIA So it seems, by giving her the cabinet.

LORD PLAUSIBLE These pendants appertain to your most faithful   120
humble servant.

NOVEL And this locket is mine—my earnest for love, which she never paid; therefore my own again—

WIDOW BLACKACRE By what law, sir, pray?—Cousin Olivia, a word. What, do they make a seizure on your goods and chattels, *vi et*   125
armis?° Make your demand, I say, and bring your trover,° bring your trover. I'll follow the law for you.

OLIVIA And I my revenge.

> *Exit Olivia*

MANLY (*to Varnish*) But 'tis, my friend, in your consideration most, that I would have returned part of your wife's portion; for 'twere   130
hard to take all from thee, since thou hast paid so dear for't, in being such a rascal. Yet thy wife is a fortune without a portion; and thou art a man of that extraordinary merit in villainy, the world and Fortune can never desert thee, though I do; therefore be not melancholy. Fare you well, sir.   135

> *Exit Varnish, doggedly*

Now, madam, (*turning to Fidelia*) I beg your pardon for lessening the present I made you; but my heart can never be lessened. This, I confess, [*indicating the cabinet*] was too small for you before, for you deserve the Indian world; and I would now go thither, out of covetousness, for your sake only.   140

FIDELIA Your heart, sir, is a present of that value, I can never make any return to't.

> *Pulling Manly from the company*

But I can give you back such a present as this, which I got by the loss of my father, a gentleman of the north, of no mean extraction, whose only child I was—therefore left me in the present possession   145
of two thousand pounds a year; which I left, with multitudes of pretenders, to follow you, sir, having in several public places seen you, and observed your actions throughly, with admiration, when you were too much in love to take notice of mine, which yet was but too visible. The name of my family is Grey; my other, Fidelia.   150
The rest of my story you shall know, when I have fewer auditors.

MANLY Nay, now, madam, you have taken from me all power of
making you any compliment on my part; for I was going to tell you,
that for your sake only I would quit the unknown pleasure of a
retirement, and rather stay in this ill world of ours still, though   155
odious to me, than give you more frights again at sea, and make
again too great a venture there, in you alone. But if I should tell
you now all this, and that your virtue (since greater than I thought
any was in the world) had now reconciled me to't, my friend here
would say 'tis your estate that has made me friends with the world.   160

FREEMAN I must confess I should; for I think most of our quarrels
to the world are just such as we have to a handsome woman—only
because we cannot enjoy her as we would do.

MANLY Nay, if thou art a plain dealer too, give me thy hand; for now
I'll say I am thy friend indeed. And for your two sakes, though I   165
have been so lately deceived in friends of both sexes,

> I will believe there are now in the world
> Good-natured friends, who are not prostitutes,
> And handsome women worthy to be friends;
> Yet, for my sake, let no-one e'er confide   170
> In tears or oaths, in love or friend, untried.

Exeunt

Epilogue

Spoken by the Widow Blackacre

To you, the judges learned in stage laws,
Our poet now, by me, submits his cause;
For with young judges, such as most of you,
The men by women best their business do.
And truth on't is, if you did not sit here,° 5
To keep for us a term throughout the year,°
We could not live by'r tongues—nay, but for you
Our chamber-practice would be little too.
And 'tis not only the stage practiser
Who, by your meeting, gets her living here; 10
For, as in Hall of Westminster
Sleek seamstress vents, amidst the courts, her ware,°
So, while we bawl, and you in judgement sit,
The vizard-mask sells linen too i'th'pit.°
Oh many of your friends, besides us here, 15
Do live by putting off their several ware.°
Here's daily done the great affair o'th'nation;
Let love, and us, then, ne'er have long vacation.°
But hold! Like other pleaders, I have done
Not my poor client's business, but my own. 20
Spare me a word then, now, for him. First know,
Squires of the long robe, he does humbly show°
He has a just right in abusing you,
Because he is a brother templar too;°
For, at the bar, you rally one another, 25
Nay, 'fool' and 'knave' is swallowed from a brother.°
If not the poet here, the templar spare,
And maul him—when you catch him at the bar.
From you, our common modish censurers,
Your favour, not your judgement, 'tis he fears; 30
Of all loves begs you then to rail, find fault,°
For plays, like women, by the world are thought
(When you speak kindly of 'em) very naught.

EXPLANATORY NOTES

Friedman	*The Plays of William Wycherley*, ed. Arthur Friedman (Oxford English Texts; Oxford, 1979).
Holland	*The Plays of William Wycherley*, ed. Peter Holland (Plays by Renaissance and Restoration Dramatists; Cambridge, 1981).
Hunt	*The Country Wife*, ed. John Dixon Hunt (The New Mermaids; London, 1973).
Ogden	*The Country Wife*, ed. James Ogden (The New Mermaids; London, 1991).
Revels	*The Country Wife*, ed. David Cook and John Swannell (The Revels Plays; London, 1975).
Simpson	Claude M. Simpson, *The British Broadside Ballad and its Music* (New Brunswick, NJ, 1966).
S.D.	Stage direction.
Smith	*The Plain Dealer*, ed. James L. Smith (The New Mermaids; London, 1979).
Weales	*The Complete Plays of William Wycherley*, ed. Gerald Weales (Stuart Editions; New York, 1966).

Unless otherwise stated, dates given for seventeenth-century plays are those of publication, not first performance. Shakespeare is quoted from *William Shakespeare: The Complete Works*, ed. Stanley Wells and Gary Taylor, with John Jowettt and William Montgomery (Oxford, 1986).

Love in a Wood

Title-page

    in a wood: bewildered, in difficulties (a proverbial phrase).

    Excludit . . . Democritus: 'Democritus [the philosopher] bars sane poets from Helicon [the mountain sacred to the Muses]': Horace, *Ars Poetica*, 296–7. The relevance of the epigraph is obscure. Either 'You may find some wildness and extravagance in this play; if so, it suggests that I am a true writer.' Or, alluding to the end of the Prologue, 'Poets must be mad, because they press on, with irrational optimism, despite ill-success and opprobrium.'

[Dedicatory Epistle]

    Duchess of Cleveland: Barbara Palmer, *née* Villiers (1641–1709), recently created Duchess of Cleveland; celebrated beauty, and one of Charles II's mistresses. Her affair with Wycherley began soon after the play's first performance (early spring, 1671), when she addressed him as 'a son of a whore' (wittily alluding to 1.2.326–7). While the ambiguous language of the Dedication (particularly 'favours' and 'service') suggests the intimate relationship between author and dedicatee, the references to her being excessively 'obliging' (l. 27) and the equivocal 'had enough of the play' (ll. 40–1) imply that the promiscuous duchess was tiring of Wycherley by the time the play was published (late 1671 or early 1672).

10–11 *but begin . . . themselves*: the praise which begins as praise for others always comes round to self-flattery in the end.

20 *twice together*: at two consecutive performances.

21 *Lent*: the joke implies that early performances of the play took place in March 1671.

34 *petitions*: from those who wish her to use her influence with the king and court.

43 *possible*: an acceptable alternative to 'possibly' in constructions with 'can' or 'could'.

48 *promises*: the unkept promises of courtiers and 'great' persons were a standing joke.

The Persons

13 *in distress for*: desperately anxious to secure; widows were conventionally portrayed as lustful.

22 *Prentice*: 'prentices' (Q1), but only one is required.

Prologue

Prologue: perhaps spoken by Charles Hart, playing Ranger; or, more appropriately, by John Lacy, playing Gripe: see note to ll. 24–5.

1 *cart*: the condemned criminal delivered his last speech from the cart which brought him from prison to the gallows.

3 *the damned poet . . . gone*: the playwright knows already that he's as good as dead—condemned ('damned') by the critics.

5 *fear of critic*: adapting the formula used in criminal indictments: 'not having the Fear of God before his Eyes'.

8 *counterfeiting*: an offence punishable by death, because judged to be treason against the monarch.

11–18 *You he does mean . . . than Turk would do*: the speaker indicates the self-appointed critics in the audience, customarily seated on the front benches in the pit. These hostile critics have themselves 'counterfeited' plays, trying to pass off their shoddy stuff as valuable work; they now therefore claim the authority to sit in judgement, accusing other playwrights of the very faults they committed themselves. Similarly, large-scale financiers, when faced with bankruptcy, contrive to shift their debts and obligations onto the shoulders of the smaller money-men, who end up in jail. The big men, by declaring themselves bankrupt ('breaking'), cleverly salvage enough to allow them to leave their counting-houses and adopt the life-style and status of 'gentlemen'. (Cf. Samuel Butler, *Hudibras*, 3.3.248: 'As Citizens, by breaking, thrive'.) No longer mere 'bankers', they take the lead in sneering at their former brethren, now impoverished. So the failed dramatists-turned-critics ('renegado poets') are the first to deride the struggling playwright, treating him worse than would Turkish Sultans, who secured their thrones by killing their own brothers. (Q1's punctuation of ll. 15–16—'by breaking gentlemen, are made, | Then more than any scorn,'—does not yield any very satisfactory sense.)

19 *But vent*: merely, i.e. futilely, vent.

20 *fleering*: laughing mockingly at both the executioner-critics and the subjects of the play's satire.

24–5 *And strict . . . pillory*: 'And there are single-minded practitioners of scoffing and banter who are yet alive, defying prison and pillory.' 'Strict professors' (people who unswervingly profess their faith) continues the religious imagery. The porter's lodge in the gatehouse of Whitehall Palace was used as a prison, specifically for servants of the crown, including actor-members of the King's and Duke's Companies. The actor John Lacy was sent there in April 1667, having offended the king by improvising satirical jests in an already politically dangerous play. As Weales suggests, Wycherley's allusion would be most telling if Lacy himself were speaking the Prologue.

30 *gasping credit*: their reputations, financial and literary, are at their last gasp.

31–2 *And those . . . if such there are*: those who have never tried their hands at writing would be his harshest judges; but the world is so full of scribblers that there may be no-one in this category.

1.1 s.d. *Flippant*: foolishly and impertinently talkative.

7–8 *Do not . . . virtue*: proverbially, patience is a virtue.

8 *in truly*: Wycherley's modification of the Puritan asseveration 'by my truly', i.e. indeed, verily.

16–17 *Has not . . . fire*: her late husband's scutcheon (the shield bearing his coat-of-arms) would have been painted on the door-panels of their coach, and so has circulated ('walked') about town. After the Great Fire of London (1666) many City shopkeepers moved their premises, and therefore their shop signs, to fashionable locations in Westminster.

20–1 *Have I not . . . fortune?*: have I not, most reluctantly, admitted that I am the widow ('relict') of someone in the City, so that people will believe that I'm well-off?

23–4 *Covent Garden Church*: St Paul's, Covent Garden, on the west side of the square; a well-known rendezvous.

24 *St Martin's*: St Martin's-in-the-Fields, predecessor of the present church, in the fashionable part of town. There may be a covert allusion to the City parish of St Martin's-le-Grand, the centre for the manufacture and sale of imitation jewellery.

40–1 *wenches that eat oatmeal*: the anaemic condition known as 'green sickness', affecting adolescent girls, was thought to arise from a frustrated desire for sexual experience. Its symptoms included a yearning for a diet of oatmeal, chalk, lime, and coal.

49 *like bishoprics . . . no*: a cleric elected to a bishopric was expected to decline twice, with the formula '*Nolo episcopari*' (I do not wish to be made a bishop), before accepting.

58 *were sped*: Lady Flippant means 'had met with success, had fulfilled my wishes'. Mrs Joiner takes the word differently: 'extricated from my difficulty, made an honest woman of '.

63 *port*: (1) expensive style of life, and (2) weight or burden that one carries—maintaining the childbirth metaphor.

64 *must down*: must be given up.

76 S.D. *Gripe . . . a clerk*: Gripe is the nickname given to both misers and money-lenders. An 'addleplot' is a bungling schemer; Sir Simon's alias is the Greek form of Hebrew Jonah, its Biblical associations making it appropriate for a Puritan's clerk. His dress will be a plain dark (probably black) suit, a white shirt with broad collar, and a girdle at the waist; a broad-brimmed hat (no wig); and perhaps a quill pen or two stuck behind his ear.

77–8 *as they have been*: as they were formerly.

79 *hates a vest . . . surplice*: as a republican ('Commonwealth's man': l. 88) and a Puritan, Gripe detests both court fashions and the trappings of Anglican worship. The surplice, banned during the Commonwealth, was officially reinstated in 1660. The vest was a long, close-fitting, collarless garment with short, loose sleeves, worn under a coat. It became suddenly fashionable when the king introduced a modified, vaguely oriental-looking version at court in October 1666.

87 *prying*: (1) looking thoroughly into things, and (2) peering nosily. Realizing Gripe's presence, Mrs Joiner uses neatly equivocal language.

99 *Now they are in*: they've really got going.

104–5 *you cannot . . . take him*: three proverbs signifying ingratiating behaviour and flattery for personal ends.

108–9 *terrified . . . preferment*: legislation against Dissenters included the Conventicle Act (1664), under which those attending nonconformist services could be imprisoned. Formal allegiance to king and established

403

church was required for official posts, e.g. in local government. Mrs Joiner is insincere: Gripe is an alderman.

118 *saints*: some Puritan sects so referred to themselves, i.e. as God's elect, as true believers, and as suffering persecution.

119 *fructify and increase*: Gripe's version of 'Be fruitful and multiply', Genesis 1:22 (Friedman).

120 *hand-basket*: traditional receptacle for carrying away illegitimate and unwanted offspring; Gripe perhaps intends an allusion to the baby Moses in his ark of bulrushes, Exodus 2: 3.

126 *Blushes . . . imperfection*: as Friedman notes, Gripe inverts the proverbial wisdom that blushing is a sign of virtue and grace.

129 *muffler*: (1) scarf or kerchief worn by old-fashioned women over the mouth and chin, and (2) piece of cloth used to mask the face.

130 *headband*: headscarf, sometimes worn outdoors; so 'top or high point of justice'. Perhaps also the blindfold traditionally covering the eyes of justice; it symbolizes impartiality, but Gripe literally blindfolds justice.

150 *protections*: documents issued by the king, giving immunity from arrest to his servants or agents. Gripe hates them, both as an anti-royalist and as a money-broker, since they could be used by bankrupts to claim exemption from repayment of loans or debts (Friedman).

151 *forbid*: past tense.

155–6 *Yet I durst . . . midnight*: Martha, whose biblical namesake resented her domestic, housekeeping role (Luke 10: 38), is eager to get away from home.

164–5 *bishops and wits*: bishops as symbols of Anglican authority and power; wits as foes to men of the City, always mocking them and pursuing their wives.

181 *engineer*: (1) mastermind of the plot, and (2) military engineer responsible for conducting a siege, undermining the fortress walls, etc.

201 *there's something in't*: it's pretty remarkable, there must be a reason for it.

217 *seamstresses*: often mentioned as particular (and willing) targets of rakes' attentions; a dressmaker's establishment was sometimes a front for a brothel.

220–1 *tailors . . . houses*: all guilty of overcharging; vintners regularly tampered with poor wines to improve flavour and colour.

234 *'Tis good . . . bow*: proverb, usually applied to love-affairs.

238 *a vow made at sea*: proverbially, 'Vows made in storms are forgotten in calms'.

248 *like an ass*: because his ears, normally hidden under his wig, are clearly visible in his clerk's disguise.

251 *Pardon me*: a polite disclaimer ('I'm not going to reply to that'), which he can take as complimentary, though she means it otherwise.

1.2 S.D. *Ranger*: his name signifies rake, libertine, one who goes in pursuit of sexual adventure.

38 *les douces yeux*: in English texts the phrase is normally '*les* (or the) *doux yeux*' = an amorous, languishing look, with eyes half closed. In making the adjective feminine, Dapperwit displays the ignorance he proceeds to censure in others.

40 *the lie*: telling me I am a liar, charging me with falsehood.

49 *'Tis disobliging . . . face*: Dapperwit is a false friend; a true friend is willing to point out one's faults.

63 *courage*: 'a courage' (Q1).

68 *breaking of windows*: a common nocturnal sport of London rakes and drunkards. The windows were usually those of brothels and prostitutes' lodgings.

84 *appointed her*: got her to agree.

105 *younger brother*: the laws of inheritance, by which an estate was entailed to the eldest son, often left a younger brother impoverished, and in search of a financially attractive wife.

120 *'Tis a sign . . . indeed*: she really must be a close prisoner, to be made as desperate as that.

146 *Your . . . servant*: Q1 has long dashes after each 'servant', implying appropriate gestures as Sir Simon refuses to tell.

157 *find her talk*: hold up my end in conversation.

164 *You . . . everybody*: I can trust you (though not the others) with her company.

168 *our [two] bottles*: most editors emend Q1's 'bottles' to 'bottle', but Ranger's next speech suggests that the compositor omitted the word 'two'. A man was expected to be too far gone only after three bottles (see 2.1.3).

179 *reserved . . . ladies*: kept the wit (i.e. Dapperwit) too, as my lover, just as other clever women do.

191 *words in fashion*: the word is 'forced', which needs more elegant packaging than Sir Simon can manage; Mrs Joiner shows how it should be done.

197 *small cards*: the low-value cards were not used in certain card-games, e.g. piquet and loo.

202–3 *doctor and apothecary*: during the 1660s a heated paper war broke out; physicians sneered at apothecaries (dispensing chemists) as mountebanks who presumed to diagnose and treat patients without proper training, while apothecaries accused doctors of charging exorbitant fees.

216 *Whetstone's Park*: a narrow lane between Holborn and Lincoln's Inn Fields, notorious as a red-light area.

229–30 *love . . . sweet torment*: proverbially, 'Love is a sweet torment'.

232 *'Tis a sign so*: your behaviour bears clear witness to that.

235–6 *your coachman*: a lady's affair with her coachman was a stock joke; it reappears at 4.2.12.

236 *they have . . . resignation*: I cheerfully withdraw from the contest.

241 *pray?*: Q1 has a long dash after this word, suggesting stage-business: Lady Flippant leers at Ranger and Vincent, and, without waiting for Dapperwit to answer, turns to Mrs Joiner with the vital question.

281 *park-time*: the social hour for promenading in St James's Park—around midday in winter, from dusk to midnight in summer (see 2.2.2 ff.); to a wit, 'park-time' is the time when one sets off for adventures there.

293 *pretend*: Lady Flippant means 'profess', but Ranger responds with the other possible sense, 'feign, simulate'.

305 *Those aims . . . Simon*: all those flirtatious words and looks are really directed at Sir Simon—to make him jealous.

311 *a new song*: a setting by Pelham Humphrey—a jaunty tune in 3/4 time—was published in 1684. It is reproduced in modern notation in Weales, 29.

321 *act*: (1) the legal financial settlement drawn up when husband and wife agreed to separate (such a separation, without possibility of remarriage, was often loosely called a 'divorce'); or (2) the private Act of Parliament required for dissolution of a valid marriage, a rare and costly procedure.

337 *their room*: the room they have hired for the evening. Friedman notes the allusion to the proverb 'His room is better than his company', i.e. his absence is preferable to his presence.

2.1 S.D. *at night*: on the representation of night scenes in the Restoration playhouse see Note on Staging, pp. xxiii–xxiv.

9–10 *no man's . . . whitest*: all wigs look grey in the dark. White, powdered wigs were *à la mode*.

12 *dyed*: altered in colour, shaded (women used rouge on their lips). Being less visible, the lips are less obviously expressive of disdain and pride.

12–13 *sleepy and glimmering*: half-closed, amorously drooping, and glancing seductively.

15 *miss*: discover the absence of, perceive that it's not in its right place.

[*disordered*]: the large gap in Q1 between 'the' and 'cravat' (a space which would accommodate ten characters) suggests that the compositor found his copy illegible. 'Disordered' fits the space and the context (a cravat ought to hang neatly); it is used of a cravat in Etherege's *Man Of Mode* (1676), 4.1.

19 *Something 'twas*: it's easy to see why.

28 *waits of Westminster*: a wind-band, maintained at public expense, playing on ceremonial and festive occasions, often at night or early morning. Dapperwit selects the fashionable residential side of London, including the royal residences, rather than the City.

39 *playing at bo-peep*: alternately coming into view and disappearing, as in the children's game.

48 *spoke*: Q1 has 'speak', perhaps a misreading of the manuscript's 'spoak' or 'spake'. Friedman retains 'speak', interpreting it as a present subjunctive: 'though he does speak against drinking'.

54 *beer-glass*: holding rather more than a pint; used by serious wine-drinkers.

63 *least*: the smaller of the two.

69 *I['m] come*: this edn.; 'I come' (Q1).

85 *put you to 't*: challenge you to show your mettle in self-defence.

90 *stay the push*: continuing the duelling/sexual wordplay; ostensibly, 'I won't wait for the first thrust'; covertly, 'I won't prevent or defer the sexual assault'.

99–100 *Rhenish wine and sugar*: considered a ladies' drink: sweet, and not too potent.

103 *jostling*: aggressive, taking the sexual initiative, unlike the classical nymphs who fled from lecherous satyrs. The verb 'jostle' still preserved overtones of its original meaning (to joust), so Lady Flippant's 'stand' means 'stand his ground under attack', as well as having its usual bawdy sense.

106 *forsooth*: here probably = 'madam' (see Glossary) rather than 'indeed'. Taking Lady Flippant for a whore, Sir Simon uses a condescending, unfashionable form of address.

108 *Who . . . know me?*: since both speakers are masked, and prepared for flirtation, they naturally use the vocabulary of the masquerade, the fancy-dress entertainment in which the masked participants strolled about guessing identities, flirting, and joking. The set questions and responses—'Do you know me?', 'I don't know you'—were conventionally spoken in high, squeaky tones, which Lady Flippant and Sir Simon no doubt employ.

118 *what should one ask for*: why should one bother to ask.

127 *Joan's . . . dark*: an unflattering proverb, said of a plain or ugly woman.

129–30 *put . . . question*: interrogate with force, torture her.

135 S.D. *Enter torches . . . distance*: linkboys carrying torches, and a band of fiddlers; they enter from the wings furthest upstage.

145–6 *eat, drank, run*: acceptable alternatives at this time for 'eaten', 'drunk', and 'ran'.

153–4 *pulled . . . head*: a traditional way of murdering an invalid.

155–6 *betwixt . . . cheese*: since she uses both pomatum (scented white face cream) and Spanish red (orange-coloured rouge) her complexion is as yellow as Dutch cheese.

209 *But . . . justice*: Apollo was supposed to preside over the tribunals ('Sessions of the Poets') at which literary fame was apportioned, and laurels awarded.

211 *plea to the bay-tree*: claim to a laureate wreath in recognition of your wit.

222–3 *the obligation*: for the flattering (obliging) compliment you have paid me.

237 *true gentleman . . . knight*: knighthoods, properly given for personal merit and/or public service, were too often awarded for dubious political reasons, or purchased by unworthy persons like Sir Simon (see 5.1.204).

245 *poll-wit or politic-wit*: a wit who uses his head, or one cunning in public affairs.

254–5 *combing perukes*: fops combed their wigs in public, especially in the theatre, to draw attention to their grace and good looks.

255 *ribbons*: the shoulders of men's coats, and the waistbands and outside legs of their breeches, were lavishly decorated with bunches and loops of ribbons.

259 *sets . . . ears*: incites them to quarrel. Coffee-houses were numerous in London by this date, and the drinkers engaged in discussions (often heated) and political debates; news-sheets such as the *London Gazette* were available to customers.

261 *pirates of Algiers*: merchant ships in the Mediterranean were constantly under threat from North African corsairs. The depredations increased markedly during 1671 (making them newsworthy), when Algiers, whose economy depended on piracy, had new rulers.

261–2 *Grand Signior . . . Signior*: the Sultan of Turkey and Louis XIV of France, known as 'The Most Christian King'. The growing political power of both rulers was causing concern.

273 *cooks and tobacco-men*: the leaves of unsold books were used to line baking-tins and wrap up tobacco for sale.

281 *of his form*: (1) to be ranked with him, of the same species, and (2) a companion of his on the wit's bench in the theatre, towards whose occupants Lydia could gesture.

2.2.7 *tell the clock*: count the hours, spend the time idly and tediously.

8 *keep . . . misfortunes*: 'my accounting [book-keeping] is made up entirely of my misfortunes'—with a play on 'a count' in response to Isabel's 'tell'.

31 *Mr Valentine's . . . France*: Valentine has fled the country, having injured Lord Clerimont in a duel. Should Clerimont die of his wounds, Valentine could be tried for murder, and could expect no pardon, though duelling itself was not illegal.

45 *my old second*: Lady Flippant, Isabel's assistant (as in a duel) in chit-chat and gossip.

50 *faithful shepherdess*: John Fletcher's pastoral romance, *The Faithful Shepherdess* (written *c*.1610) was a popular item in the repertoire of the King's Company. Its heroine, Clorin, is a model of chaste fidelity to the memory of her dead lover; she clearly corresponds to Christina, who is wearing mourning, and whose phrase 'my only faithful heart' has just given Lady Flippant her entry cue. Lady Flippant herself strongly resembles Fletcher's nymphomaniac Cloe. Moreover, both plays present multiple confusions among trees at night, and oppose true love to base lust.

59 *deny . . . courageously*: tell him very firmly that I am not here.

92 *superstition*: Christina's over-scrupulous adherence to the resolution that she has taken.

93 S.D. *[and Lady Flippant]*: Christina, recapitulating this episode at 5.1.409 ff., assumes that Ranger saw neither Lydia nor Lady Flippant.

179–80 *[RANGER . . . honour]*: Q1 gives two consecutive speeches to Christina. Perhaps Wycherley removed an intervening speech, but forgot to indicate that Christina's speeches should be run together. Alternatively, the compositor's eye skipped over the intervening speech (presumably Ranger's) because of its verbal similarity to what preceded or followed. Friedman offers two plausible reconstructions of the missing speech: 'Rather than that should be, madam, I would stay till tomorrow noon'; or 'I would stay here till tomorrow noon to prevent any scandal to your honour'. I have suggested a third possibility.

2.3.9 *of a term's standing*: 'fairly recently arrived'; she has not been in residence much longer than a law term, of which there were four a year.

2.4.10–11 *he and . . . life*: by prosecuting Valentine for felonious assault, or simply by seeking revenge.

15 *cock*: to cock one's hat is to wear it with the wide brim turned up, usually at the back, and fastened with a loop and button; a mark of the fashionable and jauntily showy man.

16 *ask her blessing*: when meeting or leaving their parents, or on being reunited with them after an absence or quarrel, children formally knelt to ask a parental blessing. (Children living at home would do so each morning.)

48–9 *[VALENTINE] . . . with me*: Q1 gives both speeches to Vincent. It seems unnatural for him to answer his own question. Valentine, on the other hand, is understandably jumpy and suspicious.

71 *Does she*: Q1 has a long dash before these words, indicating Vincent's comic amazement and/or some stage business, as he tries to draw Ranger out of Valentine's hearing.

108 *nor will . . . assistance*: and I won't come to ask your assistance in the event of a duel with Valentine.

3.1 S.D. *Mrs Crossbite*: to crossbite is to deceive or outwit.

13 *Pepper Alley*: in Southwark, just south of the Thames; presumably a notorious haunt of bawds and prostitutes. The text suggests that Mrs Crossbite herself lives nearer the City, perhaps in Holborn or Whetstone's Park.

36 *vacation*: between law-terms, when legal and other business was slack.

37–8 *If he . . . want it*: whatever he had, he shared with us; we didn't go without.

40–1 *the dog . . . broken up*: the guard dog which is fed titbits to keep it quiet while the house is broken into and plundered.

43 *a bone . . . to pick*: a problem on your hands, something to be sorry for (proverbial).

49 *midnight magistracy*: constables and watchmen patrolling the streets at night.

62–3 *hard name*: an outlandish name, difficult to pronounce; those which occur most frequently in the love-poems of the period are Phyllis and Chloris.

66–7 *old . . . zealously . . . charity*: Q1's initial capital-letters for these words suggest hypocritical emphasis.

86–7 *brought . . . playhouse*: 'introduced me into a theatre company'. The recommendation of an influential patron was invaluable to an aspiring actress, and could lead to further lucrative liaisons.

3.2.10 *censure my honour*: by suggesting that he is acting as pimp to his own wench.

11–12 *For as one . . . draw out another*: proverbs commonly used to illustrate the saying that 'one love drives out another'.

18–19 *young parson . . . Rome*: because the Gunpowder Plot (1605) was held to be a Roman Catholic conspiracy.

29–30 *justest . . . assignation*: absolutely punctual in keeping a date, and absolutely faithful to her lover.

39 *by—*: Dapperwit is being mysterious; he won't name the party concerned. But the phrase is not in all copies of Q1. Its inadvertent omission could have been rectified during the printing process. Alternatively, it may have been excised from later copies, having been misapprehended as a profane oath.

44–5 *rarity . . . Cross*: 'rarity' can mean both 'rare delicacy' and 'freak'. Several coffee-houses at Charing Cross exhibited 'monsters' (e.g. midgets, hermaphrodites), and showmen's booths there may have held similar sights, advertised by flags and signs.

72–3 [*RANGER . . . admit us*]: Q1 has two consecutive speeches by Dapper-wit; another case of compositorial eye-skip, resulting in the omission of Ranger's facetious retort. I follow Friedman's reconstruction, with its play on 'stirring' as (1) being up and about, and (2) sexually aroused.

74 *next your stomach*: on an empty stomach.

77 *walk to Lamb's Conduit*: a promenade popular with 'citizens' (and therefore considered unfashionable) to the fields around Lamb's Conduit in Holborn.

96 *preferred*: (1) introduced to her, and (2) esteemed more than you.

103 *in the presence*: (1) in the royal presence, or (2) in the king's presence-chamber.

111 *my partner*: as my partner.

125–6 *bring . . . to the lure*: 'to bring a young wench to the lure' (i.e. to persuade her into bed) was a cliché. A 'lure' is a gadget containing food, used by a falconer to recall a hawk; so Dapperwit's orange is *à propos*.

131 *venture . . . well*: 'the pitcher goes so often to the well that it is broken at last': Mrs Crossbite gives the proverb a bawdy application.

138–9 *join in the security*: (1) be a party to the transaction, and (2) confirm ('secure') Lucy's virginity.

146 *say*: present subjunctive.

159 *in—*: again, Dapperwit pretends mystery, withholding the name of the tavern with its private room (perhaps with a knowing glance at the audience).

168 *pawn . . . rent*: literally, 'hire me out to your friend so that you can pay your rent'; figuratively, 'sneak off and leave me to face the conse-quences' (a variant of 'to pawn someone for the reckoning', as at 5.1.163–4).

175–6 *take . . . favour*: I accept the accusation against me as a kindness, because it allows me to prove my innocence.

189 *You have . . . hostess*: you have calculated the bill without consulting your landlady, i.e. you've unwisely left me out of account. Proverbially, 'He that reckons without his host must reckon again.'

196 *Long's powdering-tub*: an establishment (run by a Mr Long?) using sweating-tubs to treat venereal disease.

218 *slave . . . coffee*: a waiter at a coffee-house.

269 *Peace . . . walls*: Gripe's version of the biblical benediction 'Peace be within thy walls' (Psalm 122: 7).

272 *Moreclack hangings*: fine and costly tapestries made in Mortlake, Surrey.

273 *China embroidered beds*: bed-covers and bed-curtains of embroidered Chinese silk.

279–80 *the wicked . . . it*: they prefer society with all its pleasures; in solitude their consciences would torment them.

284 S.D. *Turns . . . family*: Gripe draws back a shabby hanging (no Mortlake tapestry) to reveal a larder or walk-in cupboard with almost bare shelves, probably painted on the back-scene.

301 *modes and forms*: religious rituals, prescribed forms of prayer, etc., which are anathema to the Puritan.

309 *to love and be wise*: a proverbial impossibility.

323 *wine has arsenic in't*: Gripe speaks both figuratively ('it's poisonous stuff') and literally: vintners occasionally added sulphide of arsenic to wine, perhaps to help clarify it, or to improve the colour of old or thin-bodied wine.

363 *Take . . . piece*: Gripe reluctantly doubles his offers: a crown was worth five shillings (25p), a gold angel ten shillings, and a gold piece, or guinea, twenty shillings.

380 *broad-seal ring*: a wide ring, embossed with the family coat-of-arms, and used to seal Gripe's documents and bonds.

392 *kit*: a dancing-master's pocket-size fiddle, and an obvious *double entendre*.

409 *By yea and by nay*: a form of declaration, almost a mild oath, of biblical origin ('let your communication be, Yea, yea; Nay, nay': Matthew 5: 37), and therefore favoured by Puritans.

414 *die*: rape was punishable by death.

419 *Thou young . . . serpent*: 'that old serpent' is the devil (Revelation 20: 2), whose 'seed' (Genesis 3: 15) was taken by Puritans to mean all evil men and women, particularly fornicators (like Gripe).

420 *as*: to the same extent that.

423 S.D. *Aside*: Q1 marks the whole speech 'aside'.

426 *none*: 'neither'; Mrs Crossbite addresses the landlord and his prentice. Since the latter is no doubt also a party to the conspiracy against Gripe, it would be appropriate for him to approach the door, as if about to summon the neighbours and constable, and then, in response to a covert signal from the landlord, to announce (falsely) that they are coming (ll. 438–9).

428 *twenty mark*: rather more than £13. A 'mark' was a sum of money, however made up, equivalent in value to eight ounces of silver, or 13s. 4d.

446 *The instruments are drawing*: 'legal agreements are being prepared'; the trap has evidently been laid well in advance. 'Instruments' are also 'mechanical appliances': the documents are truly 'engines' (l. 444) for Gripe's persecution.

3.3.20 *make an adventure of*: (1) take a risk with, hazard, and (2) barter, exchange in a commercial transaction.

24 [*fellow*]: not in Q1; Q2 remedies the omission with 'spark', but Lady Flippant normally uses 'fellow(s)'.

25 S.D. *Leonore*: Q1 has no entry for Leonore, though she must be on stage to hear Lydia's dialogue with Ranger. Other editors place her entry at the beginning of the scene.

67 *beat him . . . pit*: 'driven him from the cock-pit', the arena where cock-fighting took place.

78 *'Tis fit . . . love*: It's only right that other kinds of affairs should take second place to those of love.

90–1 *he offers . . . liberty*: he proposes to give up his bachelor's freedom as security for the money you will bring him when you marry.

92 *a pawn . . . money on*: a pledge or security against which to borrow money.

112 *Russian . . . beating*: Russian women were supposed to love most passionately the husbands who beat them most violently.

4.1 S.D. *blue gown*: informal indoor wear, the equivalent of a modern dressing-gown, probably belted, perhaps lined with velvet or fur; its colour reflects Gripe's disconsolate state ('to look blue'), his Puritanism (Scottish Presbyterians were nick-named 'True-blues'), and the financial cost of his misadventure with Lucy: 'to come off bluely' is to fare badly, and a blue coat was worn by paupers and charity children.

6–13 *Art thou not . . . disturbs us*: Gripe implies that an informer might accept a bribe to keep silent, at least for a time, but might be beaten up once her/his informing was known. In the period 1670–1, as the authorities clamped down on religious dissent, informing was particularly lucrative.

21 *Mr Doublecap*: Nonconformist ministers customarily wore two caps, or a high-crowned hat over a black cap; Mrs Joiner will report Gripe's slander against a fellow-congregationalist to the minister and elders.

29–30 *sweet . . . cane*: Gripe, feeling unwell, supports himself on a walking-stick with a perforated metal head containing medicinal herbs.

43 *have me in excuse*: 'forgive me'; perhaps a Puritan phrase, or coined by Wycherley to sound puritanical.

58 *saints*: see note, 1.1.118.

63 *give off, a loser?*: abandon the game when you have lost your money or been defeated.

4.2 S.D. [*Another . . . house*]: Q1 has '*Enter* Sir Simon' with no change of scene. But 'sitting at a desk' suggests that both characters are 'discovered' on stage as the back-shutter for the previous scene is slid open.

22 *coy*: 'playing hard to get'; Sir Simon's obtuseness is total.

23 *crevice*: gap or space. He stretches out his hand to indicate the line she must not cross.

34 *You'll*: 'You' (Q1).

39 *What ail you?*: in what way do you ail?

70–1 *the last . . . water*: the latest wash for the complexion, prepared from mercury; it would irritate the eyes.

82–4 *the playhouse . . . Fields then*: by 'playhouse' Lady Flippant means the Drury Lane theatre, where *LiW* is being performed. Her brother abominates and avoids playhouses; since he is ignorant of their locations, Lady Flippant can innocently substitute Lincoln's Inn Fields, a highly fashionable residential district, but also the site of the rival theatre occupied by the Duke's Company.

87–8 *look to my hits*: look after my own interests and fortunes.

104 *the . . . gentleman*: Sir Simon is lost for a superlative.

129–30 *your women . . . anything*: 'Fools with money are lured into marriage and ruined by prostitutes on the make; all the unmarried men about town are penniless'; once again Sir Simon has gone too far.

134 *modish distemper*: syphilis, known as the 'French disease'.

135 *French chirurgeon*: not necessarily French-born, simply a specialist in the 'French disease'.

136 *Has his . . . much?*: has he been so much his own worst enemy?

4.3.41 *as an old woman, that*: the start of an overarching but uncompleted simile into which Dapperwit ambitiously inserts the subsidiary similitudes of the gamester and the bully.

54–5 *egress, and regress*: legal right of leaving and re-entering a property.

63 *the door*: the one by which Ranger has just left the stage.

4.4.9 *so old . . . faculty*: so professionally experienced and expert a person.

28–9 *to love . . . jealous*: proverbially, 'Love is never without jealousy'.

32–3 *she'll not miss this*: she'll not fail to be there tonight too.

38 *between the scenes*: backstage, where gallants and fops hung around to chat up the actresses.

68 *campaign*: Turenne's rapid conquest of Flanders (1667), or Condé's even more rapid occupation of Franche Comté (1668).

obliging: the Frenchman, as *valet de chambre*, has gratified his English employer by his smooth servility; cf. *GDM* 1.2.71, where the French footman comes over to 'oblige' the English. In both cases there is probably a snigger at homosexuality.

86 *calls me a fool*: because, according to the proverbs, 'Fools only are fortunate', and 'Fortune favours fools'.

90–1 *I have none . . . dedicatory*: I don't receive any of those short notes, half of their space taken up by names and elaborate forms of address, like the dedications in Spanish books, that list in pompous detail all the titles of the dedicatee.

105 *parson*: Q1's 'person' is a spelling-variant of 'parson'.

107 *to be revenged . . . friends*: to disappoint her relatives of their financial expectations; they would prefer her to remain single.

134–5 *to keep . . . countenance?*: save me from embarrassment.

194 *the patience of an alderman?*: the long-suffering of a cuckolded City worthy (a common jibe); possibly also the patience to listen to endless talk: a meeting of the Court of Aldermen could be boringly tedious.

199 *The blessing's . . . quickly*: proverbial: 'He gives twice who gives quickly'.

5.1.58 *wight*: 'man'; an archaism, with overtones of jocular contempt.

72 *bishop . . . friars*: bishops (see 1.1.164) and Roman Catholics ('friars') are alike anathema to Gripe.

80 *due to*: your love was the tribute (the due) which my merit naturally deserved.

81 *Sir Simon's original*: the original of which Sir Simon is an inferior copy.

111 *this mode*: Gripe has changed his tune: cf. 3.2.301.

114 *as it were the dark*: perhaps a joke about night scenes, which have to be well enough lit for the audience to follow the action. Gripe could gesture wryly towards the lights in the auditorium or those over the stage.

125–6 *above six . . . hundred*: the maximum legal rate of interest was 6 per cent.

134 *as fine as fippence*: 'smartly dressed, showy'; a proverbial tag (fippence = fivepence).

139–40 *I have heard . . . maintenance*: the husbands complain that their wives, of independent means, won't grant them any separate maintenance allowance.

163–4 *pawned . . . reckoning*: left to foot the bill when his companions absconded.

172 *mongrel light*: half-light, neither light nor darkness.

176–7 *I can . . . find*: proverbially, 'He that gropes in the dark finds that he would not' (i.e. that which he would prefer not to find).

192 *That's . . . neighbours*: proverbially, 'He dwells far from neighbours that's fain [obliged] to praise himself.'

194 *see the knight; well, but*: so Q1, and cf. 'Well, but if I had thought' at 5.2.64. It is possible, as Friedman suggests, that the semi-colon should go after 'well'.

200 *else*: if you don't believe me.

204 *title . . . laundress*: the absence of regulations about registering titles with the College of Arms made it easier to assume a knighthood and bribe the relevant officials. Sir Simon's laundress must have acted as a go-between.

205–6 *clothes . . . paid for*: a stock joke; the upper classes never paid promptly (if at all) for their clothes.

207–8 *let the jest . . . earnest*: the jingling contrast of 'jest' and 'earnest' was a common formula.

210 *knight in earnest*: Sir Simon unwittingly puns on 'earnest' as 'money paid by way of deposit', i.e. his purchase of his knighthood.

255 *natural*: 'genuine', but also alluding to the phrase 'a natural fool' = a congenital idiot.

256 *ruined . . . Cavalier!*: the 'old Cavaliers' were Royalists who had fought for the king during the Civil War. Some of them subsequently organized ineffectual conspiracies to overthrow the Commonwealth—by assassinating Cromwell, seizing London, and so on. The plotters were usually arrested or forced into hiding.

257 *plot of prevention*: a plot to forestall and thwart their marriage plans.

432 *contract*: a formal and binding betrothal.

519 *drawn*: as in a lottery, or from a bran-tub.

531–2 *blot . . . game*: the game is backgammon, in which 'to make a blot' is to expose a piece to capture by one's opponent. Lydia has taken considerable risks in her attempts to test Ranger's affections.

5.2.11–12 *I and . . . estate*: he has spent all his inherited money (estate) in wife-hunting; his annuity is now likely to suffer the same fate.

35–6 *unbid . . . welcome*: trying to salvage the situation, Dapperwit contradicts proverbial wisdom: unbidden guests are most welcome when they have departed.

44 *(to Vincent)*: at the end of the preceding line in Q1. It is very unusual for one character to be directed to laugh 'to' another; I suspect that Wycherley meant the direction to apply to the first sentence of Dapperwit's speech—he desperately addresses his only possible ally. The printer, realizing that he had omitted the direction, inserted it as near to Dapperwit's words as he could manage, rather than re-set the whole speech.

Fools . . . things: 'unhappy' means nasty, mischief-making. The proverb which Dapperwit rephrases is ironically appropriate: 'A fool may sometimes speak to the purpose (or tell the truth).'

88–91 *Our ladies . . . sure of them*: Christina and Valentine are already contracted in marriage, so further promises are unnecessary; but Wycherley wants his gentlemen to have a politely elegant last word together.

99 *Fortune our foe*: the popularity of the Elizabethan lament 'Fortune my foe, why dost thou frown on me?' had given its opening phrase proverbial status. The melancholy tune (for which see Simpson, 227), was also used for a monitory poem beginning 'Aim not too high in things

above thy reach', and ballads about the unhappy ends of criminals. If Dapperwit half-sings his couplet it will gain in comic resonance.

114 *away with*: put up with, endure.

119 S.D. [*Exeunt*]: Q1's omission of a final *Exeunt omnes* is probably not significant—unlike the end of *CW* where there is real point in having the characters on stage during the Epilogue.

The Gentleman Dancing-Master

Title-page

non satis . . . virtus: 'It is not enough to make your audience's mouths open wide with laughter—though there is also a kind of merit in doing just that' (Horace, *Satires* I. x. 7–8); a modest claim for the comedy that follows, which had not been a success in the theatre.

The Persons

The Persons: Q1 provides no cast-list for the first performance, but the dialogue at 3.1.46 ff. indicates that Wycherley intended Monsieur de Paris and Don Diego for the two principal comic actors of the Duke's Company, James Nokes and Edward Angel—brilliant individually and as a comic duo. Thomas Betterton, the company's leading actor, may have created the role of Gerrard, so giving special point to the admission 'I could never dance' (2.2.372); according to Anthony Aston, Betterton 'was incapable of dancing, even in a Country-Dance' (*A Brief Supplement to Colley Cibber* [1747?], 4). Mary Betterton, excellent as both coquette and sweet young girl, could have played Hippolyta, with Henry Harris as Martin, and Elinor Leigh, famous in comic, elderly roles, as Mrs Caution.

8 *Spanish merchant*: engaged in the English/Spanish trade, from a base in Spain.

Prologue

Newly after . . . Court: the Duke's Company opened in their spacious and splendid new premises, the Dorset Garden Theatre, on 9 Nov. 1671; *GDM* was the third play of their first season. Salisbury Court is south of Fleet St., just inside the City of London boundary. Both Prologue and Epilogue exploit the contrast and antagonism between the mercantile City and the fashionable West End ('t' other end o'th'town'), between solid 'cits' and lively 'wits'.

2 *come to you*: to a new theatre (*LiW* had been produced by the King's Company at Drury Lane), and to a rather different audience and locale—a locale which (with the exception of 1.2) provides the play's setting: a merchant's house somewhere in the City.

4 *substantial*: (1) ample in size, and (2) full of people of substance.

21 *ticking gentry*: among other things, gentlemen could purchase theatre tickets on credit.

1.1 S.D. *Hippolyta*: the huntress queen of the Amazons.

3 *fourteen*: the age at which a woman could legally take control of her estate and fortune.

8 *Ponchinello*: ancestor of 'Mr Punch'. The most celebrated Italian puppet-show, based on *commedia dell'arte* figures, was at Charing Cross, but Prue may be thinking of similar shows in Moorfields, north of the City, and at Bartholomew Fair, Smithfield.

- *Paradise!*: a working model of the Garden of Eden, on show in a house in Hatton Garden.

9 *park*: probably St James's Park, more popular than Hyde Park for amatory adventures.

10 *Gar'n!*: intended as a slightly cockneyfied, or at least non-standard pronunciation. But Wycherley is more likely to have heard it in Hampshire, during his boyhood, than in London.

11 *Tatnam Court . . . Islington!*: rural villages (the former clustering round the manor of Tottenham or Totten Hall), within easy reach of the City, popular (but not fashionable) for walks and refreshments. Prue's pleasures are consistently below Hippolyta's on the social scale.

14–15 *Prince in the Sun!*: probably one of the several Sun Taverns in the City (or perhaps the one further east, in Shadwell), its sign a golden face surrounded by rays.

17 *organs and tongs*: unsophisticated (or burlesque) music played on pipes or recorders ('organs') and firetongs clattered on the floor or rattled with a stick or key.

17–18 *Gun in Moorfields!*: Moorfields was a popular open space for sports and walks, adjacent to the mustering-ground of the London militia and the Artillery Company's training-ground. There were naturally several Gun Taverns in the area.

22 *maids*: her bridesmaids.

33 *a monsieur*: the stock joke that Frenchmen are effeminate, unmanly, frivolous, etc.

62–3 *hold out . . . oatmeal*: the diet of a sexually frustrated adolescent girl (cf. *LiW*, 1.1.41); 'lime' = mortar.

68 *new Protestant nunnery*: in 1667, and again in 1671, Edward Chamberlayne proposed the establishment of a boarding academy, to be run on strict religious lines, for young single women. His argument, on which *GDM* casts an ironical light, was that many girls were 'corrupted and debauched' before marriage by having 'too much liberty'.

73 *Hackney School*: the village of Hackney was conveniently near to the

City. Its boarding schools for girls provided instruction in cookery, household management, dancing, etc.; the one run by a Mrs Perwich was particularly celebrated.

106 *conveniently*: agreeably—a Gallicism (*convenablement*).

113 *mon foi*: 'by my faith', 'upon my word'; Monsieur uses this incorrect form (despite his three months' residence in Paris), as well as *ma foi*.

115 *de belle humeur*: good-tempered, cheerful.

121 *if I think it*: 'if I think so'; i.e. 'it must be so, since it's my opinion'.

123 *within Ludgate*: in the area between Fleet St. and St Paul's; not a fashionable location, but (significantly) in the City.

125 *English eating-house*: serving plainer food than a modish 'French house', with its more elaborate (and expensive) cuisine.

132 *snuff-box*: *à la mode* in France, but still rare in London.

136–9 *St Peter's . . . Roi*: the standard tourist attractions. The buildings of the Escorial, north-west of Madrid, comprise palace, monastery, church, and mausoleum. An equestrian statue of Henri IV was erected on the Pont Neuf, built by his direction, in 1614; additions to the palace of the Louvre, notably the colonnade on the east front, had been completed in 1670. The Grand Roi is Louis XIV.

155 *Foi de chevalier*: on the word of a gentleman.

209 *Ship Tavern*: the name (a fairly common one in the City) appropriately suggests mercantile trade.

215–16 *his own*: the (unpalatable) truth about himself, exactly what I think of him.

250 *Just as . . . agree*: proverbially, 'Youth and age seldom agree', and old age is traditionally 'crabbed', i.e. peevish, bad-tempered. Perhaps a reminiscence of 'Crabbèd age and youth cannot live together', from *The Passionate Pilgrim* (1599; sometimes attributed to Shakespeare).

284–5 *a vision*: a waking dream or hallucination (which might turn out to be real).

290 *Throng of Temptations*: parodying the solemn language of Puritanism.

300–1 *virgins but in masquerade*: passing themselves off as chaste. But masquerade costumes may have included nuns' habits (as in the early eighteenth century), so giving further point to the gibe.

302–3 *The children . . . fathers*: proverbially, 'It is a wise child that knows its own father': you'd have to be superhumanly wise to be absolutely sure of your paternity.

308–9 *the Temple . . . night*: entertainments of music and dancing were frequently held at the Inns of Court during the winter months. The law-students and their friends would want more stylish company than a 'City dame'.

319 *taking me up!*: 'capping my remarks'.

1.2.3 *enjoyé*: a blend of English 'enjoy' and French *enjoué* (vivacious, sprightly)

4 *enfinement galliard*: extremely lively. Monsieur means *infiniment*, as at 3.1.9.

5 *'La boutelle ... glouglou'*: 'The bottle ... glug-glug'; presumably the first line (or the refrain) of an actual drinking-song from Northern France (*boutelle* is a provincial form of *bouteille*).

18 *'Arthur ... Norfolk'*: to match Monsieur's drinking-song, Gerrard chooses two traditional ballads associated with rural celebrations. 'Arthur of Bradley' concerns a rustic wedding to which one and all are invited; 'I am the Duke of Norfolk', though its words have not survived, seems to have been a harvest-home song: 'To serve the Duke of Norfolk' is a proverbial phrase meaning to make merry.

61 *obliged*: gratified: for a similar bawdy use cf. *LiW*, 4.4.68.

67 *abuse the Dutch*: the Third Anglo-Dutch War officially began on 17 March 1672, some six weeks after the (probable) date of the play's première. But relations between the two countries were already strained, and acts of hostility had been committed. The City, however, saw Catholic France, England's ally in the war, as ultimately a greater threat than Protestant Holland. Moreover, measures recently taken to finance the forthcoming war were causing hardship in the City. Wycherley is exploiting his audience's mixed feelings.

70 *swabber*: Monsieur is sneering at Dutch traders, captains of cargo vessels, etc. (The Dutch word *swabber* = sailor of the lowest rank.)

73 *disobligé*: a cross between 'disobliged' and *désobligé*.

83 *never honeste ... drunke*: proverbially, 'In wine there is truth': men speak the truth when they are drunk.

89 *de toad in Irland*: St Patrick was said to have expelled all toads (supposedly venomous) and snakes from Ireland.

89–90 *on' chevalier*: a single 'person of quality'; *on* is Monsieur's emphatic blend of English 'one' and French *un*. The predominance of its energetic and prosperous bourgeoisie would make Holland appealing to the City.

91 *rebel*: because Holland had achieved independence from the Habsburg Empire in the late sixteenth century.

97–8 *chandeleer*: grocer, provision merchant; a blend of English 'chandler' and French *chandelier*.

98 *chandels*: French *chandelles* (candles), but with the final 's' pronounced.

99 *witer hands*: not a compliment, but a sneer at Dutch frugality (a standing joke); the candles are a dirty yellow colour, being made of cheap tallow, not expensive wax.

lady: ladies, the 's' being silent, as in a French plural.

100 *stringing*: threading on strings, ready for smoking.

101 *So-o-o! And*: 'So—h—and' (Q1); either a mock-sigh, in pretended sympathy with Monsieur's disdain, or a long-drawn-out 'Soh!', expressing disgust.

104–6 *dere master . . . greater rebel*: Cromwell, a 'greater rebel' than the Dutch in having overthrown his king, became their 'master' in 1654, when he imposed harsh terms at the end of the First Anglo-Dutch War.

137 *French qualification*: syphilis was known as the 'French pox' or 'French disease'.

174 *pay myself*: by having sex with her gratis.

182 S.D. *Flounce and Flirt*: to 'flounce' (used at *LiW*, 3.2.99 of a periwig) is to curl or fluff up, referring perhaps to her hair-do; 'flirt' implies pertness and flightiness. But, names apart, the women are indistinguishable.

188 *hot service*: (1) under heavy fire, so suffering injury, and (2) having sex with carriers of venereal disease.

208 *for one . . . shop*: to claim the acquaintance of a female customer, in a shop selling silks, velvets and other expensive materials, could lead to paying for a gown.

209–11 *He has spoken . . . words*: he has said that he won't lose the honour of your acquaintance; so you could hold him to his word and get a meal out of him while you're here (he's a regular customer), or force him (punningly) to eat his words.

212–13 *She does . . . dishabilè*: Monsieur interprets Flounce's reference to the mercer's shop as a broad hint; she is wearing only an informal wrap or 'nightgown'. 'Dishabilè' is his version of French *déshabillé* (= informal dress), and the word's first recorded appearance in an English text. The standard spelling eventually became 'dishabille'.

249–50 *can't you . . . meat?*: proverbial phrase, said of someone imprudently announcing a piece of private good fortune.

252 *The silent . . . grains*: proverbial.

264 *D'e tinke*: Q1 has 'Deè, you tinke.' 'Deè' is one of its several abbreviations of 'do ye' (e.g. 'what deè call't' at l. 24 above). The compositor perhaps mistook a mark or flourish in the manuscript for a comma, and then inserted the redundant 'you'. Holland interprets 'Deè' as 'Monsieur's stab at pronouncing Dieu'; but it seems too wide of the mark to be easily understood by an audience. Moreover, Monsieur likes to repeat his oaths: he nowhere else uses *Dieu*.

267 *curtoise*: English 'courteous' combined with French *courtoise*.

296 *Or ça, à manger*: Now then, we'd like to eat.

297 *cram schiquin*: crammed chicken, fattened by being force-fed with a dough of wheatmeal and milk; considered a delicacy.

310 *extrêmente*: for *extrêmement*, extremely.

323 *Mustard Alley*: perhaps a specific street (in the Charing Cross area?); more probably a deliberately suggestive name (cf. 'hot service' above).

Crooked Billet: a thick, untrimmed stick; a not uncommon tavern sign, but the phallic symbolism would make it a suitable sign for a brothel.

371 *fort bon*: excellent.

2.1 S.D. *Spanish habit*: tight-fitting, buttoned-up doublet or quilted jacket; leather girdle; skin-tight breeches to below the knee, with visible fly-buttons; white stockings, possibly with additional net stockings over them; flat-heeled shoes; no wig; hat either flat-crowned with a small brim or a high-crowned 'sugar-loaf'.

32 *for it*: to acquire wisdom.

40 *Spanish whiskers*: moustache, and beard cut square and full. Englishmen at this period were almost all clean-shaven.

2.2 There is no scene-division in Q1. The preceding dialogue between Don Diego and Mrs Caution could have been played on the forestage, in front of the set and props for Hippolyta's room, and accepted by the audience as taking place in some unspecified part of the house.

29 *bench*: backless benches provided the only seating in theatres.

53 *I—ah—am*: 'Ih—am' (Q1); Gerrard takes a deep breath to steady his nerves.

59–60 *For blushing*: as for, to account for, my blushing.

85–6 *of your own head*: of your own accord.

93 *fiddling*: (1) fussing about trifles, and (2) impertinently familiar.

135 *questions and commands*: a parlour game involving the asking of inventive and audacious questions, or the imposing of similar commands, with subsequent forfeits.

152 *a*: not in Q1.

158 *'Tis in vain . . . Fate*: proverbial.

194 *la gaillarda*: a lively dance. Diego blends Spanish *gallarda* with French *gaillard*.

209 *pray . . . blessing*: a child would customarily ask a parental blessing after a period of separation.

212 *mi mal, mi muertè*: my plague, my death.

217 *Traidor . . . honra*: traitor, thief of my honour.

219 *you mistake your man*: formula used in response to an insult, and preceding a challenge: 'I'm not a person to be insulted with impunity'; here also, 'I'm not the guilty party'.

244 *confess . . . hanged*: proverbially, 'Confess and be hanged'.

252 *forsooth*: 'ancient madam' (see Glossary)—condescendingly archaic, to the antiquated lady.

253 *does't*: 'do'st it' (Q1).

290–1 *At the Surgeon's . . . springtime*: the juxtaposition of young man and surgeon usually betokens venereal disease. Mrs Caution hints that Gerrard lodges with a quack-doctor who can keep him in good repair during the season for love-making. She refrains from naming the street or district lest Gerrard should latch on to it, but she could look slyly at the audience.

304–5 *the mother . . . oven*: proverbially, 'If the mother had never been in the oven [place of ill repute], she would never have sought her daughter there.'

305 *A word to the wise*: this proverbial tag—'A [single] word to a wise man is enough'—is comically inappropriate to the tattling Mrs Caution.

311 *Santiago para mi*: 'St James [the apostle] for me!' He swears by his name saint, Diego being a variant of Jago.

348 *seeing your legs*: lifting her skirt to check the position of her legs and feet.

399–400 *had taken it up*: 'had it taken up' (Q1).

405 *after-game*: a second game played in order to reverse the outcome of the first one; hence, an expedient brought into play to retrieve a situation.

416 *spirit*: an abductor or kidnapper of children, servants, vagrants, etc. Such people were lured or forced on board ships, for sale in the plantations of the West Indies and North America.

477–8 *the new song*: a setting by John Banister (a seventeen-bar melody, repeated three times), appeared in John Playford's *Choice Songs and Ayres* (1673), and is printed in modern notation in Weales, 169.

505 *lawful wench*: a legal prostitute.

S.D. *steps to the door*: Q1 regularly places directions at the ends of speeches, even when the designated action obviously precedes or accompanies the words. It is unclear whether Prue moves only after having heard Don Diego off-stage, or whether, as she approaches the door (to show the singer out?), she hears him and turns back to Hippolyta.

510–11 *But . . . new slavery*: Q1 has a comma after 'free', and a semicolon after 'slavery'. But the parallel in thought with *LiW*, 5.1.78 ('to avoid slavery under [my father], I stoop to your yoke') suggests that Hippolyta's final couplet is a single entity.

3.1.15 *Mal . . . putains!*: 'plaguy whores'. Spoken half-aside: Monsieur assumes that Hippolyta won't understand French.

19–20 *subject or property*: 'subject-matter or accessories'. But also 'lines to speak or stage-props'—a compliment to the comically expressive limbs and features of James Nokes, playing Monsieur; they are put to good use later in the scene.

42 *Italian Academy*: the Comédie italienne, currently performing *commedia dell' arte* to great acclaim in Paris.

43 *Signior Scaramouchè*: Tiberio Fiorelli (or Fiorilli), principal actor of the Comédie, known as Scaramouche for his brilliant playing of the role, that of a cowardly, foolish boaster.

44 *Angel*: see note on 'The Persons'.

55 *matrès*: Monsieur's pronunciation of *maîtres* (masters, instructors) will be comically close to 'mattress' (Holland).

65 *Fools have fortune*: a common variant of the proverb 'Fortune favours fools'.

66 *So . . . Sénèque*: Monsieur is practising one-upmanship; though Seneca was a standard source of quotable maxims, he seems never to have cited this adage.

75 *Well—vel*: Monsieur quickly corrects his lapse into plain English.

76–7 *the conclusion . . . sad*: cf. such proverbs as 'The end of mirth is heaviness', and 'Leave jesting while it pleases, lest it turn to earnest'.

142 *Spanish hose*: his close-fitting breeches, in marked contrast to Monsieur's culottes-like pantaloons.

146 *contraries*: with a subdued pun on 'countries': it was a commonplace that the French and Spanish were diametrically opposed in their dispositions, social behaviour, dress, and deportment.

149 *Formal*: the name implies a man stiff and stately, unduly ceremonious, living according to rigid rules of behaviour.

154 *nedèr*: Monsieur's version of 'neither'; i.e. 'do not call me Parris either'.

159 *bien trové*: bien trouvé, 'that's a good phrase'.

165 *Ridicule*: ridiculous. This meaning of 'ridicule' is first recorded in print in 1672; Monsieur is being affectedly modish.

174 *gabacho . . . gusto*: frenchified fool who has bad taste; Q1 has the meaningless 'gavanho'.

214 *riband upon de cravat*: the cravat was held in place by a length of black or coloured ribbon, usually tied in an elaborate bow which framed the loose knot of the cravat.

215 *matress*: for *maîtresses*, mistresses.

228 *voto*: Monsieur uses Diego's favourite oath, either deliberately and tauntingly, or accidentally, in which case he will regret his error with comic grimaces.

231 *my*: not in Q1.

246–7 *by my ... snuff-box*: Spaniards were commonly said to swear by their beards, and to be addicted to snuff.

253 S.D. *followed by the Blackamoor*: Q1 gives no exit for Diego's black servant; he needs to be off-stage by l. 276, when Diego calls to him and his fellow-servant.

276 *Pedro, Sanchez*: the names which Diego has given to his young black servants.

281 *Dear belte! Dear sword!*: in May 1670 Nokes acted at Dover before the English and French courts; he wore the Duke of Monmouth's broad waist-belt and sword, lent to him for the better caricaturing of the similarly equipped French. The delighted Duke presented the sword (and, one supposes, the accompanying belt) to Nokes, who no doubt sported them as Monsieur.

282 *chapeau retroussé*: his cocked hat, its brim showily pinned up; it is probably decorated in the French manner, with loops of ribbons and an outsize plume.

garn!: trimmed with bows of ribbons at the toes and ankles, and laced with further fancy ribbons.

352–3 *honour the king*: perhaps, as Friedman suggests, 'save your protestations of honour for the king; stop prating'. There may be an allusion to the injunction 'honour your partners', the customary bow and curtsey at the beginning of a dance (so 'your honour' at 4.1.666).

355 *a-fiddling*: Diego unwittingly invokes two other meanings of 'fiddle': to cheat, and to take liberties with a woman (Weales).

355–6 *all that ... impertinency*: Proverbially, 'Fiddlers, dogs, and flies come to feasts uncalled [uninvited]'.

398 [*GERRARD*]: 'One ... toes' is given a separate line in Q1, but no speech-prefix. It is not Diego but Gerrard, using his newly acquired 'canting', who gives Hippolyta instructions by numbers. 'Turn out your toes' was a basic rule in dancing.

403 *fall*: not in Q1.

411–12 *You, a Spaniard*: a true Spaniard would be vigilant and suspicious, sensitive to any threat to his family's honour.

468 *whining*: using the extravagant language and gestures of romantic adoration.

488 *the use ... doctrine*: a preacher would expound the significance of his sermon text, its 'doctrine', before proceeding to explain its 'use' or practical application. Gerrard comes very quickly to the point.

514 *not a man ... coachman*: a neat twist of the standing joke about ladies' affairs with their coachmen (for want of anyone better).

553 *roundly together*: all of it, smartly and without more ado.

4.1.10 *double*: thickly quilted or padded.

17 *Spanish ear*: following the Spanish mode, Monsieur is 'without a peruke'; but his ears are more clearly visible even than a Spaniard's, since his head will have been closely cropped to accommodate his wig.

22–3 *new title of honneur*: knights are stock figures of fun in Restoration Comedy; cf. *CW*, 3.2.110 ff. and note.

29–30 *unite France . . . now*: the Treaty of Aix-la-Chapelle (1668) concluded hostilities between France and Spain, with France retaining some of the frontier towns captured in the Spanish Netherlands. If Monsieur's 'Spanish hat' is of the sugar-loaf shape (see note on S.D. at head of 2.1), his holding it in front of his pantaloons will transform it into a grotesque codpiece.

43 *countree capitaine*: captain of the local militia, swaggering among the yokels.

55–6 *you wash . . . white*: a variant of the proverb 'To wash the Ethiop white': to undertake a fruitless task.

56–7 *an English monsieur*: glancing at James Howard's comedy, *The English Monsieur* (performed 1663, published 1674); the character Frenchlove lives up to his name in his 'fashion, discourse, and clothes'.

58 *taken . . . ply*: become set in their French ways.

142–3 *verdadero . . . Castilian*: the authentic bearing, grace, and gravity of a genuine Spanish gentleman. The ancient kingdom of Castile considered itself superior to other parts of Spain.

148 *horns*: cuckolds' horns.

151 *grandees . . . Spain*: Spanish noblemen of the highest rank were privileged to wear their hats in the king's presence.

156–7 *the hood . . . skin on*: two proverbs (the second deriving from Aesop) asserting that appearances do not create realities.

190 *bonnets*: usually brimless caps; perhaps here a form of turban.

202 *to*: 'too' (Q1).

203–4 *do thus . . . hand*: the contemptuous gesture is probably the 'Spanish fig', the fist extended, with the thumb protruding from between two fingers.

212 *it*: not in Q1.

291 *dreams . . . contraries*: proverbial wisdom.

295 *a brick unburnt*: a yellowish-grey colour, before being baked red in the brick-kiln.

330 *Nothing . . . love*: conflating two proverbs: 'Love will find a way', and 'Nothing is impossible to God' (or 'a willing heart').

354 *But I . . . upon me*: I'm deeply grateful to you—as the future husband of the woman whose honour you have gallantly not compromised.

381 *it shall . . . but I'll*: I shall most certainly.

410 *[I] know him*: Q1's omission of 'I' looks like an accident; Monsieur is now speaking standard English.

436 *So, there . . . you*: he is even with you. Gerrard is fooling you (if you did but know it), while you protest at the fooling about that is going on.

464–5 *the troth-telling . . . of old*: Cassandra, daughter of Priam, warned of the fate of Troy; her prophetic words were heeded too late. 'Troth' is (1) what is going to come true, and (2) plain, honest speaking.

506 *yet*: still, as you were before.

615 *Hold . . . woman*: this sentence is given to Gerrard in Q1. But 'silly woman' is Diego's way of addressing Mrs Caution (e.g. 5.1.308): Gerrard, at his most irate, would not so insult Hippolyta. Perhaps Wycherley prefaced Diego's following questions with the direction 'To Gerrard', but placed the word 'Gerrard' in such a way as to mislead the printer.

634–5 *Avoid, Satan*: 'begone Satan', a tag deriving from Coverdale's translation (1535) of Matthew 16: 23. The Authorized Version's 'Get thee behind me, Satan' is more familiar.

673 *make no bones*: have no scruples about, don't hesitate to (proverbial).

5.1.43 *don't be troubled . . . helped*: proverbial advice: 'Never grieve for what you cannot help'.

74 *dance*: Here, and throughout the dialogue that follows, Q1 gives an initial capital-letter to this verb (also to 'sing', l. 101), to indicate taunting emphasis.

85 *hanging*: the punishment for killing one's opponent in a duel.

92–3 *hit in the teeth . . . with*: constantly and painfully reminded of.

102 *you two?*: 'you too' (Q1); but Hippolyta is simply dismayed to find them quarrelling at all: she pursues her enquiry at l. 159.

126 *malicious . . . plague does*: malicious = vindictive, revengeful; remembering the Great Plague of 1665.

130 *(to take . . . love)*: if you leave his infatuation out of account.

146 *give losers . . . speak*: an opportunity to voice their resentment (proverbial).

154 *Wittols*: (1) half-wits, and (2) contented cuckolds, those who tamely accept their cuckoldom.

197–8 *for most men . . . warned*: Prue rephrases the proverb 'Forewarned, forearmed' so as to make the customary joke about horns.

199 *Plain dealing . . . honesty*: 'Speaking frankly is one sort of virtuous, honourable behaviour.' Proverbially, 'Plain dealing is a jewel'.

229 *Spanish and Guinea force*: Juan, the 'old withered Spanish eunuch' (4.1.190), and the two servant boys from the west coast of Africa.

352 *look to my hits*: keep a watchful eye on my own interests.

379 *my great-great-grandfather*: in Q1 Diego persists in referring to his 'great, great, great Grandfather' (so also at ll. 381 and 384); this suits his pompous ancestor-worship, but doesn't square with Monsieur's account of the genealogy.

390 *Canary merchant*: specializing in the import of wine (mainly light and sweet) from the Canary Islands.

393 *tuns . . . canary*: wine-casks on a bright yellow background (punning on Canary wine). There were several London inns called the Three Tuns.

396–7 *Great . . . Yard*: Great St Helen's, near Bishopsgate, notable for numerous splendid monuments (inside the church) to important City dignitaries (aldermen, Lord Mayors, merchants) of the sixteenth and seventeenth centuries. The tombs of more humble citizens are in the churchyard.

410 *'Tu quoque, Brutè'*: the last reproachful words allegedly uttered by Caesar as Brutus stabbed him; Shakespeare's *Et tu, Bruté* is another version.

412 *Don Quixote*: madman.

498 *for a fly*: merely in order to save the bait; proverbially, 'You must lose a fly to catch a trout.'

508 *blessing*: his formal approval of their marriage.

510 *What*: why, for what reason.

551 *We fiddlers . . . unsent for*: groups of fiddlers would tout for custom when any festivity was going forward; cf. 3.1.355–6, and note.

569 *two . . . bargain*: both parties must agree (proverbial).

588 *'Flirt coach'*: constantly on the go, flitting from one place to another.

589 *the park*: Hyde Park, favoured location for evening coach-drives; she will be admired and accosted as she rides slowly along.

608 *take no acquaintance . . . abroad*: don't claim to know me, or behave fondly towards me, in public.

609 *any*: anyone.

618 *Queen Elizabeth*: traditional, old-fashioned.

633–4 *flame-colour . . . Indian*: bright reddish-orange gown or négligé, made of imported Indian chintz.

634–5 *contented . . . twelvemonth*: would have managed happily for a whole year without craving any of the aforesaid luxuries. But the syntax of the other items in Monsieur's catalogue suggests that Wycherley forgot (or the compositor omitted) to tell us what she would have had instead.

636 *St George for England*: there were several popular ballads with this title, celebrating the knight's exploits.

636–7 *The Knight of the Sun*: the hero of Ortuñez de Calahorra's *The Mirror of Princely Deeds and Knighthood* (a sixteenth-century Spanish romance), and a byword for extravagant chivalry.

637 *The Practice of Piety*: Bishop Lewis Bayly's immensely popular devotional and didactic treatise, first published sometime before 1612.

638 *sending*: ordering to be sent.

659–60 *you know what I mean*: Jerry Blackacre uses the same parenthetical phrase to signal a *double entendre* (*PD*, 3.1.367), but perhaps Monsieur refers only to Hippolyta's headstrong wilfulness. Or at 'these heads' he may gesture towards the audience: the trading interests of the City aren't to be thwarted by the cunning of Spain or any other country.

Epilogue

25 *sparks . . . are gone*: some hundreds of gentlemen volunteered to fight against the Dutch.

26 *Into the pit*: occupying the customary seats of the wits and literati.

29 *Lumber Street*: though Lombard St was commonly so pronounced, the unflattering asociations of 'lumber' (worthless rubbish; to blunder heavily about) are no doubt intended, as a joke against City financiers.

30 *between our scenes*: backstage, flirting with the actresses.

33 *jumps*: thigh-length loose coats, particularly associated with Presbyterian ministers—hinting at the nonconformist sympathies of the City.

   gold chains . . . gowns: the badges of office worn in public by aldermen.

34 *broad cocked hats*: see note on *LiW*, 2.4.15.

35 *Your satin . . . cravats*: a City man usually wore a skull cap over his own hair, and narrow, plain shirt cuffs (as against the gentleman's wig, and his wide, deep, laced cuffs), while a broad 'falling band', rather like an oblong bib, sometimes replaced the usual cravat.

37 *gilt shillings*: a silver shilling (5p) could be gilded and passed off as a gold guinea (then worth £1).

38 *break our windows*: rakes frequently amused themselves by breaking the windows of brothels and prostitutes' lodgings, or similarly revenged themselves on fickle mistresses.

43 *camlet*: fabric of silk and camel-hair or wool; costly, hard-wearing, and favoured by City men.

The Country Wife

Title-page

   Indignor . . . posci: 'I feel offended when critics censure a work of literature not for having been written crudely and inelegantly, but simply for having been written recently, and when they demand, for writers of earlier ages, not just indulgence but honour and glory': Horace, *Epistles* II i. 76–8. Wycherley may be asking for a fair hearing for his new, sharply satirical manner, or for his inventive use of a plot-device borrowed from the *Eunuchus* of the Roman dramatist Terence.

The Persons

15 *Quack*: an unqualified, back-street physician.

Prologue

5 *late . . . scribbler*: alluding either to the fact that Wycherley's previous play, *The Gentleman Dancing-Master*, ran for only six performances, or (perhaps) to the rejection of the first version of *The Plain Dealer* by the London theatres: see p. vii n. 1. above. 'Baffled' = humbled, humiliated.

10 *Kastril*: the would-be bully-boy in Ben Jonson's *The Alchemist*; his idea of picking a quarrel is to declare, 'You lie'.

11 *our Bayses' . . . fought*: Charles Hart was celebrated for superman roles, notably Almanzor, the arrogant, bloodthirsty hero of Dryden's *The Conquest of Granada* (2 parts, 1670, 1671). Though, as the following line makes clear, Q1's 'Bayes' is plural (= dramatists), the audience would think at once of Dryden, the poet laureate. As 'Mr Bays' he was the principal character and butt of the dramatic burlesque *The Rehearsal* (1672), by the Duke of Buckingham and others.

16 *Bays (within)*: the author, standing in the wings, directing the first performance.

25 *We set no guards*: an open invitation to rakes and men-about-town which flouts attempts, including royal edicts, to check their activities behind the scenes, both during and after performances.

1.1 S.D. *Horner*: one who makes cuckolds, the traditional wearers of horns.

1 *as fit for*: as suitable to be.

2 *both*: the quack and the midwife; but 'both' could sometimes mean 'all'.

7–8 *orange-wenches*: oranges were the principal refreshment in theatres; the orange-women were notorious for retailing gossip, and expert in setting up assignations, for themselves and others.

9 *this end of the town*: Westminster, the fashionable, residential West End of London, as opposed to the mercantile City. Horner's lodging is in Russell St, near Covent Garden Piazza.

10–11 *tire-women*: either ladies' maids, or dressmakers and vendors of gloves, cosmetics, etc; both categories could be relied on to spread gossip.

17 *great ones*: the great (or French) pox, i.e. syphilis; the spelling 'pox' derives from an original plural form 'pocks'.

18 *Aniseed Robin*: a hermaphrodite who sold aniseed-water (used medicinally) on the London streets earlier in the century. He was reputed to have given birth to two children; the prudish City ladies would be shocked.

22-3 *English-French disaster . . . chirurgeon*: the French pox caught from an English prostitute, and drastically cured by an English surgeon specializing in venereal ('French') disease, or (in view of Horner's journey abroad, l. 27), by an English surgeon working in France.

47 *no, not in the City*: not even in the City, the happy hunting-ground of Restoration libertines.

51 S.D. *Sir Jasper*: ironically named: Jasper is the English form of Caspar, one of the three Wise Men who journeyed to Bethlehem.

   S.D. *Dainty*: her name means both 'fastidious' and 'choice, pretty'.

54-8 *My . . . sister sir*: by omitting the commas before the 'sirs' in Sir Jasper's first speech (and at l. 64), Q1 nicely suggests his gushing insincerity. Horner's 'sirs', marked off by punctuation, are evidently sardonic.

74 S.D. *(Makes horns)*: either holding the first with two fingers extended, or (more probably) holding a fist at each temple, with the index fingers stretched out, like an animal's horns.

75 *Mercury*: men of fashion commonly wore their hats indoors, so Horner, making horns, looks like the god Mercury with his winged hat on. Additionally, 'sweet' mercury was used to treat venereal disease. But the jest is neater than Sir Jasper realizes: Mercury was the patron of thieves and cheats, and representative of quick-wittedness and trickery.

84-5 *new postures*: new pornographic prints. Horner alludes to the notorious 'Aretine's Postures' (early sixteenth-century engravings for which Aretino provided accompanying poems), perhaps also to *La puttana errante* (The Wandering Whore) published *c.*1660 over Aretino's name, and detailing many more 'postures'.

85 *the École des filles*: a bawdy guide to lovemaking, published Paris (1655, but suppressed), and 'Fribourg' (i.e. Amsterdam?, 1668). There were various reprints, but no second part.

104-5 *The Council*: probably the Privy Council, the king's advisory body.

106-8 *wise, Mr Horner . . . impotent*: Q1 has no commas after 'wise' and the two 'impotents', making them simultaneously both nouns and adjectives.

126-7 *done . . . women*: ruined yourself for good in their eyes.

139-40 *an old . . . unwillingly*: Q1, followed by many editors, punctuates 'an old one, and of all old debts; love when' etc. But 'of all' is naturally capped by 'the most'.

160 *Not so new neither*: in Terence's *Eunuchus* a young man disguises himself as a eunuch to gain access to a girl.

431

167–8 *a great-bellied actress*: an obviously pregnant actress shamelessly playing the role of a virgin.

175 *'tis pity but*: it would be a good thing if.

196 *country*: with a quibble on 'cunt' (Ogden).

209–10 *Ay, wine ... wine*: the repetitions and punctuation suggest that Dorilant is pretending to be tipsy.

216 *Sparkish*: the name implies a young fellow who would be thought elegant and witty.

222 *he cannot drink*: he doesn't enjoy a drink because he can't hold his liquor. Cf. Dapperwit in *LiW*.

224–5 *like the worst ... companies*: the common complaint that bands of fiddlers were always pushing their services.

232 *signifies no more to't*: contributes no more to it; has no further significance in relation to it.

233–4 *Sir Martin ... music*: the celebrated comic scene in Dryden's *Sir Martin Mar-all* (1668); Sir Martin serenades his mistress from his balcony in dumb-show, while his servant sings and plays the lute in the adjoining room. The deception collapses when the servant's signal to stop goes unheard.

236 *us that ... plot*: we, who know his false pretensions to wit (like Marall's), are guilty of having encouraged him, for our own amusement (Revels).

247 *ebony cane*: the doctor's badge of office.

268–70 *fine new ... believe*: Sparkish means shop-signs; Horner deliberately understands inn-signs.

288 *I*: not in Q1.

294 *Go to him again*: 'go back to your earl.' Q1 has 'Go, to him again', which Holland interprets as Harcourt's urging Dorilant to press home his verbal attack. But 'again' would be more relevant after, rather than before, Sparkish's reply, and Harcourt's next 'go to him' (l. 298) clearly refers to the earl.

316 *the Dog and Partridge*: assuming that Sparkish's list is in descending order of cost and propriety, this is probably the Setting Dog and Partridge in Fleet St., frequented by rowdies and prostitutes.

317 *a*: not in Q1.

320 *wits' row*: a bench near the front of the theatre pit, the preserve of the critics and wits.

321 s.d. *Pinchwife*: 'pinch' is (1) harass, afflict, and (2) restrict, confine.

331 *five thousand pound*: as marriage dowry—a substantial one.

334 *a cracked title*: not a good investment; literally, the right of ownership is

not entirely secure. 'Cracked' could also mean 'bankrupt' and 'soft in the head'.

344–5 *deceitful . . . jade*: a horse of poor condition deliberately fattened up for sale at Smithfield, the London market for livestock, notorious for fraudulent dealers; figuratively, a disreputable 'woman of the town' passing herself off as a fine lady.

349 *Wales*: representative of utter rusticity and remoteness from civilization.

350 *cousins*: Q1 has 'cozens', perhaps a variant of 'cozeners' = cheats, but more probably a spelling-variant of 'cousins' = man-friends, intimates (with a hint of 'cozening' too).

justices' clerks: Q1's 'Justices, Clerks' would mean that Justices of the Peace are as much given to lechery as parish clerks. But the latter are not usually referred to simply as 'clerks'; on the other hand, a JP normally employed a clerical assistant, who might well have had time on his hands.

350–1 *chaplains . . . coachmen*: a lady's relationship with her chaplain and/or coachman was standard material for jokes and gossip; cf. 4.1.86 below.

355 *He talks . . . grazier*: he uses the same kind of sales-talk as the farmer who has brought his fattened sheep and cattle to market.

358 [*HORNER*]: '*Har.*' (Q1) is an understandable misreading of '*Hor.*' Horner is the tormenting interrogator, and his are the 'instructions' (l. 362) which Pinchwife fears. From Pinchwife's entry up to l. 366, when Horner brings them into the conversation, Harcourt and Dorilant are merely commentators.

359 *breeding*: (1) the manners of polite society, and (2) how to conceive a child.

412 *broke*: (1) stripped of cash, and (2) past it, incapable of sex—introducing the bawdy analogy between ruined gamblers and would-be lechers.

427 *eighteen-penny place*: the middle gallery of the theatre, above the boxes and pit; frequented by citizens' wives and daughters, waiting-women, apprentices, prostitutes, and men who didn't want their companions to be too visible. Horner would have had the best view of Mrs Pinchwife from a side-box.

449 *Hampshire*: in Restoration Comedy 'Hampshire' stands for provinciality and unsophistication, all that is outside the orbit of London. But the Pinchwifes actually live there (2.1.115).

454 *Cheapside*: centre of the cloth trade, retail and wholesale.

455 *Covent Garden wife*: either the City man has married an upper-class woman who likes good company, or his wife has insisted on moving from Cheapside to a more modish area, full of temptations. Cf. *GDM*, 1.1.307–8.

2.1 S.D. *Alethea*: her name (from the Greek) signifies 'truth', her commitment to her 'word and rigid honour' (4.1.30).

6–7 *town?... yesterday?*: Q1's ungrammatical punctuation suggests Margery's petulant tone.

34 *bud*: a term of endearment, usually to a child. As applied to Pinchwife the word has overtones of cuckoldry: a 'bud' is a newly-weaned calf, and an animal's horns are said to 'bud'.

196–7 *true lovers ... stock-blind*: proverbially, love is blind; but 'stock-blind' means stupid as well as totally blind.

223–4 *jealousy ... of it*: proverbially 'Love is never without jealousy'; cf. *LiW*, 4.4.29 and *GDM*, 5.1.210.

232 *No, now ... head*: by speaking of 'interest' he has raised a doubt that his intentions are mercenary.

236–7 *in necessity... cloak*: that you are marrying either because you are pregnant, or to provide yourself with a respectable cover for your intrigues.

264 *True*: she is right: Harcourt has been sincerely 'making love' to her. Or Harcourt may be complaining that Alethea is a 'true' or typical woman; cf. *PD*, 2.1.719: 'True perfect woman!'.

284 *What, what?*: angrily challenging Harcourt to acknowledge what he has said about Sparkish's 'parts'.

287–8 *Nay ... honour*: Alethea is on the point of admitting to herself that, if her honour did not forbid it, she could reciprocate Harcourt's love. Q1 marks only these four words as spoken aside, though the direction clearly applies to the first part of the speech also.

291 *after all*: finally, in short.

306 *no judge ... trimmings*: a judge only of the actors' costumes, with their frills and ribbons; once in the pit, among the critics, he becomes a judge of the play's merits.

311 S.D. *Squeamish*: prudish, coy.

343–5 *since wives ... jealous*: neglected by their husbands, the women are free to have affairs; but husbands have no need to be jealous, because their wives are also neglected by their potential lovers.

347–9 *That men ... creatures*: the king's relationships with Moll Davis and Nell Gwyn (the latter had previously consorted with Lord Buckhurst) were only the most notorious instances.

400 *dear of honour*: dear to me because of your honour (Revels).

413–14 *Mr Tattle ... Limberham*: Lady Fidget's escorts, the 'two old civil gentlemen' of l. 479 below. Limberham = supple of leg, hence obsequiously bowing and scraping.

416 s.d. *(Whispers ... Fidget)*: although she knows that Horner is (supposedly) impotent (1.1.97–8), she still has to be persuaded to allow herself to be seen with such a disreputable fellow. But the whispering is clearly a dramatic device to get the Fidgets to one side while Horner and Dorilant board the other women.

446 *In sober sadness*: seriously, I insist.

456 *Great Turk's*: the Turkish Sultan's.

457 *ombre player*: one of the duties of a lady's escort or 'gentleman-usher' was to make one at the card-table. Since 'ombre' comes from Spanish *hombre* = the man, there was perhaps a standard joke that the male ombre player was not a real man; cf. 4.3.212 ff.

471 *mortified ... wether*: the 'French disease' has reduced Horner to the condition of a castrated ram. 'Mortified' = (1) dead to sensual pleasure (as Horner is), and (2) made tender by hanging or pickling (as the ram's flesh is).

477 *drolling*: either 'facetious, unserious,' or 'ridiculous, comical'.

481 *other*: others (an uninflected plural).

489–90 *Those whom ... make fine*: if we cannot keep men as our lovers and admirers ('hold' = occupy an official position), we can at least make them pay to be released from our service. Wycherley seems to be conflating two similar expressions: (1) 'to make fine': to obtain release, e.g. from captivity, by a money payment; (2) 'to fine': to pay a fee in order to be excused from taking up an official post, e.g. as sheriff or alderman, with its attendant expenses and responsibilities.

535 s.d. *(Whispering to them)*: again, dramatically necessary, so that Lady Fidget and Horner can converse. Since Dainty and Mistress Squeamish also know the official line, Sir Jasper persuades them of Horner's advantages as a tame, rich escort, partner at cards, etc.

549 *tailors*: Q1's 'Taylors' may be either nominative plural ('we dare trust you no more than your tailors can': gentlemen notoriously left their tailors' bills unpaid), or genitive plural ('your words are as unreliable as those of your tailors'), in which case it would allude to the proverb that 'There is knavery in all trades, but most in tailors'.

554 *save you harmless*: Horner means 'ensure that your reputation suffers no harm', but his use of a technical legal phrase (usually 'to save and keep harmless') gives his promise a sharp edge. The phrase was employed in deeds of gift, etc., as a safeguard against further claims, and as an indemnification against previous ones.

559 *obscenely*: either she's making a little joke ('you'll tell' is not the expected obscenity), or she prudishly labels all frank, down-to-earth speech as obscenity.

3.1 s.d. *Alethea*: having just returned from the theatre (l. 58), she will be wearing outdoor clothes, pointing up the contrast with the housebound Margery.

12 *ninepins*: a variant of skittles; a man's game, considered rather strenuous and unfashionable.

20 *grease . . . teeth*: a well-known stable-boys' dodge; with its teeth greased, the horse can't eat the hay which its owner has paid for.

22–3 *good precepts . . . us*: cf. the proverb 'Examples teach more than precepts'.

58 *'Tis just done*: the performance would have finished at about 6.30.

3.2 S.D. *New Exchange*. The back-scene (perhaps also the wings) represents shops and stalls, together with shopkeepers ('these [women] of the Exchange', ll. 71–2) and customers. Other 'walking-on customers' probably circulate in the course of the scene. Clasp the bookseller (whether male or female is unclear) could sit at a free-standing booth, or behind a window-opening in the back-scene.

23 *Yes*: heavily scornful; but perhaps a misprint for 'Yet', as Harold Love suggests (*Yearbook of English Studies*, 15 (1985), 295).

24 *set out . . . only*: simply keep your hand occupied with a glass.

26–7 *tosses . . . ure*: plays a practice game of dice with a scorekeeper, just to keep his hand in.

34 *'tis but*: this edn.; Q1 has 'But 'tis', which would involve a rather harsh change of tone, uncharacteristically censorious and downright for Dorilant.

43 *Lewis's*: a tavern or 'ordinary'; but Lewis was the common English form of Louis, so he may be the proprietor of a smart 'French house'.

46 *sack and sugar*: dry Spanish (or Canary) white wine sweetened with sugar was a drink for women (cf. *LiW*, 2.1.98–100) or the unsophisticated.

63 *brother . . . weather*: the woodcock migrates to Britain for the winter, returning to Scandinavia in the spring (going away when the cold weather does). The bird is easily snared, so woodcock = simpleton, dupe.

81 [*HORNER*]: again, Q1 has 'Har.' for *Hor.* (cf. 1.1.358). It is Horner who replies to Sparkish's taunts.

93 *I'm*: 'I'am' (Q1); since Horner later says 'I'm sure' (5.4.24–5), Wycherley probably intended the same colloquial form here.

97 *Phyllis*: probably the most popular name (it was Wycherley's own favourite) for the subjects and addressees of love-poems.

100 *jealousy*: proverbially, 'Love is never without jealousy'.

110–11 *And indeed . . . a knight*: Sparkish has a point: Sir Martin Mar-all, Sir Simon Addleplot (*LiW*), Sir Oliver Cockwood and Sir Joslin Jolly (Etherege, *She Would if She Could*, 1668), Sir Simon Softhead (Ravenscroft, *The Citizen Turned Gentleman*, 1672) are only the most obvious examples. A character in John Dover's *The Mall* (1674) comments that knights in real life are mockingly called 'Sir Martin, Sir Nicholas, and forty other ridiculous names' taken from 'the newest comedies'.

124–5 *readers . . . uncourteous*: 'Courteous (or gentle) reader' is a cliché of literary prefaces.

132 *the king . . . supped*: the public was often admitted to the Banqueting Hall of Whitehall Palace to watch the king dining.

136 *his doctors . . . dogs*: Charles II was careful of his health and fond of his dogs, notably his spaniels.

142 *CLASP*: ironically named, after the fastening of the cover of a large and expensive volume; Clasp's wares are cheaper.

143 *Covent Garden Drollery*: published 1672, and subtitled 'A Collection of all the Choice Songs, Poems, Prologues, and Epilogues . . . Written by the refined'st Witts of the Age'. The 'Songs' and 'Poems' are mainly love-ditties and often bawdy; among them is the song from Act 2 of *GDM*.

144 *Tarugo's . . . Maiden*: *Tarugo's Wiles* is an unfunny and unsuccessful comedy by Thomas Sydserf (or St Serfe), published 1667; Sir Robert Stapylton's confused tragicomedy *The Slighted Maid* (1663), equally unsuccessful, had recently been burlesqued in *The Rehearsal*. The joke is many-layered: the bookseller is prominently displaying old, non-selling lines, in order to get rid of them; Margery's enthusiasm reveals her lack of critical sophistication—the titles alone attract her. But in fact both plays are very relevant to her situation: the principal plot of *The Slighted Maid* hinges on sexual jealousy, while the heroine of *Tarugo's Wiles* is rescued from the custodial oppression ('unjust slavery') of a jealous brother who at one point threatens her with a dagger (cf. Pinchwife's behaviour in 4.1 and 4.4), and the play finally asks, 'Can a woman's will be fettered?'

176 *seamstresses*: in the milliners' and dress-shops of the Exchange; regular targets of rakes' attentions.

238 *None to a gentleman for*: there's no-one to equal a gentleman when you want.

262 *last*: lowest, meanest. So Q1; some editors prefer Q2's 'least'.

269 *since—before*: so Q1; the dash probably represents a pause for greater emphasis ('especially since he says it to your face') rather than an interruption of her thought.

299–300 *Fortune fools*: proverbially, 'Fortune favours fools'.

320 *friends*: alluding to the proverb 'Kiss and be friends'.

declaration: Sparkish unwittingly invokes the legal meaning of the word: a formal statement of grievance or complaint.

328 *frank and free*: (1) sincere, unreserved, and (2) generously trusting (a set phrase).

331 *menial*: belonging to the household, so 'intimate' or 'one of the family'.

338 *the first day*: at a première.

349–50 *canonical gentleman*: clergyman; a jocular cliché.

357 *Must, sir?*: Q1 has 'Sir—' (as at l. 359); Harcourt probably begins to draw his sword, sheathing it during his next speech.

457 *this*: this same kind of.

512 *legion*: multitude; alluding to Christ's casting out of the unclean spirit, who declares 'My name is legion, for we are many' (Mark 5: 9).

516 S.D. *oranges and dried fruit*: figs, dates, and prunes were imported from the Eastern Mediterranean. Horner's present is lavish and meaningful; an orange-woman in the theatre normally arranged an assignation under cover of a gift of fruit from a gallant to a lady in the audience.

525 *squeezed my orange*: colloquially, 'enjoyed my woman'.

526 *City patience*: the forbearance of a City husband suffering cuckoldom in silence.

536 *I hope*: Pinchwife now pulls his wife towards the 'street' door, and so is out of earshot when Sir Jasper calls Horner his 'eunuch'; but Mrs Pinchwife won't leave before she has stowed away her presents in the unfamiliar reaches of her male disguise.

555 *strapper—*: a well-built, robust woman; the word often implies sexual vigour. Q1's dash suggests a rather physical leave-taking.

4.1.1 *Well—*: another of Q1's pauses for stage-business: Lucy puts the last touches to Alethea's dress and (as in the 1993 RSC production) her coiffure and jewellery.

4 *second-hand grave*: reopened for a second burial.

41–2 *arrant natural to*: absolute born fool compared to.

68 *high sheriff*: a Crown appointee, with (at least nominally) heavy and tying responsibilities for all aspects of his county's administration.

71–2 *Lincoln's Inn . . . Mall*: three very fashionable areas, with many fine residences of the nobility and gentry. St James's Fields is the present St James's Square and neighbouring streets.

92–3 *before . . . past*: before noon. The marriage service could legally be performed only between 8 a.m. and noon.

98 *sneaking*: servile, toadying.

112 *that's all . . . for't*: that's all the proof you have.

113 *by the same token*: as circumstantial evidence, to corroborate the fact.

117 *they are . . . story*: their accounts tally.

123 *clammy palm*: a sign of lasciviousness. In the RSC production Harcourt flipped open his Bible, from which Lucy deftly extracted the proffered bribe of a bank-note.

138 *meet . . . so to do*: alluding to the Communion Service in the Anglican Book of Common Prayer: 'It is meet and right so to do'. As Ogden notes, these are the words not of the officiating priest but of the congregation— a subtle indication that Harcourt is no clergyman.

158 *'tis late*: Q1 places these words at the end of Lucy's (following) speech. They are more plausibly spoken by the urgent Sparkish. Perhaps the phrase was squeezed into the margin of the manuscript, and misinterpreted by the printer as belonging to Lucy.

163 *Ay, pray*: Q1's 'I pray' is retained by some editors. 'I' is a common spelling of 'Ay'; Lucy is adding her smirking encouragement.

4.2.9 *the house next to*: the tavern next door to.

57 *little monster*: Cupid.

90 *Then I'm satisfied*: a set formula: 'I accept your argument, that's an end of the matter'; but also 'I'm pleased to be writing'.

93 *bare 'Sir'*: 'In her innocence Margery probably provokes her husband further with the prospect of a bare sir' (Hunt).

156 *for him*: to satisfy him; just because he tells me to.

167 *a hint at bottom*: the postcript which Horner reads aloud at 4.3.281 ff.

176–8 *Here . . . given him this*: 'that' and 'this' both refer to the second letter: 'that', when in her confusion she is about to hand it to him, 'this', when she clutches it safely out of his sight. 'I had been served' = 'I'd have been in trouble, I'd have caught it.'

198 *and a frontier town*: proverbially, 'A fair wife and a frontier castle breed quarrels', where the 'castle' stands for personal honour. But Pinchwife is also directly comparing Margery to a frontier town, vulnerable to enemy infiltration and assault.

4.3.12 *pallets*: the straw mattresses in the antechambers adjoining the ladies' bedrooms, or even in the bedrooms themselves, slept on by the chambermaids whose roles Horner is taking over.

16 *squab*: chubby; *OED* has a single late seventeenth-century quotation with the sense 'quiet, shy', which would also be relevant.

23 *giving*: giving grounds for.

24 *kept player*: see note to 2.1.347–9.

24–5 *pulpit comedian*: hypocritical chaplain—the stock joke once again; 'comedian' is simply 'actor', not necessarily a comic one.

31 *screen*: the quack probably uses the most forward of the wings, or the proscenium arch, to conceal himself.

46 *I don't understand you*: because in her hard-headed way she sets no store by the language of romance.

48-9 *to a younger brother*: since the elder brother normally inherited the estate, the impoverished younger one would find talk of money painful.

79 *buying china?*: an activity fashionable since the early years of the seventeenth century.

86 *pies and jays*: idle chatterers (like noisy magpies) and fops (jays, as well as being noisy, have colourful plumage).

87 *forbidden fruit*: proverbially 'Forbidden fruit is sweet (or sweetest)'.

100-1 *Why, d'ye think*: either 'Why, would you believe it?' or possibly (since Q1 has no comma after 'Why') 'What do you think!'

109-10 *plain . . . jewel*: blunt (or honest) speaking is a precious thing (proverbial).

173 *Biddy*: diminutive of Bridget.

174 *as ever . . . voice*: an Italian castrato singer. Such singers could be heard in London at private concerts and in the theatre.

180-1 *prettiest pictures*: of the imported kind referred to at 1.1.84.

182 *toiling and moiling*: a set phrase, = labouring, working hard. 'Moil' is often used for drudging in wet and muddy conditions.

218 *that remedy . . . torment*: proverbially, 'The remedy is worse than the disease'.

220-1 *picture in little*: a portrait miniature.

255 *kiss me*: kissing between men was restricted to very intimate friends, and was considered rather frenchified.

261 *all one . . . wont*: 'just the same with one another as we used to be'; 'all one' echoes the sound (but not the sense) of the preceding 'alone'.

262-3 *as shy . . . Locket's*: the wealthy City dignitary suspects that the polite courtier seeks a loan (which he may never repay), or an introduction to his wife.

284 *squirrel*: a fashionable pet.

292 *art thou*: you are indeed.

311 *reason*: (1) sense (Horner is being giddily facetious), and (2) satisfaction.

315-16 *you have mistaken . . . man*: playing on the literal sense—'you've got the wrong person'—and the formula used to threaten or challenge to a duel, i.e. 'I'm not the person to tolerate an insult'.

325 *No . . . hinder me*: with a disbelieving glance at Pinchwife's sword.

337 *you*: the dashes in Q1 after 'you' and 'welcome' (l. 339) probably represent Horner's mockingly formal bow, answered by Pinchwife's curt nod.

345 *love you*: a dramatically justified misquotation; the letter has 'love me', which would sound odd on the Quack's lips.

350 *Grand Signior*: the Sultan of Turkey.

351 *that I say*: 'that's what I say', answering Horner's 'What say'st thou to't?'

360 *all the Common Prayer*: the full form of the marriage service, as prescribed in the Book of Common Prayer.

365 *Thy wedding?*: Horner knows already that Sparkish is to marry Alethea (1.1.329 ff.), but Wycherley now needs to give Pinchwife reason to suspect that Horner is interested in her.

371 *any ill by her?*: anything to her discredit; 'by' also = 'brought about by', as in Horner's response.

408 *over the pale . . . briars*: 'pale' = fence; figuratively, a moral boundary, as in 'to leap the pale', to indulge in extravagant, licentious behaviour. 'Out of the briars' = out of danger, trouble, or a predicament.

4.4.53–4 *first stake of love*: the first round in the love-game.

56 [*PINCHWIFE*]: Q1's '*Mrs. Pin.*' must be an error. Pinchwife is giving the orders, and Q1's dash after 'No' suggests that, as in the RSC production, he pushes Sparkish away.

68 *comes with a fear*: being afraid of it helps to bring it on.

73–4 *now you . . . concerned*: now that it concerns you too, as a married man.

78 *breeds for her*: he grows his cuckold's horns before she gives birth to the illegitimate child, and as a direct result of her illicit behaviour.

5.1.38 *She might think*: she must have thought.

84 *yet*: as yet, at the moment.

109 *Come . . . up*: Pinchwife leads her to the door. She passes in front of him, as if to go in. But as he releases her hand, and reaches for the door-knob and key, she dodges round behind him, ready to be led away as Alethea.

111 *for*: instead of.

5.2.17 *cracked . . . for 'em*: (1) ruined himself by extending credit to courtiers, and (2) lost his good name by being cuckolded.

33 *Pshaw!*: Horner expresses disgust and annoyance, assuming that Pinchwife has brought him a prostitute.

81–2 *we are talking of*: 'that we were discussing earlier'—at the beginning of the scene. 'Were talking' would be more intelligible to an audience. The present tense, and Horner's use of the same phrase at l. 32, before Pinchwife's entry, suggest that we have here an unrevised vestige of a first draft, in which Sir Jasper appeared immediately after the cuckold topic had been aired.

92 *knot, gang*: both words mean group or band, but 'knot' was especially used of conspirators, and 'gang' of drinking companions.

5.3.1 S.D. *the letter*: the one completed by Margery (in 5.1) with Alethea's name.

26 *by that time*: just as soon as.

34 *a gentleman . . . town*: a set phrase, usually commendatory.

38 *by*: to judge from.

72 *servant, servant*: the second 'servant' is either mockingly ceremonious (accompanied by an excessively deep bow), or, as Ogden suggests, it sarcastically emphasizes that Sparkish is no longer her 'servant', i.e. lover, admirer. In the RSC production Sparkish, having furiously spat at Alethea, concluded his speech with an obscene gesture.

5.4 S.D. *[Chairs,] . . . bottles*: The table and chairs are already in place—'discovered' when the scene changes. The ladies enter carrying bottles of wine, fruit, etc. As they bustle in from one side of the stage, Horner, taken by surprise, enters from the bedroom on the opposite side.

2 *new—*: so Q1, the dash indicating either business (he adjusts his clothes?) or that he pauses before deciding how to label Mrs Pinchwife.

22–3 *for truth . . . found*: proverbially 'There is truth in wine'; people speak sincerely when they've had a drink.

42–3 *lay't on . . . shape*: go to it, and never mind our figures (Revels).

49 S.D. *[Drinks]*: the drinking-scene begins with the passing round of a single brimming goblet.

55 *as it were*: what amounts to the same thing.

57 *French chirurgeon*: a specialist in the treatment of syphilis; cf. 1.1.22–3, and note.

71 *neat*: trim, attractive without being showy; perhaps also, free from infection.

79 *common house*: (1) public restaurant, and (2) brothel.

97 *a duck, or rabbit*: the flesh of wildfowl and rabbits being superior in flavour to that of farm-reared creatures.

125 *you allow . . . say?*: you'll permit me to speak frankly?

139 *receivers*: officials appointed to receive money; here, servants (especially chambermaids) who expect bribes.

140 *to pass your grants*: to go beyond the formal approval you grant to your admirers, and to make love to you.

141 *hearts*: punning on the suit of cards.

142–4 *for your honour . . . takes up*: in exchange for the reputation ('your honour') which you commit to your gallant's keeping, he pledges his word (his honour) to obtain credit with the shopkeeper, who will not be slow to demand payment. So your gallant, paying for all your expensive purchases (to take up = to buy wholesale), pays handsomely for the privilege of lifting up your skirts.

150 *telling-ripe*: ready to be told the secret.

174 *Harry Common*: Harry is Horner's first name (see 1.1.256); 'Common' = stud, on the analogy of 'common woman' = prostitute; cf. Dol Common in Jonson's *The Alchemist*.

219 *weak place*: poorly fortified town.

236 *I am . . . to speak*: it's only that I'm rather reluctant to intervene.

249 *a Christmas pie*: a mince-pie, Sparkish's substitute for the proverbial green cheese.

270 [*HARCOURT*]: 'Hor.' (Q1), but the speaker must be Harcourt, the 'him' of Horner's next speech.

319 *Soh!*: either an expression of contemptuous disgust at being interrogated by this silly cuckold, or (in view of Lucy's offer of help) the desperate sigh of the cornered man.

320 *her . . . she*: Mrs Pinchwife.

330–1 *man of conduct*: skilful manager of affairs (= 'you clever fellow'), perhaps punning on 'conduct' as the leading or escorting of Margery to Horner.

346 *a censorious world*: scornfully harking back to Lady Fidget's words at 4.3.57–8.

359–60 *They'll swear . . . apoplexy*: doctors will perjure themselves (for a fee) to hush up fatal injuries inflicted in duels. Duelling, though not uncommon, was against the law, and a combatant could expect no pardon if his opponent died. 'Apoplexy' was loosely used for haemorrhaging.

386 S.D. *Dorilant . . . Mrs Pinchwife*: an opportunity for comic dumbshow, as Dorilant tries to persuade Mrs Pinchwife that she must somehow be mistaken about recent events in Horner's bedroom, and that, if she's looking for a lover, he, Dorilant, is the better man. Alternatively, Dorilant has begun to suspect the truth (like Sparkish in the preceding scene), and seeks confirmation from an expert witness.

408–9 *Doctor . . . maskers?*: we have been given no indication that the Quack might bring along a troupe of masked dancers. (Horner's vague invitation, 'Doctor, anon you too shall be my guest' (5.2.105) hardly qualifies as a hint to the audience.) But no other character on stage can plausibly introduce the dancers. Wycherley probably hoped that the audience would not notice his sleight-of-hand.

421 S.D. *A dance of cuckolds*: the dancers could wear head-dresses of horns, as in the 1977 National Theatre production, and dance (as Weales suggests) to the traditional, well-known, and sprightly tune 'Cuckolds all a-row' (for which see Simpson, 146).

425 *First . . . despised*: Q1 has no final *Exeunt*. It would be appropriate for the characters to remain on stage: Horner's last speech leads directly into the theme of the Epilogue, and his presence would give point to ll. 23–4, where his phrase 'women's men' is picked up. The presence on stage of the female characters would similarly reinforce the final line of the Epilogue.

Epilogue
  Mrs Knepp: playing Lady Fidget. So Q2; Q1 has 'Mr Hart', but the resounding last line could only be uttered by Lady Fidget.

 3 *if in place where*: 'if you were in the right place' (a set phrase).

 4 *'Come out'*: (1) 'leave the theatre with me', and (2) engage, as in a duel.

15 *buckram maidenheads*: figments of the boasters' imaginations. Wycherley alludes to Shakespeare's *1 Henry IV*, 2.2 and 2.4: having robbed a group of travellers, Falstaff and his gang are in turn robbed of their booty by their 'friends', Poins and the Prince. Later, Falstaff excuses his cowardice by a story of a valiant fight against 'eleven buckram men', i.e. men wearing protective suits of stiffened cloth or coarse linen. More literally (and bawdily) 'buckram maidenheads' would in any case resist the attempts of these fumbling 50-year-old braggarts.

22 *Flanders mares*: (1) finely built and costly horses, used for drawing coaches, and (2) expensively dressed mistresses.

27 *kiss the cards*: a piece of modish gallantry.

The Plain Dealer

Title-page
  The Plain Dealer: someone free from dissimulation and subterfuge, straightforward and downright in dealings with others. Several proverbs current in the seventeenth century are relevant: 'Plain dealing is a jewel' (to which is frequently appended 'but they that use it die beggars'); 'Plain dealing is praised more than practised'; 'Plain dealing is dead, and died without issue' (i.e. we now live in an age of hypocrisy).

  Ridiculum . . . res: 'Generally speaking, a joke can decide important issues more efficiently and more satisfactorily than severity': Horace, *Satires* I. x. 14–15. Either (1) the play's comic satire on hypocrisy, abuses in the legal system, etc., is more effective than a grave, moral denunciation would be, or (2) Manly, the humourless plain dealer, goes about things the wrong way.

[Dedicatory Epistle]
  my Lady B——: 'Lady' or 'Mother' Bennett, proprietress of a well-known London brothel.

1 *favour*: (1) sexual satisfaction, and (2) syphilis; the first of a string of *double entendres*.

6 *out*: to the end.

15 *great, noble*: Q1 has initial capital letters, for ironic emphasis.

29 *in spite . . . teeth*: notwithstanding his denial (proverbial phrase).

35 *hanging*: rape carried the death penalty.

40 *not the first day*: not even at the opening performance, before its subject-matter was known, and when no one could have accused you of prurience.

42 *as Mr . . . his*: in Buckingham's *The Rehearsal* (1672) the playwright Bays (alias Dryden) claims that 'my play is my touchstone': those who praise it reveal (of course) their good sense and judgement (3.1).

44 *'touchstone'*: a word to set dirty minds to work; Weales cites 'touch-trap' and 'touch-hole' as slang for penis and vagina respectively.

52 *procurement*: contrivance, with a play on sexual procuring.

58 *watermen*: Thames boatmen, notorious for hurling scurrilous jokes at river passengers, who usually took them in good part and replied in kind.

62 *to halves*: perfunctorily, ineffectually.

69–70 *Nihil . . . sumunt*: 'There is nothing to equal the effrontery of those women who are caught in the act; their very guilt endues them with anger and arrogance': Juvenal, *Satires* vi. 284–5. The lines are very relevant to Olivia's behaviour in 5.1.

88–9 *Elles . . . règle*: in Montaigne (*Essais*, iii. 5, first publ. 1588) it is men (not women) who 'send their consciences to the brothel, and keep their countenances prim and proper'. Montaigne is protesting against lying and dissembling; he himself will be open and sincere.

97–8 *like our plantations . . . women*: among those transported to labour in the plantations of North America and the West Indies were whores, vagrants, and thieves.

101 *your own*: the plain truth about yourself; the phrase usually implied an unpalatable truth.

102 *communicative*: (1) accessible, sociable, and (2) passing on venereal disease.

107–8 *jilted . . . lives*: continually deceived for the rest of their lives.

108–9 *unbewitched*: the widowers are not infatuated and lured into second marriages, but satisfy their desires in the brothel.

115 *like blowing . . . fire*: in the Great Fire of 1666, and in subsequent conflagrations (including that in January 1672 which destroyed the

Theatre Royal), houses were demolished by gunpowder to check the spread of the flames.

115–17 *Nimirum . . . extinguitur*: 'Undoubtedly incontinence is necessary to secure continence; fire is put out by fire': Tertullian, *De Pudicitia* [On Chastity], I. xvi—but Wycherley's source (including the misquotation: 'extinguitur' for Tertullian's 'extinguetur' (will be put out)) is the Montaigne essay from which he has already quoted.

121 *French authors*: Corneille and Racine furnished their published plays with critical prefaces.

128 *fraternity of Parnassus*: the brotherhood of writers.

129 *may go*: be offered, and accepted, as payment.

liberties: domains, with a pun on 'liberty' as licence, immoral conduct.

for guineas: in place of guineas. A guinea (a gold coin then worth twenty shillings, or a modern pound) was the price of one of Mother Bennett's girls (l. 153); a short poem might be sold for as little as sixpence (2.5p).

134 *playhouses*: playwrights were normally offered free admission.

141 *dunghill*: territory, i.e. the theatre. Proverbially, 'The cock is master (or is bold) on its own dunghill.'

146 *lead by the nose*: easily make a fool of (a proverbial phrase).

147–8 *the Scythian . . . him*: another borrowing from Montaigne's essay, which is much concerned with the 'natural violence' of female desire. The Scythian women blinded their male slaves and prisoners of war 'so as to use them more freely and privately'.

154–5 *lie . . . house*: stay the night free of charge—but the servants would expect handsome tips.

157–9 *which in . . . allowance*: it was widely believed that the brothels in Rome were authorized by the Pope, and contributed to the revenue of the Vatican.

176–7 *Après . . . vertue*: 'After pleasure comes pain [*peine* is also suffering, remorse, penalty], and after pain, virtue.' The lines are probably proverbial, or from a popular song, and the 'solid [serious and scholarly] French author' a joke.

The Persons

2 *Dutch War*: presumably the Third (and most recent) Dutch War, 1672–4.

22 *Letice*: abbreviation of Letitia.

Prologue

1 *act*: Q1 has 'Act' (as also in l. 40), the initial capital giving extra emphasis to the verb; Manly's role is a theatrical artefact, with no parallel in the outside world.

6 *faint . . . damn*: a crisp variant of the proverb 'Faint praise is disparagement'.

26 *limning*: writing truthful character-sketches; a limner is a painter specializing in portraits.

29 *too, here*: here (in the theatre) also.

30 *Lely's*: the studio of Peter (later Sir Peter) Lely (1618–80), the fashionable portrait painter; his sitters included aristocratic beauties, and the admirals involved in the Second Dutch War, shown holding their commanders' batons ('truncheons').

36 *men . . . age*: smart, well-to-do young men (a set phrase).

38 *only . . . just*: faithful only to social forms.

50 *friends at court*: people with influence; proverbially, 'A friend in court is better than a penny in purse'.

1.1 s.d. *Plausible*: flattering, smoothly ingratiating.

10–11 *tug on . . . behind*: 'dragging a load, like a horse in a team, and (in the usual fashion) servilely following its leader'; 'faction' is (1) an approved course of conduct, and (2) a clique. 'Kissing behind' alludes to the phrase 'kiss my arse' = show humble respect.

69 *I know . . . think*: I can't detect your real thoughts (whether you would find me tiresome or not) under your veil of politeness.

93–4 *those that get . . . hulls*: Charles II made presents of obsolete or badly damaged naval vessels to court officials and others, who could then sell them for scrap.

95 *almost to a longboat*: the ship's longboat was a large rowing-boat, stowed on board and used for trips to shore and between vessels; l. 133 below suggests that it was not always kept in good repair. So: 'until the ship is dismasted and leaking, virtually reduced to the condition of a longboat'.

122 *out of any discontent?*: 'away from all sources of vexation': Manly's natural element is irritable dissatisfaction.

123–4 *an old tarpaulin . . . captain*: the Third Anglo-Dutch War had brought to a head the antagonism between professional seafaring captains ('tarpaulins') and 'gentlemen-captains' (derided as 'butterfly captains'), often young and inexperienced, but well-connected; with influential patrons at court they were able to secure 'good voyages', carrying plate and other valuables, and with opportunities for lucrative trading. Wide-legged and beribboned pantaloons, modish in town, would be impractical on board ship.

127 *a new . . . hats*: sailors received their pay in their hats.

131 *no near!*: the command to the helmsman, if the ship was in danger of being driven on to rocks, to steer no nearer the wind; Manly's temper has to be carefully watched.

135 S.D. *Freeman*: his name suggests one who is easygoing and outgoing, open-minded and spontaneous.

141 *hob*: games of quoits were popular with sailors; perhaps here a kind ơ chuck-farthing.

160 *as ill . . . horse*: a stock joke against sailors.

209 *latitudinarian*: a tolerant and liberal-minded churchman, not discriminating against fellow-worshippers on narrow doctrinal grounds; Freeman will accept anyone as a so-called friend.

253 *bought his employment*: military commissions were normally purchased.

261 *hired*: the aristocratic poetaster ('the scribbler of honour') merely puts his name to a ghost-writer's production.

283 *doctors differ*: 'There are two ways of looking at it'; a jocular tag ('doctors' = divines, learned theologians).

286–7 *Exchange . . . Whitehall*: the 'people' are, respectively, merchants, lawyers, and courtiers.

288–9 *rehearse . . . dance*: in Act 5 of *The Rehearsal*, Bays directs a 'grand dance'—a medley of ill-assorted characters—to be staged, as part of his new dramatic spectacular. As Smith notes, 'rehearse' (= repeat) alludes to the title of Buckingham's burlesque.

290 *door-keeper*: a great man's porter had absolute power to admit or refuse a visitor.

291 *jack-chain*: the heavy chain used to turn the kitchen roasting-jack; sneeringly applied, with its menial associations, to the gold chain worn by an alderman as a badge of office.

314 S.D. *Fidelia*: the name connotes faithfulness and sincerity; some seventeenth-century romances have a Fidelia as their heroine.

316 *volunteer*: as opposed to a 'pressed' or conscripted sailor.

328 *Fame . . . liar*: 'fame' = gossip, rumour; proverbially, 'Common fame is a liar.'

332 *cushion-bearer*: toadying sycophant; literally, a servant who looks after the great man's physical comfort.

333 *probation sermons*: preached as show-pieces by candidates for ecclesiastical offices or church livings.

339–40 *purser . . . place?*: since the purser dealt with the ship's accounts, a fraudulent one could easily line his pockets; the job was worth purchasing.

360 *coffee-house . . . writer*: writers of news-sheets frequented coffee-houses in search of material; they were likely therefore to print gossip and misinformation.

384–5 *like two . . . another*: proverbially, 'One knife whets another.'

388–9 *seaman's . . . Office*: the Navy Office, near Tower Hill, handled official Admiralty business, including claims for the payment of bounties to widows and orphans of seamen.

389 *Blackacre*: a plot of ground; an arbitrary or fictitious name used in legal cases.

399 *Norfolk*: Norfolk men were proverbially contentious and litigious.

401 *Easter term*: one of the four law-terms during which the courts sat; it began on the seventeenth day after Easter.

406 *Inns of Chancery*: eight hostels, affiliated to the Inns of Court, providing accommodation for law-students and junior members of the legal profession.

410 S.D. *mantle*: the widow's loose, sleeveless cloak is both outdoor wear (she is a 'woman of business') and the nearest she can get to a lawyer's gown.

426–7 *Chancery . . . law*: Chancery Lane is close to the Inns of Court; 'towards the law', an archaic set phrase, means engaged in legal practice, connected with the law. The women are probably shopkeepers selling law-books, legal stationery, etc.

441 *seamstress*: the stock joke that seamstresses are the easiest pick-ups.

449 *John-a-Stiles*: 'John who dwells by the stile': a fictitious name for a party in a law-case.

451 *one*: already an hour past his normal dinner-time.

456–70 *There are first: Fitz, Pere, and Ayle . . . the per*: Fitz, Pere, and Ayle are law-French for son, father, and grandfather. The convoluted case concerns Ayle's rightful possession in perpetuity ('seised in fee') of a piece of land (Blackacre), and his subsequent dispossession by John-a-Stiles. Ayle begins proceedings for repossession, during which Stiles dies. Pere then resumes ownership (re-enters), which suggests that Stiles had taken possession on his behalf. But it is Fitz who actually moves in (enters). Ayle, to remove Fitz, brings a writ 'in the *post*', alleging that Fitz is a false claimant without original right to the property, and with no connection to Stiles, the deceased dispossessor. Pere meanwhile moves a writ 'in the *per*', against his own son as the heir to the dispossessor (himself). But Pere could proceed by a simple writ of entry; for those really in the know, Wycherley may be indicating that the Widow's legal expertise is shakier than she thinks. Most of the audience, admittedly, would have thought it all gibberish. (At l. 470 Q1 has 'Pere', which Q2 corrects.)

481 *Master's*: the twelve Masters in Chancery, headed by the Master of the Rolls, were assistants to the Lord Chancellor.

495–6 *livery . . . turf*: 'livery of seisin' (commonly corrupted to 'livery and . . .') is the ceremonial transfer of property rights. The vendor hands over the deeds and a representative bit of the property (e.g. a piece of turf). The Widow herself should dig the turf; 'Jerry's inaccuracy makes possible the *double entendre*' (Weales).

496 *watch your waters*: 'keep a close eye on you': from the diagnostic inspection of a patient's urine.

514–15 *by the way*: in the course of his voyage to the East Indies.

575–6 *French maxim*: not traced.

2.1.15 *talked . . . man*: linked in gossip with some particular man (Smith).

18–19 *And if . . . tells*: the chambermaid might spread gossip to get her own back on an ungenerous mistress; a not-very-veiled threat.

23 *aversion*: with the meaning 'object of repugnance', *aversion* was a newly fashionable word.

76 *trusting . . . widow*: her late shopkeeper husband has allowed courtiers and court hangers-on to run up credit for clothes, jewels, or whatever, and has died a bankrupt; a sardonic stock joke.

77 *Holborn*: an unfashionable, shabby district.

90–1 *dreams . . . contrary*: proverbially, 'Dreams go by contraries', while almanacs notoriously make wrong predictions. Dutch news-sheets, particularly during the recent war, were derided as very untrustworthy, minimizing their own losses, etc.

123–4 *rail at . . . ill of*: the proverbial injunction is 'Speak well of the dead.'

149 S.D. [*Exeunt . . . Servants*]: Q1 provides no exit for Letice, though she re-enters at l. 655. This seems the best moment for her to leave the stage (shooing out the other servants once the company has been settled), as in the 1988 RSC production.

166–7 *old Grecian . . . banquets*: an Egyptian custom, described by Herodotus; at the end of a great feast ('banquets' = desserts) an attendant would carry in an effigy of a corpse in a coffin, as a *memento mori*. Wycherley's source was probably Montaigne, *Essais*, i. 20.

168–9 *eating with . . . Libertine*: in Act 5 of Thomas Shadwell's recent drama *Don John, or, the Libertine Destroyed* (1675), based on the Don Juan story, Don John's servant Jacomo is terrified when the statue of his master's victim invites his murderer to dine at his tomb. In the final scene ghosts offer Don John, and the still terrified Jacomo, glasses of blood instead of dinner.

196 *City bride*: overdressed, to display her father's mercantile wealth.

206 *Mr Lely's*: see Prologue, note to l. 30.

226 *taking . . . mouth*: depriving someone of a living by fierce competition (proverbial).

250 *fop-corner*: probably one of the side-boxes nearest the stage: spectators there would be easily seen, and heard, by the rest of the audience; or

perhaps the 'wits' row', a bench at the front of the pit occupied by would-be wits and critics.

275 S.D. *kisses him*: it was usually only fops, aping French fashion, who would kiss one another in front of mixed company.

315 *City security*: being of sufficient wealth and standing to act as surety for another in business dealings; a set phrase.

323-4 *at the back-end . . . coach*: as a mere lackey; footmen rode on the platform at the rear of their master's coach.

329 *conventicle gallant*: a conventicle is a nonconformist meeting-house (often a private residence); so Lady Goodly's is not frequented by true worshippers of fashion. Plausible, placing the adjective 'gallant' after its noun, in the French manner, probably gives it a French pronunciation.

353 *Gridelin*: French *gris-de-lin* (flax-grey), an indeterminate pastel shade, usually grey tinged with purple; it implies a poor complexion and an insipid personality.

363 *As proud . . . wife*: claiming social precedence in the community.

380 *after the first day*: after the première, when the play's bawdiness had become common knowledge.

388 *over-captious*: so Q2; Q1 has 'over-conscious'. Wycherley may have used the spelling 'capscious', and the compositor may have misread it as 'conscious' (though Wycherley's 'p's are very distinctive). 'Over-captious' is certainly the right adjective for the censorious 'fool'. But 'over-conscious' (revealing a too obviously guilty knowledge, aware of something naughty) exactly fits the 'lady' who appears later in the sentence (l. 390), and the phrase 'an over-conscious lady' would nicely balance 'an over-captious fool'. Perhaps 'over-conscious' was an after-thought, inserted in the margin of the manuscript, and misinterpreted by the compositor of Q1 as a replacement for 'over-captious'.

393 *white and red*: face-powder and rouge, the latter used on the lips as well as on the cheeks.

408 *Horner*: the cuckold-maker who has himself reported impotent in order to accomplish his sexual ends. Horner's name signifies that he produces horns on other men's heads; Olivia in effect re-names him 'Horned'. Like Lady Fidget, she thinks Horner's 'very name obscenity' (*CW*, 2.1.570).

430 *china*: in the notorious 'china scene' of *CW* (4.3), 'china' stands for love-making, sexual potency, male sperm, etc.

438-9 *pictures . . . countries*: erotic and pornographic prints, particularly those associated with the name of Aretino; cf. *CW*, 1.1.84-5 and note.

442 *put . . . conceit*: make me displeased.

462 *rhyme*: the serious heroic plays of the period were written in rhyming pentameter couplets; with very rare exceptions, prose was the norm for

comedy. Only Mr Novel could propose a rhymed version of *CW* (Smith).

469–70 *outcasts . . . shops?*: (1) in their tawdry finery they resemble heaps of dressmakers' scraps, and (2) even seamstresses, not notably choosy, reject them as lovers.

471–4 *Faith . . . men only*: Freeman quotes Manly's words from 1.1.559 ff.

494 *doing his business*: getting himself seriously wounded, and so proving himself a hero.

496 *the staff . . . France*: the commander-in-chief's baton.

497 *gazette*: the *London Gazette* carried reports of naval battles during the Dutch Wars, with details of officers killed and wounded in action.

506 *fanatical hatred*: the hatred of a religious 'fanatic' or dissenter, specifically a Quaker; being no respecter of rank or birth, a Quaker would decline to remove his hat in any man's presence.

517 *Thames Street!*: on the north bank of the river, between Blackfriars and the Tower of London; the site of Billingsgate fish market, and numerous warehouses and wharves.

520 *musk-cats*: perfumed fops (like the animals from which musk is obtained); the word was also applied to courtesans, so it suggests effeminacy and pimping.

562 *well-trimmed . . . scent of it*: a modish man's gloves would be trimmed with ribbon, lace, or fur, embroidered with gold or silver thread, and perfumed.

568–9 *red breeches . . . sword*: the usual appearance of an officer (naval or military).

570 *Thy courage . . . sword*: Novel's ornate sword-belt (probably a broad shoulder sash, embroidered, and with lace edges) is only too visible; his drawn sword is never likely to be so.

577–8 *gunpowder spot*: bluish beauty-spot, usually on the hand, produced by means of gunpowder.

578 *jewel . . . ear*: fops sometimes wore ear-studs or earrings.

599 *tailor*: proverbially timid, un-manly, and small of stature.

600 *training day*: the citizen militia trained and drilled usually four times a year.

607 *Bartholomew Fair*: a two-week-long carnival held at Smithfield, London, in late August, with acrobats, jugglers, mountebanks, etc; synonymous with crude entertainments.

622–3 *you presume . . . urge me*: either 'in provoking me you know that your effeminacy will shield you', or 'you count on your effeminacy to make me hold my hand' ('to urge' can mean to constrain or restrain).

630–1 *your respect to her*: your self-respect in her eyes.

637–8 *we'll go . . . bedchamber*: following the aristocratic French custom of entertaining company at cards and conversation in a lady's bedroom.

639 *Captain*: not simply sneering at a naval captain's rough manners; the title 'captain' was sometimes assumed by rakes and bully-boys.

642 *my windows*: a jilted lover might thus revenge himself, implying that his mistress was no better than a whore; smashing the windows of brothels and prostitutes' lodgings was a common sport of rakes and rowdies.

643 *suburb . . . Tower*: 'suburb' was equivalent to 'red-light district'. The riverside areas east of the Tower of London (e.g. Wapping and Limehouse) were full of sailors.

647 *for*: as for.

655 S.D. *Enter Letice*: Smith suggests that Olivia has coolly summoned her during the climax of Manly's tirade.

701 *there's no . . . destiny*: a common Restoration formula: cf. the proverbs 'No flying from fate', and 'Destiny may be deferred, not prevented'.

S.D. *Aside*: placed at the end of the speech in Q1, as if applying to the whole of it. But Q1's long dash after 'woman' suggests that Manly turns furiously away from Olivia at that point, having delivered his first bitter words directly to her.

738 *disappointments*: either the gallant will fail to keep his assignations, or his performance will disappoint her when he does.

753–7 *being made . . . at least*: being captured by love, which like a pirate ship makes its attack under cover of a false (friendly) flag; when, endeavouring to escape, you have run your ship aground and wrecked it, the nimble pirate ship ('picaroon') pulls away, turning into the wind ('luffing') to avoid the same fate. So love captivates ('takes you') by a show of affection, but the false woman ('picaroon' is slang for cheat and whore) leaves you as soon as you have spent all your money on her. In either case your ruin saves you from enslavement—the corsairs of North Africa made galley-slaves or domestic servants of their prisoners.

765 *an end . . . suits*: because a married woman was unable to bring legal actions in her own name (cf. 5.2.455 ff.).

768 S.D. *Oldfox*: a crafty old man, but also an ex-military man: an 'oldfox' is an old-fashioned, broad-bladed sword.

770–1 *for the last . . . in law*: having just met Manly off-stage, the Widow has served him a second time with her subpoena. But the first 'service' (at 1.1.477) was perfectly valid, despite Manly's having thrown the subpoena away. Once again, the Widow's legal knowledge seems faulty.

781 *a younger brother*: the elder brother would normally inherit the entire family estate, leaving the younger one short of money and on the look-out for a lucrative marriage.

795 *no person*: either Oldfox is about to say that she is no person to be trifled with (his next two speeches are similarly capped by Freeman); or the Widow is no 'person' in the contemptuous sense which the word sometimes had—the heavy-handed quibble would be typical of Oldfox.

797–8 *arm her*: escort her, take her arm.

803 *turned red breeches*: an officer's cast-off trousers, repaired or altered, and now worn by the sort of rake who called himself 'captain'.

a broad back: sexually vigorous, lusty—a common euphemism.

816 *ann'... prim'*: 'in the eleventh year of Charles I's reign', i.e. 1636. The Widow spontaneously employs the language used to date legal statutes. She claims to be 40; in what follows Wycherley establishes her age as about 45.

818 *very servant*: true and faithful admirer (archaic).

824–5 *How appears*: Q1 begins a new line with these words, giving room for some comic business; the Widow perhaps consults a law-book, or signals to Jerry to produce one from his bags.

826 *time out of mind*: from time immemorial (proverbial).

830–1 *widow's ... equity*: 'whether she judges by strict legal canons, or looks on me more tolerantly'; equity involves recourse to general principles of justice, allowing them to modify or soften the actual provisions of the law.

833–4 *snap up ... first*: 'seize and devour (like a bird of prey) this tender morsel now, once and for all'. A 'snap' is also a cheat, and snap up can mean speak snappishly to, 'shut him up'.

862 *scorched trencher*: wooden platter, heated for use as a bed-warmer.

863 *Scotch warming-pan*: jocular tavern slang for 'a wench to go to bed with'. A traveller in Scotland (so the story went) asked for his bed to be warmed; the chambermaid obligingly undressed and got into it.

869 *peppercorn rents*: nominal rents. It was a stock complaint against guardians that they granted long leases on land and property at rents unfavourable to their young wards (Friedman).

879 *action of the case*: usually 'action upon the case', a legal process to obtain damages or restitution for wrongs not brought about by physical violence, not carrying specified penalties, and with no prescribed form of suit. Slander was one of the most frequent subjects of such actions.

896 *guineas*: gold coins, first minted 1662, as opposed to 'old gold' (l. 894), the earlier 'broad piece' or 'Carolus'. That coin, larger than the guinea, was also originally worth 20 shillings, but because of the rising price of gold had become rather more valuable.

907 *pay 'em*: reward them, with venereal disease, for an adulterous liaison.

916 *estate personal*: chattels, movable possessions.

918–19 *betwixt... Wapping*: 'from one end of London to the other': the Hercules' Pillars Tavern, near Hyde Park Corner, was at the western extremity of London's built-up area. Wapping, at the other extremity, was full of sailors' lodgings; the Boatswain may have been an actual pub, or Wycherley's apt invention. But another Hercules' Pillars, on Fleet St., was popular with lawyers: in that case Jerry would mean 'between your nautical haunts and my legal ones'.

920 *my trees*: unscrupulous guardians were commonly criticized for felling timber on their wards' estates to make a quick profit.

925 *lath-backed*: with a slender, fragile back, hence = undersexed (cf. 'broad back', l. 803 above).

926 *Norfolk*: naturally her favourite county: see 1.1.399 and note.

927 *King's Bench bar*: the goal of ambitious barristers, because, as the supreme court of common law, the King's Bench dealt with serious crimes.

935–6 *old... purchase*: a valuable estate, with the manor house thrown in to make the terms of sale particularly attractive.

3.1 S.D. *Westminster Hall*: the representation of the interior of the great hall, on the back-scene and wings, may have included painted figures of black-gowned and black-capped lawyers, and their clients. The back-scene would also have depicted some of the stalls, selling books, haberdashery, trinkets, etc., which lined the walls; the bookseller's stall could be free-standing, or (so as not to impede movement on the stage) a window-opening cut in the back-scene (cf. *CW*, 3.2, where the New Exchange scene has a similar stall).

S.D. *two Sailors*: Manly's unconventional servants from Act 1, named Tom and (predictably) Jack. In this Act their role is to assist Freeman in his love-intrigue.

6 *This... thought*: either 'those who revere the law would naturally think this place to be', or (though less likely) 'the respected members of the legal profession would have us think this place to be'.

9 *black guard*: (1) bodyguards, henchmen, usually those of a despot, e.g. the Turkish Sultan or the devil; (2) a gang of street urchins, living off their wits; (3) lawyers in their black gowns.

10–11 *own halls... time*: the Christmas Revels at the Inns of Court included feasting, dancing, and serious dice-play open to all comers.

11–17 *fools bring... old ones*: fools who come to Westminster Hall to recover money by legal process suffer the same fate as those who seek a fortune at gaming during the Revels. The gambling fools lose little by little ('drop away') their money 'on both sides', i.e. all the players lose to the 'Christmas-box' or house bank kept by the young lawyers who organize the Revels. (The comparison of the law and lawyers to a

Christmas-box, which always shows a profit, was traditional.) The litigious fools also lose 'on both sides': defendant and plaintiff alike pay legal fees into the money-boxes of the established ('old') lawyers in court.

20 *making false musters*: entering fictitious names, and/or those of absent or deceased men, on the ship's roll, so as to draw their pay and allowances.

23 *limb of it*: a 'limb of the law' was a shady or crooked lawyer, on the analogy of 'limb [agent] of Satan'.

62–3 *there's venturing . . . stealing*: stealing carried the death penalty if the value of the stolen goods exceeded one shilling.

137 *not to*: so as not to.

138 *reference*: the proposal to submit a dispute to the Masters in Ordinary of the Court of Chancery for arbitration. This 'would rob the Widow of her fun' (Smith).

140–1 *Serjeant Ploddon*: his name suggests a studious porer over legal records and law-books. As a serjeant he belongs to the highest order of barristers, distinguished by their learning, experience, and dress—a shoulder cape and hood.

145 *splitter of causes*: a lawyer who divides a case into a number of separate suits, so increasing his business and his fees.

156 *Quaint*: (1) ingenious, and (2) elaborately rhetorical.

159–60 *the decree . . . queen*: the judgement in Chancery of the Lord Chancellor (as presiding judge) in the thirty-fourth year of Queen Elizabeth (i.e. 1591/2); since none of the few recorded decrees of that year seems appropriate, this may be another joke at the expense of the Widow's bogus learning.

161 *matter of fact*: the factual aspects of a case, as distinct from matters of inference and opinion.

170 *Billingsgate*: London's principal fish-market was a byword for foul, abusive language.

191–2 *your judgement . . . ands*: the court's decision in your favour shall not be held up by your adversary's attempting to raise doubts and suspicions. 'Ifs and ands' (a set phrase) = suppositions, false expressions of doubt. If proceedings were successfully 'arrested', the case would be dismissed and the defendant acquitted.

194 *Exchequer*: the court for hearing cases involving treasury and financial matters, fines, etc.; the presiding judges were called Barons of the Exchequer.

219–20 *a brass half-crown*: a forgery; genuine half-crowns were silver.

231–2 *a cuff . . . courts*: the penalty for an act of physical violence in Westminster Hall while the courts were in session was life imprisonment and forfeiture of one's estate.

236 *the Council*: the king's Privy Council, before which certain types of legal case, e.g. involving wardships and property, might be heard.

242 *five pound fee*: a barrister's normal fee.

266–7 *who s' will*: who so will, i.e. whoever wishes to.

269 *Splitcause*: cf. 'splitter of causes', l. 145 above.

271 *Quillet, Quirk*: a quillet is a verbal quibble, and a quirk an evasive cavil or bit of hair-splitting. 'The quirks and quillets of the law' was a set phrase.

283–4 *lozenges . . . corns*: booksellers also stocked patent medicines.

291–2 *Culpeper . . . Midwife?*: taking the Widow for a midwife or bawd (or both), the boy offers her three medical treatises dealing with conception and childbirth, books also read more widely for their mildly scatological interest: Nicholas Culpeper's *Directory for Midwives* (1651); *The Problems of Aristotle*, a sixteenth-century compilation of physiological and philosophical material, and *The Compleat Midwife's Practice* (1656), by Thomas Chamberlayne and others.

293–4 *Dalton . . . Wingate*: prolific legal writers; they produced between them nearly forty standard, and regularly reprinted, guide-books and manuals of the law, collections of statutes, etc.

304 *pen*: unwittingly bawdy; 'pen' = penis in seventeenth-century slang.

305–6 *St George . . . England*: Q1 has a comma after 'or', suggesting that Jerry is quoting not two separate titles, but title and subtitle. He is confusing, and conflating, two popular works: the ballad *St George for England* (of which there were several versions), and Richard Johnson's *The Most Famous History of the Seven Champions of Christendom* (1596), in which St George heads the list of champions.

307 *The Young Clerk's Guide*: compiled by Sir Richard Hutton (1649, subsequently enlarged and reprinted); a collection of legal precedents to help the trainee attorney in conveyancing work.

318 *queen of the stage*: an actress playing royalty, but with a pun on 'quean' = whore.

320–3 *Mr What-d'y'-call-him . . . fees*: a crooked lawyer is luring the Widow into the illegal practice of champerty (l. 328)—offering her a substantial share (£500) of the proceeds of one of his cases, in return for her initial help with the legal expenses and fees. The penalty included three years' imprisonment and a fine.

349 *at age*: having attained his majority, at 21.

358 *look to themselves*: manage their own affairs.

359 *man of myself*: an independent person, my own master.

364 *Inn*: Inn of Chancery: see 1.1.406 and note.

365 *cut down my trees*: selling the timber to raise money for her dowry.

384-5 *dancing of the ropes*: dancing on tightropes, by men, women, and monkeys, was a feature of the London fairs.

398 *Jack of All Trades*: a shop selling a wide range of cheap knick-knacks.

400 *my blow at*: maintain my assault on.

411-12 *news-book secret*: an item published in a news-sheet would be no secret worth whispering.

415 *reader's dinner*: the sumptuous Inns of Court banquet held at the time of the twice-yearly 'readings' (commentaries on the statutes) given by an invited senior lawyer. The guest-list was very select; Manly's presence implies his social standing.

419 *reformed . . . Tavern*: before 1650 the sign of a tavern called The Salutation, of which London had several, would have depicted the Annunciation. The sign was 'reformed' (both redrawn and secularized) under the Puritans, to show two men politely bowing to one another.

428 *ungracious bird*: Oldfox's little joke: Jerry is graceless and wicked, the owl unlucky, boding misfortune (an archaic sense of 'ungracious').

432-3 *commodities*: (1) purchased goods, and (2) benefits, things worth having: the phrase 'all profits, commodities and advantages whatsoever' was common in legal transactions.

443 *in order to*: with regard to, so as to further.

459 *due benevolence*: (1) voluntary repayment of money, and (2) sexual satisfaction (slang).

489-90 *felo de se*: guilty of self-murder: a suicide's possessions were forfeit to the Crown.

490 *choose a guardian*: a male child whose father had died could legally do so at the age of 14.

491 *felo de ses biens*: a witty coinage by the Widow: 'committing a felony against his property and possessions, by putting them into the wrong hands'.

494 *a saying*: perhaps Wycherley's own invention.

497-8 *action . . . trover*: a writ of detinue is brought to recover goods wrongfully detained by one to whom they have been entrusted; a writ of trover, for goods which the finder refuses to relinquish.

502 *a making-water while*: a short time (more commonly 'a pissing-while').

521 *make no bones on't*: have no hesitation in doing it.

529-30 *but if . . . not*: but I suspect it was.

571 *Edgehill officer*: a veteran of the Civil War: Edgehill was its first major battle, 23 October 1642.

581 *field at Bloomsbury*: Southampton Fields (roughly the present Russell Square) was both a duelling ground and the scene of pitched battles between rival gangs; Oldfox's scar may not be very honourable.

591 *the picture of ill luck?*: an image or symbol of misfortune (proverbial).

595 *broadsword*: with a broad, heavy blade, in contrast to the fashionable small (or dress) sword.

598 *holiday captains*: splendidly accoutred, as though on holiday rather than ready for active service; or perhaps officers of the citizen militia, which normally assembled and drilled on public holidays.

599 *martinet rogues*: drilling their men according to the rigid system evolved for the French army by Lieutenant-Colonel Jean Martinet. The English army was gradually introducing more formal drill.

607–9 *for he was . . . field*: Oldfox was on both sides in the Civil War. Though on the muster-roll ('list') of the Parliamentarian army, he failed to earn his pay because he was too cowardly to fight; he was therefore in effect a supporter of the king.

616 *by your wits*: since 'great wits' proverbially have bad memories, only stupid people have good ones.

638 *go thy ways*: so Q2; Q1 has 'go this way', which is possible (Manly directs or pushes the lawyer), but awkward.

651 *in forma pauperis*: literally, in the manner of a poor man. A claimant with possessions valued at under £5 was entitled to free legal aid, with costs waived.

655 *Bumblecase*: liable to bungle his cases.

669–70 *tell me—Truth*: 'tell truth, and shame the devil' (proverb).

679 *thirty in the hundred*: charging 30 per cent interest on his loans; the maximum legal rate was 6 per cent.

680 *setter*: dog used by huntsmen to find game and drive it towards them; hence (1) pimp, and (2) agent of a con-man, marking out his victims.

684–5 *land security*: investing in property, rather than lending money or trading.

694 *'tis the better for't*: both the Second and Third Anglo-Dutch Wars were largely undertaken to suppress Dutch maritime trade.

701–2 *laced coffee*: laced with sugar or spirits or both.

708–9 *City security*: a guarantee backed by known assets.

738–9 *nick . . . mother*: win his mother from him by cunning or fraud.

742 *no herald, or poet*: the herald would draw up a handsome genealogy, devising good family connections; the poet would dedicate his next book to the great man in glowing terms (and so earn several guineas).

744 *the old philosophy*: acceptance of scriptural authority as absolute, and of Nature as a subject for metaphysical speculation only; the 'new philosophy' (particularly associated with Thomas Hobbes) was materialistic and rationalistic.

755 *common dessert*: the usual end to the meal is gambling.

756 *without going to twelve*: gamblers' slang, of uncertain meaning; perhaps 'matching the great gamblers' high stakes' (jocularly derived from the fact that twelvepence was the highest stake in certain games).

763–4 *two and thirty . . . veal*: a facetious saying (the number of bits varies), meaning that only two of the pieces of meat are actually good to eat.

764–5 *bribe pie*: perhaps a witty distortion of 'bride pie', an elaborate concoction sometimes served at weddings, consisting of several pies baked in one huge dish, the central pie containing live birds or a snake.

765 *law-French wine*: not good burgundy, but adulterated and impure wine, as law-French is a debased form of French.

766–8 *Temple Round . . . post*: the broad ambulatory of the round Temple Church contains the mutilated and time-worn effigies of thirteenth-century knights and other notables. The church, its cloisters, and the walks in the grounds of the Middle and Inner Temples were used for legal consultations, and professional perjurers and false witnesses plied there for hire. Q1 has 'Rounds', but both church and ambulatory were normally referred to as 'the Round'.

772–3 *Three . . . hall*: Westminster Hall was formerly the banqueting-room of the palace of Westminster, and English kings had held elaborate feasts there at Christmas, Pentecost, etc.; Charles II did so only at his coronation.

4.1.44 *yet?—*: the dash (as in Q1) implies business; Manly could begin to draw his sword, causing Fidelia to shrink back even as she calls him a coward.

53 *I'll kiss thee*: close comrades-in-arms, and intimate male friends, might kiss, but usually only in private.

80 *under a confinement*: either 'debarred by their parents from male company' (like Hippolyta in *GDM*), or 'shut up in a convent'.

92 *they only keep*: are the only promises they ever keep.

123 *in that nature*: in that particular way.

152–4 *Oh go . . . of it*: Q1's punctuation conveys Fidelia's anguished urgency.

183–5 *fools . . . Fortune!*: elaborating the proverbs 'Fortune favours fools', and 'Desert and reward seldom keep company'.

186 *like Fortune, are blind*: proverbially, 'Fortune is blind'.

244 *Apollo and Littelton*: poetry (of which Apollo was god and patron) and law: Sir Thomas Littelton, the eminent fifteenth-century jurist, was still the authority on property law.

246–7 *letter . . . country*: perhaps, as Friedman suggests, glancing sarcastically at the Earl of Shaftesbury's *Letter from a Person of Quality to his Friend in the Country* (1675), written in protest at discriminatory pressure against the nonconformists.

254 *Coffee-houses*: at the end of 1675 a royal proclamation ordered the closing of London coffee-houses as hotbeds of sedition and political gossip. In January 1676 a second proclamation sought to ban 'scandalous' papers from coffee-houses. There was a public outcry, and neither order was enforced; Oldfox, as usual, is behind the times.

263–4 *Inns of Chancery*: see note, 1.1.406.

270 *huckster's hands*: huckster = a grasping mercenary person; 'to be in huckster's hands' (slang) is to be in desperate straits.

285 *hot cockles*: a rustic, and mainly children's, game: one player, lying face down, or kneeling blindfolded, is struck in turn by the others, and tries to guess the identity of the striker. 'Cockles' may already have acquired the slang meaning of female genitalia; at all events, the Widow would fear what the game might lead to.

286 *though . . . behind*: even if I had shown you the humblest filial respect; cf. 1.1.10–11.

298–9 *ravishment . . . Second*: a famous statute of 1285, known as Westminster the Second, laid down severe penalties for the abduction of an heir in ward ('ravishment de gard'). The Widow is Jerry's legal guardian until he reaches the age of 21, or chooses another.

308 *squeeze wax*: place yourself under a legal obligation—by setting your seal to a document.

329 *amble . . . judges*: accompany the judges on their leisurely progress from one assize court to the next.

346–7 *bastard eigne*: the illegitimate son—born before their marriage—of her late husband and herself; eigne was pronounced 'ain'.

367 *Prerogative Court*: where cases involving disputed inheritance, wills, and probate, were heard.

375 *though*: a mild intensifier ('even the devil . . .') much used in dialect speech.

377 *Whitefriars*: run-down area between Fleet St. and the Thames, enjoying the privilege of sanctuary for criminals, and so the haunt of debtors, sharpers, bent lawyers, etc.

4.2.21 *noble*: 'Noble' (Q1), indicating a sneering emphasis.

26 *in bed . . . lady*: married to her. Wedding-guests normally saw the married couple into bed, and visited their bedroom next morning. Plausible deliberately misunderstands.

40 *of all things*: especially, above all.

46 *But the*: Q1 begins a new line with these words, giving time for Novel to take out his comb; cf. *LiW*, 3.2.95 ff.

64 *by way of ombre*: as a stake in a game of ombre which Novel has allowed Olivia to win.

102–3 *Go then . . . you of:* either Olivia is sending the boy well out of the way, east, west, and north, on pointless errands, or she is putting off her other lovers with false messages about meeting them in the royal drawing-room—as Novel has already surmised (ll. 93–4).

110 *game-cocks:* cocks bred and trained for fighting, with a bawdy reference to male organs ready for sex.

111 S.D. *Varnish:* his name (which the audience learns only at the end of the play) signifies a specious gloss or hypocritical display of virtue.

S.D. *as from a journey:* wearing a cloak or long riding-coat, boots, a short 'travelling-wig' and broad-brimmed hat.

113–14 *Your haste . . . kindness:* a variant of the proverb 'He giveth twice that giveth in a trice'.

147 *I'll lead . . . nose:* dupe him, twist him round my little finger; proverbial (cf. Epistle Dedicatory, l. 146), but here echoing Iago's harsh comment on Othello (*Othello*, 1.3.393–4).

171 *the last:* the latter, i.e. pleasure.

182–3 *like a devil in a play:* unidentified; perhaps a version of Marlowe's *Dr Faustus*—either for the public theatre or at one of the fairground booths—expanded the scene with Helen of Troy.

217 *Saracen . . . sign:* the inn-sign of the Saracen's Head (a common one in London) conventionally portrayed a large, fierce, and ugly face, with wide mouth and thick lips.

239 *for it:* for its sake.

241 *pulls . . . pillow:* a traditional way of hastening the death of an invalid.

262–3 *to be revenged . . . disappoint her:* the way to get your revenge is to disappoint her lust—by leaving.

265 *keep the door:* guard the door, as in a brothel.

285 *That . . . out?:* 'so that you must devise new tortures, not experienced by anyone else, to punish me with?' Q1's punctuation ('That, untried tortures, you . . .') is retained by many editors, but involves a clumsy change of addressee; Fidelia's complaint is to the heavens, the 'you' of the next line.

305 *run my fortune:* share my dangerous lot.

324 *spirits:* the brandy-bottle is available to revive her lovers, but also for her own secret drinking.

343 *their tattling:* the indiscreet boasting, and betraying of confidences, of the old lovers.

366 *the tables turned:* a set phrase (from the turning round of the table in backgammon) for a complete reversal of a state of affairs or relationship.

378 *to guide . . . suspicions:* to show me the escape route, so that I would avoid your suspicions.

400 *shut*: fasten securely, hinting (like Manly at l. 265) at the brothel doorkeeper.

5.1.26–7 *That you deface . . . real*: the criticism refines upon a couplet in Molière's *Le Misanthrope*, 3.4, where Célimène reports what the world says about Arsinoé. The RSC production gave heavy-handed emphasis to Eliza's comment by having her model a little nude figure in clay throughout this conversation.

85–6 *I have bespoken . . . betimes*: I have ordered supper to be postponed for a while.

103 *matter*: the space after this word in Q1 suggests a deep, half-mocking curtsey by Eliza, and Varnish's answering bow.

5.2.55 *as riches . . . gentleman*: proverbially 'Money makes a gentleman,' though 'good manners' is usually a second ingredient. 'Riches' could be singular or plural in the seventeenth century.

65 *surest*: 'sure' (Q1, first state).

73 *called*: 'call' (Q1).

74 *cocking*: strutting, cocky; Q1, first state, reads 'coaching'.

80 *grinning honour*: the honour accorded to a man killed in action. Falstaff, standing over the body of Sir Walter Blount on the battlefield of Shrewsbury, declares 'I like not such grinning honour . . . Give me life' (*1 Henry IV*, 5.3.58–9).

80–1 *never . . . honour*: because honour in the sense of worldly reputation, a good name and title, will always find succour.

87 *Nay . . . satisfied*: a set formula: 'that's an end of the matter'; there is no possibility of Freeman's serving again under Captain Manly.

88 *run the . . . fortune*: undertake the risky course of action.

158 *from me*: as though I sent you.

170 *to your teeth*: to your face, in defiant confrontation.

192 *push in guard*: make a thrust without exposing yourself to a counter-thrust, i.e. fence with care and by the book.

196 *allegory*: extended metaphor; Restoration wits generally considered allegorical writing old-fashioned (like Oldfox) and puerile.

204 *close hunks*: stingy miser.

211 *betwixt . . . exactly*: 7.30 precisely.

220 *cutting . . . hangings?*: slashing the table linen, hangings, and curtains in a tavern dining-room.

227 *breaking windows!*: cf. note on 2.1.642 above.

241 *quibbling*: playing on words was frowned on by good conversationalists.

247 *You rail . . . himself*: the satires of the Greek poet Archilochus drove one of his victims to commit suicide out of shame.

248 *satyr*: (1) satirist: Oldfox has no satirical wit, and (2) the mythological creature, part-human and part-goat, notably lustful, and often depicted as leering: Oldfox can only manage lecherous looks.

251 *fool . . . memory*: a bad memory was proverbially compensated by a strong intellect (cf. 3.1.615–16).

306 *blind, bearing office*: the cuckold's role is to shut his eyes to his fate, and passively suffer his wife's infidelities. The phrase echoes the allusion in the Dedicatory Epistle (ll. 147 ff.) to the Scythian women blinding their slaves, and also suggests the fate of Samson, betrayed by Delilah, blinded and enslaved by the Philistines.

355 *house*: tavern.

363 s.d. *Knights of the Post*: the RSC production costumed these petty crooks to resemble highwaymen, with three-cornered hats and dark grey cloaks.

408–9 *riding a widow*: (1) managing her affairs; (2) mastering, controlling her; (3) copulating with her (slang).

410–11 *like leaping . . . before*: quasi-proverbial; cf. 'A low hedge is easily leaped over.' 'Leaping' is another colloquial metaphor for copulating.

423 *acrostics*: a distinctly outmoded poetic form.

s.d. *constable*: recognizable by his staff and lantern, high-crowned hat, and long (probably grey) coat.

425–6 *gaping . . . today!*: with her mouth forced open by the gag, the Widow looks as she is yawning from fatigue.

432–4 *We arrest . . . pounds*: Q1 has initial capitals for all the significant words in this speech, suggesting the emphatic accents of officialdom.

435 *choke-bail action!*: where the sum sued for is so large that bail is unlikely to be granted.

457 *is*: not in Q1.

462 *durante beneplacito*: 'while you continue to give me satisfaction (in every sense)'. Certain high legal appointments were officially made for the 'duration of the good pleasure' of the sovereign, rather than for life.

472 *settled exhibition*: a legally protected maintenance allowance.

nag of assizes: a horse of good quality, up to standard. A mild joke, since assize regulations set trading standards for goods, but not for livestock.

473 *the common*: land belonging to the whole community, and therefore over-grazed.

473–4 *ingress . . . regress*: rights of entry, exit, and re-entry; a legal phrase.

476 *fair words . . . cabbage*: Jerry's variant of the proverb 'Fair words [mere promises] butter no parsnips'.

5.3.9 *fits*: Fidelia's pretended epilepsy (see 4.2.331 ff.).

28 *forbid*: past tense.

28–9 *I mentioned . . . came*: proverbially, 'Talk of the devil, and he is sure to appear.'

41 *happiest minute*: most opportune moment. But 'happy minute' was also a euphemism for sexual climax.

59 *there I'm right*: there *is* a lover here.

60 S.D. *runs . . . behind*: attacks him from the rear, with the sword she had earlier declined to draw in self-defence (4.2.352 ff.). The RSC production had Fidelia (without a sword) jump on Varnish's back to impede his movements.

65 *But I think . . . 'tis he*: Olivia thinks that Fidelia is victorious ('he has the better'). Groping forward in the darkness, she touches Manly's sash (see 2.1.598), mistakes it for Fidelia's, and is then convinced of the latter's success.

106 *refusal*: what she has refused or turned down; Manly had given Olivia the original refusal of his love—the right to accept or decline it.

106–7 *a sacrifice . . . love*: as a sacrificial offering on the altar of your love, my heart, tainted by my former love, would only profane it.

125–6 *vi et armis?*: forcibly (literally, by force and arms); a legal phrase, used in indictments for cases involving violence.

126 *demand . . . trover*: a demand is a legal claim for recovery of property. The Widow advises a writ of trover (see note, 3.1.498), because Novel and Plausible could be said to have found the jewels on the floor, and could be sued for wrongfully withholding them.

Epilogue

5 *sit*: (1) be in session, as judges in court, and (2) sit on the foremost benches of the auditorium, as critics in the theatre.

6 *To keep . . . term*: (1) preside in court throughout a law-term, and (2) attend the theatre regularly during the season.

12 *seamstress*: well-known to be of easy virtue.

14 *linen*: her sexual services.

16 *putting off*: (1) selling, (2) passing off fraudulently, and (3) taking off, removing.

18 *long vacation*: when the law courts are not in session, during the summer months. The London theatres were also normally closed from early June to October, so the actresses will be on the look-out for amatory engagements.

22 *Squires . . . robe*: lawyers and law-students: the latter were regular theatre-goers (cf. 3.1.316–18).

24 *templar*: a lawyer occupying chambers in the Inner or Middle Temple. Wycherley was admitted to the Inner Temple in October 1659, but never qualified.

26 *Nay*: so Q2; Q1 has 'And'.

31 *Of all loves*: a phrase of strong entreaty: 'by all that's sacred'.

GLOSSARY

à d'autres 'tell me another'

above more than; 'gone': *PD*, 5.2.358

abroad out, out of doors, out of the house (opposite to 'at home'), be seen in public

abuse deceive, laugh at, make a laughing-stock of

action acting

adad mild oath (variant of 'By God')

address skill, dexterity

admiration wondering approval, astonishment

admire marvel at, with foolish naïvety

adonde where

advice considered statement of opinion

affected with partial to; tainted with

affection partiality

again in reply, in return, back

agree make up a difference, settle a price, draw up a contract

agreeable delightfully, agreeably, suitably

ague malarial fever

alcove recessed part of bedchamber where bed is placed

alderman member of the governing body of the City of London; loosely, a City worthy or businessman

all a case exactly the same thing

all one neither here nor there, 'it amounts to the same thing', just the same

allay *n.* check; *v.* dampen, spoil one's pleasure

alley street in red-light district

allow approve

allowance toleration, approval

amuse delude

and if

anon by and by, soon

an't if it

apish affected

apostle spoons silver spoons with figures of apostles on handle-ends

appertain belong by right

appoint arrange

apprehend fear, be frightened of; grasp, appreciate

apprehension fear, suspicion, notion, understanding

apprenti apprentice

appurtenances (legal) appendages of a piece of property

arithmetical fussily precise, pedantic

arrant downright, notorious, utter

articles legal conditions and terms

as equally, suchlike

assured certain, confident

attorney lawyer empowered to draw up legal documents and prepare client's case for counsel in a court of common law

awful terrifying

babies dolls

back on the return voyage

backward back, at the back of the house

baffle perplex, hoodwink, humiliate

ball party

ballet pantomime with dancing, the subject often exotic or bizarre

banquet refreshments, especially dessert of fruit and wine

barefaced needing no concealment, not ashamed of itself

barely without corroboration, as a mere assertion

base illegitimate

basilisk fabulous reptile, half-cock, half-serpent, whose look was fatal

bate subtract from the agreement

bawd *n.* brothel-keeper, pimp, go-between; *v.* play the go-between

beakers goblets

bear endure

beastliness disgusting behaviour; monstrous shape

beat up pay an unwelcome visit, disturb

beaux garçons male escorts
become be appropriate to, suit
beef-eater pampered servant
beetle-headed dull
begar mild oath, 'By God', conventionally used by non-native speakers
behind (stage direction) speaking or watching from a place of concealment
beholding obliged
bel esprit clever fellow, wit
belie misrepresent, slander by lying
bellman town-crier patrolling streets at night and calling out the hour
bellyful one's fill; be with child
below downstairs
bespeak ask as a favour, order, book
betimes early
bien mise well turned out, very presentable
bilked cheated, defrauded out of due payment
bill advertisement
bill in Chancery formal indictment or bill of complaint
bite dupe, cheat
black-pot beer mug
blade good fellow (implies rumbustiousness)
bloody bloodthirsty, cruel
boar-cat tom-cat
bob taunt
boggle hesitate, demur
bona-roba high-class prostitute
bond legally binding agreement, written guarantee
bonnet brimless cap worn by servant
bookseller publisher and vendor of books
bordel brothel
borracho madman (literally, drunkard)
bougre brute
bound acting as joint party or guarantor in a bond, e.g. as security for a loan
Bow-dye scarlet-coloured
box (1) theatre box: the first tier of seats above the pit; the most expensive seats, mainly occupied by women of quality; (2) dice-box; (3) the 'bank' at the gaming-table into which go the house share and lost stakes; (4) vagina

braggadocio braggart
brandenburgh man's winter overcoat
branch embroider with figures of speech
brave n. hero, warrior; adj. fine, handsome
bravely well, excellently
breed educate, bring up; bear a child
breviate compendium; lawyer's brief
Bridewell prison and house of correction for bawds, prostitutes, vagabonds, etc., in Blackfriars
brimmer glass full to the brim
brisk vigorous, sprightly, forward with women; witty, clever
briskness pertness, impudence
broke, broken ruined financially, penniless
brother brother-in-law; a weak/unperforming brother an undersexed or impotent man (a jibe at the Puritan use of 'brother' as fellow-believer; cf. sister)
brutal brutal person
bubble n. gullible fool, dupe; v. cheat, trick into giving something up
bueno very well
buffle-headed foolish
buffoon fairground jester, clown
bulk stall or bench set up outside a shop
bully (1) stout fellow, rowdy gallant, ruffian; (2) term of address expressing admiration and affection ('my fine fellow'), often used ironically
burgundy man drunkard
business matters requiring attention; one's political, financial, mercantile, or sexual affairs
busk about (nautical) change tack
bustles struggles
by the by 'as we go along'
by-walks hideaway
cabinet casket for keeping and displaying jewels
cailles quails
canaille barbare uncouth riff-raff
canonical clerical
canting jargon; using religious language hypocritically
capon castrated cock, eunuch
carelessly with seeming indifference

carking worry

carriage conduct, behaviour

carry win, go with, take; **carry it** behave

cast throw of the dice or coin; sample, specimen

catcall squeaking whistle or pipe

catch part-song

caterwauling chasing women

caudle-maker one who prepares an invalid's drink (caudle = warm gruel, sweetened, with wine and spices added)

cause legal action, case

cavalier, cavaliero courtly, well-born gentleman

cellar cheap, low-class alehouse

cerecloths waxed cloths used as winding-sheets

certes indeed

chaffer barter

chair sedan chair, carried by two **chairmen**

chamber bedroom, private apartment

chamber-counsel lawyer who gives his legal judgements in private chambers, not in court

chamber-practice legal practice in private chambers; affairs of the bedchamber

Chancery principal court of equity (in effect an appeal court, to moderate the rigour of the common law), already notorious for protracted cases and legal quibbling

chandler grocer

Change see **Old Exchange**

changeling idiot

chanson à boire drinking song

chapman customer, purchaser

character brief prose sketch, usually satirical, of a class or type of person

charge duty, responsibility, burden, trouble, expense; part in a plot

chargeable expensive

chariot light carriage for two persons, less grand than a coach

charm n. spellbinding attraction; v. cast a spell over, transform by magic

Chateline's fashionable French restaurant in Covent Garden

checked rebuked

Chelsea village on the Thames, noted for its gardens and good air, popular for outings

chemist alchemist

chequered cellar cheap alehouse

chewed stale

china house shop specializing in porcelain and other goods from the East, much used for assignations

China orange sweet juicy orange, sold as a refreshment in the theatre

chirurgeon surgeon

chopping big and healthy

chouse n. swindler, impostor; v. cheat

cinder-woman employed to rake out and collect cinders for re-use as coke

circumstance circumstantial detail, particular

cit(s) contemptuous abbreviation of **citizen(s)**

citizens inhabitants of the City of London (financiers, entrepreneurs, merchants, artisans, shopkeepers, etc.) usually as distinct from those of the residential West End

civil respectable, well-bred, polite, respectful, courteously compliant (with sexual implications)

clap attack of gonorrhea

close covered

closet small private chamber, usually opening off a bedroom

clownish uncouth, stupid

club join forces, associate

coat coat-of-arms

Cock well-known tavern in Bow St., Covent Garden, frequented by wits (including Wycherley) and men about town; famous for food and notorious for drunken debauches

Colby proprietor or catering-manager of the **Mulberry Garden**

combination conspiracy

come off manage to extricate oneself

come up come from the country to visit London

come-off (military) satisfactory conclusion of an action against heavy odds

comfortable pleasant, consoling

coming forward, eager to meet advances, flirtatious

comment explanatory gloss

Common Pleas court for hearing of civil cases; only **serjeants** could plead there

common woman prostitute

companion fellow (used disparagingly)

complacent delightful

complaisance, complaisancy courtesy shown by compliance; wish to please others, meek acquiescence

complaisant accommodating, disposed to please, fawning

composition settling of a debt or claim; terms of an agreement

con licentia 'if you'll forgive my saying so', 'if you wouldn't mind' (literally, with permission)

conduct discretion; skilful manner of handling things

confidence self-assurance, boldness, impudence

confident bold, impudent, brazen

conjure entreat, charge

conning studying, learning by heart

conscience sense of what is right and reasonable, fair play; moral scruple (ironic at *LiW*, 3.2.121)

conscientious making much of one's duty and conscience

conscious guilty, sharing a guilty secret

consideration (1) (legal) the *quid pro quo* or recompense which makes a contract binding; (2) reflection, pausing for thought before taking action

constable officer appointed to keep the peace, especially on the streets at night, and to apprehend criminals

constitution disposition, sexual proclivities

contemn treat with contempt, look down on

contemptibly contemptuously

control curb, check

conventicle nonconformist meeting-house

converse keep company

conversation company; sexual intimacy

convict of compel to acknowledge

convoy escort vessel; captain of such a vessel

copy manuscript or picture from which a printed book or copy is made

coquin rascal

correspondency relationship

counsel secret

coupee dance step, passing one foot backwards and forwards while resting on the other

courante fashionable French dance in triple time, with running or gliding steps

course procedure, normal practice

coursers pursuers

coursing hunting hares with dogs

cousin (1) relative, often = niece or nephew; (2) male or female 'friend'; (3) mistress

Covent Garden fashionable and expensive residential area, including the **Piazza** and adjacent streets

covert-baron a married woman's legal status, under her husband's authority and protection

coxcomb vain, silly fool

coy unsociable, standoffish, disdainful, resistant

cozen cheat

cravat ancestor of modern neck-tie: length of lace or linen, tied in bow or held in place with ribbons, its ends (usually fringed) hanging on chest

crazy on their last legs

credit do credit to, give credence to

crediting naively trusting

cringe servile bow

cringing obsequious, excessively deferential

crocodile hypocrite (the crocodile was said to shed tears in order to lure men to their deaths, and to weep while devouring its prey)

cross of a sword the junction of hilt, blade and crossguard

cross or pile heads or tails

crossbite defeat by superior cunning

crowd fiddle

cuddens born fools

cuerno mild expletive, 'damn it'

cuisinier chef

cully dupe, stupid associate, tame fool, cuckold

curious wonderfully

curiously nicely, cleverly

curmudgeon miserly, morose person

curst savage, disagreeable (usually of animals)

cuz abbreviation of **cousin**, used in familiar address

da indeed, 'so there!'

daggled bedraggled, dishevelled through haste, slovenly

dainty fussy, choosy; precious

damn condemn, by hostile critical reception

dark-lantern (1) lantern fitted with shutter for dimming the light or focusing it, e.g. on an adversary; (2) (slang) servant (usually at court) who can be bribed

dauber crude, unskilful artist, especially a painter of signboards

daubing crude portrait-painting; dissembling (because using paint or cosmetics)

day-pinner close-fitting cap with long flaps pinned to the dress or to the cap itself; for informal wear indoors

de grâce 'I beg you', 'spare my blushes', 'for heaven's sake'

debauch corrupt, lead astray, entice away from one to whom allegiance is due

declaration (legal) the plaintiff's statement of complaint

decree a judgement given by an equity court, specifically the court of Chancery

defend forbid

definitivo categorical

depending awaiting settlement

desertless undeserving, devoid of merit

design *n.* plot, scheme; *v.* plan, plot, scheme to another's detriment

die reach sexual climax

difficulty reluctance

diffide in mistrust

diffidence distrust of, doubts about

diffidency circumspection

diffident suspicious, mistrusting

dilapidation (legal) wilful neglect of property, usually ecclesiastical

dipped mortgaged, involved in debt

discover reveal, reveal one's identity, give oneself away, betray; recognize

discovery revealing of a secret, demonstration

disgust dislike, loathe

disgust to dissatisfaction with

disgustful displeasing

disobliging impolite

disparage bring dishonour upon; specifically, degrade one's family by marrying a person of inferior rank

distemper disease, disorder

distinguished distinct, clearly audible

divertise (accented on second syllable) amuse, entertain

divertisement entertainment, sexual satisfaction

doctor instructor, learned clergyman

doctrine religious instruction, moral precept

documents lessons

dogged surly, sullenly obstinate, unmovable

domine (pronounced 'dominie') sir, master (term of respectful address to a professional man)

dominion (legal) right of possession, ownership

doom legal sentence

dough-baked half-baked, soft in the head

dowdy a plain, unattractive woman

doxies prostitutes

doze stupefy, make dull

draw pull together (of horses drawing a coach); prepare legal documents

draw out remove, extinguish

drawer barman, waiter

drawing-room formal royal reception held regularly in the drawing-room of Whitehall palace, early evening

drayman brewer's delivery man

drudge *n.* slave; *v.* work hard (usually bawdy)

druggets cheap, plain woollen cloth

duenna elderly lady having charge of daughters in Spanish household

dull silly, stupid

dun *n*. importunate creditor or debt-collector; *v*. demand money importunately

dust away drink up quickly

earnest foretaste; initial down-payment; guarantee

easy obliging, compliant, gullible, indolent

éclaircissement (vogue word) elucidation, clearing up (of a misunderstanding)

edify profit spiritually, benefit from instruction

education upbringing

employ keep occupied

emulation envy, resentment at another's success

en hora mala a threatening imprecation, 'I'm warning you', 'it will be worse for you' (literally, in an evil hour)

en poste on a flying visit

end purpose

ends scraps

engagements financial encumbrances, e.g. debts and mortgages

engine instrument of torture

engrossed monopolized

enow plural form of 'enough'

entail legal document settling the inheritance of an estate

equipage retinue

errand (dialect) utter, absolute

essence perfume

even pretty nearly

ever always

examine interrogate

examplify enlarge, exaggerate

exception objection; (legal) plea by defendant to bar plaintiff's action

exceptious easily offended

Exchange in *LiW* and *CW* = New Exchange; in *GDM* and *PD* = Old Exchange

excuse apology

executrix woman (usually widow) appointed to execute a will

expedition fee gratuity for prompt arranging of a loan

expose put on public view, usually in order to sell

expound explain significance (of a biblical text)

extenuate make light of

fa' mild oath, 'faith!'

facetious witty, amusing

fadges thrives

fail of be short of

fain *adj*. obliged; *adv*. gladly, willingly I would fain I'd like to

faisan pheasant

fall on get to work (often bawdy); attack (food, the enemy)

fall to make a start on, set to work on

falling-sickness epilepsy, thought to be most common among adolescents and melancholy lovers

fancy inclination

fancying imagining, fearing

fanfaron braggart

fantastical extravagant in opinion and dress

farandine silk and wool mixture; a gown of such material

far-born born long ago

favour permission, leave

feague get the better of, 'do for'

field background of picture; battlefield

fiddle toy with, take liberties with; cheat

fiddle-faddle nonsense

fiddles band of professional fiddlers, hired to play at weddings, masquerades, etc.

finical dainty, foppish

fireship ship loaded with gunpowder, set on fire and secured to enemy vessel; (slang) prostitute (because a likely carrier of venereal disease)

firkin small cask

fisk gadabout

fit repay, punish with a fitting penalty

flippant foolishly chattering

flirt pert, flighty young woman

flounce curl

flouting scoffing

fly flee

fob small pocket in waistband of breeches; cheat

fobus trickster, impostor

foil spoil the scent for the pursuing hounds

foiled in poor shape

fond foolishly credulous

fondness foolish affection

foot-post letter-carrier or messenger travelling on foot

fop fool, often an affected, would-be modish fool; sometimes 'old fool'

for all despite; **for all her** in spite of what she says; **for all them** for all they care

for me as far as I'm concerned

for my heart emphatic exclamation, 'for my life'

forehead-piece impregnated cloth worn at night to improve complexion

foretops front locks of wig, arranged decoratively over forehead

forfeit, forfeiture fine or penalty for breaking an agreement

formal utter, out-and-out; excessively ceremonious

forsooth provincial and old-fashioned equivalent of 'madam'. Perhaps pronounced with accent on first syllable, to distinguish it from 'forsooth' = indeed. On the page it is not always clear which forsooth is intended.

forswear renounce an oath, commit perjury, go back on one's promise or word; swear not to go near: *LiW*, 5.1.163

fortunes rich heiresses

foy indeed, by my faith

franchise outspokenness

frank outspoken; generous, lavish with one's affections, generously trusting

frankly unreservedly

free spontaneous, uninhibited

freedom outspokenness, informality, taking liberties, forward behaviour

freely seriously, frankly, without inhibition, familiarly

French house expensive London restaurant and wine-bar specializing in French cuisine; specifically Chateline's

friend (1) lover; (2) relative

froppish peevish, bad-tempered

fry young fish

fulsome disgusting; over-fed

fumbling impotent; capable only of clumsy, ineffectual love-making; doddery

furniture furnishings and decorations

furieusement extremely, passionately

Gadsbodikins, Gadsnouns, Gadsprecious 'By God's (Christ's) body/ wounds/precious blood'

gallant admirer, acknowledged lover of a particular woman; one who keeps a mistress; young man about town, fine fellow

gallery corridor

galliard lively

gamester gambler; (slang) lecher

gape to open one's mouth wide, yawn

garniture decorative additions to dress, especially ribbons, jewels

garters ribbons or small sashes worn round the leg, below the knee, to prevent stockings from slipping

gaudy showily dressed, flashy, wealthy

gazette news-sheet, specifically the *London Gazette*, semi-official paper with court and foreign news

generation set of people

generous magnanimous, not mean; sincere, honest; often used as vague honorific = 'noble'

generosity magnanimity, natural nobility

genius natural inclination and aptitude

gens people, persons

gentil well-bred, nice, fine

gentle well-born, chivalrous, ingratiating

gentleman-usher companion to person of superior rank, usually a superannuated gallant escorting a lady

gentlewoman (1) woman of good birth and breeding; (2) female attendant upon a lady of rank

gewgaw cheap and showy

giddily insanely, thoughtlessly

Gifford's well-known London brothel

gill-flirt flighty, wanton woman

gipsy coquette

give the lie flatly contradict, accuse of being a liar

glass mirror

gloat make eyes at, look meaningfully

GLOSSARY

goat considered a lecherous animal

goldsmith jeweller, often acting as banker and money-lender

golilla semi-circular Spanish collar, starched and stiffened with wire, standing up behind the head

good-fellow jovial drinking companion, reveller

Good Old Cause the political programme—for a free people and parliament—of the Puritan revolution

good one expression of sarcastic approval: 'a likely story', 'listen to that'

gossip godmother to one's child; friend and neighbour; chatterbox

governante chaperon

gown (1) ankle-length dress, with low-cut bodice, elbow-length sleeves, full skirt drawn up and looped back to reveal petticoat; (2) loose robe, often of rich material, worn informally

grateful agreeable, pleasant

greasy foul with grease, dirty, disgusting

green bag in which barristers and lawyers carry their documents

green cheese inferior cheese, made from whey

grimace affected facial expression and gesture; affected politeness

groat coin, value fourpence (last minted 1662)

grum hostile, severe, grim, sullen, taciturn

grumness moroseness, glumness

guarda beware, 'take care'; 'no indeed'

gull *n.* dupe, everyone's fool *v.* dupe, make a fool of

gusto taste

habeas corpus writ requiring a person to be produced in court (usually from prison)

habit clothes, dress, outfit; demeanour

hackney *n.* horse kept for hire; hired carriage; prostitute; *adj.* hired out, worn out by use

had often = modern 'would have' or 'would'

hand handwriting, signature

handkerchief (1) woman's neckerchief: square of lace, or muslin edged with lace, diagonally folded and worn round shoulders, the ends often pinned together; (2) woman's headkerchief: headscarf, trimmed with lace, the ends tied under the chin or hanging free

hanging-sleeves loose, open sleeves in young children's frocks, used as reins

Hans-in-kelder unborn child, usually one conceived outside marriage (literally, Jack-in-the-cellar)

happy-go-lucky just as good luck will have it

hard cruel: *LiW*, 4.4.135; unpleasant: *CW*, 2.1.465

hardened emboldened (by drink); confirmed

hardly with difficulty

harlotry harlot, wretch, hussy, good-for-nothing

haut-goût stench

hawk clear the throat noisily

haycock heap or conical pile of hay

hearing counsel lawyer attending court merely as an observer and to pick up business

hector *n.* swaggering, loud-mouthed bully-boy; *v.* bully, attempt to intimidate; swagger

hemming clearing the throat with a half-cough

hey-day an exclamation of surprise or irritation

hictius doctius conjurer's formula, 'abracadabra'

hidebound constipated, unproductive

hitherto so far, up to now

hold refrain, restrain oneself, suffer in silence, wait; guard

hold out resist temptation

hollow sepulchral

hombre French form of **ombre**, the card-game

home to the point, personal, directly, straight

homely plain, unsophisticated

honest virtuous, good, respectable, chaste

honestly frankly

honour (1) high rank; (2) chastity, good reputation; (3) the bow and curtsey, or kissing of the woman's hand, at the beginning and end of a dance

honra dignity, personal honour, good name

hope suppose

hopeful promising, having good prospects; promising oneself sexual satisfaction

hopper-hipped with protuberant buttocks

hospital almshouse, asylum for the needy, aged, and disabled

hostess landlady of an inn

house tavern

housewife good, and strict, household manager

how in questions and exclamations often = modern 'what'

hoyden boisterous young woman

huddle disorder; confused mass or crowd

huddle up put out of sight hurriedly

huff boast, bluster

hugeous, hugeously (rustic, colloquial) very, enormously

humour temperament, frame of mind, good mood; **out of humour** out of sorts, bad-tempered

humoursome temperamental, moody

hurry-durry (nautical, of the weather) rough, boisterous

hurt harm, evil, wrong

husbandry management of affairs, with an eye to one's own well-being

huzzas rakes, gallants

huzza-women prostitutes

Hyde Park fashionable for coach drives, promenades, and gallantry; rather more proper than St James's Park

Hymen god of marriage

idle empty-headed, worthless

if you go thereto (provincial) if that's the way it is, if you want to know, if that's your intention

i'fac, i'fackins, i'facs mild exclamations, 'in faith!'

i'fads (low and rustic) 'in faith!'

ill *n.* evil, wickedness, immorality; *adj.* wicked, bad, awful, injurious, disagreeable, poor; *adv.* badly, injuriously

ill-favoured unattractive, ugly, nasty

impertinency insolence, sauciness, forwardness

impertinent insolent, rude, meddlesome; irrelevant, trivial; absurd

impudence effrontery, utter shamelessness, immodesty

impudent shameless, keeping nothing back

in fine in short, to conclude

in form according to formal rules of logic, by prescribed methods

in my hand completely under my influence

in present now, at once

incommode embarrassing

inconscionable without conscience, unscrupulous

inconsiderable trifling, insignificant

indecently immodestly, unbefitting a modest woman

indenture legal contract

Indies India and the East Indies, considered a region of great riches

indocile obstinately self-willed

infiniment extremely

ingenuously frankly, candidly

ingrate unkind, hard-hearted person

insensible stupid, 'blind'

intelligence news, information; report, gossip

intelligencer informer, secret agent; newsmonger

interest self-interest, mercenariness, personal advantage

intrigue (vogue word) *n.* affair, sexual liaison; plan of seduction, plot, scheme; cunning; *v.* carry on a clandestine love-affair; scheme

inward inner

i'vads (low and rustic) 'in faith!'

jack fellow, knave; common appellation for a sailor

jack-pudding low, slapstick comedian, especially the foolish servant of a fairground mountebank

jack-straw worthless fellow

jarni 'I swear', 'damn it' (from *je renie Dieu*: I deny Christ)

jaunty well-bred, genteel, stylish

jealous mistrustful, suspicious

jealousy watchfulness, vigilance in guarding possessions; fear of being supplanted in love

jeer make fun of; **you jeer** you're not serious

jeminy mild and childish oath (from *Jesu Domine*: by the Lord Jesus)

jennet small Spanish horse

jeunesse young gentlemen

jew used for any grasping, canny money-lender

jilt *n.* whore, kept mistress; false, scheming, and mercenary woman; *v.* deceive in love-matters, pretend to be in love

jilting devious

jog (colloquial) go

jointure portion of husband's estate settled on wife at marriage as security against widowhood

joker merry fellow

jostle push aside; collide

journeyman hired hand; drudge

juggled conspired, played a deceitful trick

junket cakes; merry-making

just exactly, 'your typical'

keep support a mistress; care for an animal; attend; celebrate

keep up confine, keep safely inside

keeper a man who keeps a mistress

killing fatal, overpoweringly attractive

kind generous, particularly with sexual favours; eager for sex, loving, compliant; true to one's nature

King's Bench court handling pleas of the crown, cases involving treason, loss of life, injury

knack trinket, jewel

knight of the post professional false witness, willing to perjure himself in court for a fee, and to forge documents, etc.

lackey footman, valet

ladrón thief

lambskins judges' robes, trimmed with lambskin

lamp-blacking coating with soot from lamps and torches

lampoon scurrilous satire on private individual

lanterloo popular card-game

last most recent

late recent

laurel bay-tree; its leaves were an emblem of victory in war or distinction in poetry

law-French descendant of Norman French, used in law-books and by law-students in moots and pleadings

law-meuse legal loophole

lead *v.* escort, give his arm to a woman

leading-strings reins for toddlers

leads horizontal part of roof, nearest the gutter, covered in lead sheet

leave in the lurch disappoint, leave on the sidelines

led-captain hanger-on, sycophant

lees dregs

length full length

letter of attorney legal document empowering another to act in one's behalf

levee reception

lickerish lecherous in intention

lie have lodgings; stay the night

lie down, lie in to be in childbed

lieutenant second-in-command of a ship

like alike, like the original; likely

limb adherent, close associate

linkboy boy employed to carry torch (or torches, one on each shoulder) to light pedestrians along street

lively lifelike, vivid

Locket's well-known, expensive restaurant at Charing Cross

Lombard Street (commonly pronounced 'Lumber') the City premises of goldsmiths and eminent merchants

long be impatient

loo the card-game lanterloo

look to it beware, 'watch it'

look up be cheerful, take courage

lost wasted

luscious gratifying one's lascivious taste

lusty large; lustful

machiavel unscrupulous schemer

madrigal short love-poem, usually intended to be set to music

Maecenas patron and protector, after the wealthy Roman friend and patron of poets

magdalens penitents, reformed prostitutes

magpie chatterbox

maids of honour the ten attendants on the Queen and Duchess of York, unmarried and usually of aristocratic birth

maidens (archaic and rustic) maid-servants

mainly (rustic) very much

make order to be made, provide with, arrange for; do

make a conscience of have scruples about, think it wrong

make a leg bow, with one leg drawn back, the other bent

mal à peste 'curses', 'curse it' (literally, a plague on)

malapert cheeky girl

Mall alley-walk in St James's Park, site of the present Mall

malo 'dreadful!', 'shocking!'

mammocks shreds

man manservant, footman

manet (pl. manent) remains on stage

manor landed estate

march n. step, pace; v. walk

marker scorer employed in tennis-court or gaming-house

marry, marry come up, marry gep mild exclamations (from 'St Mary of Egypt!'), expressing assertion ('yes indeed'), remonstrance ('come off it'), indignation, or contempt

mart market, fair

masque masked ball

masquerade (1) entertainment, often in a private house, with singing, dancing, and much flirtation, the participants wearing masks and fancy dress; (2) social visit by group of maskers—masked and disguised men and/or women

masty mastiff, a large and strong dog

match marriage, marriage contract, suitable marriage partner

matron married woman; midwife; bawd

meeting-house for nonconformist worship

megrim migraine; whim

merry facetious

merry grig extravagantly frolicsome person

merry pin jovial mood or disposition

mien bearing

milliner vendor of fancy wares, especially gloves, jewellery, ribbons

minutes notes, memoranda

minx lewd woman, hussy

miss (1) kept mistress; (2) term of address, usually familiar and affectionate, to young unmarried girl

mistake misunderstand

mistress (1) girl-friend, sweetheart, fiancée; kept woman; (2) term of formal address to woman, married or unmarried

modest backward, slow; undemanding

monastery convent

monkey a fashionable pet, considered a lascivious animal

monopoly price-fixing scheme

morbleu mild oath, "sdeath!' (from *Mort de Dieu*)

mortgaged pawned, left as security for a tavern bill

mortified dead to worldly pleasures

mother-in-law stepmother

motion (1) formal proposal, plea; (2) bodily exertion, excitement, desire; (3) puppet-show

Mulberry Garden at the west end of St James's Park (now site of Buckingham Palace), for public entertainment and gallantry, with walks, arbours, and refreshments

mumble maul

mummy dried flesh

mump cheat, overreach, disappoint

murrain cattle-disease, plague

muzzle give a French kiss

nanger (rustic and affectionate) make angry

Naples biscuit a type of crisp biscuit

naught, naughty wicked, good for nothing

naughtiness wickedness

477

neat trim, smart, nicely proportioned

Neat House market-garden in Chelsea, open to the public for walks and refreshments

negligent indifferent to minor details of dress, not excessively fussy

neither none

never go, never stir mild exclamations, 'believe me,' 'take my word for it'

New Exchange shopping mall on the south side of the Strand, especially for luxury items, e.g. gloves, ribbons, perfumes; galleries or walks on two floors, the lower walks favoured for rendezvous and assignations

New Spring Garden pleasure garden, with arbours and covered walks, music and refreshments (a famous cheesecake), at Vauxhall, south of the Thames, patronized by the bourgeoisie

newly shortly

next nearest; **next to** almost: *LiW*, 2.4.76

nice of strict virtue, correct; affectedly modest; hard to please

nick of time critical moment

nick upon gamble with

nightgown (woman's) long, loose gown or wrap, of silk or brocade, for informal wear, day or evening, indoors or out

nimble-chaps chatterbox (chaps = jaws)

noble a term of respectful address, not restricted to the nobility

noise company, band, usually of musicians

obliging granting (sexual) favours; polite

observe respect the wishes of

occasion opportunity; excuse, reason; need

occasional timely, just

of one's own head for oneself, of one's own accord

offer make a move, begin

offerers at pretenders to, would-be exponents of

offering at making an attempt on

offices high official positions

old acquaintance cast-off mistress, old flame

Old Exchange the Royal Exchange, City of London, the business centre for merchants and financiers; on its upper floor, galleries with shops

Old Pall Mall the present Pall Mall, street of expensive houses and lodgings of gentry and aristocracy

olio rich stew of meat and vegetables

ombre (pronounced 'umber') fashionable card-game for three players

on the tenters on tenterhooks

once once and for all, finally, at last

only merely

or ça 'well now'

ordinary public restaurant, often a dining-room in a tavern, serving midday meal at fixed and modest price, a resort of gamblers in the evening

original unique specimen, novelty

out wrong, mistaken

overlooking contemptuous

over-concerned over-anxious

owl solemn-faced simpleton

own *v.* admit, acknowledge, answer to; *adj.* independent, in control of one's own fortune or destiny

Pall Mall see **Old Pall Mall**

pampered well-fed, sensual

pantaloons very wide, knee-length trousers, lavishly ornamented with ribbons; a French fashion, worn in England by fops and gallants

pardon me polite formula of disagreement, disclaimer, or excuse

parents relatives

particular idiosyncratic

parts abilities, talents; private parts; **man of parts** clever fellow

pass safe-conduct

pass by ignore

pass upon impose upon, be believed by

passe-partout one who has free access everywhere

passionately irascibly

patch small piece of black silk or velvet worn by both men and women to show off complexion or hide

blemishes; often of fanciful shape,
e.g. star, crescent, lozenge

patent document conferring right to
property or title

paw dirty, not nice

pay get one's own back; answer,
confute: *PD*, 5.2.79

pay it make up for it

peep take a close look

peevish perverse, obstinate; spiteful,
bad-tempered

Penelope wife of Odysseus, the type
of the patient and faithful wife

pension lodging-house

penny-rent income from rented
property

periwig large, full-bottomed wig,
composed of a mass of irregular curls
reaching to the shoulder

person someone of a certain social
standing, 'somebody'

perspicuous transparent

peruke wig, sometimes specifically a
short 'travelling-wig'

petticoat trimmed and ornamented
underskirt, often of satin

pettifogger lawyer dealing with petty
cases and using sharp practice

Phoebus Apollo, the sun-god and
patron of poets

physic medicine

Piazza, Piazzo open arcades on the
north and east sides of Covent
Garden square; popular promenade
and meeting-place

pick up regain possession of

picklock skeleton key

pink most perfect, perfection

piping extremely

piquet (pronounced 'picket')
fashionable card-game for two players

pissing-clout nappy

pit equivalent of modern theatre stalls:
backless benches, occupied by wits,
critics, etc.; largely a male preserve

place employment, position as a
servant

placehouse country house and
surrounding estate

plain dealing candour, honest
speaking, sincerity

play (1) gambling, gaming with dice or
cards; (2) sword-play; (3) love-making

play fast and loose get the better, by
whatever means

player actress, actor

plea argument in support of a case

pleading-counsel barrister

pleasant agreeable, ridiculous

pledge drink another's health, as a
token of friendship

pocket-glass small hand mirror

pocky infected with syphilis

poet author, often = playwright; writer
of genius

poignant stinging, sharp

point characteristic; principle: *PD*,
5.2.297

points pieces of fine lace used for
kerchiefs, etc.

policy prudence, cunning, shrewd
self-interest

politic sagacious, shrewd

poll crown of the head

poor term of endearment (= 'dear'),
usually without overtones of pity or
scorn

porter doorkeeper

portion dowry, brought by the wife to
her husband at marriage, less
commonly by husband to wife

posed perplexed

positive inflexible

positivo *n.* man of determination; *adj.*
stubbornly opinionated, determined

post *v.* send post-haste; *adv.* with all
speed

pother to-do, fuss

powder-room ship's magazine

power (rustic) abundance

pox syphilis

practiser practitioner; one who
practises the law

prate blab, tell secrets

precise puritanical, prudish, righteous

preferment promotion (backed by
influential support)

present give a present to someone

presently at once; soon, shortly
afterwards

pressing forcibly conscripting by
press-gang; importuning; intruding

pretence pretext, claim

pretend claim, presume

pretenders suitors

pretending aspiring to, suing for

prevent be beforehand, forestall, balk, stop

private obscure, of no social rank or standing

private house tavern having private room available

probatum est tried and tested, of remedies and recipes (literally, 'it has been proved')

process legal action; mode of operation

proctor lawyer handling civil or canon-law cases

profess make no secret of, declare openly, avow one's religious faith, attachment, etc.

profuse extravagant, wastefully prodigal

project scheme, proposal (often fraudulent or harebrained) for financial gain

projector speculator, proposer of a project

projection the crucial point in the alchemical process, when powdered philosopher's stone is thrown onto base metal to effect its transformation into gold

promiscuously indiscriminately, whatever they are really like

propagated kept in a flourishing condition

proper good-looking, fine; individual

proportionable suitable

propre à tout fit for anything

propriety right of ownership

prospect appearance, sight; pleasurable expectation

publish make public

puissant mighty, influential

pullet young hen

pulvilio perfumed cosmetic powder, also used on wigs and clothes

pumps light, low-heeled shoes for dancing, also worn outdoors by fops

punctilios scruples about ceremony and honour

punctual keeping one's word, scrupulously observant of principle

punk prostitute

puny inexperienced; (legal) junior in appointment

pure (rustic and unsophisticated) fine, marvellous, out-and-out

purser naval officer in charge of ship's accounts and provisions

pursuivants state officers with power to serve and execute warrants for search and arrest

push press forward; make a thrust; gamble, especially with big stakes

pusher active promoter

pushing rash, putting down large stakes

put out lend money at interest; delete; throw an actor off his stride

put to it test, force (or give a chance) to prove

put up suffer tamely; put away, hide, sheathe

putter of cases law student learning to present legal cases in court

quality high birth and corresponding social rank; the aristocracy and gentry

quibble *n.* verbal quip, pun; *v.* joke facetiously, quip, make punning joke

quirk verbal trick, let-out

railing invective, abuse, malicious comment

raillery good-humoured banter, teasing, ridicule (often using irony); jest, jibe

railleur one who practises raillery

rakehell rake

rally banter, make fun of, employ raillery

ramble *v.* go out in search of sexual adventures, or to pick up a man or woman; digress towards dangerous topics; *n.* excursion for sexual adventure

rant make a boisterous uproar

rather with better reason; more readily

ravish seize and carry off, rape; spoil, interfere with

ravissaunt delightful

reading commentary, lecture

reason (1) **do reason to someone** do justice to, reciprocate, keep one's end up, in drinking or repartee; (2) **have reason** be right (a modish Gallicism); be a rational creature

recant withdraw

receipt-book medical guide

receipts cookery recipes

recover make good, brush up, learn properly; get back by legal process

register parish register of baptisms, marriages, and deaths

rehearse speak or recite in public

relict widow

relish give a relish to

rencounter *n.* meeting, duel; *v.* meet

renegado renegade, deserter

renounce fail to follow suit

resentment sense of loss

resolve make up one's mind; **resolve me** give me a straight answer

retirement withdrawal into seclusion

Rhenish popular German white wine

ridicule ridiculous

right *n.* justice; *adj.* lascivious, promiscuous; **a right woman** a whore; *adv.* firm, rightly, correctly

rigid puritanical, abstemious

roar rampage, 'carry on'

roaring riotous

rogue term of playful reproach or endearment

rolwagen tall cylindrical vase, usually of blue and white Chinese ware

romance fairy-story

rook (1) sharper, notorious cheat, con-man; (2) dupe, incompetent would-be gambler: *CW*, 1.1.237

roundly straight

royally absolutely, positively, for sure

rude barbarous

rudely violently, roughly

ruffs male sandpipers (a delicacy)

rummage rifle

Russell Street street of fashionable houses, coffee-houses, and taverns, running east from Covent Garden Piazza

sa sa sa fencing-cry, uttered when drawing one's sword, or thrusting at an opponent

sack dry white Spanish or Canary wine

sadness seriousness

St James's Gate Tudor gatehouse of St James's palace, at the west end of Old Pall Mall

St James's Park enlarged and beautified by Charles II, with walks among trees, and a canal; much used for clandestine affairs and pick-ups

salute greet, usually with a kiss, and usually on the lips.

saraband stately Spanish dance

satisfaction the right to satisfy one's honour in a duel; acceptance of a challenge

satyr mythical woodland creature, half-man half-goat, horned, shaggy, and lecherous

saucy insolent, presumptuous

scarf (1) woman's: of silk, lace, or gauze, worn outdoors like a shawl; (2) man's: broad sash, usually of gold or crimson silk, with fringed ends, worn at waist or over shoulder, as sign of military rank

science skill, body of knowledge

scolding wrangling, quarrelling

scour rampage

scourer roisterer, hooligan (usually drunk) rampaging about the streets at night

scribble produce quantities of mediocre literary work

scrivener moneylender (often = loanshark); broker receiving money to put out at interest

scrupulous meticulous in matters of right and wrong

scullion kitchen-hand

scuttle hatchway, small trapdoor

seat country house and surrounding estate

secure protect; hold on to; convince, satisfy, guarantee; **I'll secure you** believe me, you have my word

security depositing of money, or entering into bonds, to guarantee the fulfilment of an obligation (e.g. repayment of a loan) by oneself or another

seguramente certainly

sense feeling, perception, awareness

sensible keenly felt; sensitively aware of, conscious of

sensibly acutely

sentence sententious maxim

serjeant (1) officer of the law courts, empowered to arrest offenders and bring them before the court; (2) the most senior order of barristers, twenty in number

serjeant at arms officer of Houses of Parliament, responsible for enforcing their commands

servant lover, professed admirer, gallant

serve satisfy sexually; formally deliver a legal writ

serve one's turn suffice, satisfy one (sexually)

service position as a servant; military service; sexual relationship, giving of sexual satisfaction; act of serving a legal writ

serviteur 'your humble servant'

set off show to advantage

set one's teeth on edge (1) irritate, vex; (2) give one an appetite (physical or sexual)

set up for make a show of

several different

severally (stage direction) separately, at different doors

sham hoax, take in

sharks henchmen

sharp bent hungry, with a keen appetite

she woman

shift n. expedient, ingenious scheme, subterfuge; v. manage things, contrive, extricate oneself

shifting skilled at devising expedients

shock-dogs, shocks lap-dogs, specifically long-haired poodles

should often = modern 'would', sometimes 'may', 'might', or 'must'

show set off

shy distrustful, suspicious, wary

sign shop- or inn-sign; empty semblance: *CW*, 1.1.284

sillabub drink of cow's milk curdled with wine, sweetened and flavoured; or of cider, with sugar, nutmeg, and cream added

silly unsophisticated, inexperienced, ignorant, foolish

simile-maker portrait painter

sinecure ecclesiastical living, with emoluments but without duties

sister whore, mistress, especially one who looks respectable (sardonically alluding to the Puritan 'sisterhood' of believers; cf. **brother**)

sitting the courts while the law courts are in session

sleek smooth-tongued; plump, nicely got up

sleepiness languishing look

slur gliding dance-step

smack taste, mouthful, smacking kiss

smock woman's undergarment, chemise

smug smartly

smugged smartened

smugness self-consciously smart appearance

snack take part, have a go

snap up snap back at, 'put down'

snip small share

snub reprimand, rebuke

soh exclamation of disgust and indignation

soliciting inciting to illicit acts; disturbing

solicitor lawyer (originally an attorney's assistant) who instructs a barrister on behalf of a client in courts of equity

solvable solvent

something somewhat, rather

song short love-poem

son-in-law stepson

sonnet love-poem, song

soothes confirms, maintains

sound free from venereal disease

soundly thoroughly

soused pickled, or boiled with herbs

Spanish leg deep bow, with one leg bent nearly to the ground

Spanish wool pad of wool impregnated with rouge

spark fashionable young man, gallant; often derogatory = empty-headed young fop

spend expend, exhaust (often bawdy)

spirit abduct, specifically for sale to plantations of North America or West Indies

spleen melancholia, a fashionable nervous complaint; irritation

splotch stain

spoil do an injury to, corrupt

sponge soak up, steal

sputter *n.* clamour, fuss; *v.* speak vehemently and incoherently

square honest, above board; **on/upon the square** honestly, without cheating or duplicity; on equal terms

squeak cry out (a virtuous woman always **squeaks** when sexually assaulted)

squire country gentleman, often = young heir to country estate; male escort

stamp design (e.g. king's head) on face of coin

stand withstand

stand fair stand fast, confront enemy without flinching

stand off bargain, make terms; keep one's distance

stand to submit to

stand upon insist on

State General (properly States General) the delegates of the Dutch provinces, forming the legislative assembly

stay wait, remain, be obliged to wait, defer; prevent from leaving; appease, satisfy

stews brothel

still *adj.* attentive, usually because overawed; *adv.* always, for ever, regularly

stint limit

stock funds; capital sum or endowment, specifically for a younger son

stomach appetite, physical and/or sexual; inclination

stomachful courageous, stubborn

stout brave

straggling stray, vagrant

strange unfriendly, distant

strangeness coldness

stricken 'getting on'

studied premeditated

study think about carefully

stuffs cloth

submissions acts of deference and self-abasement

subpoena writ requiring the presence of a witness in court

such such-and-such

success result, outcome

sue out apply for grant of writ, with an eye to further proceedings

suit coat and matching waistcoat-like 'vest'; wooing, supplication

suit of knots set of ribbons (cockades, rosettes, or loops) worn by women on gown or at side of head

sullen miserable, sulky; rough

supercilious exacting, demanding compliance

supple obsequious, ingratiating

sure indeed, surely, for sure

surly imperious, rude, churlish

swanskins fine thick flannel

swingeing enormous

sympathy innate and involuntary feeling of attraction

take captivate; arrest

take acquaintance with greet, behave familiarly towards

take notice of mention, talk about

take up hire, engage; borrow; take into custody

taken up exclusively occupied by another

tale count, for stock-taking purposes

tansy strongly-scented yellow flower, used medicinally

tar, tarpaulin professional and experienced ship's officer; seaman

taste enjoy

tasteless insipid

tattle gossip, chat

tattling idle talk

tear roister, bluster, heckle

tearing roistering, loud-mouthed; notable

tell count

tennis-court roofed structure for indoor tennis; the spectators' gallery, running alongside the court, was ideal for political and other gossip

tête, têtebleu mild oath, 'for heaven's sake!' (from *tête de Dieu*)

tête non protestation or exclamation, 'I don't believe you', 'by heaven!'

that's once that's final

thereto see if

throughly thoroughly, fully

tick *n*. credit; *v*. live on credit, leave one's debts unpaid

tight watertight; smart, trim

tiring-room theatre dressing-room (usually that of the actresses)

title legal right, claim

to choose by choice, 'as far as my preference goes', 'that's my choice'

to purpose to good effect, to some purpose

Toledo sharp sword made of the best Toledo steel

tomrig tomboy; whore

tony simpleton

torch boy carrying lighted torch

tour artificial curls worn on forehead to give extra height to coiffure

touse and mouse mess about with

town fashionable London society; the ways of the world

town-bull bull kept to service cows on neighbouring farms; notorious lecher

town-woman common prostitute, woman of bad reputation

toy trinket

trace track down

traidor traitor, villain

train retinue, followers

train-bands citizen militia, formed for home defence, and regarded as something of a joke

training trailing

trangam worthless person, trinket

traverse ground move to and fro, or from side to side, in fencing

treat *n*. feast, entertainment with food, wine, and (often) music; *v*. entertain; discuss terms, negotiate

trepan (a vogue word) *n*. snare; *v*. swindle, lure

tricking titivating

trip false step, slip

trouble *n*. distress, uneasiness, troublesome or irritating thing; *v*. disturb, distress

truck cheap goods used for bartering

trust duty, office

turn away, turn off dismiss from service

tyrannical insolent

ugly disagreeable

unconscionable unscrupulous

under correction polite expression of (mock) deference to superior, 'with respect'

underwoods coppices

unfortunately with disastrous consequences

ungrateful displeasing (by one's appearance), disagreeable; hateful; hard-hearted; perverse

unmannerly rude, impolite

unquiet uneasy, anxious

unreasonable exorbitant in demanding tips (*LiW*, 1.2.132) or bribes (*LiW*, 4.1.12)

unsound unhealthy; infected with venereal disease

up upstairs (reception rooms were normally on the first floor)

upholster second-hand dealer

use be in the habit of; accustom; use to familiarize with; uses to be is normally

usquebaugh whisky

valet de chambre gentleman's personal servant

valgame el cielo heaven help me

vanidades vanities

varnish specious gloss

vaulting-school brothel

vent sell

ventre, ventrebleu 'for heaven's sake!' (from *ventre de Dieu*: by God's belly)

venture *v*. put at risk; *n*. risk; goods or money invested in a commercial speculation; a risky undertaking, usually financial; at a venture knowing the risks involved

verdaderamente truly

vert et bleu 'by heaven!' (from *vertu Dieu*: by God's goodness)

very (archaic) veritable, true, faithful

vex plague, get in the way

vexatious disposed to cause trouble, bringing legal actions solely to annoy or embarrass a defendant

vild (archaic) depraved, despicable

vizard, vizard-mask (i) black velvet or silk mask covering upper part, or whole, of face; worn in public by women wishing to remain incognito, or to allure, and as a disguise (e.g. in a masquerade) by both men and women; (ii) a person so masked; a prostitute

voto I swear, 'by heaven!'; **voto a mi honra** 'upon my honour'; **voto a Santiago** 'by St James!'

wag stir, swing open

wake be up and about at night

want *n.* deficiency, lack, need; *v.* lack, be short of, be without, have need of

Wapping hamlet on the north bank of the Thames, east of the Tower of London, largely populated by sailors

warning notice terminating a legal or business relationship

warrant improve; **I warrant** I'm sure, indeed, I believe so; **I warrant you** expression of assurance: believe me, I assure you, leave it to me, etc.

watch, watchmen constable's assistants, keeping order in streets, especially at night

water-dog one trained to retrieve shot water-fowl

wench whore, mistress, woman

Westminster Hall originally the great hall of the palace of Westminster (now the vestibule of the House of Commons), housing the law courts

whatever whatsoever

wheedle (vogue word) *v.* smooth-talk, cajole, talk round, especially in order to get someone to do something to her/his disadvantage; *n.* deceiver

whilst until

whist 'hush!', 'silence!'

Whitehall royal palace and king's residence, occupying site between Thames and St James's Park (only the Banqueting House remains); subjects of a certain standing could attend receptions in the drawing-room, and had access to the 'galleries' (corridors) to lobby and gossip with courtiers, officials, etc.

whiting's eye amorous look

whoremaster lecher, fornicator

wild boisterous, rough; dissolute, licentious; demented

willing spontaneous

wine-cooper bottler and retailer of wine

wink shut one's eyes, seem not to see

wish hope

wit (1) intellect; intelligence, acumen, quick-wittedness, especially in verbal repartee; inventiveness, literary talent, verbal dexterity; good sense, discretion; (2) one of the intelligentsia; man/woman of letters; sophisticated man (occasionally woman) about town, one of the smart set

with even with, as smart as

woman waiting-woman, maid, confidante

woman of the town (1) fashionable, sophisticated woman; (2) prostitute

wonder be amazed, marvel

word signal for attack, watchword

would wished to, desired

wrap fold

wretch (often **poor wretch**); term of tender endearment ('my little dear'), sometimes with overtones of commiseration and/or scorn

writings legal or official documents

wronged slandered

yellow jealous

your servant polite formula of greeting or farewell, also used to acknowledge a compliment, to decline to do something, to refuse to divulge information, to terminate a conversation ('I shall say no more'), or to contradict or deny ('I beg to differ')

American Literature

British and Irish Literature

Children's Literature

Classics and Ancient Literature

Colonial Literature

Eastern Literature

European Literature

Gothic Literature

History

Medieval Literature

Oxford English Drama

Poetry

Philosophy

Politics

Religion

The Oxford Shakespeare

A complete list of Oxford World's Classics, including Authors in Context, Oxford English Drama, and the Oxford Shakespeare, is available in the UK from the Marketing Services Department, Oxford University Press, Great Clarendon Street, Oxford OX2 6DP, or visit the website at www.oup.com/uk/worldsclassics.

In the USA, visit www.oup.com/us/owc for a complete title list.

Oxford World's Classics are available from all good bookshops. In case of difficulty, customers in the UK should contact Oxford University Press Bookshop, 116 High Street, Oxford OX1 4BR.